Mrs. Russell Sage

Mrs. Russell Sage

Women's Activism and Philanthropy
in Gilded Age and
Progressive Era America

RUTH CROCKER

INDIANA UNIVERSITY PRESS
Bloomington and Indianapolis

Philanthropic and Nonprofit Studies
Dwight F. Burlingame and David C. Hammack, editors

This book is a publication of
Indiana University Press
601 North Morton Street
Bloomington, IN 47404-3797 USA

http://iupress.indiana.edu

Telephone orders   800-842-6796

Fax orders   812-855-7931

Orders by e-mail   iuporder@indiana.edu

The paper used in this publication meets the minimum requirements of
American National Standard for Information Sciences—Permanence of
Paper for Printed Library Materials, ANSI Z39.48-1984.

Manufactured in the United States of America

Library of Congress Cataloging-in-Publication Data

Crocker, Ruth, date
Mrs. Russell Sage : women's activism and philanthropy in gilded age and progressive
era America / Ruth Crocker.
p. cm.
Includes bibliographical references and index.
ISBN 0-253-34712-2 (cloth : alk. paper) 1. Sage, Margaret Olivia Slocum, 1828–1918.
2. Women philanthropists—United States—Biography. 3. Charities—United States—
History. I. Title.
HV28.S1267C76 2006
361.7'4092—dc22

2006006801

ISBN-13: 978-0-253-34712-1 (cl.)

ISBN-13: 978-0-253-22045-5 (pbk.)

2 3 4 5 6 13 12 11 10 09 08

The irony here is that women who have mounted the most global critique of male privilege have typically been those with the greatest access to it.

—Nancy A. Hewitt and Suzanne Lebsock, "Introduction," in *Visible Women: New Essays on American Activism* (1993)

While it is interesting to see how men have built up fortunes, as a rule, through industry, saving, and great energy, it is even more interesting to see how those fortunes have been or may be used for the benefit of mankind.

—Sarah Knowles Bolton, *Famous Givers and Their Gifts* (1896)

CONTENTS

CONTENTS

ACKNOWLEDGMENTS

This study of what one reader has called "the upstairs long missing from women's history" began with a modest paragraph in an issue of the Rockefeller Archive Center *Newsletter* announcing that a collection of about 5,000 letters of "Mrs. Russell Sage, philanthropist (1828–1918)" had been processed by Melissa Smith and James Allen Smith and was available to researchers.[1] I went to look at the letters, which are in the Russell Sage Foundation Papers at the Rockefeller Archive Center, Sleepy Hollow, New York, and was intrigued by the problems they presented for a biographer, not least the fact that most of them were from the last twelve years of a ninety-year life and also that many were addressed to Sage, not written by her. I was surprised to find that this elite woman's career intersected with many of the debates that defined American public life in the nineteenth and early twentieth centuries—the responsibilities of haves to have-nots; the debate on coeducation and the widening sphere of women; women's construction of a public self, including their use of public space and money; voluntary associations as the seedbed of public policy; and the idea of the nation. I was especially intrigued by the interpretive problems posed by begging letters and by the ironies of benevolence in an advanced capitalist society. Since then I have been in search of Mrs. Sage, and it has been a lengthy but rewarding process.

The question of philanthropy was both more interesting than I had expected and more complicated. The philanthropic dyad (donor and donee, philanthropist and petitioner) involved a dynamic that, as a social welfare historian, I knew as the client-provider relationship, and in other ways, too, this biography took me back to themes in my previous work. In *Social Work and Social Order* (1992) I explored how Progressive-era settlement houses sought to implement reform in immigrant and black neighborhoods, modernizing families and households to fit them for industrial work and urban life. This second book, seemingly so different, presented some of the same problems: the paradox of reform as class-based intervention, gift as relationship, and benevolence as a subject position.[2]

Researching Olivia's life brought me into contact with many individuals, all of whom deserve my grateful thanks. These include conference respondents, bed-and-breakfast hosts, and more librarians and archivists than I can name. My project has involved lively stays in New York City, visits to places as different as Sag Harbor, New York; San Marino, California; Carlisle, Pennsylvania; and Newport, Rhode Island. I have worked in university archives as well as in amazingly rich local history collections such as the Onondaga Historical Association Research Center in Syracuse. Then there was the serendipity of the Bolling Memorial Medical Library, now the repository for the records of the New-York Woman's Hospital, housed unexpectedly on the top floor of St. Luke's Roosevelt, a modern working hospital in Upper Manhattan.

Much of the research for this book was carried out in New York City. I met Dawn Greeley and Susan Lederman in the Butler Library, Columbia University, where we all were working on related topics. They, along with Susan Kastan, Richard Magat, Nancy Robertson, and Susan Yohn, shared their ideas and their good company during my visits to New York. James Allen Smith of the Gilman Foundation encouraged me to write Olivia's story.

Deborah Gardner was my expert guide to New York City landmarks, including Stanford White's wonderful Hall of Fame at University Heights, now part of the South Bronx Community College, where we braved a harsh February wind and swirling snowflakes to pay homage to the bust of Emma Willard.

Professor Barry D. Karl used the Russell Sage Foundation papers in the 1970s (he recalls it was around 1977–1979) when he and Stanley Katz were writing about foundation philanthropy and when the papers were still at the Russell Sage Foundation building in New York City. Dr. Karl was most helpful in sharing with me in long informative letters what he knew about the probable disposition of Olivia's papers (see "A Note on Sources").

I received help from many people at the institutions associated with Olivia Sage. My thanks to Eric Wanner, president of the Russell Sage Foundation, for agreeing to support the publication of this biography of the woman who endowed the foundation one hundred years ago and for permission to publish the oil portrait of Olivia Sage that appears on the book's cover. I also thank the foundation's vice president and secretary, Madge Spitaleri, and publications director, Suzanne Nichols, for their help and encouragement.

The Emma Willard School in Troy, New York, has an important collection of Olivia Sage's papers. I owe a debt of thanks to librarians Barbara Wiley and Judy Mazurkiewicz and to archivist Susan Malbin, as well as to principal Trudy Hamner, for help and hospitality during my visits there. At Russell Sage College, also in Troy, Maren Stein arranged my visit and shared her knowledge of Olivia, while historian of science Nancy Slack generously gave me copies of her working notes on some of the Sage correspondence. At Hofstra, Long Island historian Natalie Naylor took me to the romantically named Far Rockaway, Long Island, to see the great "River of Life" Tiffany window at the First Presbyterian Church, given by Olivia in her husband's name, and at Cedarhurst we looked for the place where Olivia's summer home, Cedar Croft, once stood. And at the Reynolds Medical Library at the University of Alabama, Birmingham, I saw another stained-glass window given by Olivia, this one presented to the New-York Woman's Hospital and moved to Birmingham in 1918.

This project began with research at the Rockefeller Archive Center, and I would like to acknowledge the help and encouragement of Darwin Stapleton, its director, and Kenneth Rose. I also want to thank the following archivists and librarians: Bob Anderson at the Rensselaer County Historical Society; Joan Carvajal and Nancy Panella at the Bolling Memorial Medical Library at St. Luke's-Roosevelt Hospital, New York City; Alison Cornish at the East Hampton, New York, Historical Society; Carolyn Davis and Mary O'Brien at the Syracuse University Archives; Irene Lee Epstein at the Goulds' home in Lyndhurst, New York; Mike Flannery at the Archives of the University of Alabama, Birmingham; Thomas Frusciano at the Rutgers University Archives; Megan Hahn at the New-York Historical Society; Judy Haven at the Onondaga Historical Association Research Center, Syracuse; Fred Hueser and Kenneth J. Ross at the Presbyterian Historical Society, Philadelphia; Natalie Naylor at the Long Island Studies Institute, Hempstead, New York; Marilyn Petitt and Nancy Cricco at New York University Archives; Judy Harvey Sahak at Scripps College, California; Hugh Shingleton and Tim Pennycuff at the Reynolds Library, University of Alabama, Birmingham; Tom Rosenbaum and his colleagues at the Rockefeller Archive Center; Peter Wosh at the American Bible Society Archives; and Cynthia Wilson at Tuskegee University, Alabama. I also want to thank Jeff

Gottlieb of the Queens, New York, Historical Society. Finally, my special thanks to the reference librarians of the Ralph Brown Draughon Library at Auburn University for their assistance over the years. For research assistance in the Nettie Fowler McCormick Correspondence at the State Historical Society of Wisconsin I wish to thank Joan Braune.

Auburn University has been generous in supporting this project. Funding for research and travel was provided by occasional grants from the Department of History, the Humanities Development Fund of the College of Liberal Arts, and the Office of the Vice President for Research. I was awarded summer research grants from the College of Liberal Arts for research travel and writing. I also received a research travel grant from the National Endowment for the Humanities to work at the New York Public Library and another from the Presbyterian Historical Society to use its library in Philadelphia.

Earlier versions or parts of Olivia's story were shared in various forums. I was fortunate to be invited to talk at the Center on Nonprofit Organizations and Voluntary Associations, Yale University (1999) and at the Poynter Center on American Values, Indiana University, Bloomington, Indiana (2001). The Indiana University Center on Philanthropy in Indianapolis gave me an opportunity to share my ideas about Olivia as a biographical subject at the conference "Philanthropy in History" (1997), and the Rockefeller Archive Center invited me to participate in the conference "Philanthropy and the City," jointly organized with the Center for the Study of Philanthropy and the CUNY Graduate School in 2000. I also participated in a useful and enjoyable workshop on "Women, Philanthropy, and Education" at the School of Education, Indiana University, Bloomington, Indiana (December 2001), organized by Andrea Walton.

Two seminars at Rutgers University, one when I was in the midst of this book and the other right at the end, helped me develop my ideas for this project. An excellent NEH-funded seminar directed by Jackson Lears at Rutgers University in 1997, "Grace, Luck, and Fortune in American Cultural History," helped me to think more expansively about gender and money in the careers of Olivia and Russell Sage and to consider that perhaps I could deal with speculation and philanthropy as related rather than oppositional kinds of economic behaviors. Later, in April 2004, I took part in another conference at Rutgers, this one on "The Widow's Might," organized by Rudy Bell and Virginia Yans at the Rutgers Center on Historical Analysis, which provided new perspectives on widowhood and an opportunity for useful exchange with other scholars.

In addition, I have presented versions or parts of chapters at several scholarly meetings: the Organization of American Historians, the Social Science History Association, the Southern Association of American Studies, the British North American History Association, the Western Association of Women Historians (Asilomar, California), the Berkshire Conference of Women's Historians, and the Conference on New York State History. At these conferences and others, such as the Association for Research on Nonprofit Organizations and Voluntary Action (ARNOVA) and Interdisciplinary Nineteenth-Century Studies (INCS), the discussion and questions from fellow panelists, respondents, and audiences were invaluable. I especially want to thank Mary Ann Dzuback, Peter Dobkin Hall, Robert Lynn, Glenna Matthews, David H. Smith, Steven Wheatley, and Susan Yohn for their comments.

Several historians were especially generous with their time. I am deeply grateful to Eileen Boris, David Hammack, Elisabeth Israels Perry, Judith Sealander, and Marjorie Spruill, all of whom read and commented extensively on sections of this book. I also owe a debt of gratitude to the following historians who took time out from their own work to read drafts of chapters and give me their comments: Mary Blanchard, Priscilla Clemens, Cita Cook, Candace Falk, Donna Gabaccia, Caroline Gebhard, Joanne Goodwyn, Nancy Hewitt, Kristin Hoganson, Jane Hunter, Maury Klein, Jackson Lears, Kriste Lindenmeyer, Sonya Michel, Robyn Muncy, Alexandra Nickliss, Susan Reverby, Gretchen Ritter, Nancy Robertson, Lana Ruegamer, Scott Sandage, Anne Firor Scott, Kathryn Kish Sklar, Nancy Slack, James Allen Smith, Melissa Smith, Maren Stein, and Andrea Walton.

This book has been greatly improved by the generosity of my colleagues in history, English, and women's studies at Auburn University. Paula Backscheider offered the encouragement of an accomplished and prize-winning biographer as well as her assurance that this biography was worth writing. She read the manuscript in its entirety. Others who read and commented on chapters or parts of chapters were Lindy Biggs, Betsy Bishop, Donna Bohanon, Mary Cameron, Alicia Carroll, Robin Fabel, Jacqueline Foertsch, Marie Francois, Larry Gerber, Margaret Kouidis, Virginia O'Leary, Susan Roberson, Joyce Rothschild, and Hilary Wyss.

Tom Bourke, reference librarian at the New York Public Library, came out of semi-retirement to provide numerous references on Olivia Sage from the *New York Sun* "morgue" (through January 1950). My thanks to Jo Freeman, who generously (and unasked) put me in touch with this wonderful source. Independent scholar Lygia Ionnitiu illuminated the surprising history of E. Lilian Todd and offered her specialized knowledge in the field of aviation history, and Carroll F. Gray shared images of E. Lilian Todd. Bonnie Baker put me up at her home in Carlisle, Pennsylvania, during my research visit there, and James McGrath Morris encouraged me on the way to publication while sharing his own experiences of the triumphs and disappointments of authorship. At Indiana University, Larry Friedman and co-editor Mark McGarvie invited me to include a chapter on Olivia in their anthology *Charity, Philanthropy, and Civility in American History* (Cambridge, 2003).

Olivia and Russell Sage had no children, but several descendants of Olivia's brother Joseph Jermain Slocum provided access to family letters dating from the 1830s to the 1860s. The path that led me to the letters was circuitous: the obituary of Olivia's grandnephew Myles Standish Slocum (1888–1956) of Pasadena, California, described him as a bibliophile who left a collection of valuable books to Scripps College. I contacted the Scripps College librarian, Judy Harvey Sahak, who put me in touch with his descendant, Mrs. Florence Slocum Wilson, a greatniece of Olivia Sage. Her sister, the late Carolyn O. Slocum, a scientist, had transcribed and numbered many of the family letters that I read in researching this book. Mrs. Slocum Wilson gave me all the help and encouragement that she could and put me up during my two visits to her Pasadena home so that I could look at the letters and other material.

Another family member helped me greatly with this project. Mrs. Eileen Gillespie Slocum, the widow of John Jermain Slocum (greatnephew of Mrs. Sage), offered me hospitality during my two visits to Newport, Rhode Island and allowed me to read family correspondence from the 1830s to Olivia's marriage in 1869.[3] I am grateful also to John J. Slocum, Jr., of Newport and his wife Diana Roberts, to Beryl S. Powell, and to Marguerite S. Quinn, all of whom encouraged me in this project and welcomed me generously into their homes.

Sadly, Mrs. Florence Slocum Wilson died in March 2001 before this book was completed. Her daughter Lynn Rivard of Palm Springs, California, has continued her mother's enthusiasm for Olivia's story and her warm encouragement for its author.

I am enormously grateful to my undergraduate and graduate students for their enthusiasm about the transformative power of women's and gender history. A few also helped with mundane but necessary tasks. Early on, graduate student researchers Katrina Van Tassel, Kim Cantrell, and Michael Donahue found me many newspaper references on Sage. Later, Steve Murray and Rod Steward did careful editorial work on two chapters. For the most part, though, the credit and the blame for this book are mine alone.

Acknowledgments

I have depended on the love and support of family and friends. Malcolm has been patient and affirming throughout the long process of research and writing. Louise Katainen, Fran Cronenberg, Sara Hudson, and Roberta Jackel have sustained me with their friendship. Jo-Ann Chasnow reminds me of battles still to be fought and somehow keeps laughing through it all.

Finally, support for this work came from the Indiana University Center on Philanthropy. I am deeply grateful to its director, Dwight Burlingame, and to Eugene Tempel for the luxury of a semester's leave for writing and for their interest and encouragement. At Indiana University Press, editor Bob Sloan was unfailingly helpful, patient, and good-humored, as were editors Marilyn Grobschmidt and Jane Quinet. Kate Babbitt was a superb copyeditor and a wise reader.

Multimillionaires attract a lot of correspondence. Olivia Sage received so many begging letters that by 1912 thousands of them had accumulated in the closets of the Charities Building, the New York headquarters of the Charity Organization Society. In June of that year a COS official wrote to Robert de Forest (who was both Sage's attorney and a COS president), informing him that the letters had to be removed and asking what to do with them. "If they are to be preserved, they must, I think, be removed to a warehouse for storage," he warned. "Unless there is some possibility of their being studied or referred to in future they might I think, now, be destroyed. If . . . they may be put to some use in the future, of course they should be carefully preserved."[1] De Forest's reply has not survived, but we know that a portion of Olivia's papers were kept and that some remained after her death, at the Russell Sage Foundation in New York City in the building at Lexington and East Twenty-Second Street, built in memory of her husband.

They were still at the foundation in the 1960s, when Irvin G. Wyllie used them to write his biographical sketch of Olivia Sage for *Notable American Women* (1971). He described them as "unorganized and largely unused."[2] None of Olivia's papers seem to have been used to write the two-volume official history of the Russell Sage Foundation, published in 1947. Around thirty years later, Barry D. Karl and Stanley Katz examined the Russell Sage Foundation papers in the course of their research on the history of foundations. Dr. Karl remembers "a tightly packed four-drawer file cabinet . . . that was clearly the documentation left over from the two-volume fifty-year history."[3] He recalls that he and his colleague were not shown any of Mrs. Sage's papers during that visit and that they assumed at the time that most of her papers had already been "cleaned out."[4] Nevertheless, about 5,000 of Olivia Sage's letters were spared and moved to the Rockefeller Archive Center in Sleepy Hollow, New York, in 1985, along with the bulk of the foundation's papers. The original Russell Sage Foundation building had been sold after the retirement of director Shelby Harrison in 1947, and the foundation eventually moved in 1982 into the seven-story building at 112 East Sixty-Fourth Street in New York that was designed by architect Philip Johnson, which it still occupies.[5]

A sizeable collection of Olivia Sage's letters thus ended up at the Rockefeller Archive Center, where in the late 1980s they were processed by Melissa Smith and James Allen Smith. The Russell Sage Foundation Records have been organized into nine series. Three of these cover the foundation's history from 1906 to 1947: Mrs. Russell Sage's personal papers, 1886–1918; the corporate history of the foundation, 1906–1979; and early office files, 1908–1949.[6]

Olivia Sage's papers, comprising Series 1 and 10 of the Russell Sage Foundation Records, are mainly from the last years of a 90-year life, and many are begging or fund-raising letters. The petitioners who wrote them give a very full discussion of the projects contemplated and the good expected to flow from whatever it was the writer was advocating. They are a window into a hundred thousand benevolent and harebrained schemes that came before Olivia Sage in the years between 1906 and 1918. Letters to her greatly outnumber letters from her, and this presents a problem for the researcher. Like the mysterious woman painted by Velasquez in *The Rokeby Venus,* she is turned away, her face visible only as a reflection in a mirror, and even then distorted and shadowed.[7] Can we tell what a person is like by the way others address her? Work by scholars in various fields has encouraged me to think that we can. Shared values are reflected, and allusions, fragments, and memories provide many clues. In addition, many of the envelopes have notations written in her hand or by a secretary, or in some cases by Robert de Forest or her brother, Joseph Jermain Slocum.[8]

As is often the case with the papers of a married woman, Olivia Sage's papers at the Rockefeller Archive Center are not in a collection under her own name but in the Russell Sage Foundation Records, named for the foundation she set up, which in turn she named for her husband. At the New York State Library in Albany, I found one of the most revealing of her letters purely by chance among her husband's correspondence with New York governor Edwin Denison Morgan.[9]

Luckily some of Olivia Sage's papers came down to us by another route and at her own direction. Between 1912 and her death in November 1918, Olivia had the administrative assistance of E. Lilian Todd, who dealt with all the correspondence on a daily basis, working out of an office at the philanthropist's Fifth Avenue home. In June 1913, Olivia Sage ordered Todd to send all the papers "in the office" to the Emma Willard School in Troy, New York, for safekeeping. (The school was previously the Troy Female Seminary, which Olivia had attended in 1846–1847.[10]) Todd duly informed Eliza Kellas, principal of the school, "I am sending everything, with the idea that only one paper might possibly be used, yet that one might be a lost link in some series." She explained that she intended to include "some of the material obtained during the collecting of data for the book 'Emma Willard and Her Pupils,'" which might be of use were an attempt to be made in the future "to bring the book up to date in another volume years from now."[11]

Lilian was as good as her word, and as a consequence the second major collection of Olivia Sage papers is the recently organized Margaret Olivia Slocum Sage Collection at the Emma Willard School in Troy, New York. This includes the important correspondence from 1912 to 1918 between E. Lilian Todd and Eliza Kellas which sheds new light on Olivia Sage's last years and on her philanthropy. When I worked in the Emma Willard School archives I was also shown two boxes containing dozens of small envelopes packed into a large stationary box and hundreds more in a large square box. The latter contains not only Emma Willard Association material but a variety of incoming letters both to Olivia and Russell Sage from the period 1890 to about 1901. There are advertisements for book clubs, invitations to attend weddings and to lay cornerstones; there are letters from strangers begging for money, seeking a job reference, or demanding a place for a daughter at the Emma Willard School. There are dozens of letters relating to the Emma Willard Association from the 1890s and dozens more prompted by the huge alumnae survey that resulted in the publication of *Emma Willard and Her Pupils, or Fifty Years of Troy Female Seminary, 1822–1872* (1898). All these papers have been expertly inventoried by Susan L. Malbin, archivist at Emma Willard School, and her "Finding Aid to the Eliza Kellas Collection" (May 1996), and "Finding Aid to the Margaret Olivia Slocum Sage Collection" (December 1996) are necessary guides for the researcher.

If Olivia deserves belated recognition for taking steps to preserve her papers, Eliza Kellas deserves credit for keeping them. She did so over the protest of the modest E. Lilian Todd, who in 1918 begged Kellas not to file her letters or to mention her (Lilian) by name, but to write "a concise history" of the Russell Sage College. "I am more than content to be referred to as just the 'secretary,' or 'Secretary to Mrs. Sage.'"[12]

I have found some correspondence of Olivia Sage scattered in other archives, much of it related to fund-raising. An exception is her correspondence with Richard Pratt of the Carlisle Indian School in the Richard Henry Pratt Papers in the Beinecke Library at Yale, which is valuable since so few of Olivia's letters have survived from the period of her marriage. I have also looked at her correspondence with Helen Gould, daughter of Jay Gould, at the New-York Historical Society, and at Helen Gould's papers at Lyndhurst, Irvington-on-the-Hudson. A few letters to Olivia Sage also remain in the Community Service Society Archives at Columbia University.[13]

Russell Sage still lacks a biographer. A brief use of some of the financier's papers in the New York State Archives and the Huntington Library in San Marino, California, convinced me that there will be a great deal more to learn from those collections. At the New York State Archives of the New York State Library in Albany, I used the four-page handwritten autobiographical account written by Russell Sage for Charles P. Lanman, who was compiling a biographical dictionary of members of Congress. Written in a small, neat, sloping hand (Paul Sarnoff called it a "feminine hand"), the account is important and revealing.

Material about the New York City Charity Organization Society and letters and papers of Robert de Forest are in the Community Service Society Collection, Rare Book and Manuscript Library, Columbia University, as is the unpublished biography of John M. Glenn by Shelby Harrison. The Bolling Memorial Medical Library at St. Luke's-Roosevelt Hospital in New York contains the records of the New-York Woman's Hospital. Two casebooks there cover the periods 1854–1871 and 1855–1862. There are also bound printed *Reports of the Woman's Hospital of the State of New York, 1856–1869*. Letters documenting Olivia Sage's connection with the Woman's Hospital are also in Russell Sage Foundation Records, Series 10, Box 97, Folders 978–982.

Finally, transcribed family letters from the 1830s to Olivia's marriage in 1869 remain in the possession of family members, who were kind enough to let me read them.

Mrs. Russell Sage

Introduction

In the summer of 1910, Olivia Sage, the 82-year-old widow of financier Russell Sage, known to the world as Mrs. Russell Sage, set off for the airfield at Mineola on New York's Long Island to witness the first flight of an airplane designed by a woman, a plane built with her sponsorship. Its inventor E. Lilian Todd had attracted national attention at the 1906 meeting of the Aero Club of American with a model bi-plane and an airship of her own design. Olivia subsequently invested $7,000 in the project, and the plane was built by Witteman Brothers of Staten Island. This was an extremely early plane and the only one designed and built by a woman without a male partner. The *Woman's Home Companion* celebrated the achievement in November 1909 with an article by Todd, "How I Built My Aeroplane."[1]

The Mineola Flying Field was an easy drive from Lawrence on the south shore of Long Island, where Olivia Sage spent her summers at the house she called Cedar Croft, but the afternoon was windy, and she waited several hours to see the plane take off. Captain Thomas S. Baldwin, described as a "veteran aviator," was at the controls. As she watched, she remarked that she saw "no reason why women should not fly as well as men (see fig. I.1)."[2]

It was typical of Olivia Sage[3] to want to fund a woman's "first." Ever since 1906, when her husband had left her a fortune estimated at over $75 million (equivalent to about $1.53 billion in today's money), she had been busy spending the money, and a significant portion of it went

FIGURE I.1. E. Lilian Todd in her biplane, around 1910. Library of Congress.

to open new opportunities for women. By the time she died in November 1918, she had disbursed about $45 million ($917 million in 2003 dollars).[4]

The best-known philanthropists of the Gilded Age and Progressive era, Andrew Carnegie and John D. Rockefeller, Sr., gave on an even grander scale than Sage. Carnegie gave $350 million to his philanthropic foundations, and John D. Rockefeller, Sr., and his son and namesake donated around $600 million.[5] But in these same years, the daughters, wives, and widows of America's railroad barons and industrialists (at least, a few of them), were also giving away tens of millions of dollars accumulated by their male relatives in the free-for-all of Gilded Age capitalism.[6] For wealthy women who had inherited or had married into fortunes, such as Olivia Sage, Nettie Fowler McCormick (widow of Cyrus McCormick), Helen Gould (daughter of Jay Gould), Grace Dodge, or Phoebe Apperson Hearst, philanthropy opened a space for activism, institution-building, and reform.[7]

We should add women philanthropists such as Olivia Sage to the categories of activist nineteenth-century women: their roles in founding institutions and expanding state capacity have remained elusive, in part because their self-representation was often misleading or deliberately self-effacing, but also because they used different institutional settings and social spaces. Nevertheless, their giving was self-actualizing because each gift designated a cause and fulfilled an intention. Female philanthropists who launched major social and educational institutions carried on their public work from their own homes or from voluntary associations; their male counterparts had additional venues and sources of authority such as law or corporate offices, government bureaus, or research universities.[8]

The philanthropy of Olivia Sage took place in a culture ill at ease with the relation between women and money. As today, women owned far less real and personal property than men. Lee Soltow calculated that in 1860, women and children together constituted only about 5.6 percent of wealth holders and owned only 7.2 percent of all wealth. Married women's property rights were established only after 1848, and then only state by state.[9] Not coincidentally, women's powerlessness stemmed historically in part from their poverty relative to men. Women who made money or who enjoyed investment or speculation risked being considered unnatural, like New York financier Hetty Green (1834–1916), who turned an inherited nest egg of several million into 100 million and was portrayed by her biographer as an unnatural mother, deformed in body and mind by an obsession with money-making.[10]

But if it was unfeminine to make money or to speculate, the same could not be said of giving it away. A woman could always give that little bit—"the widow's mite," or she could give of herself, donating hours of volunteer labor. If charity was a requirement for all Christian people and a demonstration of stewardship, giving seemed peculiarly appropriate for women. To give money away, to sacrifice self or substance, was the essence of Christian womanliness.[11] A female philanthropist confirmed Victorian gender expectations. She was authorized to engage in this one economic activity at least: giving it away. And paradoxically she controlled her money at the moment of disbursing it. But if contemporaries accorded female philanthropists such as Olivia Sage and Helen Gould celebrity status, they did not view them as powerful figures like men of wealth. It was the scale of their giving that provoked comment, not the giving itself. In a gender system where women could still represent themselves as naturally benevolent, charitable good works appeared as no more than a timeless attribute of womanhood, and female philanthropists were good women, only more so.[12]

Serious work on philanthropic elites by a feminist scholars begins with Kathleen McCarthy's *Noblesse Oblige* (1982), a study of charitable institution-building by men and women in Chicago, and continues with her subsequent work on women and philanthropy. In *Women's Culture: American Philanthropy and Art* (1991), McCarthy explores women philanthropists' control over the gifts and briefly discusses Olivia Sage's donations to the Metropolitan Museum of Art.[13] But no biography of Sage existed, and apart from a useful biographical sketch by Irvin G. Wyllie in *Notable American Women* (1971), the early twentieth century's major female philanthropist was unknown. And if we lacked a full-length study of this important figure, we had what was worse, a caricature, the lively but untrustworthy portrait of Olivia that appears in the biography of her husband, *Russell Sage, the Money King* (1965), by New York broker Paul Sarnoff. The author knew and understood Wall Street, but his book is a mixture of fact, gossip, and innuendo.[14] Much more useful was the brief but intriguing glimpse of the relationship between Olivia and Helen Gould, Jay Gould's daughter and a major philanthropist in her own right, in *The Life and Legend of Jay Gould* (1986), a sympathetic and careful revisionist study of Russell Sage's closest business ally by business historian Maury Klein.[15]

Olivia Sage appears again (as Mrs. Russell Sage) in a work of women's history in the context of a sophisticated discussion of the class and generational politics of the New York suffrage movement told from the perspective of a historian concerned with labor reform and the rights of working women. To Ellen Carol DuBois, biographer of labor feminist Harriot Stanton Blatch, both the failure of labor radicalism in New York and the conservative turn in the suffrage movement around 1910 were associated with the leaders' appeal to women of wealth. Seen through the lens of cross-class alliances with working women, elite women appear in an uncomfortable light, even when they in fact supported women's educational achievement and citizenship, as Sage did.[16]

But if they are peripheral or worse in some feminist narratives, the careers of wealthy activist women are instructive in others. If American white women's history has been written as a grand narrative of emancipation, as Joan Scott suggests, wealthy women, too, struggled to be heard. With access to power, they were often in a position to critique male privilege, as Suzanne Lebsock has noted, and they were consequently able to articulate demands more usually associated with middle-class reformers—demands for the vote, for a voice, for educational equality, and for control over their own resources.[17]

Wealthy women were central to the history of nineteenth-century voluntary associations. In urban places of the Northeast and Midwest, women's voluntary associations were vehicles for reform and betterment in their communities, and although they often went under the umbrella term "charity" or "benevolence," there was more to "benevolence" than met the eye: voluntarism enabled activists to construct communities and pursue political and reform goals. The charitable and reform work of nineteenth-century women was politics and state-building. It was women's public work, driven both by ambition and by altruism. In this way a generation of scholars reinterpreted postbellum temperance and moral reform movements as a "quest for power and liberty" (in Ruth Bordin's memorable phrase), as critical to the self-consciousness of their standard-bearers as to the material well-being of their clients.[18]

Through it all, the class identity of these activists remained somewhat vague. Their heavy involvement in civic work suggested independent incomes and households run in their absence by servants—it suggested women of privilege, but historians generally (and generously) labeled them "middle class" rather than elite or wealthy, reflecting what Bonnie G. Smith called an "ambivalence about heroines" characteristic of an earlier phase of feminist historical inquiry.[19]

This reluctance to make elites the subject of women's history has receded.[20] Feminist historians interested in the politics of difference are revisiting the involvement of wealthy women in suffrage, municipal reform, and other social and political movements.[21] Olivia's story is part of this ongoing scholarly reassessment, and her career, which includes thirty years of voluntary and reform activity, takes on significance for American women's history, even apart from the philanthropy of her old age.[22] Like the enigmatic and paradoxical Catharine Beecher, who built a career around the ideology of domesticity, or like Emma Willard, who leveraged brainy intellectualism, feminine good looks, and fearlessness into an educational experiment of national significance, Olivia Sage conformed to many of the gender expectations of her time while subverting others. She was a formidably respectable as well as a devoutly religious woman who could be both eccentric and outspoken. Far from being the pathetic "spinster" figure of Sarnoff's misogynist imagination, she was active and inquiring. Though she received her education long before the postbellum expansion of women's higher education, she continued to display a keen interest in education into her old age, so that the author of a begging letter to her on behalf of women law students at NYU signed herself "Yours with admiration, A fellow-student."[23]

Philanthropy took up only the last twelve or so years of a 90-year life, but its roots lie much earlier. The identity of philanthropist emerged gradually, long before she had money to spend, a convergence of good intentions, a belief in Christian stewardship, feminist discontent, and an ambitious, restless temperament spurred on by a sense of social superiority.

I have divided the narrative into three life stages. In the first, "A Liminal Place" (1828–1869), Olivia obtained an education of privilege, only to witness her father's business failures and the virtual breakup of her parents' marriage. For several years she negotiated the female labor market and the marriage market while occupying the "liminal place" of the governess. In the second, "Becoming Mrs. Russell Sage" (1869 to 1906), she played the part of a benevolent and socially prominent matron, engaging in several voluntary associations and positioning herself in relation to several communities of women and against the Other (women of color, the undeserving, unbelievers, and the New Woman). As she grew older, though still without resources of her own, she represented herself as a moral authority, a person authorized to reform others and thus to define what others really needed, the emblematic "benevolent interventionist" of Gilded Age and Progressive-era reform. The third stage (1906–1918) begins with the transformation of widowhood. "I am nearly eighty years old and I feel as though I were just beginning to live!" Olivia declared as she set up the general-purpose Russell Sage Foundation with $10 million.[24] From then until her death at the age of ninety, Olivia used the socially ascribed role of widow to carry on an astounding philanthropy. Through her $10 million donation to the Russell Sage Foundation (and another $1.6 million in her will), Sage philanthropy contributed to the development of welfare thought, created the modern profession of social work, and funded Progressive reform in housing, public health, child welfare, urban and regional planning, and industrial relations.

Chapters 1 and 2 recount Olivia's early life and education in upstate New York in the 1830s and 1840s, a time of religious upheaval and economic boom and bust that is well known to historians of American revivalism and the market revolution. She was exposed to the self-conscious (and self-serving) evangelical feminism of Troy Female Seminary and its charismatic founder and principal, Emma Willard.[25] But the elitism fostered at Troy was dealt a blow by her father's bankruptcy, a setback that forced her into paid employment as a teacher, an emotionally fulfilling but low-paid and unstable position. Issues of female wage-earning and self-help are vividly illuminated for us in newly discovered family correspondence for these years (1836 to 1869), and so is her experience of family disintegration (chapters 3 and 4). As an educated daughter with a sense of vocation but with few prospects in the job market or temptations in the marriage market, Olivia experienced two decades of indecision and powerlessness that Victorian culture tended to medicalize but that seems to have resulted from unresolved conflicts relating to her work as a teacher and governess and her feelings that she was powerless to help her gifted but unreliable father or her abandoned mother. Marriage offered an escape, and when socially prominent Albany connections brought her together with the recently widowed multimillionaire financier and railroad builder Russell Sage, she agreed to marry him, becoming at the age of forty-one the second wife of one of the most powerful of the era's "robber barons." By marrying a wealthy older widower, though an old adversary of her father, she opted for material comfort and moved onto a different stage.

In New York City as Mrs. Russell Sage, she constructed a public role as a benevolent Christian woman with work to do in the public sphere. This was despite the fact that she derived her social standing solely from her relationship to Russell Sage, financial partner to the generally despised railroad baron Jay Gould.

Several thematic chapters explore aspects of Olivia's life in these middle years as a socially prominent New York matron. Without a discretionary income of her own, Olivia slid easily into the role of moral reformer. She spoke revealingly of her own circumstances, using her situation to build general principles about what women's lives were and should be: her politics came from her family drama.[26] For example, she seized on the movement for "Indian reform," the goal of remaking Indian work and family roles, because her own history had been marred by her father's unsuccessful business career. Contemplating a remade Indian family structure, she voiced her disapproval of the system that placed white women like herself in economic dependence on men, although she viewed such dependence as proper and necessary for peoples in a less-developed state of civilization (chapter 5). In the 1870s, she joined a group of elite "lady managers" at the New-York Woman's Hospital, the hospital associated with J. Marion Sims. Energized by her new position of authority, she boldly sided with the lady managers in disputes with the hospital's male governors and physicians over space and responsibilities, using a rhetoric of gender separatism (chapter 6).

In the 1890s, she helped create another community of women, that of "educated women," presiding over the Emma Willard Association, an alumnae association for Troy Female Seminary (chapter 7). Speaking as a disciple of Willard, Olivia became an advocate for political and economic rights for women of her class, including woman suffrage. Chapter 8 examines her conversion to the suffrage cause and explores the underexamined issue of elite suffragism and suffrage funding. Chapter 9 vividly illustrates how white elite women made claims rooted in racial, gender, and class identities. It shows how Olivia linked the cause of "women's advancement" to the nation and how these claims were articulated around a racialized nationalism generated by the war with Spain and overseas expansion.

Perhaps because she had no children, Olivia cultivated friendships in which she was either a teacher or a mentor to much younger women. Such was her relationship with Helen Gould (1870–1936), daughter of Jay Gould. By the 1890s, the young woman and her mentor were both involved in philanthropy, with Olivia advising Helen how to spend her (Helen's) money. In this way both women became celebrities, and inevitably the press sought out Olivia's opinion on a range of issues. She spoke on the topic of the home (a conventional feminine arena) as a confident household manager, addressing readers of her sex who were less confident and less accomplished.

In these years of married life (1869–1906) Olivia consistently represented herself as a philanthropist, though she had little money to spend. But once she inherited her husband's fortune, she brilliantly used the possibilities of widowhood, acting in the name of an always present but forever departed and lamented spouse and making large donations to institutions of all kinds in her late husband's name (chapter 10).[27]

At the same time, her impulse to spend was impeded by the changed meanings of charity associated with the Charity Organization Society (COS) and with early-twentieth-century transformations of the political economy. The traditional practice of charity involved an interaction between unequals, a gift that seemed to suspend inequality, if only momentarily, while affirming the rightness of the hierarchy that underlay it.[28] But new meanings of independence (which involved stigmatizing "dependence") troubled and complicated the charitable relation and put charitable elites on the defensive, while modernizers promoted "scientific charity" and large-scale plans for human betterment.[29]

In this context, charitable elites devised foundations as a way to put private funds to public use while insulating the giver from direct or individual appeals.[30] Such was the $10 million Russell Sage Foundation "for the improvement of social and living conditions in the United States," Olivia's most ambitious philanthropic gift and a significant funder of social science and reform in the Progressive era and after. Most accounts attribute the foundation primarily to Robert Weeks de Forest, a noted housing and charity reformer and former advisor to Russell Sage. Surviving correspondence confirms his active work in shaping the foundation; her role has to be inferred. Did Olivia help shape the foundation or was she simply its funder? What was the relationship between these two principals? Chapter 11 revisits these questions.

The remaining chapters use two major bodies of correspondence to shed light on this most active period in Olivia's philanthropy. One includes the letters in the Russell Sage Foundation Records that document her thousands of donations to organizations and causes, ranging from woman suffrage and animal protection societies to major universities. The second is newly discovered correspondence between E. Lilian Todd, the engineer-inventor whose story began this chapter and who became Sage's private secretary, and educator Eliza Kellas, principal of the Emma Willard School. Two chapters explore Olivia's gifts to higher education as she weighed the claims of the women's colleges against those of the male-only universities and the coeducational institutions (chapter 12). "'Nothing more for men's colleges'" (chapter 13) examines the politics of influence in the founding of Russell Sage College, a vocational college for women. "'Splendid donation'" (chapter 14) surveys Olivia's donations to charitable and benevolent organizations, a body of giving that invites some theorizing about the position of the giver and the recipient of charity. Chapter 15, "'Send what Miss Todd thinks best,'" reveals Olivia in old age, alternately feisty and depressed, mentally alert but vulnerable to advisors and hampered by deafness.

Anthropologists of the gift argue that possessions kept are more secure when others are relinquished as gifts and that philanthropy reconstitutes relationships of class while seeming to erase them.[31] What Olivia held on to might have been as important as what she gave away. Could I do justice to a feminism that rested on racial and class exclusions? How to explain her spending decisions? She refused the name "Sage Foundation," insisting on "Russell Sage Foundation," even though her late husband's miserliness was legendary and the foundation was her gift, not his, causing charity expert Louisa Lee Schuyler to comment to Robert de Forest, "You cannot but admire her loyalty to her husband and her desire to suppress herself."[32] At times Olivia's disappearance was complete. Announcing a gift of $15,000 from Mrs. Russell Sage to launch an organization of Audubon Junior Clubs, a press release attributed the gift to "*The wife of* the noted philanthropist" (emphasis added).[33] Could I follow up the hunch that, for a woman like Olivia, spending was a form of speaking?

Olivia could not suppress herself completely. Spending $45 million dollars inevitably left traces in many (too many) archives; decades of voluntary activities left their traces too. They enabled me to piece together her life from letters, speeches, and scattered papers. The fund-raising correspondence generated by her great philanthropy has been a major, though not the only, source for this biography.

And if (as in this case) Olivia sometimes modestly declined to use her own name, so that the public knew her only as "Mrs. Russell Sage," she nevertheless harnessed her husband's money to her own purposes. (That, at least, was her intention: the outcomes were sometimes different and unexpected.) The record reveals a subtle form of resistance and activism that was different qualitatively from the more familiar struggles of middle-class suffragists and labor activists. In her only published writing, the essay "Opportunities and Responsibilities of Leisured Women" (1905), Olivia ambitiously redefined the relationship of women of her class to the state and society. The editor of the *North American Review*, where it appeared, added her married name, "Mrs. Russell Sage," but she signed the essay "M. Olivia Sage."[34] Like their middle-class sisters in the settlement houses, elite women such as Sage were at work on the reconstruction of identities: philanthropists, too, had their own "subjective necessities," and they sometimes made their money speak critically of male power.[35]

Part I

A Liminal Place
1828–1869

One

Slocums, Jermains, Piersons—and a Sage

Among the hundreds of purchases Olivia Sage made when she inherited the fortune of her financier husband in 1906 was an investment in image and self-representation that has gone unnoticed by scholars. Along with the donations to schools and hospitals, missions and colleges, she commissioned a family history, the best that money could buy and one befitting a person who was about to become a benefactor of national stature. She employed Henry Whittemore of Brooklyn, "Genealogist and Compiler of Family and Other Histories," and Mary F. Tillinghast, a New York artist (one of many women artists to enjoy her patronage), and dispatched them to England and France to research the genealogy of her family and that of her late husband. Their labors resulted in a large illustrated volume bound in pale green leather with gold figuring. *History of the Sage and Slocum Families of England and America, Including the Allied Families of Montague, Wanton, Brown, Josselyn, Standish, Doty, Carver, Jermain or Germain, Pierson, Howell* (1908), features the liberty-loving Myles Standish, the French-sounding Huguenot Jermain clan (or was it Jourdain?), the pious Josselyns, and the learned Piersons. Having commissioned the research and writing of the book and paid for its publication, she wrote "A Gift of Mrs. Russell Sage" inside each one and distributed them widely to libraries and friends.[1]

Whittemore's *History* testifies as much to the anxieties as to the genuine aristocratic connections of its patron. True, family history had always interested her and she longed to know more about her ancestors, but equally strong was her desire to position herself in history and in her own time. As Mrs. Russell Sage, Olivia had suffered the insecurities of the outsider excluded from the homes of New York's elite because of her husband's eccentric and frugal ways. While Whittemore's compendium of genealogy, history, and myth contains many of the basic facts about her family and her life, it also attests to her ambition to unite Sage and Slocum families to the nation's racial past and to its destiny. For a biographer, it is both misleading and indispensable.[2]

Also revealing is a small autobiographical sketch which Olivia wrote when she was in her sixties for the alumnae directory of her school, *Emma Willard and Her Pupils, or Fifty Years of Troy Female Seminary, 1822–1872* (1898).[3] Written in the third person, it portrays her early years as idyllic yet claims a sense of serious purpose as well: "Through a happy childhood she grew, as a flower reaches to the light, full of the ecstacy of existence, but with a tender conscientiousness that foreshadowed an earnest womanhood." As proof, she recalled that as a young girl she had written in her diary this couplet announcing the theme of a philanthropic life:

> Count that day lost whose low, descending sun
> Views from thy hand no worthy action done.[4]

Biographies often give more coherence to a life than it had in the living, and so do autobiographies. They impose what one scholar has called "a false integration of the subject," unifying a life story marked by discontinuity and contradiction.[5] The account in *Emma Willard and Her Pupils* is an example of this. It depicts a benevolent life that is seamless and consistent—as continuous as the imperceptible opening of a flower, the simile disarming in its evocation of the natural. The biographer discovers that Sage's life was both more paradoxical and more interesting. We begin, as Olivia Sage would have liked us to begin, with the Puritans.

Puritans West

When the American Republic was barely a generation old, the westward migration of Puritan New Englanders resumed after decades of war and political upheaval. Among the families who left the villages of the Connecticut River Valley and the seaports of Long Island and migrated to western Massachusetts and upstate New York were the grandparents of Margaret Olivia Slocum and Russell Sage, whose intertwined lives are the subject of this book. William Brown Slocum, Olivia's paternal grandfather, was the youngest of four children born to a Quaker family in Middletown, Rhode Island, in 1770. He married Olivia Josselyn of Stockbridge, Massachusetts, in April 1793, and together they traveled 150 miles to Rensselaer County, New York. Slocum became a substantial farmer and dealer in livestock, rose in local and state politics, and was elected to the State Assembly in 1820. The flattering Whittemore states, "His contemporaries and co-workers were the Clintons, the Van Rensselaers, the Livingstons, and other men of that stamp, who laid the foundation of our commercial prosperity through wise legislation and public addresses."[6]

There is an oil portrait of Olivia Josselyn Slocum, Olivia Sage's paternal grandmother (see fig. 1.1). It shows a woman whose gaze is severe, her dress simple. Her grave inscription reads, "Hers was a piety deep in its veins, and holy and most benignant in its influence." A verse of her poetry, embroidered as a sampler by her twelve-year-old daughter Lucy Josselyn Slocum in 1824, attests to the triumph of evangelical culture after the American Revolution:

> Let piety, celestial guest
> With wisdom flourish in my breast;
> And virtue, lovely, heavenly, fair,
> Hold an unrivaled impress there.
> Let living faith and love divine,
> Possess this youthful heart of mine;
> That when my flesh returns to dust,
> My soul will triumph with the just.[7]

Olivia's maternal grandmother, Margaret Pierson of Bridgehampton, Long Island, was a granddaughter of Josiah Pierson and a great-granddaughter of Colonel Henry Pierson, who, Olivia liked to remind people, was a founder of New York's common school system. Margaret Pierson married John Jordan, a native of Westchester County, New York, in 1781. Jordan's parents had moved to Nova Scotia at the outbreak of the Revolution, but the son renounced both their Toryism and their name, serving in the Westchester militia and taking the name Jermain when he moved to Sag Harbor, then a major port on the eastern tip of Long Island.[8] In the War of 1812, John Jermain commanded the fort at Sag Harbor and was promoted to major. He prospered through investments in real estate and acquired interests in several ships. He had a large warehouse and dealt in hides and rum, part of the complicated network of Atlantic trading that brought enslaved Africans to the Americas, sugar

Olivia Josselyn Slocum
(Mrs. William Brown Slocum)

FIGURE 1.1. Olivia Josselyn Slocum, Olivia's paternal grandmother. She married William Brown Slocum in 1793. Henry Whittemore, *History of the Sage and Slocum Families of England and America* (New York: Published by Mrs. Russell Sage, 1908).

and rum to New England, and timber, furs, and fish to Europe. He also owned a fulling mill for finishing cloth and a store. It was said that his cellar could store a thousand barrels of rums (see fig. 1.2).[9]

The Jermains also owned slaves, their existence casually acknowledged in family stories told long afterward. Olivia later recounted how Rev. Lyman Beecher would arrive on horseback to visit her Grandmother Jermain's house. Pastor of the neighboring parish of East Hampton and the most influential Protestant of his generation, Beecher sometimes had more mundane things on his mind than theology. As Olivia recounted, after greeting the Jermains, "[H]e would say, 'Now bring me some oysters, for I am cold and hungry.' They were brought from the cellar by slaves, for then New York had not abolished slavery. Just imagine how jolly those feastings must have been."[10]

Later, her grandmother's Sag Harbor household, with its old-fashioned Sabbath observance, would provide Olivia with a model of a traditional Christian home. Her enthusiasm for the cause of Sabbath observance was rekindled when she recalled her grandmother's "old-time habit of putting away her work at six o'clock on Saturday and not resuming it until six o'clock Monday morning." And she nostalgically celebrated the "thrifty habits of the Pierson ancestors," which seemed to cast approval on her own frugal household arrangements.[11]

Margaret Pierson Jermain and Joseph Slocum

The Jermains had nine children, several of whom died in infancy. The oldest surviving son, Sylvanus Pierson Jermain, moved to Albany in 1802 at the age of eighteen and became a prominent banker and business-man. This was Olivia's Uncle Sylvanus. His sister Margaret Pierson Jermain, Olivia's mother and the youngest daughter, was born in 1804. She attended school in Sag Harbor, where her schoolbooks can still be seen at the public library donated by her daughter almost a century later and named by her the John Jermain Memorial Library.[12]

Olivia's father, Joseph Slocum, also one of nine children, was born in 1800 in Schaghticoke Township, Rensselaer County, New York, the fourth child of William Brown Slocum and Olivia Josselyn Slocum.[13] A Syracuse newspaper of 1897 recounts an American tale of restless ambition. Joseph Slocum left the farm where he had grown up "to strike out in life for himself and journeyed to Cincinnati and thence to New Orleans to seek his fortune." But he contracted yellow fever and returned home to Rensselaer county in broken health. When he recovered, he set out for the west again on horseback until he found "what he regarded as a most promising and remarkable business opening at Syracuse, by reason of the building of the Erie canal and the Onondaga salt springs," and there he settled.[14]

Joseph Slocum had arrived in a boomtown. The salt springs that had first attracted people to Syracuse had become the nucleus of a small town, and the Erie Canal spurred the town's growth even more. A boosterish city directory of 1852 proclaimed, "In less than a quarter of a century a city has sprung from a loathsome swamp!"[15]

The years between 1815 and the Civil War saw rapid economic devel-opment. First river steamboats, then canals, and finally the railroads

FIGURE 1.2. Major John Jermain, Olivia's maternal grandfather, a wealthy Sag Harbor merchant and land owner. Henry Whittemore, *History of the Sage and Slocum Families of England and America* (New York: Published by Mrs. Russell Sage, 1908).

linked regions and created regional and then national markets. The revolution in transportation hastened regional specialization, with the Northwest producing grain and flour, the Northeast providing manufactures and capital, and the South yielding staple crops of cotton, tobacco, rice, and sugar—with unfree labor.[16] Nowhere was the economic development more striking than in the northern tier of states, where the opening of the Erie Canal in October 1825 led to the rapid development of commerce along the whole corridor between western New York State and the port of New York. By 1836, the canal was transporting grain and produce from the western part of the state to the eastern seaboard. New York became the major port of the Northeast, a transshipment point for wheat and corn from the West and an entry point for imports. Tonnage from western states over the Erie Canal to New York was 54,219 in 1836. Ten years later, it had reached over 500,000 tons, and by 1860 almost 2 million.[17] East-west railroads further increased the flow of trade, especially after the Erie and Pennsylvania Canals linked the eastern seaboard with the Great Lakes and the Mississippi River system.[18] As commerce increased, so did migration into the Mohawk Valley and so also did the volume of land sales in upstate New York, Ohio, and Pennsylvania. Joseph and Margaret Slocum and their daughter Olivia were part of this migration.

Elisha Sage and Prudence Risley Sage

And so were Elisha and Prudence Risley Sage and their children. The Sage family had left Middletown, Connecticut, where Sages were a dime a dozen, and pushed West like hundreds of others.[19] By 1816 they had reached Oneida, New York. It was a year of freakish weather—three feet of snow fell in June, and ice lay thick on the crops. Elisha Sage and his pregnant wife Prudence Risley Sage made the journey with their six sons. By August, they were in Verona near Oneida, about 100 miles west of Albany, when Russell, their seventh son, was born.[20] The Sages never resumed their westward trek. Because the Erie Canal was not yet completed, good land could be bought for twenty-five cents an acre; soon it would fetch five dollars. Elisha Sage bought some acreage and began to farm. The place was called Durhamville. Nearby, the Erie Canal was being dug.[21]

Much later, when Russell Sage was about to enter Congress as a Whig, he was asked to supply an account of his career for a biographical dictionary of members. He obliged with four pages, written in a small, neat, sloping hand and with fluency of expression that reflects well on the self-educated farm boy. This is the only autobiographical account we have of the financier's early years.[22] Russell Sage described a rural childhood of hard work and ambition. He lived at home in Durhamville, attending what he described as "a common country school and part of the time only during the winter months, my parents being unable to give me any better advantages." At the age of twelve, he left the family farm

FIGURE 1.3. Margaret Pierson Jermain Slocum, Olivia's
mother, as a young married woman. Courtesy Florence
Slocum Wilson.

and made his way to Troy, where he worked as an errand boy and then
clerk in the grocery store of his oldest brother, Henry. He proudly recalled
his efforts to improve himself: "I availed myself of all the leisure I could
get, without neglect of duty, to read, to attend miscellaneous lectures
and debating societies until I was eighteen years of age."[23]

Thirty miles to the West, Joseph Slocum was in at the beginning of
the history of Syracuse. A section of the Erie Canal opened on October 8, 1823, and the first packet boat, the *Montezuma*, soon arrived at
Syracuse, and with it boom times.[24] For twenty years, the canal dominated the economy; the railroad would not arrive until 1840 and the
telegraph for another thirty years. Joseph Slocum acquired one of the

first lines of boats for use on the canal. With a warehouse and several stores on the south bank near the Warren Street bridge, he began to make money, acquiring businesses and land in and around Syracuse.[25]

Meanwhile, in the summer of 1823, he met and fell in love with Margaret Pierson Jermain, and they were married at Cambridge, New York, near the New York–Vermont border on May 4, 1825. Three and a half years later, on the eighth of September 1828, Margaret Olivia was born. The little girl must have taken a great dislike to her given name for she never used Margaret, always preferring Olivia. On June 24, 1833, her younger brother Joseph Jermain Slocum (who was called Jermain)[26] was born.[27] Margaret and Joseph Slocum would have no other children.

Letters written by Olivia and reminiscences of her by others suggest a high-spirited child. She was bright, vocal, and confident; her brother, more plodding, was a less-accomplished student than his sister. Yet the quick retort that made Olivia a good student in the schoolroom was labeled impertinence when it was relayed back to her mother. "Both my mother and father were very much afraid of spoiling me," she admitted.[28]

With her father often absent on business or on his travels, Olivia looked to her mother as the most important person in her life. In reminiscences told years later, she recounted several stories, all of them involving the mother-daughter relationship. She described her mother as "a perfect housekeeper" and a "perfect gentlewoman" who could also "read and write and spell beautifully" and who was "much given to hospitality, and gifted with a peculiarly sweet and generous nature."[29] She recounted tales about her apprenticeship in the household skills of sewing a shirt and knitting a stocking. "Mother would call me in from my play . . . and make me sit down to knit a stocking. I learned to turn the heel and narrow the foot, and I had to do six rows at a time before I could go. I had to finish that stocking. And I have now a piece of patch-work that I made when I was four years old."[30] Other stories told of childhood scrapes incurred thoughtlessly in an attempt to have fun or to avoid chores. In each of these, the mother is portrayed as the source of moral authority, "most kind and self-sacrificing" but "very strict," whose surveillance discovers and punishes childish misbehavior. "I must have been a very active child when I was small, and a great romp. I know I used to jump rope, and I remember climbing on a fence and falling and leaving about half my skirt there. It caught as I was getting down. . . . I can remember my mother threatening me with bed-ticking dresses . . . if I was not more careful with my clothes (see fig. 1.3)."[31]

Socialization included learning about the boundaries of family and community. She learned invidious distinctions of class and race: snobbery coexisted easily with piety, enforcement was pitiless, and there was no appeal. "I remember distinctly that one time my mother had told me that if I played with certain girls she would whip me," Olivia recalled. On one occasion she tried to escape this prohibition, squeezing through a hole in the fence to play with a forbidden girl. "I remember the girl coming for me I remember just how she looked, and I thought of what my mother had said, and that now she would punish me." Sure enough, a whipping followed. (It is fascinating to speculate about this "forbidden girl"—was it religion or perhaps skin color that made her an undesirable playmate?)[32]

Lessons about inclusion and exclusion taught at home were reinforced at church. Olivia grew to maturity in a church whose members defined themselves as sons and daughters of New England, as indeed many were.[33] But the congregation also contained "others." A meeting of the Presbyterian Society on July 9, 1832, discussed the reception of "strangers" and resolved that the trustees should "give instructions where the colored population should sit."[34] Later in life, when immense wealth gave Olivia the power to help anyone in any way, African American institutions and causes remained at the margins of her vast philanthropy, and she still felt that she was better than other people, set apart from them by education as well as by birth.

Like other Americans, Syracusans were joiners who improvised the necessary educational, charitable, and welfare associations in the absence of government provision.[35] The First Presbyterian Church of Syracuse began in December 1824 with twenty-six members—nine men and seventeen women. The building was completed in the summer of 1825 and dedicated in January 1826, and Rev. John Watson Adams was ordained and installed as pastor. By 1846 there were over 400 members.[36] Margaret Slocum joined in April 1840, "by examination." Olivia grew up in this church under the much-admired Rev. Adams. She was baptized on July 7, 1843, as she approached her fifteenth birthday, together with her ten-year-old brother.[37]

Antislavery caused an early schism among Syracuse Protestants, dividing both the Presbyterian and Methodist congregations. Opponents of slavery in Onondaga County assembled to form an antislavery society in 1835, and in 1837 abolitionist members of the First Presbyterian Church withdrew to form the First Congregational Church of Syracuse, which became a center of antislavery agitation in the region. Among the visiting speakers were William Lloyd Garrison, Stephen Douglas, Isaac F. Hooper, Samuel R. Ward, Horace Mann, and Susan B. Anthony.[38] Without its abolitionist members, First Presbyterian was a conservative church, opposed to reform enthusiasm. The exception was temperance enthusiasm, which swept across upstate New York with the Second Great Awakening. Joseph Slocum appears as one of the signers of an 1836 announcement of the formation of the County Temperance Society "on the principle of total abstinence." He had been raised a Quaker, but now he joined his wife's church. He seems to have shown little interest in organized religion, however.[39]

In 1837, when Olivia was nine, the prosperity of the region suddenly collapsed and her father's fortunes with it. Tonnage on the Erie Canal fell precipitously in one year and thousands of families were ruined.[40] Joseph Slocum's fate is recorded in a small notice in the *Onondaga Standard* of March 30, 1836, where one William Barker respectfully informs the public:

> that he [Barker] has taken the Ware House formerly occupied by Joseph Slocum in the village of Syracuse, where he will give his personal attention to the Storage and Forewarding of property committed to his care, and hopes by industry and perseverance, to merit a share of public patronage.[41]

After losing the warehouse and the commission business, Joseph Slocum tried to get back on his feet. A few months later, the same newspaper announced that he had "formed a connection with Mr. N. Jewett (late of New York) under the firm of 'Slocum and Jewett'" and that he intended to continue the dry goods, grocery, and crockery business at his same store.[42] Some accounts blamed Joseph's losses on his kindly nature. "Generous and sympathetic to a fault," Joseph Slocum endorsed notes for friends and when they went under he was forced to pay up, according to one version.[43] But an angry letter from Joseph Slocum's brother-in-law John H. Groesbeck (the husband of his older sister Mary) blames Slocum's own poor judgment. A well-to-do Cincinnati merchant, Groesbeck poured scorn on Slocum's harebrained schemes. He particularly condemned the latest business fiasco in which Slocum had purchased a quantity of wheat and shipped it to New Orleans, hoping to turn a profit. When it did not sell there, he sent it on to Antigua, and there the whole scheme collapsed. Groesbeck lost money in the affair—apparently it was not the first time he regretted lending money to Joseph Slocum. Nothing you try ever works, he told his brother-in-law, and no one is to blame but yourself. I owe you nothing, he concluded angrily. "I have never had a transaction with you that I did not loose [*sic*] by."[44]

A long, detailed sheriff's notice in the *Western State Gazette* dated August 6, 1841, tells what happened next. It states, "By virtue of several executions, to me directed and delivered, against Joseph Slocum, I have seized and taken the following pieces and parcels of land." There follows a detailed listing of Slocum property to be put up for auction—two town lots, farm lots, and other acreage altogether amounting to almost 500 acres.[45] When her father was ruined Olivia was just twelve.

One small businessman who was hardly affected by the panic of 1837 was Russell Sage. Aged twenty-one, Sage had already accumulated a sizable amount of money through a combination of careful management and imaginative entrepreneurship. When asked later in life about his boyhood, he responded, "I don't suppose I ever had any."

> It was nothing but work. After I went into my brother's store, I realized that I was lacking in education and I determined to spend a part of my small earnings in attending night school. Of the $4.00 wages I got on the first of every month, I paid $1.50 to my teacher. I soon learned book-keeping, and the more intricate problems in arithmetic. I managed to borrow some books on history and read all the papers I could get my hands on, I had no time for anything else.[46]

The self-educated Russell Sage was as frugal as he was industrious. Across the street were two vacant lots which he made up his mind to acquire. By saving every penny from his earnings and by some astute horse trading he saved $200 and purchased the lots. Russell Sage was on his way.[47] The grocery clerk continued to supplement his salary with some trading on the side. In 1835, at the age of nineteen, he took a boatload of horses from Albany to New York City, sold them on a commission basis, and returned, having cleared $700. He then went into the grocery business in Troy with his older brother Elisha (1812–1874), establishing the firm E. M. and R. Sage. Not only had Russell Sage survived the panic, but by the end of 1837 he had made enough money to buy out his brother's interest for $25,000.[48] Sage now joined forces with a wealthy wholesale commission merchant and banker, John Wilcox Bates, whose business involved shipping grain and horses and managing warehouses. Sage's interests now extended north along Lake Champlain and back toward New York City.[49]

In 1841, at the age of twenty-five, Russell Sage married Maria Winne, the daughter of Moses Winne, a wealthy Troy lumber inspector and alderman. She was just eighteen and had recently been a student at Troy Female Seminary. Sage was now ready to move into politics.[50] He was elected alderman in 1843 and reelected for the next seven successive years. He also became county treasurer in 1844 and held that office until 1851. In 1848, he headed the New York delegation to the Whig convention.[51]

"Endeavor to forget the bitterness of your disappointment"

Joseph Slocum had neither Sage's luck nor his business sense, but he was a gifted mechanic who by the 1840s had made a name for himself as an inventor and promoter of improved agricultural machinery and whose inventions drew interest at agricultural fairs. One fair held in 1845 featured his new tanning apparatus and a new kind of carriage wheel (with "two hubs, screwing together"). On display also was a model of a new cotton press, "the invention of Mr. Slocum of Syracuse, N.Y.," which could press ten or twenty bales at once. For the rest of his life, Slocum would try without success to turn his engineering and inventive talents to commercial use.[52]

For men like this, there was opportunity in Russia, a country embarking on a period of rapid economic development. Details are sketchy, but sometime after his losses of 1836–1837 Joseph Slocum made his first trip to Russia, returning with orders from the Russian government for plows and other kinds of agricultural implements. He made several subsequent visits to Russia and Switzerland and for a while took a job as a demonstrator with an American reaper company in Moscow.[53] One of his plows "was placed in the Russian National Museum as an object of great interest."[54] Some correspondence documents Joseph Slocum's preparations for a second trip to Russia in 1844. He applied to Washington for official sponsorship or a title, such as government advisor on agricultural improvement. He obtained letters of introduction from Daniel Webster to friends in Berlin and Paris.[55] He failed to get official Washington backing, however, and his brother-in-law J. H. Groesbeck refused even to try to exert some influence in the capital.[56] But Slocum was successful in obtaining a letter to Secretary of War William Marcy introducing him as "on his way to Russia, whither he has been invited under the patronage of the Emperor to aid with the advancement of agriculture," and obtaining an introduction to the U.S. chargé d'affaires in Stockholm, stating that "Mr. Slocum is on his way to Russia to establish a manufactory for Agricultural implements."[57]

Joseph Slocum set sail in the spring of 1846. He was in London by May, where he made inquiries about another moneymaking scheme, an ice-importing business. He would set up a store in London for importing "ice, butter, cheese, lard, Norway salmon, etc." from Russia or Sweden. The idea received little encouragement from his business partner, however. The latter warned, "I confess to you I regard this project in its present stage as a project, merely—an experiment—or a speculation."[58]

After a summer spent in St. Petersburg, Joseph Slocum returned via England. In the English North Country port of Hull in the fall of 1846, he received a letter from his Russian contact, a P. Chihaihef. "Some of your ingenious farm implements have been tried at the farm school with a good deal of success," Mr. Chihaihef informed him. "They will have some of them cast." He asked Slocum to send the design of the reaping machine so that his machinist could copy it.[59] But the rest of the letter was discouraging. Expect nothing more from me, Chihaihef warned Slocum, not even a letter of recommendation. His letters of introduction could not be returned, his machinery would be copied, and nothing else could be expected; in short, he advised Slocum to give up "and endeavor to forget the bitterness of your disappointment."[60] Subsequent contacts show Chihaihef writing to request plans for the improved reaping machine so that his own mechanic could copy it. Slocum then applied to the firm of Curtis, Rose and Co., Machinists of Geneva, New York, in November 1846 for a description and drawing of a Hussey's reaper and a machine for hulling rice and buckwheat, to send to "a friend in Russia."[61]

By the spring of 1847, Slocum was back in New Orleans, trying, as he explained in a letter to his long-suffering wife, "to buy something in this market that would make a profit in New York." He had developed a new kind of cotton press, but several weeks went by as he tried unsuccessfully to find a buyer.[62]

"They could no longer keep silent"

For white women of the antebellum period, who were distanced both from the market and from formal politics, voluntary associations and churches were sites for public activity outside the household.[63] Religious women such as Margaret Slocum played an important part in the life of the community. When her minister Rev. Adams called for women to nurse the sick, Margaret Slocum was one of those who volunteered. As a church historian explained, "There were no nurses except those trained by their own experience, and as the unhealthful conditions of the swampy village caused much sickness, . . . friends and neighbors, and even strangers, were called upon to assist in caring for the ailing."[64] The "History of the Ladies' Aid Society" included in the seventy-fifth anniversary history of the First Presbyterian Church (1899) claims far more than an auxiliary role for the churchwomen; indeed, its author, Mrs. Frances Wright Marlette, pointed out that the church owed its very existence to a meeting "brought about and attended only by women."[65] Subsequently, the account continues, "The Ladies Were the Managers and the Gentlemen were a Committee."[66] Historian Gerda Lerner's shrewd comment is appropriate here: the infrastructure is initially created and maintained through the voluntary association of women, "who then proceed to institution-building." The new institutions become businesses or public institutions, and "they are then headed by a man and led by corporate trustees, usually also men."

> Once institutions have reached that stage, they are noted as "existing" by historians. Thus, the community-sustaining initiative of women remains outside of history, while that of men is noticed and therefore validated.[67]

Churchwomen's contributions were financial as well as spiritual, this account insists, and Syracuse church histories record that their work created value.[68] There were sales of fancywork whose proceeds helped pay the minister's salary, fetes organized to raise money, and even a bazaar where ladies of the church dressed up in the costumes of other lands.[69] The histories name the institutions for charity, reform, and education founded and sustained by the voluntary labor of churchwomen: the Orphans Asylum, the Syracuse Home Association, the Temperance Society, the Rescue Mission. Syracuse had a Foreign Missionary Association and a Female Benevolent Society as early as 1828.[70] Women's fund-raising work even helped make possible the founding of new churches.[71]

Scholars have noticed an assertive tone in the recorded minutes of missionary societies, as if these societies provoked discussion of women's rights and wrongs in general, and not only those on foreign shores. Syracuse churchwomen seemed to find a voice as they gathered to discuss the plight of "heathen" women. As Mrs. Nathan Cobb explained in her report to the First Presbyterian Church,

> the eloquent, pathetic words of a returned missionary, describing the utter hopelessness of the long, living death, suffered by women of high caste in the Zenana homes of India, so stirred the hearts of certain women in our church, that they could no longer keep silent.[72]

Churchwoman Mrs. Nathan Cobb anticipated the carping of critics. "Do you suppose the getting together of a few women once a month is going to do anything for those millions of heathen women away off there? It is like dipping up the ocean by the spoonful," she wrote. But she dismissed such negative thoughts: "Thoreau once said, 'Cape Cod was anchored to the heavens by myriad little cables of beach grass,' and may we not say, our women's magnificent Missionary Boards are anchored to God's promises by myriad little cables of auxiliaries?"[73]

By calling the whole world their household, churchwomen enlarged their responsibilities in the public arena beyond the home and church and challenged the fiction of the home as a place apart from the market.[74] They gathered in the missionary society and the benevolent association to discuss the terrible burdens borne by heathen women of the east, a burden that resembled in some ways their own—for who did not know an American wife or mother bent under the despotism of a drunken or violent husband? Foreign mission work defined women's work as work for other women in faraway lands and assigned women a worldwide sphere of influence.[75]

Olivia was socialized into a gender system that assigned white women a "sphere of usefulness," a term that seemed to offer only vague limits on what an active female benevolence could imagine. The term was elastic enough to justify whatever women wanted to do, so long as they did it in the name of their religion, their sex, their communities, or the nation. For example, within the church, raising and handling money, organizing and running associations, and making useful and ornamental items for sale were all within women's sphere of usefulness. Moreover, the claim that women were moral superiors to men underlay these activities and authorized their action to control social behaviors that threatened their communities, especially drinking and vice.[76] This was the female world in which Olivia grew up, a society of busy, benevolent wives and matrons whose public work, in the words of historian Nancy Hewitt, "implicitly challenged the tenets of domesticity and submission" of the ideology of true womanhood.[77] Later, as Mrs. Russell Sage, she would donate millions of dollars to these female reform organizations at home and abroad.

"The best schools of that place and time"

Olivia's formal education began in Syracuse. Before this, she received her education at home, mainly from her mother, whom she described as "always a very earnest and purposeful woman."[78] Whittemore referred to Margaret Slocum as "a woman of fine intellectual gifts," and there is some evidence that as a young woman living in Sag Harbor, Olivia's mother was acquainted with Margaret Fuller.[79] Both Olivia's parents are described in several sources as learned, and the family valued the memory of their ancestors Abraham Pierson, first rector of Yale University, and educator Henry Pierson.[80]

In the handwritten response to the Troy Female Seminary alumnae survey of 1893, Olivia gave her own version of her early education. The brief account survives along with hundreds of others in the archives of the Emma Willard School, Troy, New York. It states, "Went to the best schools of that place and time, always loving study for its own sake and early mastering the elementary studies and arithmetic, studying Rhetoric, Astronomy, etc."[81] Her account was embellished for publication:

> She enjoyed in childhood and early youth the advantages of the best private schools of Syracuse, always loving study for its own sake, and readily mastering the elementary branches, so that at twelve years of age she found pleasure in Rhetoric, and pastime in the brilliant marvels of Astronomy.[82]

But "the best private schools in Syracuse" were the ones the boys went to, such as the Syracuse Academy her brother Jermain attended with his friend Andrew Dickson White, the son of another Syracuse Presbyterian family and later president of Cornell. After the academy closed down, aspiring parents sent their sons to the Syracuse Classical High School, where a pupil wrote in 1849 that the patrons of the school were in an uproar because "the teachers' *exercise is* to use the rawhide daily." He added, "What the result will be I cannot say [since] almost every one of the scholars have [sic] had experience of something besides 'moral suasion.'"[83]

Olivia later claimed that her Syracuse teachers had prepared her well for the intellectual challenge of Troy Female Seminary. "Did I study botany at the Emma Willard School? No, I had finished botany, rhetoric, and many other studies before I went there."[84] What else had she learned by the time she turned eighteen? The big lessons were hard to put into words; they involved dissonance and discomfort—the continuous worries about money, for example, contrasted with the grandiose stories of family history. Her father's swings of fortune were hard to square with his status as head of the family, its breadwinner and political representative. From her parents—the absent father, the anxious, controlling mother—she learned about the unequal political power of men and women. Hard times taught a lesson in life's vicissitudes. They revealed that the mother she admired was a dependent, perhaps even a victim. Powerless as her husband was swept along by economic currents and as he dashed from one hopeful scheme to the next, Margaret Pierson Jermain Slocum became the first exemplar for Olivia of the legal and political disabilities of a married woman in the nineteenth century. There would be an even more dramatic demonstration of this in the years that followed.[85]

All the while, Olivia's understanding of self and community was mediated by the church. She was the product of an evangelical Protestant upbringing that bred a strong sense of duty. If she were to develop an understanding of the possibilities for change, it would be from within conservative religion, not in opposition to it. Scholars have described American women of the postrevolutionary generation as meekly reentering the patriarchal household of the evangelical church.[86] At seventeen, Olivia still had to leave her father's house. Her eighteenth birthday approached, but her parents had no money to spare for the further education of a bright daughter. If she were to attend one of the newly established female academies there would be fees to pay and the money would have to be borrowed. Fortunately, affluent Slocum relatives would provide the necessary funds. And at Troy Female Seminary, Olivia would meet and fall in love with a quite different model of womanhood from the ineffectual one her mother had offered in her first seventeen years of life.

Two

"Distinctly a class privilege"
Troy Female Seminary, 1846–1847

Women are almost universally educationally disadvantaged
in comparison with their brothers, and education is, for those
few women able to obtain it, distinctly a class privilege.
—Gerda Lerner, *The Creation of Feminist Consciousness* (1993)[1]

The nineteenth century saw a dramatic growth in American higher education for girls as well as boys. By the 1880s, one-third of girls attended
high school, and by 1890, more girls than boys were graduating. The
number of women enrolled at institutions of higher education also
increased, to 11,000 in 1870 and 56,000 in 1890, by which date they
constituted over one-third of all college students.[2] But in the late summer of 1846, as Olivia Slocum prepared to leave home to continue her
education, there was little sign of this revolution about to occur. No men's
college accepted women as students, and no women's academy claimed
to offer the equivalent of the best men's colleges of the day. In fact, the
term "college" was so closely associated with an institution for men only
that when educator Emma Willard (1795–1870) appealed to Governor
Clinton and the New York State legislature for funding for women's education in 1818, she went out of her way to reassure her listeners that
her proposed ladies' seminary involved nothing so outlandish as a college for women. In her "Plan for Improving Female Education" she
expressly renounced the title of "college" as too controversial and even
likely to invite ridicule. A brilliant piece of forensic argument, it begins:
"[T]he absurdity of sending ladies to college, may, at first thought, strike
every one to whom this subject shall be proposed." But, she hastened to
reassure her readers with evasiveness and not a little irony, "the semi-

nary here recommended, will be as different from those appropriated to the other sex, as the female character and duties are from the male."[3] When the legislators did not grant her the funds, Willard turned to private sources and raised enough money from the citizens of Troy to be able to open Troy Female Seminary in 1821.[4] Several other aspiring towns in the region then established ladies' seminaries, including Hartford Female Seminary, founded by Catharine Beecher in 1827, and Mount Holyoke, founded by Mary Lyon in 1837 in South Hadley, Massachussetts.[5] Olivia was to attend Mount Holyoke. This college catered to families of modest means, keeping the fees low by requiring the students to do much of the housework, a fact which probably explains why Olivia's parents selected it.[6]

The route from Syracuse to Mount Holyoke lay due east toward the bustling commercial and river port of Troy, almost 200 miles distant by river or canal. It is a considerable journey even by car today. You strike out to the east through the splendid Mohawk Gap with the Adirondacks always visible to the north until you come to where the Mohawk joins the Hudson and the great river flows south toward New York City. Even today from the interstate highway this route is impressive. By stagecoach or canal boat in the 1840s it must have been even more so. The Erie Canal passed through the center of Syracuse, and Olivia might well have chosen this means of travel.[7]

Canal boats made fourteen landings between Syracuse and Troy. One unnamed Troy Female Seminary student from Syracuse left an account of the week-long journey at about this time. The young woman was placed in the care of the captain of the canal boat and his wife. "The start had to be made on Sunday morning, much to the distress of our pious and somewhat rigid Presbyterian parents. [To keep up the girls' spirits] the good captain would frequently take us on shore to pick wild flowers, and the boat, drawn by mules, traveled slowly, so we did not reach Troy until Saturday evening."[8]

In another account, "Margaret Olivia Slocum, always called Olivia," accompanied by her mother and father, "alighted from the Syracuse stage" in September 1846 to break her journey at the home of her Uncle Hiram Slocum and his wife Elizabeth.[9] Hiram, Joseph Slocum's younger brother, was a man of some wealth who had been elected alderman in 1838. He had moved to Troy in 1834 and become a business partner of William F. Sage. Slocum and Co., located on Troy's busy commercial riverfront at 147 River Street, was a grain and provision business dealing also in wool.[10]

But in Troy Olivia became ill, and while she recovered at the home of her aunt and uncle these relatives tried to dissuade her mother from enrolling her at Mount Holyoke. "What's thee going to take Olivia to Mary Lyon's school for?" her uncle is supposed to have asked Margaret Slocum. "I do not think thee's wise to put her to peeling potatoes and scrubbing, when the best that's to be had can be got right here in Troy." When she protested that Emma Willard's school was too expensive, he responded, "If thee cannot afford to do it, I can. And I will." Olivia went to bed crying with anxiety about the $350 required for her fees. But her aunt comforted her: "It's a good investment, anyway. So no more tears."[11] This overwrought account, entitled "Hiram Slocum's Investment," ends with a moral: not long after Olivia's graduation, her uncle failed in business "and within a few years he and his wife and children had died. Nothing remained to show for the work of his life but the diploma Olivia treasured. Yet few men have left so much!"[12]

Evidently Olivia's relatives rejected Mary Lyon's Seminary in part out of snobbishness. Mount Holyoke recruited girls from middling families, but Troy Female Seminary had the reputation of appealing to social climbers and the wealthy. It offered extra subjects beyond the standard curriculum and levied additional charges for supplies. Olivia's instruction in French would cost her Uncle Hiram an extra fifteen dollars a term and stationery an extra five.

Hiram Slocum had a more immediate reason to encourage his niece to attend college close to home: his own daughter, Olivia's cousin and namesake Olivia Slocum, was also just about to enter Troy Female Seminary, and the two cousins would keep each other company. The difference in age did not matter. Educational standardization and age grading were far in the future, and some of Olivia's fellow students would be as young as twelve, the minimum age of entry, while she, entering at eighteen, was one of the oldest.[13] So Olivia recovered her health and entered Troy Female Seminary in the autumn of 1846. She would stay for only one year. The other Olivia, her cousin and namesake, entered at fourteen and received her diploma in 1848 when she was sixteen.[14]

We have a detailed description of Troy Female Seminary at about this time. The school—college?—was already a large and successful institution with 100 boarders and over 200 day students.[15] Boarders paid $200 per year for two terms of twenty-two weeks each. "For this sum the pupil is entitled to board, and all the necessaries connected with it: such as room-rent, washing, fuel, light, etc. and to tuition in any or all of the branches constituting the extensive course of English studies."[16]

The two Olivias attended the seminary together, not as boarders but as day girls who continued to live at home—Hiram Slocum's house at 21 River Street. In this early stage of Troy's history, merchants such as Hiram Slocum and Russell Sage lived above their warehouses on River Street, Troy's busy commercial district. The Sages and Slocums were in the same business and political circles, and it is likely that as the eighteen-year-old niece of Hiram Slocum, Olivia was introduced to the emerging entrepreneur-politician Russell Sage while she was still attending college, as later accounts insist.[17]

"In all essential respects, it was a college"

Troy Female Seminary resembled a college, despite Emma Willard's modest disclaimers. With its science teaching where pupils were encouraged to perform experiments and its emphasis on modern languages, the seminary's curriculum and pedagogy were equal to those of contemporary men's colleges and in some ways superior, historians now agree.[18] The seminary offered a remarkably advanced curriculum that was certainly the best available to young women in the 1830s and 1840s. All subjects were taught except Greek and advanced geometry. Modern historians agree with John Lord, Emma Willard's biographer and her contemporary, that "[w]hatever name her school may go by, yet in all essential respects it was a college."[19]

The seminary's science curriculum provides evidence of Willard's ambitious and progressive vision. Emma Willard herself had studied with Amos Eaton, professor at Rensselaer College, and she continued to pursue her own scientific work, notably her research on the circulation of the blood, which she published in 1849 after years of work.[20] Willard also secured Amos Eaton's services at the seminary as a part-time lecturer in science, thus achieving for a few years the effect of the "coordinate college" like the much later pairing of Barnard and Columbia.[21] Eaton died in 1842, but the curriculum in zoology which he had designed especially for the Troy students remained. Almira Hart Lincoln Phelps (1793–1884), Willard's younger sister and a scientist, was also an early important influence on the college's science teaching, though she left in 1831 to get married.[22]

The frank teaching of physiology and anatomy at the seminary was also remarkable for the time and drew adverse comments from the public. Olivia later recalled that several teachers "reported that visiting mothers on examination day left the room in a body when the exam in physiology was called."[23] The school's response to this controversy was to have teachers paste thick paper over the illustrations of the human body in the physiology textbooks so as to protect the girls' modesty. When the Troy seminary graduates became teachers, however, they introduced the teaching of physiology in their own schools. An important strain in Victorian feminism emphasized frankness as part of progress toward a healthier, freer society, and the early twentieth century's "repeal of reticence" was already under way during the Victorian era at women's colleges such as Troy.[24]

The school catalogue for the academic year 1847 to 1848 records the books that were Olivia's required texts. These included: Kame's *Elementary Criticism* through 1810; Playfair's *Euclid; La Vie de Washington;* and a French grammar. The second term's studies included study of Dugald Stewart's *Intermediate Philosophy* (4 volumes); *Philosophy of the Mind;* another French grammar; and composition.[25] Sewing was not part of the Troy curriculum, a remarkable omission for the time. Willard had stated defiantly, "Needlework other than useful I should regard as a waste of time."[26] Moreover, although Emma Willard spoke much about preparing girls to be mothers, and pupils were responsible for keeping their rooms clean and their beds neat, her regimen did not include instruction in housework. Instead, the school's mission was to train girls to earn their own living and thus to ensure their financial independence.[27]

Historians have seen such institutions as the all-girl boarding school as part of a Victorian "female culture" of affectionate relationships between girls and their teachers. Olivia kept up a correspondence with her former teacher Harriette Dillaye until the latter's death in the 1890s. She still recalled Miss Dillaye in 1897. When she addressed the girls graduating from the Emma Willard School (the school had recently been renamed after its founder), she praised her teachers, especially Miss Dillaye: "Tenderly in after years her beautiful spirit was breathed into mine, inspiring a love for teaching, refining and etherealizing everything," Olivia rhapsodized.[28] But although Olivia chose to remember her relationship with "my loving and beloved teacher" in personal and sentimental terms, in fact her connection with Dillaye was of a somewhat more practical nature, involving what today we would call mentorship and networking, and it would serve Olivia as a link to a job a few years after graduation.

Not all the students at Troy were resigned to a world without males. Elizabeth Cady Stanton, who attended a few years later than Olivia, remembered the all-female school with distaste. "The thought of a school without boys, who had been to me such a stimulus both in study and play, seemed to my imagination dreary and profitless," she recalled.[29] If Olivia had reservations on that score, we have no record of them. Yet stray bits of evidence suggest that her relations with her peers were not the best. Some remembered Olivia as "bright and interesting," but other evidence suggests a more contentious personality.[30] She later described herself as "an industrious pupil," and perhaps academic work secured for her the approval and affection from teachers that was withheld by her peers.[31] Called on to summarize her schooldays for the alumnae directory *Emma Willard and Her Pupils* (1898), she provided another piece of evidence about difficult relationships: Emma Willard was a comfort to the lonely, Olivia recalled, who "seemed always to have a place in her heart for the numerous and changing family in the Seminary, the youthful members of which she was accustomed to call her 'grand-daughters.'" She continued, "Her word of commendation or sympathy often marked a red-letter day for some timid, home-sick maiden, whom her quick eye had noted and her timely caress had comforted."[32]

Gerda Lerner has pointed out that historically, higher education was distinctly a class privilege for girls, and the seminary's culture of refinement encouraged even more the sense that Troy girls were specially favored.[33] Olivia was motivated by a sense of social superiority, and an unfortunate snobbishness formed part of her education. Combined with the highly self-conscious character-building of Troy Female Seminary, this produced in her a heightened sense of mission and a self-consciousness that people saw as arrogance. It seems likely that Olivia herself was one of these "home-sick maidens" suffering from self-imposed isolation.

By all accounts, Olivia was smitten by the powerfully feminine Willard. By the time she entered the seminary, its founder was back from what one account tactfully described as "her temporary retirement in Connecticut, where she had been residing for a few years." In fact, Willard was returning after a scandalous episode that would have ruined the career of a less confident woman. In 1838, at the age of fifty-one, she had entered a disastrous second marriage to Troy physician Christopher Yates, her devoted first husband and backer Dr. John Willard having died in 1825. Yates was soon exposed as an adventurer whose interest in her was purely mercenary—one account states that he refused even to pay for the wedding breakfast—and in 1843 Willard obtained a divorce from the state of Connecticut. In her absence, the school was run by her daughter-in-law, Sarah Lucretia Willard, and her son, John Hart Willard. When Emma Willard returned to Troy, she settled in a small detached house next to the seminary on the corner of Second and Ferry Streets. Here she remained, an important presence but no longer a teacher, except for those specially privileged few girls invited to visit her. Olivia was among that select few.[34]

In all her later references to her girlhood, Olivia insisted on the

FIGURE 2.1. Troy Female Seminary, around 1840. Olivia Sage attended from 1846–1847, while living with her uncle Hiram Slocum.

supreme importance of Troy Female Seminary and its "queen," Emma Willard. Looking for a parallel as she addressed the anniversary class of 1897, she compared Emma Willard to the famous English educational reformer, Dr. Thomas Arnold of Rugby School. "Emma Willard was to the girls of America what Dr. Arnold was to the boys of England."[35] Emma Willard's idea of female power was not a feminism that included women's right to vote; indeed, Willard's admiring biographer described her as "frank and acute—feminine and powerful, without any tincture of those 'women's rights' which neither the Gospel nor Nature, nor experience, recognizes." And Willard herself was said to have called suffragists "hyenas in petticoats (see fig. 2.2)."[36]

Instead, Willard's feminism involved performance, public activity, and moral authority—performance above all. Contemporaries often dwelled more on her physical appearance and demeanor than on her ideas. One pupil recalled "a woman of proud bearing, who in her trailing gown of black velvet or satin, set off by the rich, soft, creamy laces of her head-dress, her neck-ruff, and her hand-ruffles, was to our youthful fancy the very embodiment of courtly grace and elegance and the oracle of all knowledge."[37] Elizabeth Cady Stanton remembered Willard as a woman with a "fine and developed figure, well-shaped head, classic

FIGURE 2.2. Emma Willard, around 1840.
Mrs. A. W. Fairbanks, comp., *Emma Willard
and Her Pupils, or Fifty Years of Troy Female
Seminary, 1822–1872* (New York: Published
by Mrs. Russell Sage, 1898).

features, most genial manners, and a profound self-respect (a rare quality in woman) that gave her a dignity truly royal in every position."[38]
She also described Willard as "queenly," a term reserved "for the powerful women Stanton came to admire: her mother, Emma Willard, the
abolitionist Lucretia Mott, and in her old age, herself."[39] For both Stanton and Sage, Emma Willard became an exemplar of a powerful but still
feminine woman, who, as Anne Firor Scott points out, referred to herself as Mrs. Emma Willard and never as Mrs. John Willard.[40]

One incident vividly illustrates Emma Willard's public persona, which was so remarkably at odds with the modest precepts of her teaching. When General de Lafayette, aged hero of the Revolution, visited Troy during his American grand tour in 1824, he made a pilgrimage to the famous girls' seminary. Here, he was accorded a hero's welcome. A local historian describes the scene. The young women had constructed an arbor

> reaching from the street across the small park to the front of the Seminary Building, and with their own hands they had covered it with evergreens and decked it with flowers. On an arch at the entrance was the motto: "America Commands Her daughters to Welcome Her Deliverer, La Fayette." The ladies were drawn up in ranks on each side of the arbor, and as the General entered it, he was met by a committee of nine ladies.

A speech of welcome was then read. The General was "then conducted up the arbor to the front of the edifice, on the steps of which the principal of the Seminary, Mrs. Emma Willard, was waiting to receive him." If the old war hero was the nation's visiting celebrity, Emma Willard was the city's resident celebrity, and she received him as if she were a royal personage granting an audience to a fellow monarch, with equal measures of charm and condescension.[41]

If theatricality and performance were part of her public persona, Willard made an unassailable claim for women's role in public life by encouraging intellectual ambition and advocating women's public roles. Historian Anne Firor Scott identifies in Willard a mixture of radicalism and caution. The educator "combined an appeal to the prevailing view of woman with a revolutionary emphasis upon women's intellectual capacities and with proposals to expand women's sphere to include professional work," she writes.[42]

Pageants and rituals at Troy Female Seminary such as commencement and public examinations, both of which were open to members of the public, illustrate Willard's ambitious vision. A "Poem on Female Education," delivered at the seminary's annual commencement in July 1858, expressed a confidence in women's intellectual abilities in every field.

> In the great art of Teaching we shall find
> Its best exponent is a female mind
> In all that wins by manner or address,
> As in scholastic discipline no less;
> In varied knowledge, oratoric sway,
> The ready pen that knowledge to convey;

> The skill all sciences to understand,
> Grapple abstrusest problems, hand to hand;
> Our Trojan Willard stands aloft confest
> By all, the wisest, noblest, and the best.[43]

All these elements—performance, feminism, public activity—can be seen in one of Emma Willard's famous innovations, the seminary's system of twice-yearly public examinations that were part entertainment and part advertisement for the school and its founder. We have an account of the examinations in 1845, a year before Olivia arrived. This public event lasted nine days and covered the following subjects:

> Various branches of pure and mixed Mathematics
> Botany
> Ancient and modern Geography and History
> Latin French German
> Grammar [and] Rhetoric
> Moral and Intellectual Philosophy
> Music, Painting, Drawing

Both the aesthetic and intellectual aspects were noted by the observer of the examination in geography and history. "From their blackboards ornamented with beautiful maps, drawn entirely from their memory, they gave us a beautiful description of the countries of antiquity, and a history of the renowned events of the old world, alike creditable to themselves, their teacher, and the author they studied."[44]

"To break down that mysterious barrier"

Some critics condemned the public examinations on pedagogical grounds. Alma Lutz, author of *Emma Willard, Daughter of Democracy* (1929), recorded the notes of an anonymous and dyspeptic critic who denounced the public examination as "pure memory work—each young lady assigned part in farce played off before public—that their judgement could not comprehend meaning of author—but could memorize as Greek or Sanskrit." Lutz also recorded the rebuttal, which stated that the examinations were not a "systematic plan of fraud on parents and public. . . . no conspiracy between pupils and teacher—[but a] searching exam."[45] A published report issued by the school's Committee on Examinations reassured the public that "[t]he exam was eminently thorough and impartial."[46]

Others criticized the custom because it required young ladies to speak in public, destabilizing constructions of gender and threatening the ideology of spheres, already so precariously maintained that they were honored mainly in the breach.[47] For several months in 1857, a controversy would rage in the columns of the *Troy Daily Times* and other newspapers between Willard and prominent Presbyterian clergyman Henry A. Boardman over the seminary's public examinations. For Boardman, the public event "violated the true (because the Scriptural) conception of the proper social sphere of the weaker sex."[48] In defense of Emma Willard's work, her daughter-in-law, Sara Lucretia Willard, who with her husband presided over the seminary from Emma Willard's retirement until 1872, maintained that the seminary gave "experimental proof that the most highly cultivated intellect is perfectly compatible with feminine gentleness and grace, and that a judgement strengthened and enlightened by severe study conduces to the successful performance of the minor offices of the domestic station." Such an education did not threaten the traditional duties of women who were serving as "the patient and useful dispensers of domestic comfort, and the joy and ornament of social life," she wrote.[49]

In June 1847, after two terms at Troy, Olivia faced the ordeal of the final examinations. The candidates for examination stood before a crowd of pupils, teachers, and visitors. Essays were never orated by the author herself, "as this would have been too much a strain on the modesty of the young ladies."[50] Instead, girls being examined faced the torture of having their essays read aloud by another pupil. The audience was large and, according to one observer, appreciative. This witness noted, "All of the compositions bore the decided impress of minds that have drank [sic] of the deep wells of substantial and abiding literature."[51] M. Olivia Slocum of Syracuse had written on the subject "Modern and Ancient Troy" and "beautifully alluded to the many moral and social advantages possessed by modern Troy over the Ilium of the ancients— although the latter may boast of its lofty walls and the glory of its military heroes." The author "paid a just and honorable tribute to the character and devotion of a few of our distinguished inhabitants who spend their wealth in deeds of charity."[52]

It is tempting to find in this speech an archetypal myth for the student Olivia Slocum, later to become Olivia Sage the great philanthropist, just as Jane Addams's autobiography tells how as a child in Rockford, Illinois, the future social worker played with a little house and rehearsed her life mission of founding a settlement house in the midst of the slums.[53] For biographers, stories like these resonate because they work to create a unity for the life. For Addams biographers, the story allows childhood to be seen as preparation for Hull House. For Olivia, this youthful speech on the theme of charity, which has been unremarked by scholars, serves the same purpose, prefiguring her later philanthropy. Her privileged upbringing as the older child, her aptitude for study, her sense of calling and religious duty all would converge in an ideology and practice of benevolence that permitted a public life.

Graduation was the first of three milestones in her life, she later told an audience of young Troy Female Seminary graduates; teaching and marriage were the others.[54] She recalled that public and dignified ceremony when, dressed in white muslin with pink ribbons, she stood with her fellow graduates before the assembly of pupils, teachers, and visitors until it was time to step forward and receive their diplomas. Her diploma, signed by J. H. Willard and Sara S. Willard, was "awarded to Miss M. Olivia Slocum for that thorough acquaintance with a prescribed course of study and the propriety of deportment which entitle her to the highest honors of this institution."[55]

Olivia's college experience had lasted only one year, yet it was a major influence on her development. She saw the rest of her life as seeking to fulfill the principles she had learned at Troy. She often referred to her time at the seminary, calling up memories that were as fresh in the 1890s as if they were yesterday. Remarkably, during the 1894 suffrage campaign, she told a reporter that because she had attended the Troy Female Seminary, "I was early enrolled as a believer and worker in a small way for the great cause of womankind."[56]

The two most important women in her life, her mother and Emma Willard, presented competing models of womanhood. Margaret Slocum symbolized the piety, learning, and industry of the Puritan goodwife. But Emma Willard, powerfully feminine yet unquestionably subversive of gender hierarchy, came to hold a dominant influence over Olivia, who saw in her own mother an admirable woman but one needing sympathy and protection. Willard was very different; she did not advocate women's dependence on men and had taken the unusual precaution of drawing up a prenuptial agreement protecting her rights in her property (including the seminary itself) against her second husband, so that when the marriage failed she did not suffer materially and the divorce did not endanger the property rights of her son. In *Morals for the Young, or Good Principles Instilling Wisdom* (1857), Willard wrote, "In making her calculations for the future, . . . every young woman is wise to prepare herself to become independent, useful, and happy, without marriage;

although her education should always fit her for those high and holy duties, which result from marriage and maternity."[57]

Conducting a bold experiment in women's education by preparing young women for paid careers while celebrating maternity, Emma Willard had the widest possible influence in antebellum America. Feminist historian Anne Firor Scott has argued that Troy Female Seminary, the institution Willard established, was the center of "an ever-widening circle" of feminist influence that played a part in the development of an American national culture.[58] Willard enlarged opportunities for women while claiming that she was doing no such thing. Teaching itself reflected these contradictions. Emma Willard groomed her students for public roles and public speaking, brushing aside conservative prohibitions: "St. Paul has said . . . [women] must not speak in churches, but he has nowhere said they must not speak in school houses," she wrote.[59] She also insisted that women respect themselves. "Is it not perfectly true everywhere that a woman who respects herself will be respected by others?" she demanded. The purveyor of Victorian female modesty and self-effacement was also the apostle of that late-twentieth-century invention, self-esteem.

Olivia would continue to be powerfully influenced by Harriette Dillaye and by Willard herself. As she moved into adulthood, the two educators—Willard and Dillaye—became sainted figures who seemed almost to blur in her memory into a single template of beautiful, noble womanhood. Yet Olivia might have been troubled that Dillaye, the female intellectual, had cultivated her mind while first deferring and then renouncing marriage and motherhood and that Willard had almost wrecked her health and reputation in an attempt to combine both.

Intellectual preparation was important, but even more important was resolving the contradictions between the lives and words of these female intellectuals. This, rather than science, philosophy, or French, constituted for Olivia the legacy of the seminary. As a model of womanhood, Willard's example was inspiring, but adhering to it would finally prove a handicap for the star pupil of 1847. Olivia would have been better off had she questioned more insistently the contradictions in Emma Willard's representation of her school and her person, contradictions that played into stereotypes of female subordination while seeming to subvert them.

Marriage was supposed to come next. In *Portrait of a Lady* (1909), novelist Henry James explained how it was supposed to be:

> She was intelligent and generous; it was a fine free nature; but what was she going to do with herself? This question was irregular, for with most women one had no occasion to ask it. Most women did with them-

selves nothing at all; they waited, in attitudes more or less gracefully passive, for a man to come that way and furnish them with a destiny.[60]

Olivia defied the marriage plot. She began her adult life by breaking off an engagement and turning instead to that last resort of Victorian middle-class white women: wage-earning.

Three

"I do enjoy my independence"
1847–1858

The longed-for happy event never occurred, and the 21-year old
Olivia stoically prepared for her destiny—that of an old maid
doomed to spend her life at her mother's side.

—Paul Sarnoff, *Russell Sage, the Money King* (1965)

If I had married the first man who proposed to me I suppose I would
now be on a farm. . . . But I would not like that at all. It would
be too narrow a life for me. I would prefer single blessedness.

—Margaret Olivia Sage (1899)[1]

Graduation was now behind her, but Olivia stayed on in Troy where she
had relatives and friends. She was still at her Uncle Hiram's house when
her father stopped off on his way to New York, where he was to embark
for another business venture. At Troy, he heard unexpected and disturbing news. "I learned with surprise from both her Uncle and Aunt
that [Olivia] had been in correspondence with C. Foster, that he had
visited her and that previous to her leaving home she had been under
an engagement to him," he wrote to his wife. "As this was wholly
unknown to me it could not fail to excite surprise and anxiety and was
evidently a source of deep anxiety to her Uncle and Aunt. They seemed
to think favorably of the young man but urged as an objection . . . that
his father had been convicted of crime." Slocum continued, "From the
little that I have seen of young Foster I had formed a favorable opinion
of his manship and general intelligence but my acquaintance with him
is very slight."[2]

Joseph Slocum was under no illusions about a parent's power either to bring about or to prevent a match. Parents should never interfere with their children's choice of a marriage partner, he insisted. "Marriages in many cases are lotteries in which the most flattering prizes often prove to be worse than blanks," he continued dryly. "[Marriage] should therefore be left to the unbiased choice of the parties." He left the decision "entirely to your better judgement and Olivia's sense of duty to herself." Since Olivia was young and the decision so momentous, "especially to the female," he advised that she should postpone marriage "for a season."[3]

Olivia may have been relieved. Young women were under relentless pressure to marry, but novels and advice literature also warned of the consequences of a bad match. Perhaps she was mindful of Emma Willard's disastrous second marriage—a hasty liaison with consequences all the more dreadful because no one spoke of them. Perhaps because of her mother's fear of being left alone or because of the young man's unsuitable family, the mysterious C. Foster was turned down and the engagement lapsed.[4]

"I am to be the sport of a crule fate"

Meanwhile, the Slocum family fortune hung by a thread as Olivia's father prepared for another overseas business "adventure" (his word). Before embarking for Europe, he wrote a self-pitying letter to his wife and son. "With those sad and gloomy feelings which I have so often experienced I seize the first moments of leisure to say to you that I have shipped my articles on board the London Packet Hendrick Hudson and shall tomorrow embark on board of her to once more cross the Atlantick [sic]."

> Most gladly would I be spared the crule sacrifice which these sepparations from all I hold dear on Earth cost me, but it seems that I am to be the sport of a crule fate and that I am not to be permitted again while I live to consult either my present comfort or future happiness. I ought not, I will not conceale from you that I have strong misgivings as to the nature of this adventure, yet duty to you urges me to leave no experiment untried nor any sacrifice of personal comfort or feeling prevent me from braving any danger or encountering any hardship for your sake.

He feared failure that would "rather aggravate than alleviate the privations, and sufferings to which my misfortunes have subjected you." Still, he promised that as long as his health endured, he would strive to accomplish "the only object for which I now have any desire to live that is to release you and our children from the position from which my misfortune has thrust you."[5]

The gloomy, self-blaming tone would characterize Joseph Slocum's letters to Olivia and other family members over the remaining sixteen years of his life. They reveal a man often depressed and chronically in debt. In reply, Olivia's letters are breezy and confident. She tries in vain to comfort him as he continually moves from place to place. In one exchange, dated May 1854, she writes expressing sorrow at a letter in which he told her that he had "no hope for the future" and tries to offer him the consolation of religious faith.[6] A year later, she responds to his letter from Cartersville, Georgia. "I felt very much the disappointment that you expressed in your last letter, still could think of no way in which to soothe or alleviate it."[7]

After College, What?

With the prospect of early marriage put aside, Olivia returned home to Syracuse to find herself the emotional and financial support of her mother and younger brother, aged fourteen. She exchanged the lively, youthful peer culture of Troy Female Seminary for the dull routine of home, becoming again the "family possession."[8] Olivia's situation was typical. Few Troy Female Seminary graduates became teachers straight out of college; most returned to their parents' homes to run the household and wait for marriage.[9] Often the wait was a long one. Despite Emma Willard's claim that her seminary prepared young women to be the wives of wealthy men, graduates of Troy Female Seminary married later, were more likely to work for pay, and were less likely to have children than their contemporaries, according to historian Anne Firor Scott. Scott found that of the 769 alumnae who left Troy Female Seminary between 1843 and 1852 and who responded to the alumnae survey of the 1890s, one-fifth had never married and one in four had married but had no children. Of those who remained single, just over one-third worked for pay, mostly as teachers.[10]

Olivia experienced several periods of hardship and uncertainty. The 1837 panic had been devastating for her father. He was forced to sell his land and even to lease out the barn on Church Street, retaining just one stall for a cow and storage in the loft for its winter feed.[11] By the end of 1850, both the store and the family home had been mortgaged.[12] Her mother was said to be unable to afford even one servant.[13]

The family's economic distress must surely have been worsened by their decision to pay for a private education for Olivia's brother at Syracuse Academy and subsequently at Ballston Spa near Saratoga Springs. He attended both institutions with another Syracuse lad who would later be famous as the first president of Cornell, Andrew Dickson White.[14] The Slocums and the Whites attended the First Presbyterian Church, and Andrew's letters home from Geneva College throw light on the values shared by these earnest Protestants; they were very much calculated to reassure his mother and reflected the anxieties of a careful evangelical upbringing. "I stick to my coffee and tea pledge," he wrote in March 1849; three days later he reported that "Mr Gough the celebrated temperance lecturer has been here. I attended on Friday evening and was *very* much interested." (This was not enough to reassure his mother, who wrote back, "Your father is much disturbed for fear . . . you will take something *more ardent* than water. He says it would kill him if you should take to drink or any other vice.")[15]

"A hotbed of radicalism"

The 1840s was a turbulent period in the history of Syracuse and its region. The disturbances associated with the Second Great Awakening caused outbreaks of religious perfectionism in congregations all over upstate New York, the "burned-over district." Passionate advocates of immediate reform embraced antislavery, temperance, and women's rights and often all three. Visiting lecturers introduced new fads and touted panaceas to the gullible. A schoolfriend writing to Andrew Dickson White in 1849 about recent happenings in Syracuse recounted that "Drs. Dods, Wieting, and Fowler have each successively expounded the doctrines of Psychology, Physiology, and Phrenology."[16] Spiritualism, too, was in vogue. Clara White informed her son in 1850 that "the mysterious knockings have at length arrived at Syracuse—but as I have not heard them I cannot say much about them."[17]

Temperance gained new adherents as men and women sought to establish community in the midst of rapid social change. Attendees at a temperance meeting held in Syracuse in 1842 offered a resolution condemning the fact that there were "more than 70 places in this village where intoxicating liquors are sold as a beverage, which are prolific sources of pauperism, crime, litigation, taxation, and premature deaths, and ought not to be suffered by law, nor suffered to exist in a civilized community."[18] And in 1852, a mass meeting of the Friends of Temperance held at the Presbyterian church drew an estimated twelve to fifteen hundred persons to hear speeches, declarations, and prayers and be entertained by a "temperance vocalist."[19] The First Presbyterian Church the Slocums attended remained aloof from abolitionism and all enthusiasms. A church history described Dr. Canfield, successor to Rev. Adams, as "a logician, a learned theologian, a scholar of earnest Christian character, and a man of great firmness in preaching the truth. In time of laxity of religious opinions, he stood immovable, and dealt with what he believed to be serious error with a heavy hand."[20] When Charles Finney visited Syracuse in 1852 at the urgent invitation of an abolitionist minister, he found the cause burning bright only in the small Congregational Church, which was "mostly composed of persons of very radical views in regard to all the great questions of reform." He reported, "The Presbyterian churches, and the other churches generally, did not sympathize at all with them."[21]

Temperance was one thing, women's rights was another. When a gathering of Quakers and abolitionists took up the issue of women's rights at Seneca Falls, less than fifty miles away, conservative Protestants such as Olivia's parents were horrified. The Seneca Falls "Declaration of Sentiments," issued in 1848, is considered the founding document of the liberal women's rights movement in America with its radical demand for the vote for women. Although Olivia is not among the signers of the famous declaration, she evidently followed the controversy surrounding it closely.[22] Years later, she told a reporter that she "had been interested in the woman's rights question since 1848."[23]

An inhabitant of Syracuse or its surrounding region in 1852 would have been acutely aware of the ferment over women's rights. Controversy came over the role of women's organizations in the campaign against alcohol. When the New York State Temperance Society held a large public meeting in June 1852, the gathering erupted into a noisy debate over the right of women to take part in its discussions. The New York Woman's Temperance Society demanded to be included as one of the affiliated societies, thus admitting women as voting participants in the state society. Was Olivia in the audience when a Rev. Mandeville of Cayuga made a motion to exclude the woman's society on the grounds that he "desired to keep females in their proper sphere" and was supported by another speaker who pointed out that "if we co-operate with the Woman's Society, we should be obliged to admit their delegates to seats upon this floor, and the right to vote and take part in the deliberations of the Convention"? Did she hear Syracuse's most famous abolitionist, Unitarian minister Rev. Samuel May, make a motion "that the ladies present as delegates be allowed to vote and take part in the deliberations of the Convention"? Was she present on June 18, 1852, when Susan B. Anthony of Rochester stood up to speak and was ruled out of order, so that in the end, "the ladies, although rising to vote, were not counted"?[24]

The next day, a meeting was called at the Methodist church "by the friends of 'equal rights,' to give the lady delegates a chance to defend the rights of the human race in general, and women's rights in particular." Susan B. Anthony "demanded for her sex all the rights enjoyed by the sterner sex, even to the ballot box." Perhaps Olivia's long acquaintance with Anthony began at this time.[25]

Syracuse was also the site of the Second National Woman's Rights Convention three months later, with speakers that included Anthony, Lucy Stone, Antoinette Brown, and Harriet Hunt. The event provoked sharply divided reactions. The *Daily Standard* announced that "some of the most able women in the country will be present, and the discussion can not fail to be particularly interesting." But the *Daily Star* greeted the event with ridicule: "The women are coming! They flock in upon us from every quarter, all to hear and talk about Woman's Rights. The blue stockings are as thick as grasshoppers in hay-time, and mighty will be the force of 'jaw-logic' and 'broom-stick ethics' preached by the females of both sexes."[26]

Whether the press supported or opposed the new cause, they recorded the impassioned speeches of the feminists and their detractors. The *History of Woman Suffrage* would later record that the debates were "unusually earnest and brilliant," but contemporary newspaper accounts include less stellar performances. The *Onondaga Standard* included the lewd predictions of a Rev. J. L. Hatch that if the advocates of sex equality had their way, whenever someone was "suddenly stricken down by death in our streets" it would be necessary to have an anatomical examination "before we can decide whether [the corpse] . . . belonged to a man or a woman!—nay, rather—but which of those two equally and awfully unnatural, and monstrous objects the deceased had been, *a male woman, or a female man!*"[27] The chair of the meeting censured Rev. Hatch for indecent speech. But the questions he raised about bodies and identity show the radical challenge to the foundations of morals and civil society the woman's rights conventions presented.[28]

All these events took place just a few blocks from where Olivia kept house for her mother, visited her friends, or perhaps sat reading or sewing with her seminary education and its debates still fresh in her mind. Her parents discouraged her attendance at these noisy conventions, she later told a reporter. "I was brought up to look with horror on anything that savored of so-called women's rights. My father, Joseph Slocum, who was a silver grey Whig, and my mother, who was the most conservative of women, were not at all in sympathy with the state of things."[29] Despite this, the 20-year-old may well have attended the public meetings, for the *Tribune* reported that the hall was packed every day with "a deeply interested and intelligent audience" and that the crowd was large notwithstanding a 25-cent admission fee.[30] The speeches and resolutions were fully reported in Syracuse newspapers, and Olivia was conversant with debating points on both sides, for she later used some of them to support suffrage for women. Antoinette Brown, a recent graduate of Oberlin Theological School, disputed the doctrine that St. Paul had forbidden women to preach; Olivia would later use the same argument on behalf of women's public speaking.[31] The Syracuse newspapers carried Lucy Stone's protest "that the rights of the most enlightened and cultivated mother and sister are inferior, by your political arrangements, to those of the most drunken and degraded foreigner." And they reported Stanton's letter to the convention calling on women to refuse to pay their taxes until they received political representation.[32]

Joseph Slocum, New York State Representative

Meanwhile, Joseph Slocum had returned from his travels with a prize in the shape of a silver medal from the Society of Arts in England "for the introduction from America of various agricultural implements."[33] In 1850 he briefly held office in the Syracuse City Tract Society and was a supporter of temperance. But his main concern was to recoup his fortunes, and for this he looked to the newly created western state of Wisconsin.[34] Since 1846, when Congress had made a generous grant of land to the Fox River and Western Improvement Company, entrepreneurs had been flocking to Wisconsin. Among them was Troy, New York, financier and politician Russell Sage.[35]

Sometime in 1849, Joseph Slocum and a partner, Charles Wheeler, had entered into a business deal with Russell Sage, joining a new commission business in Milwaukee formed by Sage and a Scottish immigrant, Alexander Mitchell. Sage, who put up the capital, was already a rich man with interests in wholesale produce and banking, as we have seen.[36] Among the immediate payoffs of Slocum's association with Sage, it was said, was Slocum's election in 1849 to the New York State Assembly representing Onondaga County, District Three. (His father, William Brown Slocum, had also served in the State Assembly in 1821.)[37] At Albany he promoted the town's salt-manufacturing industry and backed a bill to amend the Syracuse city charter.[38] He took part in national as well as state politics, voting with the majority to condemn "the existence of prisons for the confinement, and marts for the sale of slaves, at the seat of the national government" and calling for their abolition.[39]

A collection of letters from constituents and others shows Slocum's preoccupations as a state representative. There were matters involving the regulation of roads and bridges and water works. There were requests for positions and favors, political and otherwise. One ambitious applicant for a job was brevity itself. He wrote:

> Dear Sir,
>
> I wish you would procure for me the appointment of Indian agent for the Onondaga tribe.
>
> Yours truly, Lewis T. Handley.[40]

A crisis over the Fugitive Slave Act of 1850 thrust Olivia's father into a prominent role. Abolitionist fervor erupted into violence when a group of Syracuse citizens staged a daring rescue of an escaped slave, the so-called Jerry Rescue. After the rescuers were arraigned under the Fugitive Slave Act, opponents of the act rioted to demand that they be set free, while others demanded that the law be enforced. Rev. Samuel May thundered against a government that would punish citizens for "giving a man his inalienable rights." And black abolitionist preacher Jermain W. Loguen denounced a government which had "transgressed constitutional and natural limits."[41] We don't know whether Joseph Slocum invited Daniel Webster to come to Syracuse as mediator in this crisis, but come he did, and he lodged at the Slocum house. Olivia was then twenty-two. What were the arguments, what the evasions, when the dinnertime conversation turned to the fate of the escaped slave, the punishment of those who defied the law on the grounds of conscience, or the institution of slavery itself?[42]

After this incident, Joseph Slocum secured an appointment from President Fillmore as a mail agent to convey the mails to and from California—and California would draw him back several more times.[43] All the while he kept up a correspondence with his family that was full of sadness and self-recrimination. "I felt grieved to read of your feelings in relation to our future that the thought of it should cause you so much sorrow," the nineteen-year-old Jermain wrote to him in April 1852.[44] Jermain's own future was uncertain. After leaving school, he worked for a few months in his father's store, but this was sold in December 1849. In this crisis, the longsuffering John Groesbeck came to the rescue, and Jermain left Syracuse for good to become an apprentice in the Cincinnati business of his uncle and his Aunt Mary, Joseph's older sister.[45]

With her husband away and her son gone, Margaret Slocum urged her daughter to come and live with her. But Olivia had other ideas. She took her first paid position as a teacher in a small country town not far from Syracuse. "I lived in the house where the school was held," she recalled later, "and my room was small—no bigger than a New York hall bedroom now is, and I shared it with two other girls." Still, living away from home had its compensations: "In spite of our cramped quarters the three of us had a good deal of fun in that little room." Teaching suited Olivia's temperament well. She was outgoing—talkative, opinionated, and humorous.[46] But when her father left for the California gold rush in the spring of 1852, Olivia returned to Syracuse, obtaining a position at St. Paul's Parochial School in order to be near her mother.[47] Her husband's business reverses and his prolonged trips abroad had made Margaret Slocum anxious and demanding.[48] She even discouraged Olivia from forming romantic attachments. Olivia later claimed that several potential husbands were turned away because her mother "did not like diffcrent people, and when I found out she did not like them I did not like them."[49]

Syracuse now bore little resemblance to the village of her childhood. Local historian Joshua Clark recorded in 1849 that "districts that once contained only a small number of inhabitants, have recently become populous, and where the school was attended by a score of children, it has increased ten fold." New schools and churches were needed and sometimes one building was used "for schools, religious meetings, town hall, and for almost every public purpose." St. Paul's, built during the 1840s, had about 200 pupils by 1850.[50] Olivia was employed as one of three teachers at the school, in charge of about fifty pupils. Soon she was promoted to assistant principal, and her salary of approximately $350 per year was raised accordingly.[51] A grainy photograph in a Syracuse newspaper shows her in a class photo of "St. Paul's Female School," dated 1852 (see fig. 3.1).

Feminist historian and biographer of Susan B. Anthony Kathleen Barry suggests that "teaching allowed women to establish their own identities and to gain economic independence. As a result, many of them never married at all."[52] Yet Barry's assessment seems overoptimistic. Pay for female teachers was so low that the idea of economic independence was illusory. Tales of early hardship frame the legend of Mrs. Russell Sage, the philanthropist who came from near-poverty to unimaginable wealth. One of

FIGURE 3.1. St. Paul's Female School, Syracuse, N.Y., 1852. Olivia is a teacher, probably at the far left, third row from the bottom. Collection of the Onondaga Historical Association, Syracuse, N.Y.

these involved Jenny Lind, the "Swedish songbird," whose celebrity tours drew thousands. According to one version, elderly Syracusans recalled that when the singing sensation visited the town in 1851, Olivia Slocum, too poor to afford a ticket to the concert at the First Baptist Church, sat on the steps of her "rather humble" house next door, enjoying the lovely voice for free. "As the little girl sat watching the more fortunate file into the church for the concert, she thought of all the underprivileged people of the world and how much she would like some day to help them."[53] Such stories suggested that the fulfillment of old age was the reward for earlier deprivation. (Olivia told her own, less romantic, version of this incident: she had attended the concert, she recalled, with a male friend, John L. Newcomb, and still had a worn ticket to prove it.)[54]

Before long, Slocum was back east again, trying his luck in Virginia, and two fragmentary letters show his difficulties with business partners. An 1852 letter from one Zenus Barnum of Barnum and Company, Baltimore, to a Captain J. W. Smith from Culpepper County, Virginia, tells about Slocum's difficulties with a business partner, who "is not disposed to comply with his agreement which was that he was to move off as soon as he could gather his crops [illeg.] share of which was to be delivered to Mr. Slocum."[55] A letter written a week later that accompanied a bank draft for $250 addressed to Slocum at Wilderness, Virginia, may have represented the result of this deal. Slocum seems to have found it hard to stand up to more-determined and less-principled men.

The story was the same with the Milwaukee warehouse deal. In 1853, Slocum and Wheeler discovered they had been swindled by Russell Sage and Alexander Mitchell. Sage had persuaded the pair to hand over $10,000 to be used to bribe Mitchell into giving up his claims against the owner of a large warehouse in Milwaukee. But later they learned that Sage had made a secret deal with Mitchell. Although Sage compensated the pair with $16,000, he and his partner made $107,000 on the sale of the warehouse. Slocum and Wheeler then sued Sage in District Court in Wisconsin. The lower court found for the plaintiffs, ruling that Sage had swindled his own partners. The case would continue to drag through the courts until 1863.[56]

It was at this time, as the deal with Sage began to sour, that Joseph Slocum renewed his Russian contacts; he secured a commission from the Russian government to collect examples of improved farm technology, arranged for their manufacture and shipment to Russia, and traveled to Russia to demonstrate their use.[57] An unnamed American visitor to Russia in the 1850s recorded an impression of Slocum, a "tall, thin man, with a thoughtful countenance" going about his work at an agricultural college. "He spoke nothing but English," the visitor noted, "and could hold no communication whatever with those around him, except through the medium of signs and gestures." He had brought with him a number of "improved instruments of agriculture, such as were never seen before in Russia," and he demonstrated these "Yankee contrivances" to the admiring pupils. "He perfectly astonished the natives with his long straight furrows, his clean-cut sward, and his gigantic strides with the mysterious cradle." One day when he came upon students winnowing grain by throwing it up into the wind, he "constructed a winnowing mill, out of such materials, and with such tools as happened to be at hand. It worked beautifully, and the maker was rewarded by the young barbarians with the most profound respect." When his term of employment in Russia was over, Slocum was rewarded by being elected an honorary member of the Imperial Society for the Improvement of Agriculture.[58]

By 1854, he was back in the United States. Correspondence shows him in Pendleton, South Carolina, in 1854. By 1855 he had moved on to Cartersville, Georgia, then in 1858 he was again in Virginia, trying his hand at farming.

Meanwhile Margaret Slocum had left Syracuse for good, beginning a sixteen-year wandering between the homes of various relatives. At Watervliet, near Albany, she made her home with her older brother Silvanus. At Williamsburg, New York, she stayed with her sister Julia Ann, who was married to Rev Nathaniel Prime, pastor of the Presbyterian church in Cambridge, New York, and principal of the town's academy. She also made visits to her parents' farm at Lansingburgh, New York, to Albany, and to Rymertown, New York, home to two sisters of Joseph Slocum: Maria, who was married to Clark Perry, and Almira ("Alma"), who was unmarried. Every now and then, as at Christmas 1853, she returned to Syracuse, staying with friends.[59]

"A stranger in Philadelphia"

In 1853, with a year's teaching experience behind her, Olivia decided to take advantage of her Troy connections to accept a position farther from home, and with the help of her former mentor, Harriette Dillaye, she obtained a post at Philadelphia's Chestnut Street Female Seminary, one of many seminaries spun off by Troy. The Emma Willard network enabled many Troy graduates to find employment as teachers. Anne Firor Scott has explained: "[T]hroughout the Union the simple certificate of scholarship signed 'Emma Willard' served as a passport to almost any desirable situation, notwithstanding the seminary lacked the seal of an incorporated and endowed institution." Emma Willard extended credit to any Troy student who agreed to go into teaching, the student agreeing to repay the debt from future earnings. Willard thus established a kind of "teacher placement agency with Emma Willard's signature the mark of teacher certification."[60]

Chestnut Street Female Seminary, which had been established in the fall of 1850 by Harriette Dillaye and Mary L. Bonney with just six boarders and twenty day scholars, had become a fashionable establishment by 1853.[61] The two associate principals represented the best intellectual and moral traditions of their alma mater. Mary Bonney had taught for a year each in three different schools in New York and New Jersey, then for several years in South Carolina.[62] Dillaye had attended the seminary from 1833 to 1835 and had also taught in the South for several years. She returned to New York State to take positions at an academy in Cortland and then, at the invitation of Emma Willard, to teach at her alma mater in 1845. It was here that Olivia came to know her as a teacher and friend and later as a mentor.[63] Dillaye and Bonney provided the Chestnut Street Female Seminary with a direct link to Emma Willard that was as inspiring as it was good for business, judging from the seminary's publicity materials. One publication, dated 1850, carried an endorsement from the great educator: "Miss Bonney and Miss Dillaye are Teachers of uncommon ability and faithfulness. This I know from personal observation. Mrs. Emma Willard."[64]

The regime of the Chestnut Street Female Seminary replicated features of its mother institution, including Willard's "Monday talks" on "morals and manners," which were long remembered by alumnae. Dillaye cultivated the same mixture of awe and affection as Willard had done.[65]

It makes us doubt Olivia's judgment that she found the Chestnut Street seminary so delightful. For this was a snobbish and exclusive institution where the prospective boarder was "required to supply herself with table and toilet napkins, and silver fork and spoons," and fees were $350 a year for tuition in English, Latin, and French, equivalent to a year's wages for common labor.[66] Extra fees were charged for "meals carried to the room" and for laundry, while instruction in oil painting, music, and piano also cost extra. Harp instruction cost twelve dollars extra per session, the more lowly guitar only five. Even the obligatory church attendance involved expense; pew rent varied from $5 to $8 per session.[67]

But Olivia was favorably impressed with her new surroundings—was it the educational mission of the seminary that impressed her or the allure of exclusivity and refinement? Whichever it was, she later proudly described the school as "among the leading educational establishments of the country."[68] (After 1883, the Chestnut Street Female Seminary would move into even more impressive quarters, occupying Jay Cooke's magnificent mansion outside Philadelphia, Ogontz, and becoming the exclusive Ogontz School for Young Ladies. Its fortunes soared and it attracted fashionable endorsements, including one from President Cleveland. Anna Gould, younger sister of Helen Gould, was later a pupil.)[69]

Historians have traditionally viewed paid work as the key to the entrance of nineteenth-century white women into public space and new roles, but more recent analyses expose the gendered identity of the nineteenth-century breadwinner and show how the culture constructed the female wage-earner as a secondary earner or temporary worker.[70] No wonder contemporary nineteenth-century discussions of middle-class women's paid work are characterized by evasion and contradiction. Typical of these evasive narratives, biographical sketches of Olivia mention her paid work as a problem, a temporary derangement of the proper order of things. Stories of how, as a young woman, she sacrificed a life of leisure to support her family by wage labor supplied a satisfying preamble for the fulfilled life of one who later spent her time and money on the needs of others.[71]

Paul Sarnoff's biography of Russell Sage had this to say of Olivia's young adulthood: "The longed-for happy event never occurred, and the 21-year old Olivia stoically prepared for her destiny—that of an old maid doomed to spend her life at her mother's side."[72] But Olivia's letters challenge this sarcastic interpretation and suggest that in the decades of the 1850s and 1860s, Olivia was not a woman who would eventually be married and famous: she was a single woman for twenty-two years. Where earlier narratives portrayed single women as pathetic castoffs, unqualified through looks or disability for the marriage market, contemporary women's writing reveals examples of women who chose "single blessedness" even though they were advised to "get married the first good chance."[73] Newly discovered correspondence also authorizes a reassessment of these years of young adulthood. Olivia's letters to her father reveal that she thoroughly enjoyed teaching and the independence it promised.[74] In one, dated November 1853, she describes herself as relieved that as a teacher and "a stranger in Philadelphia," she was free from the tedium of social visits. After six weeks of teaching, she was "very busy and often very tired," but "I find teaching more delightful than I anticipated and I am improving myself intellectually every day."[75] In another letter she portrays herself as "so continually busy that I have no time to think except at night, and then I go to sleep from fatigue." She was relieved to be "in a position where society has no calls upon me. . . . I have not entered any other house than the Seminary since I came to Philadelphia."

> But I do enjoy my independence and [am] relieved of the humiliation of being dependent on relatives and indeed . . . it is a blessing to be called on to rely on oneself. I am improving every day intellectually.[76]

Olivia's letters to her father were relentlessly cheerful. "I am resolved to be happy and find sunshine everywhere and like the spot I am in the best," she wrote in January 1854. She did not miss Syracuse at all, she reassured him, "and I think it is fortunate that trials come to teach us what a little dependence place is."[77] A few months later she described herself as "very happy in my present position, and . . . conscious of a continual development of all my faculties which is the highest possible enjoyment." She didn't see "poverty as a trial," she went on. "I am happier than two thirds [of the people] I am brought in contact with."[78]

But the teaching load was exhausting. In the fall of 1853, her responsibilities included grammar, mathematics, geography, and French; in the next term, they also included chemistry, physiology, geography (two

FIGURE 3.2. Margaret Olivia Slocum in the 1850s when she worked as a teacher and governess in Philadelphia. Courtesy Florence Slocum Wilson.

classes), arithmetic, and French translation. The unremitting labor soon wore her down. After just a few months she was complaining of dyspepsia and sore throat, and she was still suffering from sore throats in May 1854. Despite that, she planned to return to the seminary in the fall because, as she told her father, "I have had a pleasant and useful home here."[79] But when school resumed for the September term, she was dismayed to find that her duties were "much more laborious than they were the last," and the last straw was that she was forced to share her room with some of the boarding children, ages five to seven. In December, she described herself as "more or less disabled for a month, by my throat." She briefly considered accepting a position in Savannah for its milder climate and because it would bring her closer to her father, who was in Pendleton, South Carolina, but rejected it because of the low salary.[80] Worn out and plagued with sore throats and fever, by April 1855 Olivia had decided she would have to give up at the end of the school term "and rest a while." "Teaching has not yet permanently injured my constitution, still I have less strength, and another year, without an interval of rest, would be a permanent injury."[81]

Asked later whether she regretted all the things in life she had left undone, Olivia launched into a self-righteous account of her Philadelphia years. Rather than leaving things undone, she had tried to do too much! In the classroom she was conscientious. She liked to communicate, to explain, and persuade. "I had been taught that unless one could give expression to one's knowledge and could be able to impart it to others, one could not really be mistress of what one knew," she insisted. "I worked earnestly as a teacher, going into the classroom with the lesson in my head; I didn't hear it mechanically out of a textbook."[82] She even taught on Sundays. She would get up early on Sunday mornings, she recalled, walk to church, where she taught a class of girls, then stay to morning service, return home for lunch, then "[g]o back to teach a class of younger children the catechism, and later, at 5:30, there was a Bible class in the house. . . . I think now I did too much," she concluded. "My health broke down suddenly, but I enjoyed everything that I did."[83]

The Invalid Woman

Scholars have argued that we should always read illness in the context of culture, and I earlier wondered whether the illness of these young adult years had more to do with a crisis in life stage than with any pathology. I speculated that Olivia's illness might have been a way to resist the impossible and conflicting demands of her family and society.[84] This was a society where male and female roles were being renegotiated, for antebellum reform questioned sexual as well as racial hierarchies and the debate over abolition, temperance, and women's rights formed the background for Olivia's more personal and family difficulties. In the notorious Syracuse "Man-Woman Case" of 1856, Syracuse newspapers kept readers on the edge of their seats. The female whose impersonation of a man was declared a crime received a prison term that gave her ample time to reflect on the fragility of socially prescribed gender differences and the rashness of those who transgressed them.[85]

I earlier leaned toward the psychological explanation of Olivia's illness suggested by scholars such as Diane Herndl and Carroll Smith-

Rosenberg. They showed how the role of invalid could play into Victorian gender stereotypes of feminine weakness while offering the sufferer an arena of autonomy. As Diane Herndl observed, "In the nineteenth century [invalidism] meant a state of weakness or a predisposition to illness. Invalidism therefore referred to a lack of power as well as a tendency toward illness."[86] The Victorian notion of illness "allowed mental and physical conditions that were only marginally dysfunctional to be medicalized."[87]

The family letters make such an interpretation less plausible—and less necessary. Olivia had suffered from sore throats since at least 1847, and the condition was made worse by teaching.[88] Moreover, the biographical sketches of teachers in *Emma Willard and Her Pupils* contain many similar examples of teachers who ended their careers in ill health, exhaustion, and breakdown as well as poverty. Harriette Dillaye would suffer a complete collapse of her health that forced her to take temporary retirement in 1860 from the seminary which she and Mary Bonney had directed for ten years.[89]

A commonsense explanation of Olivia's difficulties is that teaching under nineteenth-century conditions *was* exhausting and stressful. It involved large classes; poorly heated, unhealthy schoolrooms; unremitting labor; and disturbed sleep. Olivia endured several less-than-ideal teaching positions, all the while experiencing pressure from her mother to give up and return home. Meanwhile, her friends married and moved away. Her Troy cousin, seminary classmate, and namesake, Olivia Slocum, married immediately after leaving Troy Seminary in 1849, moved to Montreal, and had four children.[90] Andrew Dickson White, once rumored to be a romantic prospect, married a young Syracuse woman, Mary Amanda Outwater, in 1857 and moved on to a distinguished career.[91]

Anxiety about her mother's situation made everything worse. Margaret Slocum's letters to her daughter have not survived, but they must have been full of complaints and recriminations about the loss of her Syracuse home, an event she blamed on her husband's brother Hiram. Olivia complained, in turn, to her father. In 1854, she wrote accusing her father of causing her mother's suffering. Mother's plans were "very indefinite," she reminded him in March. "None of us have bitterer trials than she, in her separation from a home, and its comforts." She ended melodramatically: "Mother has lived a life of continual sacrifice."[92] A few months later, commenting sarcastically on having to be the financial support of her family, she wrote: "[A]nother year my expenses will not be so heavy, having but one brother to marry off (see fig. 3.3)."[93]

FIGURE 3.3. Joseph Jermain Slocum, Olivia's brother,
as a young man. Courtesy Florence Slocum Wilson.

Into this miserable, unstable, and scattered family came a piece of surprising good news. Jermain was to marry Sallie L'Hommedieu, from a prosperous and respected Cincinnati family. Both were only twenty-one years old. Sallie's father, Stephen S. L'Hommedieu, was owner-manager of the Cincinnati *Gazette* and president in 1851 of the Cincinnati, Hamilton and Dayton Railroad, to which he would add in 1863 the Dayton and Michigan Railroad. Moreover, he and his brother were originally from Sag Harbor, her mother's birthplace, a place that loomed large in Olivia's imagination.[94]

Olivia attended her brother's wedding at Riverside, the L'Hommedieu home in Cincinnati, and sent a glowing account to her father.

Nearly 500 guests attended, she informed him, and the ceremony was performed by a bishop. "Everything about the house and the grounds were in the most complete order, and I was very much pleased with *all* that I saw in Mr. L'Hommedieu's family." Afterward, she was escorted back to New York by Jermain's father-in-law, Stephen L'Hommedieu, "and I found him a most attractive and delightful traveling companion." She also sent an admiring account of her new sister-in-law. "Sallie is a very interesting and mature character, and seems in every way calculated to be a help to him."[95] Neither of Jermain's parents attended the wedding. Joseph Slocum did not even know about it and sent his blessing only when he found out. Jermain apologized with a lame excuse, "I am very sorry that I could have been so thoughtless in not sending you a paper containing my marriage notice but none were preserved. . . . I felt I could not make a letter interesting, after working all day with a pen in my hand."[96]

Less than a year later, on April 25, 1855, the young couple's first child, Herbert Jermain Slocum, was born. Another son, Stephen L'Hommedieu Slocum, followed in four years, on August 11, 1859.[97]

Joseph Slocum was now prospecting for gold in Cartersville, Georgia, a town on the Etowah River in the northwestern part of the state. He had picked a bad time to begin. Georgia had seen gold rushes earlier in the century, but after 1849, the mining industry had slowed and miners had flocked to California. There was a revival of interest in hydraulic mining in the 1850s, but it collapsed with the crash of 1857. Joseph Slocum seems to have done poorly here, as in all his enterprises.[98] While in Cartersville, he lodged with a Dr. and Mrs. William H. Felton, but six months later the failed prospector left his lodgings without paying his board bill. Fifty-eight years later, Olivia would pay her father's bill with interest. A short piece in the newspaper explained: "Believing that John Slocum, a prospector who was befriended by Dr. and Mrs. William H. Felton in 1855 was her father, Mrs. Russell Sage of New York has sent to Mrs. Felton a check for $2,500 to cover, with interest, a board bill which John Slocum was obliged to leave unpaid when he left Cartersville (see fig. 3.4)."[99]

By September the failed gold prospector was back in Syracuse, and from there he wrote imploring his wife and daughter to join him in lodgings, but both refused. There was little to attract her to Syracuse now, Olivia told him. She promised to visit but told him she would stay with the Barnes family to avoid the expense of boarding.[100] Margaret Slocum's letter was even more frank in rejecting her husband's proposal.

FIGURE 3.4. Hon. Joseph Slocum, Olivia's father. A grim smile and haunted eyes suggest setbacks both in business and politics, and perhaps also the tuberculosis that would end his life. Courtesy Florence Slocum Wilson.

Much as she would like to join him, she wrote, "I think your small means would soon be exhausted in boarding without some business and I should prefer to wait until you had secured the office you anticipate." Meanwhile, she reminded him, his son and daughter were both in need of money. Newlyweds Jermain and Sallie were so hard up that they still had not "gone to housekeeping," that is, set up an independent household. As for Olivia, his wife warned him bitterly, "you could not afford the expense of housekeeping as she would like to live."[101] Evidently Olivia was ambitious to live well. Material comfort was important her, as was social status, but both would remain out of reach without a good marriage.

Far from being in a position to help his son, Joseph Slocum tried to persuade Jermain to send some business in his direction from the L'Hommedieus' successful enterprises. But the young man could do nothing for him. "Now my dear Father, I have to consult two interests—yours and our own," Jermain wrote. "Were I on my own I would do anything you would want me to."[102] Olivia's father had more luck with his Cincinnati brother-in-law. In June 1857, he obtained a loan from the longsuffering John H. Groesbeck to buy a farm in Virginia, although Groesbeck prudently declined to take a $500 share in it himself. Olivia was staying with the Groesbecks in Cincinnati, and she surely helped to plead her father's case.[103] But once she returned to Philadelphia, she wrote advising her father against the idea, warning, "A farm will only add to your care, without proportionate gain."[104]

Olivia found the "long confinement" of teaching exhausting and blamed her chronic fevers and sore throats on overwork. But if she were to resign, neither her father nor brother could support her, and the family did not own any house or property where she could take refuge. Her father was now a sick man, suffering painful episodes of nosebleeds that warned of the advancing tuberculosis that was soon to end his life.[105] Meanwhile, her Troy relatives annoyed her by suggesting that she should live on less. "Uncle Silvanus thinks I ought to save a hundred dollars from my two hundred salary, each year," she told her father. "[H]e probably could do it by dint of stinting, but I cannot, and with Dr.'s bills, etc. . . . I do not save much and Mother thinks it is poor pay—so do I."[106]

For a while Olivia lived off the hospitality of friends and relations, but the round of visits proved tiring also, and it was less satisfying than teaching. In January 1856, she described her life to her father as "a very busy idleness."[107] Money was so tight that she could not even afford to travel from one hospitable household to the next, and Jermain could not help because the Cincinnati business was doing poorly. In 1857 he wrote, "We have experienced for the first time the true meaning of hard times."[108]

Only one escape was possible—a good marriage. "When someone is possessed with the insane desire to settle a few thousand dollars upon me, I think I shall settle down, or travel all the time," Olivia remarked wryly to her father.[109] But until such a wealthy man could be found willing to marry a 29-year-old schoolteacher she would have to continue to scrape by. Much later in life, Olivia recalled, "I had relatives with whom I might have lived after my father's losses, but I always believed in the dignity of labor and I searched around for a position as a teacher."[110] Family letters show that this account was essentially accurate. It was the summer of 1858, and Olivia was about to turn thirty. Weary of a life of social visiting, she decided to go back to teaching. "[I am] more sure of means when I earn it myself than when I depend upon friends," she confided to her father. This time she was resolved to find a position that would enable her to be financially independent.[111]

Four

A Bankruptcy, Three Funerals, and a Wedding
1858–1869

Olivia is now thrown upon her own exertion for support.
—Margaret Pierson Jermain Slocum (1859)[1]

By January 1858, Olivia was back in Philadelphia, boarding at the home of her pastor, Rev. Henry A. Boardman, on Spruce Street and fulfilling the duties of governess and companion to his daughter Mary. A native of Troy, New York, and a graduate of Yale and of Princeton Seminary, Henry Boardman had served as minister of the Tenth Presbyterian Church at 10th and Walnut Streets for a quarter of a century and was regarded as a leading churchman.[2] How ironic that this was the very same Rev. Henry Boardman who less than two years earlier had taken to the columns of the *New York Observer* with the broadside "Public Examinations in Female Schools," a series of attacks on the system of public examinations used at Troy Female Seminary, attacks that Emma Willard vigorously refuted over the next six to seven weeks with a series of articles in the *Troy Daily Whig*.[3] Boardman declared the practice of public examinations "adverse to that delicacy of feeling and those refined sensibilities which, next to genuine religion, constitute the charm and glory of woman. . . . The whole purport and drift of these examinations, is to break down that mysterious barrier which, though invisible itself, guards the innate modesty and timidity of the youthful female from intrusive eyes, and nourishes while it shelters her purest affections." Much as he admired Emma Willard, he would never want his own daughter to be examined publicly—unless she were intending to go on the stage or become a woman's rights lecturer![4]

Boardman took up the controversy again in December 1857 in the columns of the *Troy Daily Times*. In "Public Examinations in Female Schools: Reply to Mrs. Willard," the minister reproached the Troy educator for her published defense of public examinations. He expressed horror at her statement that "[w]e shall not in our treatment of the great subject of Examinations in Schools, encumber ourselves with useless phraseology, by confining them to *female* schools, or by the continued repetition of the adjective *public*" and at her praise of women in the ministry. Boardman's tone grew shrill as he declared, "Her ideas of woman are too *masculine* for me."[5] What must have been the effect on Olivia of reading these articles condemning Willard's ideas about women's education? Did she speak in defense of her mentor and risk offending the man who was at the same time her pastor, her host, and her employer?

Perhaps Olivia and her friend Mary Boardman, Rev. Boardman's daughter, didn't take the blusterings of the 50-year-old clergyman too seriously, for no hint of tensions in the Boardman household appears in her letters to her father. Instead, she described the holidays she had spent with friends. Her visit in Philadelphia had been "an almost perfect one," she wrote in January, because of the love and kindness of her many friends there. She worried about her position, of course: "I do not quite want to teach again, because I suffered so much in my last attempt, but still might be more careful of my health another time." The question was, should she be "occupied" or not? For the present she was thankful for "many privileges, and comforts in this truly Christian family."[6] And a few weeks later, "My privileges are so great in this lovely family."[7]

But anxiety about her own family was never far away. In the wake of the 1857 panic, Hiram Slocum, by then mayor of Troy, decided to sell the house in Syracuse that had been Olivia's childhood home. Olivia made inquiries about buying it back for her mother, but the asking price of $2,000 was impossible.[8] She wrote to her father, dismissing the idea of returning to live in Syracuse as "useless almost—pleasant as it would be" and enclosed a valentine—perhaps to soften the blow.[9]

"I must be doing something forthwith"

Olivia would certainly have taken Willard's side in the dispute over women's education. Hard choices and the need to support herself had made her cynical about the conventional wisdom that women could count on men's protection. By February 1858, she was actively looking for a teaching job, but she was not prepared, as she wrote, "to accept *any* situation." Two years' experience had shown that teaching was hard work, and she was unwilling to take a poorly paid position. But she needed money, "therefore I conclude I must be doing something forthwith."[10] March came and more happy times with friends, but "I could wish that all were bright and pleasant with some other of my loved ones, as it is I am often sad for them." And there were more-serious moments. She attended "Mr. Everett's lecture on 'Charity'"; perhaps this recalled her to questions of work and duty, for she wrote, "I shrink from teaching, because I suffered so much when I tried it, still I may *have* to do it yet."[11] She was still complaining about money in April. "I am under the most hospitable roof that ever was," she wrote to her father, "and have all the kindness that friends can give. Of course, I do not think that money is included in the hospitalities which are extended to a visitor, so I go without that. Sometimes this is hard and oftentimes very inconvenient, but I manage not to complain, feeling that you and Jermain need all that you have."[12] A few months later she reported that she was "holding teaching consultations"—we would say she was on the job market. She hoped to stay in Philadelphia, but salaries there were so low "they are hardly a compensation for the labor required."[13]

Southern schools were in need of teachers, and some paid quite well. Briefly in 1855 she had been tempted by a position in a Florence, Alabama, school that paid $500 a year "beside board and washing," over twice her salary at the Chestnut Street Female Seminary. Joseph Slocum was in Georgia at this time, so the prospect of a position in a neighboring state was attractive. But she eventually turned the offer down, although "the anxiety of deciding the question made me sick."[14] Again she considered the Alabama job, only to reject it for the familiar comforts of Philadelphia and her circle of friends.[15]

Summer brought pleasure and travel. There were invitations from friends, but "I cannot visit without money, and I have no right to expect that from any one." Somehow she found the funds to move from place to place, staying with Mary Boardman at an aunt's house in Bridgton in southern New Jersey in June, then in July going in the company of a party of twelve Philadelphia friends to Saratoga and staying twelve days to take the waters.[16] More pleasure and relaxation lay ahead, for she was invited to Newport for the month of August with the Boardmans. She happily agreed, explaining to her father that the sea air and sea bathing would "give me strength and fit me for the labors of another year." September brought a visit to Syracuse and a trip to New York for the inauguration of the transatlantic cable.[17]

Olivia had secured a position for the coming school year at Mme. Vaillant's School, an ambitious new institution that was about to open near her previous one on Chestnut Street in Philadelphia. The school evidently had a select group of students in mind, for it advertised that only French was to be spoken there. By September, Olivia was immersed in the work of planning and preparation. "It takes a great deal of patience and head work to get the machinery of a school into motion," she wrote to her father, reporting that all week "we teachers had to sit up til midnight after working all day," preparing lessons for the next day. Her experience at the Chestnut Street seminary was "invaluable to me, in my present position, in giving me plans and confidence."[18] But things did not bode well for the new seminary. "Mme. is an excellent person," she reported after a few weeks of teaching at the new school, but "entirely ignorant of the discipline of teaching."[19]

Olivia continued to lodge at Dr. Boardman's and to teach the Boardman children. Not surprisingly, the double load soon fatigued her. She was "losing strength," she complained to her father in a letter dated March 1859 in which she begged him not to return to Syracuse in the bitterly cold weather but to stay in Chancellorsville, Virginia. She put the best face on her heavy responsibilities, "I get along in peace and sweetness with Madame, and teach my classes as well as I can, without trouble to anyone, and thus far I have no expression of dissatisfaction from Madame."[20] But Mme. Vaillant's incompetence was fatal to her business, for her seminary closed after only one year, leaving Olivia without an occupation or a source of income apart from what she could earn with the Boardmans.

Joseph Slocum's financial situation continued to worsen. He had never recovered after earlier losses, and the panic of 1857 wiped him out. Now the mortgage on the house on West Genesee Street, Syracuse, was foreclosed and the house was put on the market. A letter from Margaret Slocum to "My dear Husband" cries out with indignation against the "strange conduct" of her husband's brother Hiram in "the breaking up and abandonment of our once dear home" and his insulting and callous treatment of her. Hiram had sold it to a Mr. Stoddard, "and he consented to close the bargain and give Mr. Stoddard five years to make his payments and furnish his family with a comfortable home and make his brother and family wanderers," she cried. "And Olivia is now thrown upon her own exertion for support." Olivia and Jermain "both feel what they never felt before, that they are homeless." Worst of all was that she herself had not been consulted in the matter: "I suppose that your brother has written to you in regard to the sale of your property," she wrote bitterly. "He must think I have no interest in it for he does not speak of it to me." Indeed, it was only by chance that she discovered that the house was being remodeled for resale when she happened to visit Syracuse. To witness her beloved house with its chimneys smashed in and debris raining down upon the family's few possessions and carpets was just too much to bear![21]

Perhaps in response to his wife's angry letter, Joseph Slocum returned to Syracuse to see the situation for himself. A couple of odd letters from his sister Almira express her surprise at the reappearance of a brother she had thought lost. One, dated November 1859 and addressed to "Joseph Slocum, Esq., New York," speaks of Joseph's "unexpected comming."[22] Another, addressed to him in Syracuse, expresses fear that she would "forget the name of the place where you are living"—an indication that the Slocum home was already sold and that he had taken lodgings.[23]

"I have seen and known so much of the awful reality of war"

Aged thirty in 1858, Olivia could do little but watch as her father faced business ruin and her mother stood by. Margaret Slocum's situation was a demonstration of married women's second-class citizenship, a dependant who shared the ignominy of her husband's bankruptcy and was powerless to rescue him from disgrace.[24] No wonder Olivia later named George Eliot's *Mill on the Floss* (1860) among her favorite books: her mother was George Eliot's Mrs. Tulliver, whose household goods were distrained by the fiendish financier Wakem. Like the resourceful Maggie Tulliver, who resolved to save the family name, Olivia determined at the very least to support herself.[25]

The Civil War found Olivia again working as a governess in the Brooklyn home of her cousin Margaret Burnet (a daughter of her Cincinnati uncle Groesbeck), but soon she was back in Philadelphia, living with the William Bucknells on Walnut Street. "Philadelphia is just as attractive to me as it ever was, and friends are just as kind," she wrote to her father, who was back in Syracuse and gravely ill.[26] "I see so much more of the war here than I did in Syracuse," she wrote, "and with a population between five and six thousand sick and wounded men directly in our midst one cannot easily forget it." Money continued to be a problem. She never had enough "green backs." "Still I have nothing to complain of, when I am in health, as I have been all this winter."[27]

Philadelphia offered Olivia a vivid view of the Civil War behind the lines. The entire population was mobilized in towns and villages across the North. Women formed aid associations, transformed existing church auxiliaries into organizations to aid the war effort, and went to work to manufacture and collect supplies for the Union armies. The secretary for the U.S. Sanitary Commission affiliated these local voluntary associations, creating a large bureaucratic machine to support the northern war effort.[28] One such association of churchwomen, St. Luke's Church Aid Society in Philadelphia, provides an example. When in May 1863 this society affiliated itself with the war-relief effort and became one of 394 auxiliaries, the secretary for the U.S. Sanitary Commission Women's Pennsylvania Branch duly wrote, "It gives us great pleasure to welcome St. Luke's Church Society as one of our auxiliaries and we doubt not we shall find its members most faithful coadjutants in the great work we all esteem a privilege."[29]

Women who organized in these auxiliaries made and donated cloth-ing and hospital supplies for the Union troops. Records from the Phil-adelphia Women's Pennsylvania Branch, the U.S. Sanitary Commission branch office in Philadelphia, located at 1307 Chestnut Street, indicate the scale of activities of women's war work. The office recorded the receipt on February 25, 1863, of 151 red and gray flannel shirts. Other auxiliaries sent in shirts and drawers.[30] This coordinating agency noted receipts of clothing, money, and supplies, acknowledging the patriot-ism of the donors. For example, a letter to the St. Luke's Auxiliary in June 1863 thanked the society for the supplies which would provide "the means of giving comfort to many a sick and wounded patient in the army hospitals." And a note on a receipt dated June 12, 1863, expressed thanks for a donation of apple butter and added hopefully, "Please send more whenever you can solicit it."[31]

Historian Jeanie Attie has recently argued that the large scale of women's production for the war effort changed the ways women under-stood their work and the ways they saw themselves in relation to the state. Women became critical of mismanagement by male bureaucrats and sought to control the disposition of the goods they produced. House-hold production, left rhetorically outside the money economy by indus-trialization and rendered invisible by new definitions of work, was suddenly seen as having value. To return to our Philadelphia example, that local branch acknowledged in August 1863 "a large and *valuable* contribution of clothing and Hospital stores from the St. Luke's Society Auxiliary to the Sanitary Commission."[32]

Whether or not Olivia made apple butter, sewed shirts for soldiers, or rolled bandages, her life was changed by the war. She explained this to a newspaper reporter years later, during the war against Spain. Back in the days of the Civil War she daily visited the hospitals for the wounded, she recalled. "A big hospital receiving shed was erected at the corner of Broad and Pine Streets and that was where all the sick and wounded soldiers were taken until other places were found for them."

When a carload of sick soldiers was brought to Philadelphia, the bells would ring, and all the women would know that it was a summons for them, and they would gather whatever they had in the way of needed supplies and go to the temporary hospital.[33]

The wealthy people she lived with gave her money to buy "delicacies and comforts" for the soldiers, she recalled, and she would make her way to a hospital twelve miles out of the city run by Dr. William W. Keen for men who had been shell-shocked or traumatized by war. Here she would play some quiet music on the piano. "Nothing seemed more helpful to those poor sufferers." Looking back on those years she reflected that "I have seen and known so much of the awful reality of war that I cannot speak lightly of anything connected with it," adding that she "often sat and held the hand of a dying soldier whose body was covered with vermin, which would drop from him in masses as soon as death came."[34]

Jermain and the Bushwackers

The Civil War swept Olivia's brother Jermain into new and dangerous scenes. At twenty-eight, he left Cincinnati and his wife and two young sons and enlisted for the Union, joining throngs of excited hopefuls milling around Washington, D.C., in expectation of opportunity and advancement. He was commissioned captain and commissary of subsistence by President Lincoln in March 1862, but he had more ambitious goals and wrote asking his wife Sallie to persuade her father Stephen L'Hommedieu to put in a word for him "if your father should meet anyone on the street who he thinks could benefit me."[35] Jermain was assigned to General Ormsby M. Mitchel's staff, with whom he served in southern Tennessee and northern Alabama. When Mitchel was removed from his post, Jermain became post commissary at Huntsville, Alabama. He wrote to his father and sister from Shelbyville, Tennessee, in April 1862, "I must say I like the novelty of the business, and my intercourse with all the officers is very pleasant—from the General down."[36]

Family historian Elihu Slocum's account of what followed is succinct but clear. Jermain was ordered to Murfreesboro, Tennessee, but the train he was traveling in was derailed by rebel bushwackers, and he suffered a serious head wound.[37] The scene at the Jermain estate in West Troy can only be imagined. Margaret Slocum had lost her house, her husband was a broken man, and now came the news that her only son lay gravely injured.

But Jermain survived (he would live on to the age of ninety-one, though with a metal plate in his skull). After he recovered, he was assigned to General Horatio G. Wright's staff, brevetted major, and by the time he resigned from the army in 1867 he had been commissioned colonel. Meanwhile, the demand for matériel of all kinds for the Union armies had transformed the northern economy, stimulating the development of industry and transportation. As business historian Maury Klein writes,

> A host of enterprising young men ignored the call to arms and devoted their energies to supplying the government with uniforms, weapons, blankets, shovels, wagons, foodstuffs, transportation, and other goods and services. . . . [T]hey earned for themselves not only fortunes but experience that would establish them as leaders of the postwar era.[38]

For Olivia's brother, the post of commissary charged with supplying food to the Union troops in the district had revealed some dazzling business possibilities. In a letter from the border states dated June 1862, he sounded out his father-in-law about "going into a cotton speculation in connection with some moneyed man. We will make money if you feel disposed. . . . I think $30 a bale will be an average profit."[39] These contacts proved useful after the war: the 1865 edition of *Williams Cincinnati Directory* shows J. J. Slocum a partner in Williams and Slocum Commission and Forwarding Merchants.[40]

Meanwhile, Joseph Slocum abandoned the attempt to farm in Virginia and returned to Syracuse, where he spent his last years, occasionally working as a tutor. As her father's condition worsened, Olivia returned to Syracuse to nurse him. Did Margaret Slocum relent and come as well? She was not there when Jermain wrote to the family from his unit in Tennessee in April 1862, for he addressed his letters to "My dear Father and Sister," and instructed them to send "[l]ove to Mother when you write."[41] Joseph Slocum died of tuberculosis at the Voorhees House, a middle-class hotel, on March 20, 1863, at the age of sixty-three and was buried in Oakwood Cemetery. An obituary in the Syracuse *Courier and Union* described him as "a man of large intellect, fine education, and gentlemanly attainments, and possessed of the most liberal views on all matters."[42]

A Liminal Place

During her period of mourning for her father from May to September 1863, Olivia stayed in Syracuse as a guest of the Longstreet family at Yates Castle, perhaps also as a governess. This grand home had been designed in the 1850s for wealthy businessman Cornelius Longstreet, who had made his fortune manufacturing ready-made clothing; its architect, James Renwick, boasted as an earlier design achievement the first Smithsonian Institution.[43] Olivia also worked at the home of George Barnes on James Street as governess to Miss Barnes, later the wife of Justice Frank H. Hiscock, as well as in the homes of other wealthy Syracusans, including the Leavenworth and the Hovey families, before returning to Philadelphia in the fall.[44]

The position of the governess was an ambiguous one. Part house-guest, part teacher, the governess was, as historians Leonore Davidoff and Catherine Hall have pointed out, a "liminal figure," a woman working for pay within a domestic setting and thus embodying both wage-earning independence and domesticity.[45] Cultural historian Mary Poovey agrees. The plight of the governess "thrust into prominence the instability of those middle-class assumptions about female nature and the separation of spheres on which the identity of the bourgeois subject was rhetorically and legally based," she writes. The governess was "the skeleton at the feast" of Victorian bourgeois culture, a grim reminder of the wrecked fortunes of a middle-class family.[46]

This is confirmed by the oblique language Olivia later used to refer to her work: "I was with rich people then," she stated. The terms she used were fluid, evasive even, reflecting the contradictions of her work and status. The conditions of her employment were left out, including whether or not she was paid—she may even have been a paid companion rather than a governess, for she wrote that she "stayed with" or was "in the homes of" various people during those years. And a newspaper article from the 1890s informed readers that in the 1860s "then Miss Olivia Slocum" was "a guest in many of the leading homes of Syracuse"— as if being a guest were an occupation! What is certain is that she was a refugee from the wreckage of her own family.[47]

Margaret Slocum, meanwhile, was at Hedge Lawn, the Jermain estate in West Troy that belonged to her brother Silvanus. Now elderly, Silvanus Pierson Jermain was a wealthy produce and commission merchant and banker. A sympathetic local historian later wrote that "[h]is life was devoted to the pursuit of riches but he was honest, cheerful, simple and frugal; his riches gave him neither luxury nor leisure." He would leave $1.5 million to his son when he died in 1869, a small fortune.[48]

Russell Sage

And what of Russell Sage, whose machinations had helped drive Joseph Slocum toward bankruptcy? While Olivia was living the life of the schoolteacher and governess, Russell Sage continued his breathtaking ascent in the world of railroads and finance. In 1847, when Olivia received her diploma at Troy, he was already a prosperous businessman with a reputation for financial wizardry. He was prominent in Troy politics, served as Rensselaer County treasurer for seven years, and was a member of Troy's City Council.[49] While Olivia was learning how to master a lesson plan and outwit a class of restless youngsters, Russell was buying his first railroad, and in 1853, when Olivia went to teach at the Chestnut Street Female Seminary in Philadelphia, Russell Sage was elected to Congress from Troy, New York, as a Whig. To quote Sarnoff, "He was already president of one railroad, vice president of another, and a member of the founding board of directors of the New York Central." He was reelected in the fall of 1854 by a large majority." In Congress, his only independent legislative initiative was a gesture of patriotism: he offered the joint resolution for the purchase of Mount Vernon for the nation. His patriotism also took the more self-serving form of vigorous promotion of congressional grants of land to railroads.[50]

In August 1857, when Charles P. Lanman invited Sage to submit an entry for the biographical dictionary of Congress he was compiling, Sage pleaded that he was "so occupied with my private business that I cannot give you such a narration as I desire." He added tactfully, "I shall confine myself to a brief reply to your inquiries and leave the filling up to your own knowledgeability in matters of the character." Despite this reticence, Sage produced a four-page account summarizing his career to date, including his two terms in Congress, adding proudly that he had "discharged my duties there, as well as elsewhere through life, with promptness, efficiency, and ability."[51]

In 1863, the Troy directory still listed "Russell Sage, Produce," but the Troy grocery business had become Slocum and Sage, Beef Packers, and had added a slaughterhouse. During the Civil War, the firm prospered from contracts to supply the Union army with foodstuffs.[52] But Sage's interests were far more extensive than this, and they were beginning to take off along with the nation's railroad networks. His role in the building of the Schenectady and Troy Railroad between 1848 and 1856 shows the possibilities for creative moneymaking in an era before effective state or federal regulation. While still Rensselaer County treasurer, Sage had been involved in a plan to link the Hudson River Railroad with routes to the West, thus eventually connecting New York City to Buffalo. The Schenectady and Troy Railroad, which was completed in 1848, controlled the only bridge across the Hudson and thus was a vital link to the West. It had been built by the city of Troy with the help of grants from the New

York State legislature at a cost of over $700,000. Russell Sage was its president. But Sage was also head of a committee of ten citizens appointed to decide the fate of the railroad, which was losing $100,000 a year. On Sage's advice, the city sold the railroad to his friend, politician Edwin D. Morgan, president of the Hudson River Railroad, for $200,000. Morgan then sold it to the New York Central, a consolidation of New York railroads formed in 1852. Sage was a director, as was Morgan. Sage made a fortune on the deal, but his stock with his Troy constituents plummeted. Sage and Morgan got their comeuppance in 1856 when the legislature gave a charter to the New York Central to build a bridge at Albany, downstream from Troy, diverting traffic from Troy to Albany. But the episode was still remarkable for the use of public moneys and public office to grease the wheels of private profit-making.[53]

This episode turned Russell Sage from the city of Troy's darling to its villain. Sage turned his attention to developing railroads in Wisconsin and other states. He traveled constantly—to New York and to the West and back again—to supervise his business affairs. By 1863, he was already director or president of several lines, including the Milwaukee and St. Paul, the Iowa Central, the Missouri Pacific, the Union Pacific, the Wabash, and the Texas and Pacific. He was a man in a hurry who habitually signed his letters, "Yours very truly in haste, Russell Sage."[54]

It was time to move to New York City, the vital center of commerce and deal-making, and in 1863 Sage purchased a house for $32,000 and moved there with Maria. The house was located at Fifth Avenue and Thirty-Ninth Street, near the home of his political ally Edwin D. Morgan, now the governor of New York State.[55] Maria Winne Sage may already have been unwell at this time; soon she fell gravely ill, and Russell Sage's charmed existence suffered its first major setback when Maria died from cancer of the stomach in 1867 at the age of only forty-seven.[56] She was buried at Oakwood Cemetery in Troy. On the grey obelisk that marks her grave, a simple, moving inscription states:

Maria Winne Sage, wife of Russell Sage
Born July 4, 1819
Died May 7, 1867
An affectionate and devoted wife
Her virtues and deeds will ever be cherished by all who knew her.
She believed and trusted in Jesus Christ and met death
With resignation, peace, hope, and joy.

The widowed Russell Sage now moved into New York's Fifth Avenue Hotel. Perhaps he couldn't bear to be alone in the house, with its sad

FIGURE 4.1. The eligible widower from Troy, N.Y., Russell Sage. Mrs. A. W. Fairbanks, comp., *Emma Willard and Her Pupils, or Fifty Years of Troy Female Seminary, 1822–1872* (New York: Published by Mrs. Russell Sage, 1898).

associations. Nevertheless, the hotel proved to be an excellent venue for the entrepreneurial Sage, for its lobbies and foyers were a meeting place for bankers, businessmen, and distinguished visitors from the United States and abroad. King's *Handbook of New York City* (1892) declared, "No other single hotel in the world has ever entertained so many distinguished people as have been received at the Fifth Avenue. Everybody who wishes to keep in touch with the men of the day must frequent its corridors, and on occasions of political excitement, financial crises and startling events, it is the centre of information and interest."[57] Yet Russell Sage's biographer Paul Sarnoff may be correct that Sage missed having a home and especially missed the services of a wife who could be a hostess to his politician and railroad cronies and a companion in his few hours of rest. He had also lost his mother, Prudence Risley Sage, in September 1865. His despair during his wife's last illness may explain (though it doesn't excuse) why he befriended and then took advantage of a female servant who had come from Ireland to live with her sister, an employee in the Sages' Fifth Avenue house. The consequences would come back to haunt him in the 1890s.

Russell and Olivia Become Reacquainted

Older accounts of Russell Sage's life state that he met Olivia through his first wife, who had been her schoolfriend at Troy Female Seminary.[58] But Maria actually attended the seminary in 1838, eight years before Olivia became a student. It seems much more likely that Olivia met Russell Sage when she was a student at Troy or even earlier through her Uncle Hiram Slocum and his circle.

If you walk north a few blocks from the site of Troy Female Seminary, now marked by Russell Sage College's three oldest buildings, to Washington Square, you stand at what was the most fashionable part of Troy in the 1840s. Here, successful merchants who had previously been content to live over their warehouses on River Street, were building substantial townhouses. One hundred and fifty years later, these dark and handsome brownstones formed a gloomy but authentic-looking setting for the 1993 film version of Henry James's novel, *The Age of Innocence*. Russell Sage had moved here with Maria in 1846. His house at 179 Second Street is still there, though now somewhat shabby. Only two houses away at 186 Second Street is the brownstone that Olivia's Uncle Hiram Slocum built in 1849. As I stood in the snow and looked at these houses, separated only by one other house and the width of a street, I imagined Russell and Olivia meeting here during Olivia's vacations from teaching in the 1850s, before bitter quarrels divided Hiram Slocum from his brother Joseph's family.[59] Hiram Slocum and Russell Sage were not only acquainted, not only associates in business (both had served as directors of the Troy Union Railroad Company, organized in 1851), they were Washington Square neighbors. Whittemore's commissioned history (whose writing Olivia oversaw) even states that Olivia had known Russell Sage from childhood.

Moreover, Olivia had often spent her school vacations in the hospitable surroundings of the Jermain estate at Watervliet, West Troy, a few miles south of Troy on the Albany side of the river. Hedge Lawn was the beautiful home of her Uncle Silvanus Pierson Jermain, where her mother had often stayed since 1853, and here Olivia's cousin, James

Barclay Jermain and his wife Catherine presided over receptions and parties that made the home "a center of hospitality and activity for the many brothers and sisters of Silvanus and their children."[60] Olivia loved fun and conversation amid family and friends, and legend has it that she met Congressman Russell Sage and his wife at her uncle's house and that she knew him well enough to write him a letter of condolence when his wife died.[61] Olivia and Russell also met at the home of William C. Sage, Russell's older brother by two years and a business partner of Hiram Slocum, and it was here that they were reacquainted. Russell asked Olivia to come riding on the outskirts of town. He was twelve years her senior, and here the tall, gentle man with the grey eyes and quiet wit fell for the petite, vivacious, and voluble schoolteacher.[62]

But family feuds stood in the way of a connection. By the 1860s, any ally of Hiram Slocum would have been the enemy of Olivia's family.[63] No wonder her relatives opposed the marriage. The bitterness between Olivia's mother and her uncle (and former benefactor) drove a wedge between the Slocums and Russell Sage, Hiram's ally.[64] And there was the old enmity between Russell Sage and Joseph Slocum. In 1850, opposition from the Silver Grey Whigs, of which Joseph Slocum was one, had defeated Russell Sage's first run for Congress.[65] And the dispute between Joseph Slocum and Russell Sage over the Milwaukee warehouse affair was of recent memory. The litigation had dragged through the courts until it reached the Supreme Court on appeal in 1863 (*Wheeler v. Sage*, 68 U.S. [I. Wallace] 518 [1863]), where the appellants' case was denied. The court ruled that Joseph Slocum and his associates had no right to expect redress just because their former partners had turned against them, for the plaintiffs had conspired with Sage in an illegal transaction.[66]

What Olivia felt about marrying a man who had involved her father in financial loss we do not know, but bad feelings between family members seem to have held up the marriage for a year or so. Russell Sage's reputation in Troy was that of a hard-driving moneylender who took advantage of other peoples' misfortunes. But the death of Joseph Slocum in 1863 and of her Uncle Silvanus in April 1869 seem to have removed any effective opposition.

Reader, She Married Him

Go carefully through the collections of Troy newspapers from 1869. Turn the large, stiff pages though they are dusty and disintegrating, and you will find a very small notice in the *Troy Budget* for November 24, 1869, announcing a "Wedding in High Society." The account is sparse. On November 24, 1869, at Watervliet, New York, Miss Olivia Slocum, daughter of the late Joseph Slocum and niece of Hiram Slocum, married Hon. Russell Sage, two-term congressman from Rensselaer County. The ceremony of marriage took place in the presence of a few friends at Hedge Lawn, the home of Olivia's cousin James B. Jermain, and was performed by Rev. Henry August Boardman.[67]

Did she marry him for money? For that, and other reasons. Her need for money was urgent and constant, for who could live on $200 a year? More to the point, who could live well on such a salary? As a governess in Philadelphia and Syracuse, Olivia had seen how wealthy people lived and she was impressed. Family letters state that she liked to live well—felt entitled, even.[68] By the beginning of 1869, her fortieth birthday was behind her and she could hardly expect any more proposals of marriage. She was tired of depending on friends. Moreover, she was the sole support of her mother; her brother, impaired by his head wound, was not expected to amount to much as a provider. Personal liking aside, Olivia must have been flattered to receive an offer of marriage from one of the wealthiest men in the nation—and enormously relieved to accept.

Marriage allowed her to move onto a wider stage. How glad she was that she had not accepted her very first proposal of marriage, she told a reporter from the *New York Herald* many years later. "If I had married the first man who proposed to me I suppose I would now be on a farm. . . . But I would not like that at all. It would be too narrow a life for me. I would prefer single blessedness."[69] And Olivia was ambitious, in that genteel, feminine way that Emma Willard had made respectable, and she was conscious of her talents and proud of her quick wit. As Mrs. Russell Sage, she would have money to spend. Like Willard, she had executive ability. Perhaps like Willard, she too would be queenly.

Part II

❦

Becoming Mrs. Russell Sage
1869–1906

Five

The Work of Benevolence?

Mrs. Russell Sage, the Carlisle School, and Indian Reform

Mrs. Sage's education and social position, combined with her energy,
self-assurance, and personal force, well fitted her for a public role.

—Irvin G. Wyllie, *"Margaret Olivia Slocum Sage"* (1971)[1]

The newly married pair lost no time in moving to New York. The night
boat took them down the Hudson to the city, and they moved into the
brownstone residence at 506 Fifth Avenue and Thirty-Ninth Street
where Russell Sage had lived since 1863 with Maria, his first wife.[2]

The marriage, a minor event in Russell Sage's life, marked a major
transition in Olivia's, ending a long period of indecision, restlessness,
and penury. It cured the mysterious symptoms of illness, or made invalidism unnecessary perhaps.[3] What enormous good fortune to be married, at forty-one, to a gentle, thoughtful man of business talent and
fabulous wealth, to exchange the provincialism of Syracuse, or even
Philadelphia, for New York City, the nation's financial and commercial
capital! Instead of the life of the unmarried governess, an employee in
other women's homes, enduring their regimes and their children, she
was the wife of a wealthy and powerful man, mistress of her own large
house on Manhattan's most fashionable street, free to pursue pleasure,
diversion, or good works.

She began by reuniting her family. Her widowed mother moved into
the Sage household and stayed for the next twenty-six years. An
acquaintance left a portrait of the three of them driving out in Central
Park, the old lady wrapped warmly against the cold.[4] A few years later,
in 1877, Olivia's brother and his wife Sallie L'Hommedieu Slocum arrived
from Chicago and lived nearby. Russell Sage took Jermain into the firm

FIGURE 5.1. Aimee Dupont painted Olivia Sage as a plump
and elaborately dressed matron, undated but probably soon
after her marriage to Russell Sage. Portrait at the Rockefeller
Archive Center. Courtesy estate of Mrs. Jean Leinart.

as a secretary. Jermain's sons were now almost grown. Herbert, aged
twenty-two, was at West Point, Stephen was fifteen, and their daughter
and Olivia's niece and namesake, Margaret Olivia Slocum, was seven.[5]

For Olivia, there were two small clouds on the horizon. They cast
a shadow over a letter she wrote to Jermain from the fashionable resort
town of Long Branch, New Jersey, a few years after her wedding. Long
Branch was beautiful. A promotional booklet described "its splendid surf
always rolling and singing; its miles of matchless bluffs covered with
green . . . ; its charming country; its pure atmosphere, and freedom from
annoying insects; its fine society and high moral character."[6] Gracious

resorts such as the Continental Hotel, with its 700 feet of beach frontage and rooms for up to 1,000 guests, catered to tired New Yorkers.[7] "[I]t is all very nice," Olivia wrote to Jermain, "and I am more contented than I have ever been at Long Branch though I hoped to have another room for a guest, though for mother or Olivia [her niece] I can have a cot put up and make either of them comfortable." Evidently, Olivia had discovered that her multimillionaire husband economized when it came to paying for hotel rooms and that his talent for making money involved extreme reluctance to spend.[8]

The second cloud was the realization that in gaining financial security, she had lost independence. Olivia was fascinated with family history, and this interest was heightened by a newly published genealogy of the Slocums by a Dr. Charles Slocum. "I am sorry Dr. Slocum cannot find the link that connects us to the Rhode Island Slocum's," she wrote to her brother, "and I would like to go to Providence myself and sift the matter *which I cannot very well do*."[9] As a governess and single woman, Olivia had been relatively unencumbered by social expectations. She had moved around a great deal and made her own decisions, limited only by lack of money. Now she had to observe the rituals of polite society and the conventions of ladyhood. Genealogical explorations of her family that involved poking around in New England graveyards would have to wait, and they did.

Russell Sage had prospered during the Civil War, and he continued to do so during the postwar boom, mysteriously making money even when thousands of other men lost it.[10] This was a period of business instability that would last up to and beyond the passage of the Interstate Commerce Act (1887) and the Sherman Antitrust Act (1890) and that was marked by the collapse of the system of informal business alliances called pools.[11] A veteran of railroad politics since his involvement with the New York Central in the 1850s, Sage had acquired the essential political connections in New York Whig circles, to which he added a useful ring of political allies during two terms in Congress (1853–1857). By the 1870s, his connections included Democrat Samuel Tilden as well as influential Republicans such as Grant. The cooperation of powerful lawyers such as Tilden smoothed away legal obstacles and made possible the great continental systems of transportation and communication, while political connections secured congressional subsidies for railroads. In the 1870s and 1880s, Sage and other large financiers raised the capital for railroad construction. As his financial partner and confidant, Russell Sage supplied the means for Jay Gould (1836–1892) to buy up rival railroads. When Gould consolidated control over the Union

Pacific in 1874, he completed a transcontinental network comprising over 15,000 miles of railroad. For a few years, Sage and Gould dominated the nation's communications and transportation networks, including Western Union.[12] In size, these giant enterprises rivaled or surpassed the federal government itself. In 1891, a year when the U.S. Post Office employed 95,449 (which was 61 percent of the federal workforce) and the combined armed forces of the United States totaled only 39,492, the Pennsylvania Railroad (which was in the portfolio of Gould's rival Vanderbilt) employed 110,000 workers.[13] Sage did not have to concern himself with details of management, however. These firms were so complicated that no one could manage all the financial, legal, and organizational aspects; instead, he came to rely on hierarchies of full-time salaried managers.[14]

The Trouble with Russell Sage

Russell Sage was best known for his activity on the New York Stock Exchange. Here he perfected what were called "puts and calls," and here over the next twenty years, he made and lost enormous amounts of money. Contemporaries did not know what to make of the financier. His own explanation of his career was self-serving. In his handwritten autobiographical entry for Lanman's dictionary of members of Congress, Sage ascribed his early success to "close application, upright dealing, and an energy of character not often met with."[15] He told a more magisterial version later in life: "My aim in life has been to do my share in developing the material resources of the country."[16]

But Sage's contemporaries did not all share the financier's complacent self-assessment. The press portrayed him as a man greedy for wealth and ruthless in acquiring it. Journalists had a field day with his eccentric behavior and appearance, the cheap-looking clothes, the quiet—or was it duplicitous?—demeanor, the shameful attempts to avoid spending so much as a nickel on a newspaper. They delighted in contrasting the appearance with the reality: Sage was the shabby man who owned half the nation's infrastructure; he was the Yankee hayseed come to town whose gentle manner belied a predatory aim, the hypocritical millionaire who went to church but passed the collection plate, belatedly adding some pennies he found in his pocket. He was "Deacon Sage," who seemed to have no pleasure but work, yet was named in at least one paternity suit.[17]

His close ties to Jay Gould also made him an object of suspicion. His fellow financiers admired his unerring financial instincts, and to his biographer, Wall Street stockbroker Paul Sarnoff, Sage was "the very soul of discretion."[18] But the anti-business Gustavus Myers described the Sage-Gould partnership as follows: "Sage, crafty, somber, and reclusive; Gould supplying the public audacity."[19] The press treated Gould as if he were Jewish (he wasn't), attributing to him a number of supposedly Semitic vices such as secrecy and greed.[20]

Sage called forth a different kind of cultural anxiety, an unease about wealth detached from honest work. Captains of industry such as Carnegie produced new kinds of goods in new ways, but Sage was a finance capitalist whose wizardry produced capital funds for acquisitions, takeovers, and buyouts by business partners and speculative raids on the market. His countrified Yankee appearance made the miracle of his wealth even more unnerving. His homespun philosophy contrasted with the revolution in the nation's productive power. Russell Sage's own long life spanned the beginning of this revolution and its end: early in the century, he and another lad had borrowed their fathers' horses to haul iron ore from a mine a few miles from their home to the single blast furnace then in Oneida, New York. By the century's end, the production of iron and steel was revolutionized with the creation of the first billion-dollar corporation, the U.S. Steel Corporation.[21]

It was not his wealth that critics condemned so much as the fact that it came from speculation. In 1874, Sage purchased a seat on the still-unregulated New York Stock Market and became a master of the highly speculative "puts and calls," a kind of betting on futures.[22] Sage did not invent these types of speculative operations, but he became famous for them. He allowed small operators to invest, using his own huge credit. Sarnoff, himself a money expert, described puts and calls as "magnificent devices for stock-price manipulation." Sage thus embodied a variant of capitalism that many believed to be illicit or immoral, namely the speculative or gambling aspect of business.[23] Nineteenth-century public opinion sanctified the virtues of productive work, thrift, prudence, and rationality but defined as deviant a type of gain that was "irrational and selfish."[24] "Wall Street does not produce a dollar," wrote critic John Hume. "It creates nothing. It draws its sustenance entirely from outsiders. It is a blood-sucker."[25] The New York Stock Exchange is "an evil in the land, a danger to private wealth, a disturbing force in general business, and a foe to public morals," he went on. It was an enormous devil-fish

> with a hundred-thousand arms reaching into all parts of the country, and all equipped with suckers more or less powerful, and busy, every

one of them, in extracting nourishment for the monster to which it belongs. The trouble is that its tentacles are rarely seen. They work in the dark; they have the gift of invisibility. But, oh! how many victims have they strangled to death.[26]

As for the Wall-Street broker, "He can ruin the country one hour and he can save it the next. He can blight the crops of a whole section, or he can fill the land with abundance. He can make war or can make peace, exactly as his monetary interest demands."[27]

Moral criticism of stock market manipulation was sharp: "[T]he injury done to society by those forms of gambling that are recognized and undisguised is trifling when compared with the damage done by that form of gambling which wears the mask of business," declared Washington Gladden in 1884. "Those are the pimples on the skin; this is the corruption in the blood."[28] Russell Sage's wealth seemed magical, his profits the result of mere luck. They required no payback to losers or to society as a whole: Sage gave nothing to charity because he was a gambler whose fortune came by chance—it fell into his lap despite his blatant and (to his wife) infuriating lack of interest in religious observance, shown by his reluctance to go to church. He shrugged off any suggestion that he owed a debt to society. He was a man blessed by fortune who owed no one anything and was unresponsive to the promptings of conscience or the appeals of Christian stewardship.[29]

The contrast with Olivia could not have been greater, as if Olivia and Russell represented the opposite poles—benevolence and avarice— in the late nineteenth century's ideological division of labor that assigned the moral and religious realm to women, the material to men.[30] Olivia would become famous as the embodiment of generosity and of female benevolence when she gave away to charity the money that her husband had conjured from the thin air of Wall Street. Sage philanthropy, conducted by his widow after his death and in his name, retroactively spread the blessings of Sage money and gestured toward reconciling Sage success with morality.[31]

The Sages made an odd couple in New York Gilded Age society, their eccentricity widely known. When other millionaires cruised in yachts as big as ocean liners, Russell Sage was usually to be found on Wall Street. Other great financiers and industrialists of the Gilded Age found time for their favorite pastimes. Jay Gould had Lyndhurst, the Gothic Revival mansion overlooking the Hudson that he purchased in 1880 for $250,000, where he pottered among the ferns and orchids in the great greenhouses that covered almost four acres. It was said that he sometimes spent as much as $300 for a single orchid plant—half a worker's wages for a year.[32] J. P. Morgan had his *Corsair*, a magnificent black yacht 165 feet long. He joined the New York Yacht Club and subsequently purchased one stupendous boat after another. *Corsair II*, purchased in 1890, was 241 feet long, and *Corsair III* was over 300 feet long and required a crew of seventy. These yachts offered a floating retreat where he could enjoy livelier company than that of his wife.[33]

Some of the more outrageous stories about Russell Sage's frugality originated with his enemies. In the 1890s, when William Laidlaw, Jr., who had a case pending against him, was interviewed on the subject, not surprisingly, he portrayed the financier as cruel and calculating. Unlike Jay Gould, who was concerned about his public image, Russell Sage seems to have relished press attention and even to have spread some stories about his miserliness on purpose, such as the story that he sent out for two apples for lunch at two cents apiece and that when he traveled to work on the train he picked up a newspaper left by other commuters in order to avoid buying one himself.[34]

A more reliable account of Sage's daily routine depicts him at lunch with other Western Union directors. An assistant broker who visited the Western Union office every day during the lunch hour in order to hand Sage the latest stock quotations left the following description of the financier eating lunch with Jay Gould, Collis Huntington, Cyrus Field, and other directors.

> The door was always locked and I had a signal tap that called for Mr. Sage to open it. He'd always drop his knife and fork immediately to study the market changes. Sometimes he'd casually mention changes to the others. But when he'd pencil his order at the bottom of the letter to his chief broker, he would screen what he wrote with his hand, like a gambler hiding his cards. That was always the signal for a little quiet fun for the others. Jay Gould would wink at Field and all the others would grin. But they'd never laugh out loud. And when Mr. Sage had finished his orders and picked up his knife and fork once more, the faces of the five wore no trace of the smiles that had just left them.[35]

Sarnoff's gossipy biography of Sage has a great deal of fun with the idea that the Sage marriage was a pitched battle and that Olivia was madly jealous of the first Mrs. Sage, and this view has taken on a life of its own. Sarnoff claimed that Olivia found it easy to fill the role of second wife, thanks to a polite agreement to erase the memory of the first, yet he offers no evidence for this assertion.[36]

In fact, stray incidents suggest that the Sage marriage was a contented union of two people who were nevertheless opposites in many ways. We have glimpses of happy times, such as visits to Saratoga Springs in the summer season so that Russell Sage could enjoy the racing, though as one female commentator noted, "Saratoga belongs to the world of men. Nowhere do women seem so much like appendages."[37] Perhaps early in her marriage Olivia still liked being an appendage of a wealthy man. And there were holidays with friends: a memorable visit at Craigside on the Hudson in the 1870s almost ended in disaster when Russell and Olivia set off one evening by boat to visit Olivia's nephew, Herbert J. Slocum, then a cadet at the Military Academy at West Point on the other side. Olivia later recalled: "Mr. Sage and I went in a rowboat from Cold Spring to West Point for evening parade, [and] on our way back wind and tide were so strong that the boat came very near striking the rocks off Constitution Island." Arriving back, they found that friends had feared for their safety.[38] Olivia fell in love with the Hudson River Valley with its craggy, romantic scenery. And she was thrilled by its connections to Anna and Susan Warner, sisters who lived on Constitution Island, just off West Point, and whose best-selling novel *Wide, Wide World* (1850) was her favorite.[39]

Snippets of evidence from the 1890s suggest that the couple had established a comfortable relationship. For one thing, Russell Sage valued Olivia's judgment. Interviewed for *Demorest's Family Magazine* in 1894, he described women as "remarkably far sighted in business matters," adding, "doubtless many of the immense fortunes made by men are largely due to the counsel of women." At the couple's seaside home, a visitor noticed an upstairs study: "a small room fitted with desk, bookcase, and a few chairs, where Mr. and Mrs. Sage conduct correspondence and matters of business."[40] By the 1890s, Olivia was addressing Russell affectionately as "father," although the couple had no children. This does not suggest a cold or unhappy marriage.[41]

Like many couples, they were a study in contrasts. Russell Sage was tall and thin. He was a man of few words with a dry wit. A kindly portrait of him is in Elizabeth Cady Stanton's diary. When Stanton met John D. Rockefeller for the first time, she recorded meeting "Mr. Rockefeller, the oil king, who reminds me of my old friend Russell Sage."

> Both men are so quiet and retiring, you would not think it possible that they possess such executive and tireless ability. You imagine such men must be always bustling about, continually giving evidence of activity. But John D. Rockefeller and Russell Sage offer a striking proof of what I have often remarked, that it is the quiet who are the strong.[42]

Others, too, noticed Russell Sage's quiet manner. A *Tribune* reporter who visited Sage's office shortly after the financial panic of May 1884, when Sage had been forced to pay out an amazing $8 million of his own money to creditors, found the financier looking "like a well-to-do country farmer" and was astonished at his calm good humor. "There was nothing whatever in his appearance to indicate that he had just passed through the ordeal of last week and had transferred millions of dollars from his own account to those of the numerous holders of his privileges."[43]

In contrast, Olivia was voluble. Portraits show a woman whose face betrays intelligence, humor, and strength. Her confident, animated manner reminded people that she had formerly been a schoolteacher. Later, when wealth and social prominence together with old age made her reckless, she enjoyed holding forth on topics that interested her, and no one dared to stem the torrent of her conversation.[44]

A Wild Ride Every Day

Russell Sage has "one pride—and that is his horses . . . , a good, big stable of fast steppers," a *Times* reporter noted in 1887.[45] And when it came to horses, Sage spared no expense. After spending long hours poring over financial reports, he enjoyed the wild abandonment of a gallop. At four o'clock every day, he left his office at 71 Broadway to enjoy his favorite pastime. A note hurriedly penned from his office on July 13, 1882, to a T. A. Disbrow, Esq., reveals his life's twin obsessions. Sage asks to try out another horse because "The Brown Mare I tried was not as quick or as fast as I expected." It ends, "P.S. You see the stock market is going as I told you it would."[46] Five weeks later, his enthusiasm outrunning his grammar, he wrote asking Disbrow to bring the brown horse to his stable at 37 West Forty-Third Street. "The Mare is doing nicer both in condition and looks."

> I can manage with my three Horses to get along very nicely as Neddie and Nellie drive nice together or single—the new horse is a splendid Burham Horse for single as well as for double driving.[47]

In New York's Central Park, Russell Sage could enjoy himself. This was not on the park's six miles of bridle paths which were thronged on a Sunday, for there, according to one guidebook, "the Police are everywhere to arrest fast driving" defined as over six miles an hour. But one boulevard was set aside "where men may try the mettle of their teams."[48] On a special roadway, "broad, level, and well Macadamized" racing was allowed, and here "the notable men of New York may be seen in their glory" on horses that cost as much as $50,000 apiece.

FIGURE 5.2. Helen Gould and her sister Anna, the
daughters of Helen Miller Gould and financier Jay Gould,
around 1866. Elmer Holmes Bobst Library Archives, New
York, N.Y.

Fast old men and fast young men, leaders of the bulls and bears on
exchange, stock speculators, millionaires, railroad kings, bankers,
book-men, and merchants, the bloods of the city, and all who can
command a two-forty horse, appear on the drive. All is exhilaration;
the road is full of dust; teams crowd the thoroughfare; horses tear up
and down, to the horror of nervous and timid people; fast teams race
with each other, and frequently interlock and smash up, while the
tearing teams hold on their course, carrying terror and dismay along
the whole road. Danger as well as excitement attends the drive. Some
of the fastest teams are driven by men between sixty and seventy,

who have all the enthusiasm of youth, and shout out their "Hi! hi's!" and other exclamations, so common to fast teams at their utmost speed.[49]

Gambling on the results added to the excitement. In 1887, Russell Sage bet $5,000 on one race. He won, donating the proceeds to charity.[50]

Olivia developed some friendships that would last for many years. Her relationship with Helen Miller Gould was especially close. Helen Jay Miller had married Jay Gould in January 1863, and the Goulds lived nearby at 578 Fifth Avenue with a growing family that eventually numbered six children. When the financial dealings of her husband left Helen socially ostracized, Olivia befriended her. Both women were "lady managers" at the Woman's Hospital, and when Olivia was absent from her duties there in December 1884, Helen wrote on hospital letterhead telling Olivia how much she was missed, ending, "with the dearest love and wishes for you, Helen." Olivia also taught the Gould children, and Helen, the eldest daughter, born in 1870 (called "Nellie" to distinguish her from her mother), became her favorite (see fig. 5.2).[51] Russell Sage and Jay Gould remained intimates, Gould remarkably describing Sage in a note as "one of the most lovable of men."[52]

Other neighbors were the McCormicks, who had moved into a four-story house at 40 Fifth Avenue in the fall of 1866. A fellow student of Troy Female Seminary, though not a contemporary (she had attended in 1852–1853), Nettie McCormick, too, had married an older man: Cyrus McCormick was forty-eight when the couple married in January 1858, twenty-five years her senior. Though the McCormicks soon moved to Chicago, Nettie and Olivia remained friends into old age.[53]

Making a Virtue of Necessity

Meanwhile, Olivia was forced to suffer whatever simplicity her husband decreed. Her pleasures were modest ones. She went out for a walk if the weather was fine and fed the birds in Central Park, especially a pair of cardinals that wintered there, prompting witticisms that this was a pastime that cost her husband nothing. At home, the Sages kept numerous cats and dogs, and, if we can believe Sarnoff, who claimed to have interviewed family veterinarian J. Elliott Crawford, this was an eccentric household where the death of one of the pets meant that the undertaker was called on to perform a solemn funeral which the vet and the servants were obliged to attend.[54] But Olivia also began to turn her private enjoyment of animals into public work. She joined the New York Women's League for Animals; later she would be a major contributor to institutions for the care of animals and to the movement for their humane treatment.

Alongside the world of glitter and fashion whose doings filled the gossip columns, a philanthropic elite of earnest-minded wealthy people busied themselves with charitable good works, and Olivia now joined their ranks.[55] Her evangelical Protestant upbringing pushed her toward earnest endeavor, and her own family contained a model of philanthropic womanhood in Catharine Ann Jermain, wife of her cousin James, of whom it was said when she died that "when she went forth from her home, it was most frequently upon errands of mercy."[56] Scholars have suggested that charity allowed nineteenth-century white middle-class women to enjoy a more expansive public life and to overturn some of the barriers to women's opportunities placed there by law and custom. Too old to have children, unable to spend freely because of her husband's careful regime, yet convinced that her social standing and Puritan heritage entitled her to a public presence, Olivia constructed an identity around benevolence, taking on responsibilities toward others seen as less fortunate. The self-conscious rhetoric of the mission of educated women at Troy Female Seminary also propelled her toward public work.

In 1881, Olivia traveled to Carlisle, Pennsylvania, to see for herself a famous experiment in racial assimilation, the Indian boarding school founded by Richard Henry Pratt, and she became a convert. The Sages, the Goulds, and their associates such as the Jesups and the Dodges formed an earnest Protestant circle that had been electrified by the preaching of evangelist Dwight Moody, who visited New York in 1876.[57] Reform and revivals produced in these earnest Christians both excitement and a renewed sense of purpose, especially when the object of benevolence was exotic. This was the case with what was euphemistically called "Indian reform."

Olivia was certainly familiar with the Indian reform movement from her Philadelphia association at the Chestnut Street Female Seminary with Mary Bonney, a leading force in the movement. Bonney was still active three decades later, founding the Woman's National Indian Association (WNIA) in 1879, an outgrowth of the missionary circle of her Philadelphia Baptist church. By the 1880s, under the extraordinary leadership of Amelia Quinton, the WNIA counted branches in twenty states and had eighty-three auxiliaries across the nation. Quinton's organization was part of the coalition of Protestant reformers known collectively as the "Friends of the Indian," whose Lake Mohonk conferences, held throughout the 1880s, lobbied for the federal land and assimilation policy that became the Dawes Severalty Act (1887).[58]

Pratt's scheme to civilize Native Americans started when he commanded a regiment of black cavalry in the West just after the Civil War. When he was charged with guarding seventeen Indian captives at Fort Marion in St. Augustine, Florida, he became interested in the possibilities of "Americanizing" them. St Augustine was a resort that New York's elite visited by steamer during the winter months, and Pratt's famous "trained Indians" at Fort Marion soon became one of the tourist sights.[59] He subsequently continued his experiments at Hampton Institute, and because he was a skillful self-promoter and publicist by 1879 he had managed to secure both public and private funding for an Indian boarding school at Carlisle, Pennsylvania.[60] His plan was to bring Indian children from western reservations to Carlisle, where they would come into contact with white civilization, a proposal dubbed by a recent scholar "education for extinction."[61] The Sages were among a number of wealthy people Pratt courted in an effort to raise money for Carlisle. Socially prominent New York and Philadelphia citizens were named to the school's board of trustees. He also won supporters in Washington, and soon senators, congressmen, and others were arriving by the trainload to view the civilized Indians. The politicians were impressed, and the House Committee on Indian Affairs reported favorably on a bill to appropriate public funds for Carlisle (see fig. 5.3).[62]

Carlisle also became a popular destination for excursions by wealthy eastern city dwellers, visits that were duly noted by the school paper, *Morning Star.* In June 1883, "A company from Boston 160 in number made Carlisle School one of their points of interest while on an Excursion."[63] In May 1884, the paper recorded the arrival of the Committee on Appropriations, Indian Affairs and Education and members from both houses of Congress, together with their wives.[64] For those who could not visit in person, Pratt used the *Morning Star* to encourage money donations, emphasizing the role wealthy "friends" could play in sustaining the good work and listing donations of money and equipment.[65]

Pratt insisted that the Indian was in a position analogous to that of the freedman. "The negro is from as low a state of savagery as the Indian," but "in two hundred years['] association with Anglo-Saxons . . . he has laid aside the characteristics of his former savage life, and to a great extent, adopted those of the most advanced and highest civilized nation in the world," Pratt declared. "This miracle of change came from association with the higher civilization." He went on:

FIGURE 5.3. Richard Henry Pratt of the Carlisle School with Spotted Tail, a Sioux chief, and Quaker supporters Susan and Marianne Longstreet and Rebecca Haines. Olivia admired Pratt's work at Carlisle. Carlisle Indian Industrial School Collection. Courtesy U.S. Army Military History Institute.

If millions of black savages can become transformed and assimilated, and if annually hundreds of thousands of foreign emigrants from all lands can also become Anglicized, Americanized, assimilated, and absorbed through association, there is but one plain duty resting upon us with regard to the Indians, and that is to relieve them of their sav-agery and other alien qualities by the same methods used to relieve the others."

"Help them, too, to die as helpless tribes," he declared, using a trope from the Christian theology of redemption, "and to rise up among us as strong and capable individual men and American citizens."[66]

Here was a cause calling for white Christian women to invest time and money. Evangelical women who had earlier defined it as their duty to bring civilization to their sisters in foreign lands now responded to the appeal to evangelize and "domesticate" the "alien within," a process that scholar Amy Kaplan labels "Manifest Domesticity." This involved remaking gender roles, vesting landownership in the male, and establishing a Euro-American middle-class gender division of labor and authority in a nuclear family structure. Reform in heathen lands became reform of the heathen *within* the domestic body of America.[67]

Olivia was already active in the Woman's Union Missionary Society of America for Heathen Lands, whose purpose was to send out single women as missionaries. She eventually headed its executive committee.[68] Now she joined with other women of the WNIA to support Carlisle's "civilizing" goals. For example, the WNIA donated metal-working tools for the school's industrial training program in fulfillment of their purpose to teach Indian men male-appropriate trades.[69] In 1887, along with female members of WNIA branches in New York and Brooklyn, she sponsored a visit by 140 Carlisle students and teachers to Philadelphia, New York, and Brooklyn. Points of interest included Wanamakers department store and the mint in Philadelphia, the Statue of Liberty, a public school, and the Academy of Music in New York. The trip ended with a walk across Brooklyn Bridge.[70] Thus, in one fell swoop, these young Indians were presented with the spectacle of all of America's most successful ideas made manifest: consumer society, the idea of the nation as civilizing mission, and technological progress.

At some level, associating herself with the assimilation of racial Others offered the marginalized Olivia Sage an assurance of belonging and confirmed her membership in the company of philanthropic "friends of the Indian." Religious belief further encouraged Olivia's interest in Pratt's work, for mainstream Protestant denominations had identified America's Others—Indians, Eskimos, Hispanics, and Mormons—as "exceptional peoples" and had created elaborate networks of home missions charged with assimilating them to Anglo-American culture and Protestantism.[71]

Olivia's intense concern with civilizing the Indians comes more sharply into focus when we consider that her own experience with normative white family roles had been less than ideal. Her father's inability to support his family, her mother's flight from the family home, and her brother's irresponsible early marriage before he had the means to support a wife and baby all pointed to the instability of gender relations in American society. By the 1880s, as a member of the Woman's Hospital Association, Olivia was beginning to articulate a feminist critique of white women's political and economic disabilities. But she was still unable fully to examine the problem or even to name it.[72] Nevertheless, the context of unstable roles and identities seems to have sparked her interest in Indian "rights," defined as the emancipation of Indian women within the domestic sphere and the establishment of "manly" roles for Indian men.[73] As Louise Newman points out, "[P]rimitive women's labor, and the respect it was accorded in their own cultures, presented a potential opening for feminists who were critical of their own dependency and confinement within the domestic sphere."[74] Olivia declared her passionate support of Pratt's mission, which in its focus on making Indians "men" would make other Indians "women."[75] She wrote to Pratt on the subject of one Indian girl in whom she had taken a particular interest, "[S]he needs training just as everything in nature does, and with it, I think this girl could become useful to her people."[76]

Olivia evidently understood the Indian "problem" in terms of her own family. Untroubled by the inconsistency of an Americanization that cultivated the gentle blossoms of Indian womanhood in the East while slaughtering Indians in the West, she informed a reporter that she was named for Olivia Standish, her great-grandmother, who was the great-granddaughter of Myles Standish, "the redoubtable Indian fighter."[77] Now her nephews were carrying on the Standish tradition, serving in military campaigns to crush western Indians and herd the survivors onto reservations. After attending Columbia College, Stephen L'Hommedieu Slocum entered the U.S. Army on the staff of Gen. Samuel D. Sturgis in the Indian campaign of 1878. He was then posted to the 18th Regular U.S. Infantry in Montana as lieutenant, where he saw action against the Nez Perce at Canon Creek. By the 1880s he was stationed in Montana.[78] His older brother, Herbert Jermain Slocum, entered West Point in 1872.[79] In 1876, he was assigned to the 7th Regiment U.S. Cavalry (Custer's regiment) as lieutenant, and by 1880 he was stationed at Fort Totten, Dakota Territory.[80]

Russell Sage's interest in Indians and the West was that of developer and despoiler, even though Jane Remsen, author of an uncritical (1938) biographical essay on Sage, stated that he "played with redskins as a boy, and never to the day of his death lost interest in their welfare and advancement."[81] As a partner with Jay Gould and Sidney Dillon in the takeover of the Union Pacific in 1874, Sage helped secure the triumph of continental Euro-American domination and the destruction of the Plains Indians, epitomized in Gould's comment on hearing about the battle of Little Big Horn in 1876: "The ultimate result will be to annihilate the Indians and open up the Big Horn and Black Hills to development and settlement and in this way greatly benefit us."[82]

At the same time, the West, remote and savage, intruded its unwelcome presence in the shape of artifacts, vividly and even offensively present in the cluttered bourgeois interior of the Sage home in New York. In addition to maps of his railroad holdings and tenement houses with which Sage decorated the house, according to Sarnoff, he "covered the parlor with buffalo robes—gifts from Indian chiefs—that he draped sloppily over the furniture. Mrs. Sage just couldn't stand the moth-eaten stinking things."[83]

Meanwhile, Olivia and Russell became personal friends of the Pratts and their growing family. In January 1882, Olivia wrote enthusiastically to Pratt, after reading in the paper that he was in Washington, "I see . . . that you are making your usual earnest appeal for the *rights* of the Indian," and assured him, "I am sure those rights will soon be theirs, and while the time seems to *lag*, in reality there has been most speedy work I think, in the matter of public interest and sentiment." She described herself as "tenderly impressed with the subject," adding, "my heart warms toward the pupils at Carlisle." Olivia sent small donations ranging from twenty to fifty dollars. In 1882, she sent a box of books for "a New Year offering" with a note voicing concern that the reading level might not be challenging enough for the more advanced students.[84] In 1883 she wrote to Pratt to express her impatience with the pace of reform. "A lady friend of mine asked what she could do in the way of small giving to the Indian work at Carlisle," she wrote to Pratt, "but . . . the work to me seems now so *great*." She ended by inviting herself to visit Carlisle again "and renew my pleasant acquaintance with Mrs. Pratt, and see the 'darling Baby' as well as revive the ardor of my interest in your Indian work."[85] She kept in touch with him, writing in 1886 to describe a meeting of the Indian Rights Association she had attended in New York.[86]

Legend has it that Olivia persuaded Russell Sage to pay for the education at Carlisle of over forty students.[87] She certainly acted as a conduit to Carlisle for donations from wealthy friends.[88] Sending a $30 donation from Mrs. John P. Munn (the wife of Russell's physician) and adding twenty of her own in 1884, she wrote to Pratt, "I never lose my interest in your work, which I consider the pioneer in the regeneration of the Indian. I trust the good work will grow until every Indian is a law abiding citizen of the United States."[89]

Gail Bederman and others have shown how the goal of civilizing

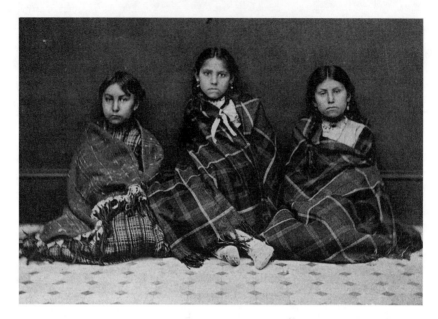

FIGURES 5.4A AND 5.4B. These before and after images of Native Americans were intended to demonstrate the successful Indian assimilation at such institutions as Hampton and Carlisle. Olivia Sage wrote of such a photo that was "constantly picked up by visitors, always with the remark, 'Surely they are not Indians,' to which I would reply, 'Surely they are Indians.'" a. On arrival at Hampton, Va. Peabody Museum, Harvard University Photo #H5634. b. Fourteen months after, Hampton, Va. Peabody Museum, Harvard University Photo #5635.

"lesser races" abroad and at home intersected with and supported the emancipatory project of Euro-American white women.[90] For women such as Olivia Sage, a benevolent interest in the Indian helped to bring into focus a new view of progress, one where gender equality in white society could be heralded as a marker of progress that further distanced white Americans from barbarian peoples. Membership in the "Indian reform" movement thus sharpened Olivia's awareness of gender inequality in her own society while allowing her to enjoy the romance of a connection with the continent's wild inhabitants, whose nameless, unconquered spaces were now crisscrossed by her husband's railroads. In November 1889, when Pratt sent her a photograph of the graduating class at Carlisle, she thanked him for the graphic demonstration of Carlisle's work of assimilation: "As it lay on the table in my country home at Lawrence, Long Island, it was constantly picked up by visitors, always with the

remark, 'Surely these are *not* Indians,' to which I was very proud to reply, 'Surely they are Indians.'"[91] As her husband symbolized material progress for his role in consolidating the nation's infrastructure of railroads and financial markets, Olivia represented the "benevolent empire" of Protestant missions and white Christian womanhood. For both, Native American culture was a barrier to progress.[92]

"Add just this one more position to your list"

Though she still signed her letters "M. Olivia Sage," to most people she was "Mrs. Russell Sage," a member of the benevolent elite and a sought-after board member for voluntary and reform associations. Such work offered mental stimulation, moral validation, and emotional attachment, and although Olivia sometimes told any journalist who would listen that she admired the simple home lives of her ancestors, she chose to spend her time laboring over the reports of reform organizations and reading the newspaper with an intensity remarked on by several observers. At her summer home a reporter noted that downstairs there was "a reading room, where the leading papers of the city are spread out." Here, she pursued reform issues that interested her. A perceptive reporter commented, "She belongs to the strongly defined New York type of well-to-do committee-working church women."[93] In December 1886 a friend wrote, begging her to "preside at and guide our Executive Committee meetings," adding, "I cannot help hoping that you may be able to add just this one more position to your list."[94] As an escape from a dull marriage and a chance to use her considerable powers, voluntary work had much to offer. It brought association with socially prominent women and access to their circles. For example, the Indian Rights League and the Woman's Hospital brought her into contact with Mrs. John Jacob Astor III.[95] As historian Irvin Wyllie noted, "[Olivia's] education and social position, combined with her energy, self-assurance, and personal force, well fitted her for a public role."[96]

Through Indian reform, Olivia had begun to engage not only with the nineteenth century's representation of bourgeois domesticity and civilization but also with the class and gender contradictions of her own position. The chapters that follow describe how she continued to exploit the possibilities of benevolence as a "subject position" that conferred authority over others and authorized public work.[97] By the 1880s, Olivia had found a new and absorbing interest as a lady manager and board member at the New-York Woman's Hospital. Here she began to articulate an understanding of herself in relation to a different community of women and to speak out in the name of suffering womanhood.

Six

"I live for that work"

Negotiating Identities at the New-York Woman's Hospital

For nineteenth-century women the characteristic form
of political activism was participation in a voluntary association.
—Suzanne Lebsock, "Woman and American Politics, 1880–1920" (1990)[1]

This chapter examines Olivia Sage's involvement between 1871 and 1900
with the New-York Woman's Hospital, a combination public-private
institution for the treatment of women's diseases. For modern feminist
historians this institution is profoundly troubling. The surgeries that made
it famous had been developed in the 1840s by physician J. Marion Sims
through experimental surgery on the bodies of female slaves. Moreover,
by the 1880s the hospital had become known for what now seem bar-
baric surgeries such as Battey's operation, a procedure that surgically
removed the ovaries as a treatment for emotional or nervous symptoms.
Yet in these same decades the hospital became an arena for the benevolent public work of leisured white women, Olivia Sage among them.
As fund-raisers, patrons, and day-to-day managers, these upper-class
women increased their confidence, negotiating public identities that
enabled them to challenge (though unsuccessfully) men's control over
the hospital and its therapies. Privileged women thus participated in the
subordination of other women at the same time as they enlarged their
power in public life.[2]

Soon after she arrived in New York, Olivia joined the Woman's Hospital Association, a group of wealthy women who served as lady managers[3] for the hospital and formed its lay governing authority. The role
of benevolent volunteer helped Olivia negotiate a public identity and
find new meanings for womanhood in Gilded Age New York. But the

hospital showcased as its chief surgeon the controversial J. Marion Sims, whose experimental surgeries on slave women later earned him the title of "the father of gynecology." Between 1855, when the hospital was founded, and 1900, the prestige of science, the meanings of professionalism, and the techniques of gynecological surgery all underwent significant change.[4] In attempting to understand these changes, scholars have replaced an older victimization model of women's disease and its treatment with a multidimensional model. For example, in a recent essay, scholar Nancy Theriot proposes that nineteenth-century medical discourse was multivocal, with proponents of gynecology differing from advocates of alienism (psychological explanations of disease), and with women physicians differing from male doctors, who also disagreed among themselves. Patients, too, "were active participants in the process of medicalizing 'woman,'" she suggests.[5]

The present chapter listens to another voice in nineteenth-century medical discourse: that of the lady managers who formed the hospital's lay governing authority. Volunteers with no qualifications except an eagerness "to escape the routine pattern of their lives and a familiarity with genteel standards of household organization," these socially prominent women took the initiative and organized a hospital where physicians could treat and define ("construct") the diseases of women. How did Sage understand her place in supporting the work of the Woman's Hospital, and how did the experience change her?[6]

"A class of unspeakably painful complaints"

The history of the New-York Woman's Hospital and of its famous chief surgeon, J. Marion Sims, has been expertly told by Deborah McGregor and needs only a brief summary here.[7] A South Carolinian, Sims had built up a practice in Montgomery, Alabama, where his work in a private clinic included bold experimentation on his twelve female slaves. Through treatments that he carried out between 1845 and 1849 on three of them in particular, Betsey, Lucy, and Anarcha, Sims perfected the surgical techniques to repair the tears caused by childbirth known as vesico-vaginal injury. All of the women on whom Sims operated underwent numerous operations without anesthesia; Anarcha submitted to thirty. He later claimed, "They [his patients] implored me to repeat operations so tedious and at that time often so painful that none but a woman could have borne them."[8] Sims went north to New York City in 1853 to seek a cure for his malaria and to start up a new medical practice, but

his position was initially so precarious that he relied on his wife's earnings from boarders and the money raised by the sale of his slaves. The
charismatic southerner who had recently published "On the Treatment
of Vesico-Vaginal Fistula" (1852) was received like a celebrity by the
city's leading medical men, several of whom offered him assistance in
setting up a practice.[9]

And so did a group of upper-class women led by Sarah Platt Doremus (1802–1877), the wife of a wealthy merchant and a prominent figure
in numerous charitable and reform organizations. Doremus headed the
Women's Prison Association and was a founder of the New York House
and School of Industry and the Nursery and Child's Hospital. She served
on the boards of the City Bible Society and the City Mission and Tract
Society and was president of the nondenominational Woman's Union
Missionary Society of America for Heathen Lands.[10] In this capacity,
she supervised the collection of money offerings from sister societies
throughout the nation, and Olivia, who headed the Ladies Missionary
Society at her church, probably knew her through this connection. It is
easy to imagine how Sara Doremus might have invited this newcomer
to join the Board of Lady Supervisors, for her famously rich husband
could become a valuable friend of the institution.[11]

Wealth and social prominence did not protect women such as Mrs.
Doremus from chronic ill health. Untreated conditions of all kinds among
women were common, as educator Catharine Beecher discovered when
she conducted a survey of health among her friends in a number of cities
and towns. Sara Doremus's experience of frequent childbearing and mis-
managed illness was typical. She married at nineteen and gave birth to
eight daughters between 1822 and 1838, five of whom died in her lifetime, two while young. Her biographer describes her as "in fragile health
during most of her married life."[12]

The records of the Woman's Hospital Association state that when
Sara Doremus and her associates learned that J. Marion Sims had developed a surgical treatment for "a class of unspeakably painful complaints
under which many a poor broken spirited woman had sunk into an early
grave," they decided to establish "an Institution, which should place that
pearl of great price, *health*, within the reach of the poorest sufferers."
On February 10, 1855, they met to establish the Woman's Hospital Association, adopted a constitution, and established a 35-member Board of
Lady Managers. They also resolved to ask for public money, petitioning
the Common Council for $5,000.[13] Several of these lady managers were
themselves ill as a result of too-frequent childbearing or suffered from

diseases of the reproductive system. For others, such as Elizabeth Cullom, a granddaughter of Alexander Hamilton, benevolence was the obligation of class as well as gender.

Appealing for funds before the New York State Assembly in 1856, Dr. John Francis made a powerful case for public support of the hospital. Disease stalked woman at each stage of her life, the doctor warned. "The Virgin may suffer from a long catalogue of the most painful maladies, the Wife may be worn down with untold miseries, growing out of the marital relation; and the Mother, giving birth to her offspring often sustains such horrible lacerations and injuries as to render life unbearable; Old Age as well as Maturity has its thousand female sufferings calling for sympathy and aid, while cancerous and malignant diseases of women require special investigation." Women's chronic susceptibility to disease threatened domestic happiness, the physician warned New York's male legislators. Left alone, her complaints would go from bad to worse, "till they completely shatter the nervous system, embitter existence, poison the sources of domestic happiness, and drive their victims to the madhouse."[14]

Caroline Thompson, a recovered patient, also addressed the legislators in language that stressed the cultural understanding of woman as weak and dependent.

> Gentlemen—to your noble hearts, your generous nature, your chivalry and your gallantry I appeal. To your strength of mind and firmness of purpose, I bring my weakness and dependence. At the feet of your manly nature, I lay the self-devotion—the womanly hearts of my sex. In woman's weakness lies her truest strength.[15]

Such appeals to contemporary "social knowledge" of sex and gender roles were effective in eliciting public funds. The state legislature at Albany granted $50,000 in 1859, provided that the backers could find $100,000 from other sources, and the city's Common Council gave $2,500 for equipment and supplies.[16]

Sara Doremus and her associates gave the New-York Woman's Hospital social acceptability and enlisted the support of influential husbands, who secured funds from the city and state. The hospital received far more public support and funding than the struggling New York Infirmary for Women and Children established by Elizabeth Blackwell in 1854 that was staffed by women doctors.[17] And when the lady managers secured incorporation by act of the state legislature they overcame their own disenfranchisement as they created a legal "person," a corporation with rights that as married women they did not have.[18] In May 1856, they leased a house at 83 Madison Avenue, Thomas Doremus footing the bill.[19] Then, in a remarkable act of assertiveness, the lady managers inserted a clause into the constitution providing that the surgeon's assistant "must be a woman."[20]

The Woman's Hospital became known for surgery before antisepsis had arrived to make surgery safe or anesthesia to make it bearable. Anesthesia did not come into general use at the hospital until about 1865, and assistant surgeon Thomas Addis Emmet, who as Sims's rival had an axe to grind, chose to recall two features of the hospital: the surgeon's "remarkable display of patience and dexterity" and the screams of the patients.[21] But by the time Olivia Sage arrived in 1871, the hospital had gained a reputation as an up-to-date institution that represented the latest scientific knowledge and medical practice. Patients were admitted regardless of class and race and charged according to ability to pay. They came from far and near and even from abroad.[22]

"The surgeon's assistant must be a woman"

From the first, the institution had a complicated governing structure. An all-male Board of Managers was created in 1856 in addition to the Board of Lady Managers. The practicing physicians formed a third body, the Medical Board. Difficulties between these bodies arose almost immediately. Sims simply ignored the provision that the assistant surgeon should be a woman, appointing Dr. Thomas Addis Emmet, a Virginian untrained in the diseases of women.[23] Several female physicians could have filled this position. Emily Blackwell, who had trained with the Scottish obstetrician and gynecologist Sir James Simpson and the French surgeon Hugier, was well qualified, as was Marie Zakrzewska.[24] The clause was subsequently reworded to reflect a fait accompli—"The Surgeon's Assistant shall be such a person as the exigencies of the case require"—and Emmet remained at the hospital until 1900.[25] Decades later, Olivia was still angry about this setback to womanhood and women practitioners.

During the war, the Woman's Hospital was at a low point. Its southern patients withdrew. It was so short of money that patients had to be turned away, and plans for expansion were dropped. Disputes over the appointment of medical staff resurfaced during Sims's frequent absences in France, where he was enjoying fame and fortune with a clientele that included the empress Eugenie. Emmet was appointed surgeon-in-chief in Sims's absence.[26] Sims continued to travel between the United States and France, where his wife Theresa and their nine children had settled.

In 1870, he served as chief surgeon for an Anglo-American ambulance corps during the Franco-Prussian War. He returned to New York in 1871.[27]

This was also the year that Olivia Sage became a lady manager, beginning a connection with the Woman's Hospital that would last over thirty years. Perhaps her interest in the hospital came from consulting J. Marion Sims as a patient, or perhaps Russell Sage had consulted Sims in the 1860s when his first wife was ill.[28] Wealthy New Yorkers had begun to visit Sims for advice about infertility at this time. Weary of the surgery on vesico-vaginal tears that had made him famous, he was exploring other applications for his surgical sleight of hand. He became interested in the problem of sterility, publishing *Clinical Notes on Uterine Surgery with Special Reference to the Management of the Sterile Condition* (1866) and treating numerous cases of infertility. Sims's experimental and surgical treatments to help childless couples brought him to the edge of respectability and beyond: rumors told of husbands and wives ordered to rise immediately after sexual intercourse so that Sims could retrieve the sperm from the wife for examination under a microscope. News of these activities spread abroad. A writer for the (London) *Medical Times and Gazette* spelled out for readers the doctor's scandalous conduct: "Fancy a respectable husband quitting his bed hastily, and leaving his palpitating spouse to be examined in less than a minute after the nuptial mysteries."[29]

Did Russell Sage seek Sims's advice early in his second marriage? His first had been childless, and his new bride was already over forty. It would not be far fetched to imagine that the Sages were among the couples who consulted him about their chance of having children. Sarnoff's statement that their marriage was never consummated cannot be summarily dismissed in part because he claims to have interviewed Dr. Carl Schmuck, Olivia's personal physician in her last years.[30] Moreover, even though Olivia sometimes embraced a modern frankness in her speech, the product of training in the Troy Female Seminary approach that physiology should be taught openly and completely, she might have had difficulty satisfying her more experienced husband. When his extramarital affairs became public knowledge in the 1890s, Olivia kept her silence. But as he approached ninety she decided to discuss the issue, writing obliquely about sex in her essay "Opportunities and Responsibilities of Leisured Women" (1905). Her analysis of the problem of prostitution in this essay contains a clue about the sexual side of the Sage marriage. The way to combat vice was to provide full and free sex education to boys and girls, she argued. Husbands only resorted to prostitutes to find the sexual pleasure that their wives couldn't provide. The remedy was more sex education. "This teaching must be candid, drastic. Half of the difficulty attending it comes from a very natural, but very cowardly, sense of delicacy about discussing such topics. One should remember that any subject can be discussed with dignity by a lady."[31] This belated call for more knowledge of and openness about sex suggests (though it does not prove) that her own marriage had sexual difficulties and that this accounts for her interest in the Woman's Hospital and its work as early as the 1870s.

The whole premise of the new specialization of gynecology was its rejection of "delicacy" as false modesty that prolonged women's suffering. At a time when "ladies" were not permitted to write or speak frankly about the human body, medical discourse provided a context for the discussion of delicate and hidden matters.[32] Sims and his colleagues connected childlessness in women ("inactivity") to a predisposition to disease. They subscribed to the reflex theory of disease, according to which a whole range of symptoms, including emotional and psychological ones, were connected to "disturbances" in the reproductive organs.[33] As one historian of medicine explains, "The theory of reflex irritation posited that nervous connections running along the spine joined all the organs of the body together, including the brain, and that in this way irritations in one part could cause derangements even in distant sites."[34]

Such ideas would surely resonate for Olivia. Could her reproductive "inactivity" during the years she was a teacher have been the cause of the sore throats that had mysteriously plagued her year after year?[35] Certainly her experience of chronic ill health affected her understanding of the Woman's Hospital. The sore throats went away—we hear no more about them—but Olivia was not to become a mother. She would have been unlikely to have children at the age of forty-three, and she resigned herself to that reality. She referred elliptically to the fact in a letter to her brother when she recalled her Aunt Almira, a single woman in her eighties, and repeated the comment of another of her aunts, Mary Groesbeck, that "the best people . . . die out."[36]

Whatever the exact reason that drew Olivia to the hospital, the lady managers found her ready to give when they approached her for a donation in 1871. The hospital had reorganized in 1868, and since that time the ladies had been responsible for their own budget and fund-raising. Announcing themselves sick of organizing "sanitary fairs," bake sales, and bazaars (the usual techniques of women's fund-raising), they set about recruiting women of wealth with a Century Fund Drive. "The Managers, anxious to avoid in future the yearly recourse to some public entertainment to raise the necessary funds to sustain so costly a charity . . . turn with perfect confidence to the women of wealth in this great city and state." Sage responded with a donation of $100. Newly married, Russell Sage was not yet in a position to refuse his wife.[37]

Olivia became a lady manager in 1872, and by 1877 she was treasurer of the ladies' board. The role of lady manager had a lot to offer. Newly arrived in New York, Olivia would have been expected to begin the round of formal social visiting that occupied Gilded Age women of wealth, a practice she thoroughly disliked.[38] Voluntary work was an alternative, an opportunity to serve others but also to satisfy a restless curiosity that sought out new knowledge. Here was a chance to organize, manage, and persuade, skills she had acquired as a classroom teacher. Here was training in fund-raising and administration and a ready-made social circle of wealthy respectable women who thought as she did. Here perhaps was also a work of Christian evangelism. The hospital supplied an arena where she could discharge the charitable duties of her class and play the role of benevolent friend to less fortunate women. It offered another way of performing gender.[39]

In taking up voluntary work, Sage followed the example of thousands of other middle- and upper-class women of her day who organized to do the work left undone in an age of reluctant government, creating numerous specialized institutions for cultural, benevolent, and educational goals and claiming a fuller participation in public life than their mothers. As Anne Scott writes, "Constrained by law and custom, and denied access to most of the major institutions by which the society governed itself and created its culture, [women] used voluntary associations to evade some of these constraints."[40]

But the integrity of this woman's sphere was hard to maintain. The hospital's move to a new site in 1868 coincided with a bureaucratic reorganization that reduced the power of the lady managers. The Woman's Hospital Association (formerly the sole governing body), now resembled an auxiliary to the 27-member Board of Governors, on which no women sat.[41] The hospital was occupying a new site at 49th Street and Lexington and was undergoing expansion on land donated by the city. (Its backers had persuaded the City Council to grant the land rent free in exchange for the hospital's agreement to provide twenty-five free beds.)[42] The Wetmore pavilion was completed in 1868, and a second facility, the upscale Baldwin pavilion, opened in 1877. However, the Wetmore was found unsatisfactory and was never used. Difficulties stemmed from the unhealthy site, which had previously been a potter's field, while noise and smoke from nearby Grand Central Terminal caused numerous complaints. Thus, the move to 49th Street did not slow the effort to find a better site, and by 1882 funds amounting to $100,000 had been collected for a new building.[43]

This was a period of conflict at the hospital. Emmet was surgeon in chief and Sims was more a legend than an everyday presence, though he was still senior consulting surgeon. Professional rivalries divided him from physicians Peaslee, Emmet, and Thomas, and struggles over control of space, personnel, and medical therapeutics divided him from the lady managers. The governors sometimes took one side, sometimes the other. Olivia began to take the lead, speaking for the lady managers as they attempted to control the appointment of medical personnel and thwart Emmet, whom they disliked for reasons that had little to do with medicine. Sage preferred the charming southerner Sims to the prickly Emmet, especially since Sims was a fellow Presbyterian, Emmet a Catholic. Emmet's impression of the lady managers was jaundiced. He noted in his memoirs, "[T]here are certain positions for which women are not fitted, for experience teaches they are partisans."[44]

"A domain where ladies do not belong"

Between the 1870s and 1900, space and responsibility at the hospital was divided between male governors and female managers. The Board of Governors had responsibility for grounds and controlled the building fund. The twenty-six women on the Board of Lady Supervisors, as the Board of Lady Managers was now called, had charge of provisioning the hospital, with oversight over linens and housekeeping as well as religious services. Having relegated housekeeping in their own homes to servants, these socially prominent women offered themselves as the public housekeepers of the city's public-private institutions. At the same time, they used the defensive rhetoric of spheres to maintain their position. The Victorian gender system, which overlapped and conflicted with the division between laypersons and professionals, rhetorically divided space and responsibilities between men and women in ways that corresponded to public and private spheres. Lady managers such as Sage also made decisions about admissions and personnel and had a say in the appointment of medical practitioners, matrons, nurses, and supervisors. These issues drove them beyond their sphere and into conflict with the governors.

At one point in her now-classic essay "'Separate Spheres, Female Worlds, Woman's Place': The Rhetoric of Woman's History" historian

Linda Kerber asks, "But why speak of worlds, of spheres, or of realms at all?"[45] Why indeed? Except that nineteenth-century women themselves did so. A single letter dated May 19, 1882, from M. Olivia Sage—how interesting that she chose this form of her name—to New York governor Edwin D. Morgan, filed with her husband's correspondence to the governor, reveals the balancing act that Olivia Sage and the lady managers performed as they negotiated managerial identities.

Olivia's letter informed Governor Morgan of mismanagement at the Woman's Hospital and hinted at the waste of public monies. Taking a didactic tone, she confidently demonstrated her understanding of the physical operation of the furnace—how useful Emma Willard's practical science teaching had proved to be! "At the meeting of the Executive Board on Wednesday, Mr. Bell the [hospital] Engineer, made a requisition for coal, and previous to the meeting I went into the cellar and saw that there was only enough for about ten days use," she began. "The traps that return the hot water to the boilers are too small to do the work, and consequently the hot water passes off into the cellar. . . . The hospital can hardly afford any waste in the present state of its finances." She concluded by appealing to the need for economy. "I know that the business of attending to the traps belongs to a committee, and I would not have mentioned it to you, only to explain the drain upon the coals, *and I trust in this connection I have not intruded upon a domain where ladies do not belong.*" The letter invokes the woman's sphere while in fact breaching it.[46]

The lady managers also attempted to retain some control over who got admitted as patients.[47] Those who gave a small money donation had the right to recommend a patient for a free bed. One letter from a patient thanking Sage for a bed illustrates how hospital admittance was a gift given at the pleasure of the donor. "Such kindness from a stranger, on whom I have no claim, is a new experience," she wrote. Other correspondence shows Superintendent LeRoy deferring to Sage on the assignment of beds.[48]

Charged with the internal ordering of the hospital, the lady managers joined in January 1874 (in Sims's absence) with the Board of Governors to pass two resolutions, one ruling that no cases of cancer should be admitted to the hospital, the other that no more than fifteen spectators should be allowed to view an operation. The ban on cancer patients reflected the contemporary belief that cancer was contagious.[49] Both resolutions showed a determination to dictate the terms on which Sims could use the hospital and to protect the privacy of female patients. The lady managers complained about crowds of medical men tramping upstairs at the hospital to view operations, disturbing the peace and violating the privacy of the patients. For the lady managers, the hospital was a woman's space, a place of rest and moral regeneration. For Sims, it was an arena for his heroic surgeries, a testing ground of surgical technique and new knowledge.

Sims, now a celebrity, fought back, attacking what he called "the tyrannical course of the Board of Governors" in establishing these rules. He ignored them, continuing to admit patients with cancer and inviting flocks of medical men to view his surgeries. In November 1874, he chose the occasion of the annual anniversary meeting of the hospital, usually a pleasant occasion for taking stock and self-congratulation, to attack the managers' rules, impulsively offering his resignation, which was accepted.[50]

Hospitals were changing, and the scientific prestige of medical practitioners was overtaking the social prestige of wealthy funders who formed the hospitals' boards. Medical professionals, whether male or female, accepted a bacteriological explanation of disease and rejected as sentimental the views of moral reformers and separatists.[51] The ladies' board, created as a separate entity and charged with "feminine" concerns, resulted both from the maternalist assumption that women were morally superior and from the efforts of male governors and physicians to marginalize women whom they believed to be sentimental and thus hostile to professionalization.[52] The lady managers struggled to keep costs down and to find new sources of funds while continuing to explain their work for this public-private institution as a kind of genteel housekeeping in an enlarged "sphere of usefulness." They tried to raise money by levying fees and by petitioning the Board of Governors to include more paying patients. Accordingly, the new pavilion made provision for paying patients using a sliding scale; the first floor housed those who paid fifteen dollars a week, the second floor the eight-dollar patients, and the top floor those who paid only six.[53] They solicited subscriptions from businessmen and competed with the governors for bequests.[54] Money donations often carried a freight of sentimentality, with subscribers encouraged to feel that they were part of a larger project of redemption. When she sent her donation to Sage, one woman wrote,

> You seem to rise above the sordid things of earth, through which we are all passing, standing firmly for the principles—religious—of our noble forefathers. The work you are doing uplifts and raises one toward heaven. God bless the Woman's Hospital.[55]

Another excused herself in terms Olivia would understand only too well: "Had I the means of my husband who has passed away I would gladly send a *very* liberal amount for the good work."[56]

Lady managers were often called on for personal donations. Olivia's correspondence from the 1880s includes hasty notes from the superintendent alerting her to shortages of supplies or provisions. For example, in January 1886, he informed her that the hospital was almost completely out of furnace coal.[57] Numerous requests were for stimulants. "The matron reports to me that the brandy is nearly gone," the superintendent wrote on September 30, 1887. Two months later, Sage was informed that "Mrs. Dobson [the matron] reports that we shall need both whiskey and brandy on Wednesday 30th."[58] On January 27, 1888, Sage received another request from the superintendent for brandy and whiskey, followed by others three days later. A few weeks later still, a request for champagne was added, and on March 9, LeRoy wrote, "Champane [sic] is needed and I send John. This is for Mrs. Barker Sect. 3."[59]

The ladies' board was also in charge of the recruitment and management of nurses. Nurses had earlier been quite untrained, such as Margaret Brennan, who had worked at the hospital for many years, and Mary Smith, who enters the record in the Hospital's Register of Cases with the annotation, "Cured and made a nurse in the hospital."[60] The Crimean War and Civil War experiences had produced important reforms in the training of nurses and in the design of hospitals, and the Woman's Hospital reflected these changes. For example, during the Peninsular Campaign of the Civil War, it was considered perfectly appropriate to recruit Caroline Lane, one of the lady managers, to serve as a superintendent of nursing on board a floating hospital ship bringing the wounded from the Virginia campaign to northern hospitals.[61] Now at the Woman's Hospital in the 1870s and 1880s, Sage worried about the quality of the institution's nurses (in December 1887) and about whether the abandoned Wetmore pavilion should become a nurses' home. The following year, the lady managers sent a formal request to the Board of Governors "desiring them to cooperate in obtaining a better class of nurses."[62] As late as 1899, a prospective matron for the hospital was interviewed at Olivia's Fifth Avenue home.[63]

Lady managers also visited patients in the wards. Contemplating her hospital work from the distance of old age, Olivia remembered these duties in a self-dramatizing letter to a friend:

> [T]here were many, many times that I was about to leave that work and often my strength seemed well nigh gone in the thirty years that I labored through summer heat and winter cold for conscience sake and by the will of God to maintain the Hospital's needs for the sake of the sick under its roof.[64]

Minutes of the Woman's Hospital Association show that several times she was present at meetings of various boards in the summer when others were away. In August 1889, she was the only member of the Board of Governors to show up for a meeting.[65] However, some correspondence from the 1880s suggests a more casual connection with the hospital. "Mrs. Eldredge and Mrs. Oakley are pretty frail but not critically so," the superintendent wrote to Sage in March 1888. "It would hardly be necessary for you to come on purpose to see them. I think tomorrow would do nicely."[66] If it was occasionally troublesome, hospital work nevertheless allowed Olivia Sage and women like her an opportunity to construct what Kathleen Sander has called "quasi careers," fulfilling and visible public roles.[67]

An earlier generation of feminist scholars condemned the Woman's Hospital as the institutional setting where male physicians developed the surgical techniques that resulted in medicalizing women's somatic disorders. They argued that cultural ideals about gender were the primary determinants of surgical intervention on women's bodies.[68] They saw Sims's use of the speculum as emblematic of a misogynist medical therapeutics that laid women's bodies open to the male scientific gaze. Had not Sims written, "I saw everything, as no man had seen before"?[69] Moreover, Sims and his colleagues regularly operated on women whose symptoms were psychological and displayed no other evidence of disease. And they performed surgeries that now seem useless. The "Register of Cases" contains much detail about the operations performed, with such notations as, "Miss W____. Removal of clitoris. Pathological conditions: dysmenorrhea."[70] Deborah McGregor explains Battey's operation (ovariotomy), which was routinely performed at the hospital in the 1880s, as a procedure that "removed the ovaries, but not in response to any organic disease of the organs: the ovaries themselves were normal, except that they supposedly elicited one or several nervous symptoms, such as insanity, epilepsy, or dysmenorrhea."[71] Although holistic clinical practice was regarded as old-fashioned, and disease was increasingly localized to specific organs or systems, the theory of reflexivity still held sway. Emotional symptoms in women were still viewed as originating in an imbalance in the reproductive system and treated with the removal of ovaries or uterus or both.[72]

Moreover, information about the surgery they were to undergo was routinely withheld from patients. For example, in the case of cervical incision, which was used to correct infertility, Sims admitted in a revealing interview for the *Lancet* that he proceeded regardless of whether the patient consented. "I am opposed to operating on any rational being without first explaining what is to be done, and the wherefore," he stated. "In the cases alluded to [cervical incision for sterility] the operations were performed at the suggestion and earnest wish of the husbands, who feared that they might not be submitted to if fully explained."[73]

For the first decades, there is nothing in the record to suggest that the lady managers were critical of the surgeries carried out at the Woman's Hospital on uninformed, often unconscious (etherized) female patients—or, earlier still, on fully awake patients. Why did upper-class benevolent women such as Olivia Sage support a hospital where such techniques were practiced? New work on the development of scientific knowledge, medical practice, and professionalization supplies some answers. One is that once anesthesia became generally available, patients came forward to demand abdominal surgery to relieve them from chronic, painful conditions.[74] And invasive surgery was favored not just by male practitioners: professionally trained women doctors such as Brooklyn surgeon Mary Dixon Jones were just as likely to remove ovaries and tubes for "reflexive symptoms" as male doctors.[75] As Ornella Moscucci warns, "The rise of this operation cannot be seen simply in terms of scientific progress, nor can it be regarded as an expression of medical misogyny and male oppression."[76] Gynecology was becoming a medical specialty; significant improvements in surgical technique and the rising prestige of professionally trained practitioners made the field more attractive to physicians. And yet pathological science lagged behind, so that organs were removed without biopsy or even without being examined after extraction for evidence of disease.

Without the support of professional knowledge, the lady managers had no reason to oppose such surgeries, so they continued to bestow an aura of Christian benevolence and respectability on the hospital and its work. Patients' adherence to secrecy about their ailments increased the power of medical professionals. One thanked the hospital staff for the care she had received, but noted, "The work which you have generously undertaken is of such a nature that it cannot be proclaimed from the house-tops, and thus secure to you the plaudits of the world. It is a work which must necessarily, to a great extent, be done in secret."[77]

There is some evidence that the lady managers began to question the craze for abdominal gynecological surgery.[78] In May 1887, the ladies' board notified the Board of Governors that the operations being performed at the hospital were "very objectionable."[79] But other complaints focused less on the procedures than on the exclusion of women physicians from the hospital, and a motion of 1886 to admit female practitioners might have originated with the lady managers. The Medical Board

responded to this request by unanimously rejecting it as "highly detri-
mental to the interests of the Hospital."[80] Perhaps it was not coincidental
that it was at this point that the ladies' board began complaining bitterly to the governors about shortage of funds. In July, they informed
the governors that they were $3,000 in debt and had no money to pay
their bills. A few weeks later, another communication informed the governors that they were "in urgent need of money."[81]

At the same time, in their public pronouncements, the members of
the Woman's Hospital Association sometimes reimagined the hospital
in a way that supported their vision of the hospital as "moral universe,"
a place of moral and religious regeneration.[82] At other times, they referred
to it as a "home" in need of skilled household management.[83] The association's logo, printed on the covers of its published annual reports,
depicts relationships between lady assistants, physicians, and patients
as a triad of three figures arranged vertically in a pyramid. At the low-
est level is the female sufferer, the patient. Reaching down to her in sympathy is a kneeling woman, the lady helper, with Christ the physician
hovering over both, his hand uplifted toward his Heavenly Father, the
source of healing, forming the apex. Despite the overwhelming technical and scientific prestige of medical men and the superior political rights
of male governors, genteel upper-class women represented the hospital
as a domain where they were necessary intermediaries between their suffering sisters, medical professionals, and the healing salvation of Christ.
With ministers as allies, they went into the wards to make women of
other classes and conditions objects of their redemptive kindness. Patients thus became recipients of an influence as transformative as physical healing.

In reality, though, the inner-outer division between men's and
women's work was as unworkable as the fictive division between public
and private. The lady managers were already occupying roles in public
life. For example, in seeking state funding for the hospital in 1865, Mrs.
Doremus had traveled to Albany to meet with the state comptroller. They
continually disputed the boundaries of their sphere with male medical
staff and the Board of Governors. For example, in 1884 they declined
to go along with the governors' request that they pay the superintendent's salary from their own funds.[84] Plans to construct an administration building produced more conflict between the two boards. Finally,
in April 1885, the Medical Board and Board of Governors met in special session and resolved "in view of the clashing and misunderstand-
ing which result from the complex organization of the Hospital," that
a committee of three governors, three medical men, and three ladies

should meet to report "some plan to promote greater harmony and greater efficiency in the conduct of the Hospital."[85] In a sideswipe at the Medical Board, the lady managers complained in their report to the governors that the physicians "in the opinion of the Ladies devoted too much time to playing lawn tennis." They lost the battle, and were reduced to skirmishing over trivia.[86]

Outargued

In 1886, Olivia became the spokeswoman for the lady managers when she, along with eleven other women, was added to the Board of Governors, which now consisted of twelve women and thirteen men. The board, which had previously held its meetings at the male-only Union League Club, now met at the New York Academy of Medicine. Olivia later recalled how, in practice, "[t]he male portion of the Board was made up of lawyers mainly, and at Board meetings the women were outargued by them, and voted as they did."[87] Disputes continued over which board was responsible for which expenses. In February 1887, the lady managers wrote to the governors, insisting that they should not have to pay the Croton water rate.[88] But the board decided "that the tax was a part of the running expenses of the Hospital and should be paid by the Ladies Board."[89]

In January 1888, the governors, impatient with the continuing intransigence of the lady managers, called a conference to discuss amending the hospital's constitution. Olivia took a leading role in speaking for the women. Her experience as treasurer, her social standing as the wife of a multimillionaire, and her sense of moral authority authorized her leadership role. With her allies Maria Jesup and Emily Johnston de Forest, Olivia met with Dr. Agnew from the Medical Board.[90] She later recorded that the ladies present at this meeting disagreed with Dr. Agnew's opinion that the hospital "would be under better management with a smaller and united Board" and felt that "very much would be lost of value in reducing the Board of Supervisors." Her appeal ended, "The peculiar character of this Hospital, would seem to make it especially 'Woman's Work for Women.'"[91]

The reorganization proceeded anyway. The hospital's charter was amended by act of the state legislature, and the Lady Supervisors were replaced by a Ladies Assistant Board of twenty-five members, with Olivia as chair. The Board of Governors was to have fourteen male and thirteen female members. The minutes state that the Board of Governors resolved unanimously "that those members of the Board of Lady Supervisors who are not members of this Board be appointed an assistant board and that to them . . . be assigned the charge of the internal affairs of the Hospital."[92] Sage's account of this move in an 1892 speech left no doubt that this change was carried over the opposition of the women.[93] Moreover, the "reform" merely attempted to restore the division of labor of 1868. Historian Linda Kerber's comment seems apt here. She wrote, "The evidence that the woman's sphere is a social construction lies in part in the hard and constant work required to build and repair its boundaries."[94]

To Olivia Sage, the episode came to stand for more than just a bureaucratic fix. Instead, the events of the hospital's early years, in particular Sims's refusal to hire a woman as assistant surgeon, now took on a new significance—one more piece in the gathering evidence that the lady managers had not been given their due as founders. Although the outrage had occurred forty years earlier and before she had arrived in New York, Sage knew about it and referred to it in a speech written in 1894 on the occasion of the hospital's anniversary.[95]

And so did Dr. Mary Putnam Jacobi, an ally of Olivia in the suffrage movement of the 1890s. Although (or perhaps because) Jacobi rejected woman's separatist institutions and believed in gender-neutral, laboratory-based medicine, she recognized the discrimination women physicians faced. Both for Sage, the moral separatist, and for Jacobi, the integrationist, Sims's arrogant refusal in 1855 to appoint a female surgeon became an archetypal act of male wrongdoing against womankind. "Emily Blackwell was the woman who should have been chosen," Jacobi wrote, in her essay "Woman in Medicine" (1891). "She had an education far superior to that of the average American doctor of the day, a special training under the most distinguished gynecologists of the time." Sims selected his medical assistant "upon grounds extraordinarily frivolous," Jacobi concluded.[96]

Nor was Emmet, who replaced Sims as chief surgeon, any more progressive. In his 1879 textbook, *The Principles and Practice of Gynecology*, he interspersed his conservative views of woman's nature among the scientific discussion of disease and the statistical tables.[97] Like Edward Clarke, whose *Sex in Education* (1873) he defended, Emmet made a huge jump from a theory of the etiology of disease to cultural practice: "The various symptoms of ovarian disorders are but an evidence that nature's laws have been put at defiance, and that the nervous system has been overtaxed," he wrote.

> Who are the sufferers? The young girl who has had her brain development out of season; the woman disappointed or crossed in love by

a man not worthy of her; those who have been ill-mated, and, often, the unmated . . . ; the prostitute; and she who degrades herself and sacrifices her womanhood by resorting to means to prevent conception. In all of these the nervous system has first been abused.[98]

Not surprisingly, he also opposed woman suffrage. In his memoirs he wrote, "I have never yet met a woman who, in my judgement, should have a vote, except as a figurehead, or ever take part in the election of a medical man for a hospital appointment, nor should she be placed in a jury-box, for the same reason."[99]

Such views as these in the man who was the chief medical officer at the hospital may help to explain why in 1879 Olivia Sage presented two heavy leather-bound volumes to the governors. These were the "Reports of the Woman's Hospital in the State of New York" for 1856–1869 and 1870–1878. The dedication reads: "The Board of Lady Supervisors present with their compliments these two volumes of Annual Reports to the Board of Governors," a none-too-subtle reminder for the male governing body of the lady managers' past achievements and continuing efforts.[100]

Arguing Back

In a series of speeches delivered as reports of the Ladies Assistant Board at the annual meetings of the Woman's Hospital Board of Governors between 1888 and 1901, Olivia condemned the reorganization of 1888, which reinforced the auxiliary and inferior role of women in managing the institution. Protected by her status as the probable heir to the Sage millions (Russell Sage was eighty in 1896), and thus as the hospital's most likely benefactor, Olivia waged a one-woman battle against the authority of the governors and the strictures of "the sphere." Sage defended women's role in governance. "[D]ollars, as well as Doctors are important factors in every well managed Hospital," she declared in an address to the Board of Governors in 1892, but "a third factor should be women through whom all the work shall have impulse and direction." She framed the hospital as a woman's space. It was a "home" and patients were "guests"—the metaphors are those of domesticity, not science or bureaucracy.[101] Hospital work was an expression of the Christian duty of leisured women to their unfortunate sisters, work that would go on forever, "so long as suffering calls and humanity demands our help," she declared.[102] The hospital is "women's work for women," she insisted in 1888. "For forty-two years, woman as a patient has filled this Hospital, while women as 'ministering angels' have fostered this grand pioneer institution."[103] She invoked women's special mission even as their lay authority at the hospital slipped away and the tired prescriptions for woman's place and phrases such as "woman's work for women" sounded increasingly formulaic and old-fashioned.[104]

She reached back into the institution's early history to retell the story of the founders of the Woman's Hospital Association, not only J. Marion Sims, but Mrs. Doremus, the institution's founding mother, a model of selfless Christian love. And she invoked the long tradition of commitment from mother to daughter—all the women who had "soothed the weary ones, who as guests in this Hospital Home received their loving sympathy."[105] "For the first ten years only women managed and governed, and the Ladies' Assistant Board to-day has those in it whose mothers were 'charter members'; and within the past year a granddaughter has come into the work, leading her daughter, who will be a great-granddaughter of this institution." "Dollars and doctors" were important, she declared, but equally important were the efforts of these "honorable women." From this it followed that women should be on the boards of all institutions for their sex.[106]

In another speech, written for delivery to the Ladies Assistant Board in November 1894, a year of excitement over the Susan B. Anthony amendment in New York State, Olivia again returned to the slight shown to women forty years before by Sims's refusal to appoint a female surgeon. She began by praising the progress made at the Woman's Hospital, the foresight of the women who had placed it in such a central position—now the very center of Manhattan. The hospital had indeed kept up with modern science and surgery. "But what has become of the 16th Article of its first Constitution, 'The Surgeon's Assistant must be a woman'?" she demanded, adding rather lamely, "But ~~we will~~ let us not agitate this question now." Sage then moved from memories of division and betrayal to more conventional sentiments, thanking the Ladies Assistant Board "which has maintained order and completeness in these buildings" [correction in the original].[107]

Olivia's own position was becoming increasingly irksome. As the treasurer for the hospital's building fund, she was charged with soliciting funds from others, but she was unable to get more than a few dollars from her husband, now believed to be one of the wealthiest men in the nation. True, she devoted many volunteer hours to the hospital, but how much better if she could give it a large endowment and see it move into splendid new buildings.[108] By 1899, the building fund for the hospital had reached $320,000, close to its target of $400,000.[109] Then, suddenly, Russell Sage agreed to donate $50,000. And just as suddenly, he withdrew the offer. Alice Northrop, Helen Gould's niece, later recounted the incident. Calling on Olivia Sage one day, Alice found her upset. It seemed that on the strength of a promise from her husband, Olivia had obligated herself for $50,000 toward a new hospital building. And now that the pledges were being called in, Russell Sage had suddenly become evasive. "'I can't even face the women of the Board,' Olivia wailed. 'And I don't want to resign either. Alice, I live for that work.'"[110]

Alice Northrop was resourceful. Bumping into Russell Sage on the way out, she cried, "Oh, Mr. Sage, I have just heard the news. I think you are perfectly wonderful." "Eh, What's that?" "Your gift to the Woman's Hospital. It's perfectly wonderful." And Helen chimed in, "Oh, yes indeed! Dear Mr. Sage is so generous. What an inspiration he is to us all!" Outmaneuvered, Russell Sage wrote the check for $50,000. The donation is recorded for 1899 in the ledger book of the Woman's Hospital. (So is his donation two years later: "Mr. Russell Sage, 1 barrel apples.")[111] But in the same year that the Vanderbilts were put down for a subscription of $2,000, Olivia Sage herself was again listed at the humiliating level of $25.[112]

A black-and-white photograph from the 1890s, preserved in the archives of the New-York Woman's Hospital, portrays Olivia's isolation in this period. By the time this photograph was taken, Olivia had long been a woman who presided, gave speeches, and graciously opened meetings with prayer. She was deferred to, she could speak with authority on a range of public issues, and she had begun to make a few scattered money donations. Here, she sits alone in a room arranged for a meeting, but whether the meeting has just adjourned or is about to start, we do not know. The room is furnished in heavy late-Victorian style, with palms and draperies. A marble bust of physician J. Marion Sims strongly suggests that this is a room at the Woman's Hospital or perhaps at the New York Academy of Medicine. Papers, perhaps plans for the new building, cover two tables and have displaced a large vase of flowers, which has been set temporarily on the floor. Sage sits swathed in a tight-fitting, fur-trimmed costume, muffled up to the neck and wrists. Her hat is at a jaunty angle but her expression is sad, her eyes hooded. Alone in the center of the room, facing the rows of empty chairs, she looks like a specimen placed under glass. The camera angle looks down on her, isolated in the center of the picture: the benevolent matron, Bountifulia Americana (see fig. 6.1).

A disagreement over relocating the hospital to a site far to the north at 110th Street and Amsterdam Avenue set Olivia and Russell Sage against the Board of Governors and its president, John E. Parsons. Olivia

FIGURE 6.1. Olivia at the Woman's Hospital, around 1890. Bolling Memorial Medical Archives, New York, N.Y.

supported a plan to enlarge the existing pavilions and improve the site at 49th Street and Lexington Avenue. Money was collected for this purpose.[113] But the board made the decision to move. Parsons referred to the disagreement in his remarks to the board in 1897. He had "overheard a lady say that if something were not done or were done, she would leave the hospital. Mrs. Sage will recognize the remark." Parsons continued confidently, "You could no more shake her away from this hospital than I can pull the sun down from the heavens. . . . Mrs. Sage's remark was a mere figure of speech, and she knows it."[114]

But he spoke too soon. As Olivia later explained, Russell Sage accused the board of mismanagement of funds, "and when asked if he would give his money, answered calmly, 'I will when I see what use you will make of it.'" In the ensuing row, Olivia had to sever all connection with the hospital. This was in November 1904. Later, she dramatized the incident in a letter to a friend, "Our lives are part of a plan and that part of my life in the Hospital closed when with tears I drove out of that gate and said farewell to dear friends with whom I had labored and sick ones whom I had loved," she wrote. "It was the 'parting of the ways' over which I cannot return."[115]

But Olivia left some solid reminders of what it had all meant to her. I have mentioned earlier that she collected and bound the annual reports of the Woman's Board. In another large leather-bound volume edged with gold, she placed photographs of the women pioneers of the hospital. It has a heavy metal clasp with wrought metal decoration and gold leaf. The volumes remain in the Bolling Memorial Medical Archive at St. Luke's Hospital in Morningside Heights with the other records of the Woman's Hospital, material remains of a women's history that imagines laywomen as equal and complementary partners with male professionals in healing humanity.[116]

It is tempting for biographers to construct a linear narrative where each part of a subject's life prepares the reader for what follows. By the 1890s, Sage was a veteran of decades of struggles at the hospital. Battles over turf and responsibility had made her highly critical of men's governance of women's institutions. She had helped created a woman's sphere of influence, only to then experience its fragility and its limits.[117] From now on, she would insist that women sit on the governing boards of their own institutions whether these were colleges, hospitals, or schools. Moreover, she was beginning to connect what she did to the wider movement of "women's advancement." Her voluntary work had led her to challenge the disabilities of women as a sex. This consciousness would carry over into her work in the Emma Willard Association and in the suffrage movement. But she had learned her first, and hardest, lesson at the New-York Woman's Hospital. In gratitude, she would leave it the magnificent sum of $1.8 million in her will.

Olivia's emancipation should be seen for what it was, a sign that white middle- and upper-class women were gaining more rights and more self-consciousness by the end of the nineteenth century. Yet if evidence is still needed that white women's rights sometimes rested historically on the immiseration of other women, the New-York Woman's Hospital provides that demonstration. Without access to the bodies of enslaved black women, Sims could not have perfected the surgical techniques that made him famous. Sims and his successors subsequently depended on the lady managers for the hospital's everyday running. The medicalization of women's bodies and the founding of a new medical specialty, gynecology, rested, at least in part, on the work of these benevolent ladies.[118]

Seven

"Some aggressive work"

The Emma Willard Association
and Educated Womanhood, 1891–1898

> Mrs. Sage is anxious to lead us to some aggressive work.
> —*Third Annual Report of the Emma Willard Association* (1893)[1]

In the 1890s Olivia became involved with two women's organizations, both of which provided an arena for useful work and a way to speak out on public issues: the Emma Willard Association and the New York Exchange for Women's Work. These organizations had different constituencies and different goals. The first was an association of graduates of Troy Female Seminary. They came together to form a community of middle class, educated women, compiled a directory that was both institutional history and group biography, and organized a Chicago reunion that linked the alumnae project with national commemorations surrounding the Columbian Exposition of 1893. They also planned for new buildings that would expand and update their alma mater and commemorate its famous founder.[2]

Bound by the snobbish conventions of her class yet impelled by a sense of grievance, Olivia seized on educator Emma Willard as a powerful model of womanhood who combined intellect with orthodox religious belief and conservative demeanor, respectability with a powerful femininity. Olivia in her sixties was still a "self in hiding"—hiding behind the apotheosized Willard. Through Willard, Sage gave voice to her own discontent, and she went beyond personal complaint to articulate a vision of a nation where women of her class and race shared moral and cultural leadership with men.[3] Leadership of the Emma Willard Association gave Olivia Sage a public role independent of her husband and made her a symbol of a movement of activism among elite women that is not adequately described by the terms philanthropy or benevolence.

The second association, the New York Exchange for Women's Work, consisted of female wage-earners, small businesswomen, and professionals, most of them teachers, but it also appealed to the wealthy women who were its patrons. Both organizations criticized men's management of public life and supported women's advancement into paid work and the professions. Nineteenth-century middle-class women had wrapped their public work in the language of benevolence.[4] The generation that followed added demands for women's economic rights and livelihood as well as political rights. For both generations, education formed an unassailable argument for full citizenship. Since the Civil War, women had continued to enter institutions of higher education, and by 1890, 56,000 of them were enrolled in colleges and universities, making up almost 36 percent of all students enrolled.[5] Both organizations allowed Olivia to give vent to a displaced and largely unacknowledged annoyance with her husband, whose behavior, even more than his origins, resulted in her exclusion from New York's most desirable social circles.

The New York Exchange for Women's Work

Founded in 1878, the New York Exchange for Women's Work was a producers' cooperative for women's home-produced work, selling "any marketable object which a woman can make." Consignors paid $2 a year to belong (or $5 for three years) and agreed "to fill orders under all circumstances."[6] The exchange, with its proclaimed goal of helping women become financially independent, seems to have appealed to Olivia's image of herself as a woman who had supported herself in difficult circumstances. She served on the board of managers from 1893 to 1899, then as a vice president from 1894 to 1899.[7]

Whatever its impact on the struggling craftswomen whose products it brokered, the exchange served the needs of its wealthy patrons, and its published reports offer a clear statement of elite women's feminist dreams and frustrations in this decade.[8] Its goal was to help just that class of women with whom Olivia could identify: "the educated poor," the déclassé, respectable daughters of the well-to-do who had fallen on hard times. The class identity of its clients was spelled out in the printed materials of the exchange. For example, in 1887, the association announced plans to build a boarding house for "gentlewomen obliged to support themselves." It was to be "a real home for women of refinement and cultivation and of limited means."[9] There are laws to protect people from violence, from dishonesty and slander, but "no laws to prevent the brutal treatment and desertion which well-bred women bear in silence," one report stated.[10]

The New York Exchange for Women's Work also sought to rescue women whose lives had been wrecked by the business cycle. Its annual reports—narratives of male failure and female rescue and resourcefulness—detail the tragic insecurity and grinding poverty of the abandoned wife, echoing familiar themes of nineteenth-century life and fiction.[11] One case history explained the plight of a woman "accustomed once to a most delightful home, living with her three little children in most uncongenial and cramped quarters, with a mothers' old cook-book her only capital . . . and their sole dependence the orders she is able to fill by working at all hours of the day and night." The writer added, "This is not an extreme case, but the history of many."[12]

The women's exchanges provided a way for elite women to talk about women's economic dependence and suggested that women's weakness lay not in their delicacy but in their lack of political rights, their disadvantaged position in the wage economy, and their exclusion from lucrative professions. By 1898, eighty-three exchanges were operating in the United States, a sure sign (according to one report) that they were needed, and would be, "so long as *sudden changes in fortune* oblige women to become self-supporting."[13]

How such language must have resonated with Olivia, who as a young woman had witnessed her father's ruin. And just a few years earlier in the panic of 1884, she had watched as her husband was forced to pay out $8 million dollars to creditors in just a few days after the collapse of the Wall Street firm Grant and Ward.[14] Although she was now a "lady of leisure," she and other wealthy women felt keenly their dependence on the good fortune that had thrown them into the arms of a wealthy man. Read together with the correspondence she was receiving from former Troy Female Seminary pupils and retired teachers (to be described shortly), the case studies in the exchange reports speak eloquently of women's need for education to fit them for fields other than teaching. Later, Olivia would address these issues by making large gifts for women's vocational and higher education.

But for now, she was confined to a grim but silent war on several fronts. Already in her sixties, Olivia had several reasons to be annoyed with men in general and her husband in particular. There was her recent bout with the Board of Governors at the Women's Hospital in 1888. And embarrassing parodies of her husband kept appearing in the press.

One humorous piece had Russell Sage and his partner Cyrus Field looking out from Sage's business office, which adjoined Trinity Church. The two financiers passed the time grimly reading to each other from the tombstone inscriptions. One went,

> Here lies old 33 percent
> The more he made the more he lent;
> The more he got the more he craved;
> The more he made the more he shaved.
> Oh, Lord! Can such a one be saved?

Another:

> The wretched man who molders here
> Cared not for soul or body lost.
> But only wept when death drew near;
> To think how much a tombstone cost.[15]

When Russell Sage was accorded space in a magazine or newspaper it was as an eccentric, a "type" among the varieties of urban life. A biographical sketch of him in World's Work in 1905 was titled, "A Man of Dollars. The Story of a Life Devoted Solely to the Chill Satisfaction of Making Money for Its Own Sake."[16] Another, a tongue-in-cheek piece called "A Bashful Millionaire" that appeared in the Brooklyn Eagle in 1897, poked fun at Sage's miserliness.

> All his charities are done so quietly that not a soul hears of it. . . . Those who have seen him turn aside from the selfish throng, and going to some thinly dressed man shivering in a doorway, clap him on the shoulder and say, "Here, old friend, I'm sorry you lost in that deal with me two years ago. Here's [money] to go and get a meal at the 'Bavaria,'" have always noticed that when he did this he always turned up his collar and escaped down some side street for fear he would be chided for too lavish use of money. Even in the matter of lighting his elevated trains and paying taxes he refrains from an unseemly haste for that gives the impression of throwing his money around in a prodigal and thriftless way that would teach bad manners to the poor.[17]

If his charities were so discreet that they were nonexistent, his sexual affairs were shouted from the rooftops in a series of lawsuits in which several women complained of sexual advances while Olivia suffered in silent humiliation. A long drawn-out lawsuit by Sophie Mattern, a divorcee and an artist, kept the Sage name in the papers with titillating accounts of an affair between Russell Sage and Sophie Mattern that was relayed to the public in almost daily installments. The case arose from Sophie Mattern's claim that she had entrusted Sage to invest on her behalf in an occasional "flutter" on the stock market but that he had actually lost money for her. The press account harped on two themes: the dubious investment skills of the female sex in general and the physical attractiveness of the plaintiff. Sophie Mattern "appeared to advantage" when she came to prosecute her case, according to one account. "[A] tallish woman of perhaps 195 pounds, which was tightly encircled with a fur-trimmed ulster. A costly bonnet of iridescent blue feathers glittered above her abundance of iron gray hair, and her steely blue eyes snapped and flashed intermittently. Her face wore an air of determination and a pink flush."[18] As the suit dragged on, press coverage supplied detailed descriptions of the plaintiff's dress ("Miss Mattern wore a wonderful sage green velvet dress, that peculiar tint of green being peculiarly appropriate") and disparaging remarks about her judgment—her lawyer was quoted as saying "My client was ignorant of her legal rights. Ladies are not supposed to know the law."[19] Sage succeeded in having the case dismissed, but not before the public was treated to passages such as the following:

> During the testimony [Sophie Mattern] laughed outright on two occasions, and glancing over at Uncle Sage caught him doing the same thing. Then a beautiful spirit of sympathy seemed to attract the plaintiff to the defendant and they both laughed together, a free, gladsome laugh, utterly unsuggestive of finances.[20]

The press also alleged that Sophie Mattern subsequently paid a call on Olivia Sage, who received her "very coldly at first" but afterward grew friendly. The wronged wife and the slandered artist evidently had much in common. (Olivia later became the patron of many female artists, but Sophie Mattern was not one of them).

A further scandal erupted in 1902 that linked Sage with a Marchioness Gregorio D'Ajuria, a lady of dubious origins who claimed that the financier had promised to give her property in return for her agreement to drop charges of sexual assault against him.[21]

Russell Sage made occasional efforts to improve his public image. In "The Boy That Is Wanted," a piece in the *Ladies' Home Journal* (1891), he promised "to all boys . . . fame and fortune for them if they are made of the right sort of stuff." But such platitudinous stories tying character to success did little to convince people that his own fortune was deserved.[22]

Transitions

Frugality and his wish to stay close to New York City dictated the choice of Long Island for a summer home in 1888. The Sage summer house was not in fashionable Newport, which had overtaken Saratoga as a resort for the wealthy, but at Lawrence, Long Island, in what today we would call a bedroom community. As one reporter explained, "[M]any of the public men of New York . . . go [there] nightly after their day of toil is over to rest and gain refreshment by inhaling the pure ocean ozone, dipping in the briny waves, and riding for an hour or two behind their spirited horses. The dawn of day finds them again seated behind the iron steed [the train] on their way to the hot, dusty city for another day of toil."[23]

The house, called Cedar Croft, had belonged to a retired Englishman who had tried to replicate the design of an Indian bungalow, with porches, verandas, and other features designed to open the rooms to ocean breezes.[24] Here Olivia settled in for the summer months while her husband labored on Wall Street. Elizabeth Cady Stanton, an occasional visitor, commented approvingly in her diary, "We found the great financier and his wife in an unpretending cottage with a fine outlook on the sea. Though possessed of great wealth they set a good example of simplicity and economy, which many extravagant people would do well to follow."[25]

Lawrence was a far cry from Newport, where the very rich spent the summer season in their splendid clifftop mansions and where Olivia had enjoyed a happy summer before her marriage. At Cedar Croft, her favorite haunt was "a snug, square balcony, low-roofed and reached from a door from one of the sleeping rooms," which gave a view out to sea. Here she marked the passing of ocean ships, studied the newspaper lists of sailings and arrivals, and learned to recognize the ships by their funnels. "This is a favorite spot with Mrs. Sage," a visitor noted. "Standing there with a field glass, she can sweep the ocean for full forty miles. At her right [toward the south] . . . she can see the dim mass of the Jersey shore. Before her is a salt meadow stretching nearly a mile away to Lawrence Beach, whose bleached sands shine like a white ribbon against the dark blue mass of the ocean."[26]

There is something wistful about the description of Olivia scanning the distance. She peered out to the horizon, yet her view of the world remained parochial and uninformed by foreign travel. It was the imaginary of the American missionary, benevolent, enthusiastic, and reformist but uncertain about what lay beyond America's shores. Even her travels at home were mostly limited to New York State. She never went south, she would visit Chicago on only one occasion (in 1893, to attend the World Columbian Exposition), and would travel west for the first time only in 1910, when she was over eighty.

On top of the embarrassment caused by her husband's lawsuits and scandals came a series of personal losses. In July 1891, Olivia's mother died at Cedar Croft at the age of eighty-seven. A few months later, Russell Sage's favorite nephew and heir, Russell Sage, Jr., died of tuberculosis in his fifties. The newspapers described him as "an old bachelor, a gentleman of ease," a crack billiards player and witty raconteur who spent his time lounging in the Windsor Hotel lobby from which hotel, it was reported, he once did not emerge for six months.[27] Russell Sage lost an important ally and business partner in 1892 when Jay Gould died, also from tuberculosis.[28] Finally, in September 1895, Olivia's sister-in-law Sallie L'Hommedieu passed away at the age of sixty-two. The loss drew Jermain closer to Olivia. Sister and brother would remain in almost daily contact for the next twenty years.[29]

On December 4, 1891, Russell Sage was the target of a spectacular assassination attempt. On that day he received a visitor at his office in the Arcade Building at 71 Broadway. Henry P. Norcross of Boston, "a man of unbalanced mind," gained entry with a forged letter of introduction from John D. Rockefeller and demanded a sum of $1.2 million. When Sage refused, Norcross dropped a dynamite bomb on the floor. The explosion blew Norcross to bits, killed one of the clerks, and wrecked the entire office. Russell Sage was hurt, as were four others, but he soon recovered sufficiently to be able to make an identification of the bomber for the police—though all that remained of Norcross was the head.[30] William Laidlaw, Jr., a broker's clerk, then sued Sage, claiming that at the instant the bomb went off Sage had seized him and used him as a human shield, causing him to suffer serious injuries. To the press the incident proved that Russell Sage was a calculating and heartless man who would sacrifice another's life to save his own skin. Charges against Sage were initially dismissed, but $25,000 was awarded on appeal after a second trial in April 1894. The case went through two more trials before the plaintiff abandoned the attempt to get Sage to pay damages, and in 1898 the Court of Appeals reversed the original verdict. Sage's biographer concludes in his usual overwrought style that although Sage was partly exonerated in the courts, "to the world-at-large he was guilty— guilty of being the meanest, most miserly skinflint that ever lived."[31]

Scandal again splashed Russell Sage's name across the headlines in 1893 when he was sued for $100,000 damages by Delia Keegan, the sister of a cook employed in the Sage household decades earlier. Keegan

FIGURE 7.1. Russell Sage. Henry Whittemore, *History of the Sage and Slocum Families of England and America* (New York: Published by Mrs. Russell Sage, 1908).

alleged that Russell Sage had made sexual advances to her during Maria Sage's last illness and that after first agreeing to marry her, he had "ruined" and then abandoned her. Now she had an adult son in his twenties to prove it. "Russell Sage Made Love; That, At Least Is the Complaint of Delia Keegan," chortled the *New York Times*. But Sage's lawyers managed to portray Delia Keegan as a blackmailer, a drunkard, a deranged person, and "lewd," and the case was dismissed.[32]

That winter of 1893 Olivia sought relief from chronic ill health and personal sorrows (and who could tell where one ended and the other began?) at a Hudson River resort, perhaps Kirkside, the Goulds' home at Roxbury in the Catskills. Harriette Dillaye, her old teacher from Troy and former principal from Philadelphia's Chestnut Street Female Seminary, must have been reading the newspapers, too. News of her former pupil's troubles prompted her to write Olivia a note of commiseration, from one "semi-invalid" to another.[33] After the bombing, Russell Sage avoided public appearances. He maintained a bodyguard and no longer kept the clockwork routine of his daily walks for fear of assassins and blackmailers. He had suffered a hearing loss in the explosion and this increased his isolation. When Nettie McCormick sent him a hearing aid, Olivia wrote back, "Both Mr. Sage and my Brother are quite astonished with the distinctiveness it gives to conversation; 'quite like a telephone,' my Brother says."[34] Sage remained remarkably spry. "He is tall of stature, spare of frame, with thick, iron gray hair, and bushy eyebrows over a pair of shrewd, steel gray eyes," a writer for *Muncy's Magazine* recorded. "Though his step has lost much of its elasticity, at seventy-eight he is still a notable instance of well preserved energy (see fig. 7.1)."[35]

"These days of light and liberty for an aspiring sisterhood"

For all Russell Sage's millions, New York society remained as impenetrable as ever. When Mrs. Astor made up her guest list of 400 with its inner circle of 273, the crème de la crème, the Sages were not on either list (neither were the Goulds or the Harrimans). And when New York's wealthy departed to escape the summer heat, the Sages moved only as far as Lawrence, Long Island, still close enough to the city for Russell to travel to Wall Street each day. Socially isolated and without a discretionary income that would enable her to keep up with fashion in dress or furnishings, unable to travel abroad, and reduced to using a hired carriage or a borrowed one, Olivia felt hard done by. She sought an outlet in earnest and thrifty activities.[36]

The Emma Willard Association, an alumnae association for the Troy Female Seminary alumnae that was headquartered in New York City, was founded on November 4, 1891, and incorporated on February 2, 1892. Olivia was its president from the time it was organized until her death twenty-seven years later. The association supplied a language for her discontent and offered a community of like-minded middle-class white women, mostly educated wives and wage-earning women. The association's goals were "to revive old associations and to perpetuate the name of Emma Willard," to plan a presence at the Columbian World's Fair, to raise money for scholarships, and to erect a statue of Emma Willard. (Willard had died twenty-two years earlier.)[37] Olivia already harbored more ambitious plans. She hoped to persuade Russell to put up the money for a new Troy Female Seminary campus and she was beginning to dream about a women's university in the East to match the newly founded University of Chicago, where female students were being educated on equal terms with men.[38]

At a time when some of the most powerful arguments for women's public activity were articulated around motherhood, the identity of 'educated woman' suggested an alternative identity, one based on merit, that was especially appealing to women such as Olivia Sage who had no children. She, along with the others of the Emma Willard Association, celebrated Emma Willard's intellectual accomplishments and made their education a basis for distinction. Their racial and class privilege remained invisible to them.[39]

Moreover, for all the talk of education, the organization focused a great deal on personal style, bearing, dress, and demeanor. Emma Willard had the power to signify the feminine, and at Emma Willard Association meetings during the 1890s those present celebrated not only her brains but her physical presence and demeanor, a combination of beauty, celebrity, and class that added up to cultural power. Willard's career demonstrated that self-support and intellectual achievement could be combined with respectability, these matrons agreed. "Her presence was queenly," one aged teacher recalled, "made attractive through mingled dignity and courtesy."

> Her dress, in harmony with her character and the occasion was appropriate, often elegant, always picturesque. She had recently returned from her European travels; her school was in the high tide of success and peerless among the female seminaries . . . of the world. She was then in the full enjoyment of "the youth of age," with finely developed physique, and her mind distinguished for vigor and versatility. . . . No other woman ever impressed me so deeply.[40]

Though she had opposed suffrage and disparaged the language of woman's rights, by the 1890s it hardly mattered what the historical Willard had done or said: her actual life was eclipsed by her legend, her name enlisted for causes she had opposed. In the Emma Willard Association, as scholar Mary Poovey remarks of Florence Nightingale, another major and enigmatic nineteenth-century figure, Willard was "displaced by her own image."[41]

Some Creative Philanthropy?

One way to open professions and institutions that had been closed to their sex was to endow college scholarships and fellowships for younger women, and this retired teacher Harriette Dillaye urged Olivia to do.[42] A two-year postgraduate fellowship at Middlebury College would be "beautifully appropriate," for it was at Middlebury that Emma Willard had felt "as never before," the injustice of depriving young women of higher education, she wrote. A few months later, she wrote: "An *advocate* is wanted, who is in sympathy with what Willard stood for, and acquainted with modern methods and ideas."[43] But Olivia, as always, was strapped for cash. She donated just $100 each to the scholarship and the statue funds; for the most part she played the role of fund-raiser, angling for the money of others. When fellow alumna Nettie McCormick endowed a scholarship fund at the school, Olivia assured her, "[T]he girl (or girls) who in the Future will reap the benefit, may not know how good you have been, but 'He who knoweth all things, will have this in remembrance.'"[44]

Meanwhile the association spawned a number of public activities to advance women. These included planning the Willard exhibit at Chicago's Columbian Exposition, compiling a biographical record, enlarging and modernizing the school, and placing statues of Emma Willard at Troy and Albany.[45]

Chicago, 1893: Reunion and World's Fair

Soon after its founding, the Emma Willard Association announced plans for a great reunion of former pupils of the Troy Female Seminary at the 1893 World's Fair in Chicago.[46] They obtained permission of the powerful Bertha Honoré Palmer to mount an exhibition on Emma Willard in the Woman's Pavilion, which was to house examples of women's achievements. What a showplace this would offer for the achievements of the great educator![47] Olivia asked Nettie McCormick to organize a committee of alumnae in Chicago for this event and to hire a secretary, perhaps in order to relieve her, Olivia, of work.[48] The exhibit documented the life and achievements of the famous educator. There were portraits; views of the old seminary (which had recently been removed to make way for new buildings) and of the old assembly room and the new Gurley Memorial Hall, a symbol of progress. There was a watercolor drawing of the famous examination room and a reproduction of Emma Willard's ingenious chart "temple of time and English Chronographer," catalogues of Troy Female Seminary from 1822 and 1824, architects' drawings of the projected Russell Sage Hall, and a copy of John Lord's *Life of Emma Willard* (1873). There were also copies of the numerous books written and published by Emma Willard.

Clearly the display had a serious educational purpose, but its sponsors soon discovered that the public came to Chicago to be diverted, not lectured to. Emma Willard Association members who visited the display complained that after all the tiresome arrangements the results were disappointing. Not enough space had been allotted to the Willard exhibits, they complained; the materials they had shipped to Chicago had been "arranged with no reference to the instructions which had been sent" and were "poorly arranged and unattended." One association member who visited the fair complained to Olivia that the Emma Willard material was hidden away.[49] Many felt it was a mistake to have a separate Woman's Pavilion at all; one of the Connecticut organizers remarked that the Woman's Pavilion "did not accomplish what it promised. . . . Like a woman's life, it seemed to be full of things which did not count."[50]

When the association's members gathered that summer at the Woman's Pavilion, they were even more disappointed. The walls of the Assembly Hall were hung with pictures of noted women, "intended, doubtless, as a galaxy of our sex, but Mrs. Willard's luminous face being absent, its brilliancy (to us at least), seemed clouded." Accordingly, the exhibit was moved to a more desirable section, "handsomely furnished and set in order." And during the course of the exposition, over 300 former pupils signed the registry, one-third from the West and South "showing how far the seed sown by Emma Willard is scattered."[51]

In an unusual departure from routine, Olivia traveled to Chicago in the summer of 1893 to see the fair for herself. Her close companion on this trip was Helen Gould (1870–1938), the eldest daughter of Jay Gould. Olivia had been a private tutor to all six children in the Gould home and she was particularly attached to Helen, so much so that after Helen's own mother died in 1891, Olivia stepped into the role. Over the next decade, as Helen embarked on some large-scale philanthropy, Olivia assumed the role of her protector and mentor.[52]

The party that traveled to Chicago also included Helen's niece, Alice Northrop Snow, Virginia Orton (daughter of Western Union's first president), a nurse, and a housekeeper, Miss Terry. They occupied a suite of rooms at the Beach Hotel on Lake Michigan, where cooling breezes wafted through the rooms. When three days of sightseeing left them all feeling fatigued, Alice Northrop Snow suggested that they should all rent the wicker "rolling-chairs" pushed by strong young men that were a popular way of seeing the fair. After first declaring that she would "never get into one," Olivia agreed and so did all the others. History does not record what she made of the midway with its exotic dancers, Samoan "natives," and other displays meant to heighten the contrast between "primitive peoples" and the civilization of the "White City."[53]

While in Chicago, Sage also attended and presided at an Educational Congress session devoted to Emma Willard. The elderly Susan B. Anthony delivered a speech written, in time-honored fashion, by Elizabeth Cady Stanton, which ridiculed critics who claimed that intellectual work harmed women. "I doubt whether as many women die annually from writing essays on induction and deduction as from over-production!" she quipped.[54] Olivia Sage as president then addressed the assembly. "We meet to pay a tribute of love and honor to a woman who ninety years ago gave the first great impulse to the cause of Woman's Higher Education in this country," she declared. Although the association was only two years old it already had 700 members, and fund-raising for the Middlebury College fellowship was under way. With God's blessing, they could hope to see "the old seminary rebuilt and the work begun by Mrs. Willard perpetuated."[55] Later the association held a reception at the McCormick house on Rush Street, "this sumptuous home adorned with pink roses and sweet peas," where "soft music mingled with the perfume of a thousand flowers, and over all rose the cheerful hum of friendly voices."[56]

Banquets and Reunions: From Cleopatra to Emma Willard

After the excitement of Chicago, meetings of the Emma Willard Association settled into a routine of polite sociability. The sixth annual banquet held in November 1896 was typical. Printed cards invited ladies to assemble at eleven o'clock "for social intercourse" before the banquet, which was to begin at one o'clock. The menu, though relatively simple, spoke of refined taste.

Consomme in Cups
Tournado [*sic*] of Bass, Lobster Sauce
Filet Mignon
Chifonnade Salad
Fancy Ices and Assorted Cake

Olivia Sage delivered the address of welcome, then Mary Jane Fairbanks gave a progress report on the alumnae directory (the "Biographical

Record") of which she was editor. The main speeches then began. After an address by Mary Alice Knox, principal of the Emma Willard School, a Mrs. Teall spoke on "The Power of Influence," then Harriot Stanton Blatch spoke on "Higher Education."[57] Other meetings were held in the Sage home. At one, educator Ezra Brainerd spoke on "Mrs. Emma Willard's Life and Work in Middlebury." Some concentrated on British heritage and history: a meeting in February 1895 featured a talk on Robert Burns and was enlivened with Scottish songs.[58]

Despite their rhetoric of empowerment and their efforts to historicize women's struggle and document women's progress, associations such as the Emma Willard Association, while they provided meaningful activity for their members, did little to forward real educational equality for women.[59] We can see this when we compare the Emma Willard Association to a rival association, the Emma Willard Educational Society, which announced its more far-reaching goals: "the opening of all great universities to women, the equal division of all school offices, the equal pay of same, the forming of [affiliated] loyal leagues among the school children." Olivia Sage alerted Nettie McCormick about this organization, enclosing the clipping from the *Woman's Journal* with her letter and condemning the group's approach as "undignified."[60]

Press coverage of Emma Willard Association events framed the meetings as fashion, not feminism. The *New York Daily Tribune* described the graduation ceremonies at the Emma Willard School in June 1897 under the heading "Boudoir Chit-Chat" and described Olivia Sage's Worth gown as "a triumph of the modiste's art." Yet Sage's address to the eighth annual banquet at the Windsor Hotel in New York City in November 1898 included a rousing evocation of "these days of light and liberty for an aspiring sisterhood,"

> when women's colleges are an accomplished fact, and an "open sesame" is written over the gateway of every profession, when a Mothers' Congress at our capital publicly considers the physical culture of children.

It now seemed "ancient history," she continued, to recall the days "when the study of physiology was prescribed for our grandmothers as indelicate and . . . higher mathematics was omitted from their curriculum."[61]

Among its own members the Emma Willard Association worked a quiet revolution that we might call consciousness-raising. One grateful alumna described how Emma Willard's rhetoric of history had awakened her own feminism (though she did not use the term). Late in life, this woman confessed, "I studied her Universal History which brought the world's events into continuous order, and I there learned the potency of woman and her influence inspiring and directing progress."[62]

Though it reported verbatim these rousing words (as well as Harriot Stanton Blatch's call for an end to militarism, voiced at the same banquet) the *Tribune* did so under the heading not of "Pacifist Protest" or "Women's Equality Proclaimed!" but "Black Velvet Hats Trimmed With Ostrich Feathers." Framing the speeches in the context of a gathering of fashionable women, the newspaper contained and sanitized the Emma Willard Association's feminist rhetoric.[63]

The Biographical Record: Creating the Community of Educated Women

Olivia Sage directed and paid for the alumnae survey, the association's most significant achievement. The plan was to record the lives of all the graduates of one of America's pioneer women's colleges. Questionnaires were sent out to all former pupils, their friends, and their descendants. The result, the 800-page quarto volume *Emma Willard and Her Pupils, or Fifty Years of Troy Female Seminary, 1822–1872*, documents the careers of 3,500 alumnae of the more than 12,000 women who attended the seminary during the period 1822 to 1872.[64] Administration of the questionnaires and assembling and editing the data were assigned to a committee. Mary Jane Fairbanks (class of 1845) had the task of writing the historical sections and compiling the biographies from her home in Providence, Rhode Island.[65] Olivia sent a monthly remittance for her editorial work and in return received deferential acknowledgment.[66]

Olivia received correspondence from hundreds of alumnae in connection with the directory. Some letters were 20-page sagas describing their careers or the careers of their mothers. There were requests for information, orders for the book, and, after it appeared, the inevitable complaints from women whose names had been misspelled or whose mothers' biographies had been mysteriously and unforgivably omitted. Many of the letters forcefully outlined women's economic dilemma. One alumna, Alice Bryant, wrote asking for a position. "What such a position might be is a matter of conjecture because I belong to that large and sad class who are not trained in any one direction."[67] Some letters echoed the radicalism of an earlier era. Octogenarian alumna Mrs. M. M. Cummings identified herself as "a 'Daughter of the Revolution'—the Revolution which Mrs. Willard effected in a warfare for her sex."[68]

Olivia wrote sections of the book herself. She certainly wrote the

"Prospectus" and sent it to Mary Jane Fairbanks, who suggested some changes.[69] The biographical sketches show Olivia's influence also. The detailed and admiring biography of Harriette Dillaye, which runs over four pages, suggests Olivia's authorship, as does the brief and understated biography of Maria Winne (1838), the first Mrs. Sage.[70] *Harper's Bazaar* praised "the notable volume recently prepared by Mrs. Russell Sage." Another press notice stated that although Mrs. Sage's name did not appear as the author, "she is doubtless the author and compiler of the volume." The title page lists "Mrs. Russell Sage, Publisher."[71]

Editing this volume of alumnae biographies must have had a powerful effect on Olivia. As she surveyed her generation of students and teachers, wives and mothers, she could not help noticing that there were other kinds of marriage, partnerships that looked more egalitarian than her own. Her friend Nettie Fowler McCormick, for example, wife of Cyrus McCormick, enjoyed wide administrative discretion over the great McCormick fortune, and her husband shared business and financial affairs with her. Imagine Olivia's feelings as she read and edited the "Nettie Fowler" entry:

> At Mr. McCormick's death, in 1884, Mrs. McCormick was made one of the executors and trustees of the estate. Being familiar during her husband's life with all the details of his large business, her sound judgement and experience have proved important factors in fulfilling the duties of that important trust.[72]

The Emma Willard Association leaders used the powerful male-dominated American Tract Society, with headquarters in New York City and branches in Boston, Philadelphia, Chicago, Cincinnati, San Francisco, and Troy, to distribute the directory.[73] And they yielded business decisions such as whether to have one large volume or two smaller ones to their husbands, men experienced in securing cost estimates and in producing and distributing the printed materials of their own fraternal and patriotic organizations. Mr. Fairbanks wrote to Russell Sage suggesting as a model for the Emma Willard volume the *Year Book of the Sons of the Revolution of the State of New York* and advising him about printing costs.[74]

Cultural Work: The Work of History

As a self-conscious attempt to simultaneously designate and create a community of educated women, the biographical directory, which was completed and published in 1898, provided incontrovertible evidence of

women's advancement in education and the professions. Elizabeth Cady
Stanton saw its power to make women's achievements visible. She
advised Olivia, "[I]f you have not already thought of it . . . place the
Emma Willard Volume in the libraries of all our Universities and Colleges, not forgetting the Teachers College Columbia, etc. etc."[75] Writing and compiling the biographies had been "a herculean work . . . a labor
of love," Olivia told members of the association at their November banquet in 1897. The *New York Daily Tribune* article reporting this event
quoted the book's preface:

> To trace the history, not only of the alumnae of the school, but of all
> the pupils who had belonged to it during that half-century which began
> seventy-five years ago; to find and identify some seven thousand
> women, scattered all over our broad land, most of whom had taken
> new names—some of them more than once, and half of whom had
> passed away from earth—this was a task, the like of which was prob-
> ably never before undertaken, and one far greater than its originators
> had ever dreamed.[76]

But while the association signaled elite women's self-consciousness
it also reveals how their vision was narrowed by class. This was a project
to shore up by continual reaffirmation the hegemony of Anglo-Protestants. Its "usable past" was the past of the Pilgrims and the *Mayflower,*
with Pilgrim Mothers added to the familiar story. Meetings of the Emma
Willard Association were the occasion to tell and retell this past, to evoke
an alternative version of American biblical—indeed, world—history,
one with female heroines, queens, and warriors. Through the Emma
Willard Association, white elite women "wrote themselves into the
nation's history."[77] A typical banquet speaker regaled her listeners with
a recitation of the great women of the past: Cleopatra, Naomi, Maria
Theresa, and Catherine the Great. Queens, empresses, and biblical heroines thus joined in the procession which culminated in the enlighten-
ing vision of their own dear Emma Willard. Mrs. Jane Bancroft
Robinson's speech on Emma Willard at the 1893 reunion evoked a progressive history of women beginning with medieval times, when women
were "as compassionate as they are brave, as gentle as they are masculine" so that they were made "regents of kingdoms, heirs of crowns, joint
managers of princely estates."[78]

At another reunion, members heard a talk about the Pilgrims
through which those far-distant ancestors were made to shed a sanctified
and sanctifying glow on the present. "In your President, Mrs. Sage,"
the speaker declared, "a direct descendant of Myles Standish, we see

the same race traits of character, the desire of doing good and pleasing everyone, the strength of convictions, and the ability to hold her own council."[79]

Olivia Sage's attitude of reverence toward her country's history, real or imagined, contrasts with the shameless rewriting of history by her more practical feminist contemporary, Elizabeth Cady Stanton. The contrast is worth making. Here is the account, from Stanton's published memoirs, of an annual "Pilgrim Mothers' Dinner," from December 22, 1893:

> This afternoon we had our annual Pilgrim Mothers' Dinner. Lillie Devereux Blake presided and opened the speechmaking with an excellent toast to "Our Forgotten Foremothers." I came next with "Christmas, 1620–1893, Contrasted." My account of Christmas on the *Mayflower* was mainly a fancy sketch mixed with historical facts. But everybody accepted it as genuine history. A young lady came up to me at the close of the dinner and asked me where she could see "the posthumous family papers" of the Brewers. And I told her I feared only in the arches of my brain.[80]

These Emma Willard Association celebrations of the past, typical of a decade when at least fifty patriotic societies came into being, draw attention to the awakened confidence of elite women who are often assumed to have "sat out" Progressive-era realignments of class and gender.[81]

When the Emma Willard Association gathered in Chicago for their memorable 1893 reunion, a few at least had in mind something more substantial than the enjoyment of each others' company and the pleasure of viewing Nettie McCormick's Rush Street home completely bedecked in pink flowers. Philanthropy that was solid meant buildings, and the Emma Willard Association women vowed to revive the seminary as a boarding school (it had languished since the death of Sarah Willard).[82] The first of three new buildings was donated by Troy civic leader Lewis Gurley at the cost of $60,000 and was dedicated on June 8, 1892. Olivia attended the ceremony and, at her urging, so did Elizabeth Cady Stanton.[83]

But an attempt to take control of their own institution by placing four women on the Emma Willard School board of trustees was turned back by a veto from New York governor Roswell Flower in April 1894. At a noisy meeting in her home, Sage voiced her outrage at this setback: "If women could vote, they would decide the question of whether women should be members of the Board of Trustees of a girls' school, or whether men alone should be members," she declared. "Oh! No! He won't be elected again!" the women shouted back.[84] A compromise was announced later that year at a meeting of the association in New York, when the 200 guests were informed that a bill allowing four female trustees had passed the state legislature. This would eliminate the mayor of Troy "who, it was said, was not always an educated man," a remark that drew laughter. To her great satisfaction, Olivia now became one of three new female trustees.[85] But the episode reinforced Olivia's conviction that women needed the vote because it amplified how women as a sex were disadvantaged, regardless of their class, race, or education. It gave impetus to the movement of women like Olivia toward the suffrage, a movement that in the first decade of the twentieth century would fill the NAWSA's coffers while pushing it away from its associations with radical and working-class allies.

Meanwhile, Olivia had managed to extract a promise from Russell Sage to give the school a new dormitory, and construction had begun.[86] This was his first-ever substantial philanthropic donation, and he evidently had second thoughts when it came to writing the check. Olivia was able to get him to carry through on his promise only by a subterfuge involving his crony, fellow Western Union director Chauncey Depew. Interviewed much later for the *Syracuse Post-Standard*, Depew explained how Olivia had engineered the gift and produced what appeared an aberrant act of generosity by the man known in the press as "the skinflint of the great Yankee nation."

Some months earlier, Depew had received an invitation from Olivia Sage to give an address at the Emma Willard School. She told him she was going to give the school a large check for a building (in fact, this was untrue), and she invited him to be present. When he declined on the grounds that he was too busy, she fired back an urgent message. "Russell is going to give $120,000. . . . This is Russell's first endeavor in this field. Don't you think he ought to be encouraged?" Depew made the speech, Russell Sage gave the $120,000, and Sage Hall was dedicated at a ceremony in 1895 attended by alumnae and friends.[87] Addressing the crowd, Depew teased the reluctant philanthropist and struck a surprisingly progressive note when he declared that the greatest questions of the age were presented by "the accumulations of wealth and the use which should be made of it. 'Where did he get his money and what is he doing with it?' are the crucial questions. The press asks, the pulpit inquires, the platform orator wants to know what the rich man is doing with his money that he should receive for it the protection of the state."

The answer was, they were giving it to universities. There was Rockefeller's gift to the University of Chicago, Ezra Cornell's to Cornell University, and most recently Seth Low's to Columbia.[88] Called on to make some response, Russell Sage recounted to the assembled pupils, teachers, and friends the time when, as a freshman congressman about to set off for Washington, he had received a call at his house from Emma Willard. Instead of asking the newly minted politician to do her some political favor, the educator "made him an offer of her personal services to help him in his work as a legislator," since "her position and her pen had given her a personal acquaintance with many of the prominent men of the country, and if Mr. Sage wanted aid either through her pen or to make acquaintances she would be glad to serve him."[89] For us, the incident reveals Emma Willard's mode of operation and her supreme confidence: the voteless woman offering to advance the career of the male politician.

Russell Sage continued in a spending mood, comparatively speaking, for in October 1897, Olivia and Jermain traveled to Syracuse for the dedication of a window at the First Presbyterian Church in memory of their parents. Designed by New York artist Mary Tillinghast and costing over $10,000, the window also showed Olivia's new interest in patronizing women artists.[90]

The dormitory was a start. Troy Female Seminary was now renamed the Emma Willard School, "thus bringing the school into close touch with its famous past and associating it even in name with its illustrious founder."[91] And Russell Sage Hall completed a trio of new school buildings. These might now "form a nucleus around which we fondly hope may one day cluster the proud structures of a well endowed university," the association's secretary declared in 1893. "Mrs. Sage is anxious to lead us to some aggressive work," attendees of the Chicago reunion of the association were told.[92] "I would very much like to rebuild and have endowed our own dear Troy Female Seminary," Olivia had confided to Nettie McCormick in 1891. "At any rate something fine must be done to honor such a woman as Mrs. Willard and perpetuate her memory in educating women. Statues may be built but a more lasting work must be carried forward."[93]

Harriette Dillaye encouraged Sage to think seriously about founding a women's national university. She was impatient for the day "when the Emma Willard College or University, amply endowed, can take its place in the sisterhood of Vassar, Wellesley, Smith, Bryn Mawr, and other colleges with every department crowned with able educators."[94] At the fifth Emma Willard Association reunion she offered a resolution "that

FIGURE 7.2. Unveiling the statue of Emma Willard at the dedication of Russell Sage Hall in Troy, N.Y., 1895. Courtesy Rensselaer County Historical Society.

we look forward to the development of the Troy Female Seminary into a College or University for Women, bearing the name of Emma Willard." She continued, "Shall it be Troy College—or University, taking its place with Vassar, Smith, and Bryn Mawr—with Barnard and Radcliffe?"[95]

The ambiguous legacy of Emma Willard became a permanent monument in December 1895 when a statue of the great educator costing $8,000 collected from Emma Willard Association members was erected outside the new buildings in Seminary Park, Troy, where it remains to this day. A photograph captures the alumnae gathered around the massive bronze figure. The enigma of the large seated figure is explained by a former pupil. Willard would always remain seated when delivering a public address, this alumna recalled, because she did not believe it proper for women to make speeches. The speech thus became "merely conversation and therefore appropriately feminine (see fig.7.2)."[96] Olivia also attended the dedication in May 1899 when the association placed a bust of the educator in the State Library at Albany, making a space in New York's civic culture for this monument to female achievement.[97]

In June 1897, when Olivia Sage traveled to Troy to attend the fiftieth anniversary of her graduation she drew out her original diploma before an astonished audience.[98] Women's advancement was her theme at a subsequent meeting of the association. Although the lovely young women she had seen recently at the anniversary celebration looked just like the girls of her schooldays, looks were deceiving, for young women had made enormous progress over the last half-century, she declared. "[Their] brains have the ascendancy now." Woman had achieved that "perfect symmetry" which allows her, with God's help, to lift up "the other half of humanity called man."[99] Her speech mirrors a shift away from the language of spheres. The idea of symmetry proposed an androgynous ideal in place of the conventional one of woman as separate creature, angel, mother, or muse.[100] Women had beaten back opponents who cited scientific and health reasons for excluding them from colleges. Now the educated woman had arrived, a more fully evolved human type, morally superior to man and equipped to wield cultural and political power. Indeed, women's nonpartisan good sense was needed in politics more than ever. With brain, body, and moral nature all balanced, woman was the perfect instrument for God's plan of advancing the nation and uplifting the morally unevolved male half.[101]

As the decade drew to a close, confident assertions that morality and education were more important for citizenship than other attributes (such as physical strength) received a rude shock. The war with Spain showed that brute strength counted after all and that the virile civilizations were the ones that could fight and win.[102] And wealthy women had not rallied around the idea of an Emma Willard University by giving substantial amounts of money. Dues to the Emma Willard Association remained pitifully low at one or two dollars a year, and receipts for 1899–1890 were only around $1,500; the idea that such an organization could produce an endowment for a new university for women was risible. Russell Sage Hall had enabled Troy Female Seminary to restart its boarding program, which had been discontinued since 1872. But it was far from the dreamed-of Willard University. Stanton, more realistic, expressed doubt that women could ever command the wealth to endow a university. She declared, "The most fitting monument we can rear to Emma Willard is a generation of thoroughly educated women."[103] And Olivia, now seventy, informed the association that it was time for her to retire, "to sit down at home and knit stockings." She had been president for seven years and now she should be "laid on the shelf," she told them. But the association returned her as president by acclamation, signaling that she

FIGURE 7.3. Olivia Sage. Bolling Memorial Medical Archives, New York, N.Y.

was indispensable either as guiding spirit or as potential angel. Russell Sage could not live for ever, and the Sage millions might yet become the endowment they needed.[104]

As for Olivia, she did not lose interest in endowing a university, but she began to entertain a proposal from a very different source: Chancellor Henry MacCracken of New York University had bold plans for expansion, and Olivia's young friend Helen Gould was one of his staunchest supporters. In 1895, Helen, a multimillionaire since the death of her father in 1892, pledged funding for the administration building and the library at University Heights.[105] Helen was not interested in directing her philanthropy toward women's education, but Sage could think of little else. When she learned that MacCracken's plans for New

York University included an uptown campus with a Hall of Fame displaying 100 busts of great Americans, she determined that women should be included, especially Emma Willard. In 1905, almost sixty years after her graduation from Troy Female Seminary, and with remembrances of college days in the 1840s still fresh, she took pale pink writing paper and wrote fifty letters to the trustees, urging them to nominate "Emma Willard, Teacher" for the Hall of Fame. "[Willard] was not only a great teacher, but an educator, an author, and in a vital sense a reformer," Olivia wrote. "Few other women named upon the list can rank with her. Many of them entered their life-work because of her, they rose to eminence on the foundation she had laid."[106]

One year later, Olivia was a widow with her husband's vast fortune at her disposal. Suddenly it seemed as if the New York University scheme might become the dreamed-of Willard University, a great and concrete monument to Emma Willard. Now Olivia could fulfill her duty not only to class and nation but also to the undying ideal—Mrs. Willard's ideal—of educated womanhood. How she longed to perpetuate the memory of "The Sage of Troy"! But whether this "Sage" meant Russell Sage or Emma Willard was the question. Perhaps even Olivia herself did not know.

In the Emma Willard Association, Olivia and women like her achieved a significant transformation of their consciousness about women's place in the nation. Historians of the suffrage movement have described how the National American Woman Suffrage Association (NAWSA) approached women of wealth during the 1894 New York campaign, forging an alliance that helped the campaign's finances and propelled it toward victory.[107] This chapter reveals that wealthy women such as Olivia Sage were moving toward suffrage even before the suffragists moved toward them and that if NAWSA was successful in securing their support, it was because some, Sage among them, had already undergone their own feminist transformations.

Eight

Converted!

Parlor Suffrage and After

Women of the leisure class need freedom, too.
—Jessie Ashley, *Woman's Journal*, April 22, 1911[1]

Women like me need the ballot to teach us to think
of other women and to help them.
—Alva Vanderbilt Belmont (1910)[2]

In 1897, the fiftieth anniversary of her graduation from Troy Female Seminary, Olivia received a presentation copy of a slim pamphlet, *The Parable of the Ten Virgins*,[3] from fellow alumna Elizabeth Cady Stanton.[4] The
gift had been carefully chosen. Stanton, now over eighty and retired from
the presidency of NAWSA, was a veteran woman's rights activist who
advocated a wide range of reforms, from easier divorce to the vote. She
was also an outspoken critic of religious traditions that oppressed women,
of denominations that collected churchwomen's offerings to send young
men to colleges from which they and their daughters were excluded, and
of churches that barred from the pulpits their most rational and brilliant
speakers on the grounds of sex.[5] In 1892, she had published the distilla-
tion of her feminist individualist philosophy, "The Solitude of Self," and
more recently she had co-authored the *Woman's Bible* (1895).[6] Stanton's
religious radicalism was seen as a political liability by the delegates to the
NAWSA convention of 1896, who passed a resolution disassociating
the organization from the publication for fear of causing a break with the
evangelical women of the temperance and purity crusades who were coming in large numbers to the suffrage cause.[7]

Olivia might well have taken offense at Stanton's choice of a text.

"Watch, therefore, for you know neither the day nor the hour" seems an unkind reminder to a woman approaching seventy that the time to act on her principles was now or never. Moreover, Stanton intended this to be advice of a secular kind. She brushed aside the standard interpretation of the parable that Christians should always be in a state of readiness for the Heavenly Bridegroom. Rather, this was a "very simple parable" which "seems to apply much more clearly to this life than to that which is to come," Stanton wrote. One must have the courage of one's convictions or be guilty of "the sin of neglecting and burying one's own talents, capacities, and powers." She went on to attack the whole basis of women's subordination to men. Foolish virgins were like women who "have never learned the first important duty of cultivating their own individual powers, using the talents given them, and keeping their own lamps trimmed and burning." Wives, especially, were at fault: "The idea of being a helpmeet to somebody else has been so sedulously drilled into most women that an individual life, aim, purpose, ambition, is never taken into consideration." The parable was "a lesson for the cultivation of courage and self-reliance."[8]

Olivia was one of those evangelical wives who found herself more and more drawn to the suffrage cause. This was a time of moral reform fervor when celebrity preachers such as Rev. Charles Parkhurst of Madison Square Presbyterian Church and Rev. De Witt Talmage of the Brooklyn Tabernacle drew large crowds. Parkhurst, the organizer of the Society for the Prevention of Crime and founder of the City Vigilance League, became famous for sermons that denounced the evils of ancient Babylon and the Babylonian excesses of his own time, and his personal investigations of sinful activities in New York's dives and slums gave him celebrity status. Olivia enjoyed Rev. Talmage's sermons and several times succeeded in persuading Helen Gould to accompany her to hear him speak (they occupied a box with Mrs. Talmage).[9] "His talk was of his travels in the Holy Land," 22-year-old Helen reported to her father after one such sermon, "and he spoke in stirring language of the profligacy and great wickedness of some of those old cities, and how suddenly ruin had come upon them. Then he denounced New York and warned the people."[10]

Millennial change was in the air and revelations of political corruption and vice shocked public opinion. Campaigns for temperance and purity, the crusade against white slavery, gambling, and police corruption all summoned evangelical Christians to take up the work of reform.[11] In 1894, Parkhurst, heading a Committee of Seventy, successfully backed William Strong as reform candidate for mayor of New

York. The minister pulled no punches in his attack on the Tammany-led administration, which he described as "polluted harpies that, under pretense of governing this city, are feeding day and night on its quivering vitals. A lying, perjured, rum-soaked and libidinous lot."[12] Strong defeated the Tammany candidate and initiated a three-year cleanup of the city's brothels, dives, and gambling dens, only to be defeated in 1897.[13]

Since her marriage Olivia had tried out, one by one, the available roles of the New York matron with an interest in public affairs but without disposable income of her own: wife, benevolent lady, committee woman. She encouraged an image of herself as a philanthropist long before her significant philanthropy began, writing of herself in the third person in *Emma Willard and Her Pupils*, "Her benefactions have been unstinted, and her executive ability in her public philanthropies have already passed into history."[14] But as she added new layers of responsibility in voluntary associations for missions and temperance, Indian reform, and protection of working girls, the fact of her disfranchisement became ever more irksome. As an enthusiastic churchgoer and strict sabbatarian, Olivia had come to see women's advancement as part of God's plan for world redemption. Helen Gould shared this view. Writing to Olivia from Cairo, the eighteen-year-old confided, "It makes me sad to see the women veiled and to think of the harems. I think I should be dreadfully jealous if I were one of several wives."

> They are not allowed to worship in the mosques, and if you call on a musselman you are not allowed to ask after his family. How much Christ has done for us women and how grateful we should be to Him! One's life is a poor return for the light and liberty and hope he has given us.[15]

If Olivia agreed with Helen on the imperialistic mission of white Christian women to the Moslem world, and I believe that she did, on the issue of women's rights she was closer to Elizabeth Cady Stanton and her commitment to women's advancement. Earlier, Stanton had warned her women's rights colleagues to beware the new recruits brought to the suffrage by the temperance crusade, but now she actively sought their endorsement and their financial backing.[16] In her diary she wrote, "Men and women of the conservative stamp of the Sages can aid us greatly at this stage of our movement."[17] So she agreed when, in 1892, Olivia begged her to attend the dedication of a new building at the Troy Female Seminary. In her address to the assembled students, Stanton stated frankly that she no longer knew any of her peers from the class of 1832, "and if I did, probably our ideas would differ on every subject, as I have wandered in latitudes beyond the prescribed sphere of women." But her speech, a strong defense of women's equal educational and professional opportunities, met with Olivia's hearty approval.[18] The two women met again in 1893 when Olivia visited Stanton's summer retreat at Glen Cove, Long Island, and persuaded her to deliver a speech at the Emma Willard Reunion in Chicago. Stanton returned the visit in August when she came with her son Theodore to spend a few days with Olivia and Russell Sage at their seaside home. As the little party sat looking out over the marshes to the Atlantic where steamers bound for New York could be seen far out on the horizon, the discussion turned to suffrage.[19] Stanton's diary entry for October 1893 records victory. "Mrs. Sage has just been converted to woman suffrage," she wrote, "and she tells me that she is drawing Mr. Sage in the right direction."[20]

"Converted"—the word was apt. Olivia had gone through a transformation shared in the 1880s and 1890s by thousands of evangelical women who no longer trusted the old standby of "woman's influence" in politics but demanded the ballot for themselves.[21] Many of them were Woman's Christian Temperance Union (WCTU) members. Spurred on by president Frances Willard's "Do Everything" slogan, they believed they were "called by God out of their homes into active temperance agitation," and many became suffragists.[22]

Olivia's conversion was also precipitated by events in her personal life. A handwritten fragment in her writing is revealing. Scrawled and undated it reads, "'Private greifs [sic] must not stand in the way of public duties,' Emma Willard." As she often did, Olivia let Emma Willard speak for her. I have described how Olivia underwent a number of "private griefs" in the 1890s. During that decade, she sought solace in public activity, including suffrage activism.[23]

Between 1887, when Congress first debated a woman suffrage amendment, and 1914, when the amendment again reached the floor of the House, leaders of NAWSA courted different constituencies: college graduates and professionals, black and white clubwomen and church members, immigrants and working women. As a result, the movement grew, in the words of political scientist David McDonald, from "an embattled group of iconoclasts on the fringes of mid-Victorian society into a conservative movement with closer ties to the mainstream of middle-class Protestants, and finally into a movement capable of reaching many sectors of the state's huge immigrant population."[24]

Some scholars have read this as a narrative of declension, where "the ideals of the pioneer suffragists were gradually diluted over time by elitism, racism, and expediency."[25] They have pointed particularly to the effort to attract socially prominent women who might become suffrage funders. Three interconnected but nonetheless distinct themes signal suffragists' approach to women of wealth: first, proposals relating to the "educated vote"; second, proposals for a franchise based on wealth; and third, themes of race and nation. By the 1890s such themes had become more insistent and more blatant as New York suffrage leaders relinquished the goal of full suffrage in favor of municipal suffrage for taxpaying women.[26]

The key to the transformation of the suffrage movement in this decade was the sleight of hand that allowed upper-class women to represent themselves as "educated women." The history of the Emma Willard Association has shown how, by framing the suffrage movement as a movement for an "educated suffrage," leaders could make it attractive to women such as Olivia who would otherwise have seen it as socially disruptive and morally suspect. By 1893, NAWSA leaders were appealing to the idea of the "educated vote." Their convention of that year resolved

> That without expressing any opinion on the proper qualifications for voting, we call attention to the significant facts that in every State there are more women who can read and write than the whole number of illiterate male voters; more white women who can read and write than all negro voters; more American women who can read and write than all foreign voters; so that the enfranchisement of such women would settle the vexed question of rule by illiteracy, whether of home-grown or foreign-born production.[27]

In January 1894, in "An Appeal to the Women of New York," Stanton declared that the suffrage cause could hope for nothing from "the devotees of fashion and the victims of want . . . those enervated by luxury or benumbed by ill-paid toil and ceaseless suffering. But intelligent, thinking women will certainly spare no effort to relieve themselves from the disgrace of being classed in the political category with idiots, lunatics and criminals."[28]

Suffrage leaders also invoked stereotypes of race to underline the claim of white native-born women to full citizenship. In the West, Carrie Chapman Catt raised the specter of government by racial Others. Who would be the rulers of the Dakotas once the Sioux (she meant men of the Sioux tribe) were allowed to vote, she demanded in an early speech, portraying Indians as cruel savages.[29] Women such as Olivia who had represented themselves as benevolent patrons of racial and class inferiors and the natural protectors of Indians and women of heathen lands were indignant to find themselves in a position of being "protected" by male immigrants and by men of color who had exercised the right of franchise since 1870.[30]

In 1894, Olivia gave her first newspaper interview on why women should vote. The paper ran the piece under the heading "Views of a Millionaire's Wife," but Olivia significantly represented herself as one of "a class of thoughtful women," many of them "women of means, widows and spinsters . . . throughout the state." These independent women think it is "not only unreasonable but unjust" that they pay taxes but have no vote. She declared her "earnest desire" for "the privilege of the ballot" and her belief that women's votes would purify politics and raise moral standards.[31] Olivia had been appearing in public as a suffrage advocate in different venues. In 1894, she and Stanton shared a platform when the latter addressed a girls' physical education class at the Horace Mann School. The topic was dress reform. "Just think how easily they [men] can go up and down stairs in those suits!" Stanton declared. "I don't believe men know what a terrible time women have going upstairs with a bundle. Why, I remember when I used to want to carry a baby upstairs—and you know I had plenty of them to carry—I had to take my petticoat in my teeth and go up that way."[32] By linking women's rights with an iconic healthy motherhood, suffragists helped deflect accusations that suffrage meant sex antagonism and race suicide.

NAWSA's approach to wealthy and socially prominent women had scored a notable success in Colorado with the suffrage referendum of 1893. Now the same strategy would be tried in New York.[33] At the center of the New York campaign of 1894 was the attempt to collect enough signatures to persuade the elected members of the state's constitutional convention to remove the word "sex" from the state constitution. During the five months of the campaign, over 100 meetings were held in different places—parlors, churches, political clubs, settlement houses, and labor halls—and by one estimate, 600,000 signatures were collected.[34] Elite suffragists politicized new space as they turned fashionable meeting places into sites for suffrage discussion and organizing. One of these was described as "a fashionable caterer whose shop is the rendezvous of the Equal Suffragists; there men and women go to sign petitions to the Constitutional Convention for the elimination of the word 'male.'" The "antis," she reported, told the proprietor they would go somewhere else for their ice cream and cake.[35]

In March 1894, suffrage leader Lillie Devereux Blake informed readers of the *Woman's Journal* that the campaign was gaining adherents among the rich. "Fashionable women are taking it up, and one set of ladies of wealth and position have taken headquarters at Sherry's, the fashionable caterer's quarters on Fifth Avenue and 37th Street," where they would be handing out petitions and suffrage literature on Saturday mornings.[36]

A writer for the *New York Sun* also noted the change. "The suffrage has finally enlisted the active aid and support of the most cultured and intelligent women in the community, and has even attracted the attention of the so-called society women."[37] Suffrage headquarters was at Sherry's, "a resort of fashion," another noted, and not in a place "with which radicalism or eccentricity is associated."[38] Another account, under an illustration of well-dressed women signing the petition, helpfully explained to its readers that society leaders had only just become aware of the movement for women's rights. Earlier they had opposed it, thinking that suffragists were "chronic fault-finders, who held meetings chiefly for the purpose of scolding their husbands."[39]

Olivia Sage was associated with the political action committee of wealthy Republican women, which included Josephine Shaw Lowell, Mrs. Robert Abbé, and Mary Putnam Jacobi, dubbed the "Sherry Committee."[40] Elite women transformed their parlors, spaces that signified both domesticity and respectability, into arenas for political discussion. One reporter supplied a telling detail of this transformation: "Two-story tea-tables of mahogany, satinwood, and marquetry have been cleared of old china and silver, and suffrage materials, for sale, substituted," he wrote.[41] Space at these meetings was limited, and competition for invitations was intense. The New York State Woman Suffrage Association (an affiliate of the NAWSA) reported that "the greatest desire was aroused to get in, among hundreds of people who had not occupied themselves with the suffrage question in the least." Two thousand people crammed into the general meeting in space designed to hold 700; many were turned away.[42] Acknowledging that the petition drive had attracted many women of wealth, the suffrage leadership presented statistical proof of their success that included the amount of taxable property estimated to belong to women in the state (it was $350 million).[43]

Parlor suffrage activity continued through the spring. In May, Stanton reported that the city was still "at white heat on the suffrage question," with "fashionable women about equally divided between the two camps."[44] The New York State Woman Suffrage Association organizer's report drew a revealing parallel with an earlier female mobilization. "The situation recalled for me the days of the great religious revival which followed the panic of 1857," she wrote.

FIGURE 8.1. "A Woman's Suffrage Meeting in Mrs. Russell Sage's Drawing Room," 1894. A reporter described Sage as "an ardent advocate of woman suffrage who presided with dignity and a great deal of self-possession." Mrs. Robert Abbé, scrapbooks of newspaper clippings and other material relating to woman suffrage, microform, 1894–1921, 26 v., New York Public Library, New York, N.Y.

> As then I remember even school girls saying, "I do not see why I should not have a prayer-meeting at *my* house"—so now, women, *during the spring freedom from a great pressure of social engagements,* were ready to be carried off their feet by any wave of social feeling, and cried on many sides, "I don't see why I may not have a parlor meeting."[45]

In April 1894, Olivia Sage held a "political equality meeting" at her home, and 200 "women of fashion" attended and warmly applauded her address, according to a newspaper reporter.[46] She was "an ardent advocate of woman suffrage who presided with dignity and a great deal of self-possession," he wrote. Unaware that he was describing a former teacher, he expressed surprise that she had "no notes at all and was not in the least embarrassed." Chairs were scarce, and listeners crowded in—some even sat on the stairs. "Chairs were uncomfortably close together," another reported, "there was a little overflow gathering in the hall, and new-comers crowded in every now and then throughout the afternoon."[47]

Fortunately, someone present sketched the scene that day, and the drawing found its way into Mrs. Robert Abbé's suffrage scrapbook, now in the New York Public Library. Under the caption "A Woman Suffrage Meeting in Mrs. Russell Sage's Drawing Room," it shows a matronly figure standing to address elegantly clad women seated on sofas and chairs who lean forward in their seats to hear her words (see fig. 8.1).[48]

Olivia began by reassuring her listeners that being suffragists would not render them unfeminine. The vote would not compromise womanliness or threaten the institution of marriage. Women wanted the vote and they wanted to be trustees of their own institutions. "But we want to do these things in a womanly way. We do not want to do them in a man's way."[49] These words offered reassurance that giving women the vote would not erase sexual differences. Radicalism still clung to the suffrage cause from the days of Garrisonian idealism, fears captured in a series of cartoons that were also preserved in the Abbé scrapbook. The artist portrays a disordered gender regime: bearded male ballerinas in tutus, henpecked husbands with overbearing wives, and aggressive female politicians, orators, mail carriers, even sea captains.[50] The drawings vividly illustrate the fear that voting women would be mannish women and that voting itself would bring the purer sex to sites of pollution and danger, the polling places where men drank, smoked, and swore (see fig. 8.2).

When Troy Female Seminary's custom of public examinations had come under fire from conservative clergy, principal Emma Willard had defended the practice by reinterpreting the father of women's silencing, St. Paul. Olivia now used the same technique, turning to the Bible for endorsement of woman suffrage and women's citizenship rights.[51] The former Sunday school teacher had done her homework. "I have been looking this subject of woman's rights up in my Bible recently," she declared, referring her listeners to an obscure passage in the twenty-seventh chapter of the book of Numbers. "There was a man named Zelophehad, who died in the wilderness. He had five daughters, and when his lands were to be distributed they went to Moses and said, in substance, 'Our father was not in the company of them that gathered themselves against the Lord; therefore give us a possession among our brethren.'"

> You would think Moses would have said immediately, "of course, that is your right." But he was afraid to decide alone, and he went right to the Lord, and said, "What shall we do in this matter?"
>
> The Lord told Moses to let them have their rights, for it was right that they should. And the men did not dare say one word, but gave them their share of the land.[52]

FIGURE 8.2. Dangerous Diversions: anti-suffrage cartoons. Mrs. Robert Abbé, scrapbooks of newspaper clippings and other material relating to woman suffrage, microform, 1894–1921, 26 v., New York Public Library, New York, N.Y.

According to the *Times* reporter, Olivia made "quite a hit by her reference to the first mention of woman's rights which came in the twenty-seventh chapter of Numbers." She then turned to the New Testament, and scornfully dismissed St. Paul.

> Christ lifted woman out of the heathen degradation to be the equal and companion of man. St. Paul says, in the Epistle to the Romans, that when he had an important message to send he would send it by the hand of Phebe. He said: "Let the women keep silence," but he showed that he did not mean anything [by it] when he sent the message by Phebe.[53]

To read Olivia's speech is to be aware of a teacher's voice: brisk, humorous, and businesslike. The arguments and examples are from the scriptures, but the point is not spiritual truths so much as present politics. New York governor Roswell Flower, who had refused to appoint women trustees to the Troy Female Seminary, was one of her targets. Declaring "He won't be elected again!" Olivia drew laughter and applause.[54] Male politicians had long been unresponsive to the interests of women. "The Emma Willard School tried to get an appropriation years ago," she reminded her listeners, "but, though money was given to colleges for men, they would not grant it for the women."[55] Give women the vote, and they would clean up the cities and improve public health—women had strongly supported a street-cleaning bill in the state legislature at Albany, she reminded her listeners. But instead of acknowledging women's superior good sense in matters of cleanliness, male politicians had defeated the bill. Olivia referred to this as "another grievance women had suffered at Albany." Defining female political power as a force for good, she implied that men's opposition to it was irrational. "Men would rather have sickness in their city than let woman have her way." Male politicians would never do what was right until the ballot was in the hands of women.[56]

Attention then turned to the grievances of working women when Olivia introduced Harriot Stanton Blatch, daughter of Elizabeth Cady Stanton and a woman's rights and labor activist. Blatch, just back from England, spoke about the need for reform of industrial conditions.[57] Appealing to her listeners, some of whom, like Olivia, could remember a time when they had been struggling wage-earners, Blatch reminded them that men's support of women was not a given and that even wealthy women were just a husband or a father away from destitution. As one suffragist pointed out, married women "are not contented because they are aware that their only security lies in the character of the men on whom they rely."[58] These married women adopted the rhetoric of self-reliance, just as men did, while at the same time they shared in the language of struggle with working-class women. "Self-support," which had echoes of self-possession versus slavery and dependence, resonated for women of all classes, providing them with an effective political language.[59] (Where class was concerned, elite women were guilty of obfuscation. They exaggerated when they compared their disabilities to those borne by working women. Similarly, Harriot Stanton Blatch and other "self-supporting women" in fact had independent incomes and many could be defined as upper rather than middle class.)[60]

It is easy to parody the parlor suffrage meetings, and contemporary criticism was sharp. "There is a degree of exclusiveness at these meetings that seems to be incompatible with the object to be achieved," one reporter noted.[61] It was useless to apply for an invitation, a writer for the *Evening News* reported, and several women who had expressed interest in being invited complained of being brushed off by haughty organizers.[62] Socialists were scathing about the "gilt chair" suffragists' "snobbish truckling to the women of influence and social position."[63]

The significance of the parlor suffrage meetings will remain elusive until we restore the context of this transformation as upper-class women opened their houses to political activity for the first time. By politicizing private space, elite women exposed the fiction which undergirded nineteenth-century domestic ideology of the home as a place apart. Parlor suffrage momentarily transformed the home into political space as surely as another contemporary institution, the settlement house, transformed the home into a women's community and urban studies institute. Both became sites of transformed identities and consciousness. Both enabled a new politics and were part of the wider reorientation of class and gender of the Progressive era.[64] For suffragists, as for settlement workers, the idiom of "home" supplied a rich trove of images and possibilities for women's political action.[65] And parlor suffrage meetings were, like the settlements, a "creative solution" to the boundaries set by culture on woman's politics. Later, when suffragists took to the streets or rented halls (with funds donated by these same wealthy suffrage supporters), parlor meetings were no longer necessary, but for the 1890s they were a kind of indispensable "female public sphere," one where socially elite women could comfortably engage in political activity.[66]

When NAWSA organizers, always on the defensive against the charge that suffragists were man-haters, sought the endorsement of pro-suffrage husbands, Russell Sage was ready. Interviewed in January 1894, the "millionaire and financier" enthusiastically supported his wife's stance: "I believe when women vote we shall have wiser government, cleaner politics, more ballots, and fewer bullets," he declared.

> When men and women labor together there is compact, new completeness, thoroughness, in the result that is often wanting when the sexes work separately. If men have experience, women have insight; if men use logic and reason, women use instinct and intuition; if men are hasty, cruel, brutal, women are diplomatic, merciful, refined. Combine these qualities and you have a unit that approaches perfection.
>
> Women look at suffrage through the spectacles of morality and spirituality; but men, being more practical, very naturally see the question from a material, a financial, point of view.[67]

Such a declaration gave the movement reason to hope that Russell Sage's endorsement would be followed by an equally generous donation to NAWSA. Stanton kept in touch with the Sages, familiarly reminding Olivia in December 1898, "Tell Mr. Sage to look for my stocking on his bedpost Christmas night."[68]

As for Olivia, a reporter expressed wonder that "Mrs. Sage has shown herself as valuable in the good cause as she was formerly reticent. . . . No one dreamed she would become one of the leading advocates of woman suffrage."[69] Olivia herself reflected on the change. "I am a recent convert," she confessed to the reporter who called at her house in May 1894. "I was led to think as I do now by Mrs. Elizabeth Cady Stanton. She was my guest not long since and during her visit she led me captive in the cause and now I feel that I cannot do enough to make up for that which I did not do before."[70]

"Their sacred rights at the mercy of a masculine oligarchy"

The New York State campaign of 1894 ended in failure. The Anthony amendment, as it was called, would have been an amendment to the New York State constitution barring discrimination in voting on the grounds of sex. When it came to a vote before the male legislators sitting as a constitutional convention in August, it was defeated by ninety-seven votes to fifty-eight. Stanton commented in class as well as gender terms: "It is very humiliating for women of education to have their sacred rights at the mercy of a masculine oligarchy, especially when this oligarchy is made up largely of inferiors."[71] By 1910, even Harriot Stanton Blatch had accepted literacy qualifications for the vote, although she had earlier argued against them.[72]

But Olivia's "conversion" was permanent, and when the parlor suffrage activities of the spring revived around the issue of municipal reform, with Josephine Shaw Lowell launching the Women's Municipal League to assist Rev. Charles Parkhurst with his anti-vice campaign, Olivia took out a life membership in the league for $250.[73] Ostensibly a moral reform and municipal improvement association with no suffrage agenda, the league was nevertheless a political organization that aimed to unseat Tammany and bring more women into public life.[74] The original "Sherry Committee," now enlarged to thirty members, was reconvened for November 1894 to discuss "political equality work." In the discussion of cleaning up after men, women found a political language that was more persuasive and less threatening than a language of rights. In an interview for the *New York Times*, Olivia argued:

> When women vote there will be a national housecleaning such as no
> nation ever saw. Once armed with the ballot, then the mop, the broom
> and the bucket will be decidedly more in evidence in the places in
> which they are most needed.[75]

The suffrage was necessary because times had changed, she asserted.
Woman had advanced in education, the professions, and business and
she was now man's intellectual equal.[76] Framed in this way, the suffrage
no longer seemed to pose a threat to respectability; rather, it seemed evo-
lutionary within a progressive vision of history that was also a vision of
Christian perfectionism.

Olivia continued to speak out publicly for the suffrage. The morning papers, with their daily reminders of woman's demeaning treatment
at the hands of men, kept her seething. She was enraged when she read
that Cambridge University had decided not to confer degrees on women.
"The attempt to place women on an equal footing with men has just
had a miserable onslaught at the greatest of English colleges. . . . After
twenty years, Cambridge has rejected women as they would a beggar who
did not know her place," she declared in a speech at the Emma Willard
School.[77]

Olivia even predicted that a "general suffrage uprising" of the
women of New York would occur by the time of the next constitutional
convention, in 1915.[78] Then, "[T]he necessary amendment to the constitution, urged by a monster petition of women who own property, will
be passed by the legislative bodies of New York State." The franchise
would be limited to women of property and then all the other states would
follow suit.

> Meanwhile it seems too bad that the women who own real estate and
> pay taxes are not allowed to cast a ballot. Why, the men of this coun-
> try went to war because of taxation without representation. The women
> of New York state alone pay taxes on one billion dollars' worth of real
> estate, yet they are not allowed a voice in the practical government
> of the state to which they contribute so much revenue.[79]

Interviewed in 1905, she declared, "A rich woman is not different from
a poor woman, except in the matter of money."[80] But she contradicted
this democratic ideal when she called for a property qualification for
the vote. As the nation's largest taxpayer after 1906, Olivia's demand
for representation would take on a new urgency. She was not alone.
New York suffragists had been entertaining the goal of a taxpayer fran-

chise since the 1890s, and by 1900 they were ready to relinquish the goal of full suffrage in favor of municipal suffrage for taxpaying women.[81]

In her campaign for the suffrage, Olivia found an ally in wealthy Republican physician Mary Putnam Jacobi. Jacobi was founder in 1894, along with Josephine Shaw Lowell, of the League for Political Education, which Lowell's biographer calls "a pro-suffrage advocacy group."[82] She was a well-known champion of sex equality who had won the gratitude of educated women for her spirited defense of women's education against the hysterical imprecations of Edward Clarke, author of *Sex in Education* (1873). Jacobi's response, *The Question of Rest for Women during Menstruation,* had scored a notable victory over Clarke and was awarded Harvard's Boylston Prize in 1876.[83] The leading female physician in the United States and the author of over 100 scholarly articles, Jacobi strongly advocated women's entry into nontraditional fields such as medicine.[84] However, she was also a snobbish woman who deplored the fact that women, "no matter how well born, how well educated, how intelligent, how rich, how serviceable to the State," were the political inferiors of all men "no matter how base-born, how poverty stricken, how ignorant, how vicious, how brutal." She ridiculed the idea of "women of property being put aside by their hired servants."[85]

In a little-known incident at the NAWSA convention of 1900, Olivia Sage joined with Jacobi and Stanton to try to derail the candidacy of Carrie Chapman Catt, whom Anthony had picked as her successor for president, supporting instead Lillie Devereux Blake, president of the New York State Woman Suffrage Association from 1879 to 1890 and of the New York City Woman Suffrage League from 1886 to 1900, a gifted speaker and fearless activist.[86] For this, her first intervention into NAWSA politics, Olivia shed "Mrs. Russell Sage," the name by which she was known to the public. As delegates entered the Washington, D.C., church where the NAWSA convention was being held, they were handed a circular endorsing Blake's candidacy signed by M. Olivia Sage, Elizabeth Cady Stanton, and Mary Putnam Jacobi.[87] The flyer urged the election of Blake on the grounds of her talents and her long service to the suffrage cause and credited her with a number of important legislative reforms for women, including school suffrage, joint guardianship of children, the right of a wife to make a will independently of her husband, and provision of seats for saleswomen. Blake was also given credit for obtaining civil service pensions for war nurses and for female police matrons and census enumerators.[88]

But when it became known that the revered Anthony opposed Blake's nomination, the delegates threw strong support to Catt. Blake withdrew her name before the voting took place "for the sake of harmony in the Association," and Olivia's brief attempt to influence the succession was over. After that, her engagement with the suffrage was that of donor, patron, and symbol.[89]

The momentary disloyalty of 1900 could not be allowed to chill relations between NAWSA leadership and Olivia Sage, a potential funder of great wealth. In 1905, Olivia sent the aging Susan B. Anthony birthday greetings along with a press clipping from the New York *Evening Telegram*, "fully half the lines being underscored." Her communication ended with "I am yours affectionately, Mrs. Russell Sage." The 85-year-old women's rights leader responded, urging Olivia to give to the cause she claimed to love.[90]

> I remember that you had an article some years ago saying that at the next Constitutional Convention in 1914 action should be taken. I think the time has come when the suffrage women in all the different societies and clubs of the State should unite and petition the Legislature for the striking of the word "male" from the suffrage clause of the constitution.

"Why won't you, Mrs. Sage, lead off in this matter?" she challenged, adding pointedly,

> It is very sad indeed that rich women do not feel the importance of helping the cause, and I want to appeal to you and to Mr. Sage to do something handsome in the way of an appropriation of money to be used in the next State campaign of 1914. . . . If both of you really feel the force of what the Telegram says editorially you will want to help the campaign and carry to success the mighty work that was begun in 1894.[91]

Her letter also contained news of the death of Mrs. Samantha Lapham Vail, a mutual friend from Troy. Anthony drove the point home: "Mrs. Lapham, although really feeling that she loved the cause of woman's freedom as much as you or I or anyone, nevertheless died without making any bequest."[92]

A year later, Anthony was dead and so was Russell Sage. Now Olivia was free to make significant money donations to all her favorite causes, including the suffrage. But she had raised expectations among the suffrage leadership that would be hard to satisfy. Changes in the movement, as well as her own advancing age, would increase her uncertainty and limit her role as suffrage patron. In 1907, a year when she created a sensation by setting up the $10 million Russell Sage Foundation, she began the strange dance of avoidance and equivocation that would characterize her philanthropy to the woman suffrage cause.

Olivia's suffrage career supports the notion that a quiet revolution had occurred in the political consciousness of elite women by the turn of the century. Often described as "ladies of leisure," these women were nevertheless keenly aware of the ways in which the rise of wage earning, higher education, and the professions had altered the context of women's lives. And they shared this consciousness with suffragists from whom they differed in style and perhaps in goals.[93] Shaped by the best education of the antebellum period, a self-supporting wage earner and mainstay of her family in her young adulthood, cast into the role of society matron in Gilded Age New York, Olivia Sage became an enthusiastic suffrage advocate and activist in the 1890s.

That the conversion was permanent can be seen in "Opportunities and Responsibilities of Leisured Women," an essay that she published in November 1905 in the *North American Review* under the name M. Olivia Sage. The parable of the talents, which Stanton had forcefully drawn to Olivia's attention a decade earlier, was now replaced by the story of the laborers in the vineyard: "God has put woman with these tools into His vineyard and commanded her to work." The parable was a different one, but the point was the same.[94] Women like herself, who possessed "time, money and executive ability," had a duty to engage in public work, Olivia explained. "Twenty-one years ago, I did not think women were qualified for suffrage; but the strides they have made since then in the acquirement of business methods, in the management of their affairs, in . . . civic matters, and the way in which they have mastered parliamentary methods, have convinced me that they are eminently fitted to do men's work in all purely intellectual fields."[95] Despite the biblical language, the essay, with its argument for a redefinition of women's citizenship, was significantly more secular than her views cited earlier in this chapter, and it was buttressed by historical and contemporary data about women's advancement in education, the professions, and public life.

Alva Belmont, multimillionaire widow and passionate suffragist, made a similar pronouncement: "Women like me need the ballot to teach us to think of other women and to help them."[96] She became a major suffrage leader. In claiming the suffrage for women of their class, Sage and Belmont positioned themselves as superiors who stood ready to take up their responsibilities for poor and working women. Only "leisured women," not powerful men, could act for, and in the name of, other women, they asserted.[97] Such benevolence, assuming responsibility over others, constitutes a kind of elite power and contradicts feminism's emancipatory and democratic potential. It helped suffragists come to terms with ideas of national mission, racial exclusion, and moral uplift.[98] The next chapter shows how the symbols of an imagined American colonial past proved irresistible to Sage and other white upper-class women who anxiously sought pedigrees and other forms of distinction. Nativism and racism continued to undergird these women's claims on citizenship as the suffrage campaign entered the twentieth century. They reinforced Olivia's commitment to the vote and formed the context for the astonishing philanthropy of her old age.

Nine

"Wiping her tears with the flag"

Mrs. Russell Sage, Patriot, 1897–1906

God had a purpose in planting high-toned and good
women in American soil, both North and South.

—Margaret Olivia Sage (1905)[1]

I saw many a woman wiping the tears from her eyes with the flag
she had brought out to wave in farewell to the departing soldiers.

—Margaret Olivia Sage (1898)[2]

Individuals construct meanings and fashion identities in the spaces and
with the language and dreams available to them at a given time in history. Middle- and upper-class white women, who were still barred from
many public arenas at the turn of the century; classed as less than full
citizens by enlightenment notions of the rational, self-standing male subject; and trammeled by the conventions of the lady, nevertheless created new spaces in public life and dreamed new dreams. For elite women
such as Olivia Sage, this remaking of identities turned on discourses of
race and nation as well as gender.[3]

I have described in an earlier chapter how Olivia Sage and the other
aging alumnae of the Emma Willard Association defined themselves in
the 1890s as "educated women" who deserved more say in public affairs.
The educated woman would not bring "women's particularity and emo-
tionality to the public sphere," they promised. She was rational, informed,
and steady, with none of the fickleness and variability associated with
females. Educated women had helped reconcile the nation after the Civil
War: now they stood ready to lead a reformed nation into the new century.[4] They refashioned the memory of Emma Willard to fit this new

vision of women and the nation. In her 1896 presidential speech to the association, Olivia held up Willard as the archetype of republican womanhood, "the illustrious woman who three quarters of a century ago saw into the possibilities of womanhood, as her Creator had planned her, the moulder of a race."[5]

Thinking nationally and racially in this way meant discarding the ideology of spheres. Emma Willard Association member and suffragist lecturer May Wright Sewall explicitly rejected the notion. Identifying herself as one of the younger generation of women who had been "permitted to go to college," Sewall declared that the spirit of Emma Willard meant simply that "'You can come into the sphere where man is.'"[6]

The "sphere where man was" was national expansion, and the reorientation of white women in regard to the nation was precipitated by war. American public opinion, aroused by the Cuban uprising of 1895 and the sinking of the *Maine* in February 1898, prompted Congress's joint resolution of April 20, 1898, and inaugurated a popular war to free Cuba.[7] The war with Spain raised in an acute form the question of women's relationship to the state and the nation. Unable to vote or fight, they were challenged to redefine their place relative to the public and the political.[8] In the Civil War–era Sanitary Commission, they had shown their capacity for organizing and self-sacrifice, and in the years that followed they had labored in dozens of voluntary and reform associations. But such work was not, in itself, sufficient basis for a claim of suffrage or equal citizenship rights, for it was easily naturalized as an instinctive response to suffering that owed little to education or even to rationality. It has been left to present-day historians to name nineteenth-century women's benevolence a form of politics.

As America prepared for war in the spring of 1898 and as nationalism became an insistent theme in American life, elite women intensified what Kristin Hoganson calls the search for a new political language.[9] Addressing the Women's National War Relief Association (WNWRA), a group of ladies assembled to organize aid for the armed forces, Ellen Hardin Walworth declared, "In the time of war we have a peculiar and an urgent duty. It appears to me that no other opportunity than the state of war allows us to prove so clearly that the national life throbs in our veins—that the nation is ours by right of our womanhood."[10]

Olivia embraced the idea that women's advancement was part of God's plan for America. "God had a purpose in planting high-toned and good women in American soil, both North and South," she wrote in 1905 in "Opportunities and Responsibilities of Leisured Women."[11] Women's power for good had helped heal the wounds of sectional strife, and for decades their influence had been spread far and wide through charitable and missionary endeavors. They had raised tens of thousands of dollars and sent out hundreds of missionaries to the "exceptional peoples" of the United States—Indians, freedmen, Mormons, and Hispanics. Olivia was familiar with this work through the Presbyterian Woman's Executive Committee. Imposing order on multifarious peoples, the Protestant mission project had generated new nationalism and new ideologies of race. Now the nation picked up this mission impulse, transmuting it into a messianic foreign policy that aimed to spread American culture abroad, extending the rule of the United States and Christ over savage and heathen nations.[12]

Elite white women rallied to men of their class in the imperialistic atmosphere of 1898. Interviewed by the *Brooklyn Eagle*, Russell Sage declared he would stand by the flag, "and so will other rich men."[13] Olivia, too, embraced nationalism and America's manifest destiny abroad with a letter to the editor of the *New York Daily Tribune* on how to increase patriotism, but her solution offered little more than flag-waving. For the "large class of unthinking people, who learn from impressions. . . , the American flag is an object lesson wherever it is seen," she wrote. "I do not think we can ever see that flag too often. No matter where it appears, it is an evidence of patriotism." There were several occasions "like milestones along my path through life," when the sight of our flag "filled my heart with so much of love for its every star and stripe." The most recent was when the 69th Regiment marched down Fifth Avenue: "I saw many a woman wiping the tears from her eyes with the flag she had brought out to wave in farewell to the departing soldiers."[14]

Helen Gould and the Women's National War Relief Association

Both Olivia and her young protégée Helen Gould enthusiastically supported the WNWRA. The organization was launched in April 1898 by Ellen Walworth with an appeal "To the Daughters of the American Revolution, and other Patriotic Women of the United States, concerning a National Corps of Sanitary Volunteers to aid our officers, soldiers, and sailors, in time of war."[15] Olivia headed the New York branch. On April 25, the secretary of the navy accepted the WNWRA's offer to equip a hospital ship, the *Solace*. WNWRA branches sprang up and fundraising began. Substantial donations were gathered up and given to the navy to purchase supplies for the comfort and health of the nation's fighting forces.[16]

Her tender conscience stung by reports that men were dying in the camps because of bureaucratic bungling before they could be shipped to Cuba, Helen arranged for the purchase of large quantities of fresh food and other needed supplies for the encampments. In August 1898, she was sending to San Diego for shipments of lemons and arranging for deliveries of peaches and plums to the malnourished recruits.[17] Olivia encouraged her in this patriotic and charitable work. Having taken for herself the title of vice chairman of the Executive Committee and member of the Board of Directors, she insisted that Helen accept the title of assistant director-general, which involved organizing the receipt of aid from New York City while the indomitable Mrs. Walworth ranged "in the field."[18] Taking charge of a meeting was a new departure for Helen. "Presiding in our small directors' meeting yesterday did not seem so difficult as I had imagined," she confided to her brother Frank. "Mrs. Sage seemed quite proud and delighted and thought I had been very business like."[19] A few days later she reported, "Thirty-five ladies came here to sew and to listen to our reports."[20] Helen appreciated the mentorship of the more experienced woman and often told people that Olivia had been "like a mother to me" after the death of her own mother in 1891.[21]

The published reports of the WNWRA document the huge amount of aid given personally by Helen Gould—one estimate is $100,000—and (at her instigation) other elite women during this brief national emergency.[22] (To organize the written report, Ellen Hardin Walworth employed as secretary a Washington-born businesswoman-inventor, E. Lilian Todd, who would later become Olivia's private secretary.)[23]

Performative Philanthropy

For Olivia, the national emergency presented the opportunity to do something for the nation. Her patriotism took a practical turn in the fall of 1898. Shocked to hear about the poor conditions of veterans at Montauk Hospital, Olivia wrote to President McKinley offering the government a hotel property near Washington for a convalescent hospital. The official reply was disappointing:

> This beautiful property if located nearer to the seacoast and a line of railroad, would be very desirable for hospital purposes, but it does not appear to me to be advisable at present to establish a hospital so far from the coast and from the different encampments occupied by our troops.[24]

Although her offer was rejected, the fact that it was made at all suggests that she had more discretionary power over money in the 1890s than has previously been thought. When her philanthropy blossomed after 1906 it would include patriotic and civic causes, with large gifts to the nation, the region, and her own city. But in the years before 1906, she was mainly reduced to acts of civic commemoration and national pride that cost little or nothing. Too elderly for strenuous volunteer work, Olivia instead carried on a kind of performative philanthropy as she visited troop encampments and navy vessels.[25] She was in the public eye, doing her duty as a patriotic Christian woman without spending large amounts of money, which Russell Sage still forbade. And excursions to inspect the nation's forces at military camps, on docks, and on shipboard were gratifying, even thrilling, to Olivia, who rarely traveled far and had never been overseas. While Helen complained of exhaustion, Olivia relished the adventure of excursions to cheer on the brave fighting men. One such outing took them on board the transport ship *Thomas* as it prepared to leave for Manila with 1,610 men on board. It was, a newspaper reported, "a bleak, cold, raw sleety day at the end of October," but Olivia gamely made her way over the wet and slippery decks to inspect the men's quarters for their 60-day voyage. When the tour was completed, Helen begged to know "if there wasn't something more they could do for the comfort of the soldiers," at which the officer in charge replied that there was nothing they could do "unless you go with us as our guests."[26] A journalist who sailed on the *Thomas* that day recalled how the benevolent pair stood together on the deck of the tugboat "and waved their rain-beaten handkerchiefs in answer to the cheers and the hundreds of waving hats of the soldiers as our big ship swung into the channel and began her long voyage."[27]

"Give up the Philippines? Never!"

When Spain surrendered in August 1898, American public opinion divided over whether to take control of her colonies. Both political parties stood for taking up the "burden of empire," which was strongly opposed by a passionate group of anti-imperialist intellectuals and politicians. Republican senator Orville H. Platt spoke for the expansionist cause when he described Admiral Dewey's warship in Manila Bay as "a new Mayflower . . . the harbinger and agent of a new civilization."[28] Olivia supported this position. "I am one of those who believe that all we took should be ours," she wrote in the *New York Daily Tribune* in August 1898. "Give up the Philippines? Never!" Long committed to the project of missions at home and abroad, Olivia was confident in the power of Protestantism to evangelize and civilize new peoples. In the 1880s she had condemned as "a burning disgrace to this nation" the act of Congress barring all Chinese immigration, not because it was racist or a betrayal of the American promise but because it excluded those who might otherwise enter the United States and convert to Christianity. She saw the Philippines as an analogous case: "God has brought these far-away nations to us now. Let us keep them, govern them, and keep their people as Christians should."[29] These "far-away nations" would get a large slice of Russell Sage's money once Olivia had control over it: Christian missions, schools, and colleges from Korea to Persia and from Turkey to Guam would all benefit from her generosity after 1906.

In calling for conquest and absorption of a multiracial empire, Olivia differed both from anti-imperialists Josephine Shaw Lowell and Jane Addams (who were raised in abolitionist traditions) and from Harriot Stanton Blatch. Representing a younger generation of activists, Blatch deplored the militarization of the country, telling a *New York Daily Tribune* reporter that "she thought Americans might much better turn their attention to improving the roads than looking after territorial expansion, and loading up the great Republic with inferior races."[30] In contrast, Olivia found no contradiction between the anticolonialist legacy of the American Revolution, symbolized for her by her grandfather John Jermain, and the nation's imperialist expansion. She endorsed the idea that the United States should rule and Christianize the "lesser races." She believed in trusteeship and the white man's burden.

Visits to the troops that had begun with the war did not end with Spain's surrender in August 1898 or with the Treaty of Paris in December of that year. Olivia continued to involve herself in national issues. Perhaps she went along in December 1898 when Helen Gould and some friends visited a gun factory to inquire into the nation's preparedness. Show these ladies "all favor consistent with army regulations," Representative George Southwick instructed the officer in charge. "Miss Gould and her friends are desirous of inspecting the wonders of your great gun-factory."[31] And in 1903, Olivia and other members of the Mayflower Society went out on launches to President Roosevelt's boat *The Mayflower,* moored in the Long Island Sound. Here, "leaning on the barrel of one of the rapid fire guns," she saluted the sailors and petty officers. "My ancestors came over on the Mayflower, among them Captain Myles Standish," she declared. "Your ancestors and mine helped make this country what it is, and helped to make you the good, brave men that you should be." Turning to the officers present, she announced that she and Helen Gould intended to open on-shore depositories where sailors could bank their paychecks "instead of spending them or having them stolen."[32]

Better guns and larger ships were not sufficient to make America ready for its overseas role. Also important was the moral character of the men themselves, and this prompted Olivia's largest donation to date: a gift of $150,000 in March 1904 to the American Seamen's Friend Society for a Sailors' Home and Institute in New York City. When completed, the building had six stories and housed 225 men.[33]

As she contemplated the nation's overseas responsibilities, Olivia recalled the achievements and struggles of her own family members. Her brother Jermain had risen to colonel during the Civil War, and both his sons had made their careers in the military. Olivia was indignant that her two nephews, who were serving their country in the army and the diplomatic service, were so poorly provided for, and she complained about the housing and salaries of diplomatic service officers. The *Troy Daily Times* reported a conversation with an acquaintance about Russell Sage's favorite nephew, Captain Stephen L'Hommedieu Slocum, who had just been appointed army attaché to St. Petersburg. "How much do you think a young man in his position ought to have to be properly provided for?" she demanded. "At least $10,000 a year," the acquaintance replied. "My, my," she exclaimed, for this was a far greater salary than he was getting. And Russell Sage commented that the young man would be better off staying at home.[34]

Both nephews served in the territories taken from Spain in 1898: Herbert Jermain Slocum, a career officer in the United States Army, was posted to Havana in 1907. Stephen L'Hommedieu Slocum, who had been appointed military attaché to Portugal and then to Vienna in 1899 (and subsequently to St. Petersburg), was ordered to the Philippines on the army's general staff in 1902.[35]

Character as Blood: The Society of Mayflower Descendants

Family ties supplied one reason to think about the nation and its far-flung responsibilities. Working-class insurgency and its threats to property provided another. These were the years of the Pullman Strike and Coxey's Army, when every year a million immigrants entered a nation that white native-born Americans thought of as their own. In July 1897, Olivia gave an unusual interview in which she condemned the " misguided agitator" Eugene Debs.[36] Still, in the nation at large, the 1896 Republican victory over Populist and third-party challenges, along with the return of prosperity, abated fears of social disorder, while anxiety that still lingered tended to be displaced onto issues of gender and race. Nationalism fueled the growth of patriotic societies such as the New

York Society of Mayflower Descendants, which Olivia now joined. Snubbed by New York high society on the one hand and thwarted in her philanthropic ambitions on the other by the stingy old miser whose good health in his eighties drew astonished comments, she sought moral authority in a New England identity traced through her mother's family. (Russell Sage was not immune to these insecurities either: he joined the New York Genealogical Society at this time).

Her public work, which during her middle years had focused on New York and such associations as the hospital, was now redirected to nationalist ends and expressed through participation in patriotic and ancestral societies. The Society of Mayflower Descendants was emblematic of turn-of-the-century commemorative societies that linked character with blood and associated both with canons of respectability.[37] But Olivia and other female members of the Mayflower Society who assumed that family descent would guarantee their membership in the society on equal terms with men soon learned that the war had released a new gender conservatism: soon they were being "disinvited" to the society's meetings, which had come to resemble men's smokers.[38] Smoking marked male territory and was a message that women were unwelcome.[39] Olivia complained bitterly that at the annual dinner of the New York Society of Mayflower Descendants at Delmonico's in 1902, the society's presiding officer took advantage of her absence to announce that "as the lady who objected to smoking at the last dinner was not present, and no one else objecting, he thought they might use cigars." "Men all over the room took advantage of the privilege, with the result that three women were taken ill and obliged to retire," the *Daily Tribune* reported. Olivia interpreted this as a snub to herself and an attempt to oust the women members of the society, and she let her membership lapse (but later renewed it).[40]

Unlike the Society of Mayflower Descendants, the Pilgrim Mothers Association was a female-only organization. Founded by suffrage leader Lillie Devereux Blake in December 1892, it emphasized women's contribution to an imagined Pilgrim past, with banquets designed to commemorate, as Blake put it, "those noble women, who are apt to be overlooked at the celebrations in honor of the Pilgrim Fathers."[41] By 1900 these had become an annual affair that attracted hundreds of socially prominent women.[42]

Not everyone went along with the deception and the snobbery. Under the title "Mrs. Catt Gives Chill To 'Pilgrim Mothers' by Slur on Their Birth Claims," the *New York Journal* reported in 1908 that suffrage leader Carrie Chapman Catt "created a tense and frigid atmosphere" by noting in one public meeting that she had met so many people in America who claimed their ancestors came on the Mayflower, that the Mayflower "must have been as big as the Lusitania or a whole fleet of modern steamers."[43]

If such ancestral associations helped Olivia publicize her family history and prove her patriotism, they also held up a socially conservative view of family that was at odds with her parallel advocacy of the suffrage. Olivia did not seem too bothered by the inconsistency. Her remembered New England past featured her mother and the "old-time ways" in Sag Harbor, with its strict observance of the Sabbath and its cast of faithful household slaves to provide for the family's wants.[44] She had long been fascinated with stories that portrayed her family as once wealthy and prominent. This was in some earlier, happier time, before her father's bankruptcy, her mother's collapse, and her brother's disabling Civil War injury. Olivia once wrote to her brother, "I have heard Aunt Mary Groesbeck say that her Great Grandmother rode in a coach and four. I hope this was not all in the imaginations of our Aunts."[45]

There was another personal and unacknowledged dimension to Olivia's interest in the patriotic societies. In celebrating her mother's ancestors, she suppressed another genealogy, that of the undistinguished Sages. It was Olivia's mother's antecedents—the Piersons, Jermains, and Standishes—who provided a link to Puritan New England and Huguenot France. They constituted a kind of American aristocracy, their ideology a blend of patriotism, learning, moral rectitude, respectability, and material success. Hadn't the Jermains chosen to transport their mahogany dining table when they moved west from Sag Harbor after Olivia's grandmother Olivia Josselyn had declared that "she would never eat off pine"? A century later, the incident glowed for Olivia with the patina of founding myth.[46] In this way, the "deep forgetting" which had fallen over the descendants of New England conspired with the imaginative legerdemain of genealogists for hire to transform the colonial past into a flattering prelude to the present.[47]

"Even the loneliness vanishes"

But when she tired of nationalist dreaming, Olivia woke to the reality of approaching old age and unfulfilled hopes. Russell Sage continued to be as dear to her as he was infuriating: fit as a fiddle at eighty-five, still fond of a good-looking woman, and a legend for his miserliness. By the late 1890s, Olivia clearly felt that she had little room for maneuver. A reporter who interviewed her in September 1897 described "an elderly woman, whose face, while sweet, shows the delineations of a strong character and noble purpose; bright eyes that reveal the keen intelligence behind, but which now and then dim as if weary."[48]

At Thanksgiving 1898, with the "splendid little war" with Spain just concluded, Olivia wrote to thank Nettie McCormick for sending roses on her anniversary. The letter expressed gratitude, but also sadness. Reflecting on the times "as our beloved land stands the chosen of God among the nations of the earth," Olivia reflected also on her own situation. It was the twenty-ninth anniversary of her marriage: "Truly you have made this Thanksgiving day very rosy, *even the loneliness vanishes*," she wrote to her friend.[49] Isolated because of her wealth yet unable to spend it, she agonized as the press mocked her husband.

Her pronouncements now took on a more peevish tone; her public statements show her preoccupied with efforts to improve the image of her own family and reform the behavior of others. Sometimes her comments were no more than the querulous complaints of a woman who had lived into an age she didn't understand or particularly like. Recollecting the small salary she had earned as a teacher years before, she launched into an ill-tempered recital of the faults of the modern age. "The tendency nowadays is all toward luxury and personal ease and indulgence," she complained. "Many a school teacher and trained nurse has as many silver backed brushes and silver etched bottles and hand painted toilet appliances on her dressing table as any spoiled woman of fashion."[50]

But there were still flashes of fresh observation and self-deprecating humor. She lectured friends and strangers alike with a self-assurance that came from years in the classroom and in voluntary associations. Arthur Gleason, who wrote a revealing essay about her, summed her up as "a Puritan and a schoolteacher."[51] Reckless and unconventional in her old age, she developed the habit of lecturing complete strangers. A newspaperman who was attending Collegiate Church with some colleagues to hear a well-known preacher experienced her chastening influence:

> Through the four verses of the first hymn we were worshipful, but not vocal. We planned the same tactics for the second hymn. But Mrs. Sage was seated directly behind us. She made a collection of hymn books, and proceeded to deal them out. "Let me hear you sing," she said to the group at large.

After the service, she approached the group.

"You men don't sing," she said, good naturedly but definitely; "I wish you'd sing when you come to church. Make a try at it." The effect was exactly as if the Colonel's wife had "called down" the regiment . . . or as if the nurse were rebuking the patients who swore by her.[52]

On another occasion, as she waited at the Mineola Flying Field on Long Island to watch a test flight of E. Lilian Todd's plane—the plane designed and built with her sponsorship—she was interviewed by journalist Elizabeth Hiatt Gregory. Gregory described her as "quite chatty" and "interested in my career," but she was put off when Olivia told her she "should not work on the Sabbath."[53]

> As we talked, a peanut boy made a sale of a bag to her. She wanted to know the exact profit and whether the youngster spent his money for cigarettes, lecturing him on the evils of tobacco. "What do you think I am going to do with these peanuts?" she asked the boy. "Eat 'em," he said. Then she told him she would go to the park and feed them to the squirrels.[54]

"Mrs. Russell Sage, indeed! Just who is she?"

Alice Northrop, Helen Gould's niece, recorded a more gossipy account of Olivia and Russell Sage in these years. She began diplomatically, "We rather thought of them as being characters, though the word seems generally reserved for persons in other stations of life." But then she went on to describe several incidents during her visit to the Chicago World's Fair that reveal that Olivia could be arbitrary and snobbish. A dispute erupted when Olivia complained to Alice Northrop that Helen was too familiar with her servants. "She spoils them. Even associates with them. Why, it's shocking! What can she be thinking of anyway—having Miss Terry at the table? And sitting in the parlor!" (In fact, Miss Terry had been with Helen for several years during the loss of both of Helen's parents and was more a companion than a servant.) When Alice defended her aunt's more democratic treatment of her staff—Helen didn't even like to use the word "servant"—Sage got into "a towering huff, . . . rose decisively from her chair and stalked away," saying that she would put Miss Terry "in her proper place" if no one else would. "I thought, a few minutes later, that Miss Terry would have a stroke," Alice continued.

> Purple of face, she came running in to me. "Oh, that woman!" she choked. "Mrs. Russell Sage, indeed! Just who is she? Just what was Mrs. Russell Sage before her marriage? I'll tell you! A schoolteacher!

A common, ordinary schoolteacher—that's what! . . . Well, anyway, Mrs. Sage was poor, just plain poor, before her marriage. She needn't be putting on airs with me!"[55]

Another incident, again related by Northrop, illustrates Olivia's insecurities. Wealthy New Yorkers rented boxes at the newly built Metropolitan Opera House for what one scholar calls "display and spectatorship." In the opera box, a wealthy woman was legitimately in public and subject to public display, a surveillance disciplined by etiquette books and manners manuals.[56] So popular was the opera in this period that the new opera house had three tiers of thirty-six boxes each. But Olivia could not persuade Russell Sage to rent a box, and if they could not beg space in the Goulds' box, they had to stay home.[57] On one occasion, Alice Northrop recounts, Olivia was annoyed when she saw that Helen's carriage had not been provided to take her to the opera, and when she found out that Helen's box would not be available, she refused to go altogether. Northrop added that Olivia afterward offered apologies and explanations "for months afterward." She characterized Olivia as "at heart, illimitably good, and absolutely genuine."[58]

As Olivia aged, her eccentricity increased. Her love for animals was well known but its application was inconsistent. Wealthy, elegant suffrage leader Lillie Devereux Blake and her friends were startled one night when Olivia arrived at a meeting at their home, soaked by a downpour. "She smiled at us all and said, cheerfully, 'I had to come in the horse-cars. I couldn't take the horses out on a night like this.'"[59] In her anxiety to protect her own horses from a drenching, she had used public transport—though it was also horse-drawn.

Her religious enthusiasm was well known. Its theological basis, so far as we can ascertain, reflected the stern mandates of that branch of Protestantism known as the Reformed Tradition, especially an insistence on human depravity and the need for obedience to an all-powerful God. She gave no quarter to those she suspected of heterodoxy and moral backsliding. Others found that her religiosity bordered on the excessive. Helen Gould, ever tactful, hinted at this when she wrote to inform her father about a New York society wedding she had attended. She explained that the Sages did not attend because "Mrs. Sage told me she did not approve of the wedding being on prayer meeting night."[60] Olivia was also known for her running campaigns against Sabbath violations. In March 1886, Helen wrote to her from the family's 230-foot yacht *Atalanta*, then cruising the Caribbean in an attempt to restore Jay Gould to health (he would die of tuberculosis a few years later). From Havana ("a large and dirty city belonging to the Spaniards") she wrote to Olivia, "I am sure you would not approve of the way they keep the sabbath, for in the morning there was a bull fight, in the afternoon the carnival, and a ball in the evening. Of course the people are Roman Catholics."[61]

Helen Gould at twenty-one was a genuinely kind and unpretentious person, despite her great wealth. In a revealing 1891 letter to her father, she mused "[H]ow good Mother was to everyone. She was always a Lady and did not limit her kindness to those who had social position or money." She went on, "I did not suppose ladies and gentlemen were unkind to people if they behaved themselves. Perhaps sometimes we say 'lady' or 'gentlemen' when *snob* would be much more appropriate and truthful. Is it any wonder they do not reform the world when their hearts are full of vanity, coldness and self?"[62] Could she have had Olivia in mind?

Defining an American Womanhood

If Populist insurgency, marches of the unemployed, and the demands of labor had haunted the 1880s and 1890s, threats from racial Others formed the background to the turn-of-the-century reconstruction of American culture. Earlier, Olivia had based her public work on claims of women's moral superiority over men. But more dangerous times called for elite women to align themselves with men of their class, holding immigrants and others at bay in the name of an expansive nationalism.[63] Emma Willard was once again crucial to Olivia's reimagining of the polity, and her image proved adaptable to more patriotic times. Willard had compared her work of training teachers and mothers (supposedly the same women) to that of the Founding Fathers in devising the Constitution. Now the antebellum rhetoric of republican motherhood was revived.[64] Olivia declared,

> A perfected humanity must combine the most exalted qualities of both men and women, and lack of refinement in women but delays the coming of that better day when they shall walk together, one in soul, mind, and purpose.[65]

But who had the right to represent womanhood?[66] The Emma Willard Association naturally claimed this honor for Emma Willard, who was described by one of the members in 1898 as "the acknowledged exponent of gracious, perfect womanhood."[67] But a new generation, symbolized by the "New Woman," was behaving in ways that flaunted this conservative ideal. The New Woman was breaking the rules and expanding society's notion of sanctioned public activity for women in restaurants and hotels, travel, and sports. The dispute over decorum was illustrated by an incident at a NAWSA convention in Washington, D.C.[68]

It was a political blunder for President Taft, who addressed the delegates to the NAWSA convention of 1910, to tell them "frankly" that "he was not altogether in sympathy with the suffrage movement." Taft's speech began well enough by endorsing "popular and representative government, because every class . . . who are intelligent enough to know their own interests, are better qualified to determine how those interests shall be cared for and preserved than any other class." But then he added a deadly rider:

> [T]he class shall be intelligent enough to know its own interests. The theory that Hottentots, or any other uneducated, altogether unintelligent class is fitted for any government at once, is a theory I wholly dissent from.

Instantly there was hissing. The president had compared American-born women to uncivilized peoples. The convention hall filled with the sound of "feminine hisses . . . as if a valve on a steam engine had broken."[69] The hissing caused a sensation and horrified the defenders of polite womanhood. A newspaper reporter gallantly excused the behavior by alleging that it originated with people in the audience who didn't belong there, though he gave no hint as to who these might be. Apologies were offered to the president, NAWSA president Anna Howard Shaw responded to Taft's objection that the suffrage would enfranchise "the less desirable class" by assuring him that woman suffrage did not mean doubling the ignorant vote. She would "draw the voting line horizontally, not diagonally, and exclude from the privilege of voting not only ignorant women but also illiterate men."[70]

A generation or more separated the women of the Emma Willard Association and the New Woman. Both had achieved the highest education available to them, both welcomed the entry of women into paid work and the professions and supported the suffrage. But there the similarities ended. Calling for self-support, women such as Olivia found that they had unwittingly endorsed New Woman freedoms and behavior that they could never condone. In the debate over womanhood, battle lines were drawn over issues of refinement and behavior, over the propriety of public disputes and speeches versus ladylike self-control, and over the question of what signified the feminine. In a graduation speech to Emma Willard School girls in 1897, Olivia declared, "We are proud of the fine intellectual attainments of the new generation, while deprecating some things that have developed with it." She lectured them on deportment and character, which she defined as "a perfectly educated will," adding, "I commend from my own experience of life the cultivation of manners and sound common sense."[71] The progress women had made was threatened "in the close of the nineteenth century . . . when some women smoke, haze, and seem to outdo their brothers in ways that right-minded people condemn in men."[72] A *New York Times* reporter aptly described Olivia as "the friend of woman's advancement, while severely deprecating the 'advanced woman' in the accepted sense of the term."[73]

She continued to advocate women's public roles, praising simple housekeeping and making a virtue of her own economical regime: "If I had the care of a great many servants, I should not be able to devote the time to important outside work that I do now," she wrote. A large staff was just a nuisance. Why, she could manage with just a handful of servants, and if her cook left, she would manage on her own! This was no idle boast, and visitors to 506 Fifth Avenue were sometimes startled when the front door was opened by the mistress rather than by the expected maid.[74] She defended her eccentric household management, calling it "absurd to suggest that women who have a talent for music or literature or art should be enslaved by domestic drudgery, while the struggle for civilization of the world is going on."[75] Yet she also voiced concern about the changes that were transforming the work of the home—commercialized food preparation and the apartment houses and hotels that offered temporary lodging to city dwellers. "I shall be sorry if we, as a race, get to living in the homeless way that some people do, going to a restaurant for this and a hotel for that," she declared, adding melodramatically, "I would rather live in a shanty on the rocks than to give up my home. Everything is a tavern to me that is not my own home."[76]

These were the years when middle-class women reformers were making a remarkable entry into public life. Working for reform of industrial conditions or municipal reform, for safe milk or better schools, they took on the challenge of "doing the nation's work."[77] Yet suffrage seemed stalled: after Colorado (1893), a decade went by before another state west of the Mississippi gave women the vote. Women of wealth such as Olivia Sage and Helen Gould had another means of influence: they could use their money to leverage change. Reform of married women's property laws had gone far toward protecting their right to contract, bequeath, and gift.[78] Moreover, their religious traditions encouraged stewardship and taught that wealth was to be used wisely and responsibly.[79] An Emma Willard Association speaker stated the obvious when she declared that women would never be in a position of equality so long as their husbands controlled all the nation's wealth. Wives and daughters of wealthy men could purify this money, she declared, removing its taint as they spent it to make the world a better place.[80] Women of wealth could invest in civic, patriotic, or educational institutions if they wanted, in feminism or in furs. They might still be waiting for the ballot, but until they had it, their money would speak for them.

Helen Gould Takes the Lead

When Helen began her philanthropy Olivia was by her side (Helen would not marry until 1912). Correspondence from the 1880s reveals Olivia playing the part of spiritual guardian and financial advisor, with Helen the affectionate and grateful mentee. Helen was a serious girl. Facing yet another ocean cruise in her father's yacht in 1887, the seventeen-year-old wrote to Olivia, "I can't understand why crossing the ocean should seem so solemn to me unless because it reminds me of death—crossing the sea to the unknown land of which we have heard so often."[81] Religion was a comfort to her, and she thanked Olivia for bringing her to an experience of religious conversion the year before. From the Gould yacht off the Bahamas she wrote, "I am so glad, Mrs. Sage, that I took the step I did before I left home, and I hope God will help me to be a good Christian."[82] She continued, "[E]ver since you have known me I feel that it has meant a great deal in my life, and if I ever become a good woman it will have been in great measure due to you."[83] Later, she again thanked Olivia: "Since Mother's death you have been like a mother to me, and I am warmly grateful for all your kindness, for the teaching that has been such a help in piloting my course, and for the loving friendship that has been so sweet (see fig. 9.1)."[84]

After her father's death in 1892, Helen prepared to manage her own affairs. She enrolled in the Woman's Law Class sponsored by New York University (NYU) and first taught at the university in 1890–1891 by Belgian-born Emilie Kempin, a graduate of the law school of the University of Zurich. She graduated in 1899, after passing what was referred to as a "severe" exam. She then became vice president of the Woman's Legal Education Society.[85]

Helen Gould was not some anxious undergraduate but a prospective donor of breathtaking wealth and generosity, just the kind of donor NYU chancellor Henry MacCracken was trying to cultivate as he contemplated a major expansion of the university. There had already been informal contacts between the Gould family and the MacCrackens. The

FIGURE 9.1. Helen Gould, around 1913, the year of her marriage. Courtesy New York University Archives.

families' summer homes in the Catskills were adjacent, and in the 1880s friendships had developed between the children.[86] Chancellor Mac-Cracken had been encouraged when Jay Gould gave $25,000 for NYU's new undergraduate college in University Heights in the Bronx and promised more.[87] Helen continued her father's interest in NYU, enlarging his donations with spectacular philanthropic gifts. She was not put off by Chancellor MacCracken's vision for NYU's expansion, which called for a new male-only undergraduate campus—unlike Olivia, who constantly voiced her support for women's education. Helen viewed her donations to this campus as contributing to a nationally significant project, assuring Chancellor MacCracken that she intended to find "some opportunity of being of assistance *to the nation* in these troubled times."[88] Helen paid for the library and the administration building at the new uptown campus and for a stately Hall of Fame designed by Stanford White. Together with subsequent donations to the Engineering School, the School of Pedagogy, and the Medical College, her gifts to NYU in these years would total $2.5 million.[89] Gratefully, the university conferred on her an honorary Master of Letters degree in 1902.[90]

Olivia stood, often literally, at Helen Gould's side as the younger woman gave away millions of dollars. She spoke up in public for the self-effacing Helen in her clear, schoolmistressy voice. And she continued to advise Helen on her various philanthropies that included YMCAs and YWCAs, colleges, and foreign missions. A photograph of Helen Gould in her thirties shows a kindly looking, plumpish woman entirely without pretensions. Her large correspondence reveals her to have been a tireless and meticulous philanthropist. Olivia relished her role as mother-advisor and took pride in the philanthropy they planned jointly. She surprised a visitor to her Fifth Avenue home in May 1906 when she confided to him that Helen Gould was her "spiritual daughter and gives here and there at her direction and advice."[91]

"A wife should have an allowance"

In 1903, the Sage household moved from 506 Fifth Avenue to a house at number 604 opposite St. Patrick's Cathedral. Here, they soon reverted to a life of quiet routine. They were not on the list of the "Four Hundred" drawn up by Ward McAllister, the self-appointed arbiter of New York society.[92] Nor were they in the social set described by Edith Wharton as the new people "whom New York was beginning to dread and yet be drawn to."[93] Russell Sage was still occasionally portrayed in the press as a financial baron of immense and sinister power, but one journalist described him as, "broken in body under the overreaching task set by his cold, grim hunger for innumerable dollars."[94] "Men have asked Russell Sage what his ambition is," the writer continued. "He has answered with a set of copy-book phrases about simple, just, and godly living. He has never said that his ambition from the beginning of his life has been to prove the superiority of his persistence and shrewdness over other men by accumulating the worldly tokens of worldly effort—dollars."[95] Sage brushed aside such criticism. "So long as some men have more sense and self-control than others, just so long will some men be wealthy," he remarked. He relished press discussion of his frugality, ascribing his fortune to a lifetime of small daily economies and claimed in a 1902 essay entitled "The Injustice of Vacations" that he had never taken a day off work, even on his birthday.[96]

Others treated him as a figure of fun. "Russell Sage Is Growing Younger," declared one writer with tongue in cheek, describing how the financier "whom the infirmities of age seem to have overlooked" had discovered he could read without his glasses.[97] Russell Sage seemed oblivious to public derision, but Olivia suffered dreadfully. "Mrs. Sage has been more sensitive to the ridicule and the envy which have grown up around her husband than he is himself," a journalist noted in 1905. "What a woman can do by tact and perseverance and marvelous ingenuity, she has done to make the name of Sage known for generosity and for charity."[98]

But associating the name Sage with charity was difficult while the old man lived. Russell Sage's unwillingness to part with even a few dollars involved Olivia in some humiliating negotiations. For example, the Sages remained friendly with Carlisle Indian School principal Richard Pratt and his family, though Pratt was now no longer associated with Carlisle and a new Indian policy ruled in Washington. Sometimes the Sages and the Pratts went together to see the famous Carlisle football team. On one such occasion Olivia was reduced to begging daughter Anna Pratt for free tickets to a game which they were all to attend together—"though I think ~~we~~ I ought to pay."[99] On another occasion, a tapestry Olivia had donated to the New York City Mission and Tract Society was returned with a curt note from the secretary saying that "[t]he poor with whom we work have no way of using such things to advantage." How to perform the role of philanthropist if she had nothing worth giving away—if even the donated furnishings from her shabby-genteel home were rejected as unusable by the guardians of the poor?[100] People close to her described her as suffering from "nerves."[101]

In a revealing interview with a reporter for a Syracuse newspaper in 1903 on the subject of marriage, Olivia held forth on the question not of love, but of money.

> Very often . . . have I been asked what, in my opinion, is the most frequent cause of unhappy marriages. After years of observation among different sorts and conditions of people I have come to the conclusion that the answer is: the absence of individual incomes.

> A wife should have an allowance—not only a standing order at her grocer and her milliner for whatever she wants . . . but a regular cash allowance to do with as she chooses.

"A man can hardly realize the galling position in which thousands of wives are placed in begging their husbands for money," she continued recklessly.

> A man does not realize that a woman needs a certain amount of independence for her happiness, and so he goes on patting himself on the back as a model husband whose wife can have most everything she wants by going to this or that store and ordering it on credit.

For example, she knew a young wife who had turned over management of her money to her wealthy husband only to find that she had to "scrape along on a mere pittance of pin money which she has to beg from him." The well-meaning husband had reduced his wife to "a pauper."[102]

"Beggar," "pauper," "pittance"—this is bitter language! Ostensibly a discussion of marriage in general, the piece had turned instead into an embarrassing public airing of Olivia's own grievances. With her good intentions standing unused and old age staring her in the face, she longed to put Russell Sage's money to good use. At the same time, she resented her narrow and scraping lifestyle and used the interview to voice her frustration. She enjoyed beautiful clothes and travel—in fact, she deserved them! But Russell Sage's passion for work and only work deprived her of her due.

The First Gifts

The newspapers continued to speculate about how long the old man would last. "Who Will Get His Money?" rudely asked a reporter for the *Troy Daily Press*. "Russell Sage, the millionaire, has twenty-eight relatives in the city of Troy. He has about $60 million and the larger part of this will come to his Troy relatives. . . . There is little reason to believe [Mrs. Sage] will inherit anything like the bulk of the estate," the reporter speculated.[103]

Previous accounts have suggested that Sage philanthropy began only after Russell Sage's death.[104] In fact, Olivia made several significant donations to charity before this date. Her donations to Troy Female Seminary (1893), the Woman's Hospital (1899), and the American Seamen's Friend Society (1904) have already been noted. Now, as Russell

Sage approached ninety, she began to plan some major gifts. She also began to be pursued by creative fund-raisers such as Henry MacCracken of NYU and James M. Taylor, president of Vassar.[105] When John D. Rockefeller, a Vassar trustee, promised to match every dollar raised by the college before June 1904, up to $200,000, Taylor appealed to Olivia to match Rockefeller's challenge grant: "I know of your general interest in the education of girls," he began. Olivia responded with a check—we do not know the amount.[106] In another donation, Olivia gave Radcliffe $500 for the library in 1905 on condition that the gift be credited only to "A Friend and Pupil of Emma Willard." Since she had no personal or family ties to Radcliffe, this suggests that she was starting to give to women's colleges, including those outside New York State.[107]

Then there were some more-personal gifts. In 1903, she put a memorial window in the Home for the Friendless in Helen's honor. Helen thanked her: "It will be a sweet memorial to the warm friendship that has existed between us for so many years. You have been a very dear friend to me a big part of my life."[108] Family ties prompted a donation of $500 for an endowed room at a Presbyterian convalescent home to a woman lucky enough to have "Jermain" in her name, perhaps a relative. "You know I am Jermain Stoddard Duncan's Mother in Law," the begging-letter writer confided. "Will give $500 not $5,000," Olivia wrote on the envelope.[109] It was 1905, and in the magazine the *World's Work* the author of a muckraking essay, "Our Financial Oligarchy," described Russell Sage as still a factor in the money market, a man who "commands more cash than any other man."[110] If so, his hold on the cash was loosening.

A Teachers' College for Syracuse University

Olivia now turned her attention to her birthplace of Syracuse and especially to Yates Castle, sometimes called Renwick Hall. She felt a sentimental connection with the grand building where she had lived in the 1850s as governess to the Longstreet family.[111] In the fall of 1905, she informed Syracuse University president Rev. James R. Day that she was ready to defray the cost of buying Yates Castle to house a teachers' college for the university, and in November she sent the university a check for $150,000, enabling it to purchase the building and the surrounding property. The building was designated the new Teachers' College.[112] The action was significant. Olivia had begun to act independently of Russell Sage in a project that combined her attachment to Syracuse, her self-identification as a teacher, and her commitment to women's education. It was a measure of her assertiveness and her sense of possibilities at this time that she agreed that the college should be named after her: the Margaret Olivia Slocum College for Women Teachers. Although she would go on to spend $45 million in philanthropy in the next decade, never again would she permit any building for which she provided the money to bear her name.[113]

Part III

❦

"Just beginning to live"
1906–1918

Ten

"A kind of old-age freedom"

We might begin by defining a widow as a woman,
at a particular cultural and historical moment,
caught in a situation of complex and complicating transformation.
—Allison Levy, "The Widow's Cleavage" (2004)[1]

On May 11, 1906, James D. Phelps, secretary and financial administrator for Syracuse University, was in New York on personal business: his
wife was going to Philadelphia to visit her sister and had to change trains
in the city. Phelps accompanied her to New York, then he set off toward
the Sage brownstone at 604 Fifth Avenue on another mission, one aimed
to raise money for the university.[2] Syracuse University was facing a financial crisis and a crisis of identity. Its chancellor, Rev. James Day, wanted
to raise his institution to the first rank of American universities, but problems pressed on him from every direction. Cornell, sixty miles to the
south, was a thorn in his side. Larger than Syracuse and favored by the
state legislature in funding, it was developing into a major research university. Equally disturbing were tendencies in universities across the nation
toward liberal religion. The nineteenth-century college knew that its
mission was to produce Christian gentlemen of character. But now denominational institutions such as Syracuse were under pressure from
forces working to homogenize American institutions and articulate them
with the needs of business.[3] Chancellor Day's applications to the
Carnegie Foundation for the Advancement of Teaching had been
repeatedly rejected because of his university's Methodist ties (Day himself was a Methodist minister). The foundation's letter of rejection cited
the university's "narrow sectarianism."[4]

Then there was the problem of "tainted money." John Archbold,
vice president of Standard Oil and a prime target of muckraking and

reformist journalists such as Upton Sinclair, was president of the university's board of trustees, and the chancellor had to endure jibes about "Chancellor Day and his Standard Oil University." Yet Archbold was the most active and vigorous friend the university had; in fact, Archbold bailed out the university year after year. It was all most galling.[5]

Chancellor Day urgently needed money for buildings and programs. Phelps decided to show some initiative and go to where the money was. Clutching a bundle of photographs of Syracuse University, he made his way to visit Mrs. Russell Sage. He would seize the moment and pull off a coup for the university. Phelps might have felt some nervousness as he approached the Fifth Avenue brownstone. Russell Sage sat atop a vast financial empire that included some of the nation's major transportation and communications networks. He was director and officer of numerous railroad companies. For over thirty years he had been one of the most powerful men on Wall Street, and now his wealth from railroad, timber, and shipping interests was estimated at between sixty and one hundred million dollars. Would the great man be busy making decisions affecting the fate of millions, pondering weighty business decisions, concluding multimillion-dollar deals?

To his surprise, Phelps found Olivia at home and eager for company. Russell Sage, who was almost ninety years old, was ill in bed, she explained. Phelps's patience was rewarded when Olivia stated that "she intended to do something for Syr. Univ. but had not made up her mind what. She said she would like to make up her mind independently . . . she would do something worthy of her position if she gave." Olivia looked with interest at the photographs, asking to keep the one of Yates Castle (Renwick Hall).[6] She had been planning a large gift to Syracuse for some time, but she wanted to satisfy herself that its female students did well in a coeducational system, and she grilled the university official for an hour on the subject. When Phelps finally made a move to leave, she asked him to call again and keep her posted and to send her "anything of interest concerning Syracuse University." From his hotel the next day on Twenty-Seventh Street he wrote informing Chancellor Day that Mrs. Sage had promised to help the university. "Her husband is 90 years old and is ill in bed. She is looking after the business."[7]

Phelps's letter shows that Olivia was anticipating how her position would be changed by her husband's death, which seemed imminent. Mentally alert, she was seeking ways to act independently with her money. It shows her interest in higher education for women and confirms her sense of agency as she pondered her next move—"something worthy of her position."

Russell Sage was sinking fast. He had been mentally incapacitated for several months, and though he insisted on going to his Wall Street office each day, his visits had become perfunctory.[8] For some time he resisted well-meaning attempts to persuade him to retire, but in early July he agreed to go to Cedar Croft, the house by the ocean. Here, after suffering "numerous spells of weakness," he died on July 23, 1906, of "general debility and old age."[9] A reporter for the *Troy Record*, quoting Sage's physician, Dr. Schmuck, recorded that his last word was "Olivia." But Paul Sarnoff claimed that his last words were "Marie, Marie!"[10] His body was borne by private railroad car to the family plot at Troy's Oakwood Cemetery and buried "with the same simplicity that characterized his life," a reporter noted, next to his first wife, Maria Winne Sage. Twenty mourners accompanied the coffin, which was six feet four inches long and encased in a burglar-proof vault of chilled steel. Sage was so unpopular in Troy that his impressive mausoleum, a copy of the Parthenon, bore no inscription, reportedly because of fear that the public would deface it.[11]

When the will was read, it was revealed that the financier had left everything to Olivia after the payment of $25,000 each to his nephews and nieces.[12] At seventy-eight she found herself in possession of a fortune of over $75 million, more than $1.5 billion in 2004 currency.[13] Obituaries for Russell Sage were respectful, leaving a lot unsaid. "Like many another American, he knew how to accumulate money but not how to distribute it," one wrote tactfully.[14]

Dissatisfied with their legacies, two of the Sage nephews decided to fight to have the will set aside on the grounds that their uncle had been mentally incompetent.[15] One of them, James H. Sage of Sage and Gaffey, a wholesale and retail fruit, fish, and vegetable dealer of Troy, declared he had made up his mind to get "that to which, as a blood-relative of Russell Sage, I am entitled." He also challenged the provision that any beneficiary who disputed the will "shall be absolutely barred and cut off from any share in my estate." Olivia responded by doubling the bequests to all the Sage relatives, and the challenge fizzled out.[16]

To Olivia, Russell Sage's death came both as the tragic loss of her companion of almost forty years and a longed-for release. It would have been difficult for her to disentangle these two, and it is impossible for us. However, she did leave some clues. At the funeral she wept quietly while the coffin was being lowered, then she directed that a cluster of lilies of the valley from the garden at Cedar Croft be placed in the grave on top of the casket. She "walked to the head of the grave and stood in deep meditation and wept." Her brother then led her away, and they

FIGURE 10.1. After the death of Russell Sage, Olivia Sage
was said to own twelve fur coats. Here she is pictured in one
of them. Henry Whittemore, *History of the Sage and Slocum
Families of England and America* (New York: Published by Mrs.
Russell Sage, 1908).

left by the evening train for New York City, where she was reported to
have taken to her room in a state of collapse.[17]

But by January 1907 she had made a decision that suggests that her
feelings toward her deceased husband were deeply contradictory. She
gave directions for herself to be buried next to her mother and father at
Oakwood Cemetery in Syracuse, not in Troy next to Russell Sage and
his first wife.[18] James D. Phelps of Syracuse University agreed to act for
her in this matter. At her request, he had new headstones made for her

parents' graves, and in the depth of winter he visited the gravesites and sent her a report and photographs:

> The sun was shining dimly and the cemetery seemed quiet and beautiful though covered with snow. The tops of your memorial stones were covered with several inches of pure white snow which at a distance looked like white crowns. I brushed the snow from the footstones and read the words, "Father" and "Mother," words that must mean more to you than to anyone else.[19]

Nothing was too much trouble for Phelps if it pleased the elderly donor who had purchased Renwick Hall and the surrounding property for the university. In June, Phelps mailed her a picture of her own gravesite. "I had all the old soil, a foot in depth, removed and then replaced with fresh earth. I also had the lot leveled, and newly terraced, sodded, and seeded," he informed her.[20]

"In leaving his fortune to Mrs. Sage, Mr. Sage has left it to charity"

The busiest years of Olivia's life now began. At the age of seventy-eight and a multimillionaire, she turned her hand to managing her affairs. Public expectations were high. As Mrs. Russell Sage, she had mobilized the image of the benevolent Christian woman whose generous impulses were restrained only by her tightfisted husband. A writer in *Outlook* praised Russell Sage's decision to leave his fortune to his wife, "who has the reputation, among those who know her, of being at once charitable in her sympathies and wise in her judgements." Another described her as "a woman of strong charitable instincts."[21] "The turning of the great estate over to Mrs. Sage was most natural," another editorialized. "For years she has been her husband's advisor in gifts to charities, and has shown herself familiar with the responsibilities and obligations of large wealth."[22] Now the nation held its breath. Dr. Schmuck, a family friend, commented, "In leaving his fortune to Mrs. Sage, Mr. Sage has left it to charity."[23]

But how free would Olivia be to spend her money? The question of charity had become enormously complicated since the Civil War as Americans rethought the relationship between wealth and work. Populist-era denunciations of monopoly joined with Progressive-era antitrust rhetoric until those with large fortunes seemed a threat to the republic and philanthropy seemed no more than a guilty gesture of repentance by the owners of ill-gotten wealth.[24] Olivia's widowhood coincided with new controversy over whether people of conscience should accept donations from those named by President Theodore Roosevelt the "malefactors of great wealth." In fact, public interest in Rockefeller philanthropy peaked in 1905, with thirty-six articles in the *Tribune* and forty-six in the *New York Times* in that year alone.[25] Social Gospel minister Washington Gladden coined the term "tainted money" to describe the charitable donations of industrial giants such as Andrew Carnegie and John D. Rockefeller, Sr. Should a church or a university accept donations from such a source, he demanded? "Is this clean money? . . . Can any man, can any institution, knowing its origin, touch it without being defiled?"[26]

Stereotypes about gender and age protected Olivia from this antitrust rhetoric. No one saw Sage money as a threat to republican institutions as they did Rockefeller money. Contemporaries could understand a woman who gave away money since they understood the benevolent impulse to be feminine, just as the acquisitive instinct necessary for business was masculine. "The very process of accumulation unfits a man, as a rule, for its expenditure," Abram Hewitt had declared in 1892. "Every faculty of his mind and body is absorbed in adding to his wealth, so that he has no time or even inclination left to distribute it according to the demands of society or the judgment of his fellows."[27] At a time when debate raged over tainted money, writers depicted Russell Sage's money in the hands of his benevolent widow as somehow purified and rededicated, "a link in the chain of gold which is lifting the world up to God," as one correspondent put it, acknowledging Olivia's gift of $10,000 for the American College for Girls in Constantinople. By spending Russell Sage's money, his widow would be "wiping her husband's name clear."[28]

Reaction in the press was awe mixed with pity for the widow's large responsibilities. Stereotypes of the elderly widow as pitiable, dependent, and passive competed with images of her as powerful and independent. For an elderly woman to have such large responsibilities was both unnatural and inappropriate, commentators suggested. She would have to relinquish "the ease, leisure and mental repose and contentment that are the cherished privileges of old age," one wrote. In their place, she would be besieged by advisors "just jam full of panaceas."

> From now on these professionals will unmercifully pelt and bombard Mrs. Sage with schemes and suggestions as to the best and most adequate way of getting rid of her surplus millions. . . . Professional Christians, professional patriots and professionally charitable people will ransack the vocabulary . . . in their hunt for persuadable and alluring sentences with which to picture to Mrs. Sage the monuments which will be erected to her memory if she follows their advice.[29]

FIGURE 10.2. An oil portrait of Olivia Sage on a rustic seat probably in New York's Central Park, feeding squirrels. Later, she would give hundreds of thousands of dollars to protect birds and other wildlife. Courtesy Rockefeller Archive Center, ref: 1059 RSF.

There was some truth to all of this. In a letter to her friend Maria Jesup, also recently widowed, Olivia complained that she could not visit in "this sad and sorrowful time of both our lives." She was pestered by "Job's comforters"—"would-be friends," coming "from the ends of the earth" with their "needless applications for help."[30] Nevertheless, press reports that she was "a prisoner in her own home," besieged by clamoring petitioners, seem more an attempt to contain her in the public realm than a description of her life.[31] Correspondence gives a glimpse of a more carefree widow. "I will close this hurried note and go for my morning stroll as the day is beautiful," she wrote to her friend Mrs. Aldrich, from Lawrence, Long Island (see fig. 10.2).[32]

When news of her inheritance leaked out and the Sage brownstone began to receive over 300 begging letters a day, the press sounded a note of caution. Charity had become part of the "social question," and a penny passed to a beggar signified a position on what one class owed to another. Mrs. Sage had been studying "the charity problem . . . hard and for thirty years," notes the author of "Mrs. Russell Sage and Her Interests," an article that appeared in *World's Work*. The public need not expect from her a "picturesque and spectacular overflow of sentimental good-will."[33]

But would the elderly widow be able to manage her own philanthropy? When John D. Rockefeller, Sr., had tried to handle his donations single-handedly he had found the task altogether beyond him. "I am in trouble," he wrote to Frederick W. Gates in 1891. "[T]he pressure of these appeals for gifts has become too great for endurance. . . . I am so constituted as to be unable to give away money with any satisfaction until I have made the most careful enquiry as to the worthiness of the cause. The investigations are now taking more of my time and energy than the Standard Oil itself." Rockefeller put Gates in charge of several of his philanthropies.[34]

Olivia, too, was simply drowning in begging letters. A reporter who visited her New York home around the turn of the century described her library as "a vast and gloomy apartment which seemed to have been struck by lightning—one could barely discern mountains of papers and tomes, piled helter-skelter in corners and over tables and chairs."

> On one long table were the letters—merely the morning mail begging for everything under the charitable sun. . . . One correspondent was declaring in a highly dramatic epistolary style that if he did not receive a thousand dollars before sundown he would blow out his brains. Another wrote a tear-faded letter about departing this life on an empty stomach, and another threatened the addressee with dire consequences if she did not obtain and forward him information about certain railway securities.

Olivia informed the reporter that she always handled her correspondence herself, but he noted that "a weary expression about her mouth accentuated the slightly pathetic tone."[35] An acquaintance offered to help: "It must be a great nuisance to have so much troublesome mail as you have," she wrote to Olivia, after a mutual friend mentioned "that immense pile of letters you showed her in your parlor."[36] In 1905, Olivia had employed Catharine Hunter as a private secretary to handle her correspondence. But with the announcement of Russell Sage's death, the stream of letters increased to an avalanche. As Rockefeller turned to Gates, Olivia now turned to her husband's firm of attorneys, the de Forest brothers.[37]

Robert Weeks de Forest

Robert Weeks de Forest (1848–1931) and his wife Emily were old acquaintances. In Robert de Forest, Olivia had an experienced advisor who had long been a member of New York's charitable elite. Emily de Forest was, like Olivia, a lady manager at the New-York Woman's Hospital and a friend.[38] Robert de Forest was a patrician reformer of independent means who often invested his own money in schemes of betterment. An example of his philanthropy was the Provident Loan Society of New York. In the 1880s, he set up the society, raising money from wealthy friends. A quarter of a century later, it was loaning out more than $30 million a year.[39] In 1901, he established and partially funded the first School of Philanthropy for the training of social workers.[40] His friend and colleague John Glenn later said of him, "Certainly no man in America ever recognized more selflessly and more devotedly the duty of noblesse oblige which birth and inheritance and personal character imposed on him."[41] De Forest had entered his father's law firm in 1872 after graduating from Yale, and in 1893 joined with his brother Henry to form the De Forest Brothers law firm on Broad Street, specializing in corporation law. In this capacity he had organized the legal department of the Central Railroad of New Jersey (his father-in-law's company), and at some time, probably in the 1890s, he put his knowledge of railroad law at the service of Russell Sage.[42] Aside from his law practice, de Forest was also an officer in the Hackensack Water Co., the Dolphin Jute Mills, the Metropolitan Life Insurance Co., and other corporations (see fig. 10.3).[43]

He was also president of the New York Charity Organization Society (COS), a group of elite charity experts and modernizers. Before this date, Olivia's connections with the COS had been limited to whatever modest annual subscriptions Russell Sage could force himself to part with. For example, in 1884 the couple each separately subscribed $10. In 1885, "Mr. and Mrs. Russell Sage" were listed as having subscribed $25, and the same amount was listed under "Mrs. Russell Sage" in 1896. In contrast, John D. Rockefeller, Mrs. William E. Dodge, and Cornelius Vanderbilt all contributed over $500 a year.[44] Such subscribers may have been motivated by more than admiration for the society's reforming spirit.

FIGURE 10.3. Robert Weeks de Forest, around 1907. De Forest, Olivia's attorney and advisor, became a trustee and first president of the Russell Sage Foundation from 1918 to 1931. John M. Glenn, Lilian Brandt, and F. Emerson Andrews, *Russell Sage Foundation, 1907–1946* (New York: Russell Sage Foundation, 1947).

Labor strife and even class warfare were the threats conjured up by ministers at New York's fashionable churches. Rev. John R. Paxton, D.D., minister at Olivia's own West Presbyterian Church, energetically endorsed the society: "No cause appealing to the public in this generation of unrest, strikers, paupers, communistic ideas, and *trouble ahead* deserves more help and encouragement than the charity organization society," he wrote. "I am heartily in favor of it."[45]

Historian David Hammack describes the years 1886 to 1903 as a transitional period in New York City politics "between the merchant-dominated polity of an earlier era and the Tammany-managed city of the first third of the twentieth century," a period when "a changing coalition of disparate economic, political, charitable, and labor elites" challenged the dominant Tammany and Republican organizations.[46] De Forest was part of this reform challenge. Deeply critical of politicians who used public relief to solidify the loyalty of their immigrant constituencies, reformers launched several self-styled "citizens' movements": the People's Municipal League (1890), the Committee of Seventy (1894), and the Citizens' Union (1897, 1901, 1903). The last, the Citizens' Union, led by Elihu Root and J. P. Morgan, won the mayoral election in 1901 and put into office Seth Low, who as mayor of Brooklyn in the 1870s had carried through the ultimate charity reform: a complete ban on publicly funded aid (outdoor relief).[47] Low's administration signaled reform in the areas of housing, public health, and civil service administration. He appointed Robert de Forest to the office of tenement house commissioner.[48] But after 1903, when Low lost the mayoral race to a Tammany candidate, de Forest was again looking for sponsorship for his reform activities. His voluminous correspondence documents his administrative ability and astounding capacity for hard work. "I am driven so rapidly, in so many directions, that my head is somewhat dizzy, and I have a realizing sense of the necessity for either longer work hours or less work," he confided to a friend.[49] As Olivia's charity advisor, de Forest would have a chance to invest some substantial amounts of money to implement the modernization of charities, public health, and housing.

Olivia was not a stranger to business or businesslike values. Her role at the Woman's Hospital had been that of treasurer and fund-raiser, and her evangelical ideals suggested stewardship and careful financial accounting.[50] Moreover, she managed her own investments. In the fall of 1906 she was making large investments in New York real estate. In December, she loaned $1.2 million at 4.5 percent on the New York Hippodrome. A week later she made another huge loan, $1.5 million on Wall Street property, and ten days later another half-million-dollar loan on real estate. Her investments in Manhattan real estate in the six months after Russell Sage's death totaled about $10 million. A few years later, when she refused to give a donation to the New York Exchange for Woman's Work, it was not on personal or sentimental grounds but on the grounds that she was "no longer familiar with property values."[51] Her philanthropy would be investment, not largesse. Shaped by COS principles, it would not mean a redistribution of wealth to the poor.

Nevertheless, the fact that she had millions to spend and was inclined to spend it seems to have produced anxiety in the circle around her—her brother, her secretary, the de Forest brothers. Protecting her privacy became their task. Breaching it became the goal of hundreds of fortune-seekers, letter-writers and self-described long-lost relatives.

De Forest's ideas on charity were those of the New York COS. The society's methods offered the very best solution to "the much vexed problem of how to make the poor better," he wrote in its third annual report.[52] Its goal was to end outdoor relief and to turn relief-giving over to private charities. No aid was to be given before thorough investigation (a home visit) by a "friendly visitor" who could assess the family's needs and identify resources they might call on. The society's main concern was to protect donors from fraud: it was a clearinghouse for charities, not a distribution point for relief. Advocates of "scientific charity" were confident that private charities run efficiently by men and women with no financial incentive to be dishonest could meet the legitimate needs of industrial society. Determining need was not seen as problematic, and neither was the assumption that the poor suffered from moral as well as material deficiencies.[53]

COS reformers such as de Forest fascinate us for their combination of Christian stewardship and class bias, complacency and idealism. Representing themselves as secular modernizers, members of the COS movement enacted the same search for order in the field of philanthropy as the merger movement in American business, and its technique of casework was an important new instrument for measuring need and prescribing relief.[54] Earlier, the central tenet of charity organization had been the ban on material relief. "The Society will not dispense alms in any form," the 1883 constitution declared. But by the early twentieth century, this prohibition was being modified in practice. The 1896 constitution was revised to read: "The Society will not dispense alms in any form from its own funds," and COS general secretary Edward Devine admitted in 1896 that the society's position had "always been, that we believed in relief, and plenty of it in the particular cases in which, after investigation, it seemed clearly wise to give it, and we have always acted as intermediaries in obtaining it, either from relief societies or from individuals."[55] A survey of charity organization societies in 1897 found that many routinely gave relief from a special fund. One charity organization secretary answered a survey about relief-giving by acknowledging that she had disbursed $17,000 in relief funds during the previous ten months. "No public appeal is made. Funds are replenished by a small number of donors in a quiet way."[56] Other major changes were on the way. The society relied increasingly on district agents, who were seen as more professional than the volunteer "friendly visitors" of earlier years.

The COS even began to grant small pensions to deserving widows and deserted wives. Yet all COS aid continued to come from private sources, and all the clients who received it had to be found deserving.[57]

I have described the COS in some detail because of the role the society played in handling Olivia's giving to individuals after 1906. What is evident is how the COS's purpose, to educate and curb private givers, represented a rebuke to the older charity—personal, sentimental, discretionary—represented in the figure of the philanthropist. COS publications sounded the theme that charity should be more than sentimental, more than a kind gesture of someone "with a soft heart."[58] To COS advocates, impulsive, thoughtless giving was as bad as not giving at all, for charity needed to be based on investigation and careful diagnosis of each case as well as efficient administration. As the historian of the COS points out, organized charity "defined givers as part of the problem of pauperism."[59]

The Sage Fund

In the closing months of 1906, Olivia took steps to establish some systematic way of handling her philanthropy. Following Robert de Forest's advice, she began three different types of giving which would continue simultaneously over the next twelve years. They were first, charitable donations to individuals; second, giving through the foundation; and third, philanthropy to institutions.[60] I turn in the remainder of this chapter to describe the first of these, Olivia's private charitable giving to needy individuals.

In October 1906, Robert de Forest set up the "Sage Fund" to deal with the begging letters addressed to Olivia from individuals. She was to pay the NYCOS $10,000 a year (just over $203,750 in 2003 dollars) for its agents to screen her incoming letters from New York and to disburse money to the needy. Letters asking for contributions for institutions or claiming personal acquaintance were sent on to her secretaries.[61] COS officials investigated the individual appeals, sorting requests according to "personal wants," "family wants," "vicarious wants," and "public wants" and needs into "means of support, aid in business, payment of debts, purchase of home, means of education, means of medical treatment," and so on.[62] Every time the fund got down to $1,000, Olivia replenished it with a personal check for $10,000. By 1914, her donation had increased to $10,000 every six months.[63]

De Forest divided those who appealed to Olivia as individuals (rather than on behalf of institutions) into two different categories. There were "strangers," people whom she did not know and who therefore had no claim on her. Appeals from these were either refused or were redirected to the agents managing the "Sage Fund." One category of individual appeals, those with a connection to Emma Willard, were referred directly to Olivia. But even then there was no guarantee of a favorable outcome. To a request for aid on behalf of a needy mother with two children, a former employee of the Emma Willard School no less, secretary E. Lilian Todd replied that Mrs. Sage "does not take up cases of this kind, as her benefactions are on lines that prevent her taking up individuals in this manner."[64] Letters with Emma Willard connections were still sent to Olivia for decision.[65]

Olivia's use of the COS represented a practical solution to the problem of the begging letters. Correspondence between COS official W. F. Persons and Robert de Forest provides a glimpse behind the scenes. In November 1906, Persons sought direction from de Forest in dealing with the fifty to sixty begging letters that were coming in every day.[66] Some of the requests were easily dismissed. "I only ask you kindly to devide some of your fortin with me," one hopeful correspondent wrote. Another, a man in Portland, Tennessee, explained he "thot a too thousand dollar check would set me up in the world and you would never miss it." Another, from two female nurses "both thirty years of age, self-supporting for fifteen years," asked for "a sum sufficient to provide for a trip to Europe, with a chaperone or an alternative of an annuity of $1,000 each." The COS agent annotated these "absurd."[67]

But many were from people who were "apparently meritorious," Persons reported. "Some are extremely pitiful." Would the usual COS rules of investigation apply, he asked de Forest? Should he assume that no aid would be given without investigation? "Should investigation be limited strictly to the class of cases in which it is the province of the COS to extend assistance; or should we inquire into applications for payments of debt, payment of mortgages on the homes of elderly people, means of education, admission to home for the aged and pensions where the beneficiaries are not resident within this community?" To what extent should investigation be carried on in distant places and how much should be spent on investigation?[68]

De Forest replied to each of Persons's questions. Don't discard letters from outside New York, so long as they are from cities with corresponding COS societies, he instructed. The COS network of information and referral would deal with these. When the writer lived outside the range of investigation by the NYCOS or one of its affiliate charity organization societies, the recommendation was "no action; inaccessible."[69] Correspondence with regional charity organization societies shows the system in operation. For example, when begging letters came postmarked from Buffalo, Persons screened them, referred about one-tenth for investigation back to the Buffalo COS and its corresponding secretary Porter R. Lee, and discarded the rest. Screening and investigation were conducted in strict secrecy.[70]

Olivia agreed to this arrangement, but she did not want it known that she was using the COS. As Persons explained to Richard H. Lane, secretary of the Montreal Charity Organization Society, "Mrs. Sage has a very sympathetic regard for the writers of these letters." She felt that misleading reports in the newspapers of her intentions had encouraged large numbers of unfortunate people to write to her. "She would regard it as particularly unfortunate if it were to reach the newspapers that she has distributed the letters among various charity societies." Publicity would only attract more attention and more letters.[71]

Sometimes she was kept in the dark. "We ask particularly that no letters or reports be sent to Mrs. Sage and that those who have appealed to her be discouraged from communicating with her," Persons instructed Baltimore COS secretary Mary Richmond in October 1906. COS agents were sometimes not told that a case they were investigating originated in a letter to Olivia; not surprisingly, the investigations were often met with "frigidity," as the COS was intensely unpopular. It proved impossible in practice to hide the reason for the investigation. Families in need "at once surmise that the call is in response to their appeal to Mrs. Sage," Persons warned.[72]

In October 1910, de Forest instructed Persons to send a package of letters relating to YMCA work in Puerto Rico to Olivia at Sag Harbor in an envelope "without endorsement on the face, so that they will reach her just as they were intended to reach her by the writers without indication to her or to any one that they passed through the C.O.S."[73]

For a charity expert, de Forest could be remarkably callous. Asked by Edward Devine for advice about a Miss Adams, who had applied to Olivia for paid work—(Devine had written, "She has a nice, honest face and perfectly straight story seemed to me a person who deserved help to get work, though I don't consider myself a judge of character")—de Forest directed Devine to reply as follows:

Dear Miss Adams,

I will send your note to the COS. Finding work is matter of personal effort. I advise you to continue doing what you can. The relief of immediate distress can be relied upon.

Sincerely yours,
Robert W. de Forest[74]

The note reveals de Forest's aristocratic aloofness and recalls the comment of a former colleague, Clare Tousley, that she had never known him to come into direct contact with any poor person.[75]

Olivia Sage Breaks the Rules

Was Olivia a COS enthusiast or was she the benevolent lady of legend? The essay "Mrs. Russell Sage and Her Interests," which was published in November 1906 in *World's Work*, seems intended to negate the image of Lady Bountiful. Olivia is quoted as holding to a strict COS line: "Helping the poor does not mean giving them money. In the majority of cases that would be the very worst thing to do."

> In order properly to help the poor they must be brought to a frame of mind from which they now seem to be very far, although they are approaching it as the years pass. This frame of mind must be a willingness to help themselves; in a word, it means that the poor must learn the meaning of responsibility.[76]

But this interview, given soon after Russell Sage's death, might have been intended expressly to discourage begging letters. In practice, Olivia quite frequently broke the "rules." In a letter that shows she managed to retain some discretion over the kinds of cases relieved by the Sage Fund, Persons confided to a colleague, "Mrs. Sage is not averse to extending aid of a character not usually dealt with by a COS." So far, the COS had been able to hold the line and keep to the rules. If the agent on the spot should recommend certain kinds of aid, however, "it is probable that the funds will be forthcoming; particularly in cases where it is advisable to place aged persons in homes or to provide medical treatment."[77] The agent in charge sometimes agreed to increase the amount of relief or add services. In 1908, Persons was using some Sage Fund moneys to pay the salaries of probation workers and a visiting nurse to serve needy cases that had been brought to light by begging letters. Persons informed de Forest that investigating the cases of these individuals who had appealed to Olivia was costing the society $125 a month.[78]

When she could, Olivia broke free and spent as she felt inclined. In 1908, she gave instructions that money from the Sage Fund should be used to help the unemployed. In a strict COS regime, "outdoor relief" of the unemployed required a work test—that is, a stint of make-work in the COS-run woodyard.[79] Olivia sidestepped this phase with her request. By 1914, $400 a month was being paid from the Sage Fund into the General Provident Relief Fund for the direct relief of distress and without the usual investigation, over de Forest's objection.[80] The Sage Fund was being used "for cases which do not come exactly within the Society's power to help," one COS agent admitted in 1918.[81]

COS agents handling the Sage cases sometimes balked as the rules were stretched and the criteria of worthiness set aside. The comment of a social worker in charge of distributing some of the Sage Fund money in Manhattan illustrates why the COS was hated by the poor. She wrote to Persons that the disbursement of such a large sum of money seemed to her "a very serious proposition." She opposed giving money to men of her district, most of whom were Italian or Bohemian immigrants and were seasonally unemployed. These men would be much better off being sent to labor on truck farms. The family should at least be made to pay the rent, she went on.

> This is usually a fair test as to the real desire to keep the home. Food can usually be secured in so many ways without any effort on the part of the adults, for instance the man can always be provided by a free lunch counter in a liquor store through the payment of five cents. *The woman can always secure broken food by begging from door to door.* It is a very large question and it seems that it might be well to give it longer and more serious consideration.[82]

Olivia also gave generously to the Salvation Army, even though its charitable practices broke COS rules that no relief should be given without investigation of need.[83] The Salvation Army even pandered to donors' enjoyment of charity as spectacle. The wholesale giving of gifts to poor children was staged annually at Madison Square Garden. Wealthy donors paid to attend, watching from the balcony as hundreds of poor children filed forward to receive toys and sweets. Robert de Forest expressed his bitter criticism of the practice in *Charities Review* (the COS organ). He praised charity that was "personal service, not mere largess," and questioned whether the children really needed the sweets and toys.[84] The Salvation Army ignored its critics, continuing these mass distributions of relief. In December 1913, Olivia was invited by Evangeline Booth to attend a similar spectacle: "The distribution of four thousand baskets on Christmas morning, at 10 o'clock in the Ninth Regiment Armory, 14th Street. *It will be a sight you will never forget,*" Booth wrote.

> You are also invited to attend the entertainment that will be given to 3,500 poor children and the distribution of 6,300 toys and Christmas goodies. . . . Special seats in the balcony will be reserved for our subscribers. The enclosed card will admit you and your friends.[85]

Olivia sent a money donation, and Evangeline Booth's acknowledgment allowed her to enjoy vicariously the sensation of reward for this old-fashioned charity. "I wish so much that you could have witnessed the gratitude of the desolate and starving to whom your bounty went," Booth wrote.[86]

If Olivia didn't agree with strict COS principles, why did she hand over her begging-letter correspondence to the society? The answer lies in the sheer bulk and number of the letters. A report on the "Sage Letters" submitted by Persons to de Forest reveals why the screening process was necessary: 29,124 letters had been received by February 9, 1907. Of these, he described 22,611 as "not read" and only 6,513 as "read and classified." Of those read, 18,500 were from individuals and about 4,000 from institutions. In total, 4,628 were declared "read but not to be investigated," 601 "read, investigated and aided," 139 "under investigation," and 109 "read and under treatment."[87] On August 1, 1907, Persons' next report stated that 39,696 letters had been received to date, 9,972 since his report in February.

> The whole number of letters read [carefully] during the period ending July 31 [examined and forwarded to other societies] is 14,202; letters not read 24,894. The letters read may be classified as follows:
>
> Letters relating to institutions 7,512
> Letters relating to personal wants 6,690
>
> Of the letters relating to institutions . . . 6,486 required no attention whatsoever. Of the 6,690 letters read and abstracted—relating to personal wants—5,460 have not been investigated; the remaining 1,230 have either been investigated or are now under investigation.

A further 5,460 claimed personal acquaintance with Olivia; "abstracts of these letters are now in your hands."[88]

Painstaking though the report was, de Forest wanted more detail. Acknowledging Persons' "very complete and satisfactory report with regard to the applications," he wrote back requesting further clarification. "[Y]ou say letters read 14,000 etc., letters not read 24,000, etc. Am I right in supposing that you mean to distinguish between letters carefully read and letters glanced at sufficiently to make it manifest that careful reading was unnecessary?" He went on, "You say that of the 6,690 letters relating to personal wants read and abstracted, 5,460 were not investigated, and the remaining 1,230 have been investigated. Am I right in supposing that you mean that the contents of the 5,460 made it apparent that further investigation was unnecessary or futile, and in the case of the 1,230 further investigation outside of the letter was made?" Persons' reply has not survived.[89]

Suffrage Cross-Currents, 1907–1910

If giving to the poor was fraught with difficulties, giving to the cause of woman's suffrage should have been simple. Scholar Carolyn G. Heilbrun has seen in widowhood a vantage point that confers "a kind of old-age freedom for women."[90] Widowhood can be a time to speak out, a time when respectability is unassailable or irrelevant. A vocal advocate of suffrage for a decade, Olivia now stood ready to become the campaign's biggest funder.

Her new wealth coincided with a revival in the suffrage movement. In reaction against the increasing conservatism of the NAWSA-affiliated New York State Woman Suffrage Association, Harriot Stanton Blatch founded the Equality League of Self-Supporting Women (later the Women's Political Union) in 1907. The new organization aimed at a closer alliance with immigrant working women and adopted a more lively style and methods than those of NAWSA.[91] In addition, for a while, a remarkable alliance held between working women in the Women's Trade Union League (WTUL) and wealthy sympathizers.[92] Working women's activism culminated in the shirtwaist workers' strike of 1909–1910. But the resulting settlement failed to secure either union recognition or labor reforms, and the Triangle Shirtwaist Company fire shortly thereafter in 1911 not only dramatized employer indifference to worker safety, it also revealed the gulf between workers and wealthy suffragists.[93] After 1910, NAWSA leadership sought a winning strategy by distancing itself from labor and marginalizing women of color. Even Blatch now moved toward women of wealth and accepted the illiberal nativist arguments she had condemned a decade earlier.[94]

Meanwhile, Olivia had joined the rival association of Mrs. Clarence (Katherine Duer) Mackay, the Equal Franchise Society, formed in December 1908. Its members dubbed themselves "suffragists" in distinction to the "suffragettes" who were adopting the daring methods of the English feminists. They would win the vote, but in ladylike ways. "Certain wealthy, and fashionable and intelligent ladies," members of the Four Hundred, "have undertaken to play Royalty to the Equal Suffrage cause," the *New York Evening Journal* commented. They had decided that taxation without representation is "tyranny now, just as it was in the days before '76."[95] Wealthy suffragist Gertrude Foster Brown later recalled that "suffrage had taken on a new tone."[96]

The Equal Franchise Society wed suffrage principles to fashion. "Mrs. Mackay and her fashionable friends have put the cachet of style upon a woman thinking for herself," one editorial noted.[97] Another described wealthy women "flocking" to suffrage events in response to invitations designed by Tiffany, "as gorgeously got up as smart wedding cards," and another revealed that the menu at a January 1909 Political Equality Club meeting included as a dessert "glace en ballot box" (ice cream in the shape of a ballot box).[98] There was also a corresponding Men's League for Woman Suffrage made up of "a number of men of wealth and social influence."[99]

When Olivia attended the society's Suffrage Bazaar held at the Martha Washington Hotel in New York, the papers accorded her the status of celebrity suffrage patroness (though the prize for enthusiasm went to Mrs. Mackay, who bought no less than ten boxes from which she and her friends watched the proceedings).[100] The *Woman's Journal* reporter outdid herself with enthusiasm, describing as "sensational" the fact that the list of patronesses "marked the first entrance of woman suffrage into New York's Four Hundred. The names Vanderbilt and Goelet were for the first time publicly associated with woman suffrage. Mrs. Russell Sage, the heaviest taxpayer in New York, headed the list."[101]

The Suffrage Bazaar included attractions both entertaining and novel. Along with the palm reading and phrenology booths were exhibits of technology designed to free women to exercise their political rights. Inventions by women included "The Twentieth Century Kitchen," with a "domestic electrical display which showed how a woman could go to the polls and at the same time have everything in her house from washing dishes to rocking the baby moving like clockwork by electricity."[102]

Newspaper coverage depicted wealthy patronesses as "attractions" in their own right—celebrities, in other words. The *Woman's Journal* writer recounted the flamboyant generosity of Mrs. Mackay, who "came in, with a laundry bag, and purchased items for 50 cents, each time paying with five dollars, until it was full."[103] The suffrage celebrity was as brilliant in her arguments as in her dress: "Mrs. Montgomery's gown of pink and green silk was a dream, but her discourse was not," one commentator wrote. "In the latter, she placed her dependence on cold facts. Mrs. Montgomery had facts, figures, and history at her tongue's end."[104] Olivia came in for the same treatment. People were flocking to the Suffrage Bazaar expressly to see her, one reporter suggested. "It was generally believed that Mrs. Sage was at the fair and could be seen there at any time, along with other marvels. Yesterday a German woman asked for several things in broken English. 'I want to see Mrs. Russell Sage,' she said, 'and the frying pan, and where we touch a spring and the fish turns itself over to be browned.'"[105]

By representing elite women as celebrities and by focusing on the minutiae of what they wore and bought, media coverage downplayed the political consciousness that inspired their suffrage activism, disguising the strength of conviction that drove these conservative women to support the suffrage cause. In fact, the Equal Franchise Society and its offshoot, the Collegiate Equal Suffrage League, also sponsored educational lectures that drew large audiences and helped quicken the momentum toward suffrage after 1908. When Ethel Arnold, granddaughter of the British educator, addressed the league on "The Progress of Women in Europe" at the Berkeley Theater in December 1908, Olivia sat on the stage along with Blatch, Dean Ashley of the NYU Law School, and Carrie Chapman Catt.[106] And she continued to play the role of sponsor, patron, and celebrity at suffrage events, attending those organized by the Equal Franchise Society as well as by the Collegiate Equal Suffrage League. At a monster meeting to oppose the antisuffragists' claim that college women did not want the ballot, she rented a box. The box made her a spectator at this political event, but like the opera box, it symbolized both solidarity and distance—solidarity, because the occupant was present at the meeting, but distance because it indicated the large donation of the patron who was literally elevated above ordinary attendees.[107]

"Their policy frankly is publicity"[108]

Meanwhile, a younger generation of suffragists had come under the influence of the British leader Emmeline Pankhurst, whose visit in October 1909 electrified the American movement. Subsequently Blatch and her followers adopted tactics that took the suffrage protest out of the parlor and into the streets and public meeting halls.[109] Wealthy suffragist Gertrude Foster Brown has left an account of these sensational activities that turned suffrage into front-page news but dismayed more-conservative supporters. At one demonstration, designed to draw attention to the superiority of educated American-born (white) women over immigrant voters, groups of university women attended Naturalization Court wearing their caps and gowns. "They sat in silent protest as some thirty foreigners, including Russians, Serbs, Turks, and Persians received their final papers, new citizens from whom American women had to beg the vote."[110] On another occasion, Gertrude Brown recounts, she and some friends, dressed in their most beautiful gowns and hats, addressed packed crowds from the stage of a vaudeville theater. She had never set foot in such a place before, let alone stood on the stage. Other actions of these bolder suffragists used the element of surprise to attract an audience. Brown and her friends would drive to various parts of Manhattan in an open automobile, stand up in the back, and deliver impromptu speeches on woman suffrage. Such action conveyed what DuBois calls "a militant challenge to femininity."[111] At other times, fashionably dressed suffragists rode the public transit system all day, holding large signs advocating votes for women. No stunt was too daring if it put the suffrage cause in the newspapers and before the male electorate.

> Even the Goddess of Liberty was enlisted. A yacht full of women held a pageant on her island, and when an actress demanded dramatically, "What says the Goddess?" the statue answered hollowly, "Votes for Women."[112]

"You could be our guardian angel"

Olivia had gone from suffrage advocate to patron, to suffrage celebrity. But would she become the movement's largest donor? She had begun to feel quite detached from the cause. Stanton had died in 1902 and Anthony in 1906, and Olivia was unfamiliar with the new leadership. In May 1907, she subscribed $25,000 to the Susan B. Anthony Memorial Guarantee Fund, but the gift was hedged with conditions. The sum was to be paid at the rate of $4,000 each year from 1907 to 1911 inclusive and was donated "upon express condition that the fact of my subscribing this amount shall remain absolutely confidential to yourselves and to me, and that it shall appear in any published statement as coming simply from a friend."[113]

After 1908, she refused to allow suffrage organizations to use her name on their letterhead.[114] In January 1910, she met Carrie Chapman Catt for the first time and was sufficiently impressed to give her a check for $2,000 toward the campaign in New York State, but she disliked the flamboyant style and tactics of Alva Belmont and suffragists influenced by Pankhurst's Women's Social and Political Union. And she refused Catt's invitation to appear as guest of honor of the Woman Suffrage Party of the City of New York. It was safer to designate her donations for rent than to give discretionary amounts that might be used to produce sensational or shocking displays.[115]

Catt pressed Olivia to come out boldly in support of suffrage. "You have done more for us this year than any other one person," she wrote in 1910, "and we wish to acknowledge that fact publicly."[116] Subsequently, when the suffrage leadership came begging to Olivia, it was for the rent on their headquarters. In 1912, Mary Garrett Hay wrote, "Just now you cannot help us with work, but my dear Mrs. Sage, you could be our Guardian Angel and give us the roof over our heads, while we do this work for all womankind."[117] In November 1913, Catt appealed for $5,000 to cover the rent "until the campaign is over in November 1915."[118] "If bad men do not cheat us out of our victory we are surely going to win in 1915," she added, instructing Olivia's secretary, "Tell Mrs. Sage I sincerely hope that she may have the privilege of casting the first women's vote in New York."[119]

Granted that Olivia might have been confused by new issues that arose within the suffrage movement in this period and by the demands of different factions, her insistence that her gifts to suffrage organizations be anonymous presents a puzzle. Perhaps it was simply a matter of giving discreetly so as not to encourage more begging letters. But if so, then why did she allow her other gifts—to universities, hospitals, and so on—to be made public? Could it be the case that she wanted to keep her support of the suffrage secret not from the press but from Robert de Forest or from her brother? No correspondence from Robert de Forest advocates a gift to any suffrage organization; dozens from him discuss gifts to other entities. Moreover, in the months following Russell Sage's death, de Forest was moving ahead with a grand plan to put Sage money to work. Suffrage organizations and other competing causes would distract the elderly donor at a time when de Forest needed her undivided attention. The grand plan and its results are the subject of the next chapter.

Eleven

Inventing the Russell Sage Foundation

1907

You cannot but admire her loyalty to her husband
and her desire to suppress herself.

—Louisa Lee Schuyler (1907)[1]

The commonly accepted view of the origins of the Russell Sage Foundation divides credit between its brains (Robert de Forest) and its heart (Olivia Sage). "It is fortunate that those who, like Mrs. Sage, have the means and the desire to benefit others, can be reached by men like yourself who can wisely counsel and direct philanthropy into the most effective channels," a colleague wrote ingratiatingly to de Forest in March 1907, attributing intellect and will to de Forest and relegating Olivia to the "natural," the instinctive but untutored benevolence of the essential woman.[2]

In correspondence with Olivia dating from the end of 1906, de Forest proposed a "benevolent trust," a foundation incorporated under state or federal law and administered by trustees appointed for life. Foundations were modeled on business corporations, but unlike corporations organized to make steel, refine petroleum, or sell insurance, they were designed for public purposes.[3] There were several recent precedents, memorials created by the new rich with perpetual funds dedicated to charitable or benevolent purposes. Some, like the Peabody Education Fund, founded in 1867, were devoted to a single purpose such as improving education or building model housing. When Caroline Phelps Stokes drew up her will in June 1893, she directed that her money be placed in the Phelps Stokes Fund and the interest used to build tenement houses "for the poor families of New York City and for educational purposes in the education of Negroes both in Africa and the United States, North American Indians and needy and deserving white students."[4] Others proclaimed a more general purpose. The General Education Board was set up by John D. Rockefeller, Sr., in 1903 to promote education in the United States "without distinction of sex, race or creed."[5] De Forest was already a trustee of two such foundations, Phipps Houses, dedicated to building model tenements, and the Burke Foundation, a more general-purpose foundation which funded convalescent homes.[6]

This chapter revisits the origins of the Russell Sage Foundation and suggests that given all we know about Olivia Sage's life before 1907, particularly her ethic of stewardship and her commitment to public roles for educated women, it makes sense to reimagine the Russell Sage Foundation as a two-parent foundation. Both Olivia and de Forest believed they were stewards for the public at large; both believed they were called to public service. De Forest may have been an "aristocrat," as McClymer says, but he positioned himself as an enlightened middle between irresponsible wealth and wretched poverty. Olivia, too, had no sympathy with "paupers" but neither was she tolerant of the idle rich, and in her essay "Opportunities and Responsibilities of Leisured Women" (1905), she offered a keen-eyed assessment of her own class: "[M]issionaries are needed among the idle rich more than in any other class," she wrote. "A rich woman is not different from a poor woman except in the matter of money, and one of the greatest barriers to her usefulness as a missionary among her less fortunate sisters is her failure to realize this truth."[7] Both principals were reformers by temperament, impatient of delay and optimistic about results. Neither looked to democratic sources of change such as formal politics; both assumed it was the duty of those with money, leisure, and education to invest private wealth to improve public life. Olivia was religiously observant, de Forest less so, but both supported material as well as moral improvement, or rather, they elided the two. The foundation would result from their collaboration.

Russell Sage's bequest could not have come at a better time for Robert de Forest. A philanthropist in his own right and the architect, with Lawrence Veiller, of New York's 1901 tenement house laws, de Forest was at once a social expert, a benevolent aristocrat, and a patrician Progressive with what Judith Sealander calls "a fierce kind of optimism we now find peculiar" and a belief in fact-based policymaking that left little room for skepticism about what facts were or who got to decide.[8] President of the New York Charity Organization Society and former president of the National Conference of Charities and Corrections, the nation's umbrella association of public and private social work organizations, de

Forest was a prominent figure. As discussed earlier, the COS of the early twentieth century, though still run with private monies, had moderated its ban on relief-giving and in other ways reflected a shift toward environmental theories of poverty and to collective rather than individual explanations, a shift long seen by scholars as the hallmark of progressivism. The COS, its personnel, and its ideas would be central to the foundation's early years.[9]

A year or two earlier, in a series of letters to associates such as former New York reform mayor Seth Low, de Forest had proposed an ambitious program of social betterment. He invited Low to join him and a group of friends who would conduct large-scale investigations, "watch experiments and profit by results."[10] In correspondence with COS secretary Edward Devine and other social-welfare experts, he sketched out a large project for the improvement of social conditions. Reform was urgent but it was also within reach, thanks to new techniques for producing and disseminating social knowledge such as the social survey (for "fact-gathering"), and the public exhibition (to disseminate social knowledge). "[A] more flexible, continued medium of information is imperative to make available the underlying facts of social conditions which affect the right living and well being of the community," he wrote.[11]

De Forest viewed poverty as the symptom of a social malady that could be diagnosed, treated, and cured—with sufficient knowledge. Relief was all very well, but "the most effective work is to strike at those conditions which made these families needy, and, so far as possible, remove them," he wrote in January 1907.[12] Easily blending moral and scientistic language, de Forest recommended setting up a new "charities" committee in the COS to put people like himself, with experience and "right thinking," in touch with "those who know first-hand." He envisioned a national network of social investigators, surveyors, settlement workers, and field agents ready to "share their experience and institutions, their methods and their painfully won facts."[13]

"Assume $50 million"

Surviving correspondence allows us to trace how the idea for the foundation evolved. Olivia had already embarked on a spectacular private philanthropy that could wipe out her fortune within a few years. In October 1906, she gave a whopping $294,000 to New York University, and she was planning large gifts to Rensselaer Polytechnic Institute and the Emma Willard School.[14] De Forest would have to move fast. Confident but with a sense of urgency, he began to canvass members of his reform and charity network for suggestions as to how to spend her money. "It has fallen to me to advise Mrs. Sage," he confided to Jeffrey R. Brackett (a director, with Zilpha D. Smith, of the Boston School for Social Workers, founded in 1904). "Assume 50,000,000 dollars, of which 10,000,000 or 15,000,000 is to be devoted distinctly to one purpose, national or local, as a memorial; what would you do with it to accomplish the most good?" Brackett's reply, dashed off by hand in the Boston Union Club, began with an elaborate endorsement of neighborhood houses as "centres of education and social life," with rooms for "all sorts of meetings, for gymnasia, for approved games, with selected caretakers and instructors." These social centers could eventually be taken over by the city.[15] He also suggested an institution on the lines of the Carnegie Institute and the Rockefeller Institute for Research in Medicine "with the aim of getting and spreading knowledge for decreasing human ignorance and ills."[16] De Forest also polled Baltimore COS leaders, including liberal intellectual Daniel Coit Gilman and charity reformer John Glenn. And he sent a draft proposal for a foundation to Edward Devine, who praised the plans as "convincing, comprehensive, and far sighted."[17]

Then he turned to Olivia Sage. His ever-so-patient, ever-so-tactful correspondence with her provides almost our only window on the origins of the foundation. On December 10, 1906, de Forest drafted a twelve-page memorandum called "Suggestions for a Possible Sage Foundation." This now-well-known position paper displays all of de Forest's lawyerly powers of persuasion. There were encouraging precedents for such a foundation in John D. Rockefeller's General Education Fund and the Carnegie Institute, he began. But what should be the object of a Sage foundation? "What sphere of benevolent activity most commends itself to you?" He ruled out founding a new university ("there are enough already"). Did he know that in the 1890s, Olivia and her Emma Willard associates had talked of founding a Willard University, a national university for women in New York City? "Religious propaganda" was also summarily dismissed. If Olivia wished to fund home or foreign missions, she could do so through the church boards (she would, indeed, give millions to these boards in the next few years and in her will).[18]

De Forest proposed a fund that could put its money to work in many different ways, building housing for profit or as a charity; constructing and maintaining community centers; setting up cooperative stores like those in England, "where the necessaries of life . . . might be supplied to the poorer classes at cost, plus a reasonable profit of say six percent"; creating privately funded insurance schemes for workers; or building tuberculosis sanatoria or convalescent homes. It could establish children's playgrounds or institutes for industrial education or build exhibition halls for art or industrial exhibits.[19]

But there were serious objections to a single-purpose foundation. Who could predict what programs would be needed in the future? A foundation "most needed and most beneficent a quarter of a century ago might now, with the shift and change of social conditions, be comparatively useless." Many once-useful schemes became "useless and worse than useless . . . with the constant change and shift of social conditions, and extension, or it may be contraction, of the sphere of government activity." A foundation must be "sufficiently elastic in form and method to work in different ways at different times." The best solution was to secure "the united judgement of the wisest men and women . . . and to put them in a position to carry out whatever plans may seem to them . . . to be wise to meet differing and varying needs."[20]

De Forest then laid out a plan for a "Sage Foundation" for "social betterment." Its task would be "to investigate and study the causes of adverse social conditions, including ignorance, poverty and vice, to suggest how these conditions can be remedied or ameliorated, and to put in operation any means to that end."[21] How much did this reform blueprint represent de Forest's own views rather than Olivia's? He wrote to her, "*Your inclinations, as you have expressed them to me,* have rather tended toward social betterment—improvement of the hard conditions of our working classes; making their homes and surroundings more healthful and comfortable and their lives happier; giving more of opportunity to them and their children." Evidently there had been discussions between them about how she might use her money to bring about improvements in the living and working conditions of ordinary people. "With all her heart she desires great things," journalist Arthur Huntington Gleason reported in November 1906, "[and] to deal wisely and sanely by the trust committed into her hands."[22]

Had Olivia seized on the idea of large-scale philanthropy, a vision she now shared with de Forest and that his letter now reflected back to her? Or was de Forest presenting Olivia with plans for the foundation that were his alone, merely pretending to endorse her views ("your ideas for a Russell Sage foundation"), flattering and soothing the elderly woman on whose goodwill he depended but who in turn depended on his legal expertise and his connections?[23]

Two important but overlooked contemporary accounts suggest some answers. The first, a journalist's account of his visit to her home in 1906, shows Olivia weighing schemes to put her money to work, preparing herself for large-scale philanthropy by reading up about all kinds of ideas for social betterment, social experiments, and plans of educational reform. "Her rooms look like the city room of a newspaper," this author wrote. "They are the abode of a worker—full of letters, pamphlets, newspapers, and magazines. There is also a filing system for letters, and drawers for newspaper clippings on woman suffrage, . . . [experiments in school reform], *Journal* editorials, and the triumphal progress of Miss Helen Gould. . . . She is more than a reader, she is a student of the daily paper," he noted.[24]

Olivia was reading voraciously. Along with the New York newspapers, the *Woman's Journal,* and the evangelical mission magazines, she collected the annual reports of dozens of reform and charitable organizations—and later donated them to the New York Public Library.[25] She was also devouring the ideas of bold new thinkers such as the anthropologist and sex radical Elsie Clews Parsons, whose first book *The Family* would be denounced by the *New York Daily Tribune* in November 1906 for its "disgusting theory" about open marriage. In *Charities and the Commons,* the social work journal, Olivia read the debate over idle women and girls, including Elsie Clews Parsons' much-discussed essay, "A Plan for Girls with Nothing to Do." The essay struck a chord with Olivia, who was immersed in reading about schemes for girls' trade schools and the general problem of helping unmarried women to become self-supporting.[26]

The second source, Olivia's essay "Opportunities and Responsibilities of Leisured Women," confirms the 1906 portrait. In this essay, which she wrote as her husband slipped into senility and signed "M. Olivia Sage," she declares her intention to put her resources to use for the public good: "[W]oman is responsible in proportion to the wealth and time at her command. While one woman is working for bread and butter, the other must devote her time to the amelioration of the condition of her laboring sister. This is the moral law."[27] "Opportunities and Responsibilities of Leisured Women" has not been taken seriously as a blueprint for Sage philanthropy, but perhaps it should be compared to Carnegie's essay "Wealth" (1889) or John D. Rockefeller's *Random Reminiscences of Men and Events* (1909). It offers a window into her motivation as she began her philanthropy. Even the title, "Opportunities and Responsibilities," nicely captures the dual aspects of Sage philanthropy as both self-realization and duty.[28]

In February 1907, Robert de Forest sounded an anxious note in a now-famous memo "intended to supplement previous letters on what may be called your philanthropic problem." Her recent donations amounting to over $2 million were no more than the yearly income from her fortune, de Forest warned her, advising, "You can readily afford to give two or three millions, or even a larger amount, each year." Several broad categories of need demanded her attention: first, "the personal and family wants of strangers"; second, demands from relatives, acquaintances, or people claiming connection to the Emma Willard School; and third, institutions, 4,000 of which had already appealed to her. The begging letters from "strangers" were being handled by the Sage Fund, he reminded her, while the demands from organizations and institutions had been abstracted to help her decide which to fund. She should continue her private philanthropy and keep on giving "slowly and deliberately as you have been doing during the past few months."[29]

But all these worthy causes paled before the great opportunity for philanthropy of the kind they had discussed, namely "*to carry out your idea of a Russell Sage Foundation*, placing in the hands of a benevolent society, which you found, and in which you associate with yourself certain select persons as advisors, a large principal sum, the income of which is to be used for the improvement of social conditions."[30] "Your wishes would determine the application of that income during your lifetime," de Forest assured her. "Organizing the Foundation is a matter for your lawyer. Choosing the charities is your own affair—and in my opinion, the hardest part of the whole undertaking."[31]

This was misleading, to say the least. De Forest was at the same time sounding out the social work and reform communities for *their* recommendations. He canvassed experts in New York and beyond, including charity expert Frederick Wines; Superintendent of Chicago Charities Ernest Bicknell; Robert Hill, secretary of the New York State Board of Charities; and housing reformer Lawrence Veiller.[32] To Edward Devine, de Forest wrote asking for a list of suggestions for projects the foundation should undertake, "preferably numbered in the order in which you give them importance." He promised Devine that the foundation "could be made, within the national sphere, the same center for charitable and philanthropic information as the C.O. societies makes [sic] for the city of New York." The foundation would fund the social work journal *Charities and the Commons* (Devine was editor), which in turn would publicize the foundation's work.[33]

The next step was to select the trustees. In the 1890s, Olivia had complained about the male governors of the Woman's Hospital. And she had scornfully dismissed the tradition of an all-male board of trustees for the Emma Willard School.[34] Now she had the right of refusal of trustees for the foundation, and she would use it. She blocked the nomination of Levi P. Morton, a former business partner of her husband's, and demanded instead Robert C. Ogden, president of the Southern Education Board, a trustee of Tuskegee Institute and Hampton Institute, and president of the Southern Educational Association.[35] It was March before de Forest had a list of the names that Olivia had "definitely approved."[36]

Since Olivia's influence over the direction taken by the foundation in its first decades followed partly as a consequence of her choice of trustees, it is worth taking a closer look at them. Most were members of the New York charity elite: de Forest himself, Cleveland Dodge, Gertrude Rice, Louisa Schuyler, and Helen Gould. Baltimore attorney John Glenn and Daniel Coit Gilman completed the Russell Sage Foundation (RSF) board.[37]

Gilman, president of Johns Hopkins University and an early member of the American Social Science Association, president of the Slater Fund, trustee of the Peabody Education Fund, and first president of the Carnegie Institution, was chosen for his intellectual weight and expertise. Other trustees were chosen for more personal reasons. Cleveland H. Dodge, the foundation's treasurer, was the son of Olivia's old friend Sara Dodge and the inheritor of a family tradition of noblesse oblige. He was the grandson of William E. Dodge (nicknamed "the American Shaftesbury" in acknowledgment of his philanthropic activities) and heir to the huge copper conglomerate of Phelps, Dodge, and Company, which was capitalized in 1908 at $50 million.[38] He was vice president of the New York Chamber of Commerce; president of the board of trustees of the YMCA; a trustee of Princeton University, the Carnegie Institution, and the John F. Slater Fund; a member of the governing board of the New York chapter of the American National Red Cross; and a trustee of the Museum of Natural History.[39] Ties of affection linked the Dodges to the Sages, and so did overlapping charitable commitments. Cleveland Dodge's sister, Grace Dodge, had launched her public career in 1876 under the tutelage of Louisa Schuyler in the State Charities Aid Association and was now associated with Olivia Sage and Helen Gould on the International Board of the YWCA. Cleveland and Grace Dodge were supporters, like Olivia, of the American College for Girls at Constantinople. Olivia Sage and Sara Dodge had jointly pledged over half a million dollars in private funds for the 28th Street Y, international headquarters of the YMCA.[40]

Other trustees were veterans of social service work. John Glenn had long been a leader in the Baltimore COS and served as president of the National Conference of Charities and Corrections in 1901. Gertrude Rice and Louisa Schuyler, both now in their seventies, were women of impressive administrative experience in New York public and private charities. Louisa Schuyler had first become prominent in public life as a leader in the Civil War–era Woman's Central Association of Relief at the age of twenty-four. Mannish and commanding with her "erect figure and rather formidable manner," she struck people as "a great personage."[41] Both Schuyler and Rice had served on the Central Council of the NYCOS in the 1880s with Robert de Forest, and their State Charities Aid Association wielded so much power over private and public welfare agencies that they were known (along with Josephine Shaw Lowell, who had died in 1905) as the "Big Three" of New York charity.[42] Adding Helen Gould ensured that the foundation would have an unusually large number of female trustees. Yet evidence of Gould's participation in the foundation is elusive. She was out of the country when it was being set up, and a long letter that she sent Olivia from Luxor, Egypt, is full of details about sightseeing on the Nile and her plans to go with some Christian missionaries into the homes of Egyptian women. Did she have the foundation—or evangelical missions—in mind when she wrote to Olivia in March 1907, "I am so grateful to you for interesting me in work that is sweet and good and sensible"?[43]

Historian Nancy Hewitt reminds us that particular philanthropic ventures are shaped by "gender, racial, ethnic, and class relations rooted in structures of social, political, and economic power."[44] The interconnected charity elite of New York, Baltimore, and Boston formed the intellectual context for the Russell Sage Foundation, and the all-male clubs such as the University Club, the Union Club of Boston, and the Century Club of Baltimore formed its social context.[45] But so also did the parlors and drawing rooms of upper-class benevolent women such as Olivia Sage and genteel experts and activists such as Gertrude Rice, Louisa Schuyler, and Josephine Shaw Lowell, women who had entered public service during and after the Civil War and who in the years following remained outside formal politics while working through the COS and similar semi-public organizations.[46]

Once the foundation's bill of incorporation went to the New York State legislature in April 1907, a confident Robert de Forest drafted "Mrs. Sage's Statement for the Press," and began to write to prospective trustees, formally inviting them to serve.[47] The Russell Sage Foundation was subsequently incorporated under the Laws of the State of New York, 1907, Chapter 140.[48]

John Glenn's response was ecstatic. "My dear Bre'r Rabbit," he wrote to de Forest, "I cannot possibly express my joy, I would like to have a chance to hug you. . . . It is delightful to think of being closely allied with you in such a splendid opportunity and responsibility."[49] Glenn accepted the post of director and secretary of the foundation at $8,000 a year. His wife, Mary Willcox Brown Glenn, general secretary of the Baltimore COS, also joined the foundation staff, bringing with her social work expert Mary Richmond to head the foundation's Charity Organization Department.[50]

Louisa Schuyler's response to de Forest's invitation was much more tentative: she was not sure she was the right person for the job, she wrote modestly, for her work had always been "assisting public service through voluntary aid," as in the United States Sanitary Commission. But she welcomed the chance to work with Gertrude Rice, for they had been "friends and fellow workers all our lives."[51]

Religious antecedents went unacknowledged in the foundation's mandate and its public image, for the act of incorporation stated its purpose in broadly secular terms, but the evangelical tradition was strongly represented by the Glenns, by Gould and Dodge, and by Olivia herself. John Glenn, whose earlier philanthropic work had included Protestant home missions work in West Virginia, exemplifies how the foundation linked reform networks with distinct philanthropic traditions and experience. His biographer Shelby Harrison explained: "Glenn liked that aspect of the American missionary movement, home and foreign, which had traditionally combined some material aid and lifting of the general standard of living with the teachings of faith and religion." Of Mary Willcox Glenn, a colleague wrote, "Her activities for social work were part of her religion."[52] Historian David Hollinger characterizes these hybrid Progressives as men and women who believed in "the moral efficacy of social science."[53]

Foundation decision-making is often characterized as informal and closed, and in the years before the reforms associated with the Patman inquiry of the 1960s it was even more so.[54] Insularity characterized the RSF in its first decades, and a feeling of informality, of a small group of old friends coming together for one more project, adheres to the account of the first trustees' meeting on April 19, 1907, the meeting to adopt the constitution and organize the corporation. Here, in Olivia's Fifth Avenue home, the trustees adopted the charter offered by Robert de Forest and its statement of purpose, namely, to maintain a fund and apply the income to "the improvement of the social and living conditions in the United States of America . . . to use any means for that end which from time to time shall seem expedient . . . including research, publication, education, the establishment and maintenance of charitable or benevolent activities, agencies and institutions, and the aid of any such activities, agencies or institutions already established."[55]

The meeting began decorously enough with the saying of the Lord's Prayer. But it ended in a most uncharacteristic outburst when the foundation's president, Mrs. Russell Sage, declared, "I am nearly eighty years old and I feel as though I were just beginning to live"![56] The exclamation of pleasure and anticipation was also one of relief. She had set aside $10 million to endow a foundation for social betterment. The legal papers were complete, the trustees were selected, the foundation was incorporated, and the work could begin. No wonder she was thrilled.

But the letter of gift of the same date transferring $10 million in securities and cash from Sage to the foundation contained two significant changes from earlier proposals. The letter retained the instruction that the principal was to be invested and the income applied to "the improvement of social and living conditions in the United States of America."[57] But it specified that no less than one-quarter of the income at any time could be applied to "the needs of my own city and its vicinity"—this concession to Olivia's desire to concentrate on New York was a departure from de Forest's wish to create programs with national impact.[58] A close reading of the letter also shows a disagreement between the two over investment of RSF funds in income-producing schemes, so-called investment philanthropy, which de Forest favored. In an unusually blunt expression of dissent, the donor stated:

> I have had some hesitation as to whether the Foundation should be able to make investments for social betterment which should themselves produce income, as for instance small houses or tenements. . . . I realize that investments for social betterment, even if producing some income, may not produce a percentage as large as that produced by bonds . . . and that the income of the Foundation might be therefore diminished by such investments.[59]

But then she conceded, "If I fail to give the Foundation powers in this respect it may be unable to initiate or establish important agencies or initiatives."[60] Having aired her disagreement with de Forest in the letter of gift, she went on to grant the foundation this power anyway, with the condition that these activities should yield at least 3 percent and that no more than one-fourth of the principal should be invested at one time. (De Forest had wanted the trustees to be able to invest one-half of the capital.)

This provision allowed the trustees to experiment with model housing that would bring a modest return on investment along with a more significant social return. It allowed de Forest to launch Forest Hills Gardens in Queens, New York. Looking back from 1947, the foundation's historians recalled the plan's idealism: "to exemplify some of the possibilities of intelligent town planning," to create a new community with "healthful, attractive and solidly built homes . . . convenient thoroughfares, quiet domestic streets, and ample public spaces."[61] But Forest Hills Gardens "entirely failed . . . to earn any profit for the foundation (in fact it lost about $300,000)," according to historian David Hammack. The experiment would absorb as much as one-quarter of the foundation's capital by 1922.[62]

No political row erupted in the nation over the incorporation of the Russell Sage Foundation like the one that marked the struggle over the Rockefeller Foundation a few years later.[63] Messages of congratulations poured in, though not always from disinterested sources. "Allow me to join with the nation in thanking you for your great gift toward making this world better and hastening the millennium," Syracuse fund-raiser James Phelps wrote to Olivia Sage.[64] Experts and intellectuals penned enthusiastic testimonials in the RSF-funded organ *Charities and the Commons*, a whole issue of which was devoted to the foundation (May 11, 1907).[65] De Forest made a revealing comment. "I had expected criticism on the grounds of vagueness of purpose," he confided to Veiller. "The truth is, the vagueness of purpose was the very fundamental idea of the Foundation." At the same time the level-headed de Forest admitted that he felt "appalled" by the great task ahead, "[v]ery enthusiastic about the possibilities, and at the same time sober with regard to the responsibilities."[66]

In the months that followed, the trustees went about inventing the foundation, constructing an organization, and deciding on the grants. They established Departments of Child Hygiene, Recreation, Education, Statistics, Child Helping, Southern Highlands, Remedial Loans, Charity Organization, Industrial Studies, and Surveys and Exhibits. They launched an Editorial Department, renamed the Publications Department in 1917.[67] The Russell Sage Foundation made external as well as internal grants, sometimes charging its own staff with research tasks, at other times using outside experts. The most famous of its investigative studies, the Pittsburgh Survey, was a remarkable demonstration of the use of social science research to document the impact of industrialization on a whole region.[68]

"Her desire to suppress herself"

De Forest later claimed that "having established the Foundation and turned over its management to trustees of her choice, [Olivia Sage] never thought to direct their action, except in a single instance, and that was in urging that a permanent home be built for the Foundation."[69] Did he downplay her role? Scholars have suggested that a major goal of the Progressives was a rewriting of history that emphasized the rupture between their modernist project and the past and that for men such as de Forest, Glenn, and Devine, foundation funding meant independence not only from corrupt politicians but also from the traditional purveyors of charity, the "ladies bountiful" whose giving was too often prompted only by sentiment, not guided by science.[70] These twin enemies of progress could endanger the cause of scientifically based reform, de Forest warned Devine in March 1907: "There is a real danger to our cause from a union of mushy philanthropy and self-seeking politics."[71]

Progressives such as de Forest dismissed the tradition of female voluntarism and benevolence that had funded both the foundation and its significant projects. Gendering charity as female (disorderly, sentimental, and labile), they condemned modes of giving that were traditionally women's and consigned the Lady Bountiful figure to the past. When Paul U. Kellogg had to choose a name for a new journal of social work in 1906 he rejected the title "Charities" as appealing primarily to "spinsters and society ladies," and chose *The Survey* instead.[72] As the authority of social science increased, the contribution of Olivia Sage faded from memory. A remarkable cartoon illustrates this disappearing act. It shows Paul Kellogg approaching the foundation, which the cartoonist personifies as Glenn, an old man seated on a kind of throne labeled "Sage." It graphically illustrates Olivia's near-disappearance from the foundation's official history (see fig. 11.1).

Olivia herself was partly to blame. Shown a draft copy of "Suggestions for a Possible Sage Foundation" in December 1906, she added in pen, "Russell" making it "Russell Sage Foundation."[73] Urged to reconsider, she insisted that the foundation was a memorial to her husband and that it should bear his name only. De Forest commented to Louisa Schuyler, "You cannot but admire her loyalty to her husband and her desire to suppress herself."[74]

Olivia had more influence than the cartoon or de Forest's statement suggests. She held the title of president of the foundation from 1907 to 1918. And meetings of the executive committee during 1907 and 1908 took place at her New York home or, in the summer, at Lawrence, Long Island.[75] She usually presided at these meetings even when de Forest was present, as in April 1910. She also chaired the committee in his absence in March and April 1908. (From October 1908 to the spring of 1910 she was away in Sag Harbor and the minutes included the formulaic "Mrs.

FIGURE 11.1. Cartoon showing the Sage Foundation personified by John Glenn, with Paul Kellogg the persistent applicant. Note the disappearance of Olivia Sage. Paul Kellogg Supplement Collection, Social Welfare History Archives, University of Minnesota.

Sage sent regrets.") Glenn described the process of decision-making at the foundation as personal and informal. No detailed or formal records were kept of the discussions of this small coterie of friends, many of whom had worked together for decades, and the committee's minutes are a bare summary of attendance and decisions reached.[76] Minutes do not seem to have been kept for the executive committee meetings during the summer of 1907, for example, even though the trustees decided on expenditures totaling $71,300. Without a record of these discussions it is even more difficult to assess Olivia's contribution.[77]

Where evidence about trustee discussions has survived, we see Olivia taking part in the decision-making. At one meeting she moved to recommend a request from the State Charities Aid Association for an appropriation of $5,000 for ambulance and hospital service in New York City.[78] At the May 1908 meeting, she made a motion to recommend an appropriation of $5,000 for the Committee on the Prevention of Blindness of the New York Association for the Blind. And she prevailed on the foundation trustees to hold in trust two favorite institutions, Susanna Hospital in Guam, to which she gave $10,000, and the Russell Sage Institute of Pathology located on Blackwell's Island, which she endowed with $300,000. The institute focused on research into the diseases of old age and served a mainly indigent population.[79]

We now know that Olivia followed the activities of the foundation even in her very old age and considered its work an extension of her own personal philanthropy. For example, by appointing Helen Gould and Cleveland Dodge as trustees she had taken steps to integrate the moral reform mission of the YMCA and YWCA movement into the foundation itself. The education and moral training of young men and women now became a matter for the experts at the foundation: the economists in the Statistics Department, the recreation specialists in the child hygiene department, the cost-of-living and industrial relations experts in the Industrial Studies Department. Her private donations to the Ys fell off proportionately. In response to an appeal on behalf of the YMCA in 1917, her secretary replied that "as she has given something more than a million to them she feels it is impossible to take the matter further."[80]

She encouraged the activities of the Playground Association of America headed by Luther Gulick, director of the RSF Department of Child Hygiene from 1909 to 1912, and pursued a parallel program in her private philanthropy in Sag Harbor, using foundation experts.[81] When Gulick's successor Joseph Lee appealed to her for help setting up a separate million-dollar foundation devoted just to recreation, she refused on the grounds that she already supported the cause of children and playgrounds through the foundation.[82] The foundation's moralistic "play philosophy" coincided with Olivia's views, which included distaste for vulgar commercial entertainment and enthusiastic sponsorship of civic pageants and commemorations. Foundation programs under Gulick and Lee promoted recreation as part of a civic religion. Their efforts to develop playgrounds and organized recreation laid the groundwork for state-sponsored, tax-supported children's recreation in the 1920s and after.[83]

Another of Olivia's favorite causes, girls' education, also received some support from early foundation grants. When she was polled by de Forest in April 1907 about where the foundation should direct its efforts, Gertrude Rice suggested investment in girls' trade schools as "these would appeal to Mrs. Sage." Accordingly, the trustees made a grant of $10,000 to the Manhattan Trade School for Girls in January 1908.[84] Higher education was specifically excluded from the foundation's mandate, however, and Olivia's giving to colleges and universities took place entirely through her private philanthropy.[85]

Other RSF grants and activities show the enthusiasms of the various trustees. Investigations into women's working conditions conducted by Mary van Kleeck's Department of Industrial Studies, Women's Work, for example, and Margaret Byington's investigation of Pittsburgh households for the Pittsburgh Survey, *Homestead: Households of a Mill Town* (1910), were significant reform efforts.[86] The foundation's Remedial Loans Department, a pet project of de Forest, was a development of his Provident Loan Society, although the idea of teaching thrift to the working classes situates the RSF in an older charity tradition than, say, the Twentieth Century Foundation, which recognized the importance of consumer credit for middle- and working-class people.[87]

One of the foundation's first grants went to the New York Association for the Blind, a cause passionately embraced by John Glenn as well as by Louisa Schuyler.[88] De Forest favored support for tuberculosis prevention work, and the first RSF grants for tuberculosis education were made as early as May 1907.[89] Support for housing and urban planning stemmed from the reform commitments of de Forest, Alfred T. White, and Lawrence Veiller, as did the work of the Surveys and Exhibits Department (founded in 1912).[90] Other trustees, notably Robert Ogden and John Glenn, directed foundation interest toward education in the South. Louisa Schuyler recommended aiding the Public Education Association of New York City, which was promoting kindergarten and industrial training, and the State Charities Aid Association of New York, which Schuyler headed, received nearly $900,000 between 1907 and 1947.[91] Still other initiatives sprang from the minds of idiosyncratic progressives such as Leonard P. Ayres, director of RSF's Division of Education, and John C. Campbell, director of the Southern Highlands Department, with a variety of outcomes, from triumphant demonstration projects to ill-conceived fiascos.[92]

De Forest's own ambitious and expensive projects were generously funded. When it was proposed in 1909 that the foundation should loan the enormous sum of $1.4 million at 5 percent to a newly created Sage

Foundation Homes Company, the minutes record a discussion only on the matter of the project's name, a decision graciously left up to Olivia. On this issue, de Forest accorded her only a symbolic role.[93]

To California!

An outpouring of generosity such as Olivia had shown should leave the giver contented, fulfilled, at peace. Instead, Olivia was anxious and restless. Early in February 1910, she left New York for California by train for a rest and change of scene, accompanied by her nephew, Stephen L'Hommedieu Slocum. In Pasadena she enjoyed daily outings, walking to the golf course or watching tennis, according to one account; others reported her suffering from a "nervous condition."[94] On the return journey, she carried out a sort of philanthropic mission for Robert de Forest: her purchase of a collection of Navajo textiles from a Pasadena dealer and another of Navajo blankets at the Grand Canyon on her way home were probably at his urging, for when she returned to New York in May she immediately donated them to the Metropolitan Museum of Art. The secretary to the museum who politely acknowledged her gift was none other than Robert de Forest.[95] Even on this vacation she gave several philanthropic donations, including gifts to the Pasadena Associated Charities (the COS) and the Pasadena YWCA. It was her only journey west, so far as we know, and it was probably her last trip of any consequence.[96]

Perhaps this travel was too much for her, for in January 1911 she was reported to be ailing. Thinking the end was near, de Forest fired off a letter to Harvard's President Lowell. If you are hoping for a donation for the university, he wrote, "frankly I would move as quickly as possible."[97] But Olivia rallied. Newspapers reported that she was not gravely ill after all, and soon she was spotted in Central Park, feeding the squirrels and birds as usual—the habits of a time when thrifty pleasures were the only ones available.[98]

And Olivia now found the strength to stand up to de Forest over the question of a building for the foundation, which he had consistently opposed. Up to this point the foundation had occupied two offices at 30 Broad Street—the law offices of the de Forest brothers. Olivia wanted the foundation to be housed in a building that would memorialize her husband.[99] A letter to an old friend who had recently been widowed suggests that she was missing her husband and supports the idea that she sought a public memorial to him. "[T]o have one so loved and loving torn from you is the saddest, saddest blow on earth. Do I not know it and in knowing am I not fully prepared to feel for you?" she wrote.[100]

By the winter of 1911–1912, de Forest could no longer ignore her pleas. The site, at Lexington Avenue and East 22nd Street, one block from the United Charities Building, was purchased in February 1912 at a cost of over $200,000. Grosvenor Atterbury designed the nine-story building, which was realized in the Italian Renaissance style. Carved panels held symbolic figures: over the front door stood Service, flanked by Study and Counsel. Other figures symbolized, on one side of the building, Religion, Education, Civics, and Justice, and on the other, Health, Work, Play, and Housing. The building would eventually absorb about 8 percent of the foundation's original capital.[101] All the departments moved there, except the Southern Highlands Department, in December 1913. The building also provided space for other foundation-supported charitable and social service associations such as the New York Association for the Blind and for public meetings. The two top floors were set aside for a specialized library for social work and social science. Collections belonging to the COS and the State Charities Aid Association were combined, and by 1917 there were almost 17,000 bound volumes. The library became a major resource for social scientists and social workers, with 50,000 volumes and 200,000 unbound items.[102]

There is no record of Olivia attending an executive committee meeting after October 1910, but fund-raisers and perhaps also the public continued to see the foundation as an expression of her intentions. "I have often wished to tell you how much our secretaries depend upon Mrs. Glenn and Miss Van Kleeck for advice and help in our various problems," a YWCA leader wrote to Olivia, interpreting foundation support of reformed recreation as a direct expression of the founder's wishes. Without correspondence between Olivia and van Kleeck or the other trustees, these connections remain elusive.[103]

Gender and Policymaking at the RSF

The Russell Sage Foundation was among a handful of foundations established by and presided over by a woman, and in its first decade it seemed a "feminized" foundation, with Olivia Sage its president and four female trustees chosen by her—more than served on any other foundation board.[104] In addition, several notable women were hired to head its departments. Mary Richmond directed the Charity Organization Department and Mary van Kleeck headed the Industrial Studies Department.[105] The RSF also hired female experts to conduct research investigations as a preliminary to reform; for example, the brilliant Crystal Eastman, a Ph.D. economist who authored *Work Accidents and the*

Law for the RSF's Pittsburgh Survey before moving to an RSF-funded position at the New York State Commission on Employers' Liability Insurance (and later into feminist and pacifist circles in Greenwich Village). Social scientists Margaret Byington and Elizabeth Beardsley Butler each produced a volume for the Pittsburgh Survey.[106]

At a time when most academic research positions were closed to women and as the settlements (significant loci of reform activism earlier) became increasingly marginalized in the 1920s, the RSF provided an institutional home for female social scientists in the Progressive era and after World War I, when in many institutions the tide was running against them.[107] Mary Richmond stayed for most of her professional life, as did Mary van Kleeck, who worked there for forty years until her retirement in 1948. Moreover, female experts who came into the foundation brought with them contacts with women's voluntary and reform associations. The foundation thus put resources into schemes associated with the women's reform agenda labeled by scholars as "maternalist."[108] The authors of the Pittsburgh Survey volumes showed particular interest in women as victims of industrialization. *Homestead: Households of a Mill Town*, authored by Margaret Byington, argued for protection of working girls and mothers and imposed a middle-class, male-breadwinner model on poor families.[109]

Yet no generalization covers the various women associated with the foundation as trustees or as experts. They were of different generations and different life experiences. In 1907, Schuyler and Rice were in their seventies, Richmond was forty-six, Eastman twenty-five, van Kleeck twenty-four. Several, such as Mary Willcox Brown Glenn and Mary van Kleeck, exemplified the combination of religious idealism and belief in social science.[110] Van Kleeck, who began her reform career in Social Gospel and settlement activism, would evolve through Taylorism to the Stalinism of her later years.[111] Both Rice and Schuyler rejected same-sex separatist organizations. Schuyler wrote, "I like . . . the plan of having men and women working together on the same Board. I have always worked so, all my life, and it works well."[112] Mary Richmond exemplified the new female professionals who rarely explained their policies in terms of gender, though they often used female networks and support. Even those who were female-identified worked with male allies.

Yet their careers significantly advanced the opportunities for other women. Richmond's work, for example, would make possible professional careers for a significant number of women as social workers and social experts. They would enter the Social Service School of the University of Chicago and other academic departments of sociology or economics, find paid positions in government agencies such as the Children's Bureau, and join foundation staffs.[113] In the 1920s, when antistatism fueled antifeminism and conservatives attacked female-dominated institutions such as the U.S. Department of Labor's Children's Bureau, the RSF was still a beachhead of female social scientists, with Mary van Kleeck, Mary Richmond, and Joanna Colcord still on staff.[114]

How the presence of women trustees and social scientists at the RSF affected the topics studied and projects funded, and consequently the production of social knowledge, and how gender affected policymaking are questions that require a fuller discussion than belongs here.[115] Others have explored the consequences for social science of women's entry into the paid professions in the early twentieth century.[116] They have shown how female practitioners helped shape gender because as experts they prioritized different definitions of the social good, whether from conviction, from personal experience, or, as seems likely, from opportunism, namely that on certain topics (such as children's welfare) their knowledge was seen as legitimate, their voices heard. Gender thus affected policymaking, and social policies in turn shaped gender.[117]

Here it is enough to note that although the foundation's first trustees were benevolent aristocrats and genteel charity reformers, in staffing the research and other departments they drew a younger generation of social experts from other reform communities—not only the COS, but also academic social science, the settlements, and Social Gospel reform circles. The foundation thus amplified communities of women reformers, funding many of their schemes and giving them a base outside the state and outside academia from which to develop social programs for workers and their families.

As the original trustees died or retired, men replaced women. Louisa Schuyler and Gertrude Rice remained trustees until their deaths in 1926 within a few months of each other. Helen Gould stayed. On January 22, 1913, she had married Finley Johnson Shepard. Both were in their forties. The couple subsequently adopted three orphans, two girls and a boy, and raised a second boy as a foster child. Helen continued her activities in dozens of benevolent, charitable, religious, and patriotic societies, remaining an RSF trustee, but an increasingly conservative one, until February 1936, a few months before her death.[118]

The foundation's importance is clear 100 years later. By funding investigations of social and industrial conditions, initiatives in urban planning, child welfare, and public health, the Russell Sage Foundation played a significant role in the development of America's welfare state in the years before the New Deal. Foundation funding also set up the framework of modern social work education and professional practice. It launched and subsidized *The Survey,* the major publication for social work professionals. The charter of the RSF specified its purpose in very general terms as "the improvement of the social and living conditions in the United States of America," and if this broad mandate did not mention working conditions, the omission was corrected when the RSF took up and funded the investigation of industrial work, beginning with the Pittsburgh Survey, an investigation into the impact of industry on the lives of the steel workers and their families and communities. Energized by an overoptimistic and very typical turn-of-the-century expectation that exposure would produce reform, RSF-funded research investigations often seemed destined to remain just that—investigation.[119] Nevertheless, the RSF brought experts and researchers together to gather and publish data that would form the basis for regulation of wages and hours, workers' compensation, pensions, and collective bargaining. Its work contributed to improving health and safety conditions in workplaces and communities.[120]

Progressivism as a label is notoriously elusive, but optimism, the sense of urgency, the willingness to look at new institutional forms and new techniques, the faith in experts rather than in democratic or grass-roots impulses would meet most common definitions of early-twentieth-century Progressivism, and by that measure, this old/new institution, incorporated under the laws of New York and dedicated to public purposes but with its roots in nineteenth-century voluntarism, was undeniably Progressive.[121] And in the next generation, as social experts replaced benevolent philanthropists and as nonsectarian agencies came to outnumber religious agencies, the structure of the think tank remained: part of the new institutional arrangements where social scientists could shape society, not just explain it.[122]

The Russell Sage Foundation, Olivia Sage's most significant achievement, emerged from her collaboration with Robert de Forest between October 1906 and April 1907. De Forest was charming, considerate, discreet, supremely confident in his knowledge of the law and finance, and in his class position. Each depended on the other: he needed the Sage millions to achieve his reform goals, she in turn depended on him to put her money to work. Socially insecure and emotionally "needy," she was no match for de Forest—she would be overwhelmed in the end, not so much by his bullying as by his consummate charm. It was a sign of what was to come when, as early as February 1908, she amended her will (written the previous October) to bequeath over one-seventh of her entire estate to the foundation, making it her largest institutional legatee. The foundation would receive $5.4 million when the will was probated in November 1918. This increased its endowment to $15 million.[123] She also gave the foundation Marsh Island, Louisiana, a bird sanctuary with an area of 75,000 acres which she had purchased in August 1913 and which later proved a godsend to the foundation when oil and gas were found there.[124]

But this is to get ahead of my story. For now, with the foundation established, Olivia Sage, restored to health and strength, launched into the delightful business of spending what remained of her money without the intermediary of the foundation, its trustees, or its experts. It was the spring of 1907, and at seventy-nine Olivia felt she was "just beginning to live."

Twelve

"Women and education—there is the key"

If we use our plant and professors somewhat as Radcliffe
College uses Harvard or Barnard College uses Columbia you
could tell Mrs. Sage to organize here the best woman's college
in the world.

—Henry M. MacCracken (1898)[1]

At the same time that the Russell Sage Foundation was being established, Olivia began to respond to the thousands of appeals directed to her. What causes would she support? The public expected the widow of Russell Sage to give large amounts to good causes of all kinds, but especially to women's education. One sympathetic observer believed he had the answer: "Women and education—there is the key."[2] Olivia's essay of 1905 had repeated the view common among advocates of the suffrage: that educated women would provide the moral leadership abdicated by men and that women's entry into full citizenship by means of the suffrage would transform the public sphere.[3] Because Olivia was known as an advocate of women's advancement, expectations were high that she would make some significant donations to women's education. She believed that women's education was as necessary for the general reform of society as woman suffrage: educated women would provide the moral leadership abdicated by men, just as enfranchised women would bring maternal values into public life.[4]

And indeed within just a few weeks of her husband's death, Olivia had made three large donations for education: $294,000 to New York University in October 1906, $1 million to the Emma Willard School in December 1906, and half a million to Troy Polytechnic (Rensselaer Polytechnic Institute, or RPI) in January 1907. After thinking about it for a while, she doubled her gift to RPI. There were also several large gifts to Syracuse University. These were all gifts that expressed sentiment, memorialized family ties, or rewarded long associations. The donation of $1 million to the Emma Willard School was an expression of her "personal relations of long standing with the Emma Willard School as pupil and trustee," she explained in the letter accompanying the donation."[5] The money enabled the school to build an entirely new campus on a site overlooking the city of Troy—the beautiful Gothic Revival campus that is there today. The Emma Willard School moved there in 1910.[6]

But as she considered which other universities, colleges, and schools to support, Olivia faced a bewildering array of choices. Should she found a single great institution, a Sage University for Women in the East, as the University of Chicago was Mr. Rockefeller's university in the West? Should she support the coeducational universities like Syracuse and Cornell, limit her gifts to women's colleges like Vassar, or support coordinate colleges like Barnard, founded in 1889 as the female coordinate of Columbia? And what about all the trade and professional schools for women that were clamoring for money? In an earlier chapter, we saw that when the financial officer from Syracuse University called on her in May 1906, he found her anxiously weighing these questions. He reported to the university president, "She inquired very minutely about the working of coeducation with us."[7]

"This is the best work women of wealth can do"

Historian Margaret Rossiter has described how some wealthy women made their donations to universities conditional on the admission of women or in other ways tried to use philanthropy to leverage new opportunities for women. Some examples of such "creative and coercive spending" will be familiar to readers, and they were familiar to Olivia Sage.[8] Philanthropists funded the era's most famous reform institution, Hull House. Its major financial supporter in its early years, apart from Jane Addams herself, was her friend and partner Mary Rozet Smith. Another female civic leader and elite reformer, Louise de Koven Bowen, gave the settlement house $297,777 between 1904 and 1914.[9]

Wealthy female donors also supplied funding for fellowships to help younger women pursue careers in new fields as juvenile court officers, visiting nurses, and social workers.[10] The Association of Collegiate Alumnae supplies an example of such creative philanthropy by educated women of means. The association supported several women scientists and social scientists studying for their doctorates in Germany at a time when no American graduate school would admit them.[11] Mary van Kleeck, who would become a leading social expert at the Russell Sage Foundation, was a beneficiary of such a scholarship.[12]

Another example of how women's philanthropy could serve as an entering wedge into higher education occurred in Baltimore, where a group of wealthy women formed a committee in October 1891 to promote women's education and gave $119,000 toward a medical school where women should be "admitted upon the same terms which may be prescribed for men." When this sum proved insufficient, Mary Elizabeth Garrett gave the Johns Hopkins Medical School an additional $306,977 in 1893, making a total endowment of almost half a million dollars.[13] Less-well-known efforts were common. According to Rossiter, even small-scale philanthropy (donations of $50,000 and under) was quite effective in fostering science institutions that included women.[14]

Among Olivia's immediate friends, such ideas were commonplace. Mary Putnam Jacobi had recently been involved in trying to leverage women's entry to Harvard Medical School. Together with Marie Zakrzewska and other female doctors, Jacobi had tried unsuccessfully to use philanthropy to "purchase" entry for women into Harvard Medical School.[15] Elizabeth Cady Stanton, who was better known as an advocate of coeducation, also urged women to financially support their own institutions. Speaking at the sixtieth anniversary class of the Troy Female Seminary in 1892, Stanton appealed passionately to women to endow college scholarships for girls. It seems likely that Stanton was aiming her remarks at Olivia, who shared the speakers' platform with her at Troy that day. Addressing her remarks to the wealthy women in the audience rather than to the assembled pupils, she declared, "This is the best work women of wealth can do, and I hope in the future they will endow scholarships for their own sex instead of giving millions of dollars to institutions for boys." If an example was needed, there was Harvard. "After all the bequests women have made to Harvard, see how niggardly that institution, in its 'annex,' treats their daughters."[16] At a parlor suffrage meeting in New York City in April 1894, Stanton again appealed for money for women's colleges. If there were any rich women present who were soon to make their wills, let them leave their money for the advancement of their own sex, she declared. Yale and Harvard "had received millions from women but very, very little had been done for the education of deserving girls."[17]

But which system of higher education best served women—coeducational universities, women's colleges, or perhaps that compromise, the coordinate college? Stanton had sent two sons to Cornell and her daughters to Vassar. We find her in the 1890s pressuring Olivia to give to Cornell but to designate her gifts to the university's female departments. When Stanton and her son Theodore spent some days with the Sages at Cedar Croft in August 1893, the conversation again turned to education. Learning that the president of Cornell was trying to interest Russell Sage in endowing a civil engineering chair, Stanton declared that he "should help the girls and not the boys."[18] But did coeducation really help women? Should they not have their own colleges? When Olivia and Stanton lunched with Annie Nathan Meyer, founder of Barnard in October 1893, the topic came up again. Stanton's diary records, "We had some very lively conversation on Cornell and coeducation, on Barnard College and segregation, and on the comparative merits of these two systems for girls."[19]

But Stanton would die in 1902 and Jacobi a few years later. Sage embarked on her educational philanthropy without the support of these feminist friends and mentors, and with the influence of her lawyer and advisor Robert de Forest in the ascendant.

Just how ascendant is revealed in the memo de Forest wrote to Olivia Sage in 1907 that advised her how to proceed with her philanthropy to institutions. De Forest brushed aside the claims of most of the 4,000 institutions that had already applied to her, confidently asserting that the institutions to which she would want to donate were those that had *not* applied.[20] Charity Organization Society officials, who were dealing with much of Sage's incoming mail, evidently approached their task with little regard for her wishes. For example, in submitting his report on Sage's incoming letters to COS president de Forest in August 1907, COS official Frank Persons added the breathtakingly dismissive annotation, "Letters relating to institutions . . . 7,512. Of the letters relating to institutions . . . 6,486 required no attention whatsoever."[21]

Several pieces of evidence point again to the role of Robert de Forest as gatekeeper to the Sage fortune. When Harvard president A. Lawrence Lowell sounded out a friend on how best to approach the elderly widow to request money for undergraduate buildings, his informant, who "knows Mr. de Forest very well," warned him that de Forest "does not like to have his territory trodden on by outsiders."[22] But mail could and did get through to Olivia when she was in Lawrence or in Sag Harbor, at the eastern end of Long Island, where she had taken to spending her summers since Russell's death. Fund-raisers soon learned to approach her during these summer months. De Forest admitted as much when, advising the president of Yale about an appeal to Sage in 1909, he urged him to write to her while she was at her summer cottage. The Yale president took his friend's advice, and the astounding results will be described shortly.[23]

New York University

Olivia Sage's donation of almost one-third of a million dollars to New York University is significant not only because of its size but also because it was her most ambitious philanthropic investment in women's education and its failure was the most deeply disappointing.

Olivia's interest in New York University had developed in partnership with Helen Gould while Russell Sage and Jay Gould were still alive. Helen's donations to NYU expressed her belief in stewardship, and they were unconditional.[24] In contrast, Olivia intended her donation to open the doors to women. New York University would provide a test case. Indeed, in NYU, Sage believed she had found a worthy recipient of her money: a progressive New York institution that was friendly to women— far more so than Columbia, whose president, Nicholas Murray Butler, had declared that women would enter over his dead body.[25] But Henry MacCracken, NYU's chancellor since 1891, was an imaginative and ruthless fund-raiser. While pursuing a masculinist vision of undergraduate education, he was mindful of the need to cultivate the goodwill of wealthy men and women who were potential donors. His experimental Woman's Law Class, launched in 1890, won him friends among some of New York's wealthiest families, including the Goulds and the Sages. As mentioned earlier, Helen Gould was a graduate of the first class and subsequently was vice president of the Woman's Legal Education Society. Mary Putnam Jacobi was on its board.[26] In this year, the university began to admit women as students to professional programs in law and pedagogy at the older Washington Square campus in lower Manhattan.[27] A group of wealthy women paid the salaries of instructors, notably Emilie Kempin, a doctor of laws from the University of Zurich. As one of the attendees explained, the class did not "aim to prepare students for the practice of law, but to give to women who are likely to have responsibility for the care of property, or who for any other reason desire to have fuller knowledge of the laws . . . the opportunity to study the fundamental features of modern American law."[28] By 1901, forty-seven students were enrolled, among them Margaret Olivia Slocum, Sage's 27-year-old niece, who received a certificate in 1897.[29] MacCracken also appointed Olivia and Helen to a new Women's Advisory Committee that was charged with preparing "plans and recommendations for the advancement of the University's work for women."[30] Olivia served from 1896 to 1906, and the chancellor encouraged her to feel that she was part of an important experiment in women's education, writing to her as "my official associate in the work of New York University for higher Christian education."[31]

But coeducation was not part of MacCracken's plan for educational excellence. His new "up-town campus," a modern undergraduate campus at University Heights in the Bronx, was for male undergraduates only. NYU reflected a national trend, at least in the sciences: a three-decade process of feminization beginning in the 1870s was followed by a "rather brutal" process of defeminization under the guise of higher standards in the 1890s.[32]

For a decade, chancellor Henry MacCracken had attempted to interest Russell Sage in giving to NYU, using mutual acquaintance Dr. John P. Munn, the wealthy physician retained by both Russell Sage and Jay Gould.[33] On one occasion, MacCracken invited Russell Sage to accompany him and Dr. Munn "to glance at the New Laboratory on the corner of First Avenue and 26th Street." But nothing came of this excursion, and the Sages were not among fifty donors of large gifts who contributed to the purchase of the University Heights property for NYU between May 1891 and February 1898.[34]

In 1897, a bold new proposal landed on the desks of the members of the University Council. This was a petition from a Mrs. Vanderpoel "for leave to submit a plan for the formation of a Woman's College to be carried on at University Heights in connection with the University."[35] The council ignored the petition, but MacCracken evidently thought it worth pursuing, if only a donor could be found to underwrite the new undergraduate College. He turned to the Sages for a large gift, writing to Russell Sage in December 1898:

> I remind you of your general promise to me, since 1892 to do somewhat for New York University. It is more than ever a great and growing enterprise which helps City and Nation and Christian Civilization. We have 1,717 students this year, but the work is too great for our means. Come and help.
>
> 1. Civil Engineering
> 2. Mechanical Engineering
> 3. Industrial Chemistry, are still unnamed and unendowed.[36]

But then he broached the idea of a woman's college. "No better place exists in the world for a new woman's college than University Heights," he wrote boldly. "If we use our plant and professors somewhat as Radcliffe College uses Harvard or Barnard College uses Columbia you could tell Mrs. Sage to organize here the best woman's college in the world."[37]

In the years that followed, the chancellor laid careful siege to Olivia. He agreed to include a bust of Emma Willard in NYU's grandiose new Hall of Fame at her request.[38] And he persuaded the University Council to grant Olivia an honorary master of letters degree. Her letter accepting the honor, dated May 31, 1904, shows surprise and genuine delight. But Olivia continued to use Emma Willard to speak for her: she was still a "self in hiding":

> With great diffidence I take my pen in hand to reply to your letter of April 30th. That an Institution so famed should choose to give me a Degree was quite incomprehensible, hence my hesitation in replying, as an acceptance seemed doubtful. But my loyalty to my own Alma Mater and to its Founder Mrs. Emma Hart Willard, induces me to write my acceptance and to thank the Corporation of New York University for the great honor they have done me.[39]

The chancellor's plans for the uptown campus took on a new urgency with the death of Gustav Schwab's widow, the owner of the property needed for expansion.[40] The chancellor prepared a statement for potential donors, arguing the need to preempt "the establishment of some undesirable institution, probably some Catholic asylum or school."[41]

In the spring of 1906, MacCracken called on Olivia at home, ostensibly to discuss with her an inscription for the Emma Willard bronze tablet in the Hall of Fame, but in fact to discuss the Schwab property. Olivia demurred at the asking price. The university again approached her in August—only weeks after the death of her husband.[42] Well aware that Russell Sage's death removed the last obstacle to her gift to the university, MacCracken, returning from a trip to Europe, "made a call of friendship upon Mrs. Sage," again on the excuse of talking about the Emma Willard memorial. Finally, on October 9, 1906, Olivia informed MacCracken that she intended to give the land to the university "if it could be acquired at an acceptable price." The gift amounting to $294,250, and thus the largest donation to date in the university's history (apart from Helen Gould's gifts), was formally offered on November 9, 1906.[43] But Olivia attached a condition to her generous donation. It was that "[s]ome part of the property at least will be used by New York University as a center for women's working and living, for a women's building, or for other University activities in connection with women."[44]

This poorly drafted clause was vague and unenforceable. MacCracken at first attempted to get the council to meet some of Olivia's conditions by expanding its facilities for women students, and in 1907, women students attending summer school were lodged in two buildings on the property.[45] But his attempt to get the university to fulfill the donor's wishes was voted down by the board of trustees, who insisted that the needs of the engineering school came first. An undated typed memorandum from about 1907 shows that the university had imposed its own restrictions on the gift. The "Olivia Sage College," set up to "carry out those ideas and principles which have been expressed and advocated by Mrs. Sage," would be opened by New York University only after the university had obtained a sufficient endowment to place it in a financial position comparable to that of "Bryn Mawr, Simmons, Smith, or Vassar Colleges," the memo stated. When MacCracken retired in 1910, nothing had been done about the terms of Olivia's donation. He bequeathed the embarrassing situation to his successor, Elmer E. Brown.[46] Chancellor Brown not only failed to fulfill the condition of the gift, he continued to approach Sage for money for other purposes. Brown tried everything. He wrote her flattering letters about Russell Sage and about her Standish ancestors. And he attempted to use Colonel Richard Pratt as an intermediary. Pratt, the retired principal of Carlisle Indian School and an old friend of the Sages, relished his role as go-between, confiding to Brown that several university and college fund-raisers were trying to get to Mrs. Sage through him and proudly repeating Robert de Forest's remark about him, that "if any man could get Mrs. Sage interested, he [Pratt] could."[47]

Brown also tried to use Olivia's brother Jermain Slocum as an intermediary. Writing to Jermain in November 1917, the NYU chancellor admitted that he had heard about "the unfortunate situation which had arisen, in which Mrs. Sage had expected a woman's college to be erected on the Schwab property and had been disappointed in this expectation." Brown assured Slocum that he had "always been in hearty accord with this plan" and had "the utmost sympathy with everything which has to do with the higher education of women." Nevertheless, he informed him, the university had decided to erect an engineering building on the Schwab property, although "we have not given up hope of having eventually a college for women on the magnificent property which Mrs. Sage has made available."[48] The NYU chancellor continued to beg Olivia for money right up to the end. Just three months before her death, Brown wrote appealing to her in the name of the national emergency. He even sent the NYU men's glee club to sing for her at Christmas in a badly bungled piece of public relations.[49]

Olivia's NYU episode shows how difficult it was for female donors to use their money to advance opportunities for women in general or to retain control over their gifts. The shadow of the NYU fiasco hangs over the rest of Olivia Sage's philanthropy to education. It was infuriating that the university refused to honor her condition with the excuse that they had insufficient funds, while they spent millions of dollars on other programs which excluded women.

Her friends Helen Gould and Nettie McCormick offered a model of a different kind of philanthropy. Both women were spectacular philanthropists but neither specified that their gifts should support women's causes or institutions. Gould gave generously to all kinds of civic, religious, educational, and benevolent institutions. McCormick, a Troy Female Seminary alumna (1852–1853) who had inherited the McCormick Harvester fortune on the death of her husband Cyrus McCormick in 1884, made a dazzling series of donations to McCormick Theological Seminary, built Fowler Hall at Northwestern University and The Virginia Library in Richmond, and donated funds for needy students. She was a leading benefactor of the Presbyterian church and a major donor to dozens of colleges and universities whose gifts to educational and religious institutions are estimated at $8 million.[50] McCormick drew Olivia into some joint philanthropy, writing in 1908 to urge her to join with herself and three other friends in a donation to the College of Wooster in Ohio. Make some inquiries about the institution first, she suggested, "and if the investigation is satisfactory . . . take an interest with us in this cause."[51] Olivia also gave money to found scholarships in the McCormick Theological Seminary—for male seminarians.[52] The women's friendship continued into old age, sustained by visits, letters, and gifts. Philanthropy and affectionate tokens were intertwined. In 1913, Lilian wrote to McCormick on Olivia's behalf, sending thanks for "two beautiful shawls, and the slippers," and conveying a promise from Olivia to send "the check for the fifteen hundred dollars additional that is required for the scholarship [at Fowler Theological Seminary] over the one thousand she gave you a few days ago."[53]

"Something for women's work"

Many fund-raising appeals to Sage continued to include promises of "something for women's work." Her donation of $150,000 to Syracuse University to purchase a building and fourteen acres of land for a teachers' college encouraged her correspondents to believe that her interests were in women's education above all.[54] Her gifts to Syracuse were conditional on the university using them to help women, and she sought assurances that her intentions were being carried out. In September 1909, she instructed Henry de Forest to let Chancellor Day know that she wanted to give the university $50,000 on her birthday. "Mrs. Sage's interest, as you know," de Forest wrote to the chancellor, "particularly attaches to woman's work and she asks me to write you to inquire in connection with what special line of woman's work such gift would be the more acceptable."[55]

Chancellor Day, whose university had already received $200,000 from Sage since 1905, responded with an ambitious proposal. Would she be "interested in a proposition of segregation here at the University?" he asked Henry de Forest. He suggested a women's coordinate college consisting of Renwick Hall plus an additional large building, "the College to be the Margaret Olivia Slocum College for Women or Woman's College." The opportunity existed to found a college that would be "more prominent and equally useful with Radcliffe, Barnard, Wellesley, and Vassar," he suggested. The idea was not taken up.[56]

A year later, Chancellor Day was angling for Sage funds for a dormitory to house the Teachers' College students. This was necessary "because of our snowy country in winter," the chancellor informed Henry de Forest. "Four hundred and fifty-two students have been in attendance . . . , almost all of them women. It is really a woman's college," he added.[57] Another Syracuse official, writing in June 1912, informed her that Syracuse University was training three times as many teachers for the public schools as any other institution in the state. "There are over 400 students in the Teachers' College, nearly all of whom are women." He hoped that "the Teachers' College should be made one of the great factors in giving an opportunity to women, and training them for service as educators."[58]

"A few strategic educational institutions of national scope"

But philanthropists often prefer to give to the most prestigious, not the most needy, entities.[59] In the same year that she donated $150,000 to the Teachers' College at Syracuse, Olivia gave Yale over half a million. And she consistently gave more to men's institutions than to women's. Partly this was because Robert de Forest controlled access to her while nudging her philanthropy toward institutions that he favored. He suggested, reminded, and cautioned but never dictated: he was the soul of tact. Olivia respected his opinion, sometimes using it as an excuse for inaction. For example, in July 1910 her secretary answered an appeal from Cornell, "She will have to postpone the consideration of it . . . as Mr. de Forest is not here now, and she would like to talk with him about the matter."[60] Occasionally, de Forest even suggested the dollar amount of a donation. In response to an appeal for a "Colored Chautauqua" near

Nashville "where they are gathering the different ignorant negro cler-
gymen from different parts of the South for some elementary and I imagine very useful instruction," he advised Olivia, "I would not give more
than $5,000. I would not give less than $1,000. I think $2,500 would be
deemed a very liberal contribution."[61]

De Forest's role in guiding Olivia's philanthropy is well illustrated
in the maneuvering that produced her gift to Yale. A Yale alumnus, de
Forest was strategically placed to direct a large chunk of the Sage fortune toward his alma mater. The elderly widow's vulnerability seems quite
palpable as fund-raisers conspired with her own closest advisor.

The correspondence between de Forest and Anson Phelps Stokes,
Jr., secretary of the Yale Corporation, reveals de Forest alternately
confident and despairing about his ability to direct her giving. Stokes's
plan was to play on Olivia's pride in her family's descent from Rev. Abraham Pierson, Yale's first rector in 1702. In the spring of 1907, even before
Russell Sage's estate was settled, Stokes wrote to Sage about Yale's needs,
enclosing a photograph of a statue of her eminent forebear. Intrigued,
she wrote back, requesting a sample signature of Rev. Pierson. De Forest confided to Stokes, "I think you have planted good seed, but it may
disappoint you to know that the harvest is not yet. She has been giving
very liberally of late, as you are aware, and I know she does not wish to
give to Yale at the moment."[62]

De Forest's description hardly conveyed the enormous spending
activity that was going on at 604 Fifth Avenue following Russell Sage's
death. Stokes's suggestion that de Forest grease the pipeline by donating to Yale himself—"a contribution from you would be an evidence of
appreciation of Yale's great needs which might have some weight later
with Mrs. Sage"—was cavalierly dismissed, and December found Stokes
again consulting de Forest about how best to proceed.[63]

Emboldened by delay, Stokes addressed Olivia Sage directly in a letter
dated April 7, 1908: "I see by the papers that Mr. Sage's estate has been
settled—which you implied was a condition precedent to seriously considering Yale's needs," he began. He went on to lay out for her consideration Yale's two most pressing needs, first, the purchase of the thirty-acre
Hillhouse Estate ("which represents the University's only opportunity
for large future expansion"), and second, dormitories ("statistics and
reports show that the intellectual and moral standards of men in college dormitories here average higher than those of men in private lodgings about town"). Stokes concluded: "The great need of our country
today is the strengthening of a few strategic educational institutions of
national scope which stand for scholarship and high Christian ideals."[64]

Stokes was well advised to quote statistics to the woman who continued to keep a clipping file on educational reform, even in her eighties. And his language captured well the conflicting purposes of the American university in transition between older moral verities and the new social sciences.[65] De Forest urged him to act without delay while Olivia Sage was at her summer cottage. "Why not write a line to the lady yourself at once, addressing her at Sag Harbor, where she is and where she will be likely to read any mail that comes to her?" he urged. "Bring up the whole question of opportunity; . . . give any reason you please for bringing it up again now."[66]

The timing was just right. Olivia agreed to give the university the huge sum of $650,000, enabling it to purchase the Hillhouse property, and the end of December found Stokes thanking her for the "wonderful offer" which had "put a new spirit in us all and a renewed determination to make the university stand truer than ever to its ideals of democracy, public service, and Christian faith."[67] But subsequent contacts with Olivia were less profitable for Yale. She turned down the invitation to attend the graduation ceremony in June on the grounds that crowds fatigued her, and she gave no more to Yale, even after Stokes managed to confer an honorary degree on her former pupil, Mary Boardman, a move de Forest called "a stroke of genius."[68]

"Start in by giving to those that are distinctly women's colleges"

Olivia had made huge gifts to Yale, New York University, Syracuse University, Rensselaer Polytechnic, and the Emma Willard School, and people were wondering when she was going to start giving to women's colleges. There was still a general expectation that she would do so, and letters of appeal continued to pour in. In July 1910, Robert de Forest addressed a memo prompting the elderly philanthropist, "If you have in mind to do something for women's colleges, as you have several times suggested," he wrote, "I think in your place I would start in by giving to those that are distinctly women's colleges, such as Wellesley, for instance . . . $100,000, $50,000, or even $25,000 apiece . . . would undoubtedly be a great boon."[69] These amounts were significantly lower than she had been giving to men's colleges. Not until 1911 did Olivia make her first large donation to a women's college. (Her early donations to Vassar and Radcliffe had been modest and, in some cases, anonymous.)[70] In this year, she gave $150,000 to Vassar for a dormitory to be named Olivia Josselyn Hall for her grandmother, adding another $50,000 the following year.[71] President James M. Taylor's letter of thanks was carefully crafted: "I have recently reviewed Emma Willard's 'Address,'" he confided, "and more than ever I am admiring her work, her ideals, and her progress beyond her age."[72]

The administrators of the women's colleges such as Wellesley were on a roller coaster of anticipation and disappointment. In February 1908, Wellesley president Caroline Hazard had optimistically hailed Mrs. Sage's new wealth. "By the providence of God you are placed in a position in which you can grant great things," she wrote to Olivia.[73] But Wellesley's request for half a million dollars went unanswered even after the college lost its main building in a disastrous fire in 1913. "Wellesley in trouble is like a friend in distress," wrote one supporter to Sage, "and I hate to think of her splendid work crippled." But Olivia sent only $25,000.[74] De Forest gently reminded her again in 1914: "Has it possibly occurred to you to anticipate your future intentions toward Wellesley by giving them something now when their main building has burned down?" He advised against giving to Harvard (which had "a larger and richer list of graduates than any other university in the country") and suggested "balancing Harvard's needs and resources as against the needs and resources of other universities, notably women's colleges, gifts to which you have been considering in the past."[75]

Other correspondents compared the situation at Wellesley unfavorably to that at Harvard. "Shall we have our girl students unhoused, scattered, and with imperfect supervision, or shall we be able to place them in such a Hall as now rejoices the boys of Harvard?" asked William Lawrence, bishop of Massachusetts, an officer of Harvard as well as a trustee of Wellesley. Referring to Standish Hall, the dormitory recently completed with Sage money at Harvard, he asked for "a girls' Standish from you." Emma Willard alumna Euphemia Worthington, a mathematics instructor at Wellesley, wrote to her, "Now [after the fire] there is an opportunity for someone to give where there is really urgent need, in fact almost to refound the college." Finally, in 1914, Olivia gave Wellesley $250,000.[76]

Why was Sage so slow to help Wellesley? Perhaps she was uneasy about the direction the women's colleges were taking. Wellesley abandoned compulsory chapel attendance in 1900, and by 1914 it had become a "secular liberal-arts college for women," in the words of one historian.[77] A letter from Helen Gould to Mary Wooley of Mount Holyoke in 1903 expressed displeasure that an instructor in the chair of biblical study which she, Gould, had endowed was using critical analysis, "being destructive in her criticism and sweeping away faith without putting anything in its place."[78] Vassar, too, was changing. Helen Gould was so dissatisfied that Vassar had become "too liberal" that the college returned the money she had donated for four scholarships. A $40,000 endowed chair at Mount Holyoke (set up in 1902 with Gould money) was later transferred to the Department of Romance Languages, and a $50,000 endowment of the Wellesley Biblical Department was withdrawn and reassigned to the Department of Mathematics![79] Ten years before, Sage had seen Vassar, a women's college in New York State, as her dreamed-of "Willard University." In those days, she thoroughly approved of its commitment to uphold Christian ideals and prepare women to be schoolteachers. Now she wasn't so sure.

An additional explanation for her failure to support the all-women's colleges comes to light in a February 1914 letter from her secretary, E. Lilian Todd, to Barnard College president Virginia Gildersleeve. In informing Barnard's president why Mrs. Sage refused to consider a gift to the college, Todd explained, "She feels that her gift to the Emma Willard School is her contribution to women's education, and the few buildings given elsewhere were merely special cases."[80]

Disappointed by the NYU debacle and distracted by numerous appeals, Olivia nevertheless continued to fund scholarships and fellowships for girls. Her years as a struggling teacher and governess in the 1850s had convinced her that the best education for a young woman was a practical course of training leading to paid work. Dozens of examples of such donations are scattered throughout her correspondence, from a gift in November 1909 of $10,000 to the New York State Federation of Women's Clubs girls' college scholarship fund to a $125,000 donation to the New York School of Applied Design for Women in 1916.[81] In acknowledging a $2,500 donation to the Pennsylvania School of Horticulture for Women, its director assured Sage that "the school . . . will benefit many women in teaching them to earn their living in healthful occupations." She went on, "Your name is so connected throughout the country with projects for helping women to help themselves."[82] Sage also gave to industrial high schools. At Lawrence, Long Island, she endowed the Margaret Sage Industrial School with $150,000 in August 1907. The school offered recreational and cultural activities as well as vocational training for boys and girls.[83] Another industrial school that received a large donation was the Idaho Industrial School. Whether it was because Olivia approved of this self-described "absolutely non-sectarian but thoroughly Christian" school for poor white students or because its principal, E. A. Paddock, wore her down with solicitations and visits over several years, she gave the school $25,000 in 1910, $20,000 in 1916, and a legacy of $200,000 in 1918.[84]

A lifelong interest in Protestant missions and admiration for the work of evangelist Dwight L. Moody prompted Olivia's donations to Northfield Training School. This Presbyterian missionary center (consisting of the Mount Hebron School for Boys and the Northfield School for Girls) had been founded by Moody in 1879. Northfield received one of her first major gifts ($150,000) in 1907. She subsequently endowed five scholarships at Northfield for women in 1912 at a cost of $25,000.[85]

Personal connections seem to account for Olivia's surprising financial support of two educational institutions for African Americans. Perhaps Tuskegee and Hampton appealed to her because both represented themselves as conservative institutions, identified with industrial education and self-help.[86] But the recommendation of her friends Andrew Dickson White and Robert Ogden seem to have been decisive. A well-placed word from her old friend Andrew Dickson White served to bring Booker T. Washington's institution to Sage's attention. Another word from White brought Washington to a conference with Robert de Forest in New York City, and Tuskegee received its first gift from Olivia, of $20,000, in May 1908. On her death, it was one of the colleges selected to receive an $800,000 share of her estate.[87] Another friend, Robert Ogden, seems to have prompted Olivia's support of Hampton Institute. A newly appointed trustee of the Russell Sage Foundation, Ogden was also president of the Hampton Board of Trustees and a trustee of Tuskegee. He energetically promoted the requests of President H. B. Frissell in his correspondence with Sage, and she responded, giving $25,000 in February 1908. But after Ogden's death in 1913, Olivia's secretary refused to forward Frissell's letters to Sage, even though his proposal for a training school for nurses at Hampton would probably have appealed to her. "Mr. Carnegie has promised $300,000," Frissell wrote, but his rather blunt appeals to Olivia went nowhere. "*I'm* not going to give this to Mrs. Sage," Lilian wrote to Jermain, Olivia's brother. Fortunately for Hampton, the school already stood to benefit from a change in her will. The new codicil of February 17, 1908, assigned the college one share of her legacy, or $800,000.[88]

Olivia had also donated to interracial Berea College, and a remarkable letter of thanks for a gift of $25,000 to the college has survived from two Minneapolis women "as representatives of 40,000 Colored Club Women of America." But later appeals from Berea's President Frost were ignored.[89]

The theme of many carefully crafted appeals to Olivia was the need to protect the morals and improve the living standards of female undergraduates in these days of dancing, smoking, and other "New Woman" behaviors. Colleges that invested in new dormitories, dining halls, and chapels supported a paternalistic vision of a college that supervised student morals and protected student well-being.[90] For example, in appealing to her for funds to build a dormitory at Cornell, Andrew Dickson White alluded to the dangers of housing female undergraduates in lodgings. A new dormitory would allow them to benefit from the care of "an excellent and accomplished Lady Dean exercising a direct and most happy influence upon them." They would be fully integrated into the university's academic life but housed apart, for their protection.[91] White also invoked Emma Willard's vision of civic womanhood. Writing to Olivia in January 1911, he described Cornell as

> a great educational center . . . sending out through the whole country young women unaccustomed to luxury, but brought up in respectable families, under good influences, instructed here under the advantages of a thoroughly equipped University, and going out year after year into the homes and schools of this and surrounding states.

These female graduates "seem to me to give us one of the best grounds of hope which we have for our country," he added.[92] Two weeks later, Olivia gave Cornell the enormous sum of $300,000 for a women's residence hall.[93]

At a time when a backlash at Chicago and other universities threatened to remove female students from the classroom even though—or perhaps because—they were showing themselves to be men's academic superiors, White was defending the integrated classroom on the grounds that the presence of women students was good for male undergraduates. He described his administration at Cornell as a successful experiment in coeducation: "None of the evils which were anticipated by many good people have ever arisen from [women's] admission here," he informed Olivia in 1910.

> There have been no troubles nor scandals arising from them. Their presence has promoted decency and order as it does everywhere. My experience shows me that the difference between college lecture rooms where women are present and where they are absent is like the difference between a church and a political meeting, or between the smoking car and the car back of it.[94]

The mixed classroom afforded female students an opportunity to civilize their male counterparts and by extension the entire campus. The admission of women to Cornell had been "good—good for them, good for the young men, good for the community at large," he informed Olivia. "[The] lecture rooms, laboratories, libraries, and public rooms of every sort, are far more quiet and orderly and civilized than they would be if only men were admitted." She responded through her secretary, pleased that the civilizing presence of women was at work and remarking that their influence would be even more effective once they had the vote.[95]

Olivia's gifts to institutions of higher education continued to be highly personal and idiosyncratic. Her interest in Cornell was a result of old friendships. Andrew Dickson White was, like her, a native of Syracuse, and the families had been close. Now both were elderly. White, who at seventy-seven was younger than Olivia, appealed to her pointedly, "I can think of nothing which would be a greater satisfaction to me on leaving all earthly scenes than the knowledge that these young women and those succeeding for hundreds of years are to be suitably housed." His offer to name the dormitory after her mother and father was hard to resist: "There could be no more beautiful and appropriate monument standing in the midst of this beautiful lake region in the very heart of this great State with which your honored husband and father were identified."[96]

Naming decisions show her wish to venerate the women of her family. She named the new dormitory Prudence Risley Hall for her late husband's mother, commemorating the achievements of the women of her family, as she had done at Vassar, and those of her husband's family. For the new Teachers' College at Syracuse, she vetoed the names Slocum and Sage College, choosing the name Caroline Longstreet College for Women Teachers over the objection of Dean Jacob Street, who asked her to remove the word "women" since 25 percent of the students training there were men![97]

But other motives and influences came to outweigh her support for women's education. One such was her determination to salvage her husband's reputation. What better way to rescue the name Russell Sage from public opprobrium than to link it with some prestigious college or university? And if her husband's millions had been amassed by dubious means, if he had been born in obscurity and received only a meager schooling, at least his name would be linked after death with the nation's finest universities.[98]

Other gifts confirm that Olivia wished to draw attention to her descent from Mayflower ancestors, a motive historian Kathleen McCarthy calls "tribalism" (but one that can also be called snobbery). By giving to prestigious universities, she conferred prestige on the Slocum, Jermain, and Pierson families. For example, in donating to Vassar and naming the building she donated Olivia Josselyn Hall, she advertised her descent on her mother's side through Josselyn from her colonial ancestor Myles Standish.[99] Similarly, large gifts to Yale, Harvard, Princeton, and other prestigious all-male universities were given in the name of various relatives.

Correspondence in the papers of Harvard president A. Lawrence Lowell reveals how easy it was for fund-raisers to persuade Sage to donate to prestigious universities, all of which excluded women. In a letter to President Lowell, Harvard trustee Major Henry Lee Higginson told how he netted an enormous gift from Sage. Princeton fund-raiser John Cadwalader "had gone to Mrs. Sage, not knowing her, and asked her if she would put up a building for the students of Princeton."[100] To his surprise, she immediately agreed to donate $250,000 for a building that was then (after additional gifts totaling over $165,000) named Holder Hall after Christopher Holder, a seventeenth-century ancestor.[101] Higginson recounted how Princeton had secured the additional amount for the building, which was larger than initially planned. Cadwalader "returned to her and showed her what part of the building she had built, being one side of a quadrangle. She asked: 'Why not the whole?', and he said, 'Because the whole cost more money than you furnished,' whereupon, after consideration, she gave the rest." She had no prior connection to Princeton.[102]

"My feminine name did not seem suitable"

President Lowell was cheered by the news. "It is encouraging to hear that Mrs. Sage has given money to a dormitory at Princeton, for she may be willing to do the same for us," he wrote to Higginson.[103] He appealed to Olivia to support his plan of building student dormitories to provide "the opportunity of exerting on them a strong moral influence" and was granted an interview with her in March 1911. Higginson had already warned him that she would want to have a protracted conversation, but "I know you are as patient as you are eloquent."[104] In July, Henry de Forest informed the Harvard president that Mrs. Sage was "inclined . . . if you so desire, to make donation of *say $225,000,*" or half the cost of a dormitory.[105] To J. P. Morgan, Jr., a trustee and go-between, the Harvard president wrote, "I suppose there is no use in trying to persuade Mrs. Sage further, and *as we have no claim upon her,* I feel that her giving this amount is very generous, and I am exceedingly grateful for it."[106]

A year later, Henry de Forest informed him that she had agreed to give a further $125,000. He went on, "She suggests that it be called the

'Russell Dormitory,' that being the first name of her late husband and the middle name of Mr. James Russell Lowell."[107] President Lowell now had an excuse to correspond with Olivia and perhaps to visit her at her summer home. She encouraged him: "My Secretary is off on her vacation," she informed him, and Mr. de Forest was in the south of France.[108] Then followed a curious discussion of a name for the new building. Since Harvard already had a Russell Hall, she should name the new building after herself, he suggested.[109] Olivia recorded her reply. "I then told Mr. de Forest I would give the new dormitory the name of 'Standish Hall' if there was no other building with that name, for my feminine name did not seem suitable for a boys' building, the boys might resent being 'womanized' to coin a word in these 'new woman' days." In choosing Standish as an alternative, she went on, she was naming the building "for my great Grandmother 'Olivia Standish.'"[110]

Naming decisions were difficult for Olivia; for us they are revealing. Olivia's letter to President Lowell shows her confusion over purpose and identity. Giving to a university that excluded women, she refused even a female name for the dormitory while substituting another name that appeared unmarked but in fact commemorated a female ancestor! Males were already embattled in "these 'new woman' days," she argued. They should not have to submit to the additional slight of occupying a dormitory named for a woman!

Standish Hall gave Olivia much satisfaction. She wrote to the Harvard president expressing her approval of the colonial style of architecture. "I am sure Captain Myles would say 'Well done.' Ancestral names attract me, and with 'Standish Hall' in Cambridge, and Holder Hall at Princeton, my ancestors could well hold up their heads and be proud as I am of their works." She signed the letter, "Margaret (Olivia Standish) Sage."[111]

Personal connections also explain her gift of $1 million to RPI, a memorial to her husband.[112] Some of the moneys were designated for a Russell Sage Laboratory commemorating Russell Sage's favorite nephew and adopted heir, Russell Sage, Jr., who had studied at the institute from 1856–1859 and had died in 1892.[113] These donations helped establish departments of electrical and mechanical engineering. They also made it possible for RPI to become one of the nation's first postgraduate schools of engineering.[114] A further donation to RPI of $100,000 for a dining hall in 1915 was also a memorial to this nephew, as were two fellowships at $15,000 each.[115]

By May 1910, RPI's President Palmer Ricketts was asking for another $1.2 million "because of Mr. Sage's position in the school and of your interest."[116] In 1912, he informed her about his plans to build dormitories at the east end of a piece of land "in a part of the city particularly free from bad influences . . . and practically in the country." Olivia replied, agreeing that dormitories were needed and noting that "the problem of sleeping and eating is now being solved at Princeton and Harvard most satisfactorily."[117]

Affection for the memory of her father prompted many gifts to Syracuse. She donated over $250,000 to Syracuse University to build the Joseph Slocum College of Agriculture to honor her father, the clever promoter of agricultural improvement.[118] The university's officials must have perked up as September 8th approached each year, when they could expect a letter informing them that she was giving another $25,000 or $50,000 on her birthday in honor of her father. In September 1912, she gave $83,000 to correspond to her age, leaving its spending to the discretion of the university.[119]

For those who wanted to help women's advancement by donating for women's education it was certainly ironic that at the very moment when Olivia Sage and women like her were poised to spend the fortunes reaped by their husbands and fathers in the great free-for-all of late-nineteenth-century capitalism, the universities were being redesigned to keep women out or to relegate them to special programs or units. University administrators, even at Chicago, where there was an initial commitment to coeducation, were beginning to draw back and to talk about professionalism in ways that conflated rising academic standards with male-only student bodies, constructing as "scientific" those disciplinary discourses from which women's voices were absent.[120]

The new colleges of engineering were the most obvious sign of this transformation. University presidents such as RPI's Ricketts measured progress by the distance their universities put between themselves and the classically oriented universities of the nineteenth century. And because science had developed within what David Noble has called a "priestly culture," the "capture" of the universities by science and engineering meant that they would be even less hospitable than before to female students and faculty. Sage philanthropy to RPI and NYU helped sustain institutions that would exclude her sex until the mid-twentieth century or even later.[121]

Educational philanthropy can shore up elite institutions or fund alternatives. It can effect transformations of curriculum, engineer a more diverse faculty body, or support a more inclusive student population.[122] Olivia Sage remained a fierce advocate of women's advancement, but she pursued this goal inconsistently. She found it hard to resist appeals from colleges and universities when the connection seemed to flatter her own family or offer national recognition, and many of these institutions were for men only. Her educational philanthropy has an air of improvisation. In the end it was a scattershot affair that divided her splendid inheritance into many small donations and had no single impact like that of Rockefeller or Carnegie. It reflected not so much any one philanthropic vision as it did the competing pressures of a number of determined fund-raisers on an elderly donor swayed by flattery and made vulnerable by age and isolation.

Thirteen

"Nothing more for men's colleges"

E. Lilian Todd and the Origins of Russell Sage College, 1916

I am sorry not to help you, but Mrs. Sage . . . has told me repeatedly
that she was going to do nothing more for men's colleges.

—Theodore C. Janeway (1916)[1]

In 1916 Olivia announced her determination not to give any more money
to men's colleges, turning down an appeal from male-only Rutgers College, even though it was affiliated with her own Reformed Church. That
same year, she founded Russell Sage College, a vocational college for
women in Troy, New York, designed to aid women's entry into the professions and other well-paid work. If her gift to New York University
had been emblematic of her early philanthropy, her refusal of funds to
Rutgers marks its endpoint. Founding the Russell Sage College reaffirmed
her belief in women's advancement. But opposition from Robert de Forest and Olivia's own advancing years prevented her from taking steps to
establish the college on a firm financial basis.

 Disappointed with the broken promises of New York University,
Olivia Sage became suspicious of university fund-raisers in general. One
sign of her increasing unease was that she began to make inquiries about
whether the conditions of her earlier gifts were being met. Doubts
extended even to her favorite causes. In September 1912 she wrote to
Chancellor James Day of Syracuse University to inquire about the scholarships she had endowed five years earlier. Were they still open to
women, as she had specified? The chancellor reassured her: "We intend
to keep the doors open to both men and women and to give scholarship
assistance to any woman who wishes to pursue agricultural instruction
as they do at the State Universities like Wisconsin, Purdue, etc."[2]

Olivia was right to distrust promises like these. Correspondence between fund-raisers shows their lack of interest in the donor's intentions. In January 1911, Harvard trustee Henry Lee Higginson recounted to President Lowell the story of a visit by mutual friend John Cadwalader to Olivia Sage. Cadwalader's mission was to raise money for Princeton. He "went in to see her, not knowing her, and she had much to say, and talked an hour steadily," the fund-raiser reported. "I did not say a word, and let her have her say, and then told her what I wanted." Notable about this account is that the fund-raiser does not bother to record what Olivia had to say—if indeed he listened.[3]

At Pierson High School in Sag Harbor, the high school she had funded in 1908, Olivia still had a say. To a request from Grover C. Hart, the school's principal, she instructed her brother to respond:

> Dear Sir:—
>
> At the request of Mrs. Sage, I answer your letter to her, dated August 24th, regarding a scholarship. Mrs. Sage directs me to say that *boys* have no scholarship in the "Pierson High School." The only institutions for scholarships for boys, are the Moody School at Northfield, and Cornell. I would advise you to address either one in regard to the same, in reply to your inquiry.
>
> Yours truly,
(Signed) J. J. Slocum[4]

Appeals from schools, colleges, and universities of all kinds continued to come in. By 1916, Sage was ready to say no to appeals from any college that excluded women students. Rutgers, a male-only college in New Jersey, provided a strong test of her resolve because it was connected to her own Reformed Church (two-thirds of the trustees were required to be communicants in that denomination), and this connection made its president hopeful that he would be able to get her to part with some money.[5] The correspondence with Rutgers is typical of other fund-raising correspondence I have examined of the period. The letters, written by and between a cast of characters—Sage herself, Robert de Forest, secretary E. Lilian Todd, university officials, and a group of often terminally frustrated university fund-raisers, churchmen, trustees, and friends of the university—co-conspirators in the attempt to pry the money loose from the multimillionaire—provide a measure of drama that begs for a Molière or a George Eliot.

The Rutgers Connection

Rutgers fund-raisers began corresponding with Olivia promptly after the probate of Russell Sage's will. In January 1907, Dr. Sleght, a friend of the university, wrote informing the newly inaugurated president, William Demarest, of "the advisability of urging upon Mrs. Sage the claims, hopes, and aspirations of our Rutgers, now that at last our denomination holds one who holds the strings to so large a purse."[6]

Overconfident because of this church connection, President Demarest rushed in with a direct appeal to Olivia Sage in a brief and inelegant begging letter ending, "The college sorely needs a Chemistry building" and asking permission to call on her and press his claim in person.[7] When there was no response, Demarest attempted to reach Sage through her pastor, Rev. Dr. Donald Sage Mackay (she attended his Collegiate Church at Forty-Eighth Street.) Another go-between, Rev. Andrew Hageman, promised the president that he would try to find an opportunity to approach her at church and find out "whether there is any tender spot in her heart for Rutgers."[8] In September 1911, on the heavy, stiff stationery of the De Forest Brothers law firm came a one-sentence response that spelled the death of Rutgers' hopes. "Mrs. Sage has never spoken of Rutgers either to my brother or myself, as yet," Robert de Forest informed Demarest. He could recommend action on behalf of Rutgers only if she brought the matter up first.[9]

Demarest became increasingly frustrated, yet mysterious gifts from Olivia Sage to Williams and Knox Colleges—donations that came as a surprise to the recipients (so they claimed)—kept his hopes alive. How did Mrs. Sage come to give $75,000 to Knox? "I feel it was the Lord's doing," Knox's president confided smugly to Demarest.[10] Rutgers fund-raisers did not give up. But when Rev. Hageman again tried to approach Sage on behalf of Rutgers in 1916, he was told by Dr. Theodore Janeway, "I am sorry not to help you, but Mrs. Sage takes very little interest now in helping the education of men, and has told me repeatedly that she was going to do nothing more for men's colleges."[11]

Two subsequent attempts also failed. The first took Hageman to the doorstep of the Sage Fifth Avenue brownstone, where Jermain Slocum barred the way. The second took him to Cedar Croft. Here he was intercepted and turned back by her physician, Dr. Carl Schmuck. "No one sees her," the physician warned. Hageman reported back to the president that Schmuck "told me some things which prove to me that all further effort along such lines is hopeless." Was he hinting that Olivia was ill or senile or that she already had her philanthropic giving planned out? We have no way to know.[12]

A New Start: Russell Sage College

Olivia was eighty-eight in 1916, but she was mentally alert. In the year that Andrew Hageman went away empty-handed, she established Russell Sage College, a brand-new women's college, using the Troy Female Seminary buildings which had been vacant since the Emma Willard School moved to its new site in 1910. The new college fulfilled Olivia's ideal of establishing a college for women in Troy, the home for many years of her late husband, yet it owed its existence to the concerted lobbying of two extraordinary women. These were her secretary, E. Lilian Todd, and Eliza Kellas, principal of the Emma Willard School.

This book began with the dramatic story of E. Lilian Todd and her biplane. In 1909, Todd and her plane had attracted national media attention and Sage was her financial backer.[13] Yet by January 1911, in what seems to a modern reader a remarkable (and disappointing) change of fortune, Todd, the engineer and inventor, was working out of an office at 604 Fifth Avenue, New York, as her sponsor's private secretary. She later confided to Eliza Kellas that she had become a secretary "by accident, not by training or inclination, or intention."[14] She ruefully shared with Kellas her sense that she was a "self-made" woman whose talents were going to waste.[15]

E. Lilian Todd was from a modest background that made it necessary for her to earn her living. Born June 10, 1865, in Washington, D.C., and educated in that city, she had taught herself to type and had trained as a stenographer, finding employment with a firm of patent attorneys. She subsequently seems to have set up her own firm. In her words, "I had years of experience in my own office, and I touched upon almost every line of business in existence, plus science and invention, architecture and law, even medicine and chemistry."[16] Todd came to the attention of the socially prominent Olivia Sage and Helen Gould in the 1890s when she was a member of the first Woman's Law Class at New York University, and Gould subsequently employed her as secretary to the director-general of the Women's National War Relief Association in 1898.[17] In 1903, Todd was hired as a secretary for the Louisiana Purchase Exposition in St. Louis (the 1904 World's Fair), probably again on the recommendation of Helen Gould, a board member of the fair. Todd was entranced by the airships she saw at the fair. She recalled:

Captain Baldwin and his dirigible balloon, and the Ville de Mandes of France were in St. Louis, and my windows overlooked the enclosure where the airships were stationed. That was sufficient to fire my mind with a desire to conquer the air.[18]

In the next few years she designed a dirigible which flew successfully, founded the Junior Aero Club of the United States, and built numerous successful flying models of planes and balloons. She received national attention as an inventor with several firsts to her credit. Interviewed for *Woman's Home Companion* in 1909, she described how she had begun work on the design of a heavier-than-air biplane in 1906 after seeing a sketch of a proposed aeroplane in a Paris newspaper. "I immediately set to work to evolve a [plane] which I considered much superior to the pictured design."[19] Now, she announced, "the machine is completed, and ready to prove to the world that a woman's machine is quite equal to a man-made flyer, and far more practicable in some respects than many he has made."[20] One of "her boys" from the Junior Aero Club took her plane on its trial flights in 1910.[21] But Todd needed a wealthy backer, and this role Olivia enthusiastically played. The elderly woman made several trips to Mineola to see progress on the plane. In July 1910, when she visited Mineola "especially to see Miss E. L. Todd's aeroplane," she was asked by a reporter whether she would continue to provide financial backing "for a successful machine should this one fail." Olivia replied that she would. "I have known Miss Todd a long time. . . . I have always been interested in her because I think she is a capable woman and I like to see women do things."[22]

We do not know why Todd was unable to use this sponsorship to develop her career further as an inventor and aviator. She was forty-five years old in 1910, and, in an odd reversal of the stereotyped idea that typing was peculiarly suitable for women, she told an interviewer that she couldn't crank the plane because years of typing had weakened her fingers! "I expect to operate the machine myself, when I have fully mastered the intricacies of the engine, but at present I have not strength enough to crank it, my hands having weakened from the long, hard strain at the typewriter."[23]

By July 1912, this brilliant and frustrated "self-made" woman had replaced Catharine Hunter as secretary to Olivia Sage. To begin with, she enjoyed a warm relationship with her employer, signing a note to Olivia, "Lovingly, Lilian," Olivia writing back to her, "Most affectionately, M. Olivia Sage."[24] Lilian had free access to her elderly patron,

FIGURE 13.1. Eliza Kellas aged around fifty, the age at which
Olivia persuaded her to become principal of the new Russell
Sage College. Courtesy Emma Willard School.

and she used this access to encourage Sage's philanthropy to a woman's
college designed to help talented women of modest means—women
like herself.

The third figure in this story, educator Eliza Kellas, also had a remarkable career, though in a more traditional field. As a young woman, she

was described as "her father's constant companion, the son of the family." She trained as a teacher at Potsdam Normal School in upstate New York, graduating in 1889, then taught at Plattsburgh State Normal School. In 1898, she attended the University of Michigan, and in 1905 she secured a fellowship to Radcliffe, graduating with a B.A. in 1910 at the age of forty-six. She became principal of the Emma Willard School in 1911. Like Lilian Todd, she never married, but made her home with her sister (see fig. 13.1).[25]

Kellas advocated professional schools for postgraduate women. "Truly this is a time of specialized training," she wrote to Todd, "and if young women are to fit themselves thoroughly to succeed they must have an opportunity for careful and thorough training." The Russell Sage College would be this type of institution.[26]

A previously unknown correspondence between Todd and Kellas sheds new light on the origins of the college, Olivia's last major philanthropic gift. A friendship had grown up between the two single women, both in their early fifties (Kellas was just one year older than Todd), each of them dependent in different ways on the elderly philanthropist, an acquaintance sparked initially by a meeting at the Emma Willard School commencement in June 1914, then sustained by letters, formal to begin with and then increasingly frank and affectionate, and by occasional meetings in Troy and New York City.

Kellas first broached the idea of a new women's college to Lilian in June 1914. She had invited Lilian up to Troy to attend the Emma Willard School commencement as Sage's representative.[27] Recalling their meeting a year or so later, Lilian wrote, "I can give the day, and almost the hour, that the suggestion [for the college] was made,—it was our first talk in the Library of the School."[28] And then another time: "You spoke to me of wishing to start some sort of classes in those buildings, when I saw you—something that would bring certain forms of education within the reach of girls who could not afford to go to the main school."[29] After that first discussion, Kellas wrote a long letter to Olivia, summarizing the arguments in favor of using the three buildings on Second Street in Troy (Russell Sage Hall, Gurley Hall, Anna Plum Hall). Acknowledging this "full and interesting Report," Olivia agreed with her secretary that the abandoned buildings should be put use. "I think as Memorials there should be some educational work for them."[30] Returning to New York, Todd prepared a proposal for a new college and presented it to Olivia Sage.[31]

But November came and there was no response. Lilian wrote to Kellas, "I have done all I could to suggest to Mrs. Sage that she aid you in your project."[32] Subsequently, Kellas and Todd met in New York and drew up some more detailed plans and a budget. But presenting these to Olivia was no longer as easy as before. Lilian now had to go through Mrs. Sage's nurse Ruth Simpson, a recent addition to the household.[33] Simpson soon proved to be a useful ally, however, and so by the end of 1915 did Henry de Forest, who expressed his "absolute approval" of the idea.[34] Some days later, Kellas was summoned by telegram to come down to New York City to consult with Mrs. Sage. She found the elderly woman in the second-floor room where she now spent most of her time, "a quiet little figure sitting in a great circular window commanding a view up and down Fifth Avenue."

> She was a still, white little person . . . with her white hair, and her white hands crossed on her black dress. Because of her deafness it was extremely hard to talk with her, and she had a personal dignity that one could not offend—though she was gracious and really friendly.[35]

Kellas, the Radcliffe graduate and school principal, felt like a schoolgirl as she obeyed instructions to pull up an ottoman and sit close by the old lady's chair. "I never tried to persuade her to any course: one does not argue with a woman who is very old and stone deaf!"

Olivia's first question was, "What shall we do with the Second Street buildings?" Plum, Gurley, and Russell Sage Halls were standing empty, as they had been since 1910. The thought saddened Olivia, for she remembered persuading Russell Sage to pay for the hall twenty years earlier— how hard it had been to get him to part with the money! Lilian had prepared Eliza Kellas for this question, and she was ready with an answer. She didn't know what would become of the buildings, she replied, "unless you or someone else will give money to found another educational institution there."[36]

The interview ended without a decision, and Kellas returned to Troy. But Lilian continued to raise the subject whenever she could. Russell Sage Hall, donated by her late husband to the old Emma Willard School in 1895, was empty and overrun with rats and mice, she told Olivia. Then why not put the hall and the other abandoned seminary buildings to use? Why not found a new women's college in Troy?

Two weeks later Kellas received another summons to the Sage home in New York. Here, Olivia announced her decision to use the buildings as the nucleus of a new vocational college. And she wanted Eliza Kellas to be the president! The news fell on Kellas like a bombshell. As she protested that she already had her hands full with the Emma Willard

School, "Mrs. Sage listened, leaned back in her chair, and replied wearily, 'Well then, we shall have to give it all up. I am old, and tired, and I cannot go over all this thinking with someone else. We shall just have to give up the idea.'"[37] Kellas begged for some more time to consider. Eventually and reluctantly she agreed to head both institutions.[38]

On December 16, 1915, Lilian received a note from Olivia: "Mr. de Forest came yesterday for my consent to [the] Technical School, so Miss Kellas can do her best, and she is truly capable."[39] Olivia then informed the trustees of the Emma Willard School of her decision to establish the Russell Sage School of Practical Arts "or such other appropriate name as I may choose to designate," with an initial gift of $250,000. The governing board would have five members, four of whom were to be also members of the Emma Willard School board.[40] A clause in the deed of gift directed to the trustees of the Emma Willard School stated: "The standard of work and study at the school shall be at least equal to the standard maintained at similar schools, say at Simmons College, Boston, and the Pratt Institute in Brooklyn."[41]

The college opened in September 1916 with 300 students divided between departments of secretarial work, household economics, and industrial arts, with a curriculum that reflected the belief that modern women must train to earn their own living in the professions and business.[42] Olivia still got indignant when she thought about the low salary she had received as a teacher sixty years earlier. She had earned $200 a year plus board, she told Lilian.[43] Now graduates of Russell Sage college and similar colleges would have an alternative to the overcrowded and underpaid field of teaching. The college was a great success. The first class that assembled in September 1916 was fully subscribed, with 117 registered students (not counting extension students), Kellas informed Robert de Forest.[44] The next year was the same. By March, every place was taken for the next year, and applications still came in every day.[45]

Behind the scenes, Lilian begged Kellas not to publicize her role in the project. "You alone will get the credit," she promised.[46] In a memo to Robert de Forest she called the college "Mrs. Sage's greatest and crowning work."[47] Olivia, on the other hand, embarrassed Lilian by instructing her to inform prominent supporters in Troy that she was only giving the college because of Troy's connection with her husband, "that she was not interested in Troy personally, that it was not her home and she only had done what she had for it because it had been Mr. Sage's home, he had lived there, made part of his money there, been elected from Congress there." Needless to say, such publicity hurt fund-raising efforts among the Troy public.[48]

Worse still, it was already apparent to Kellas that the initial gift of $250,000 left nothing for an endowment or for acquiring additional properties, while rapid wartime inflation made her job almost impossible. The overworked principal of a school who now had the additional responsibility of running a college without proper funding, she was in despair. Although she drew a salary as principal of the Emma Willard School, she worked at the Russell Sage College for nothing.[49] Lilian Todd and Eliza Kellas favored replacing the moribund Emma Willard Association with an alumnae association that would raise money for scholarships and for an endowment for the new college. Lilian actively helped defeat the Brooklyn/New York–based EWA, encouraged Olivia Sage to resign as president, and then created a new Margaret Olivia Sage chapter in Troy. Sage then gave money to this new branch.[50] Aided and abetted by Nurse Simpson, Kellas and Todd also continued to work behind the scenes to get Sage to increase her gift. When Kellas showed Lilian a progress report about the college, Lilian warned her that it was too optimistic: "I am not going to pass your letter [to Mrs. Sage]. I do not wish you to leave the impression that the College is 'progressing so finely' that it most runs itself."[51] And she complained, "Had Mr. [Robert] de Forest taken a little more personal interest, your troubles might have been less. . . . Had it been anything he wanted,—it would have been another matter. I am sorry, because Mrs. Sage has given more to other institutions, and this is so individually her own, it seems too bad not to make it the best."[52] Kellas noted with satisfaction that Mrs. Sage's gift was "fulfilling one of Mrs. Willard's fondest hopes, as well as helping girls of merit to fit themselves thoroughly to do their part of the world's work." It was gratifying that graduates of Emma Willard School and Vassar were returning to Russell Sage College "for their technical training in household economics."[53]

This was Olivia's ninetieth year. Funding for the new college was still insufficient, and it was becoming apparent that the elderly woman was no longer able to grasp what had to be done to make it financially viable, "although she has been really remarkable in thinking of as many things as she has under existing circumstances," Lilian noted generously. She added, "I blame Mr. de Forest, because Mrs. Sage would have given any amount he advised."[54] In May 1918, when Kellas put forward another budget request, de Forest blocked it, "in view of which," Lilian wrote to her, "you may be interested to know that the one who turned it down as excessive, is this morning putting in an appeal of his own for the Red Cross."[55]

For Lilian, the satisfaction of having founded the new college was not followed by more personal satisfactions. When Kellas invited her to "come and see the schools at work," she responded, "If I could come up and make you take a day off and forget both schools for a whole twenty-four hours, I might think about it."[56] In the college's second spring of operation, Lilian wrote, "I wish I might run away with you and take you on a trip somewhere South, if one could be found that would include a really warm place." But burdened with the double responsibility of the school and the college, Kellas had neither the time nor perhaps the inclination to accept.[57] Meanwhile the two women, one in Troy, the other in New York City, waited to find out whether Olivia Sage would alter her will and provide an adequate endowment for the college that bore her husband's name.

Fourteen

"Splendid Donation"

May I have a splendid donation from you?
—Harriet P. James, YMCA fund-raiser (1914)[1]

[We are] wondering if you would feel inclined
to put us in a state of ecstasy again.
—Marie Haines Bradwell, YWCA secretary (1911)[2]

Earlier chapters have described the great dramatic gifts that made Sage philanthropy famous—the endowment of $10 million to the Russell Sage Foundation, the millions more to universities, colleges, and schools. In addition to these donations, Olivia gave generously to organizations and causes of all kinds, carrying on a complex private philanthropy that embraced children and youth, health and safety, home and foreign missions, the humane treatment of animals, and conservation. There were donations to civic institutions and to institutions for dependent persons such as the aged, orphans, and the chronically ill. There were gifts to clubs for working girls and professional women, a donation to the Music School Settlement for Colored People in Harlem, and others to the Prison Association of New York and to the Anti-Saloon League of Lawrence, Long Island. She gave to Protestant-run causes but also to Catholic charities such as the Home for the Aged run by the Little Sisters of the Poor in the Bronx and to the United Hebrew Charities for playgrounds. And there were donations for disaster relief, for flood relief in Mississippi (1912) and for earthquake relief in Persia (1915). There is a life membership in the New York Peace Society for $100. One estimate put her lifetime gifts to religious, charitable, and educational organizations between 1907 and 1918 at around $40 million. Her bequests total another $35 million.[3]

270

Our window into this large and complex philanthropy is the collection of approximately 5,000 fund-raising letters and appeals addressed to Sage and now preserved at the Rockefeller Archive Center in the collection that bears her husband's name, the Russell Sage Foundation Records.[4] Unlike the foundation, which took into account the general welfare of society, the private philanthropy was personal giving which rewarded specific institutions and individuals that were favorites of the donor. This chapter explores how Olivia responded to these appeals and reexamines the assumption that once she had set up the foundation she had a relatively free hand. I show how in practice Sage's spending was modified under pressure from a circle of advisors that included her brother, the De Forest Brothers law firm, and her secretaries. Fund-raisers put pressure on her, as did her friends.

We begin with a unique episode in Sage's philanthropy, the attempt between 1907 and 1912 to play a Lady Bountiful role in Sag Harbor, a village at the eastern end of Long Island with connections to her family.

Lady Bountiful of Sag Harbor

The Sag Harbor philanthropy was a small-scale but ambitious effort that aimed to rebuild the town's cultural and educational institutions and effect the moral reconstruction of the small community. It combined Progressive projects of social reconstruction with old-fashioned largesse, even including a traditional dole of money "for the poor of the town," which she distributed through a friend. And it was quirky. A local newspaper reported, "She gave the local fire company money to buy ten new suits (Mrs. Aldrich also contributed)—together they fitted out all the men in suits, blue with light trim, double-breasted coats and peaked hats." A letter of thanks from the Phoenix Fire Company, Sag Harbor, remains among her papers.[5]

Sag Harbor was dear to Olivia as her mother's birthplace, and while Russell Sage was still alive she purchased her Pierson grandparents' house at Sagaponack near Bridgehampton, Long Island, "out of her own pocket money as a surprise to him," according to a friend.[6] In 1902, she bought the colonial-era house of John Jermain on Main Street known as the Luther Cook house, built in about 1790, and restored it.[7] After she was widowed, she purchased the Huntting House, a columned neoclassical mansion built in 1845 for a wealthy merchant with interests in whaling at a cost of $40,000, then a huge amount. According to preservation consultant Alison Cornish, "Mrs. Sage purchased the building

FIGURE 14.1. Harbor Home, Olivia's summer retreat at Sag Harbor, Long Island, around 1900. Courtesy Nassau County Museum Collection, Long Island Studies Institute, Hofstra University.

in 1908, restored it, moved nearby houses to create a larger grander area, and dubbed it 'Harbor Home.'" She subsequently lived there during her summer visits to Sag Harbor between 1908 and 1912 (see fig. 14.1).[8]

Olivia's interest in the old whaling town was fed by nostalgia for her ancestry and the region. Her enthusiasm included the area's Native American history: she supported publication of *Indian Place Names* (1911) by local scholar William Wallace Tooker; she collected mementos of her ancestors, including documents about Captain Charles L'Hommedieu and John Jermain;[9] and she worked at discovering her family's roots, searching out their gravesites and quizzing elderly Sag Harbor residents about their memories.[10]

These personal preoccupations worked side by side with a benevolent reformism. She also took an interest in the immigrant population that formed the workforce of Fahy's, a watchcase factory that was the town's major employer.[11] Sag Harbor had fallen on hard times since the collapse of the whaling industry and the loss to fire of its textile manufacturing plant. Olivia wanted to revive the town by investing in community-building institutions. She supplied the funds for a new "scientifically designed" park with modern equipment and amenities, hiring the New York landscaping and architectural firm of Samuel Parsons.[12] Mashashimuet Park, built on property that was formerly a race track and fairground, symbolized moral renewal because the land had been converted from vulgar amusements to activities that would improve people's character. In a rare example of direct overlap between private and foundation philanthropy, Olivia drew on the experts of the Russell Sage Foundation, incorporating some paid foundation staff into plans for the little seaport. The park director was Lee F. Hanmer, director of child hygiene for the Russell Sage Foundation. Hanmer in turn hired Robert K. Atkinson, a field secretary of the Playground and Recreation Association of America, as director of recreation at the Sag Harbor park.[13] She even underwrote the programs of supervised recreation, including folk dancing and uplifting and educational talks.[14] This philanthropy reflected the thinking of the play movement reformers who sought "to organize the recreational life of the children of the poor and to use local public schools as the focus of neighborhood life."[15] Olivia also gave the community a new high school. Pierson High School, named for her ancestor Abraham Pierson, was completed in 1908 at the cost of $102,000. Another donation made possible a domed public library of grandiose style, the John Jermain Memorial Library, named for her grandfather, which opened in 1910.[16] She gave over $13,000 to repair the steeple of the old Presbyterian church, known as the Whalers' Church, whose spire, one chronicler noted, had long been "the first glimpse of home caught by many a sailor who has been afloat for three or five years."[17]

This emphasis on building a community's educational and recreational institutions was a hallmark of Progressive-era reform. At the same time, the Sag Harbor philanthropy was personal, steeped in the donor's imagined historical relationship to Long Island. And it put her in a Lady Bountiful relationship to a whole community. When night-school classes were started for factory workers, one journalist reported, "Mrs. Sage will personally direct the work." He was wrong, but the misstatement reveals the general perception that the donor was personally involved.[18] It helps explain why the Sag Harbor philanthropy was ultimately unsuccessful. The whole episode ended in recrimination, with the community in revolt against the reformers' uplift plans and with Olivia abandoning her summer home there and withdrawing from the town in anger in 1912 after it was revealed that the contractors for the high school had cheated her by substituting inferior building materials for the expensive ones she had paid for. One observer described Sag Harbor's inhabitants as "unappreciative," reported complaints that Sage had "pauperized" the community (by making it unwilling to shift for itself), and described vandalism against fixtures in the park.[19] Such personal philanthropy to a single community by its wealthiest resident was beset with problems and it was coming to seem archaic as well as undemocratic. Yet Olivia's affection for Sag Harbor outlasted her dispute with its city fathers. According to a friend, in the winter of 1914 and 1915 she read in a New York paper that the workers at Fahy's were experiencing hardships because of strikes and unsettled working conditions growing out of the world war, "so she sent a thousand dollars secretly for relief."[20]

"Institutions to which you can wisely give"

As early as the beginning of 1907 Olivia felt overwhelmed by appeals for money. Her cry for help (or it might have been one of complaint) to Robert de Forest is lost, but we have his response. Four thousand organizations had already applied for funding, he noted, advising her to select institutions "to which you can wisely give in sums of fifty, one hundred or it may be even two hundred and fifty thousand dollars."[21] Offering to handle these appeals for her, he stated confidently: "I am satisfied, after reading them, that comparatively few of the institutions or causes which you will ultimately determine to help have made any application at all." He had provided her with brief summaries, and they had been numbered and filed "so that they can be readily referred to by the number of the abstract and by the name of the applicant." "Unless you are prepared to consider every small church and every small school and college, it would seem unnecessary for you to give attention to applications other than those which have been abstracted."[22] De Forest assumed that those who *had not* applied for aid were more deserving than those who had—a theoretical position which gave him a free hand to decide who *was* deserving. In July 1907, he summarized for Sage the appeals from institutions received to date. Of these, "6,486 upon examination were found either to require no attention from you or to be outside of any possible sphere of your benevolence. The remaining 1,026 have been carefully abstracted, and await your consideration whenever you feel ready to take them up."[23]

But Olivia had her own ideas. Arthur Huntington Gleason, the author of the 1906 article "Mrs. Russell Sage and Her Interests," referred to her as having "an active intellectual life."[24] For years she had been collecting materials from all kinds of reform and educational organizations, as we know from correspondence with the New York Public Library.

In October 5, 1903, the library's director, J. S. Billings, acknowledged "a collection of pamphlets relating to Women's work and a file of the recent years of the *Mail and Express,* which you are willing to donate to this Library." In May 1908 there was another donation consisting of "reports of institutions." Subsequently Billings acknowledged "a miscellaneous collection of over one thousand volumes and pamphlets, being for the most part, reports of colleges, hospitals, etc." These were not valuable books but working materials that provided the data to support an informed philanthropy.[25]

Then there was her motivation. Although she turned eighty in the fall of 1908, her belief in stewardship still burned bright and her intentions remained the same: to memorialize her husband, to demonstrate that educated women could reform public life, to exercise Christian stewardship, and to alleviate human suffering. As one fund-raiser wrote excitedly to Harvard president A. Lawrence Lowell "from the little that I have heard of her . . . she really wishes to spend it."[26]

Working from her Fifth Avenue home and in the summer months from Cedar Croft on Long Island, she answered the appeals one by one, with the help of her secretaries E. Lilian Todd and Catharine Hunter. Her increasing age added a sense of urgency, as did the fact that the money was continuing to pile up. By one estimate, it was increasing by $12,000 a day. If she was to do some good with her money, she would have to act fast. That she was able to begin to spend right away and on a grand scale was because the channels and contacts were already in place and the recipients were already picked out; in many cases the organizations were ones she had supported through voluntary work or with small donations over the years. On the other hand, the scene was now set for a struggle between the donor, connected by ties of affection and relationship to the small female-directed charities beloved of her mother's generation and the new proliferation of associations of Progressive-era women's reform, and her attorney, who had his own networks (New York reform politics, Yale alumni), his own favorite causes (the Metropolitan Museum of Art), and his belief in large-scale, income-producing philanthropic experiments such as Forest Hills Gardens, a benevolent capitalism that yielded "progress and six percent."[27]

Women's reform associations began writing to Olivia at once. Some causes she had aided with volunteer time or with small donations before 1906 now reaped the reward or, in some cases, were shocked to receive a refusal. The Pascal Institute, a sewing school for girls on Lexington Avenue, was a favorite of Olivia's. Founded in 1898, it trained women for the dressmaking trades, which was still an avenue to self-support through small business.[28] In 1906, Olivia was named as honorary president (she usually refused such titles), and it was reported that she took "the greatest personal interest and pride in the young needlewomen Pascal Institute turns out." She spoke at their graduation ceremony in 1906 and presented the graduates with copies of her favorite books: *The Cloister and the Hearth, Emma,* and *Cranford.*[29] But little more than a year later, Robert de Forest was quoting a COS investigation to persuade her that the Pascal Institute did not merit her support and arguing that "no greater burden should be assumed by you." No records of further gifts to this organization remain.[30] The Ely Club and the College Women's Club, which both appealed to Sage in flattering terms, were also refused.[31]

Olivia also began to neglect many small-scale missions, settlements, and religiously based social agencies that she had earlier supported. She had served on the board of the Gospel Settlement in New York City for five or six years previous to 1906 and, according to the director, Sarah J. Bird, had often declared that she intended to give it a large amount of money, "but that she had very little money at her disposal and that all she had went to her nephew in the Philippines."[32] The small gifts continued, but the large donation never occurred. Pathetic letters from Mrs. Bird tell the story: "I feel sure you do not receive my letters or you would give us some little encouragement in our present extremity," she wrote.[33]

Other charities were more lucky. The Loomis Sanatorium, a small tuberculosis charity that had elected Olivia to its board in May 1904, received a donation of $25,000 from her a few years later to build and equip a cottage for patients.[34] When the charity was a familiar and dear one like this, Olivia managed to have her own way. The Onondaga Orphans Asylum of Syracuse is a case in point. "Refused for Mrs. Sage and Colonel, too," wrote Lilian on the envelope of an appeal from this institution. But shortly afterward, Olivia gave $10,000 anyway.[35] And her donations rewarded other charities that did not meet COS criteria. Some, like the McAuley Cremorne Mission in New York City, were small-scale, financially shaky institutions, carried on by Social Gospel type ministers and their wives. This mission, too, had a personal connection, for it had been a favorite of her friends the Jesups. Olivia gave to it several years running.[36] Her donations to such small charities continued throughout the period 1906–1918.

Olivia also continued to give in kind as well as with money, sending donations of clothes and shoes to the Eighth Avenue Mission, a cause successfully pleaded by her "houseman" Nelson.[37] Numerous charities that gave out shoes, coal, or food or provided visiting nurses or help with housing received her support. In 1918, she gave $2,500 to the Woman's

Hospital for the purchase of coal during the cold weather.[38] And she regularly gave donations of \$1,000 to the New York Association for Improving the Condition of the Poor, an older association which helped the poor directly. In December 1907, its secretary assured Olivia that her check would "help our work among the poor and unfortunate of the city"; a few months later he wrote thanking her for a donation for the purchase of shoes with a vivid image: "We shall be able to cover the feet of nearly 500 children by means of your kind donation." Her donation of \$1,000 in the winter of 1915 would be used "at once for unemployed and sick," the secretary assured her. These all suggest that she was not sticking to the strict guidelines of the COS that tied relief to investigation of need.[39]

Friends and False Friends

Old friends were relentless in their attempts to interest Olivia in funding one scheme or another. Access was everything. "Let me come to you dear Mrs. Sage for ten minutes," wrote Maria Beebe of the YWCA, adding, "You cannot be left out of this great movement to extend the helpfulness to the five hundred thousand working girls of New York." A few weeks later she tried again, asking Olivia for \$600,000, "because you are a woman of large interests and warm impulses."[40] Former Carlisle principal Richard Pratt always had new reasons to see his old friend, and in May 1913 he found Olivia receptive, for she instructed her secretary, "Thank Brigadier-General R. H. Pratt for Report on the Indians. And ask how I can contribute *now* to the cause that I have been interested in from the time of my first visit to the Carlisle Indian Training School."[41] But mostly she was wary about social visits because guests often used them as an opportunity to ask for money. This was true even when the cause was one that she supported. When Mrs. W. A. Putnam, daughter of a former secretary of the Woman's Home Missionary Society and a friend, asked to see her about a donation to Babies' Hospital in New York, Lilian noted, "Wrote Mrs. Sage could not take up the matter, as she already contributes to Babies' Hospital and other hospitals and homes for children in New York, and did not grant interviews for the purpose of hearing details of the work."[42]

Especially upsetting were visitors who abused the intimacy of a friendly visit by launching without warning into an appeal for money. Even close friends were not to be trusted. In May 1914, Lilian warned Olivia that a Mrs. Robert Mead, daughter of Dr. Cleveland, was about to appeal to her again on behalf of the American Society for the Control of Cancer. "[F]rom what Mrs. Mead says, either Dr. Delevan or Mrs. Thompson may spring it on you over a game of backgammon. They want $5,000 now and failing to get that, they want the amount you gave last year doubled." Olivia was forewarned. When the charity appealed to her she scrawled a note to Lilian, "Had the courage to refuse to see Dr. Cleveland, suspecting his errand (see fig. 14.2)."[43]

Olivia Sage's philanthropy was "never the giving of money . . . always the giving of money after personal contact with the work," a sympathetic journalist wrote in 1906.[44] Personal involvement was no longer possible as Olivia grew older, but the letters support the idea that she retained interest in the details of her gifts. On an appeal from the Babies' Hospital for $250 for a bed, her secretary had written, "Shall I send check?" Olivia wrote a note, "Yes. I know the good work the Babies Hospital does." Her earliest recorded donation to this cause had been $10 in 1891.[45]

Still, Olivia was wary of fraud, and not all the people she had to guard against were outside the family circle. Jermain had his own reasons to try to keep people with expensive proposals away from his sister. In the will she had drawn up and signed in October 1906, Olivia had left Jermain only $10,000 in trust. But in a first codicil to the will dated February 17, 1908, she gave him $2 million dollars, and in July 1911 a second codicil increased his legacy by $5 million! Not surprisingly, after this, Jermain became even more protective of his sister and her wealth.[46]

Jermain, the de Forest brothers, and E. Lilian Todd, who together comprised the circle around her, developed a set of informal rules that people appealing for Sage money broke at their peril. Olivia established some of these rules herself. She usually refused institutions that were outside New York, and when she sent a check for $5,000 to Hull House in 1910, it was with a note to Jane Addams declining to send a larger sum because "my chief responsibilities are elsewhere than in Chicago." Similarly, a strong appeal to help working women in the "silk mills, cork and candy factories, and other self-supporting women," dated May 11, 1914, was refused, probably because it came from Lancaster, Pennsylvania.[47]

Another rule was that one donation did not set up a relationship or entitle the recipient to a stream of giving. Instead, the fiction was maintained that each gift stood alone and that each was completely at the donor's initiative.[48] But correspondence shows that beneficiaries of Sage's generosity continued to expect one gift to be followed up by another, with the first gift establishing a stream of giving and finally an entitlement.[49] William Goodell Frost, president of interracial Berea College, was regarded as a nuisance by Olivia's advisors because after Olivia

FIGURE 14.2. "Olivia Sage answering correspondence." Daniel Coit Gilman, "Five Great Gifts," *The Outlook* (August 1907).

gave several gifts to Berea and another of $5,000 in 1916, the Frosts redoubled their efforts. The secretary noted, "Dr. and Mrs. Frost have been persistent and insistent for several years in trying to see Mrs. Sage and 'tell her all about it.' Think they must have grown quite a grievance against the secretary by this time for refusing, but they undoubtedly think they can get through now." Olivia decided she could not face President Frost again, for she wrote a note to Lilian, asking her to make an excuse for not meeting him.[50]

Also against the "rules" was trying to enlarge a gift. When Chancellor Day offered to change the name of the teachers' college to Margaret Olivia Slocum Woman's College, de Forest warned him, "[Y]ou should not do so based upon the expectation that Mrs. Sage will make her gifts larger on this account. She is averse to being asked to give more where she has already given something."[51] Once she had given a large donation, further requests were viewed as an intolerable breach of etiquette. When a member of the Salvation Army independently solicited a donation from Olivia (who had given large amounts to the organization), Brigadier R. Griffith hastened to apologize, explaining to Lilian, "I am sure you will quite understand that it is not possible for the Commander to control all the members of the organization, and there is always the possibility that someone will take the liberty of writing to Mrs. Sage for help."[52]

Now elderly and often overwhelmed by the task before her, Olivia weighed competing claims, rewarding some causes and refusing others. She remained alert for fraud, using networks of friends and informants in major charitable associations to investigate the worthiness of an appeal.[53] Handwritten notes on the letters or their envelopes provide a glimpse of how decisions were made. Her secretaries, her friends, her brother, and the COS network were all mobilized to check on dubious charities; when there was doubt, money was withheld. She was about to send a donation of $150 to the Indian Association of Northern California (motto: "Only the Self-Raised Stay Up"), but became suspicious. Her secretary raised the alarm: "Wait—does not recognize the name find out more about this before giving."[54] On another occasion, when Olivia wanted to give $5,000 to the Newsboys Home Club, Lilian checked on the organization using the *New York Charities Directory* and reported that it was not such a worthy organization as the Home for Working Boys. The Newsboys Home Club "is only to keep them interested and off the street," she told Olivia.[55]

She expected organizations to be run efficiently. The New York Orthopedic Dispensary and Hospital, to which she gave an early donation of $50 in February 1902 and donations ranging from two to five thousand dollars annually afterward, wrote in 1914 to ask for a donation of $10,000. But when the organization slipped deeper into debt Sage refused to support it any further, and her secretary stopped forwarding its appeals to her.[56]

Sometimes Sage donated in response to an appeal, and some very persistent petitioners, such as E. A. Paddock, principal of the Idaho Industrial Institute, were spectacularly successful. Others got only what they requested: when the Woman's Municipal League of the City of New York, to which Olivia had subscribed for a life membership, appealed for support of its summer recreation programs for workers, Olivia sent $100.[57] At other times, she liked to take the initiative and give to an organization that had not even contacted her. Such a strategy helped to maintain the fiction that the gift set up the recipient in self-sufficiency, that every gift was the last.

Suddenly free to spend her money, Olivia thought of the organizations she had long admired. Some of these stretched back into her past. One such was the Ladies Christian Union of the City of New York, founded in 1858 with the goal of promoting "the welfare of women, particularly the young and unprotected employed in stores and manufactories."[58] In 1904, Sage was still paying a $5 annual subscription. Ten years later, she asked her secretary whether the organization still existed, as she wanted to donate $200. The request sent Lilian to the *Charities Directory*. "The Ladies Christian Union of the City of New York is still in existence," Lilian informed her. "It aims to promote the temporal, moral and religious welfare of self-supporting young women by providing boarding houses with home-like apartments. It maintains five of these in different parts of the City."[59] Satisfied that the association was worth funding, Sage sent it $200. "Not the result of an appeal," Lilian wrote on the envelope.[60]

These traditional charities were usually run by middle- or upper-class women, and they were often financially shaky. Their fund-raisers (and directors—often the same person) were often cursed by a traditional modesty. Begging letters from women's organizations were often so meek that they produced only meager donations. An appeal by Martha Talmage Wycoff (daughter of Brooklyn Tabernacle's celebrated minister de Witt Talmage) on behalf of the Ely Club at West 97th Street asked for funds "to provide a comfortable home for young women of limited means who are either studying with a view to self-support or supporting themselves on an amount not sufficient to enable them to live elsewhere." But then Wycoff blurted out: "This is going to be a begging letter for a club to which I belong, and if I never get a reply I shall know you were entirely too busy to acknowledge it for the letters you receive must be appalling." Olivia responded with only $25.[61]

"Studies of the sun"

Very different were the grandiose schemes of Charles D. Walcott, secretary of the Smithsonian Institution, who corresponded with Olivia through Henry de Forest. Walcott had large expensive projects that he wanted the philanthropist to fund. The investigation of South America "should have an endowment that would give an income of Two hundred and fifty thousand dollars a year for a generation or more," he informed de Forest.[62] When Walcott managed to obtain an interview with Sage early in 1908, he came armed with several different draft deeds of gift. But evidently the four research areas specified there (anthropological studies of North and South America, the effects of artificial light, and the causes of earthquakes) did not appeal to her.[63] He now suggested instead "The Russell Sage Fund for the Increase and Diffusion of Knowledge for the Benefit of Mankind," a general fund of "a million or more" for research.[64] Walcott also tried to interest her in other ideas. At various times he floated "a plan to rescue the poor whites of the south from their present degraded condition" (October 1908); an "all-around-the-world investigation" of earthquakes (February 1909); and a Herbarium of World Botany (December 1909).[65] In December 1909 he suggested that she might fund "studies of the sun" and the effect of variations in temperature on different crops.[66]

Walcott finally struck a chord in 1911 when he suggested that Olivia might provide major funding for the purchase of 79,300-acre Marsh Island in Louisiana for a bird sanctuary. The gift was in line with her lifelong interest in protecting birds. She bought Marsh Island after consultation with George Bird Grinnell of *Field and Stream* and Dr. Hornaday of the New York Zoological Gardens.[67] But there would be no bequest for Walcott or the Smithsonian in Olivia's will, which instead named as beneficiaries the American Museum of Natural History ($1.6 million) and the New York Botanical Garden ($800,000), both in New York City.

If she remained unmoved by grandiose scientific investigations, Olivia was clearly touched by the many associations for infants, children, and young people that wrote to her for money. She donated to day nurseries, kindergartens, playgrounds, fresh air and outings funds, homes for working boys, the Boy Scouts, the Camp Fire Girls, and many others.[68] In the case of the Camp Fire Girls, programs and ideology coincided with the recreational work of the foundation, and the foundation's Luther Gulick was the liaison.[69]

Olivia's involvement with the YWCA and YMCA movement predated her husband's death. In 1902, at a time when she still had little discretionary income, she donated $100 to the Springfield, Massachusetts, YMCA training school.[70] After Russell Sage's death, she worked through old friends like Sarah Dodge, her co-worker at the Woman's Hospital since the 1870s, and after Sarah died, with her daughter, the extraordinary Grace Hoadley Dodge.[71] She contributed to the YWCA National Training School and gave generously to help build YWCAs in other far-flung places: in Colorado Springs (1909), El Paso (1910); Los Angeles (1910); St. Louis, San Francisco, and Seattle (1912); Pasadena (1913); and even Manila.[72] The result was a network of nonsectarian urban religious institutions that protected thousands of young single women as they migrated from country to city to become workers in industry, banks, offices, and stores.[73] It is significant that when Olivia made a late donation to the Syracuse YWCA in January 1918 (she was refusing appeals from Ys elsewhere), she requested that the money be administered through the local Business Women's Committee. This was self-consciously women's philanthropy, wealthy women putting their resources together to build urban and moral reform institutions for young working women.[74]

Donations to the YMCA were larger and its goals even more ambitious: to project the ideology of American Protestantism and material betterment beyond New York and overseas.[75] The YMCA movement advocated reform of the social order itself through a redeemed and cleansed male citizenry—a goal which far transcended its earlier missionary and recreational purposes. It had become part of the Progressive-era reshaping of young men and women in the modern city.[76]

Olivia and other wealthy women combined forces—and fortunes— to found railway YMCAs for young men. She gave a $50,000 donation for the Long Island Railroad YMCA in 1907 and $250,000 for an annex to the Brooklyn Navy Yard YMCA erected by Helen Gould.[77] She and others established a Women's Auxiliary of the International Committee of the YMCA, claiming it as a "legitimate field for woman's interest and help, because it has to do with those who will determine in large measure the future of the home, the church, and the state. The direct outcome of this special effort for young men is the making of better sons, better husbands, better fathers, and better citizens."[78]

In October 1906 and again in 1907, and with a speed suggesting that she had been contemplating this action for some time, Olivia anonymously gave $250,000 for the new International Headquarters of the YMCA at Twenty-Seventh and Twenty-Eighth Streets in New York. She acted with her old friend Sarah Dodge, who gave the land while Olivia Sage gave the seven-story building. An additional gift brought Olivia's total to $350,000.[79] "Be sure to have the extra one hundred thousand dollars go through the treasury of the Auxiliary so that the Auxiliary may receive credit for it," her friend reminded her.[80] She also gave $30,000 to the San Francisco YMCA and $20,000 to the St. Paul, Minnesota, YMCA.[81] Olivia Sage was encouraged in this cause by Helen Gould. Helen was now a celebrity who traveled in what the press reported almost as a royal procession, founding grandiose YMCA buildings to protect young men from vice along the railroad lines her father had built.[82]

But after a fall in 1913, Sage refused all further requests from YMCAs. And when Emma Morgan wrote to her on behalf of the YWCA International Institute's work with immigrant girls, Lilian wrote on the envelope, "Wrote could not take up the matter: had given more than a million to Christian Association in the last few years, and felt other interests [were] now entitled to her attention."[83]

"Add this church to your list"

Donations to religious institutions in general took up a large part of her private philanthropy, which supported religious causes in a way the foundation could not.[84] De Forest continued to steer religious petitioners to her, even after she had given up reviewing personally other requests for help. In 1917, he wrote to her on behalf of Bishop Brent, "whose activities in the Philippines you have hitherto aided, and who has been rendering such efficient public service." He suggested, "[T]he practical question is whether you care to renew your previous gift of $5,000, or perhaps wish to follow the example of Mr. [J. P.] Morgan and make it $10,000."[85]

She rewarded dozens of individual churches. For example, in Sag Harbor she paid for a new bell for the Christ Episcopal Church. She rewarded the A.M.E. Zion Church in nearby Eastville with a new parsonage.[86] In Far Rockaway, Queens, New York, she built a new First Presbyterian Church in memory of her husband, including a splendid window with a tree of life design by Louis Comfort Tiffany at a cost of over $35,000. The church and its accompanying buildings were completed and dedicated in 1909; Sage added an endowment fund of $100,000.[87] She made numerous other donations to churches, including her own church in New York City and churches in her native Syracuse. In New York, she gave a pulpit to the Cathedral of St. John the Divine at a cost of more than $25,000.[88] At Forest Hills Gardens, the Russell Sage Foundation's planned community, she gave funds for a nondenominational church.[89] So well known was Olivia for her gifts to churches that a Mrs. Marion Eager from Syracuse wrote to her: "When thinking of this town, add this church to your list."[90]

Olivia had been interested in the cause of foreign and home missions since the 1880s, and there are records of small money donations from this earlier period.[91] Once she inherited her millions, she was free to invest boldly in overseas philanthropy to seminaries, mission-run colleges and schools, and foreign-mission societies. This was an era when the Progressive thrust toward betterment joined with evangelical fervor and foreign missions channeled private money abroad to modernize and evangelize foreign peoples.[92] Evangelical women were deeply involved in this movement. A brief quote from Helen Barratt Montgomery's *Western Women in Eastern Lands* (1910) conveys the sense of urgency as American women and men worked to transform societies and cultures around the world with the goal of evangelizing the world in a single generation.

In 1861 there was a single missionary, Miss Marston, in Burma; in 1909, there were 4,610 unmarried women in the field, 1,948 of them from the United States. . . . Then the supporters numbered a few hundreds; to-day there are at least two millions. Then the amount contributed was $2000; last year four million dollars was raised.[93]

Sage philanthropy supported several mission colleges abroad. She gave $75,000 to the Syrian Protestant College of Beirut, sent a check for $50,000 to Roberts College in Constantinople in January 1908, and gave to a Persian girls' school.[94] She supported a mission in Labrador for New-foundland fishermen and a Presbyterian Chapel in Manila.[95] She directly supported several missionaries, including her own cousin, Rev. Arthur Tappan Pierson, a well-known evangelist and editor in chief of the *Missionary Review of the World* who was also the founder of the Pierson Memorial Bible School in Korea. Olivia funded Dr. Pierson's mission tour, which ended only when serious illness in Seoul forced his return. He wrote: "When at your suggestion I undertook a world-tour of missions, I felt it to be a sort of sacred and hallowed partnership in service to our one blessed Lord."[96] After his death in 1911, she sent an additional $5,000 for the Pierson Memorial Bible School in his memory.[97] Olivia's gift of April 1911 to the Women's Board of Foreign Missions had been used for "a much-needed missionaries' home in Kagoshima, Japan," the director informed her.[98]

Sometimes several wealthy friends joined to support a missionary. A letter to Olivia from her friend Caroline Borden refers to the network of benevolent women who sustained the American College for Girls in Constantinople. In 1909, as president and Wellesley graduate Dr. Mary Mills Patrick prepared to return to Constantinople, where the college would begin to build on a new site donated by Helen Gould, Borden wrote to Sage, "I am rejoicing in the beautiful coterie of four women who have encircled Miss Patrick with interest in her and in her college work. . . . Sage—Gould—Dodge—Borden."[99] Letters from 1904 to 1919 document Sage's continuing support of this college: a gift of $10,000 in March 1908, one of $25,000 in 1911, another of $35,000 for a dormitory in 1912. Gratitude came in a personal letter to Olivia assuring her that "[w]e are trying to plant a spiritual and Christian leaven in the home life of the Turkish empire."[100] After the 1908 donation, Caroline Borden wrote, "It is beautiful that you have made this College a link in your chain of gold which is lifting the world up to God."[101] Olivia funded the Nile Mission Press ("to bring the Gospel to Moslems"), and gave $50,000 jointly with Nettie McCormick for a building to house the press.[102]

Spreading the American dream to heathen nations was one field of missionary endeavor; home missions was the other. Home missions to immigrants and the poor of America's industrial cities, Indians, the Hispanic peoples of the Southwest, and the Mormons had become an important part of Protestant evangelicals' charge to take the gospel to every corner of the North American continent. Hundreds of thousands of dollars in private giving, much of it from white women, supported the goal of converting the entire continent to evangelical Christianity. Scholars see these home missionary organizations as agents of assimilation aimed at absorbing the peoples whom Anglo-Protestants saw "as obstacles to the creation of a more perfect United States."[103]

Olivia had earlier served on the Women's Executive Committee for Home Missions, renamed in 1890 the Woman's Board of Home Missions, and had made small donations to the association.[104] No wonder that by 1906 numerous small city missions and settlements had expectations that she would endow them or at least reward them generously. And indeed her will, which was dated October 1906, gave two parts of her estate (each part would be worth approximately $800,000) each to the Women's Board of Foreign Missions of the Presbyterian Church, the New York City Mission and Tract Society, and the New York Female Auxiliary Bible Society.

But only sixteen months later, this will was revised in the codicil of February 17, 1908, to rescind these bequests, instead giving the American Bible Society one and one-half parts (roughly $1.2 million) and the New York Bible Society a one-half part (roughly $400,000), both to be administered through the New York Female Auxiliary Bible Society.[105] The circumstances surrounding this change are mysterious, but the beneficiaries seem to have been Jermain and the corporate-style, male-dominated, and modernizing American Bible Society, a favorite of Robert de Forest (he and his father both served on the society's Board of Managers). Olivia was persuaded to give $500,000 to the American Bible Society in May 1908, provided that the Society raised an equal amount within one year.[106]

Analysis of Olivia's gifts to animal welfare and related causes also shows her moving from support of the small humane societies and women's parallel or auxiliary societies that were typical of nineteenth-century humane reform to more modern institutions that included action at the public and national level. The humane treatment of animals had been a popular, even fashionable cause since the founding of the New York Society for the Prevention of Cruelty to Animals in 1865 brought to America the sensibility, crusading spirit, and legislative goals of the older British movement. Women, who were barred from leadership roles in these humane societies but enthusiastic in the cause, founded their own societies in Philadelphia, New York, and other cities.[107] Olivia supported the American Society for the Prevention of Cruelty to Animals, favoring its women's auxiliary. "The tender-heartedness of woman will naturally lead her to use her influence in bringing about a humane treatment of animals," she wrote in 1905. After 1906, she gave the New York Women's League for Animals $1,500 each year for its work on behalf of humane treatment of work horses; by 1915 the league was operating watering stations throughout the city that could accommodate as many as 2,000 horses per day. She endowed a Westinghouse chassis for an animal ambulance ("with three decks and a capacity for carrying three hundred dogs and cats") and gave $10,000 for an animal hospital that would provide free treatment for animals of the poor.[108]

Olivia had long been a voice for the preservation and protection of birds, and she denounced society women for the "barbarous fashion of wearing for her adornment the plumage of small birds."[109] She supported the National Audubon Society and in 1910 established the Junior Audubon Clubs with a gift of $15,000.[110] For another $10,000 donation, this time to the Wild Life Protection Fund, Olivia was awarded the society's first Gold Medal in 1917. Todd conveyed Olivia's thanks and best wishes for "the greater dissemination of knowledge among the people as to why protection is necessary, not only for economic reasons, but also as a factor in humane treatment of all living things."[111] For humane education she donated generously to the public educational mission of the New York Zoological Society, leaving it $800,000 in her will.[112]

A range of activities, from small associations and local charities to wide-ranging schemes, can be seen in her philanthropy for health and medicine. Initially, her gifts represented the societies and causes she had supported for half a century, such as the New-York Woman's Hospital. After years of involvement as a lady manager and then, in the 1890s, a funder, she was ready to reward the hospital with a grand gesture, and immediately after Russell Sage's death she gave the hospital $50,000. Then in July 1907, she considered taking over the whole financial burden on condition that the men who had opposed her husband be taken off the hospital's board. But de Forest persuaded her against the idea.[113]

The major contribution of Russell Sage's fortune to public health was of course through the foundation-funded Pittsburgh Survey, which documented the interrelated health problems of a whole region, and through the foundation's significant support of efforts to combat tuberculosis.[114] At the same time, Olivia continued to fund many smaller health-related charities such as the New York Tribune Sunshine Society and Fresh-Air Fund, which received $1,000 from her each year.[115] She supported the Robin's Nest, a home for physically handicapped children in Tarrytown, New York; sanatoria; and schools of nursing. She supported several hospitals including the Presbyterian Hospital in New York City, Southampton Hospital on Long Island, the Hospital of the Good Shepherd in Syracuse, and Susanna Hospital in Guam, which she endowed.[116]

De Forest's hand can be seen in her donation to the Russell Sage Institute of Pathology. Like Forest Hills Gardens, this was an income-yielding philanthropic investment of the kind de Forest favored. The institute was set up in July 1907 when Olivia deeded securities valued at $300,000 to the New York Trust Company (Robert de Forest was president) to be held in deposit; the income of $12,000 a year was to be used for a Russell Sage Institute of Pathology on Blackwell's Island to serve the mainly indigent population of City Hospital and the City Home. The institute was also to carry on basic research, especially into the diseases of old age, and it drew the praise of Progressives.[117] This experiment in running a government health department with private funding soon collapsed in political wrangling, however. It survived, changing its affiliation to Cornell, and reemerging with Graham Lusk, Robert de Forest's nephew, as scientific director in 1920. He wrote to his uncle, "I am one of those who believe that the welfare of the world is more largely advanced through the support of scientific work than by any other procedure."[118]

Olivia also funded institutions for orphans and other dependent persons and for the disabled. There are donations for the deaf and for the blind, though the latter population benefited most from the Russell Sage Foundation, receiving one of the foundation's first grants in 1908.[119]

Donors often seek out the most prestigious rather than the most needy recipients, and some philanthropy serves only to embellish or sanitize the image of the giver. This book began with the story of Olivia's investment in public image when she paid for research, publication, and distribution of a volume on her family genealogy.[120] Self-aggrandizement was one element of Olivia's civic philanthropy, but it coexisted with a genuine affection for her city and region. She gave significant gifts to New York's most visible monuments, such as $25,000 for the renovation of the Governor's Room of New York's City Hall. She donated to the city's major cultural institutions such as the American Museum of Natural History and the Metropolitan Museum of Art. She also gave $800,000 to the New York Public Library.[121] Gifts to Central Park expressed her affection for the refuge where she had spent time while her husband toiled on Wall Street. She made large donations to the park for rhododendrons, and for several years every employee of Central Park received a Christmas gift from her. Always hopeful about the uplifting power of education, she gave a small library of technical books to each of the 258 firehouses in greater New York.[122]

Keenly aware of the nation's history, in September 1908 Sage purchased Constitution Island off West Point for $150,000 and deeded it to the nation for the use of the U.S. Military Academy.[123] The island stirred her patriotism, for it was the site of an important Hudson River naval engagement during the Revolutionary War. But there were other, sentimental, reasons for this donation. Olivia had a particular fondness for this part of the Hudson River Valley; she had spent time there with her husband when they were first married and she still visited the area on occasion to stay with friends. She was an admirer and friend of Anna and Susan Warner, authors of popular domestic fiction, who had made their home there, and it was a condition of her gift that the surviving sister, Anna Warner, be allowed to remain on the island during her lifetime. Olivia instructed her lawyer to draw up the deed of gift from Anna Warner jointly with herself.[124]

Great wealth allowed Olivia to project the ideals and prejudices of the moral reform crusade into public life. For example, she supported the nativist campaign for a "Safe and Sane Fourth of July," a movement to replace the rowdy, dangerous festivities of working-class and immigrant communities with "rational" and dignified celebrations of nationhood.[125]

Art Philanthropy

Unlike most great donors to America's art museums, Olivia Sage had little interest in or knowledge of art. She was neither a collector nor a connoisseur. A reporter who was admitted to her house at 506 Fifth Avenue at the turn of the century later unkindly described a "homely brownstone residence upon which no stranger would waste a second glance." Its interior "might have been a boarding house," and the walls were hung with "somber wall paper interrupted by somberer pictures of clouds and chariots and things."[126] When she died, her houses and their contents were said to contain little of value, and her paintings were said to be copies. Her 1886 purchase of a life membership for $200 in the Metropolitan Museum of Art probably reflected friendship with the de Forests rather than an interest in art.[127] After 1906, Olivia occasionally donated objects to the museum, some of them of doubtful value. Kathleen McCarthy recounts how de Forest, careful not to upset Olivia, advised the museum staff not to return unwanted items to the donor. When she offered the museum an English teapot in 1914, he wrote to a staff member, "I have not attempted to pass judgement upon the teapot. It may or may not be something we care for, but I clearly want to accept any gift from Mrs. Sage."[128]

His tact paid off. In 1909, Olivia made a significant gift to the Metropolitan Museum of the Bolles Collection, 600 pieces of early American furniture valued at $100,000. De Forest may also have encouraged this purchase—McCarthy suggests "it may have generated the need for the American wing that the de Forests donated"—but it also spoke clearly of Olivia's personal interest in American colonial history and heritage.[129]

Olivia saw herself as a patron of female artists and sculptors, and some contemporaries shared this view. A newspaper article in October 1906 predicted that "Mrs. Russell Sage . . . may be [the] generous patron of the movement [who will] establish a permanent women's art club in Brooklyn or Manhattan at a cost [of] $100,000 or more."[130] In 1903, she had employed Emma Shields to paint portraits of her parents as well as of Major John Jermain, (his portrait hangs today in the John Jermain Memorial Library in Sag Harbor.)[131] She commissioned Mary F. Tillinghast to design the windows of the First Presbyterian Church in Syracuse in 1898 and later.[132] In the First Presbyterian Church at Far Rockaway she used Tillinghast again to design the windows except for the great east window, for which she employed Tiffany.[133]

I have described earlier how in 1904 Olivia gave $150,000 to the American Seamen's Friend Society (her brother Joseph J. Slocum was president) to construct a twelve-story Sailors' Home and Institute on the New York docks.[134] During World War I she invested large sums in the welfare of the armed services, working through the YMCA and the U.S. Soldiers Christian Aid Association (USSCAA). Fearful about the boredom and temptations to which the men were exposed, she donated books, calendars, portable phonographs, and thousands of "decent" phonograph recordings to the navy.[135] Through the USSCAA she responded to requests from numerous U.S. army and navy chaplains for religious materials to raise their spirits, "inspire them with hope and lift their vision to higher and holier purposes."[136] She supplied the chaplain at the New York Navy Yard with flowers for services every year until her death in 1918, provided a small library of books for the U.S. army chaplains at Fort McKinley in Maine and Fort Leavenworth in Kansas, and sent a stereopticon, records, and books to the chaplain at Camp Keithley, Mindanao, in the Philippines.[137]

Some of her philanthropic investments reflect her advancing age. Charities to help the elderly appealed to her. In March 1907, when she had been a widow for only four months, she gave $250,000 for a home for indigent women, as if facing old age without her husband in affluence made her think of those who did so in poverty. She also paid for a "Sage Memorial Room" for two elderly women at the Syracuse Home Association (a retirement home "with which my mother was associated").[138] When the president of the Presbyterian Hospital Nurses' Alumnae wrote appealing for help with the pension fund, she sent $1,500.[139]

But she also made many donations to organizations for working women. In her 1905 essay "Opportunities and Responsibilities of Leisured Women," Olivia had defined rich women's responsibilities toward female wage-workers "working for bread and butter."[140] One way to help was to fund suitable housing for single women in the city, such as the newly popular women's apartments and hotels. Olivia donated $25,000 in August 1910 to New York City's The Virginia: A Hotel for Working Girls.[141] Annual donations of between $1,000 and $1,500 to her church, the Collegiate Church of St. Nicholas, supported its Women's Auxiliary's lunchroom for working girls "who have absolutely no place to go and get a cheap noon lunch without being thrown up against strange men." The Working Women's Protective Union received $10,000 in her will.[142] In May 1915 she gave $1,000 to enable working-class women to attend the General Federation of Women's Clubs convention.[143]

As she recovered from her 1913 fall and resumed her philanthropy, a note of weariness entered into the correspondence and is reflected in the comments of her secretaries. Now that she was nearly ninety she had to abandon even favorite causes. Tactless or indelicate comments in letters were carefully screened so as not to upset her. An invitation from the Harlem Music School Settlement to a "Unique Concert of Negro Music," sent along with thanks for a donation, caused a flurry as Lilian wondered how to respond.[144] An appeal from an organization that ran free classes in manual training and domestic economy "for the poor of all races and creeds" acknowledged a gift of $200 and asked for more. The letter of appeal has the secretary's note: "As Mrs. Sage seemed uncertain about this, I did not send check."[145]

Even favorite causes were now turned down. When the Southampton Hospital board of trustees asked permission to use her name in a fund drive, Lilian drafted a reply: "She does not approve of being a member of any organization when it is not possible for her to keep herself informed as to its affairs."[146] Even the American College for Girls in Constantinople had no success when it appealed to Olivia in 1913, Lilian noting on the envelope that Mrs. Sage "did not care to hear further about this college."[147] In 1917, Lilian informed Dr. Patrick that she should no longer bother Mrs. Sage with appeals about Constantinople. "She feels at this time that this country needs some attention, and she is not inclined to take up outside matters."[148]

Philanthropy is investment and always represents choice among competing possibilities. Even the Sage fortune was not limitless, and not every cause could be supported or every appeal answered. The long imaginative proposals from Charles D. Walcott of the Smithsonian Institution to Olivia make fascinating reading today, but they didn't stir her interest, while other appeals that caused her to reach for her checkbook, such as the Nile Mission Press, seem today improbably quixotic or wrongheaded.

The problem was not peculiar to Sage. The world of philanthropy where wealthy men and women worked closely with the details of their gifts was changing. Philanthropists gradually were withdrawing from personal involvement in benevolence, and by the 1920s professional experts would expend the funds that privileged groups provided.[149] But petitioners who felt entitled to a stream of giving responded with anger when their letters were ignored or refused. Pathetic letters from Mrs. Sarah J. Bird of the Gospel Settlement seemed almost to want to force Olivia to share the pain of the embattled city missionary in the slums: "It is almost cutting my heart to do what I said I would never do ask you for money," she wrote dramatically. "But God tells me to do it now after months of earnest prayer about it."[150] Some unsuccessful petitioners directly blamed their failure on the fact that they could not see the donor face to face. Mrs. Sage had distanced herself too much from her old associates, one acerbic writer commented on a smaller-than-expected donation from Sage to the Aged Pilgrim Fund (a small New York charity). "Our aged people do not die off very fast . . . and our need increases." Her letter of thanks for a too-small sum turned nasty with the thought that the money would be used "as I am sure Mrs. Sage would wish to have it if she could go into the homes of the poor as we do and see the need."[151] Writers thus invited the philanthropist to witness in imagination emotional scenes from which she was removed, as if trying to repersonalize the gift: "I am sure it would have made you feel happy to see the joy that [the check for $10,000] gave me. I really burst into tears and I want to thank you over and over again from the bottom of my heart," wrote Ellen P. Speyer, secretary of the New York Women's League for Animals.[152] The appeals from the Babies' Hospital must also have been hard to resist:

"Your little bed is never empty, and every baby that enjoys its comfort could add very much to our thanks if it were able to speak for itself," director Mary Calvert wrote to Olivia.[153]

But if there were difficult decisions to be made, this was also a time of fulfillment as small gifts made early in her career now blossomed into huge legacies. Her donation of $25 to the New York Zoological Society in January 1906 was followed by a $1,000 gift in 1912 and an $800,000 legacy in her will.[154] A bird lover all her life, Olivia had founded Audubon Clubs across the nation and purchased an entire island as a bird sanctuary. Earlier she had supported the Woman's Hospital with volunteer hours; now she would leave it a bequest of $1.6 million. As she opened one more letter of thanks which (no surprise here!) ended with another appeal, Olivia must have felt satisfied. The principal of a missionary-run Persian girls' school wrote to her, "It only confirms my conviction that you are truly guided by God's Spirit."[155] "You are an angel of light!" another grateful writer declared. "I can only say that there will surely be one more star to your crown, dear Mrs. Sage, for your unlimited Christian charity."[156]

Fifteen

"Send what Miss Todd thinks best"

> Gift systems always have the potentiality for
> trouble brewing within them.
>
> —Natalie Zemon Davis,
> *The Gift in Sixteenth-Century France* (2000)[1]

In 1915, Olivia addressed a note to Lilian that was intended to end the demands for money from individuals and institutions in Troy, New York. From our point of view, the note is important because it is evidence that Olivia remained mentally alert in her old age. Though the writer was approaching eighty-eight the thought is cogent, the writing steady and clear. Her gift of $100,000 for a dining room to Rensselaer Polytechnic Institute in Troy was meant "as a memorial to Mr. Russell Sage's nephew Russell Sage 2nd, who was educated as an Engineer in Troy Polytechnic, and left there to help engineer and build the *Troy and Boston Rail Road* and much of the gift from me was his money well earned," she wrote. "I like the plans as presented in the Troy Times picture. . . . Just give this data to President Ricketts." She signed it, "Affectionately yours, M. O. Sage."[2]

Olivia's life continued in its seasonal rhythms: away from the city at the end of June to Cedar Croft, then back to the Fifth Avenue house at the end of October for the winter. She never returned to Sag Harbor after 1912. Her strength now ebbed and waned with the seasons. She fell ill during the winter of 1911–1912 and kept to her rooms upstairs, refusing to see even Robert and Emily de Forest for several weeks, and her illness— perhaps it was illness, perhaps depression—continued into the spring.[3] Then there was a period of recuperation at the resort town of Lakewood, New Jersey. In a gentler climate, away from the begging letters, Olivia used her time to make more inquiries about her Sag Harbor roots.[4] By the following May she was home again and well enough to resume her daily walks. Soon she was also going for daily drives in her automobile with Nelson at the wheel—"pleasure trips," de Forest called them (see fig. 15.1).[5]

Nurse N. Ruth Simpson joined the domestic staff in 1913, complicating a circle of people all trying to protect and influence the elderly woman. Recommended by John and Mary Glenn and by Helen Gould, Nurse Simpson won Olivia's affection, and soon Olivia was asking her advice about spending decisions as well.[6] When she decided to increase her gift to Russell Sage College by $250,000, Nurse Simpson was the first to know, and she phoned Lilian from Lawrence to tell her the news. Lilian then informed college principal Eliza Kellas.[7]

Old friends were dearer than ever. Nettie McCormick wrote affectionately to Olivia, her letters interweaving themes of spirituality with references to physical pleasure and bodily comfort. After one visit, she wrote recalling her friend's cold fingers and enclosed two pairs of gloves and some hose. "And you know I spoke to you of my warm hose. Will you put on one pair of these in the parcel Saturday morning. I pray you do." She ended, "*You don't know what great things I learn from you.*"[8] Another time she enclosed "a little hand-knit shoulder shawl . . . and I wish you would wear it these cool days, to keep your dear shoulders and chest from a draft of air."[9] Thanking Olivia for another gift and before leaving Cedar Croft, she wrote, "This lovely afghan is a true emblem and figure of the warmth your presence, and your rare conversation, has diffused over *my life, my spirit.* I can never forget the moments spent with you."[10]

Nettie McCormick was in New York early in 1913 to attend Helen Gould's wedding to Finley Johnson Shepard (1868–1942), a railroad executive and sportsman and the son of a minister. The ceremony at Lyndhurst was a simple affair in view of the wealth of the bride's family, especially when compared with the lavish wedding of Helen's sister Anna to a French count a few years earlier, a society sensation that nevertheless ended in divorce after five years.[11] Olivia was not strong enough to attend the wedding, but she sent a corsage of 200 white diamonds, an extraordinarily extravagant present from one who bought very little jewelry for herself.[12] Nettie afterward spent several weeks with Olivia at Cedar Croft. She returned home to find orchids and a note from Olivia along with a portrait.[13] She continued to write affectionate letters to her old friend. "I think of you every day—every morning and every day I love you more—and cherish every word you have said to me. . . . Do keep your dear hands warm," she wrote, ending, "Fondly, thine own."[14] Nettie worried that Olivia would catch cold: "I feel you are so near to

FIGURE 15.1. Olivia used her car and chauffeur for daily jaunts, but this was evidently a special occasion. She is pictured with her chauffeur and an unidentified female companion. Courtesy New York University Archives.

me," she wrote. "And when I rest under your downy pink afghan—and feel your warm heart beat beneath the Troy Female Seminary favorite color, then, oh, I think on thee—ever of thee! Dearest!"[15]

Later she wrote to Olivia of Helen's wedding, "It is a sweet fairy romance, better, indeed, than any myth or fabled story." She added, "You may *always* remember that you have been blessing and instruction to me during those weeks of privilege in Cedarhurst." Spring came, and she was still happily recalling Helen's wedding and sending tips about avoiding the cold. "I pray you may rub the warm, camphorated sweet oil (olive oil) plentifully on your *chest and back. It helps.*"[16] Intermingled with these intimate exchanges were money matters: Olivia endowed fellowships at the McCormick Theological Seminary at Nettie's urging. In February 1915, she sent Nettie an antique purse containing a check for $1,000 "for Missions."[17] Nettie's letter of thanks ends: "I love you and I am ever fondly thine own, now eighty years old."[18] With Lilian's help, the two also kept in touch by means of a "wireless apparatus."[19] In 1916, when Olivia fretted about the tragedy of war, Nettie encouraged her to visualize the good her money was doing overseas. It was comforting to think that her gifts to the YMCA had helped toward "the care of the sick and wounded in Germany and France, during the last six months, as our YMCA secretaries have worked in the prison camps, and in the Hospitals in all those countries at war, as *brothers indeed*."[20]

Meanwhile Lilian was dealing with the deluge of incoming mail. Writing replies as instructed by Olivia or sometimes on her own initiative, she saw herself as the elderly woman's protector, and she was furious when she saw how the others tried to manipulate her—Robert de Forest pushing for his own favorite cause, the Red Cross, and houseman Nelson with his inappropriate (she thought) reminders to Olivia about the Eighth Avenue Mission.[21] Frustrated with what she saw as her own loss of access to the elderly woman and Nelson's ascendancy, Lilian wrote in response to an appeal from the mission's director: "I return the letter, in case you wish Nelson to make the attempt to give it to Mrs. Sage. He takes liberties that a secretary is not entitled to."[22]

Imaginative attempts by outsiders to reach the elderly philanthropist sometimes ended in embarrassment or farce. James E. West, head of the Boy Scouts of America, wrote a profuse apology "with reference to the conduct of the scout in attempting to deliver the letter to Mrs. Sage."[23] West had already proved quite persistent, sending Olivia photographs illustrating scouting activities in July 1913 and then writing to ask whether she had received them. Olivia usually gave the Scouts $6,000 a year, but when she was pestered for an additional $10 annual subscription she lost patience. The next demand for the customary $6,000 was marked "Decline."[24]

Lilian tried to protect Olivia from all the appeals. "It is impossible for me to submit a letter of the length received . . . to Mrs. Sage," she wrote to the president of the Southampton Hospital in 1916.[25] Begging letters now upset Olivia, and Lilian often refused to send them on. On October 11, 1915, she informed Jermain that she had refused an appeal from Robert Grier Cooke of the Fifth Avenue Improvement Association. "I have turned Mr. Cooke down repeatedly, but he always bobs up."[26] Long personal letters, too, were sometimes not sent on if they ended with an appeal for money. For example, in November 1912, Lilian decided not to give Olivia a letter containing a long description of the Emma Willard Association banquet. The secretary recorded her action on the envelope: "[B]ecause of the appeal in this did not send this in but acknowledged receipt and thanked her for description."[27] Olivia deferred to her. "Do as You Think Best," she wrote on one appeal, dated November 30, 1914.[28]

Lilian typed or sometimes handwrote the decision for each letter. On the envelope of one letter which contained a detailed discussion of the needs of various New York charities, Lilian wrote, "May tell Mrs. Sage about this letter." Passionate appeals for Sage money were sometimes marked simply, "Neglect." Tactless, awkward, or indelicate matters were also screened out. A letter from Rebecca Latimer Felton regarding the Georgia Training School for Girls was withheld because, in the course of an enthusiastic and detailed description of the work of the school, it made an oblique reference to abortions performed on delinquent girls at the school. I would have sent it to "Colonel" (Jermain Slocum), Lilian noted, "but it does not treat of subjects that it would be polite to send to Mrs. Sage through him."[29]

Olivia was so weary of all the solicitations that she even instructed Lilian to refuse further demands from suffrage leaders, including educator M. Carey Thomas. But she relented after an appeal from Carrie Chapman Catt, the forceful president of NAWSA, agreeing to pay the rent on the headquarters of the Woman Suffrage Party of the City of New York.[30] Olivia paid the rent and did so again in April 1916. But she declined to support the cost of the campaign, estimated by Catt at $100,000 a year.[31] "But you told me to say no to all the suffrage folks," Lilian protested. It was so difficult to refuse Catt anything, though, Lilian added, "[S]he is one of the few. . . . of whom no one speaks ill. And the *cause* is JUST, being the Cause of *All* Women."[32] If Catt was eloquent, Mary Garrett Hay, nicknamed by her colleagues "the big boss," was more direct. One of Hay's letters, dated October 26, 1914, went as follows:

Dear Mrs. Sage,

This is the last year of the New York Suffrage Campaign; just twelve months more of hard work.

In the past you have paid our rent, and I make the same request again; that you would continue to help us in this last year of our campaign and pay the rent.

This would be the last time we would ask for money, for we sincerely hope to have victory in 1915.

Sincerely yours,
Mary G. Hay, Chairman

Lilian did not even pass this on. Instead, she typed a note to herself on the envelope: "Miss Hay asks Mrs. Sage for the rent. It is not a particularly cordial letter, and I could not pass it."[33] In her reply to Hay, Lilian put the best spin on it. She did not tell the suffrage leader that she had not even shown Olivia the appeal from the campaign. Instead she described Olivia as generally confused and overwhelmed: "Mrs. Sage now feels she is too far removed from active participation in this work to understand the new phases that have arisen, and she wearies of the multitude of details and explanations[;] each day brings with it an endless list of appeals. Nothing more could be done."[34]

Yet Olivia was soon continuing to pay the rent on the New York suffrage campaign headquarters, describing herself in the cover letter accompanying her donation as a suffrage pioneer who had been "interested in the woman's rights question since 1848."[35] A reporter covering the huge suffrage parade of 33,000 marchers down Fifth Avenue in October of that year espied Olivia Sage, a tiny white-haired figure at her favorite spot—a round second-floor window that gave her a commanding view of the street below. Mrs. Sage was "enjoying wonderful health for a woman of her years," he wrote. "She is keenly alive to subjects that are occupying public attention, but if there is one question that interests her more than anything else, it is woman suffrage."[36] The press and the public now saw her at eighty-seven as a symbol of the long campaign of American women for the vote.[37] But the 1915 referendum again failed to endorse woman suffrage, and when a suffrage organization appealed for money in the fall of 1916, Olivia wearily left the decision to Lilian. A handwritten note on the envelope states, "Mrs. Sage said to send what Miss Todd thinks best."[38] Woman suffrage finally succeeded in New York by state amendment in 1917.

As Olivia saw fewer people, the circle around her tightened and access became harder. Our window into Olivia's situation in these last few years is, again, the correspondence between E. Lilian Todd and Eliza Kellas. Their increasingly frank exchanges reveal the rumors and intrigues swirling around Olivia as she approached her ninetieth year. Lilian saw Olivia at least twice a day to discuss correspondence. We saw in an earlier chapter how Kellas and Todd conceived the project of the new women's college in Troy, the Russell Sage School of Practical Arts. In September 1917, Olivia increased her gift to $500,000, and the combined institution, renamed Emma Willard School and Russell Sage College, received a charter from the New York State Board of Regents in October.[39] Yet Kellas, in the dual role of principal of the school and head of the college, found herself in an almost impossible situation, commuting several miles daily between the school high on Mount Ida and the college below in Troy. She learned that the time to bargain is *before* accepting a position. It was clear that Robert de Forest opposed foundation investment in the college at any level. She was refused a car, which made her daily commute miserable, and even her request to foundation director John Glenn for advice from foundation education specialists on setting up the curriculum was refused.[40]

The Colonels

"Colonel" Joseph Jermain Slocum visited his sister every day, and he was a factor to reckon with. He was now working out of an office at 111 Broadway, answering correspondence on paper engraved with the letterhead "Estate of Russell Sage."[41] But he lacked judgment and even good sense. Entrusted by Olivia with forwarding a donation of $300 for the Indians to General Richard H. Pratt, former principal of Carlisle School, Slocum couldn't resist the inappropriate quip to Pratt that the amount was needed "to make your financial status straight with the *starving Indians*." He went on recklessly, "General Sherman said, as you remember, 'The best Indian, was a *dead one*.' I know you are more friendly disposed, and I suppose it is up to those who have money to keep them alive (see fig. 15.2)."[42]

In a series of frank letters to Eliza Kellas, Lilian criticized "the Colonel." He was incompetent, irascible, and worse still, he had begun to insist on making decisions that were not his to make. In 1916, he had taken responsibility for giving scholarships at the Emma Willard School without Olivia's consent. His son, Herbert J. Slocum, was also giving out scholarships.[43] Places at the school were in great demand: "Do you know the lists of our Emma Willard School closed the first of March, with every place taken for next year?" Kellas confided to Todd. "Practically every mail brings applications."[44] Olivia was a strong believer in scholarships for deserving girls, and she wanted to retain control over them. But her brother "apparently intends to assume the entire right of the scholarships for the future. (That is a confidential remark to you)."[45]

Two weeks later the scholarship quarrel was still simmering, and Lilian burst out in a bitter denunciation of Jermain and his sons, "the Colonels," as she called them. "I wonder why those men have got to mix it all up again. They think they always know so much. I do wish they would give a demonstration sometime of how much they know."[46]

Elderly, his acuity impaired by his old Civil War head injury, Jermain tended to fuss and bluster; he couldn't be counted on to get much done. And he was aware of his limitations. Passing a letter on to his sis-

FIGURE 15.2. Joseph Jermain Slocum, Olivia's brother, aged around seventy. Courtesy Florence Slocum Wilson.

ter, he wrote, "My dear sister, Shall I acknowledge or will you? You can do it better. JJS."[47] One friend of the family recalled hearing him referred to privately as "an idiot."[48] Still, fund-raisers tried to use him to get access to Olivia. When Richard Pratt wrote to advise Chancellor Elmer E. Brown about getting more Sage money for New York University, he suggested putting Colonel Slocum on the university's board of trustees, "for the Colonel and Mrs. Sage are very near to each other. To my knowledge and confidentially to you, they entertain each other almost daily."[49]

Lilian was scornful of Jermain's "downtown office." She wrote to Eliza Kellas, "Colonel, Sr., is bound to confuse everything he has to do with. . . . He is over eighty-one, nearly eighty-two, and detests anything outside of the downtown office, and I am not sure he is fond of that always." In one incident, a letter "should have been sent to Mrs. Sage instead to

any of the colonels," she confided. "Colonel Slocum, Sr., does not understand things nearly as well as Mrs. Sage and everything irritates him.
Mrs. Sage does not take kindly to *long* explanations, but it is easier to
say things to her than to her brother."[50]

The de Forest brothers were still nominally administering Russell
Sage's estate. Robert de Forest continued to play a major role as advisor, and as Olivia grew older he tried to safeguard those parts of her will
that rewarded his personal favorites: the New York COS, the Metropolitan Museum, the American Bible Society, and the Russell Sage
Foundation. Rev. McLeod, Olivia's minister, had the right idea when
he advised a fund-raiser: "The way that I would suggest is, that you get
on the good side of [Mrs. Sage's] lawyer, Mr. de Forrest [sic]. He is the
key to the situation."[51] The family distrusted de Forest's influence and
sought ways to diminish it.[52]

Isolated by her wealth and vulnerable because of her increasing deafness, Olivia was lonely. When Lilian heard that Eliza Kellas had been
in New York City on a visit she reproved her for not making a social
call. "While Mrs. Sage feels she cannot see callers, still she does like to
have them ask. It is really a lonesome matter—getting old. Little atten-
tions are missed, even while the acceptance of them sometimes is too
much exertion."[53] There were visits from Jermain's children and grand-
children, Olivia's grandnephews and nieces. John J. Slocum, who was
conveyed as a child of about six by his father Herbert Jermain Slocum,
Jr., to take tea and cookies with the ancient lady, recalled her as "a
ramrod-straight, white-haired old lady in black with lace at her throat
and cuffs." He remembered her parrot, "who had learned to call for the
maid, Delia, in accents very much resembling those of Mrs. Sage."[54]

When a daughter was born to Herbert Jermain Slocum's other son,
Myles Standish Slocum, and his wife, Isobel Bradford Slocum, in 1910,
Olivia took a proprietary interest in the new baby, her grandniece,
instructing the mother to call her Rose, "because Rose was the name of
Myles Standish's wife." Isobel, a former St. Louis belle, refused. She was
from the South, she protested, and there "only the Negroes are named
after flowers." The baby was named Florence instead. Olivia then urged
her grandnephew's wife to get the best baby-nurse available, "and she
would pay for it herself." And she did. Olivia paid for a nurse for each
of her grandnephews' babies.[55] She was also paying regular amounts to
dozens of relatives and friends, her "pensioners."[56]

Sometimes Olivia was cranky as only the very old can be cranky. An
amusing story told by John J. Slocum was that the elderly lady insisted on
having her portrait painted with her parrot by the well-known portraitist

Lydia Emmett. But when the portrait was completed she took a great dislike to it and refused to accept it, "and Mrs. Emmett, who was not accustomed to being rejected, cut out the parrot and threw the rest away."[57]

Olivia had cause to be irritable. Even visits from loved ones sometimes ended in an appeal for funds. Her brother's grandsons (her grandnephews) were chronically short of money and took advantage of her generosity. According to family legend, when Herbert Jermain Slocum, Jr. ("Jerry") was a college student at Rensselaer Polytechnic Institute in Troy, he once wired his great aunt, "Please send money. Am one jump ahead of the sheriff." Olivia's reply was "Keep jumping," and she sent no money—this time. Jerry complained that the Russell Sage connection was a liability, according to John J. Slocum. "As an experiment one day, he handed in a blank notebook for a final examination in mathematics. When the marks came in, he found he had earned a B. Outraged, he went to the president, resigned from school, and went off to New York to see his great-aunt. In his diatribe against the favoritism shown him, he concluded with the statement, 'I am nothing but the great nephew of Russell Sage.' She retorted, 'Jermain, I am nothing but the widow of Russell Sage.'"[58]

But if he found the connection embarrassing, Jerry also depended on it. He kept in touch with his aunt, sending affectionate postcards from his honeymoon trip to Europe with the lovely Marguerite Spear ("Margot").[59] When Olivia died it was revealed that he owed her the enormous sum of $400,000 on notes and her nephew Stephen L'Hommedieu Slocum owed her $127,500.[60] Of Olivia's niece, also named Margaret Olivia Slocum, we know very little. She was an exact contemporary of Helen Gould and, like her, an attendee at the NYU Woman's Law Class in the 1890s. In February 1899, at the age of twenty-nine she married Sherman Flint, son of Austin Flint, a well-known surgeon.[61] The couple had two children, Margaret Olivia, born 1900, and a son, Austin, who died in 1919 at age seventeen in a horseback accident. If she ever visited her elderly aunt, there is no record of her doing so. We hear nothing about her until the crisis precipitated by Olivia's death. Then she becomes a force to be reckoned with.

"Far from strong"

In May 1916, Lilian informed Kellas "very and most confidentially," that Olivia Sage was "far from strong."[62] By January 1918, Olivia's decline was evident. In this month, an artist named Mrs. Huntley asked permission to paint her portrait. Lilian commented to Kellas,

FIGURE 15.3. The largest grant made by the Foundation was to Forest Hills Gardens, a model suburb and the dream project of Robert W. de Forest. Here Olivia ceremonially turns over the first shovelful of dirt at the site, August 1914. Courtesy Central Queens Historical Association, New York, N.Y.

[I]f Mrs. Huntley has ever seen Mrs. Sage, it would probably be a shock to her to see her now. At nearly ninety, one does not preserve the vigor and alert appearance that those Troy people have as a recollection. She is shrunken and frail, and most of the day sits on the sofa, bundled up as most elderly people are when they are not active physically. And worse than all, she is so deaf, that she does not hear what is said, she gives answers at random, and leaves an entirely incorrect impression as to her mental powers. Like all deaf persons, she refuses to take the consequences, and admit she does not hear perfectly, and she has not learned lipreading, and won't use an instrument of any kind to help. She refuses to see strangers.[63]

One photograph of Olivia survives from this period. It shows a tiny stooping white figure turning the first symbolic shovelful of dirt at Forest Hills Gardens.[64] Early in November Olivia fell ill with pneumonia, and as her condition worsened, Helen Gould Shepard came to her side (see fig. 15.3).[65]

"Have the servants been paid? Has the Kaiser abdicated?"

Those who lived through the euphoria and the disappointment of November 4, 1918, never forgot it. Believing that the war was over, people poured out into the streets and celebrated with whistles, bells, and noise-makers. Schools closed, and in small towns and villages people turned out in the thousands for parades and celebrations. But the news of peace was premature. Later that day came to be known as "false armistice day." The United Press had circulated the false report that Germany had accepted the armistice.[66]

On that same day, Olivia Sage died at 12:15 A.M. Her last words, "Have the servants been paid? Has the Kaiser abdicated?" expressed her wish to settle her affairs and her characteristic hunger for news.[67] Lilian sent a letter off to Eliza Kellas, its terseness emphasizing her sense of crisis. Lilian's reserve broke: "The situation here is heartbreaking," she wrote.[68] The niece, Margaret Olivia Flint, had taken charge, ordering that none of Olivia's friends be allowed to view her. But Lilian challenged her authority and managed to moderate the ban. With permission from other family members and the encouragement of Robert de Forest, she sent off telegrams informing people of Olivia's death. "I did not get my telegrams off until pretty late, but they WENT," Lilian wrote to Kellas. Nettie Fowler McCormick received hers in time to send a beautiful wreath. In New York, fifty friends and relatives attended the funeral service at 604 Fifth Avenue, with Rev. Malcolm McCleod presiding.[69] Afterward, a small group consisting of close family and friends accompanied the body to Oakwood Cemetery, Syracuse, where Olivia had expressed the wish to be buried. There were Robert de Forest, Jermain, his sons Herbert Jermain Slocum and Stephen L'Hommedieu Slocum, his daughter Margaret Olivia Flint, and his grandsons, Herbert Jermain Slocum, Jr., and Myles Standish Slocum, young men in their thirties. The journey by train from New York to Syracuse was remarkable only because Helen Gould kept turning to Jermain's sons and intoning balefully, "Poor boys! Poor boys!"[70] Rev. James R. Day conducted the service for Olivia at Oakwood Cemetery. Another famous Syracusan, Olivia's old friend Andrew Dickson White, died on the same day. "I suppose more might have been . . . [at the funeral], but for Dr. White's funeral the same day," Lilian reflected.[71]

Olivia's modest grave marker is set between two others in what is now the oldest part of Oakwood Cemetery in Syracuse. As I stood there on a misty day in June amid the grandiose stone monuments of Syracuse's more self-important Victorians, I could see beyond the modern city and across farmland toward Lake Ontario to the north. But when I looked down again, the three memorials spoke more plainly than Olivia had ever dared to do. For her final resting place is not with Russell Sage but between the graves of her parents. Russell Sage lies near Maria Winne under a much more pretentious monument at another Oakwood Cemetery, in Troy, 150 miles to the east.[72]

For Lilian the debacle was depressing. Even before the will was made public she faced the collapse of her situation. In a series of self-pitying letters to Eliza Kellas, she wrote, "I shall be 'out on a cold world' shortly, and it will not be easy for one whose hair is the color of mine to obtain a position, but—I think I shall try to go overseas if I can be accepted."[73] She begged Eliza Kellas, if she came to New York, to "*let me see you* once more before the absolute 'parting of the ways.'" She ended melodramatically, "If I go abroad I never expect to return to this country, and 'never' is a very long while." Six days later, she wrote to tell Kellas about the funeral. There had been between seventy-five and eighty at the services— "Mrs. Flint (the niece) couldn't keep them all out, even if she did try. She didn't count on my opposition—I felt that Mrs. Sage had been too much of a prominent personage to be treated in such manner, or her friends either."[74]

The Will

The will, dated October 26, 1906, and subsequently amended in two codicils under circumstances that remain obscure, made a number of specific legacies.[75] Since Olivia had no children, her heirs were her brother and his descendants. Witnessed by Johnson de Forest, her physician J. Carl Schmuck, and her maid Delia Gill, it left only $10,000 and the Sag Harbor property known as the Luther Cook House to Jermain. It named "my friends, Robert W. de Forest and Henry de Forest" as executors of the estate and instructed them to hold $1 million for her brother's use during his lifetime, perhaps another indication that Jermain was not considered competent. But only fourteen months later, in February 1908, a first codicil to the will had dramatically increased Jermain's legacy to $2 million. And in July 1911, Olivia had signed a second codicil, leaving an astonishing $5 million more to her brother. At his sister's death Jermain thus inherited the enormous sum of $7 million, 86 million in 2003 dollars. He survived another six years, living with his daughter and her husband, Sherman Flint, until the age of ninety-one. His sons, Herbert Jermain Slocum and Stephen L'Hommedieu Slocum, received $128,231 and $126,750 respectively, but these legacies barely canceled out their debts to their philanthropist aunt—Herbert filed for bankruptcy only a few years later.[76] To Jermain's daughter Margaret Olivia Flint, Olivia bequeathed $100,000 to be held in trust and disbursed to her semiannually. Her daughter, also named Margaret Olivia (later Proctor), then aged eighteen, received a life interest in $100,000 and a quarter interest in the Lawrence property.[77] Relatives outside the immediate family received more modest amounts; cousins received $5,000 apiece, for example.

Altogether Olivia left $49,051,045, of which just over $1 million was owed for income tax for the current year. Olivia's "splendid donation" was her disposition of the remainder. This huge sum of over $40 million was ordered divided into fifty-two equal parts of about $800,000 each.[78] A few specially favored institutions received two parts each, or $1.6 million. These were the Troy Female Seminary, the Association for the Relief of Respectable Aged Indigent Females in the City of New York, the Woman's Hospital in the State of New York, the Board of Home Missions of the Presbyterian Church (to be distributed through its Woman's Executive Committee), the Women's Board of Foreign Missions of the Presbyterian Church, the New York City Mission and Tract Society, the New York Female Auxiliary Bible Society, the Children's Aid Society, and the Charity Organization Society of the City of New York. Other institutions receiving two parts were the Metropolitan Museum of Art and the American Museum of Natural History.[79]

Olivia had made other changes in her designees since October 1906 in addition to those that so generously benefited her brother. In the first codicil (in February 1908) she had taken both parts from the Association for the Relief of Respectable Aged Indigent Females (that is, $1.6 million) and one part each from the YMCA, the YWCA, Middlebury College, Rutgers, Bates, Northfield Schools, and Mt. Sinai Hospital and redirected the money to the American Bible Society (one and one-half parts) and the New York Bible Society (one-half part).[80] Altogether this first codicil revoked nine parts (or nine times $800,000, or about $7.2 million) and gave an additional part to Syracuse University; one part to Hampton Institute, and seven parts (approximately $5.6 million) to the Russell Sage Foundation. The foundation was thus her largest institutional beneficiary.[81]

Olivia also rewarded several of the women's auxiliary or parallel associations on whose boards she had once served. For example, she gave to the Board of Home Missions of the Presbyterian Church of America, donating an additional $1.6 million to its Women's Executive Committee. The Woman's Board of Foreign Missions of the Presbyterian

FIGURE 15.4. Today, this Cecilia Beaux portrait hangs
in the library of the Russell Sage Foundation, New York,
N.Y. Courtesy Russell Sage Foundation.

Church similarly received $1.6 million, and so did the New-York
Woman's Hospital. Yet only a few years later, the rationale for such gender separatism would be lost and along with it the institutions it had fostered, as mainstream denominations moved to consolidate control and
fund-raising in a single body.[82] Olivia did not confine her gifts to Presbyterian organizations. Also named were YMCAs, rescue missions, and
working girls' homes. The nondenominational New York City Mission
and Tract Society (Woman's Board) received $1.6 million, the New York
Bible Society $400,000.[83]

Universities, colleges, and schools were Olivia's largest beneficiaries. She rewarded seventeen different educational institutions with one

part, roughly $800,000 each, a total of $13.6 million. These included men's as well as women's institutions, and they were not confined to New York State or New England. Women's colleges named as beneficiaries were Barnard, Bryn Mawr, Vassar, Smith, and Wellesley. She also named the male-only Harvard, Yale, Princeton, Amherst, Williams, Rutgers, and Dartmouth; black institutions Hampton and Tuskegee; the religious schools at Northfield, Massachusetts; Idaho Institute, a vocational school; and the Emma Willard School. Four institutions received $100,000: Park College, Maryland; Middlebury College, Connecticut; Rutgers; and Syracuse University.[84]

Olivia Sage's benevolence aroused surprise and admiration but little curiosity. Media coverage reflected an understanding of giving as natural to women. The Presbyterian *Home Mission Monthly* treated the news that she had bequeathed millions of dollars as an object lesson in stewardship, ascribing her philanthropy to "her lifelong habit of giving a tenth of her income. In the days when she was a teacher at a salary of $200 a year she established this method of systematic giving, and when in later years large sums were at her disposal she made stewardship her business in life." Such descriptions naturalized giving: habit rather than investment, rational decision-making, or altruism explained Olivia Sage's philanthropy, according to such accounts.[85] Stereotypes of Lady Bountiful were still powerful (though jostled by the sharply competing images of the reforming professional and the New Woman), and these characterized the public reception of Sage's philanthropy. Even Robert de Forest, Olivia Sage's attorney and advisor, who was closer to her philanthropy than anyone, wrote a press release when she died in 1918 that reflected this view: "[T]he will of her husband, who had left her virtually all his great fortune, enabled her to gratify in a very large way her lifelong desire to help others." She did no more than a generous woman should, he implied; thus he both naturalized and dismissed Sage's philanthropy.[86]

Perhaps for this reason, most of Olivia's correspondence and papers (including her large clipping collection) were thrown away some time after her death and long before the foundation's records were moved from New York City to the Rockefeller Archive Center in Pocantico Hills, New York in the 1980s.[87] Fortunately for us, in 1913 Olivia had already ordered Lilian to "clean out" the accumulated papers from her New York office and send them off to the Emma Willard School, where they joined the materials from the Troy Female Seminary Alumnae survey, and where they remain to this day.

Several institutions that had secured huge donations during her lifetime received a rude shock when they learned of the clause in the will stipulating that donations made during her lifetime "were to be deemed advances" so that the legacies in the will "shall be diminished accordingly." For example, Yale was named in the will as recipient of one fifty-second part of the estate, or $800,000, but its legacy was substantially diminished because it had received $650,000 from her during her lifetime. Syracuse University, which had received $637,000 during her lifetime, got only an additional $100,000. Privately, Robert de Forest had warned the American Bible Society that "the $500,000 gift of Mrs. Sage to the A[merican] B[ible] S[ociety] will undoubtedly be deducted from its legacy." The society sued unsuccessfully to challenge this provision.[88]

Russell Sage College was left high and dry. Its supporters appealed to the Russell Sage Foundation for help with an endowment fund without success. No money could be raised in Troy, one friend of the college explained to foundation director John Glenn: "The people of wealth in Troy feel practically no interest in the institution. First, because it bears the name of Russell Sage."[89] Eliza Kellas continued to run both the Emma Willard School and Russell Sage College, living with her sister Katherine Kellas, who was dean of liberal arts, and commuting between the institutions daily until 1929 when she resigned to devote her remaining time to the school alone.[90]

And what of Lilian? A few days after the funeral, she described her situation to Kellas. First she had to stay and make an inventory of Number 604. "[B]ut when I am free I hope to make arrangements to go overseas. I am not sure I will be accepted—*Age* being a bar" (Lilian was fifty-two). Eliza invited her to Troy, but Lilian declined. "I am now out on a cold world, and must practice the most rigid economy, and cannot afford trips," she wrote. "If we do not meet again . . . rest assured I shall be one of the great number of admirers you have earned in your administration of the Emma Willard School and Russell Sage College."[91]

The terms of her employer's will revealed that Lilian's fears were well founded. Few clues exist to document how it happened that E. Lilian Todd, an inventor and engineer who had put aside her scientific work to do the work of private secretary for the twentieth century's greatest female philanthropist, ended up in such straitened circumstances. Or why relations between Olivia and Lilian cooled so much between 1915 and 1918 that in her will Olivia left Lilian only $2,500, less than the $3,000 set aside for each of her domestic servants and less even than her laundress! "E. Lilian Todd" heads the list of "servants" in the *New York Times* account of Olivia's bequests.

After her employer died, Lilian moved to California, where she made her home with Nurse Simpson. At last she found the warm climate she had longed for. And she received a small income from the foundation. As Shelby Harrison reported, "After Mrs. Sage's death, the trustees authorized the continuance of payments to certain relatives and friends of Mrs. Sage to whom she had given during her lifetime but for whom no provision had been made in her will." Miss Todd, "because of her knowledge of Mrs. Sage's affairs, was appointed by the trustees to keep in touch with these beneficiaries and distribute the checks to them monthly."[92] Lilian received $600 a year for this service. She died of cancer in Corona del Mar on September 26, 1937. Her death certificate, under "Trade, profession, or kind of work done," lists her only as "Housekeeper."[93]

Conclusion

Women's activism in the nineteenth century was not the sole possession of radicals and freethinkers, nor was it confined to working or
middle-class women. Activist women occupied different social locations
and political contexts. At one end of this spectrum, white women of
the upper class were surprisingly active in public debates. Although they
usually stayed within the boundaries of conventional gender ideology
and conformed to rules of religious observance and appropriate behavior, these elite activists nevertheless embraced a wide variety of causes.
Some weighed in against women's rights. But others supported the
expansion of legal and economic rights for women, including the suffrage.
They founded public institutions, sustained reform movements, and
engaged in politics.[1] They form the upstairs of the women's movement.

When these women got control of their own funds through marriage,
inheritance, or widowhood, they had the power to make change. From
benevolent matrons existing in the "shadow public sphere," they became
philanthropists. Speaking up and speaking out gave way to investment.
Whereas earlier their voices had registered only in obscure female-only
organizations, in the feminist press, or in domestic fiction, they now could
spend millions to make change. Spending became a form of speaking.

This book has explored the possibilities of self-making for such a
ruling-class woman in Gilded Age and Progressive-era America. A wife
who derived her social standing from her financier husband, who was
business partner to Jay Gould, Olivia Sage nevertheless created a per-

sona of benevolence that authorized a public career. In her husband's shadow for thirty-seven years, she mobilized a Victorian ideology of active reforming womanhood, and when he died in 1906 leaving her a vast fortune, she put the money to her own use, demonstrating that then—as now—money disbursed by a woman with women's advancement in mind, from a room of her own, could fund institutional change and leverage opportunities for other women.[2]

Olivia and Russell Sage exemplify what Catherine Kelly calls the "gendered dichotomies of making and spending."[3] While Olivia Sage models the nineteenth-century woman involved in the traditional charity work of the wealthy matron, the work of benevolence, Russell Sage was the robber baron or financial wizard (depending on your point of view) who helped modernize and consolidate the nation's transportation systems and its capital markets while making himself enormously rich. His career reflects themes of national and transnational development; hers seems the obverse—that of a private actor, secluded in the domestic world or its extension, the voluntary association. As a wife and later a widow, she carried out "public-private work" from her home—the parlor, the library, the upstairs room from whose windows she watched New York pass up and down Fifth Avenue, or the balcony at Cedar Croft, with its views out to sea.

Yet her story is one of emancipation and to some extent of emergence. It enables us to explore both the contours of women's private-sector activism in the nineteenth century and the limits of such benevolence-based activism in the early-twentieth-century transformation we call the Progressive era. It illustrates the impact of shifting gender ideology on a generation of middle- and upper-class Protestant women who in the years before the Civil War embraced the notion of a "sphere of usefulness" and who found in that concept an enabling rhetoric for all kinds of public work. As Mrs. Russell Sage, she performed the genteel activism of the Victorian woman of wealth, donating volunteer time, material goods, and small amounts of money. Engaging in these activities with others, she forged a self-consciousness that grew with the years. As a socially prominent New York matron, she involved herself in several significant reform communities: remaking Indian work and gender roles at Carlisle, managing an institution for the treatment of women's diseases, and constructing an educated female citizenry in the Emma Willard Association. These activities had consequences for public life. She was one of the women Mary Ryan calls "critical and creative political actors," private providers of social services and makers of culture who operated from social spaces far from the political realm.[4]

An efficient administrator who attended the first extension courses in business law at New York University and served alongside men on boards of voluntary associations such as the New-York Woman's Hospital, Olivia tested the boundaries of benevolence to gain authority and stature in Gilded Age New York. But without resources of her own until her husband died, she long remained a philanthropist with no money to spend, a moralist and a "character" rather than a leader, a person with pet peeves rather than a reformer with the long vision of contemporaries such as Jane Addams or the theoretical daring of Elizabeth Cady Stanton—a do-gooder rather than a saint.[5]

Widowhood, with its expectations of serious purpose combined with self-effacement, authorized what Carolyn Heilbrun has called an "old-age freedom." As a widow, Olivia Sage moved in public with authority so long as she signaled the absent presence of her late husband. Her philanthropy nevertheless enacted a recovery of personhood even when, like the Russell Sage College, it was named for him. Invoking his presence, she spent as she wished. It was investment, it was reform, and for the most part it fulfilled her wishes. Money made all the difference. With money, Olivia Sage the advocate for the rights of women and the responsibilities of wealth, for moral reform and material betterment, could fund the causes she believed in. Spending replaced volunteer work, and the "performative philanthropy" of suffrage bazaars and fund-raising fetes gave way to large money donations to favorite causes.

Yet as I have shown, the promise of a transformative philanthropy fell short, departing in significant ways from the "women and education" program that the public expected from this voluble philanthropist and reflecting the blinkered perspectives of her class and race position as well as the pressures of fund-raisers of all kinds. There were several reasons why this was so.

The main characteristic of philanthropy historically, and what distinguishes it from publicly funded programs, is its voluntarism and its quirkiness. Philanthropy stems from the ideals, beliefs, enthusiasms, and prejudices of the giver. What counts are the donor's intentions, not the objective qualities of the recipient. It is a matter of taste, not justice. (In contrast, state provision depends, or should depend, on a system of categorical entitlement.) Olivia's philanthropy was neither a kind of private form of progressive taxation aimed at the redistribution of wealth nor a generalized helping. It was a very specific targeting of certain institutions and individuals that the donor deemed worthy.[6]

These were numerous and varied, and although much of her spending was directed to women's institutions, hundreds of other causes competed for her support. But some of the institutions she had planned to fund—the smaller, female-only organizations and auxiliaries—were already facing merger or closing as the twentieth century opened. And because she lacked the confidence and physical stamina of fellow philanthropist and activist Alva Belmont, her plans for spending were often deflected, and she was led by connivance, flattery, or both to abandon some causes and fund others.

Moreover, her reform vision was limited. Philanthropy empowered her to make concrete her best and worst impulses, her humane ideals and her prejudices, the ample generosity as well as the narrow-mindedness. Generosity with funds coexisted with a less-than-generous outlook; benevolence with snobbery, self-righteousness, and social conservatism; religious faith with prejudice. Because she benefited from her place in America's racial-ethnic and class hierarchy and from her connections with powerful men, she did not envision democratic cross-class alliances with working women but represented herself as "a missionary to her poorer sisters." Paradoxically, her extreme wealth and her celebrity as the wife, then widow, of a powerful man isolated her and limited her freedom of action. Evangelical religion, which earlier had spurred her on to public work, became a brake on her activism and her feminism. In old age, without connections to the new leadership of the suffrage movement and surrounded by those who would both protect and control her, she lost some of her independence of action even as she worked to give away a fortune, one check at a time.

The private philanthropy totaling around $35 million is difficult to characterize. What was the impact of all this spending? Could philanthropy, even on this grand scale, ever result in anything more than "small change"? The questions lie beyond this biography but are worth asking anyway. One of the most thoughtful writers on American philanthropy, Robert Bremner, was skeptical of philanthropy's power to change society. "Was the benefactor-beneficiary relationship a denial of the equality democracy implied?" he asked in 1960 in *American Philanthropy*. "Did charity perpetuate the conditions that created poverty? Could philanthropy, tied as it was to the purse strings of the existing order, accomplish anything of importance in building a better society?"[7] Returning to the question three decades later, Bremner emphasized motivation rather than outcomes. Noting the tendency of historians to look for hidden (and presumably less worthy) motives, Bremner challenged them to reexamine their own motives. Perhaps philanthropy has no deeper meaning than that some rich people want to use their money to do good, he suggested. In the search for a good story, we should not overlook the obvious fact that sometimes people simply are altruistic.[8]

At a time in history when everything is for sale, large-scale philanthropy seems to call for a more complex explanation than this. I have shown how Olivia's philanthropy mixed altruism with other motives that included ambition, insecurity, patriotism, and nostalgia. Altruism can never be entirely explained away. Olivia had the opportunity to give and she gave splendidly—over $770 million in today's money. This, in the words of one philosopher, was "heroically altruistic."[9] Yet giving away something of great value usually means having less yourself, and this was not the case here. If Olivia gave freely, she also gave without cost, for spending did not impoverish her.[10] Finally, like many donors then and since, she often gave to the largest, most prestigious entity rather than to the neediest, and sometimes these were institutions that excluded women.

The important exception was the Russell Sage Foundation, which included women as trustees, staff, and researchers and which continues to fund social science research to this day. In her willingness to cooperate with elite reformer and charity expert Robert de Forest, Olivia Sage made her most significant donation, one that married the bold and optimistic spirit of Progressive-era social science to the tradition of nineteenth-century elite women's benevolence and took into cognizance the general welfare in an extraordinary and unprecedented way. A New York institution with national reach, the Russell Sage Foundation was a new engine for social investigation and reform, a think tank and grant-maker for urban and regional problems, and a leader in the modernization of social services and welfare thought. Its experts were drawn from the interlocking reform and charity networks of Boston, New York, Philadelphia, and Baltimore, circles of benevolent, white, middle- and upper-class women and men who had been elaborating, in the non-state sector, privately funded social services of all kinds in these same cities.

Unlike her private philanthropy with its designated outlays for direct aid to the poor, the foundation was organized to advance the study of poverty as a societal problem. It established the modern profession of social work, funded innovative research on working families in Pittsburgh (the Pittsburgh Survey), and supported investigations of labor conditions, industrial relations, work accidents, housing, and consumer economics. Elite women such as Olivia Sage were for long neglected in our histories of progressivism. Yet for a few years at the beginning of the twentieth century, a woman's money—Sage money—funded a broad spectrum of Progressive reform.

ABBREVIATIONS

Abbé Scrapbooks	Mrs. Robert Abbé, Scrapbooks of Newspaper Clippings and Other Material Relating to Woman Suffrage in New York City, microform, 1894–1921, New York Public Library, New York, New York
ANB	John Garraty and Mark Carnes, eds., *American National Biography* (New York: Oxford University Press, 1998)
Columbia	Rare Book and Manuscript Library, Columbia University Library, New York, New York
Cornell	Department of Manuscripts and University Archives, Cornell University, Ithaca, New York
CSSA	Community Service Society Archive
DAB	*Dictionary of American Biography* (New York: Scribner, 1928–)
ECS/SBA	Patricia G. Holland and Ann D. Gordon, eds., *The Papers of Elizabeth Cady Stanton and Susan B. Anthony* (Wilmington, Del.: Scholarly Resources, Inc., 1991)
EGS	Papers at the home of Eileen Gillespie (Mrs. John) Slocum, Newport, R.I.
EWP	Mrs. A. W. Fairbanks, comp., *Emma Willard and Her Pupils; or, Fifty Years of Troy Female Seminary, 1822–1872*
EWS	Emma Willard School Archives, Troy, New York
FSW	Papers at the home of the late Mrs. Florence Slocum Wilson, Pasadena, California
Harvard	Harvard University Archives, Harvard University Library, Cambridge, Massachusetts
HMG	Helen Miller Gould
Huntington	Huntington Library, San Marino, Calif.
HWS	Elizabeth Cady Stanton, Susan B. Anthony, and Matilda Joslyn Gage, eds., *History of Woman Suffrage*. 6 vols. (Rochester: Susan B. Anthony, 1881–1922; repr., New York: Arno Press, 1969)
JJML	John Jermain Memorial Library, Sag Harbor, New York
Lyndhurst	Lyndhurst Trust for Historic Preservation, Irvington, New York

MacCracken Records	Henry Mitchell MacCracken Administrative Records, 1884–1910, Office of the Chancellor, Archives, Elmer Holmes Bobst Library, New York University, New York, New York
MOS	Margaret Olivia Sage
NAW	Edward T. James, Janet Wilson James, and Paul S. Boyer, eds., *Notable American Women, 1607–1950: A Biographical Dictionary*, 3 vols. (Cambridge, Mass.: Belknap Press of Harvard University Press, 1971)
NYHS	The New-York Historical Society, New York, New York
NYPL	New York Public Library, New York, New York
NYSL	New York State Archives, New York State Library, Albany, New York
NYSM	New York Sun Morgue Collection, New York Public Library, New York, New York
NYU	New York University Archives, Elmer Holmes Bobst Library, New York, New York
OCPL	Onondaga County Public Library, Syracuse, New York
OnHA	Onondaga Historical Association, Syracuse, New York
RCHS	Rensselaer County Historical Society, Troy, New York
RPI	Rensselaer Polytechnic Institute, Archives & Special Collections, Troy, New York
RSF	Russell Sage Foundation
RSFR	Russell Sage Foundation Records, Rockefeller Archive Center, Sleepy Hollow, New York
RS Foundation	Papers at the Russell Sage Foundation, New York, New York
Rutgers	Special Collections and University Archives, Rutgers University Archives, New Brunswick, New Jersey
RW de F	Robert Weeks de Forest
Smithsonian	Smithsonian Institution Archives, Washington, D.C.
SWHA	Social Welfare History Archives, University of Minnesota, Minneapolis, Minnesota
SUA	Syracuse University Archives and Records Management, Syracuse, New York
TPL	Troy Public Library, Troy, New York
Vassar	Vassar College Archives, Poughkeepsie, New York
WHP	Woman's Hospital Papers, Bolling Memorial Medical Archives, St. Luke's-Roosevelt Hospital, New York, New York

WHSA	Wisconsin Historical Society Archives, Madison, Wisconsin
Yale, Beinecke	Beinecke Rare Book and Manuscript Library, Yale University, New Haven, Connecticut
Yale, Manuscripts and Archives	Manuscripts and Archives, Yale University Library, Yale University, New Haven, Connecticut

Notes

Acknowledgments

1. Olivia Sage's papers comprise Series 1 and 10 in the Russell Sage Foundation Records, Rockefeller Archive Center, Sleepy Hollow, New York. Series 1 is "Mrs. Russell Sage" and includes Folders 1–10; Series 10, "Personal Giving," comprises Folders 584 to 1060, arranged alphabetically by designee.

2. Ruth Crocker, *Social Work and Social Order: The Settlement Movement in Two Industrial Cities* (Urbana: University of Illinois Press, 1992).

3. John Jermain Slocum, the son of Herbert Jermain Slocum, Jr., and his first wife, died in 1997 in Newport, Rhode Island. See his obituary, "John J. Slocum, 83, Diplomat and Connoisseur of Literature," *New York Times*, September 1, 1997. His James Joyce collection was donated to Yale University. See also "At Bailey's Beach, the Ruling Class Keeps Its Guard Up," *New York Times*, July 20, 2003, 9:1–2.

A Note on Sources

1. W. Frank Persons to Robert W. de Forest, June 8, 1912, CSSA, Columbia.

2. Irvin G. Wyllie, "Margaret Olivia Slocum Sage," *NAW*, 3: 222–323.

3. Personal communication from Professor Barry D. Karl to the author, January 9, 1990 and February 9, 1998. See also David C. Hammack, "Introduction" to *Russell Sage Foundation: Social Research and Social Action in America, 1907–1947*, ed. David C. Maddox (Frederick, Md.: CIS Academic Editions, 1988). The two-volume history referred to is John M. Glenn, Lilian Brandt, and F. Emerson Andrews, *Russell Sage Foundation, 1907–1946*, 2 vols. (New York: Russell Sage Foundation, 1947).

4. Personal communication from Professor Barry D. Karl to the author, January 9, 1990.

5. David C. Hammack, "Russell Sage Foundation," in *Greenwood Encyclopedia of American Institutions: Foundations*, ed. Harold M. Keele and Joseph C. Kiger (Westport, Conn.: Greenwood Press, 1984): 439–465.

The present-day Russell Sage Foundation retains very few records from this period and none of Olivia Sage. There are typed minutes of the Board of Trustees (April 1907–May 27, 1907), including the meeting of incorporation and the constitution, and typed and bound minutes of the Board of Trustees for the period April 19, 1907 to May 17, 1921. The minutes of the Russell Sage Foundation trustees' Executive Committee are also bound in one volume that covers the period 1907–1948.

6. Series 1, "Mrs. Russell Sage"; Series 3, "Early Office Files"; Series 10, "Personal Giving," all in RSFP; Hammack, "Introduction."

7. The image can be seen at http://www.wga.hu/index1.html.

8. I discuss begging letters as historical evidence in Ruth Crocker, "'I Only Ask You Kindly To Divide Some of Your Fortune With Me': Begging Letters and the Transformation of Charity in Late Nineteenth-Century America," *Social Politics: International Studies in Gender, State, and Society* 6 (Summer 1999): 105–131. See also Scott A. Sandage, "Gender and the Economics of the Sentimental Market in Nineteenth-Century America," in ibid., 131–160.

9. MOS to Hon. E. D. Morgan, May 19, 1882, Edwin D. Morgan Papers, NYSL.

10. E. Lilian Todd to Eliza Kellas, June 19, 1913, Margaret Olivia Slocum Sage Collection, Box 3, EWS.

11. Ibid. She was referring to Mrs. A. W. Fairbanks, comp., *Emma Willard and Her Pupils, or Fifty Years of Troy Female Seminary, 1822–1872* (New York: Published by Mrs. Russell Sage, 1898), the directory of alumnae of the Troy Female Seminary.

12. E. Lilian Todd to Eliza Kellas, April 20, 1918, Margaret Olivia Slocum Sage Collection, Box 5, EWS.

13. "Mrs. Sage's Letters," Box 159, CSSA, Columbia.

Introduction

1. Claudia M. Oakes, *United States Women in Aviation through World War I* (1978; repr., Washington, D.C.: Smithsonian Institution Press, 1985), 10–11. My thanks to my colleague Jim Hansen for this citation. "The Aeronautical Society's First Exhibition," *Scientific American* 99, no. 20 (November 14, 1908): 338; "A Woman Inventor Who Plans—and Expects—to Fly: Miss Todd and the Coming Trial of Her Aeroplane," *New York Times*, November 28, 1909, 11; Lilian Todd, "How I Built My Aeroplane," *Woman's Home Companion* (November 1909): 11. "Early this Spring, Miss E. L. Todd, who has been experimenting for a number of years with models, and organized the Junior Aero Club, had a biplane built by Wittemann Brothers"; J. Suche, "At the Mineola Field," *Aeronautics* (December 1910), 197. My thanks to independent scholar Lygia Ionnitiu for this citation and for other help with aviation bibliography.

2. The reporter for *Aeronautics* noted, "Both times it was taken out it flew very well. But the controls were not balanced, and caused too much exertion in their operation." Journalist Elizabeth Hiatt Gregory leaves a firsthand account of Olivia Sage's day at Mineola. She describes Sage as "financial backer for Lillian [sic] Todd." Elizabeth Hiatt Gregory, *Show Windows of Life* (Wayside Press, Inc., 1944), 70–71. See also the newspaper clipping, August 6, 1910, "The Sage and Slocum Book," (scrapbook), Jermain Family Collection, JJML.

3. Margaret Olivia Slocum Sage never used "Margaret," preferring Olivia,

and I have followed suit. I use Olivia Slocum for the years before her marriage in 1869. Later she used different forms, but she usually signed herself M. Olivia Sage. When her usage seems to me significant, I draw attention to the fact.

4. For conversion of early-twentieth-century currency, a useful guide is John J. McCusker, "Comparing the Purchasing Power of Money in the United States (or Colonies) from 1665 to 2003," Economic History Services, 2004, available online at http://www.eh.net/hmit/ppowerusd.

Kathleen D. McCarthy divides nineteenth-century women's philanthropic giving into institution-founding, social movements, political reform, and donations "to leverage new opportunities and careers"; McCarthy, "Parallel Power Structures: Women and the Voluntary Sphere," in *Lady Bountiful Revisited: Women, Philanthropy, and Power,* ed. Kathleen D. McCarthy (New Brunswick, N.J.: Rutgers University Press, 1990), 1–2.

5. Major studies of Carnegie and his foundations are Joseph Frazier Wall, *Andrew Carnegie* (1970; repr., Pittsburgh, Pa.: University of Pittsburgh Press, 1989); Ellen Condliffe Lagemann, *The Politics of Knowledge: The Carnegie Corporation, Philanthropy, and Public Policy* (Chicago: University of Chicago Press, 1989); and Lagemann, *Private Power for the Public Good: A History of the Carnegie Foundation for the Advancement of Teaching* (Middletown, Conn.: Wesleyan University Press, 1983).

Rockefeller philanthropy is discussed in Ron Chernow, *Titan: The Life of John D. Rockefeller, Sr.* (New York: Random House, 1998); Raymond Fosdick, *The Story of the Rockefeller Foundation* (New York: Harper and Row, 1952). Judith Sealander surveys the Rockefeller philanthropies, the Rosenwald and Commonwealth Funds, and the Russell Sage Foundation in *Private Wealth and Public Life: Foundation Philanthropy and the Reshaping of American Social Policy from the Progressive Era to the New Deal* (Baltimore, Md.: Johns Hopkins University Press, 1997), a tour de force of research and writing. For an introduction to the literature on philanthropy and foundations, see Sealander, "Philanthropy and Philanthropic Foundations," in *Oxford Companion to United States History* (New York: Oxford University Press, 2001), 592–593; David Hammack, "Foundations in the American Polity, 1900–1915," in *Philanthropic Foundations: New Scholarship, New Possibilities,* ed. Ellen Condliffe Lagemann (Bloomington: Indiana University Press, 1999), 43–68; Ruth Crocker, "Philanthropy," in *Poverty in the United States: An Encyclopedia of History, Politics, and Policy,* ed. Gwendolyn Mink and Alice O'Connor (New York: ABC-CLIO, 2004), 2:533–537.

6. I am not arguing that women are more likely to give than men or that in the nineteenth century men were selfish moneymakers while their wives and daughters were benevolent dispensers of funds. Philanthropic women and men sometimes acted brutally to defend class interests, and when the chips were down industrialists' wives could behave exactly like men of their class: Sage's friend and classmate Nettie Fowler McCormick acted vigorously after her husband Cyrus McCormick died, defending class and property interests by authorizing the violent suppression of the 1886 Haymarket strike at the family's Chicago works.

She later became a great philanthropist who gave to over forty schools and colleges. Gilbert A. Harrison, *A Timeless Affair: The Life of Anita McCormick Blaine* (Chicago: University of Chicago Press, 1979), 39–40; Charles O. Burgess, "Nettie Fowler McCormick," in *NAW*, 2:454–455; "Nettie Fowler," *EWP*, 814.

7. Phoebe Hearst and Nettie McCormick married wealth, as did Olivia Sage. Grace Dodge and Helen Gould were daughters of wealthy men. Esther Katz, "Grace Hoadley Dodge: Women and the Emerging Metropolis" (Ph.D. diss., New York University, 1980); for Phoebe Hearst, see Alexandra Nickliss, "Phoebe Apperson Hearst" (Ph.D. diss., University of California, Davis, 1994); for Candace Wheeler, see Mary Warner Blanchard, *Oscar Wilde's America: Counterculture in the Gilded Age* (New Haven, Conn.: Yale University Press, 1998), 45–84; and Kathleen D. McCarthy, *Women's Culture: American Philanthropy and Art* (Chicago: University of Chicago Press, 1991), 37–56 and 67–70. See also Madeleine Stern, "Candace Thurber Wheeler," *NAW*, 3:574–576. Philanthropist Anna M. Harkness (1837–1926), another contemporary of Sage, inherited $150 million in 1888, but her spending began only after 1918. Miriam Langsam, "Anna M. Richardson Harkness," *NAW*, 2:134–135. See also Clarice Stasz, *The Vanderbilt Women: Dynasty of Wealth, Glamour and Tragedy* (New York: St. Martin's Press, 1991); and Stasz, *The Rockefeller Women: Dynasty of Piety, Privacy, and Service* (New York: St. Martin's Press, 1995). See also Edna Healey, *Lady Unknown: The Life of Angela Burdett-Coutts* (London: Sidgwick and Jackson, 1978).

8. Private sector spending has traditionally been seen as a counterweight to the absence of government spending, but Peter Dobkin Hall and others have argued that it was integral to state capacity. Social spending and service provision are not a matter of either/or, government or private. In fact, nonprofits today rely on direct government support for one-fourth of their income. The two sectors are interdependent or synergistic. Peter Dobkin Hall, "Private Philanthropy and Public Policy: A Historical Appraisal," in *Philanthropy: Four Views*, ed. Robert L. Payton (New Brunswick, N.J.: Transaction Books, 1988), 39–72.

Mary Ryan reaches a similar conclusion about women's voluntary work in the nineteenth century. This private activity was not a "derivative and residual by-product of the development of the public," she insists, but was developed "in tandem" with the public. "The Public and the Private Good: Across the Great Divide in Women's History," *Journal of Women's History* 15 (Summer 2003): 21–23; Paula Baker, "The Domestication of Politics: Women and American Political Society, 1780–1920," *American Historical Review* 89 (June 1984): 630, 647.

9. Lee Soltow, *Men and Wealth in the United States, 1850–1870*, cited in Carole Shammas, "Reassessing the Married Women's Property Acts," *Journal of Women's History* 6 (Spring 1994): 20.

10. Boyden Sparkes, *Hetty Green, A Woman Who Loved Money* (Garden City, N.Y.: Doubleday, Doren & Company: 1930), 124. Susan A. Yohn com-

ments, "Women could make money, but they could not keep it without their femininity being suspect." "You Can't Share Babies with Bonds: Gendering the Idea of Profit," 5, paper presented at the Berkshire Conference of Women's Historians, University of North Carolina, Chapel Hill, North Carolina, June 7–9, 1996. See also Janet L. Coryell, "Hetty Green, 1870–1910," in *Encyclopedia of American Business History and Biography*, vol. 7, *Banking and Finance to 1913*, ed. Larry Schweikart (New York: Facts on File, 1990), 233–239. The idea that speculation is destructive of femininity has a long history. See Hope Cotton, "Women and Risk: The Gambling Woman in Eighteenth-Century England" (Ph.D. diss., Auburn University, 1998).

11. The classic study is Lori D. Ginzberg, *Women and the Work of Benevolence: Morality, Politics, and Class in the Nineteenth-Century United States* (New Haven, Conn.: Yale University Press, 1990). Ginzberg elegantly characterizes this inherited nineteenth-century gender system as one where the dominant ideology "conflated ideas about femininity with ideas about morality itself" (1).

12. In our time, such stereotyping of benevolence still operates to make people expect women to be more compassionate and more caring than men. What has been called "the altruism gap" drew support from the earlier work of Carol Gilligan. See Gilligan, *In a Different Voice: Psychological Theory and Women's Development* (Cambridge, Mass.: Harvard University Press, 1982); Carol Gilligan, Janie Victoria Ward, and Jill McLean Taylor, eds., *Mapping the Moral Domain: A Contribution of Women's Thinking to Psychological Theory and Education* (Cambridge, Mass.: Harvard University Press, 1989); Carol Gilligan, Nona Lyons, and Trudy J. Hanmer, *Making Connections: The Relational Worlds of Adolescent Girls at Emma Willard School* (Cambridge, Mass.: Harvard University Press, 1990). In her study of women's philanthropy for women in the 1990s, Marsha Shapiro Rose emphasizes differences from masculinist styles of management and hierarchical thinking; "The Women's Funds," *Nonprofit and Voluntary Sector Quarterly* 23 (Fall 1994): 227–242. The debate over Gilligan's findings is ably discussed in Seyla Benhabib, *Situating the Self: Gender, Community, and Postmodernism in Contemporary Ethics* (New York: Routledge, 1992), 190–198. It is a nice coincidence for this present work that Carol Gilligan's research on young women's values was based on research carried out at the Emma Willard School—the former Troy Female Seminary in Troy, New York, which Olivia Sage attended in the 1840s.

A useful earlier discussion of women and altruism by four feminist philosophers is Larry Blum, Marcia Homiak, Judy Housman, and Naomi Scheman, "Altruism and Women's Oppression," in *Women and Philosophy: Toward a Theory of Liberation*, ed. Carol C. Gould and Marx W. Wartofsky (New York: G. P. Putnam's Sons, 1976), 222–247. The authors analyze the tension between altruistic qualities "which can be seen as universal values which are good for men as well as for women to possess," and altruism linked to self-sacrifice and "stemming from guilt, fear, and low self-esteem, rather than from freedom or self-love" (222). See also Margaret Adams, "The Compassion Trap," in *Women in Sexist Society*, ed. Vivian Gornick and Barbara K. Moran (New York: New American Library, 1972).

Alan Wolfe, "What Is Altruism?" in *Private Action and the Public Good*, ed. Walter W. Powell and Elisabeth S. Clemens (New Haven, Conn.: Yale University Press, 1998), 36–46 summarizes recent periodical literature in social psychology but concludes only that "most of the time what we do involves an uneasy combination of motives and intentions, some of them selfish, others altruistic" (43).

13. See McCarthy, *Women's Culture: American Philanthropy and Art*, 118, 120–121, 174–175, 262n9; McCarthy, *Lady Bountiful Revisited*; and McCarthy, *Noblesse Oblige: Charity and Cultural Philanthropy in Chicago, 1849–1929* (Chicago: University of Chicago Press, 1982).

14. Paul Sarnoff, *Russell Sage, the Money King* (New York: Ivan Obolensky, 1965), 322, 363. Paul Sarnoff's other publications indicate his expertise. They include *Trading in Gold* (1980); *Smart Investor's Guide to the Money Market* (1981); *Trading in Silver: How to Make High Profits* (1988); and, most recently, *Super-leverage: How to Make Money with Limited Risk: A Guide to Leveraged Transactions in the Financial and Commodities Markets* (New York: Woodhead-Faulkner, 1989).

Sarnoff's biography is still the only full-length study. See also biographical sketches of the Sages: James Allen Smith and Melissa A. Smith, "Margaret Olivia Slocum Sage," *ANB* 19:193–194; and George M. Jenks, "Russell Sage," in *ANB*, 19:194–195.

15. Klein portrays the women's friendship as a weird pairing of two dysfunctional personalities, with Helen Gould "a timid, painfully shy creature in whom Olivia must have seen something of herself." In Klein's hands, the relationship becomes a case study in codependency. Maury Klein, *The Life and Legend of Jay Gould* (Baltimore, Md.: Johns Hopkins University Press, 1986), 476.

16. Ellen Carol DuBois, "Working Women, Class Relations, and Suffrage Militance: Harriot Stanton Blatch and the New York Woman Suffrage Movement, 1894–1909," *Journal of American History* 74 (June 1987): 34–58. A critical view of wealthy women's participation in Progressive-era politics is Diane Kirkby, "Class, Gender, and the Perils of Philanthropy: The Story of *Life and Labor* and Labor Reform in the WTUL," *Journal of Women's History* 4 (Fall 1992): 36–51. I explored this topic in Ruth Crocker, "'Unrepresentable in Our Narratives': Women's History and Female Philanthropists," paper prepared for the Western Association of Women Historians, Asilomar, California, June 1997. The title is taken from Christine Stansell, "Memory and the Pre-War Avant-Garde: Louise Bryant Grown Old," plenary address, Berkshire Conference of Women's Historians, Vassar College, Poughkeepsie, New York, June 1993.

17. Nancy Hewitt and Suzanne Lebsock, "Introduction," in Hewitt and Lebsock, eds., *Visible Women: New Essays on American Activism* (Urbana: University of Illinois Press, 1993), 4. In a historiographical essay on women's his-

tory, Joan W. Scott describes the history of feminism as "the grand teleologi-cal narrative of emancipation." Scott, "Feminism's History," *Journal of Women's History* 16 (2004): 13.

18. A few of the more influential studies were Barbara Berg, *The Remembered Gate: The Origins of American Feminism* (New York: Oxford University Press, 1978); Barbara Leslie Epstein, *The Politics of Domesticity: Women, Evangelism, and Temperance in Nineteenth-Century America* (Middletown, Conn.: Wesleyan University Press, 1981); Ruth Bordin, *Woman and Temperance: The Quest for Power and Liberty, 1873–1900* (Philadelphia, Pa.: Temple University Press, 1981); Mary Ryan, *Cradle of the Middle Class: The Family in Oneida County, New York, 1790–1865* (New York: Cambridge University Press, 1981); Nancy Hewitt, *Women's Activism and Social Change in Rochester, New York, 1822–1872* (Ithaca, N.Y.: Cornell University Press, 1984); Anne Firor Scott, *Natural Allies: Women's Associations in American History* (Urbana: University of Illinois Press, 1992); Karen J. Blair, *The Clubwoman as Feminist: True Womanhood Redefined, 1868–1914* (New York: Holmes and Meier, 1980); Baker, "The Domestication of Politics"; Kathleen D. McCarthy, "Parallel Power Structures: Women and the Voluntary Sphere," in McCarthy, *Lady Bountiful Revisited*, 1–31.

The narrative served for the histories of free black as well as for white women. See Evelyn Brooks Higginbotham, *Righteous Discontent: The Woman's Movement in the Black Baptist Church, 1880–1920* (Cambridge, Mass. Harvard University Press, 1993); Jacqueline Rouse, *Lugenia Burns Hope: Black Southern Reformer* (Athens: University of Georgia Press, 1989); Glenda Gilmore, *Gender and Jim Crow* (Chapel Hill: University of North Carolina Press, 1996); Adrienne Jones, *Jane Edna Hunter: A Case Study of Black Leadership, 1910–1950* (Brooklyn, N.Y.: Carlson Publishing Company, 1990); Dorothy Salem, *To Better Our World: Black Women in Organized Reform, 1890–1920* (Brooklyn, N.Y.: Carlson Publishing Company, 1990); and Darlene Clark Hine, "'We Specialize in the Wholly Impossible': The Philanthropic Work of Black Women," in McCarthy, *Lady Bountiful Revisited*, 70–93.

19. In her 1987 essay, "Working Women, Class Relations, and Suffrage Militance," Carol DuBois challenged the label "middle-class" for women of wealth (177). A wise and witty appraisal of the historiography of women's history to the 1980s is Bonnie G. Smith, "The Contribution of Women to Modern Historiography," *American Historical Review* 89 (June 1984). She writes, "The wrong kind of woman worthy—a woman of privilege, for example—can be embarrassing" (728).

20. In a related movement, distaste for conservatism has given way more recently to an anxious search to understand it, in part to understand the politics of our own time. In this changed political climate, scholars are writing the histories of conservative women See "Right-Wing Women in Women's History: A Global Perspective," a roundtable in *Journal of Women's History* 16, no. 3 (2004): 106–186; Kirsten Delegard, "Women's Movements, 1880s–1920s," in *A Companion to American Women's History*, ed. Nancy A. Hewitt (Malden,

Mass.: Blackwell Publishing, 2002), 328–347; and Kim Nielsen, "Doing the 'Right' Right," *Journal of Women's History* 16, no. 3 (2004): 168–172, for a detailed bibliography.

21. "What happens when we beam questions about race and class on past crusades in which the protagonists were largely women of privilege?" Nancy Hewitt and Suzanne Lebsock ask in the introduction to Hewitt and Lebsock, eds., *Visible Women: New Essays on American Activism* (Urbana: University of Illinois Press, 1993), 6. Recent examples of this new emphasis are Nancy Robertson, "Kindness or Justice? Women's Associations and the Politics of Race and History," in *Private Action and the Public Good*, ed. W. W. Powell and E. Clemens (New Haven, Conn.: Yale University Press, 1998); Nancy Hewitt, *Southern Discomfort: Women's Activism in Tampa, Florida, 1880s–1920s* (Urbana: University of Illinois Press, 2001); Joan Waugh, *Unsentimental Reformer: The Life of Josephine Shaw Lowell* (Cambridge, Mass. Harvard University Press, 1998); Kathryn Kish Sklar, "Who Funded Hull House?" in McCarthy, *Lady Bountiful Revisited*, 112–115. See also Maureen Flanagan, *Seeing with Their Hearts: Chicago Women and the Vision of the Good City, 1871–1933* (Princeton, N.J.: Princeton University Press, 2002).

22. "For nineteenth century women, the characteristic form of political activism was participation in a voluntary association." Suzanne Lebsock, "Women and American Politics, 1880–1920," in *Women, Politics and Change*, ed. Louise A. Tilly and Patricia Gurin (New York: Russell Sage Foundation, 1990), 37.

23. "A fellow-student" to MOS, December 19, 1906, RSFR, Series 10, Box 88, Folder 850.

24. RW de F, "Margaret Olivia Sage, Philanthropist," *The Survey* 41 (November 9, 1918): 151. See also Russell Sage Foundation, "Meeting of Incorporators," in Minutes of the Trustees, April 19, 1907, Russell Sage Foundation. The incident is repeated in John M. Glenn, Lilian Brandt, and F. Emerson Andrews, *Russell Sage Foundation, 1907–1946* (New York: Russell Sage Foundation, 1947), 1:267.

25. Renamed the Emma Willard School in 1895.

26. "Mrs. Russell Sage on Marriage," *Syracuse Sunday Herald*, June 21, 1903, 29; "Mrs. Sage's Popularity," clipping, "Margaret Olivia Sage," NYSM.

27. My thinking about widowhood was clarified by the participants and commentators at the conference "The Widow's Might," Rutgers Center on Historical Analysis, Rutgers, New Jersey, April 2004.

28. The literature on the gift owes more to anthropologists than to historians. See Mary Douglas, "No Free Gifts," foreword to Marcel Mauss, *The Gift: The Form and Reason for Exchange in Archaic Societies*, trans. W. D. Halls. (1950; repr., London: Routledge, 2002); Annette Weiner, *Inalienable Possessions: The Paradox of Keeping While Giving* (Berkeley: University of California Press, 1992); Marilyn Strathern, *The Gender of the Gift: Problems with Women and Problems with Society in Melanesia* (Berkeley: University of California Press, 1988). Polit-

ical scientists, literary scholars, and historians have also explored the gift. See Lewis Hyde, *The Gift: Imagination and the Erotic Life of Property* (1979; repr., New York: Random House, 1983); Susan Ryan, *The Grammar of Good Intentions: Race and the Antebellum Culture of Benevolence* (Ithaca, N.Y.: Cornell University Press, 2003); Nancy Fraser, "From Redistribution to Recognition? Dilemmas of Justice in a 'Postsocialist' Age," in Fraser, *Justus Interruptus: Critical Reflections on the "Postsocialist" Condition* (New York: Routledge, 1997), 11–39. Recent work by historians includes Natalie Zemon Davis, *The Gift in Sixteenth-Century France* (Madison: University of Wisconsin Press, 2000). Other influential studies are Stanley Katz, *Poverty and Policy in American History* (New York: Academic Press, 1983); Gareth Stedman-Jones, *Outcast London: A Study in the Relationship between Classes in Victorian Society* (New York: Oxford University Press, 1971); Viviana Zelizer, *The Social Meaning of Money* (New York: Basic Books, 1994); Amy Dru Stanley, "Beggars Can't Be Choosers: Compulsion and Contract in Postbellum America," *Journal of American History* 78 (March 1992): 1265–1293. Contrasting contemporary views are Jane Addams, "The Subtle Problems of Charity," *Atlantic Monthly* 83 (1899): 163–178; Andrew Carnegie, "Wealth," *North American Review* 148 (June 1889): 653–664; and Carnegie, "The Best Fields for Philanthropy," *North American Review* 149 (December 1889): 682–698.

29. Nancy Fraser and Linda Gordon, "A Genealogy of Dependency: Tracing a Keyword of the U.S. Welfare State," *Signs* 19, no. 2 (1994): 308–363. The best study of scientific charity in New York is Dawn Greeley, "Beyond Benevolence: Gender, Class, and the Development of Scientific Charity in New York City, 1882–1935" (Ph.D. diss., SUNY Stony Brook, 1995). For contrasting but ambitious interpretations of these transformations in the ideology of liberal capitalism, see Amy Dru Stanley, *From Bondage to Contract: Wage Labor, Marriage, and the Market in the Age of Slave Emancipation* (New York: Cambridge University Press, 1998); and Jeffrey Slansky, *The Soul's Economy: Market Society and Selfhood in American Social Thought, 1820–1920* (Chapel Hill: University of North Carolina Press, 2002).

30. See Crocker, "Philanthropy," for definitions. Philanthropy involves organizing for improvement or for some benevolent or altruistic purpose.

31. Weiner, *Inalienable Possessions*.

32. Louisa Lee Schuyler to RW de F, March 23, 1907, RSFR, Box 2, Folder 11. Literary scholar Paula Backscheider calls this an example of women's "deliberate erasure"; Backscheider, *Reflections on Biography* (New York: Oxford University Press, 1999). In contrast, philanthropist Andrew Carnegie was so ready to speak and write for the record that his biographer calls him "the voluble, self-appointed spokesman for capitalism and democracy." Joseph Frazier Wall, "Introduction," in *The Andrew Carnegie Reader*, ed. Wall (Pittsburgh, Pa.: University of Pittsburgh Press, 1992), ix.

33. The passage reads in full: "A gift from Mrs. Russell Sage launched the Audubon Junior Clubs in 1910. The wife of the noted philanthropist was

shocked by the widespread slaughter of robins which she observed during a trip through the Southern states." "Nine Millionth Member Enrolled in Audubon Junior Club," press release, typed, n.p., RSFR, Box 1, Folder 4.

34. M. Olivia Sage (Mrs. Russell Sage), "Opportunities and Responsibilities of Leisured Women," *North American Review* 181 (November 1905): 712–721. Readers were informed that the essay is "by Mrs. Russell Sage," which suggests that the other attribution was unfamiliar. An interesting comparison could also be made with Alice James, tragic sister of a brilliant philosopher and a celebrated novelist, who famously left only one published item, a letter to the editor of *The Nation* (July 4, 1890), which she signed "Invalid." See Diane Herndl, *Invalid Women: Figuring Feminine Illness in American Fiction and Culture, 1840–1940* (Chapel Hill: University of North Carolina Press, 1993). I am indebted to Herndl's imaginative and original analysis.

35. Jane Addams, "The Subjective Necessity for Social Settlements," in Jane Addams et al., *Philanthropy and Social Progress* (New York: Thomas Y. Crowell and Co., 1893), 1–26.

1. Slocums, Jermains, Piersons—and a Sage

1. Henry Whittemore, *History of the Sage and Slocum Families of England and America, Including the Allied Families of Montague, Wanton, Brown, Josselyn, Standish, Doty, Carver, Jermain or Germain, Pierson, Howell* (New York: Published by Mrs. Russell Sage, 1908). The newspapers picked up on the results. One announced: "The forthcoming edition, which contains a vast collection of prints and plates in color . . . shows that the impetuous blood of earls, barons and even a king . . . flows through the veins of the financier's widow." "Mrs. Sage of Noble Lineage," Obituaries and Biographical Clippings Collection, OCPL.

Recent studies of public memory and remembering include John Bodnar, *Remaking America: Public Memory, Commemoration, and Patriotism in the Twentieth Century* (Princeton, N.J.: Princeton University Press, 1992); and Michael Kammen, *The Mystic Chords of Memory: The Transformation of Tradition in American Culture* (New York: Knopf, 1991).

2. Jacqueline Dowd Hall, "Open Secrets: Memory, Imagination, and the Refashioning of Southern Identity," *American Quarterly* 50 (March 1998): 109–124; Hall, "'You Must Remember This': Biography as Social Critique," *Journal of American History* 85 (September 1998): 439–465; Paula Backscheider, *Reflections on Biography* (New York: Oxford University Press, 1999).

3. "Margaret Olivia Slocum," *EWP*, 398. This volume includes brief biographies of 3,500 women who attended Emma Willard's famous school between 1822 and 1872. An appreciation of the scope and importance of the survey is Anne Firor Scott, "The Ever-Widening Circle: The Diffusion of Feminist Values from the Troy Female Seminary, 1822–1872," in Scott, *Making the Invisible Woman Visible* (Urbana: University of Illinois Press, 1984), 64–88.

4. "Margaret Olivia Slocum," *EWP*, 390.

5. Patricia Meyer Spacks, "Stages of Self: Notes on Autobiography and the Life-Cycle," in *The American Autobiography: A Collection of Critical Essays*, ed. Albert E. Stone (Englewood Cliffs, N.J.: Prentice Hall, 1981).

6. Whittemore, *History of the Sage and Slocum Families of England and America*, 12.

7. Ibid., 13. Whitney Cross, *The Burned-Over District: The Social and Intellectual History of Enthusiastic Religion in Western New York, 1800–1850* (1965; repr., New York: Harper, 1965); William G. McLoughlin, *Revivals, Awakenings, and Reform: An Essay on Religion and Social Change in America, 1607–1977* (Chicago: University of Chicago Press, 1978). On the triumph of evangelical religion in the northeastern United States and its effect on what Susan Juster calls "the reconfiguration of gender relations which characterized postrevolutionary America," see Juster, *Disorderly Women: Sexual Politics and Evangelicalism in Revolutionary New England* (Ithaca, N.Y.: Cornell University Press, 1994), 182.

8. Charles Elliott Fitch, *Encyclopedia of Biography of New York* (Boston: American Historical Association, Inc., 1916), 126. But John Jermain's Revolutionary War service in the Westchester Militia is family tradition only. Whittemore states that "owing to the loss of many important records during the War of the Revolution, the ancestral line of Major John Jermain has not been clearly established." Improvising in the absence of records he adds, "In the absence of a documentary evidence concerning the direct ancestry of Major John Jermain, his descendants may point with pride to him as the founder of the family in this country." Whittemore, *History of the Sage and Slocum Families of England and America*, 28–29; "John Jermain (1758–1819)," typescript, FSW.

9. "John Jermain (1758–1819)," typescript, 13, FSW.

10. Margaret Olivia Sage, "Homestead of Colonel Jermain," in Ladies Village Improvement Society, Sag Harbor, Long Island, *Souvenir of Home Coming Week and 25th Anniversary of the Ladies Village Improvement Society, July 2, N.7, 1912*, ed. Anna Milford (Sag Harbor, N.Y.: LVIS, 1912), 20; reminiscences of Mrs. Russell Sage quoted in Nancy Boyd Willey, *Built by the Whalers: A Tour of Historic Sag Harbor* (Sag Harbor, N.Y.: The Old Sagg-Harbour Committee, 1945); "Speech of John Jermain Slocum at the Pierson Re-Dedication," *Sag Harbor Express*, 1982, incomplete newspaper clipping, FSW; Joanne Pope Melish, *Disowning Slavery: Gradual Emancipation and "Race" in New England, 1780–1860* (Ithaca, N.Y.: Cornell University Press, 1998).

11. Olivia added, "Yet the amenities of life were not omitted." Reminiscences of Mrs. Russell Sage in Willey, *Built by the Whalers*.

12. Olivia kept a copy of her mother's botany book by Amos Eaton and her Bible question book, now at JJML.

13. Elihu Slocum, author of a family genealogy published privately in 1882, puts Joseph Slocum's date of birth at July 19, 1795. Charles Elihu Slocum, *A Short History of the Slocums, Slocumbs and Slocombs of America, Genealogical and*

Biographical (Syracuse, N.Y.: Published by the author, 1882), 214. Whittemore puts his date of birth at 1800 in *History of the Sage and Slocum Families of England and America*, 26.

14. "Woman of Force: Interesting Stories of Mrs. Russell Sage," April 11, 1897, "Margaret Olivia Sage," OnHA.

15. "A Brief History of Syracuse," *Syracuse Daily Journal City Register and Directory for 1851–'52* (Syracuse, N.Y.: Published at the Journal Office, 1852), 23.

16. Louis B. Schmidt, "Internal Commerce and the Development of a National Economy Before 1860," *Journal of Political Economy* 47 (December 1939). For a useful overview, see Douglass C. North, *The Economic Growth of the United States, 1790–1860* (New York: W.W. Norton, 1966), 101.

17. "Tonnage over Erie Canal to Tidewater from Western States and from New York, 1836–1860," Table B-IX in North, *Economic Growth of the United States*, 251.

18. The railroads were the New York Central, the Erie, the Pennsylvania, and the Baltimore and Ohio. North, *Economic Growth of the United States*, 110, 193–194; George Rogers Taylor, *The Transportation Revolution, 1815–1860* (New York: Rhinehart, 1951; repr., Armonk, N.Y.: M. E. Sharpe, 1989); Charles Grier Sellers, *Market Revolution: Jacksonian America, 1815–1848* (New York: Oxford University Press, 1991).

19. There were forty-one Sage families in the Middletown area listed in the 1790 census. Jane Remsen, "Russell Sage: Yankee," *New England Quarterly* 11 (March 1938): 4.

20. Russell Sage comments on various legends circulating about his birth in the *New York Times*, August 5, 1899, quoted in Paul Sarnoff, *Russell Sage, the Money King* (New York: Ivan Obolensky, 1965), 347.

21. Remsen, "Russell Sage: Yankee," 4–5. Unfortunately, Jane Remsen's detailed article has no reference notes.

22. Russell Sage to Charles Lanman, Esq., February 24, 1858, handwritten autobiographical notes, Charles Lanman Collection, NYSL.

23. Ibid.

24. A. J. Weise, *History of the City of Troy* (Troy, N.Y.: William H. Young, 1876), 132–133; *Syracuse Daily Journal City Register and Directory for 1851–2*, 15–16.

25. "Woman of Force."

26. I use "Jermain" for Olivia's brother, as the family did, to avoid confusion with his father and namesake.

27. Whittemore, *History of the Sage and Slocum Families of England and America*, 49. The family lived in a house at South Salina and East Washington Streets, moving when she was about two years old to one on West Genesee Street. Miss E. L. Todd to Mr. Fred Dutcher, September 8, 1915, Margaret Olivia Slocum Sage Collection, EWS. The Syracuse city directory of 1851–1852 still listed Joseph Slocum at 47 West Genesee.

28. "Mrs. Sage's Reminiscences," *New York Times*, January 20, 1897, 14.

29. Whittemore, *History of the Sage and Slocum Families of England and America*, 27. I am assuming that Olivia was interviewed for this book (which she paid for) and that she approved or actually wrote many passages.

30. "Mrs. Russell Sage Could Sew at 4: Tells the Pascal Graduates She Was Made to Knit Stockings Every Day," *New York Sun*, June 17, 1906.

31. Ibid.

32. Ibid.

33. Rev. Nelson Millard, "Remarks at the 75th Anniversary of the Church," in *Seventy-Fifth Anniversary of the First Presbyterian Society in the Village of Syracuse, 1824–1899* (Syracuse, N.Y.: The Society, 1899), 90.

34. First Presbyterian Church, *A Manual for the Members of the First Presbyterian Church, Syracuse, N.Y.* (Syracuse, N.Y.: S. F. Smith and Co., Journal Publishers, 1846); First Presbyterian Church, Syracuse, *Articles of Faith and Covenant Adopted by the First Presbyterian Church in Syracuse* (n.p., n.d.), pamphlet, Presbyterian Historical Society, Philadelphia, Pa.

35. The literature on voluntary associations in the antebellum period has swelled along with scholarly interest in civil society. Scholars disagree about whether the growth of associations was a "product of state policy" (Skocpol) or whether it was a "bottom-up" phenomenon (Putnam). Theda Skocpol and Marshall Ganz, "A Nation of Organizers: The Institutional Origins of Civic Voluntarism in the United States," *American Political Science Review* 94, no. 3 (September 2000): 527–546; Gerald Gamm and Robert D. Putnam, "The Growth of Voluntary Associations in America, 1840–1940," *Journal of Interdisciplinary History* 29 (Spring 1999): 511–557. See also Peter Dobkin Hall, *Inventing the Nonprofit Sector and Other Essays on Philanthropy, Voluntarism, and Nonprofit Organizations* (Baltimore, Md.: Johns Hopkins University Press, 1992); Lawrence Friedman and Michael McGarvey, eds., *Charity, Philanthropy, and Civility in American History* (Cambridge: Cambridge University Press, 2002).

36. A. Judd Northrup, "History of the First Presbyterian Society in the Village of Syracuse," in *Early Records of the First Presbyterian Church, Syracuse, New York from 1826 to 1850* (Syracuse, N.Y.: The Genealogical Society of Central New York, 1902), 87; First Presbyterian Church, *One Hundredth Anniversary of the First Presbyterian Society in the Village of Syracuse, 1824–1924* (Syracuse, N.Y.: The Society, 1924), 53–54, 73–76.

37. Northrup, "History of the First Presbyterian Society in the Village of Syracuse," 40.

38. First Presbyterian Church, *One Hundredth Anniversary of the First Presbyterian Society in the Village of Syracuse*, 74.

39. "Temperance Meeting," *Onondaga Standard*, December 28, 1842; "Great Temperance Mass Meeting," *Onondaga Standard*, March 6, 1844. See also Ian R. Tyrrell, *Sobering Up: From Temperance to Prohibition in Antebellum America, 1800–1860* (Westport, Conn.: Greenwood, 1979); Ruth Bordin, *Woman and Temperance: The Quest for Power and Liberty, 1783–1900* (Philadel-

phia, Pa.: Temple University Press, 1981); Paul Boyer, *Urban Masses and Moral Order in America, 1820–1920* (New York: Oxford University Press, 1982).

40. Tonnage on the canal fell from 39,000 in 1836 to 25,000 in 1837. North, *Economic Growth of the United States*, 254.

41. "Storage and Forwarding, 1836," *Onondaga Standard*, March 30, 1836, "Joseph Slocum," OnHA.

42. *Onondaga Standard*, October 26, 1836.

43. Newspaper clipping (obituary of Joseph Slocum), *Courier and Union*, March 31, 1863, FSW. This account states that Slocum entrusted a clerk with $1,500 to invest for him in cattle in the Albany market and that the employee absconded with the money.

44. John H. Groesbeck to Joseph Slocum, December 8, 1836, in "Family Letters, Rough Drafts," EGS. But John Groesbeck continued to help out his unlucky brother-in-law. He was still lending Slocum money twenty years later.

45. "Sheriff's Sale," *Western State Journal*, August 25, 1841, "Joseph Slocum," OnHA.

46. Whittemore, *History of the Sage and Slocum Families of England and America*, 9. Again, I am assuming that the Whittemore account relied on Olivia Sage's memories of her husband and the stories he told about his early career.

47. Ibid.

48. Remsen, "Russell Sage: Yankee," 6–9.

49. Sarnoff, *Russell Sage, the Money King*, 63; Remsen, "Russell Sage: Yankee," 9–10. Author's interview with Carolyn Higbee Parks, Russell Sage College, Troy, New York, March 17, 1994.

50. Remsen, "Russell Sage: Yankee," 10; "Maria Winne," EWP, 256.

51. Sarnoff, *Russell Sage, the Money King*, 45ff. The treasurer was an appointive office which became elective after 1847. Weise, *History of the City of Troy*, 286–287, 311.

52. "Institute Fair," *New York Tribune*, October 16, 1845, "Joseph Slocum," OnHA. I have not been able to ascertain where this fair was held.

53. Whittemore, *History of the Sage and Slocum Families of England and America*, 26; Slocum, *Short History of the Slocums, Slocumbs and Slocombs*, 214; newspaper clipping (obituary of Joseph Slocum); William L. Blackwell, *The Beginnings of Russian Industrialization, 1800–1860* (Princeton, N.J.: Princeton University Press, 1968), 242.

54. Slocum, *Short History of the Slocums, Slocumbs and Slocombs*, 214. Paul Sarnoff links Slocum's trip to Russia to his losses in 1857, but Slocum actually first went there much earlier. "Bitter at Sage, on whom he blamed his troubles, Slocum was forced to accept a job as a demonstrator for an American reaper company in Moscow. There in Russia, far from his destitute family, Joseph Jermain [sic] Slocum died." Sarnoff, *Russell Sage, the Money King*, 145. In fact, Slocum died in Syracuse in 1863.

55. Daniel Webster, letter of recommendation for Joseph Slocum to Henry Ledyard, Esq., Paris, France, February 6, 1843, and Daniel Webster to Henry

Wheaton, Esq., Berlin, March 8, 1843, both in "Rough Drafts of Correspondence Pertaining to the Years Joseph Slocum, Esq. was in Russia, England, etc., 1846–48," EGS.

56. J. H. Groesbeck to "Dear Brother" [Joseph Slocum], June 2, 1844, in "Letters to Joseph Slocum from Various Members of His Family," EGS.

57. David L. Seymour to Hon. William Marcy, February 4, 1846, and J. J. Greenough to Hon. H. W. Ellsworth, February 14, 1846, both in "Rough Drafts of Correspondence Pertaining to the Years Joseph Slocum was in Russia, England, etc., 1846–48," EGS.

58. W. R. Washburn to J. Slocum, October 28, 1847, in "Rough Drafts of Correspondence Pertaining to the Years Joseph Slocum was in Russia, England, etc., 1846–48," EGS. Emphasis in original.

59. Slocum had requested a letter stating that he had completed his Russian mission satisfactorily. Chihaihef to Mr. Slokum [sic], Esq., October 1, 1846, in "Rough drafts of Correspondence Pertaining to the Years Joseph Slocum, Esq. was in Russia, England, etc., 1846–1848," EGS. Two versions of the Russian name are in the transcribed letters.

60. Ibid.

61. Chihaihef to Mr. Slokum [sic], n.d., and Joseph Slocum to Messrs. Curtis, Rose and Co., Machinists, November 1, 1846, both in "Rough Drafts of Correspondence Pertaining to the Years Joseph Slocum, Esq., was in Russia, England, etc., 1846–48," EGS.

62. Joseph Slocum to Margaret Slocum and Jermain, March 3, 1847, in "Family Letters—Rough Drafts," EGS.

63. Mary Ryan, "The Public and the Private Good: Across the Great Divide in Women's History," *Journal of Women's History* 15 (Summer 2003): 10–27. Standard works on antebellum women's organizations include Carroll Smith-Rosenberg, *Religion and the Rise of the American City: The New York City Mission Movement, 1812–1870* (Ithaca, N.Y.: Cornell University Press, 1971); Barbara Berg, *The Remembered Gate: Origins of American Feminism, The Woman and the City, 1800–1860* (New York: Oxford University Press, 1978); Anne Firor Scott, *Natural Allies: Women's Association in American History* (Urbana: University of Illinois Press, 1991); Nancy Hewitt, *Women's Activism and Social Change in Rochester, New York, 1822–1872* (Ithaca, N.Y.: Cornell University Press, 1982); Mary Ryan, *Cradle of the Middle Class: The Family in Oneida County, New York* (New York: Cambridge University Press, 1981); Barbara Leslie Epstein, *The Politics of Domesticity: Women, Evangelism and Temperance in Nineteenth-Century America* (Middletown, Conn.: Wesleyan University Press, 1981).

On the voluntary sphere as political space, see Seth Koven, "Borderlands: Women, Voluntary Action, and Child Welfare in Britain, 1840–1914," in *Mothers of a New World: Maternalist Politics and the Origins of Welfare States*, ed. Seth Koven and Sonya Michel (New Brunswick, N.J.: Routledge, 1991), 94–135; Mary Ryan, "Women and Public Access," in *Habermas and the Public Sphere*, ed. Craig Calhoun (Cambridge, Mass.: MIT Press, 1992), 259–288. Essays by

Geoff Eley and Nancy Fraser in this same volume have also been helpful. See also Sara Evans, "Women's History and Political Theory: Toward a Feminist Approach to Public Life," in *Visible Women: New Essays on American Activism*, ed. Nancy Hewitt and Suzanne Lebsock (Urbana: University of Illinois Press, 1993), 199–223. Kathleen McCarthy provides a useful typology of voluntary associations in "Parallel Power Structures: Women and the Voluntary Sphere," in McCarthy, *Lady Bountiful Revisited*, 1–31.

64. First Presbyterian Church, *One Hundredth Anniversary of the First Presbyterian Society in the Village of Syracuse*, 53.

65. "History of the Ladies' Aid Society," in *Seventy-Fifth Anniversary of the First Presbyterian Society*, 52. One cannot help but wonder about Mrs. Marlette's maiden name, Frances Wright.

66. Ibid., 54.

67. Gerda Lerner, *The Female Experience: An American Documentary* (Indianapolis: Bobbs-Merrill, 1977), 190.

68. Money is a major theme of Mrs. Marlette's history. See also Hewitt, *Women's Activism and Social Change*, 67.

69. As historian Nancy Hewitt has said of churchwomen in this period, these Syracuse pioneers "converted domestic labor itself into public resources by sewing garments and baking food for sale at antislavery fairs." Ibid., 61. The bazaar was held in 1867. See also Beverly Gordon, *Bazaars and Fair Ladies: The History of the American Fundraising Fair* (Knoxville: University of Tennessee Press, 1998).

70. First Presbyterian Church, *One Hundredth Anniversary of the First Presbyterian Society in the Village of Syracuse*, 68.

71. Ruth Crocker, "'From Widow's Mite to Widow's Might': Philanthropy of Margaret Olivia Sage," *American Presbyterians* 74 (Winter 1996): 253–264; Susan A. Yohn, "'Let Christian Women Set the Example in Their Own Gifts': The 'Business' of Protestant Women's Organizations," in *Women and Twentieth-Century Protestantism*, ed. Margaret Bendroth and Virginia Brereton (Urbana: University of Illinois Press, 2002), 213–235; Lori Ginzberg, *Women and the Work of Benevolence: Morality, Politics, and Class in the Nineteenth-Century United States* (New Haven, Conn.: Yale University Press, 1990).

72. Mrs. Nathan Cobb, "The Woman's Missionary Society and Mission Work," in *Seventy-Fifth Anniversary of the First Presbyterian Society in the Village of Syracuse*, 66–72; Joan Jacobs Brumberg first explored the ways American missionary women used the issue of oppressed Moslem women to voice their own discontents; see "'Zenanas and Girlless Villages: The Ethnology of American Evangelical Women, 1870–1910," *Journal of American History* 69 (September 1982): 347–371. A contemporary statement of white Christian women's engagement with foreign women is Helen Barrett Montgomery, *Western Women in Eastern Lands* (New York: Macmillan, 1911).

73. Cobb, "Woman's Missionary Society," 70–71.

74. On the relations of home and market, see Amy Dru Stanley, "Home

Life and the Morality of the Market," in *The Market Revolution in America: Social, Political, and Religious Expressions, 1800–1880,* ed. Melvyn Stokes and Stephen Conway (Charlottesville: University Press of Virginia, 1996), 74–97; Jeanne Boydston, *Home and Work: Housework, Wages, and the Ideology of Labor in the Early Republic* (New York: Oxford University Press, 1990).

75. Patricia J. Hill, *The World Their Household: The American Woman's Foreign Missionary Movement and Cultural Transformation, 1870–1920* (Ann Arbor: University of Michigan Press, 1985).

Scholars disagree widely on the impact of evangelical religion on women's feminist consciousness. Susan Juster speaks of "the empowering influence of religious conversion on women evangelicals." Evangelical conversion helped women see themselves as individuals and allowed them to speak out, she claims. Juster, *Disorderly Women,* 201. Carolyn De Swarte Gifford also makes a strong argument for the emancipatory uses of evangelical religion in "Frances Willard and the Woman's Christian Temperance Union's Conversion to Woman Suffrage," in *One Woman, One Vote: Rediscovering the Woman Suffrage Movement,* ed. Marjorie Spruill Wheeler (Troutdale, Ore.: NewSage Press, 1995), 117–134. Lori Ginzberg is much more critical of the impact of evangelical religion on women's claims; see "'The Hearts of Your Readers Will Shudder': Fanny Wright, Infidelity, and American Freethought," *American Quarterly* 46 (June 1994): 195–226. Ginzberg explores the consequences of antifeminism in the freethought movement and describes the victory of the Second Great Awakening as a moment when women "accepted an ideology that amplified their own silence" (199).

76. Smith-Rosenberg, *Religion and the Rise of the American City*; Paul Boyer, *Urban Masses and Moral Order in America, 1820–1920* (New York: Oxford University Press, 1982). The rhetoric of "woman's sphere" suggested "a broader conception of church work than that performed by the ordained ministry," argues Evelyn Brooks Higginbotham; see *Righteous Discontent: The Women's Movement in the Black Baptist Church, 1880–1920* (Cambridge, Mass.: Harvard University Press, 1993), 75. See also Paula Baker, *The Moral Frameworks of Public Life: Gender, Politics, and the State in Rural New York, 1870–1930* (New York: Oxford University Press, 1991); and Lana Ruegamer, "Female Moral Authority in Nineteenth-Century America: Toward 'the Matriarchal Moment,'" paper presented at the Berkshire Conference on the History of Women, Vassar College, Poughkeepsie, New York, June 1993.

77. Hewitt, *Women's Activism and Social Change,* 39. See also Nancy F. Cott, *Bonds of Womanhood: Women's Sphere in New England, 1780–1835* (New Haven, Conn.: Yale University Press, 1977); Scott, *Natural Allies.* The now-classic discussion of the rhetoric of "spheres" is Linda Kerber, "Separate Spheres, Female Worlds, Woman's Place: The Rhetoric of Women's History," *Journal of American History* 75 (June 1988): 9–39.

Because nineteenth-century women were excluded from formal politics, the professions, and universities, the voluntary association was, to quote Elisabeth S. Clemens, "almost the *only* place to get things done"; Review of Anne Firor Scott, *Natural Allies: Women's Associations in American History, American Journal of Sociology* 98 (November 1992): 687.

78. "Mrs. Sage's Reminiscences," *New York Times*, January 20, 1897, 14.

79. Kenyon West (Mrs. Henry S. Howland) to "My dear Mrs. Sage," n.d., SUA. This letter followed a visit of Olivia and her mother to the artist's home in Babylon, Long Island, and includes the statement "I shall prize your Mother's reminiscences of Marg. Fuller and thank her heartily. It will be a great treasure."

80. MOS, response to the Troy Female Seminary Alumnae Survey, 1893, handwritten, EWS.

81. Ibid.

82. "Margaret Olivia Slocum," *EWP*, 391.

83. Joshua V. H. Clark, *Onondaga; or Reminiscences of Earlier and Later Times* (Syracuse, N.Y.: Stoddard and Babcock, 1849), 2:102; "Mrs. Sage Guest at Dedication of Risley Hall," clipping, n.d. [1912?], "Margaret Olivia Sage," OnHA; Andrew Dickson White to J. J. Slocum, February 4, 1911, Andrew Dickson White Papers, Cornell; emphasis in original.

84. "Mrs. Sage's Reminiscences," *New York Times*, January 20, 1897, 14.

85. Joan Hoff, *Law, Gender, and Injustice: A Legal History of U.S. Women* (New York: New York University Press, 1991).

86. Juster, *Disorderly Women*, 207.

2. "Distinctly a class privilege"

1. Gerda Lerner, *The Creation of Feminist Consciousness: From the Middle Ages to 1870* (New York: Oxford University Press), 1993, 16.

2. Barbara Miller Solomon, *In the Company of Educated Women: A History of Women and Higher Education in America* (New Haven, Conn.: Yale University Press, 1985), 46–47, 62–63; Mabel Newcomer, *A Century of Higher Education for American Women* (New York: Harper, 1959); Thomas A. Woody, *A History of Women's Education in the United States*, 2 vols. (New York: The Science Press, 1929).

3. Emma Willard, *Address to the Public, Particularly to the Members of the Legislature of New York, Proposing a Plan for Improving Female Education*, 2nd ed. (1819; repr., Marietta, Ga.: Larlin Corporation, 1987), 7; Frederick Rudolph, "Emma Hart Willard," *NAW*, 3:610–613.

4. John Lord, *The Life of Emma Willard* (New York: D. Appleton and Company, 1873), 87–91. Emma Willard opened her first school, the Middlebury Female Seminary, in Middlebury, Vermont, in 1814, subsequently removing it first to Waterford, New York, and then to Troy in 1821.

5. Solomon, *In the Company of Educated Women*, 14–26.

Accounts have concentrated on New England, but new research shows that the South, too, saw several significant female academies founded at about this time or even earlier, and with advanced curricula, according to Farnham. But because southern women were not entering professions and paid work like northern women these colleges continued to be staffed by graduates of northern seminaries such as Mount Holyoke and Troy Female Seminary. See Elizabeth Fox-Genovese, "Education of Women in the United States South," *Journal of Women's History* 9, no. 1 (Spring 1997): 203–211, a review of Christie Farnham, *The Education of the Southern Belle: Higher Education and Student Socialization in the Antebellum South* (New York: New York University Press, 1994).

6. Kathryn Kish Sklar, "The Founding of Mount Holyoke College," in *Women of America*, ed. Carol Ruth Berkin and Mary Beth Norton (Boston: Houghton Mifflin, 1979), 177–201; Sydney R. MacLean, "Mary Lyon," in *NAW*, 2:443–447; Amanda Porterfield, *Mary Lyon and the Mount Holyoke Missionaries* (New York: Oxford University Press, 1997). See also "One of the Country's Great Philanthropists," unidentified clipping, November 9, 1918, Scrapbook Collection, RCHS.

7. *Kneeland's Troy Directory, 1847–48* (Troy, N.Y.: J. L. Kneeland and Co., 1847), 1.

8. The coincidence of this pupil's journey from Syracuse makes me wonder if this was not perhaps Olivia Slocum, despite the disclaimer; she would not have wanted to have this passage attributed to her because it was critical of her parents. The passage is contained in "Fitting Tribute Paid Mrs. Olivia Sage," unidentified newspaper clipping, Margaret Olivia Slocum Sage Collection, Box 9, EWS.

9. "Hiram Slocum's Investment," *Philadelphia North American*, September 20, 1913. This account is romanticized and probably inaccurate. For example, Olivia's father was in England in September 1846, not in Troy, New York.

Hiram Slocum, younger brother of Joseph Slocum, was born in 1802 and married Elizabeth Van Vechten in 1827. In 1834, he moved to Troy and became a grain and provision merchant. He was elected as alderman of the city of Troy in 1838 and as mayor in 1856. From 1859 until his death in 1873 he engaged in real estate business in New York, New Jersey, and the West. Of their nine children, Olivia's cousins, six died before maturity. Charles Elihu Slocum, *A Short History of the Slocums, Slocumbs and Slocombs of America* (Syracuse, N.Y.: Published by the author, 1882), 122, 125, 215. See also A. J. Weise, *History of the City of Troy* (Troy, N.Y.: William H. Young, 1876), 285.

10. This information was provided by Robert N. Andersen at the Rensselaer County Historical Society, Troy, New York.

11. "Hiram Slocum's Investment."

12. Ibid. Hiram Slocum lived another twenty-five years, until 1873.

13. *Catalogue of the Officers and Pupils of the Troy Female Seminary for the Academic Year Commencing September 17, 1846, and Ending August 6, 1847* (Troy, N.Y.: Prescott and Wilson, 1847), 13; Alma Lutz, *Emma Willard: Daughter of Democracy* (1929; repr., Washington, D.C.: Zenger Publishing Company, 1975).

14. Her name is recorded as "Olivia M. Slocum." *Catalogue of the Officers and Pupils of the Troy Female Seminary*, 13; "Margaret Olivia Slocum," *EWP*, 391.

15. Henry Fowler, "The Educational Services of Mrs. Emma Willard," in *Memoirs of Teachers and Educators*, ed. Henry Barnard (1861; repr., New York: Arno Press, 1969) is a useful account.

16. Ibid. 17.

17. My thanks to Susan Kastan for information about Troy's residential neighborhoods in the 1840s. See also Weise, *History of the City of Troy*.

18. Anne Firor Scott, "The Ever-Widening Circle: The Diffusion of Feminist Values from the Troy Female Seminary, 1822–1872," *History of Education Quarterly* 19 (Spring 1979): 69–70. A useful discussion of the curriculum at antebellum female colleges is Farnham, *Education of the Southern Belle*, 11–28. Farnham found that some southern female colleges taught Greek as well as Latin, science, and mathematics. Advanced Greek and Latin were less likely to be included in these colleges' curricula than modern languages. French and German were always taught and sometimes also Italian and Spanish. Farnham comments, "One of the female college's major contributions to collegiate curricula . . . was its emphasis on modern languages" (25).

19. Lord, *Life of Emma Willard*, quoted in Scott, "Ever-Widening Circle," 86n10.

20. The full title was *Treatise on the Motive Powers which Produce the Circulation of the Blood* (1849). A favorable review is reprinted in *EWP*, 16. Other books authored by Willard were *Woodbridge's and Willard's Geography* (co-authored with William Chauncey Woodbridge in 1822 and reprinted numerous times); *History of the United States, or Republic of America; Exhibited in Connection with its Chronology and Progressive Geography, by Means of a Series of Maps . . . Designed for Schools and Private Libraries* (New York: White, Gallaher and White, 1828); *A System of Universal History, in Perspective* (Hartford, Conn.: F. J. Huntington, 1835); *Guide to the Temple of Time; and Universal History, for Schools* (New York: A. S. Barnes, 1849). For an excellent bibliography, see Nina Baym, *American Women Writers and the Work of History, 1790–1860* (New Brunswick, N.J.: Rutgers University Press, 1995), 278.

21. Rensselaer Institute was founded by Stephen Van Rensselaer in 1824 to teach men "how to put science to practical use." Eaton remained there as professor of physics until his death in 1842. Julia Patton, *Russell Sage College: The First Twenty-Five Years, 1916–1941* (Troy, N.Y.: Press of Walter Snyder, 1941), 10–11.

22. Nancy Slack, "Nineteenth-Century American Women Botanists: Wives, Widows, and Work," in *Uneasy Careers and Intimate Lives: Women in Science, 1789–1979*, ed. Pnina G. Abir-Am and Dorinda Outram (New Brunswick, N.J.: Rutgers University Press, 1987), 77–103; Anne Firor Scott, "Almira Lincoln Phelps: The Self-Made Woman in the Nineteenth Century," in Scott, *Making the Invisible Woman Visible* (Urbana: University of Illinois Press,

1984): 89–106. Phelps was at Troy from about 1823 to 1831, when she moved to Vermont. See also *EWP*, 25.

23. Carrie Chapman Catt and Nettie Rogers Shuler, *Woman Suffrage and Politics* (New York: Scribner's Sons, 1923), 10–11. A footnote identifies Olivia Sage as the source of this reminiscence by "a graduate of Troy Female Seminary."

24. Ibid.

25. "Report of the Trustees [Troy Female Seminary] to the State Regents, January 1848," handwritten, n.p., Troy Female Seminary Collection, EWS; *Catalogue of the Officers and Pupils of the Troy Female Seminary for the Academic Year, September 15, 1847 to July 26, 1848* (Troy, N.Y.: Prescott and Wilson, 1848).

26. Quoted in Lord, *Life of Emma Willard*, 72. A different view of the importance of needlework in women's lives is Rozika Parker, *The Subversive Stitch: Embroidery and the Making of the Feminine* (1984; Routledge and Kegan Paul, 1989).

27. Alma Lutz, *Emma Willard: Pioneer Educator of American Women* (Boston: Beacon Press, 1964), 48. Lutz's book is invaluable because the author included quotations from Emma Willard and her contemporaries which appear nowhere else.

28. "Commencement Honors," *Troy Times*, June 10, 1897.

29. Theodore Stanton and Harriot Stanton Blatch, eds., *Elizabeth Cady Stanton as Revealed in Her Letters, Diary and Reminiscences* (New York: Harper Brothers, 1922), 1:36.

30. Mrs. Abbie Whipple of Watervliet, quoted in "Death of Margaret Olivia Sage in the Ninetieth Year of Her Age," newspaper clipping [November 1918], Troy Scrapbook, Local History Collection, TPL.

31. "Mrs. Russell Sage," *Syracuse Herald*, September 5, 1909, Obituaries and Biographical Clippings Collection, OCPL.

32. *EWP*, 23. I am assuming that Olivia Sage closely supervised the production of this volume and that she wrote many sections of the book. The minibiographies were supplied by alumnae.

Paul Sarnoff emphasized Olivia's troubles at Troy. Either because of her "habitual snobbishness or unprepossessing appearance, Olivia soon became the target of gibes and whispers of her classmates," he wrote. Entering Troy Female Seminary, "this unappealing descendant of Miles Standish . . . was accustomed to counter the taunts of her oppressors by flaunting her father's wealth and political aspirations, her ancestry, and her promising future." When she was rejected by her fellow pupils, "It was the wise and understanding Emma Willard . . . who cushioned the actions of her unfeeling pupils by taking the harassed Olivia to her bosom." Paul Sarnoff, *Russell Sage, the Money King* (New York: Ivan Obolensky, 1965), 142.

33. Gerda Lerner, *The Creation of Feminist Consciousness: From the Middle Ages to 1870* (New York: Oxford University Press, 1993). The entire quote reads, "Women are almost universally educationally disadvantaged in comparison with their brothers, and education is, for those few women able to obtain it, distinctly a class privilege" (22).

34. "In the tranquil retirement of her Troy home, where she passed her declining years, Mrs. Willard seems to have held a patriarchal [sic] sway." *EWP*, 23, 33.

35. Mrs. Russell Sage, "Address by Mrs. Russell Sage, Saratoga, July 8, 1896," typescript, Margaret Olivia Slocum Sage Collection, Box 3, EWS. For Thomas Arnold, see "Thomas Arnold (1795–1842)," *Dictionary of National Biography*, ed. H. C. G. Matthew and Brian Harrison (London: Oxford University Press, 2004), 2:501–505.

36. Lord, *Life of Emma Willard*, 49; Rudolph, "Emma Hart Willard."

37. *EWP*, 23.

38. Elizabeth Cady Stanton, "The Influence of Emma Willard," in *Third Annual Report of the Emma Willard Association, Chicago Reunion, 1893* (Brooklyn, N.Y.: Press of the Brooklyn Eagle, 1893), 63.

39. Elisabeth Griffith, *In Her Own Right: The Life of Elizabeth Cady Stanton* (New York: Oxford University Press, 1984), 10.

40. Anne Firor Scott, "What, Then, Is the American: This New Woman?" in Scott, *Making the Invisible Woman Visible*, 60n12.

41. Weise, *History of the City of Troy*, 142–143.

42. Scott, "Ever-Widening Circle," 67.

43. Christopher C. Cox, "Poem on Female Education," delivered at Troy Female Seminary annual commencement, July 8, 1858; Alma Lutz Papers, Vassar. These handwritten notes were prepared by Alma Lutz for her biography, *Emma Willard, Daughter of Democracy* (New York: Houghton Mifflin, 1929).

44. "Exam 1845," handwritten, Alma Lutz Papers, Vassar.

45. Ibid. Punctuation in the original.

46. "Exam 1845."

47. Linda Kerber, "Separate Spheres, Female Worlds, Woman's Place: The Rhetoric of Women's History," *Journal of American History* 75 (June 1988): 9–39.

48. Rev. Henry A. Boardman, "Public Examinations in Female Schools: Reply to Mrs. Willard," *Troy Daily Times*, December 19, 1857. For Rev. Boardman's later connection with Olivia, see Chapter 4.

49. Mrs. John H. Willard, "Troy Female Seminary," in *Trojan Sketch Book*, ed. Miss Abba A. Goddard (Troy, N.Y.: Young and Hartt, 1846), 161.

50. Lutz, *Emma Willard: Daughter of Democracy*, 93.

51. The impressions of this unnamed observer were included in "Fitting Tribute Paid Mrs. Olivia Sage: Her Work for Women's Higher Education," *Troy Record*, September 27, 1916, 6.

52. Clipping in Russell Sage College, College Scrap Book, September 27, 1916, Vol. 1, 1916–1917, 7–18, quoted in Patton, *Russell Sage College: The First Twenty-Five Years*, 12. Julia Patton was a professor of English at Russell Sage College.

53. Jane Addams, *Twenty Years at Hull-House, with Autobiographical Notes*, edited and with an introduction by Victoria Bissell Brown (New York: Bedford/St. Martin's, 1999); Allen F. Davis, *American Heroine: The Life and Legend of Jane Addams* (New York: Oxford University Press, 1973).

54. "Graduated at eighteen, teaching at twenty-five, married at forty," was how she mapped her life from the vantage point of fifty years later. "Commencement Honors." Why did she lie about her age to the audience of Troy graduates? Her actual age at marriage was forty-one.

55. "Mrs. Sage's Reminiscences," unidentified clipping, June 20, 1897; "A Notable Golden Anniversary," *Harper's Bazaar*, June 12, 1897, EWS; "Commencement Honors," *Troy Times*, June 10, 1897, clipping in "Scrapbook, 1891–," EWS.

56. "A Queen Consort of Finance: Mrs. Russell Sage's Long and Noble Life. Suffragist and Patriot," *Ladies' Journal*, April 29, 1894, NYSM.

57. Quoted in Lutz, *Emma Willard: Daughter of Democracy*, 120.

58. Scott, "Ever-Widening Circle." See also Amanda Porterfield, *Mary Lyon and the Mount Holyoke Missionaries* (New York: Oxford University Press, 1997).

59. Lutz, *Emma Willard: Pioneer Educator of American Women*, 112.

60. Henry James, *Portrait of a Lady* (Boston: Houghton Mifflin, 1909), quoted in Carolyn G. Heilbrun, "Non-Autobiographies of 'Privileged' Women: England and America," in *Life/Lines: Theorizing Women's Autobiography*, ed. Bella Brodzki and Celeste Schenck (Ithaca, N.Y.: Cornell University Press, 1988), 68.

3. "I do enjoy my independence"

1. Paul Sarnoff, *Russell Sage, the Money King* (New York: Ivan Obolensky, 1965), 143; "Suppose They Had Married the First Man That Proposed!" *New York Herald*, December 10, 1899. I am grateful to Maren Stein, who drew my attention to this article.

2. Joseph Slocum to "Dear Wife and Son," July 9, 1847, "Family Letters—Rough Drafts," EGS.

3. Ibid.

4. "Suppose They Had Married the First Man That Proposed!"

5. Joseph Slocum to "My dear Wife and Son," New York, July 9, 1847. Some spellings have been corrected.

6. MOS to "My dear Father," May 12, 1854, in "Letters of Olivia Slocum Sage to Her Father, 1853–1855," EGS.

7. MOS to "My dear Father," February 27, 1855, in "Letters of Olivia Slocum Sage to Her Father, 1853–1855," EGS.

8. Jane Hunter, "Victorian Girlhood: Girls' History and School Culture," paper presented at the Tenth Berkshire Conference on the History of Women, Chapel Hill, N.C., June 1996. Hunter argues that the end of schooldays marked a break from the pleasure and incipient consumerism of girl culture.

A generation later, Jane Addams would describe the dilemma of the college-educated woman summoned to her parental home to obey "the family claim" as a cultural phenomenon of the age. After graduating from Rockford Seminary in Illinois in 1881, Addams experienced ill-defined physical and psycho-

logical complaints for about eight years. Jane Addams, "The Subjective Necessity for Social Settlements," in Addams et al., *Philanthropy and Social Progress*
(New York: Thomas Y. Crowell, 1893), 1–26. See also Allen F. Davis, *American Heroine: The Life and Legend of Jane Addams* (New York: Oxford University Press, 1973), 38ff; Victoria Bissell Brown, *The Education of Jane Addams*
(Philadelphia: University of Pennsylvania Press, 2004), 110, 115. Alice Hamilton provides another example. After her graduation, Hamilton experienced "a
struggle to find satisfying work that lasted a decade," according to her biographer, Barbara Sicherman; *Alice Hamilton: A Life in Letters* (Cambridge, Mass.:
Harvard University Press, 1984), 135–36. See also Joyce Antler, "'After College, What?' New Graduates and the Family Claim," *American Quarterly* 32 (Fall
1980): 409–434.

9. Nina Baym, "Women and the Republic: Emma Willard's Rhetoric of
History," *American Quarterly* 43 (March 1991): 21n10. Baym relies on Catharine
Beecher, *Educational Reminiscences and Suggestions* (New York: J. B. Ford, 1874),
which states that fewer than 6 percent of those educated at Troy Female Seminary to that date had become teachers.

10. Anne Firor Scott, "The Ever-Widening Circle: The Diffusion of Feminist Values From the Troy Female Seminary, 1822–72," in Scott, *Making the
Invisible Woman Visible* (Urbana: University of Illinois Press, 1984), 80. Scott
analyzed some of the more than 3,500 responses to a survey of alumnae made
in the 1890s. Of course, the lower birthrates of these graduates was part of a
larger trend in late-nineteenth-century America that has been well documented
by historians and demographers. Margaret Marsh and Wanda Ronner quote the
figure that 75 percent of the decline in fertility in this period was voluntary.
Marsh and Ronner, *The Empty Cradle: Infertility in America from Colonial Times
to the Present* (Baltimore: Johns Hopkins University Press, 1996), 80.

11. "Agreement between Joseph Slocum, William Brown, and E. R. Webster," April 24, 1849, EGS.

12. Hiram Slocum to Joseph Slocum, October 1, 1850, in "Family Letters—
Rough Drafts," EGS.

13. "Funeral of Mrs. Russell Sage Will Be Held in Syracuse Thursday Morning," *Syracuse Herald*, November 5, 1918, clipping, "Margaret Olivia Sage,"
OnHA. This account, which relied on the memories of Mrs. Sage's friends
Mrs. Charles E. Fitch (earlier Louise Lawrence Smith) and Miss Frances Gifford, incorrectly states that Olivia taught at Troy Female Seminary.

14. "Mrs. Sage Guest at Dedication of Risley Hall," clipping, "Margaret
Olivia Sage," OnHA, n.d. [1912].

15. Andrew Dickson White to Clara White, March 16, 1849, and March
19, 1849; Clara White to Andrew Dickson White, June 5, 1850. All in Andrew
Dickson White Papers, microfilm reel 1, Cornell. Emphasis in the original.

16. Charles E. Fitch to Andrew Dickson White, November 11, 1849,
Andrew Dickson White Papers, microfilm reel 1, Cornell. The religious revivals

and social realignments of this turbulent time are the subject of Whitney R. Cross, *The Burned-Over District: A Social and Intellectual History of Enthusiastic Religion in Western New York, 1800–1850* (Ithaca, N.Y.: Cornell University Press, 1950); William G. McLoughlin, *Revivals, Awakenings and Reform: An Essay on Religion and Social Change in America, 1607–1997* (Chicago: University of Chicago Press, 1978); and Nancy Hewitt, *Women's Activism and Social Change in Rochester, New York, 1822–1872* (Ithaca, N.Y.: Cornell University Press, 1984).

17. Clara White to Andrew Dixon White, June 5, 1850, Andrew Dickson White Papers, microfilm reel 1, Cornell. On the rapid spread of spiritualism, see Ann Braude, *Radical Spirits: Spiritualism and Women's Rights in Nineteenth-Century America* (Boston: Beacon Press, 1989).

18. "Temperance Meeting," *Onondaga Standard*, December 28, 1842, clipping, "Temperance," OnHA.

19. "Great Temperance Mass Meeting," *Onondaga Standard*, March 6, 1844, clipping, "Temperance," OnHA.

20. A. Judd Northrup, "A History of the First Presbyterian Society in the Village of Syracuse," in *Early Records of the First Presbyterian Church, Syracuse, New York from 1826 to 1850* (Syracuse, N.Y.: The Genealogical Society of Central New York, 1902), 107. Reverend Adams died in April 1850, having been minister for twenty-six years. Rev. Canfield arrived in 1854 and remained in Syracuse until his death in 1871 (530n46). He had been a member of the first theological class at Oberlin in 1835, but he later left the College and repudiated the Oberlin brand of perfectionism. Garth M. Rosell and Richard A. G. Dupuis, eds., *The Memoirs of Charles G. Finney* (Grand Rapids, Mich.: Zondervan Publishing House, 1989), 527–530. See also *An Exposition of the Peculiarities, Difficulties, and Tendencies of Oberlin Perfectionism Prepared by a Committee of the Presbytery of Cleveland* (Cleveland, Ohio: Smead, 1841).

21. Rosell and Dupois, eds., *Memoirs of Charles G. Finney*, 527; Keith Hardman, *Charles Grandison Finney, 1792–1875: Revivalist and Reformer* (Syracuse, N.Y.: Syracuse University Press, 1987).

22. On Seneca Falls, see Judith Wellman, "The Seneca Falls Women's Rights Convention: A Study of Social Networks," *Journal of Women's History* 3, no. 1 (Spring 1991): 9–33. My thanks to Shelden S. King, librarian at the Seneca Falls Historical Society, for supplying me with a list of the signers of the "Declaration." See also Kathryn Kish Sklar, *Women's Rights Emerges within the Antislavery Movement, 1830–1870: A Brief History with Documents* (Boston and New York: Bedford/St. Martin's, 2000); Ellen Carol DuBois, *Feminism and Suffrage: The Emergence of an Independent Women's Movement in America, 1848–1869* (Ithaca, N.Y.: Cornell University Press, 1978).

23. "Mrs. Sage, Now 87, Calls for Vote: Widow of Great Financier Tells of Interest in Suffrage since 1848," *New York Sun*, October 31, 1915, clipping, RSFR, Box 99, Folder 997.

24. "New York State Temperance Society," June 18, 1852, *Onondaga Standard*, clipping, and unidentified clipping, *Syracuse Standard*, June 18, 1852, both in "Temperance," OnHA.

25. "Address of Miss Anthony," June 19, 1852, unidentified clipping, "Women's Rights," OnHA.

26. Quoted in *HWS*, 1:517; Paul Buhle and Mary Jo Buhle, eds., *The Concise History of Woman Suffrage; Selections from the Classic Work of Stanton, Anthony, Gage, and Harper* (Urbana: University of Illinois Press, 1978), 116–137.

27. "Opposing Remarks of Rev. J. L. Hatch," *Onondaga Standard*, September 15, 1852, emphasis in the original; "Women's Rights Convention, Third Day," September 11, 1852, unidentified clipping, "Women's Rights," OnHA.

28. However, in "Garrisonian Abolitionists and the Rhetoric of Gender, 1850–1860," *American Quarterly* 45 (December 1993): 558–595, Kristin Hoganson points out how opponents of slavery reinscribed gender while challenging the institution of slavery.

29. "Woman's Right to Vote: Many Eminent Ladies Give Their Reasons for Signing the Petition," *New York Herald*, May 6, 1894. In volume 3 of Scrapbooks of Newspaper Clippings and Other Materials Relating to Woman Suffrage in New York City (1894–1921), compiled by Mrs. Robert Abbé, NYPL. This indicates that as the nation's political parties fragmented over the issue of slavery, Joseph Slocum was in the more conservative wing of the Whig Party. The Silver Gray Whigs supported president Millard Fillmore and were in favor of the Compromise of 1850, including its provision calling for the enforcement of the Fugitive Slave Act. The issue came to a head in Syracuse, where a group led by Francis Granger, whose silvery hair gave the faction its name, walked out of a Whig convention.

30. *HWS*, 1:517; "National Woman's Rights Convention," September 8, 1852, clipping, "Women's Rights," OnHA.

31. "National Woman's Rights Convention," September 8, 1852, clipping, "Women's Rights," OnHA. Antoinette Louisa Brown Blackwell (1825–1921) was born near Rochester and attended the literary course at Oberlin but was finally allowed to take the course of study in theology. She completed this in 1850 but was not allowed to graduate formally. She then traveled extensively as a lecturer advocating temperance, women's rights, and abolition. Eventually she became an ordained minister. Barbara Solomon, "Antoinette Louisa Brown Blackwell," *NAW*, 1:158–161.

32. "Drunken and degraded foreigner," *HWS*, 1:850. Lucy Stone's defense of nativism prefigured the arguments of suffrage advocates of the 1890s, of whom Olivia Sage would be one. See "National Woman's Rights Convention," September 8, 1852, clipping, "Women's Rights," OnHA; Louise Newman, *White Women's Rights: The Racial Origins of Feminism in the United States* (New York: Oxford University Press, 1999), 57–58.

33. B. W. Johnson, corresponding secretary, New York State Agricultural Society, July 8, 1848, in "Copies of Letters to Hon. J. Slocum, 1848–49," FSW.

34. *Daily Journal City Register and Directory for 1851–52* (Syracuse, N.Y.: Printed and Published at the Journal Office, 1851). Slocum was second vice president of the City Tract Society; Anthony F. C. Wallace, *Rockdale* (1972; repr., New York: Norton, 1980).

35. Paul Sarnoff, *Russell Sage, the Money King* (New York: Ivan Obolensky, 1965), 62–64. Russell Sage's letters to New York Whig politician and businessman Edwin D. Morgan begin to mention Wisconsin railroads at this time. Russell Sage to Edwin D. Morgan, August 27, 1857, includes "I am obliged to go to Milwaukee tomorrow on urgent business." See also Sage to Morgan, December 4, 1856, both in Edwin D. Morgan Papers, Box 11, Folder 6, NYSL.

36. Sarnoff, *Russell Sage, the Money King*, 63.

37. Joseph Slocum "was a successful food merchant who became a New York State Assemblyman through the good offices of his business associate, Russell Sage." Sarnoff, *Russell Sage, the Money King*, 141. I have not been able to verify this in another source.

38. *Seventy-second Session, Journal of the Assembly, State of New York* (Albany, N.Y.: Weed, Parsons & Co., Public Printers, 1849), 495, 1319. "Saltmaker" and "saltboiler" are common occupations listed in the U.S. census for Syracuse in 1850.

39. Ibid., 62–63.

40. "Copies of letters to Hon. J. Slocum, 1848–49," compiled by Margaret Olivia Proctor, FSW.

41. Samuel Joseph May, *Speech of Rev. Samuel J. May to the Convention of Citizens of Onondaga Co. in Syracuse on the 14 October, 1851, called to consider the principles of the American government, and the extent to which they are trampled underfoot by the Fugitive Slave Law, occasioned by an attempt to enslave an inhabitant of Syracuse* (Syracuse: Agan and Summers, Printers, 1851), 21; J. W. Loguen, *The Rev. J. W. Loguen as a Slave and as a Freeman: A Narrative of Real Life* (1859; repr., Washington, D.C.: Howard University Press, 1941), 394. On the Jerry Rescue, see Genevieve Favre, "African-American Commemorative Celebrations in the Nineteenth Century," in *History and Memory in African-American Culture*, ed. Robert O'Meally and Genevieve Favre (New York: Oxford University Press, 1994), 86–87.

42. May, *Speech of Rev. Samuel J. May*, Appendix, 22.

43. An Albany patron wrote to Zachary Taylor in February 1850 on behalf of "my friend Joseph Slocum of Syracuse who as a consequence of commercial embarrassments desires to get some employment under the Government." H. Baldwin to President Zachary Taylor, February 10, 1850, "Rough Drafts of Correspondence Pertaining to the Years Joseph Slocum Esq. was in Russia, England, etc., 1846–1848," EGS; newspaper clipping (obituary for Joseph Slocum), *Courier and Union*, Tuesday Morning, March 31, 1863, FSW.

44. In Jermain Slocum to Joseph Slocum, April 7, 1852, which begins "My dear Father," Jermain writes to wish his father a safe voyage as he embarks on his journey from New York for California. In "Letters to Joseph Slocum from Various Members of His Family," EGS.

45. Mary Groesbeck, born 1795, was five years older than her brother. She married John H. Groesbeck. She died in Cincinnati on September 6, 1854. Charles Elihu Slocum, *A Short History of the Slocums, Slocumbs and Slocombs of America* (Syracuse, N.Y.: Published by the author, 1882), 121, 346.

46. "Mrs. Sage the Richest Woman in America," unidentified clipping, June 29, 1906, "Margaret Olivia Sage," OnHA; "Mrs. Russell Sage," *Syracuse Herald*, September 5, 1909, Obituaries and Biographical Clippings Collection, OCPL.

47. Jermain to Joseph Slocum, Esq., April 7, 1852, in "Letters to Joseph Slocum from Various Members of His Family," EGS.

On Olivia at St. Paul's, see *EWP*, 390. A search of Syracuse city directories did not find her listed as a teacher in this period, although the *Daily Journal City Register and Directory for 1851–52* lists the following schools, with teachers and even the teachers' salaries:

> Onondaga Seminary for Young Ladies
> Cottage Seminary
> St. Paul's Female School
> Fayette Place Select School
> Syracuse Female Academy
> Syracuse Classical School

48. Even the Whittemore account—a commissioned piece of writing designed to flatter—let slip the fact that Margaret Pierson Jermain Slocum was an unhappy woman, though one who met the blows of fate with Christian stoicism. The writer praised her trust in God and her "quick faith which never wavered, even when gathering years, with their varied experiences, brought their sorrows and perplexities." Henry Whittemore, *History of the Sage and Slocum Families of England and America, Including the Allied Families of Montague, Wanton, Brown, Josselyn, Standish, Doty, Carver, Jermain or Germain, Pierson, Howell* (New York: Published by Mrs. Russell Sage, 1908), 27.

49. "Mrs. Sage's Reminiscences," *The New York Times*, June 20, 1897, Margaret Olivia Slocum Sage Collection, EWS.

50. Joshua V. H. Clark, *Onondaga; or Reminiscences of Earlier and Later Times* (Syracuse, N.Y.: Stoddard and Babcock, 1849), 2:102.

51. Evidence for Olivia holding the position at St Paul's, in addition to her brief autobiography in *EWP*, page 390, is in an unidentified clipping on the dedication of Cornell's Risley Hall, where Andrew D. White mentions her holding the position of assistant principal at the school; "Margaret Olivia Sage," OnHA. Her presence at St. Paul's was confirmed in a personal communication to the author from W. Dean Wallace, Syracuse, but I have been unable to find her listed in Syracuse city directories. See *Ormsby's Syracuse City Directory for 1853–4* (Syracuse, N.Y.: Hall, Mills and Co., 1853); *Syracuse City Directory for the Year Ending July 1, 1855* (Syracuse, N.Y.: Compiled and published by

W. H. Rainey, 1855). The school was at East Fayette and S. Warren Streets, Syracuse.

Teacher salaries are listed in *Syracuse Daily Journal City Directory for 1862–63* (Syracuse, N.Y.: Truair, Smith and Miles, Daily Journal Office, 1862), 37. The principal's salary was $1,000.

52. Kathleen Barry, *Susan B. Anthony: A Biography of a Singular Feminist* (New York: New York University Press, 1988), 39.

53. The "little girl" was in fact twenty-three. Byron F. Fellows, Jr., and William F. Roseboom, *The Road to Yesterday: Stories of Syracuse in the Long, Long Ago* (Syracuse, N.Y.: Midstate Offset Printing Corporation, 1948), 71–73. According to this account, 1,100 people packed into the church for the concert, with another 500 outside.

54. "Mrs. Russell Sage," Onondaga Historical Association information sheet, n.d., "Margaret Olivia Sage," OnHA.

55. Zenus Barnum to Captain J. W. Smith, Baltimore, November 11, 1852, and [Unknown] to Joseph Slocum, Esq., November 19, 1852, letters transcribed by Mrs. Florence Slocum Wilson, FSW.

56. *Wheeler v. Sage*, 68 U.S. (1. Wallace) 518; Sarnoff, *Russell Sage, the Money King*, 63.

57. Newspaper clipping (obituary for Joseph Slocum), *Courier and Union*, March 31, 1863, FSW.

58. [Joseph Slocum in Russia], no. 127, FSW. This letter has a typed postscript: "Found among my Father's papers. This Joseph Slocum is my Grandfather who visited Russia on business—HJS [Herbert Jermain Slocum]," FSW.

59. For Sylvanus Pierson Jermain (1784–1869) and the Prime family, see Whittemore, *History of the Sage and Slocum Families of England and America*, 26, 37; Charles Elliott Fitch, *Encyclopedia of Biography of New York* (Boston: American Historical Society, Inc., 1916), 126; Robert H. Collier, *A History of the Jermain Memorial Church Congregation of Watervliet, New York, 1814–1974* (Albany, N.Y.: Argus-Greenwood, Inc., 1976), 69.

60. Scott, "Ever-Widening Circle"; Henry Fowler, "The Educational Services of Mrs. Emma Willard," in *Memoirs of Teachers and Educators*, ed. Henry Barnard (1861; repr., New York: Arno Press, 1969), 155.

61. The seminary's opening was announced in *Chestnut Street Female Seminary, Philadelphia* (Philadelphia, Pa.: 1850) as follows: "Associate Principals Mary L. Bonney and Harriette A. Dillaye . . . will open a Boarding and Day School, the first of September next at 525 Chestnut Street." Materials about the seminary are at the Historical Society of Pennsylvania. They are printed pamphlets in the general collection; no publisher is named.

62. Mary Bonney, a native of Hamilton, New York, attended Hamilton Academy, then Troy Female Seminary from 1833 to 1835. She taught in New York, South Carolina, and (briefly) Providence, Rhode Island, then in Miss Phelps' School in Philadelphia. "Mary L. Bonney," *EWP*, 138–139. She mar-

ried Thomas Rambaut in 1888, but he died two years later. She was an active promoter of the reformed treatment of native Americans.

63. As a young girl, Dillaye had been taught at the Hamilton Academy by Helen Phelps, herself a graduate of Emma Willard's Seminary. By the age of nineteen, she headed the Ladies' Department of the Northampton Academy at Jackson, North Carolina. "Harriette A. Dillaye," *EWP*, 161–165. Letters from Harriette Dillaye to Olivia are preserved in the Margaret Olivia Slocum Sage Collection at the Emma Willard School.

64. *Chestnut Street Female Seminary, Philadelphia*, 6.

65. "Harriette A. Dillaye," *EWP*, 164.

66. The average daily wage for Philadelphia artisans in 1830 was $1.73. Allowing for seasonal unemployment and sickness, average annual earnings would rarely exceed $300 ($8,194 in 2003 dollars). U.S. Department of Commerce, Bureau of the Census, *Historical Statistics of the United States: Colonial Times to 1970* (Washington, D.C.: Government Printing Office, 1975), 1:163.

67. *Chestnut Street Female Seminary, Boarding and Day School, Philadelphia* (Philadelphia, Pa.: Henry B. Ashmead, 1855), 7–8.

68. *EWP*, 164; M. P. Slocum to "My dear Husband," September 11, 1855, "Rough Drafts of Letters from Olivia Slocum Sage to Her Father, 1855–1863," EGS.

69. Anna [Gould] to Helen Gould (on Ogontz notepaper), February 8, 1895, Helen Gould Papers, Folders "n.d." and "1895," Lyndhurst, Irvington, New York.

70. Indispensable studies of women's labor force participation historically include Alice Kessler-Harris, *Out to Work: A History of Wage-Earning Women in America* (New York: Oxford University Press, 1982); Kessler-Harris, *A Woman's Wage: Historical Meanings and Social Consequences* (Lexington: University Press of Kentucky, 1991); Jeanne Boydston, *Home and Work: Housework, Wages, and the Ideology of Labor in the Early Republic* (New York: Oxford University Press, 1990); Thomas Dublin, *Transforming Women's Work: New England Lives in the Industrial Revolution* (Ithaca, N.Y.: Cornell University Press, 1994); Jacqueline Jones, *Labor of Love, Labor of Sorrow: Black Women, Work, and Family from the Civil War to the Present* (New York: Basic Books, 1984). Recent studies include Alice Kessler-Harris, *In Pursuit of Equity: Women, Men, and the Quest for Economic Citizenship in 20th Century America* (New York: Oxford University Press, 2001); Eileen Boris, *Home to Work: Motherhood and the Politics of Industrial Homework in the United States* (New York: Cambridge University Press, 1994); and Ava Baron, ed., *Work Engendered: Toward a New History of American Labor* (Ithaca, N.Y.: Cornell University Press, 1991). Recent scholarly writings on women's labor also reflect an understanding of the ideological construction of the breadwinner role and the categories "public" and "private." Lawrence Glickman's *A Living Wage: American Workers and the Making of Consumer Society* (Ithaca, N.Y.: Cornell University Press, 1999) is a useful discussion of ideas about the wage and about independence, but his focus is mainly on the male worker. An important theoretical essay is Nancy Fraser and Linda

Gordon, "Dependency: Tracing a Keyword of the U.S. Welfare State," *Signs* 19 (Winter 1994): 309–336. See also Claudia Goldin, *Understanding the Gender Gap: An Economic History of American Women* (New York: Oxford University Press, 1990);

71. Her autobiographical sketch in *Emma Willard and Her Pupils* says that she "remained at home in Syracuse until through the financial reverses of her father she resolved to become a teacher"; *EWP,* 390.

72. Sarnoff, *Russell Sage, the Money King,* 143.

73. Lee Chambers-Schiller, *Liberty, a Better Husband: Single Women in America: The Generation of 1780–1840* (New Haven, Conn.: Yale University Press, 1984), 18. Caroline LeConte, a graduate of Mount Holyoke, wrote on August 25, 1840 to her mother in response to a query about her plans for the future, "Margaret [her sister] advises me to get married the first good chance, this of course I intend to do, but when I read in your letters of so many marriages, I think I shan't want to take up with everybody else's leavings so I shall grow up an old maid like the rest of my sisters." Jerusha Morris Bennett, "Family History," unpublished manuscript in possession of David Martin, Auburn, Alabama, 72–73.

74. A biographical account written much later states that financial disaster overcame her family in 1848, and as a result, "she resolved to take upon herself the responsibility of her own support." In other words, she claimed that she sought paid work as a daughter, not as a woman seeking independence. "Margaret Olivia (Slocum) Sage," *The National Cyclopedia of American Biography,* 10:422. The article is unsigned.

75. MOS to "My dear Father," November 9, 1853, "Letters of Olivia Slocum Sage to Her Father, 1853–1855," EGS.

76. MOS to "My dear Father," n.d. [1854], "Letters of Olivia Slocum Sage to Her Father, 1853–1855," EGS.

77. "I am surprised at my indifference to Syracuse," MOS to "My dear Father," January 25, 1854, in "Letters of Olivia Slocum Sage to Her Father, 1853–1855," EGS.

78. MOS to "My dear Father," May 12, 1854, "Letters of Olivia Slocum Sage to Her Father, 1853–55," EGS.

79. MOS to "My dear Father," May 30, 1854, "Letters of Olivia Slocum Sage to Her Father, 1853–55," EGS.

80. MOS to "My dear Father," September 26, 1854, December 18, 1854, and January 22, 1855, all in "Letters of Olivia Slocum Sage to Her Father, 1853–55," EGS.

81. MOS to "My dear Father," April 3, 1855, "Letters of Olivia Slocum Sage to Her Father, 1853–55," EGS.

82. "Mrs. Russell Sage the Richest Woman in America"

83. "Mrs. Sage's Reminiscences," *New York Times,* January 20, 1897, 14.

84. Ruth Crocker, "The History of Philanthropy as Life-History: A Biographer's View of Mrs. Russell Sage," in *Philanthropic Foundations: New Scholar-*

ship, New Possibilities, ed. Ellen Condliffe Lagemann (Bloomington: Indiana University Press, 1999), 318–328.

85. "The Man-Woman Case," in "Women's Rights" file, OnHA; see also Hoganson, "Garrisonian Abolitionists and the Rhetoric of Gender."

86. Diane Price Herndl, *Invalid Women: Figuring Feminine Illness in American Fiction and Culture, 1840–1940* (Chapel Hill: University of North Carolina Press, 1993), 2. Herndl points out that "some strategies of defining or using invalidism subvert norms (illness as a resistance to patriarchal definitions)" while others "collude (illness as an acceptance of patriarchal definitions)." See also Marilyn Chandler, "In Sickness and in Health," review of Diane Price Herndl, *Invalid Women, Women's Review of Books* 10 (July 1993): 10–11; Carroll Smith-Rosenberg, "The Hysterical Woman: Sex Roles and Role Conflict in Nineteenth-Century America," in Smith-Rosenberg, *Disorderly Conduct: Visions of Gender in Victorian America* (New York: Alfred A. Knopf, 1985), 197–216.

87. Chandler, "In Sickness and in Health."

88. "Olivia complained some of her throat but otherwise well." Joseph Slocum to "Dear Wife and Son," July 9, 1847, "Family Letters—Rough Drafts," EGS.

89. "Those who recall the delicate organization of the brave little woman, will not wonder that by this time she seemed to have reached the limitations of her endurance, and succumbed to a protracted illness that compelled her temporary retirement," Olivia wrote, in a generous appreciation of her mentor. "Harriette A. Dillaye," *EWP,* 163.

90. She died there in 1863. See "Margaret Olivia Slocum," *EWP,* 391.

91. I have been unable to verify the romantic attachment between Olivia Slocum and Andrew Dickson White that is mentioned in one or two other sources. There is correspondence relating to Olivia's gifts to Cornell after 1906. Andrew Dickson White's letter to Olivia of July 8, 1910, refers to their "auld acquaintance" but ends formally with "Most respectfully and sincerely yours." Andrew D. White to MOS, July 8, 1910, Andrew Dickson White Papers, Cornell.

92. MOS to "My dear Father," Philadelphia, March 17, 1854, "Letters of Olivia Slocum Sage to Her Father, 1853–1855," EGS.

93. MOS to "My dear Father," Philadelphia, May 30, 1854, and MOS to "My dear Father," December 18, 1854, both in "Letters of Olivia Slocum Sage to Her Father, 1853–1855," EGS.

94. The L'Hommedieu family had moved from Sag Harbor, New York, in 1810, Vol. II, FSW. When Stephen L'Hommedieu died in 1875, a local newspaper noted that he left "considerable wealth and, what is far more desirable, an honored and irreproachable memory." "The Late S. S. L'Hommedieu," clipping, Vol. II, 3–5, FSW.

95. MOS to "My dear Father," June 22, 1854, December 18, 1854, and May

12, 1854, all in "Letters of Olivia Slocum Sage to Her Father, 1853–1855," EGS. Emphasis in the original. In a September 26, 1854 letter, she reported that Sallie had joined Jermain's church.

96. Jermain Slocum to "My dear Father," August 27, 1854, in "Letters to Joseph Slocum from Various Members of His Family," EGS.

97. Slocum, *Short History of the Slocums, Slocumbs and Slocombs*, 346.

98. For example, MOS to "My dear Father," February 27, 1855, "Letters of Olivia Slocum Sage to Her Father, 1853–1855," EGS. See also David Williams, *The Georgia Gold Rush* (Columbia, S.C.: University of South Carolina Press, 1993), 118–119.

99. "Mrs. Sage Pays $2,500," unidentified clipping, n.d., "Margaret Olivia Sage," OnHA; "Mrs. Sage Pays Old Debt: $2,500 for Board Bill Incurred by Father 58 Years Ago," newspaper clipping, NYSM. It would have been out of character for Olivia to have paid this bill without ascertaining that it was genuine.

100. MOS to "My dear Father," from Albany, September 11, 1855. She enclosed a letter from her mother. "Rough Drafts of Letters of Olivia Slocum Sage to Her Father, 1855–1863," EGS.

101. M. P. Slocum to "My dear Husband," September 11, 1855, in "Rough Drafts of Letters from Olivia Slocum Sage to Her Father, 1855–1863," EGS.

102. Jermain Slocum to Joseph Slocum, August 25, 1855, in "Letters to Joseph Slocum from Various Members of his Family," EGS.

103. J. H. Groesbeck to Joseph Slocum, June 10, 1857. He loaned Joseph $500 and enclosed an additional $100 for Olivia. Olivia's Aunt Mary had died; see MOS to "My dear Father," September 26, 1854, "Letters of Olivia Slocum Sage to Her Father, 1853–1855," EGS.

104. MOS to "My dear Father," March 11, 1858, "Rough Drafts of Letters of Olivia Slocum Sage to Her Father, 1855–1863," EGS.

105. "Olivia writes that you suffered very much, bleeding profusely from the nose with pain in the head," Jermain wrote to his father. Jermain Slocum to Joseph Slocum, November 8, 1857, "Letters to Joseph Slocum from Various Members of His Family," EGS.

106. MOS to "My dear Father," April 25, 1855, "Letters of Olivia Slocum Sage to Her Father, 1853–55," EGS.

107. MOS to "My dear Father," June 16, 1856, "Rough Drafts of Letters of Olivia Slocum Sage to Her Father, 1855–1863," EGS.

108. Jermain Slocum to Joseph Slocum, November 8, 1857, "Letters to Joseph Slocum from Various Members of His Family" EGS.

109. MOS to "My dear Father," June 16, 1856, "Rough Drafts of Letters of Olivia Slocum Sage to Her Father, 1855–1863," EGS.

110. "Mrs. Russell Sage the Richest Woman in America."

111. MOS to "My dear Father," June 18, 1856, "Rough Drafts of Letters of Olivia Slocum Sage to Her Father, 1855–1863," EGS.

4. A Bankruptcy, Three Funerals, and a Wedding

1. M. P. Slocum to Joseph Slocum, June 2, 1859, "Family Letters—Rough Drafts," EGS.

2. In 1853 he was elected by the General Assembly professor of pastoral theology at Princeton Seminary, but he declined the position. In 1854, he was moderator of the General Assembly, and the next year he was elected a director of Princeton Seminary. "Henry August Boardman, D.D.," *Encyclopedia of the Presbyterian Church in the United States of America, including the Northern and Southern Assemblies*, ed. Alfred Nevin (Philadelphia, Pa.: Presbyterian Cyclopedia Publishing Co., 1884), 82b–83b.

3. Henry A. Boardman, "Public Examinations in Female Schools. Reply to Mrs. Willard," *Troy Daily Times*, December 19, 1857.

4. Ibid.

5. Emma Willard, quoted in ibid., emphasis in the original.

6. MOS to "My dear Father," January 23, 1858, and January 28, 1858, both in "Rough Drafts of Letters of Olivia Slocum Sage to Her Father, 1855–1863," EGS.

7. MOS to "My dear Father," February 11, 1858, "Rough Drafts of Letters of Olivia Slocum Sage to Her Father, 1855–1863," EGS.

8. MOS to "My dear Father," January 28, 1858, "Rough Drafts of Letters of Olivia Slocum Sage to Her Father, 1855–1863," EGS. Hiram Slocum was mayor of Troy from 1856 to 1857; A. J. Weise, *History of the City of Troy* (Troy, N.Y.: William H. Young, 1876), 279.

9. MOS to "My dear Father," February 11, 1858, "Rough Drafts of Letters of Olivia Slocum Sage to Her Father, 1855–1863," EGS.

10. Ibid.; emphasis in the original.

11. MOS to "My dear Father," March 11, 1858, "Rough Drafts of Letters of Olivia Slocum Sage to Her Father, 1855–1863," EGS; emphasis in the original. "Edward Everett," *DAB*, 6:223–226.

12. MOS to "My dear Father," April 20, 1858, "Rough Drafts of Letters of Olivia Slocum Sage to Her Father, 1855–1863," EGS.

13. MOS to "My dear Father," June 29, 1858, "Rough Drafts of Letters of Olivia Slocum Sage to Her Father, 1855–1863," EGS.

14. MOS to "My dear Father," April 3, 1855, March 11, 1858, and June 29, 1858, all in "Letters of Olivia Slocum Sage to Her Father, 1853–1855" and "Rough Drafts of Letters of Olivia Slocum Sage to Her Father, 1855–1863," EGS.

15. MOS to "My dear Father," September 10, 1858, "Rough Drafts of Letters of Olivia Slocum Sage to Her Father, 1855–1863," EGS.

16. MOS to "My dear Father," April 20, 1858, and June 29, 1858, "Rough Drafts of Letters of Olivia Slocum Sage to Her Father, 1855–1863," EGS. Nineteenth-century water cure resorts are the subject of Susan Cayleff, *Wash and Be Healed: The Water Cure Movement and Women's Health* (Philadelphia,

Pa.: Temple University Press, 1987). Kathryn Kish Sklar writes of these resorts, "The strong emphasis on exercise, massage, bathing, and general attention to the body . . . provided women with an opportunity to experience sensual pleasure"; *Catharine Beecher: A Study in American Domesticity* (New York: W.W. Norton, 1976), 207.

17. MOS to "My dear Father," n.d. [July 1858] and September 10, 1858, both in "Rough Drafts of Letters of Olivia Slocum Sage to Her Father, 1855–1863," EGS. For mid-nineteenth-century vacations, see Alain Corbin, *The Lure of the Sea: The Discovery of the Seaside in the Western World, 1750–1840* (Berkeley: University of California Press, 1994); Cindy S. Aron, *Working at Play: A History of Vacations in the United States* (New York: Oxford University Press, 1999).

18. MOS to "My dear Father," September 27, 1858, "Rough Drafts of Letters of Olivia Slocum Sage to Her Father, 1855–1863," EGS.

19. Ibid.

20. MOS to "My dear Father," March 1, 1859, "Rough Drafts of Letters of Olivia Slocum Sage to Her Father, 1855–1863," EGS.

21. M. P. Slocum to Joseph Slocum, June 2, 1859, "Family Letters—Rough Drafts," EGS.

22. "My dear Brother" from "Your Sister Alma," November 17th 18__, FSW.

23. A. Slocum to "My Dear Brother," addressed to Joseph Slocum, Esq., Onon. Co. N.Y., August 7, 1859[?], FSW.

24. For women's legal rights in the nineteenth century, see Norma Basch, *In the Eyes of the Law: Women, Marriage, and Property in Nineteenth-Century New York* (Ithaca, N.Y.: Cornell University Press, 1982); Carole Shammas and Michel Dahlin, *Inheritance in America from Colonial Times to the Present* (New Brunswick: Rutgers University Press, 1987); Joan Hoff, *Law, Gender, and Injustice* (New York: New York University Press, 1991); and Linda Kerber, *No Constitutional Right to Be Ladies: Women and the Obligations of Citizenship* (New York: Hill and Wang, 1998), 81–123.

25. Maggie took up plain sewing, which produced some income. Olivia married a multimillionaire. See George Eliot, *The Mill on the Floss* (1860; repr., New York: Oxford University Press, 1980).

26. MOS to "My dear Father," December 17, 1862, and MOS to "My dear Father," October 11, 1862, both in "Rough Drafts of Olivia Slocum Sage to Her Father, 1855–1863," EGS.

27. MOS to "My dear Father," February 23, 1863, "Rough Drafts of Olivia Slocum Sage to Her Father, 1855–1863," EGS.

28. For more about the U.S. Sanitary Commission, see Judith Ann Giesberg, *Civil War Sisterhood: The U.S. Sanitary Commission and Women's Politics in Transition* (Boston: Northeastern University Press, 2000); George Frederickson, *The Inner Civil War: Northern Intellectuals and the Crisis of the Union* (New York: Harper and Row, 1965); Robert H. Bremner, *The Public Good: Philanthropy and Welfare in the Civil War Era* (New York: Alfred E. Knopf, 1980). Jeanie

Attie, *Patriotic Toil: Northern Women and the American Civil War* (Ithaca, N.Y.: Cornell University Press, 1998); Attie, "Warwork and the Crisis of Domesticity in the North," in *Divided Houses: Gender and the Civil War*, ed. Catherine Clinton and Nina Silber (New York: Oxford University Press, 1992), 247–259. Attie describes how upper-class New York women centralized the collection of donations, founding the Women's Central Relief Association. This organization was then taken over after a few months by the U.S. Sanitary Commission, led by male physicians and professionals.

29. United States Sanitary Commission, Records of the Philadelphia [Work], #586–588, United States Sanitary Commission Records, NYPL.

30. "Philadelphia Women's Pennsylvania Branch, Articles of Clothing Made, December 27, 1862 to June 17, 1863," United States Sanitary Commission Records, NYPL.

31. Ibid.

32. Attie, "Warwork and the Crisis of Domesticity in the North"; emphasis added. On the construction of the women's paid and unpaid work, see Jeanne Boydston, *Home and Work: Housework, Wages, and the Ideology of Labor in the Early Republic* (New York: Oxford University Press, 1990).

33. Margaret Olivia Sage, "Mrs. Russell Sage's Plea," *New York Daily Tribune*, August 8, 1898, 7.

34. Ibid.

35. J. J. Slocum to Mrs. J. J. Slocum, Care of S. S. L'Hommedieu, Esq., May 27, 1861, FSW; Charles Elihu Slocum, *A Short History of the Slocums, Slocumbs and Slocombs of America* (Syracuse, N.Y.: Published by the author, 1882), 346.

36. Joseph Jermain Slocum to "My dear Father and Sister," April 27, 1862, FSW. The letter contained the following, "The darkies all through the country seem to think that the good time had come—but our army, having nothing to do with them, they begin to think that the war is nothing to them, though they all say they hope the Yankees will whip ___."

37. Slocum, *Short History of the Slocums, Slocumbs and Slocombs*, 346.

38. Maury Klein, *The Life and Legend of Jay Gould* (Baltimore, Md.: Johns Hopkins, 1986), 69. See also Klein, "The Boys Who Stayed Behind: Northern Industrialists and the Civil War," in *Rank and File: Civil War Essays in Honor of Bell Irvin Wiley*, ed. James I. Robertson, Jr., and Richard M. McMurry (San Rafael, Calif.: Presidio Press, 1976), 137–156.

39. J. J. Slocum to Stephen S. L'Hommedieu, June 7, 1862; J. J. Slocum to Joseph Slocum, November 7, 1862, both in FSW.

40. *Williams' Cincinnati Directory* (Cincinnati, Ohio: Williams and Company, 1865), 352.

41. [Joseph Jermain Slocum] to Joseph Slocum and Margaret Olivia Slocum, April 27, 1862, FSW. The letter came from Shelbyville, Tennessee, and was signed, "Your aft. Son and Brother, J. J. Slocum."

42. Newspaper clipping (obituary for Joseph Slocum), *Courier and Union*, Tuesday morning, March 31, 1863, FSW. See also Henry Whittemore, *History*

of the Sage and Slocum Families of England and America, Including the Allied Families of Montague, Wanton, Brown, Josselyn, Standish, Doty, Carver, Jermain or Germain, Pierson, Howell (New York: Published by Mrs. Russell Sage, 1908), 26–27. Elihu Slocum gives the date of death as March 25, 1863 in Slocum, *Short History of the Slocums, Slocumbs and Slocombs*, 214.

43. He later designed St. Patrick's Cathedral and Vassar's main building. "James Renwick," *DAB*, 15:507–509. The castle was sold to the Yates family in April 1867; Local History Pamphlet Collection, OCPL. For its later history, see "Hospital Won't Spare That Black Walnut Tree," unidentified clipping, June 22, 1922, SUA. Yates Castle was demolished in 1953 as Syracuse University sought room for expansion.

44. "Woman of Force," April 11, 1897, clipping, Obituaries and Biographical Clippings Collection, OCPL.

45. "A Governess and Tutor in the George Barnes family," *Syracuse Herald*, February 10, 1918; "Mrs. Russell Sage," *Syracuse Herald*, September 5, 1909, Obituaries and Biographical Clippings Collection, OCPL; "Woman of Force." Martha Vicinus analyzed the subject position of the governess in *Independent Women: Work and Community for Single Women, 1850–1920* (Chicago: University of Chicago Press, 1985). See also Leonore Davidoff and Catherine Hall, *Family Fortunes: Men and Women of the English Middle Class, 1780–1850* (Chicago: University of Chicago Press, 1987), 453.

46. Mary Poovey, "The Governess and Jane Eyre," in Poovey, *Uneven Developments: The Ideological Work of Gender in Mid-Victorian England* (Chicago: University of Chicago Press, 1988). 163.

47. "Woman of Force"; "Mrs. Russell Sage's Plea," *New York Daily Tribune*, August 28, 1898, 7.

48. Robert H. Collier, *A History of the Jermain Memorial Church Congregation of Watervliet, New York, 1814–1974* (Albany, N.Y.: Argus-Greenwood Inc., 1976), 68; Slocum, *Short History of the Slocums, Slocumbs and Slocombs*, 37; Sarnoff, *Russell Sage, the Money King*, 145. Silvanus Pierson Jermain served as first secretary of the Albany Savings Bank, organized in 1826, and was a director of the Mechanics and Farmers' Bank of Albany; Charles Elliott Fitch, *Encyclopedia of Biography of New York* (Boston: American Historical Society, Inc., 1916), 126. James B. Jermain's residence is listed simply as Albany Road in the 1869 directory; *The Troy City Directory, 1869* (Troy, N.Y.: William H. Young and Blake, 1869), 4:164. Two Jermain landholdings are marked on a contemporary map. Both run from east to west; the eastern end abuts on the Erie Canal (which there runs roughly north-south) and the Albany-Troy road parallel to the canal.

49. The office of treasurer was elective after 1847. Sage served on the following standing committees in 1847–1848: Finance, Navigation, Night Watch, Advisory Committee to the Overseers of the Poor, and Schenectady and Troy Railroad. He was also a director of the Commercial Bank of Troy. *Kneeland's Troy Directory, 1847–8* (Troy, N.Y.: J. L. Kneeland and Co., 1847), 1:12–13.

"Russell Sage," *Encyclopedia of American Business History and Biography*, vol. 7, *Banking and Finance to 1913*, ed. Larry Schweikart (New York: Facts on File, 1990).

50. Sarnoff, *Russell Sage the Money King*, 66. Sage was a member of the Committee on Ways and Means during this term in Congress; Russell Sage to Charles Lanman, Esq., Troy, N.Y., February 24, 1858, handwritten autobiographical notes, Charles Lanman Collection, NYSL.

51. Sage to Lanman, February 24, 1858; George M. Jenks, "Russell Sage," *ANB*, 19:194–195.

52. "Death of Russell Sage," *The Troy Record*, July 23, 1906; *Troy Directory for the Year 1863* (Boston: Adams, Sampson and Co., 1863).

53. The story is told with gusto by Paul Sarnoff in *Russell Sage, the Money King*, 69–81. See also John N. Ingham, ed., *Biographical Dictionary of American Business Leaders* (Westport, Conn.: Greenwood Press, 1983), 3:1234–1236.

54. For example, Russell Sage to James B. Swain, Esq., September 24, 1858, Papers of Samuel L. M. Barlow, Huntington.

55. Jane Remsen, "Russell Sage: Yankee," *New England Quarterly* 11, no. 1 (March 1938): 15. Remsen adds that Sage sold the house to P. T. Barnum for $110,000 when he purchased the one at Forty-Second Street. Sarnoff, *Russell Sage, the Money King*, 81.

56. Sarnoff, *Russell Sage, the Money King*, 129, cites the certificate of death, which is on file at the New York City Department of Health.

57. Moses King, *King's Handbook of New York City* (Boston: Moses King, 1892), 200–202.

58. The story is repeated most recently in James Allen Smith and Melissa A. Smith, "Margaret Olivia Slocum Sage," in *ANB*, 19:193.

59. Remsen, "Russell Sage: Yankee," 15. Bob Anderson at the Rensselaer County Historical Society gave me information about the houses.

60. Collier, *History of the Jermain Memorial Church Congregation of Watervliet, New York*, 69–73. Olivia's cousin James Barclay Jermain (1809–1897) studied law at Yale before joining his father's business. He married Catherine Ann Rice in 1842, and the couple had five children. James T. Myers, ed., *History of the City of Watervliet, N.Y., 1630–1910* (Troy, N.Y.: Henry Stowell and Sons, 1910).

61. Collier, *History of the Jermain Memorial Church Congregation of Watervliet, New York*, 70; "Margaret Olivia Slocum Sage," *DAB*, 16:291.

62. Several sources describe Olivia as lively and talkative. See remembrances of Abbie Whipple of Watervliet, a contemporary of Olivia at the Seminary and aged ninety-three in 1918. "Death of Margaret Olivia Sage in the Ninetieth Year of Her Age," Troy Scrapbook, Local History Collection, TPL.

63. Nathaniel Bartlett Sylvester, *History of Rensselaer County, New York* (Philadelphia, Pa.: Everts and Peck, 1880), 166–167.

64. "Russell Sage's Connection with Durhamville, Oneida County," *Syracuse Sunday Herald*, July 16, 1899, "Russell Sage," OnHA. The legend of resis-

tance from family members to the marriage crops up in several sources. Remsen pins it on Russell Sage's parents. His father, Elisha Sage, a farmer at Durhamville, near Oneida, had died in 1854. Opposition might also have come from his mother, Prudence Risley Sage, who passed away on September 26, 1865.

65. Remsen, "Russell Sage: Yankee," 11–12. On the division between the Seward Whigs and the Silver Group led by Hon. David Seymour, see Lanman to Russell Sage, Charles Lanman Collection, NYSL; Sarnoff, *Russell Sage, the Money King*, 45–60.

66. *Wheeler v. Sage*, 68 U.S. (I. Wallace) 518; Sarnoff, *Russell Sage, the Money King*, 63.

67. "Wedding in High Society," *Troy Budget*, November 24, 1869; "Marriage in High Life," *Troy Times*, November 26, 1869.

68. M. P. Slocum to "My dear Husband," September 11, 1855, "Rough Drafts of Letters from Olivia Slocum Sage to Her Father, 1855–1863," EGS.

69. MOS in "Suppose They Had Married the First Man that Proposed!" *New York Herald*, December 10, 1899.

5. The Work of Benevolence?

1. Irvin G. Wyllie, "Margaret Olivia Slocum Sage," *NAW*, 3:222.

2. Jane Remsen, "Russell Sage: Yankee," *New England Quarterly* 11, no. 1 (March 1938): 15; Paul Sarnoff, *Russell Sage, the Money King* (New York: Ivan Obolensky, 1965), 146. The smart set was already moving farther north on Fifth Avenue, however; see Edwin G. Burrows and Mike Wallace, *Gotham: A History of New York City, to 1898* (New York: Oxford University Press, 1999), 1076.

3. There is no more mention of the sore throats that had plagued Olivia. For evidence of some unidentified illness, see MOS to Captain Richard Pratt, January 13, 1882, Richard Henry Pratt Papers, Box 8, Folder 273, Yale, Beinecke; "Your (true) friend Phebe" to Mr. Jermain, October 30, 1881, FSW; Henry Whittemore, *History of the Sage and Slocum Families of England and America, Including the Allied Families of Montague, Wanton, Brown, Josselyn, Standish, Doty, Carver, Jermain or Germain, Pierson, Howell* (New York: Published by the author, 1908), 37.

4. "Gifts to First Church Here Made through Miss Gifford," undated clipping [November 1918], "Margaret Olivia Sage," OnHA.

Sarnoff puts the worst possible interpretation on Olivia's mother's arrival. Citing no evidence, he writes: "[Olivia] sent for her mother. From that Christmas of 1869 until she passed away in 1891, the hardy Mary [sic] Slocum stood steadfast by her embattled daughter's side and helped fight the Money-King to a standstill." Sarnoff, *Russell Sage, the Money King*, 148.

5. Charles Elihu Slocum, *History of the Slocums, Slocumbs and Slocombs of America* (Defiance, Ohio: Quintin Publications, 1908), 303, 313, 346; "Colonel J. J. Slocum Dies at 91 Years," *New York Times*, October 3, 1924, 21. Their daughter, Margaret Olivia Slocum, had been born August 3, 1870.

Another daughter, Caroline Ellis, died at West Point, New York, in July 1875, at the age of three.

6. *Guide to Long Branch, the Great Seaside Resort of the United States* (Long Branch, N.J.: James B. Morris, 1868), 3–4; Cindy S. Aron, *Working at Play: A History of Vacations in the United States* (New York: Oxford University Press, 1999), 86.

7. J. H. Schenck, *Album of Long Branch: A Series of Photographic Views* (New York: John F. Trow, 1868), n.p.

8. [MOS] to Joseph Jermain Slocum ["Jermain"], n.d. [1875?], transcribed by FSW, FSW.

9. Emphasis added. The letter ends, "Mr. Sage came in." [MOS] to Joseph Jermain Slocum, n.d. The transcription bears the following note: "Parts of one letter found among Granddad's papers written in ink—FSW."

10. Russell Sage to S. L. M. Barlow, Esq., June 18, 1874. Papers of Samuel L. M. Barlow, Box 94, Huntington. The letter is written in another hand, evidently by a private secretary, and signed by Russell Sage. The letterhead is Panama Rail Road Company, New York. However, another letter to the same correspondent is handwritten by Sage in a hasty scrawl and ends, "Will bear it in mind so as to protect our interest." Evidently, some things were too important to be delegated. Russell Sage to Barlow, October 22, 1881, Papers of Samuel L. M. Barlow, Box 147, Huntington. See the recent biographical essay by George M. Jenks, "Russell Sage (4 August, 1816–22 July, 1906)," *ANB*, 19:194–195.

11. A lively account of these years is in Mark Wahlgren Summers, *The Gilded Age: Or, The Hazard of New Functions* (New York: Prentice Hall, 1997), 82–85.

12. For the history of the development of the railroad infrastructure in the nineteenth-century United States, see Alfred D. Chandler, *The Visible Hand: The Managerial Revolution in American Business* (Cambridge, Mass.: Belknap Press of Harvard University Press, 1977), 159–160, 204; Gabriel Kolko, *Railroads and Regulation, 1877–1916* (Chicago: Quadrangle Books, 1967); Edward C. Kirkland, *Industry Comes of Age: Business, Labor, and Public Policy, 1860–1897* (Chicago: Quadrangle Books, 1967); Thomas C. Cochran, *Railroad Leaders, 1845–1890* (New York: Russell and Russell, 1965); John Stover, *American Railroads*, 2nd ed. (Chicago: University of Chicago Press, 1997); Naomi Lamoureaux, *The Great Merger Movement in American Business, 1895–1904* (Cambridge: Cambridge University Press, 1985). 159–160; Maury Klein, "Jay Gould," in *The Encyclopedia of American Business History and Biography*, vol. 2, *Railroads in the Nineteenth Century*, ed. Robert L. Frey (New York: Facts on File, 1988), 138–147; Sarnoff, *Russell Sage, the Money King*, 147, 151. Sarnoff exaggerates Gould's dependence on Sage, claiming that Gould owed all his success to his financier friend.

13. "The operational requirements of the new technology thus brought, indeed demanded, the creation of modern managerially operated business enterprises," Chandler, *Visible Hand*, 204, 189. On the federal government bureau-

cracy in this period, see Morton Keller, *Affairs of State: Public Life in Late Nineteenth Century America* (Cambridge, Mass.: Belknap Press of Harvard University Press, 1977), 310–311.

14. While Sage and Gould grew fabulously wealthy, the Gould system (Southwestern Lines) became "a synonym for bad management and poor equipment," according to Robert Riegel in *American Railroads*; cited in Chandler, *Visible Hand,* 183. The speculators paid almost no attention at all to operating needs, nor were they particularly concerned about the caliber of the managers operating their lines.

15. Russell Sage to Charles Lanman, Esq., Troy, New York, February 24, 1858, handwritten autobiographical notes, Charles Lanman Collection, MPJ 16481, NYSL. See also Judy Hilkey, *Character Is Capital: Success Manuals and Manhood in Gilded Age America* (Chapel Hill: University of North Carolina Press, 1998).

16. Russell Sage, in the *New York Herald,* December 19, 1897, quoted in Whittemore, *History of the Sage and Slocum Families of England and America,* 25.

17. Paul Sarnoff calls Russell Sage "a frustrated actor, who enjoyed posing as a fearful, intimidated benefactor, when in truth he was a fearless, courageous manipulator who thrilled inwardly to his own amazing successes in money, railroading and commerce." Sarnoff, *Russell Sage, the Money King,* 254.

18. Ibid., 153.

19. Gustavus Myers, *History of the Great American Fortunes* (New York: The Modern Library, 1936), 192.

20. Maury Klein, "In Search of Jay Gould," *Business History Review* 52 (Summer 1978): 166–199. See also Maury Klein, *The Life and Legend of Jay Gould* (Baltimore, Md.: Johns Hopkins University Press, 1986), 174–175.

21. "Russell Sage Connection with Durhamville, Oneida County," *Syracuse Sunday Herald,* July 16, 1899, 31, "Russell Sage," OnHA.

22. Sarnoff, *Russell Sage, the Money King,* 238.

23. Ibid.

24. Ann Fabian, *Card Sharps, Dream Books, and Bucket Shops: Gambling in Nineteenth-Century America* (Ithaca, N.Y.: Cornell University Press, 1990), 1; T. J. Jackson Lears, *Something for Nothing: Luck in America* (New York: Viking, 2002). Several scholars discuss contemporary reactions to the development of a highly speculative economy in this period; see Cedric B. Cowing, *Populists, Plungers, and Progressives: A Social History of Stock and Commodity Speculation, 1890–1936* (Princeton, N.J.: Princeton University Press, 1965); and Gretchen Ritter, *Goldbugs and Greenbacks: The Antimonopoly Tradition and the Politics of Finance in America* (New York: Cambridge University Press, 1997). See also Daniel Rodgers, *The Work Ethic in Industrial America, 1850–1920* (Chicago: University of Chicago Press, 1974).

Futures trading was the subject of a congressional hearing. See Congress, House, Committee on Agriculture, *Dealing in Fictitious Farm Products,* report no. 969, 52nd Cong., 1st. sess., 1892 (Washington, D.C.: GPO, 1892). See also

A. C. Stevens, "The Utility of Speculation in Modern Commerce," *Political Science Quarterly* 7 (September 1892): 419–430.

25. John F. Hume, "The Heart of Speculation," *The Forum* 2 (September 1886): 140. My thanks to Jackson Lears, who drew my attention to the literature on gambling in the NEH-funded seminar "Luck, Grace, and Fortune in American Society," Rutgers University, summer 1996, and who helped me think through the cultural meanings of luck and speculation in American society.

26. Hume, "The Heart of Speculation," 139.

27. Ibid., 138. How different from the hero-worship of "entrepreneurs" in the closing years of the twentieth century—at least before the collapse of Enron!

28. Washington Gladden, "Three Dangers," *Century Magazine* 6 (August 1884): 624.

29. Fabian, *Card Sharps*, 62. For contemporary anxiety about gambling, see John F. W. Ware, *The Gambling Element in Life, a Sermon Preached in the Music Hall, Boston, October 29, 1871* (Boston: Nichols and Hall, 1871). On gambling and gender, see Hope Cotton, "Women and Risk: The Gambling Woman in Eighteenth-Century England" (Ph.D. diss., Auburn University, 1998).

30. See Samuel Rezneck, "Mr. and Mrs. Russell Sage (1816–1918), A Money-Maker and His Philanthropic Wife," in Samuel Rezneck, *Profiles Out of the Past of Troy, New York, since 1789* (Troy, N.Y.: Greater Troy Chamber of Commerce, 1970), 193–197.

31. Yet, ironically, the practice of philanthropy in the late nineteenth century was moving to adopt the bureaucratized, rationalized, systematic practices of the corporation, rejecting intuition and sentimentality.

32. See the journalistic account of Gould, "A Lover of Roses," in Andrew Tully, *Era of Elegance* (New York: Funk and Wagnalls Company, 1947), 76–91. Tully writes, "There was a wilderness of roses and 8,000 orchid plants of over 150 varieties" (89). In *Life and Legend of Jay Gould*, Maury Klein argues that what the press called Jay Gould's "secretiveness" was simply the quietness of a man who was happiest when he was with his family.

33. Ron Chernow, *The House of Morgan: An American Banking Dynasty and the Rise of Modern Finance* (New York: Atlantic Monthly Press, 1990), 53, 60, 80–81.

34. See "Laidlaw v. Sage," unidentified newspaper clipping, "Russell Sage," OnHA.

35. Quoted in Sarnoff, *Russell Sage, the Money King*, 234–235, from a letter to Sarnoff from George Oslin dated April 8, 1963.

36. This version is current in Troy to this day. Sarnoff portrays the Sages as a grotesque couple, with a hideous and comic Olivia to accompany the outrageously unsympathetic Russell. Sarnoff regaled his readers with stories of Russell Sage's extramarital affairs, explaining them as a natural reaction to his wife's unattractiveness (which is not apparent in her portraits or in photographs; this seems to have been a product of the author's imagination). Sarnoff also claimed without evidence that there were no portraits of the first

Mrs. Sage because Olivia had them all destroyed. *Russell Sage, the Money King,* 147–148.

37. "Saratoga belongs to the world of men," Mary Gay Humphreys, quoted in Homberger, *Mrs. Astor's New York,* 165. Saratoga "in the early nineteenth century had been popular among the social elite of New York and the South, but in the post-Civil War years it was favored mostly by the racing set"; Maureen E. Montgomery, *Displaying Women: Spectacles of Leisure in Edith Wharton's New York* (New York: Routledge, 1998), 26.

38. MOS to Captain Traub, August 14, 1908, in MOS to the Adjutant, August 25, 1908, Constitution Island Collection, NARA RG 404, United States Military Academy Archives, West Point, New York. See also MOS to "The President," September 4, 1908, also in Constitution Island Collection. Olivia's reminiscence was contained in a letter to an inquiry from Captain Traub about her interest in Constitution Island.

39. Grace Overmeyer, "Hudson River Bluestockings—The Warner Sisters of Constitution Island," *New York History* 40 (April 1959): 154–155; Wylie, "Margaret Olivia Sage," *NAW,* 3:222; Anna B. Warner, *Susan Warner* (New York: G. P. Putnam's Sons, 1909); Olivia Phelps Stokes, *Letters and Memoirs of Susan and Anna Bartlett Warner* (New York: G. P. Putnam's Sons, 1925). For a modern appraisal of the Warners, see Jane Tompkins, *Sensational Designs: The Cultural Work of American Fiction, 1790–1860* (New York: Oxford University Press, 1985), 147–151, 176–201; Amy Kaplan, "Manifest Domesticity," *American Literature* 70 (September 1998): 581–606.

40. "A Talk with Mrs. Russell Sage," *New York Times Illustrated Magazine* (September 26, 1897), 2; *Demorest's Family Magazine* 30 (January 1894), 183–184, ECS/SBA, Reel 32.

41. "Russell Sage and His Life," *Troy Record,* July 24, 1906, 3.

42. Theodore Stanton and Harriot Stanton Blatch, eds., *Elizabeth Cady Stanton as Revealed in Her Letters, Diary and Reminiscences* (New York: Harper Brothers, 1922), 2:251.

43. "Russell Sage's Philosophic Views," *New York Daily Tribune,* May 20, 1884; Sarnoff, *Russell Sage, the Money King,* 244–255. The panic began with the collapse of the firm Grant and Ward.

44. Arthur Huntington Gleason, "Mrs. Russell Sage and Her Interests," *World's Work* 13 (November 1906): 8182–8186.

45. "Russell Sage Will Race," *New York Times,* May 14, 1887, 5.

46. Russell Sage to T. A. Disbrow, July 13, 1882, Manuscripts Division, folder 15725, NYSL.

47. Russell Sage to T. A. Disbrow, Esq., n.d., Manuscripts Division, folder 15725, NYSL. Other letters on this subject are dated July 18, 1882, August 29, 1882, and September 5, 1882. All of them end with a stock market tip.

48. Matthew Hale Smith, *Sunshine and Shadow in New York* (Hartford, Conn.: J. B. Burr Publishing Co., 1883), 362.

49. Ibid., 360. See also Roy Rosenzweig and Elizabeth Blackmar, *The Park*

and the People: A History of Central Park (Ithaca, N.Y.: Cornell University Press, 1992).

50. "Russell Sage Will Race." The report implies that Russell Sage intended to drive the four-horse team ("four-in-hand") himself, but ends by stating that another driver would do so. The proceeds went to a hospital—perhaps the New-York Woman's Hospital, Olivia's favorite.

51. Gould called his daughter "Nellie" and his wife "Ellie." Klein, *Life and Legend of Jay Gould*, 134, 212–214; Alice Northrop Snow, with Henry Nicholas Snow, *The Story of Helen Gould, Daughter of Jay Gould, Great American* (New York: Fleming H. Revell Company, 1943).

52. "To me, Mr. Sage is one of the most lovable of men"; Jay Gould to Henry MacCracken, Chancellor, New York University, April 11, 1892, Mac-Cracken Records, NYU.

53. "Nettie Fowler," *EWP*, 814; Charles O. Burgess, "Nettie Fowler McCormick," *NAW*, 2:454–455.

54. Sarnoff cites interviews with Crawford, the Sages' veterinarian between 1896 and 1906. Sarnoff, *Russell Sage, the Money King*, 322–323.

55. On the philanthropic elite, see Kathleen D. McCarthy, *Noblesse Oblige: Charity and Cultural Philanthropy in Chicago, 1849–1929* (Chicago: University of Chicago Press, 1982); Sven Beckert, *Monied Metropolis: New York City and the Consolidation of the American Bourgeoisie, 1850–1896* (New York: Cambridge University Press, 1991); Lori Ginzberg, *Women and the Work of Benevolence: Morality, Politics and Class in the Nineteenth-Century United States* (New Haven, Conn.: Yale University Press, 1990).

56. When Catharine Jermain died in 1873 at the age of fifty, her grieving husband and children published a little book in her memory in which they recorded the following: "Mrs. Jermain's residence being several miles from the city [Albany], the ordinary demands of society were not pressing upon her; and when she went forth from her home, it was most frequently upon errands of mercy." *To the Children and Children's Children and Family Friends of Mrs. Catharine Ann Jermain . . . Christmas, 1873* (Albany, privately printed, n.d.). Olivia kept this book with other treasured relics of her family into her very old age. This source claims that Catharine Jermain, née Rice, had attended Troy Female Seminary, but she is not listed in *Emma Willard and Her Pupils*.

57. Abbie Graham, *Grace H. Dodge, Merchant of Dreams* (New York: Women's Press, 1936), 50; Esther Katz, "Grace Hoadley Dodge: Women and the Emerging Metropolis, 1856–1914" (Ph.D. diss., New York University, 1980); James F. Findlay, Jr., *Dwight L. Moody: American Evangelist, 1837–1899* (Chicago: University of Chicago Press, 1969). For the impact of revivalists on late-nineteenth-century society, see also William G. McLoughlin, Jr., *Modern Revivalism: Charles Grandison Finney to Billy Graham* (New York: Ronald Press Co., 1959); Bernard Weisberger, *They Gathered at the River: The Story of the Great Revivalists and Their Impact Upon Religion in America* (Boston: Little, Brown and Co., 1958).

Later in life, Moody founded two academies in Northfield, Massachusetts, to which both Olivia and Russell Sage gave substantial amounts of money.

58. Helen M. Wanken, "'Woman's Sphere' and Indian Reform: The Women's National Indian Association, 1879–1901" (Ph.D. diss., Marquette University, 1981), 39 and *passim.* "Mary L. Bonney," *EWP,* 138–139 includes a photograph of Bonney and discusses her role in founding the Chestnut Street Seminary and her activities in the WNIA. For an overview, see Edmund J. Danziger, Jr., "Native American Resistance and Accommodation during the Late Nineteenth Century," in *The Gilded Age: Essays on the Origins of Modern America,* ed. Charles W. Calhoun (Wilmington, Del.: Scholarly Resources, 1996), 163–184. The full name of the Mohonk Conference was "Lake Mohonk Conference of Friends of the Indian and Other Dependent Peoples."

59. Carmelita S. Ryan, "The Carlisle Indian Industrial School" (Ph.D. diss., Georgetown University, 1962), 41. Other "reformers" depended on the reservation schools to achieve the same results.

60. Wanken, "'Woman's Sphere' and Indian Reform"; Everett Gilcreast, "Richard Henry Pratt and American Indian Policy, 1877–1906: A Study of the Assimilation Movement" (Ph.D. diss., Yale, 1967); Wilcomb E. Washburn, ed., *History of Indian-White Relations,* vol. 4 of William C. Sturtevant, ed., *Handbook of North American Indians* (Washington, D.C.: Smithsonian Institution Press, 1988). See also Genevieve Bell, "Telling Tales Out of School: Remembering the Carlisle Indian School, 1879–1918" (Ph.D. diss., Stanford University, 1998).

An example of Pratt's methods was his earlier campaign to house female students at Hampton. He sent out a "success story," named Bright Eyes, "to make use of her hold upon public sympathy for the permanent benefit of her Indian sisters. With this desire she offered her services to speak at the East in behalf of a project of some Northern friends of the school to enlarge its work by erecting a building for Indian girls, to cost complete and furnished $15,000. A beautiful site now adjoining the school premises, and now inclosed in them, was given as a generous send-off by a lady friend." The new building made it possible to accommodate fifty more Indian girls at Hampton, "thus effecting the desired balance of the sexes." Helen W. Ludlow, "Indian Education at Hampton and Carlisle," *Harper's* 371 (April 1881), 669.

61. David W. Adams, *Education for Extinction: American Indians and the Boarding School Experience, 1875–1928* (Lawrence: University of Kansas Press, 1995). Pratt's efforts differed from those directed at Indians on the reservation by government agents, missionaries, and teachers, and he refused funding that would have placed his boarding school in Kansas. Danziger, "Native American Resistance and Accommodation during the Late Nineteenth Century." Accounts that draw primarily on Indian voices in oral histories and interviews are Tsianina K. Lomawaima, *They Called It Prairie Light: The Story of Chilocco Indian School* (Lincoln: University of Nebraska Press, 1994); and Becky Matthews, "Wherever That Singing Is Going: The Interaction of Crow and

Euro-American Women, 1880–1945 (Ph.D. diss., Auburn University, 2002). See also Robert A. Trennert, "Educating Indian Girls at Nonreservation Boarding Schools, 1878–1920," *Western Historical Quarterly* 13 (July 1982): 169–190.

62. The bill's sponsors cited "the successful progress at the Industrial and Normal Institution of Hampton, Virginia, [which] furnishes a striking proof of the natural aptitude and capacity of the rudest savages of the plains for mechanical, scientific, and industrial education, when removed from parental and tribal surroundings and influences"; "A Bill to Increase Educational Privileges and Establish Additional Industrial Training Schools for the Benefit of Youth Belonging to Such Nomadic Indian Tribes as Have Educational Treaty Claims upon the United States." Quoted in Ludlow, "Indian Education at Hampton," 670.

63. *Morning Star* 3, no. 6 (June 1883). The school periodical appeared under different titles, including *Red Man and Indian Helper*. Lists of those who visited the school include anthropologist Alice Fletcher.

64. *Morning Star* 4, no. 10 (May 1884), n.p.

65. Ibid. The article is reprinted from one by one M. R. Vincent in the *Independent*. For example, an obituary for New York businessman-philanthropist William E. Dodge praised his "*stewardship*, a distinctively Christian principle," noting that "Mr. Dodge, while enjoying with Christian moderation the privileges of wealth, regarded himself as a trustee and administrator of wealth for the service of humanity and the interests of religion."

66. Richard Henry Pratt, "Eleventh Annual Report on the Carlisle Indian School (November 2, 1890)," submitted to Thomas J. Morgan, Commissioner of Indian Affairs, *Annual Report of the Commissioner of Indian Affairs, 1890*, quoted in Pearl Lee Walker-McNeal, "The Carlisle Indian School: A Study in Acculturation" (Ph. D. diss., American University, 1979), 112–113.

67. Kaplan, "'Manifest Domesticity.'"

68. Her church at this time was the West Presbyterian on West 42nd Street, according to Marjorie Harrison, *Margaret Olivia Sage: Philanthropist and Friend* (New York: Board of National Missions of the Presbyterian Church in the U.S.A., 1927–1928), 4. A useful study of women's missionary society activity, which includes discussion of Woman's Boards, is Lois A. Boyd and R. Douglas Brackenridge, ed., *Presbyterian Women in America: Two Centuries of a Quest for Status* (Westport, Conn.: Greenwood Press, 1983), 17, 164.

69. Ryan, "The Carlisle Indian Industrial School," 51.

70. "Our Trip to Philadelphia, New York, and Brooklyn," *Morning Star* 7, no. 5 (January and February 1887).

71. For the interactions of members of mainstream denominations with racial Others, see Susan M. Yohn, *A Contest of Faiths: Missionary Women and Pluralism in the American Southwest* (Ithaca, N.Y.: Cornell University Press, 1995); Peggy Pascoe, *Relations of Rescue: The Search for Female Authority in the American West, 1834–1939* (New York: Oxford University Press, 1990); James Axtell, *The Invasion Within: The Conquest of Cultures in Colonial North Amer-*

ica (New York: Oxford University Press, 1985). See also Edward Said, *Culture and Imperialism* (New York: Knopf, 1993).

72. This was "an irony that women of [anthropologist-reformer Alice] Fletcher's generation could never fully examine; nor could they cover it up entirely." Newman, *White Women's Rights*, 130.

73. My interpretation at this point is indebted to Karen Anderson, *Changing Woman: A History of Racial-Ethnic Women in Modern America* (New York: Oxford University Press, 1996), especially 39–40.

74. She adds, "But evolution's construction of racial progress prevented them from proceeding down this road." Newman, *White Women's Rights*, 130.

75. Karen Anderson calls this "gender-based acculturation." See the excellent discussion in Anderson, *Changing Woman*, 37–66. See also Kaplan, "'Manifest Domesticity,'" 582; Kumari Jayawardena, *The White Woman's Other Burden* (New York: Routledge, 1995); Newman, *White Women's Rights*, 128–129; Dolores Janiewski, "Learning to Live 'Just Like White Folks': Gender, Ethnicity, and the State in the Inland Northwest," in *Gendered Domains: Rethinking Public and Private in Women's History*, ed. Dorothy O. Helly and Susan Reverby (Ithaca, N.Y.: Cornell University Press, 1991), 167–180. Reformers intended Indian women to abandon their traditional work roles in favor of a Euro-American domesticity.

76. MOS to Captain Pratt, November 25, 1889, Richard Henry Pratt Papers, Box 11, Folder 273, Yale, Beinecke. Amy Kaplan writes, "The process of domestication . . . entails conquering and taming the wild, the natural, and the alien." Kaplan, "Manifest Domesticity," 582. To Olivia's disappointment, the girl couldn't be admitted to Carlisle because she was Cherokee and the Cherokee were not treaty Indians.

77. "A Talk with Mrs. Russell Sage." See also "Margaret Olivia Slocum," *EWP*, 389.

78. He did not graduate, as one account explains, "as circumstances led him to adopt a profession more in accordance with his natural tastes and inclination than would have followed a complete collegiate course"; typed transcripts, Vol. I, FSW. See also Charles Elihu Slocum, *A Short History of the Slocums, Slocumbs and Slocombs of America, Genealogical and Biographical* (Syracuse, N.Y., published by the author, 1882), 347; "Lieut. Col. Slocum Dies at Age of 74," *New York Times*, December 15, 1933, 25. The subtitle reads, "Indian Fighter in West; Commanded Troop Which Surrounded Sitting Bull's Forces When Chief Was Slain." This account states that he graduated from "infantry and cavalry school" in 1883.

79. HJS to "My dearest Mother and Father," October 13, 1875, shamefacedly records his "confinement" at West Point for some violation; Vol. I, FSW.

80. Slocum, *Short History of the Slocums, Slocumbs and Slocombs*, 346–347.

81. When he became a congressman in the 1850s, she went on, he requested congressional funds "to make and keep the peace in Oregon. Largely through his efforts, educational advantages were secured for the Indians in the Western territory." Remsen, "Russell Sage: Yankee," 12–13.

82. Quoted in Klein, *Life and Legend of Jay Gould*, 157. For the Union Pacific

takeover in which Sage, Gould, and Dillon beat out Thomas Scott and Vanderbilt, see 140–141. Jay Gould's business empire rested on the exploitation of Chinese labor as well as the extermination of Native Americans. His biographer Maury Klein writes, "[T]he problem was always to strike a balance between paring expenses and maintaining the [Union Pacific]. . . . By 1877 he had squeezed his Chinese labor down to twenty-seven dollars a month, which in his opinion was 'still two dollars a month too high.'" Klein, *Life and Legend of Jay Gould*, 157.

83. Sarnoff, *Russell Sage, the Money King*, 235–236.

84. MOS to Captain Richard Pratt, January 13, 1882, "General Correspondence and Official Papers," Richard Henry Pratt Papers, Box 11, Folder 273, Yale, Beinecke; emphasis in the original.

85. MOS to Richard Henry Pratt, March 12, 1883, Richard Henry Pratt Papers, Box 8, Folder 273, Yale, Beinecke; emphasis in the original. At the same time, Olivia was trying to secure a position as Pratt's assistant for Herbert J. Slocum, who was to be married in April 1884. She wrote that she feared that there was little hope of him obtaining the position "as long as General Sherman was in power."

86. MOS to Captain Pratt, March 12, 1883, Richard Henry Pratt Papers, Box 11, Folder 273, Yale, Beinecke; C. Augusta Astor (Mrs. J .J. Astor) to MOS [1885]; J. Hall to MOS, March 2, 1886, RSFR, Box 69, Folder 670. The speaker at this 1886 meeting was Herbert Welch. Correspondence between Olivia and Pratt spans thirty years (1881–1912). See Mrs. Edgar M. Hawkins [daughter of Richard Pratt] to Mr. Lawson Purdy, President, The Russell Sage Foundation, July 31, 1943, which referred to "Mrs. Sage's constant interest in father's views and her financial help in his work" and asked the Russell Sage Foundation to support the publication of her father's memoirs, a request that the foundation's director, Shelby Harrison, declined. Harrison to Mrs. Edgar M. Hawkins, August 2, 1943, Richard Henry Pratt Papers, Box 15, Folder 523, Yale, Beinecke.

87. The story is repeated in several places but I have not been able to verify it. See for example A. H. F., "Russell Sage," *DAB*, 16:292–293.

88. For a donation from Henry Flagler to Pratt, sent through Olivia Sage, see H. M. Flagler to MOS, May 11, 1883, Richard Henry Pratt Papers, Box 13, Folder 452, Yale, Beinecke. Flagler enclosed a note reassuring her that he had long approved the work being done by Captain Pratt and saying that he hoped "that better results may be anticipated by removing the Indian children and youth from their tribal influences and associations to the east, rather than to undertake to educate them on their reservations."

89. MOS to Captain Pratt, December 16, 1884, Richard Henry Pratt Papers, Box 11, Folder 273, Yale, Beinecke. The Carlisle paper *Morning Star* lists subscriptions and donations. See for example, *Morning Star*, June 3, 1883, which details donations from A. T. Jeanes, $500; H. M. Flagler, $100; Mrs Russell Sage, $50; Mrs John Munn, $10; Col. J. J. Slocum, $10; Dr. C. R. Agnew, $25. See also Ludlow, "Indian Education at Hampton and Carlisle," 669; Wanken, "'Woman's Sphere' and Indian Reform"; Gilcreast, "Richard Henry Pratt and

American Indian Policy." I have not found a full record of private donations to Carlisle.

90. Gail Bederman, *Manliness and Civilization: A Cultural History of Gender and Race in the United States, 1880–1917* (Chicago: University of Chicago Press, 1995).

91. MOS to Captain Pratt, November 25, 1889, Richard Henry Pratt Papers, Box 11, Folder 273, Yale, Beinecke; emphasis in the original. Laura Wexler, *Tender Violence: Domestic Visions in an Age of U.S. Imperialism* (Chapel Hill: University of North Carolina Press, 2000), insightfully analyzes such before-and-after pictures, 108–111.

92. Sadly for Pratt, though not for the Indians, his plans would never benefit from Sage philanthropy, for by the time Olivia inherited her fortune other causes had won her attention and Pratt had fallen from favor in official Washington.

93. "A Talk with Mrs. Russell Sage," 2; Gleason, "Mrs. Russell Sage and Her Interests," 8184.

94. "Add just this one more" in Jeannette Baird to MOS, December 15, 1886, RSFR, Box 91, Folder 884. The association was the Presbyterial Society. On voluntary association as "career," in addition to Scott, *Natural Allies*; and McCarthy, "'Parallel Power Structures," see also Kathleen Waters Sander, *The Business of Charity: The Woman's Exchange Movement, 1832–1900* (Urbana: University of Illinois Press, 1998). A late-twentieth-century perspective is Arlene Kaplan Daniels, *Invisible Careers: Women Civic Leaders from the Volunteer World* (Chicago: University of Chicago Press, 1988).

95. This Mrs. Astor was C. Augusta Astor, not her sister-in-law Caroline Webster Schermerhorn Astor, the arbiter of New York society and queen of its "Four Hundred." Wallace Evan Davies, "Caroline Webster Schermerhorn Astor," *NAW,* 1:62–64.

96. Wyllie, "Margaret Olivia Slocum Sage."

97. On benevolence as "subject position," see Judith Giesburg, *Civil War Sisterhood: The U.S. Sanitary Commission and Women's Politics in Transition* (Boston: Northeastern University Press, 1999); Ruth Crocker, "From Gift to Foundation: The Philanthropic Lives of Mrs. Russell Sage," in *Charity, Philanthropy, and Civility in American History*, ed. Lawrence Friedman and Mark McGarvie (New York: Cambridge University Press, 2003), 199–215.

6. "I live for that work"

An earlier version of this chapter was presented in February 1993 to the Medical History Society at the Reynolds Library of the University of Alabama at Birmingham.

1. Suzanne Lebsock, "Woman and American Politics, 1880–1920," in *Women, Politics, and Change,* ed. Louise Tilly and Patricia Gurin (New York: Russell Sage Foundation, 1990), 35–62.

2. I am grateful to Caroline Gebhard, who helped me clarify the complex issues involved here.

3. The women's board was called the Board of Lady Managers until 1868, then it was renamed the Board of Lady Supervisors (1868 to 1888) and subsequently the Ladies Assistant Board (1888–1900). To avoid confusion, I have used the term "lady managers" throughout. The significance of these changing terms will, I hope, be clear in the text.

4. I am indebted to the analysis of these developments in Regina Morantz-Sanchez, *Conduct Unbecoming a Woman: Medicine on Trial in Turn-of-the-Century Brooklyn* (New York: Oxford University Press, 1999); and Ornella Moscucci, *The Science of Woman: Gynaecology and Gender in England, 1800–1929* (Cambridge: Cambridge University Press, 1990).

5. Nancy M. Theriot, "Women's Voices in Nineteenth-Century Medical Discourse: A Step Toward Deconstructing Science," *Signs* 19 (Autumn 1993): 1–3.

6. On the motives of genteel volunteers, see Kristie Ross, "Arranging a Doll's House: Refined Women as Union Nurses," in *Divided Houses: Gender and the Civil War*, ed. Catherine Clinton and Nina Silber (New York: Oxford University Press, 1992), 101; Jeanie Attie, *Patriotic Toil: Northern Women and the American Civil War* (Ithaca, N.Y.: Cornell University Press, 1998).

Theriot draws a distinction between illness and disease as follows: "While illness is a matter of personal (and sometimes group) physiology and psychology, disease is a matter of representation. Disease is a scientific representation of illness that involves both a sorting of symptoms into discrete entities and a theorizing about causation and cure. As such, disease is not discovered but created." "Women's Voices in Nineteenth-Century Medical Discourse," 3.

7. Deborah Kuhn McGregor, *Sexual Surgery and the Origins of Gynecology: J. Marion Sims, His Hospital, and His Patients* (New York: Garland Publishing, Inc., 1989), revised as *From Midwives to Medicine: The Birth of American Gynecology* (New Brunswick, N.J.: Rutgers University Press, 1998).

8. J. Marion Sims, *Silver Sutures in Surgery: The Anniversary Discourse before the New York Academy of Medicine* (New York: Samuel S. Wood, 1858), 52, quoted in McGregor, *From Midwives to Medicine*, 61. Sims's formulation is odd here. Generally, the mid-nineteenth-century belief was that people of color and working-class people could bear more pain than others and that white men could bear more pain than women. See Seale Harris, *Woman's Surgeon: The Life Story of J. Marion Sims* (New York: Macmillan Company, 1950), 109; and Martin S. Pernick, *A Calculus of Suffering: Pain, Professionalism, and Anesthesia in Nineteenth-Century America* (New York: Columbia University Press, 1985), 155–157.

Other planters also brought slaves from the surrounding area to Sims for treatment; see McGregor, *Midwives to Medicine*, 326n90; Todd L. Savitt, "The Use of Blacks for Medical Experimentation and Demonstration in the Old South," *Journal of Southern History* 48 (August 1982): 331–348; Diana E. Axelson, "Women as Victims of Medical Experimentation: J. Marion Sims' Surgery on Slave Women, 1840–1850," in *Black Women in American History: From Colonial Times through the Nineteenth Century,* ed. Darlene Clark Hine (Brooklyn, N.Y.: Carlson Publishing Company, 1990), 1:51–60.

9. Harris, *Woman's Surgeon,* 118–119, 136–150; 395–399. McGregor, *Sexual Surgery,* 109–110. Sims's scientific publications over the course of a lifetime numbered over seventy.

10. Mary S. Benson, "Sarah Platt Haines Doremus," *NAW,* 1:500–501; *Memorial Service of the Late Mrs. Thomas C. Doremus, the Beloved and Lamented President of the Woman's Union Missionary Society* (New York: G. P. Putnam's, 1877). Thomas Addis Emmet, who opposed the lady managers on many occasions, nevertheless acknowledged Sarah Doremus as a founder. See Emmet, *Incidents of My Life Professional-Literary-Social, with Services in the Cause of Ireland* (New York: G. P. Putnam's Sons, 1911), 195.

11. Marjorie Harrison, *Margaret Olivia Sage: Philanthropist and Friend* (New York: Board of National Missions of the Presbyterian Church in the U.S.A., 1927–1928), 4; Lois A. Boyd and R. Douglas Brackenridge, *Presbyterian Women in America: Two Centuries of a Quest for Status* (Westport, Conn.: Greenwood Press, 1983), especially 17, 164; Benson, "Sarah Platt Haines Doremus"; *Memorial Service of the Late Mrs. Thomas C. Doremus*; Mrs. L. H. Dagett, *Historical Sketches of Woman's Missionary Societies in America and England* (1883; repr., Beltsville, Md.: NCR Corporation, 1977).

12. It is difficult for the modern reader to reconcile the descriptions of Sara Doremus's physical delicacy with the accounts of her heroic and exhausting deeds of self-sacrifice. For Beecher's wellness survey, see Kathryn Kish Sklar, *Catharine Beecher: A Study in American Domesticity* (1973; repr., New York: W. W. Norton, 1976), 204–205.

13. "Organization of Woman's Hospital, January 8th 1855–February 10, 1855," n.p., in WHP, Series 5, Box 133; emphasis in the original. Also in this box are the Woman's Hospital Association Minutes, February 10, 1855–November 20, 1884; Woman's Hospital Association Minutes, December 31, 1858–; "Woman's Hospital Association, 1865." I have also used Series 8, Ladies' Assistant Board, Minutes of Meetings. See also Harris, *Woman's Surgeon,* 152, 155.

An alternative account written by surgeon Thomas Emmet states that Dr. Fordyce Barker recruited the committee of ladies to run the organization from among his own patients. "I learned from the doctor himself, a short time before his death, that the selection was left to him and was made from among his own patients with the single exception of his wife, whom the ladies themselves elected as their first secretary of the Board." Thomas A. Emmet, "Reminiscences of the Founders of the Woman's Hospital Association," *The American Gynaecological and Obstetrical Journal* (April 1899): 364–365.

14. Address "To the Honorable Legislature of the State of New York," reprinted in *First Report of the Woman's Hospital Association, Presented by the Executive Committee* (New York: D. Fanshawe, 1856), 7. See also Harris, *Woman's Surgeon,* 172–173.

15. "To the Honorable Legislature of the State of New York." Useful scholarly studies of ideas about the body, gender, and illness are Cynthia Russett, *Sexual Science: The Victorian Construction of Womanhood* (Cambridge, Mass.: Harvard University Press, 1989); Mary Poovey, *Uneven Developments: The Ideological Work of Gender in Mid-Victorian England* (Chicago: University of Chicago Press, 1988); Thomas Laqueur, *Making Sex: Body and Gender from the Greeks to Freud* (Cambridge, Mass.: Harvard University Press, 1990).

16. Harris, *Woman's Surgeon*, 155.

17. For the New York Infirmary for Women and Children, see Edwin G. Burrows and Mike Wallace, *Gotham: A History of New York City to 1898* (New York: Oxford University Press, 1999), which offers a brief but useful comparison of the two institutions, 800.

18. On women and incorporation, see Ginzberg, *Women and the Work of Benevolence*; Norma Basch, *In the Eyes of the Law: Women, Marriage, and Property in Nineteenth-Century New York* (Ithaca, N.Y.: Cornell University Press, 1982). The Act of Incorporation was passed on April 18, 1857, and amended April 7, 1858.

19. Harris, *Woman's Surgeon*, 155.

20. *First Report of the Woman's Hospital Association*, 7. This report includes the Constitution of the Woman's Hospital Association, including Title XVI. Emmet, "Reminiscences of the Founders of the Woman's Hospital," 366–367.

21. Emmet, "Reminiscences of the Founders of the Woman's Hospital Association," 367; McGregor, *Midwives to Medicine*, 82n47. Emmet's account is self-serving and aims in part to discredit Sims. Sims used rigorous antiseptic procedures even before Lister publicized the practice of antisepsis in 1867. Yet he performed hundreds of surgeries without anesthesia, even though the effectiveness of nitrous oxide, chloroform, and other gases was known. Sims's practice was not so unusual as we might think. According to Martin Pernick, the discovery of reliable anesthetics by at least 1848 by no means meant that anesthesia was used in every case. Between 1853 and 1862, 32 percent of major limb amputations performed at the Pennsylvania Hospital were still carried out on conscious patients. Pernick, *A Calculus of Suffering*, 4.

On the development of hospitals in the nineteenth century, see Morris J. Vogel, *The Invention of the Modern Hospital: Boston, 1870–1930* (Chicago: University of Chicago Press, 1980); Charles E. Rosenberg, *The Care of Strangers: The Rise of America's Hospital System* (New York: Basic Books, 1987); David Rosner, *A Once-Charitable Enterprise: Hospitals and Health Care in Brooklyn and New York, 1885–1915* (Cambridge: Cambridge University Press, 1982). See also Susan Reverby and David Rosner, "Beyond the Great Doctors," in *Health Care in America: Essays in Social History*, ed. David Rosner and Susan Reverby (Philadelphia, Pa.: Temple University Press, 1979).

22. McGregor found that experimental treatments were more likely to be used on women of lower status and that Sims was more likely to use anesthetic on upper-class infertility patients than on those undergoing cervical incision and ovariotomies. McGregor, *Midwives to Medicine*, 51.

23. Harris, *Woman's Surgeon*, 164–166; Emmet, *Incidents of My Life*, 166–167; J. Marion Sims, *The Story of My Life* (New York: Appleton, 1884). This occurred in the winter of 1855.

24. McGregor, *Sexual Surgery*, 137; see Marie E. Zakrzewska, *A Woman's Quest: The Life of Marie E. Zakrzewska, M.D.*, ed. Agnes C. Vietor (1924; repr., New York: Arno Press, 1972), 225. An important reassessment of Zakrzewska is Arleen Marcia Tuchman, "'Only in a Republic Can It Be Proved That Science Has No Sex': Marie Elizabeth Zakrzewska (1829–1902) and the Multiple Meanings of Science in the Nineteenth-Century United States," *Journal of Women's History* 11 (Spring 1999): 121–142. On women physicians in the nineteenth century, see Mary Roth Walsh, *"Doctors Wanted, No Women Need Apply": Sexual Barriers in the Medical Profession, 1835–1975* (New Haven, Conn.: Yale University Press, 1977); Regina Morantz-Sanchez, *Sympathy and Science: Women Physicians in American Medicine* (New York: Oxford University Press, 1985); Morantz-Sanchez, *Conduct Unbecoming a Woman*; Ruth J. Abram, *"Send Us A Lady Physician": Women Doctors in America, 1835–1920* (New York: W.W. Norton and Co., 1985); and Mary Putnam Jacobi, "Women in Medicine," in *Woman's Work in America*, ed. Annie Nathan Meyer (New York: Henry Holt and Company, 1891), 139–205. Emily Blackwell's sister Elizabeth Blackwell was no longer able to practice by this time because of poor eyesight.

25. Quoted in McGregor, *Sexual Surgery*, 137. See also Emmet, "Reminiscences of the Founders of the Woman's Hospital," 381–382.

26. Harris, *Woman's Surgeon*, 202–208, 267–268.

27. Ibid., 278–281.

28. Paul Sarnoff, *Russell Sage, the Money King* (New York: Ivan Obolensky, 1965), 128 and note.

29. (London) *Medical Times and Gazette*, February 10, 1866, quoted in McGregor, *Midwives to Medicine*, 156. Recent studies of the cultural meanings of infertility in this period are Margaret Marsh and Wanda Ronner, *The Empty Cradle: Infertility in America from Colonial Times to the Present* (Baltimore, Md.: Johns Hopkins University Press, 1996); Elaine Tyler May, *Barren in the Promised Land: Childless Americans and the Pursuit of Happiness* (1975; repr., Cambridge, Mass.: Harvard University Press, 1995).

30. As usual, Sarnoff takes a snippet of evidence and runs with it: "The Slocum family motto was *Vivit Post Funera Virtus* or 'Virtue Outlives the Grave,'" he wrote. "In the case of the marriage of Olivia Slocum and Russell Sage, one might safely assume that Olivia's virginal virtue also accompanied her to the grave. . . . [H]is employment of his spouse was not for sexual pleasure. It was, in fact, quite the opposite. For Sage used his wife as an escutcheon of honor to hide his nefarious activities—in sex as well as business." Sarnoff, *Russell Sage, the Money King*, 146, 329. Evidence about Victorian marital sexuality is surveyed by John D'Emilio and Estelle Freedman in *Intimate Matters: A History of Sexuality in America* (New York: Harper and Row, 1988), 76–81.

31. M. Olivia Sage (Mrs. Russell Sage), "Opportunities and Responsibili-

ties of Leisured Women," *North American Review* 181 (November 1905): 721. On the Victorian sex reformers, see William Leach, *True Love and Perfect Union: The Feminist Reform of Sex and Society* (New York: Basic Books, 1980); and Hal D. Sears, *The Sex Radicals: Free Love in High Victorian America* (Lawrence: Regents Press of Kansas, 1977). On prudery and its defeat, see Rochelle Gurstein, *The Repeal of Reticence: A History of America's Cultural and Legal Struggles over Free Speech, Obscenity, Sexual Liberation, and Modern Art* (New York: Hill and Wang, 1996).

32. A reviewer in *Saturday Review* of Fanny Kemble's *Journal of a Residence on a Georgia Plantation in 1838–1839* (London: Longman, 1863) complained, "The coolness with which she prints sundry details which few ladies would put on paper . . . is quite inimitable. We never met with such minutiae in print except in the pages of professedly medical publications." Quoted in Diane Roberts, *The Myth of Aunt Jemima: Representations of Race and Region* (New York: Rout-ledge, 1994), 121. On discourses of sexual repression, see Michel Foucault, *The History of Sexuality: An Introduction*, vol. 1 (1978; repr., New York: Vintage Books, 1990). See also Leach, *True Love and Perfect Union*.

33. Morantz-Sanchez, *Conduct Unbecoming a Woman*, 129.

34. Ibid., 117.

35. For example, in 1854 she had described herself as having been "more or less disabled for a month by my throat." MOS to "My dear Father," December 18, 1854. See also January 25, 1854, and May 12, 1854. All in "Letters of Olivia Slocum Sage to Her Father, 1853–1855," EGS.

36. Aunt Almira was Joseph Slocum's unmarried sister, Almira Slocum (1797–1874) of Raymerstown, New York. MOS to Joseph Jermain Slocum, n.d. [1882?], FSW.

37. "Sixteenth Annual Report of the Board of Governors and Board of Lady Supervisors of the Woman's Hospital, State of New York, 1871 (and Pro-ceedings of the Annual Meeting, 1871)," 35; and "Seventeenth Annual Report of the Woman's Hospital [1872]," 46, both in WHP. On fund-raising, see Nancy A. Hewitt, *Women's Activism and Social Change: Rochester, New York, 1822–1872* (Ithaca, N.Y.: Cornell University Press, 1984), 249–251; Ginzberg, *Women and the Work of Benevolence*, 41–42, 46–48, 155; and see Beverly Gor-don, *Bazaars and Fair Ladies: The History of the American Fundraising Fair* (Knoxville: University of Tennessee Press, 1998).

38. See Maureen Montgomery's discussion of calling and calling cards as "access rituals" in *Displaying Women: Spectacles of Leisure in Edith Wharton's New York* (New York: Routledge, 1998), 28–30, 44–45.

39. Erving Goffman and others have written on the hospital as a place for the performance of stylized roles. Goffman, *The Presentation of Self in Everyday Life* (New York: Doubleday Anchor Books, 1959). See also Ruth Crocker, "'Widow's Mite to Widow's Might': The Philanthropy of Margaret Olivia Sage," *American Presbyterians* 74 (Winter 1996): 253–264; Crocker, "Gift, Gender and

Performance in the Career of Mrs. Russell Sage," paper prepared for the Southern American Studies Association session "Performing Gender: Creating and Recovering Women's Identities," Atlanta, Georgia, February 2001.

40. Anne Firor Scott, *Natural Allies: Women's Associations in American History* (Urbana: University of Illinois Press, 1991), 2. The literature on voluntary reform associations is large. Important studies are Barbara J. Berg, *The Remembered Gate: Origins of American Feminism: The Woman and the City, 1800–1860* (New York: Oxford University Press, 1978); Barbara Leslie Epstein, *The Politics of Domesticity: Women, Evangelism, and Temperance in Nineteenth-Century America* (Middletown, Conn.: Wesleyan University Press, 1981); Evelyn Brooks Higginbotham, *Righteous Discontent: The Woman's Movement in the Black Baptist Church, 1880–1920* (Cambridge, Mass.: Harvard University Press, 1993); Dorothy Salem, *To Better Our World: Black Women in Organized Reform, 1890–1920* (Brooklyn, N.Y.: Carlson Publishing, 1990); Kathleen McCarthy, "Parallel Power Structures: Women and the Voluntary Sphere," in McCarthy, *Lady Bountiful Revisited*, 1–31; Anne Meis Knupfer, *Toward a Tenderer Humanity and a Nobler Womanhood: African-American Women's Clubs in Turn-of-the-Century Chicago* (New York: New York University Press, 1996); Cynthia Neverdon-Morton, *Afro-American Women of the South and the Advancement of the Race, 1895–1925* (Knoxville: University of Tennessee Press, 1989); McCarthy, ed., *Lady Bountiful Revisited*; Ginzberg, *Women and the Work of Benevolence*.

Scholarly discussion of women's voluntary associations takes place within a debate about Victorian feminism and women's culture. Scholars such as Karen J. Blair argue that nineteenth-century women's voluntary associations fostered feminism, functioning as political training grounds even when they did not advocate suffrage; *The Clubwoman as Feminist: True Womanhood Redefined, 1868–1914* (New York: Holmes and Meier, 1980). See also Lana Ruegamer, "Female Moral Authority in Nineteenth-Century America: Toward the 'Matriarchal Moment,'" paper presented at the Berkshire Conference on the History of Women, Vassar College, Poughkeepsie, New York, June 12, 1993. Others see claims of benevolence as a cloak for emancipatory projects (Ginzberg, *Women and the Work of Benevolence*) or a movement away from equal rights feminism. Ellen Carol DuBois, "Politics and Culture in Women's History: A Symposium," *Feminist Studies 6* (Spring 1980): 26–64; Ellen Carol DuBois, *Feminism and Suffrage: The Emergence of an Independent Women's Movement in America, 1848–1869* (Ithaca, N.Y.: Cornell University Press, 1978). For recent discussions of a variety of voluntary-sphere work, see Lawrence Friedman and Mark McGarvie, eds., *Charity, Philanthropy and Civility in American History* (New York: Cambridge University Press, 2003).

41. There was also a four-man executive committee of the Board of Governors and a six-member Board of Managers of the Lady Supervisors. I rely here on McGregor, *Midwives to Medicine*, 120, 170–171.

42. Harris, *Woman's Surgeon*, 174.

43. 40. Emmet, "Reminiscences of the Founders of the Woman's Hospi-

tal," 378. Hundreds of bodies had to be removed before construction began; the site may have proved unhealthy for this reason. No reason was ever given for closing the Wetmore. McGregor writes, "Some quietly protested the loss of more than $100,000 in the construction of a now worthless pavilion"; *Midwives to Medicine*, 193–194, 211–212.

44. Emmet, *Incidents of My Life*, 335–336.

45. Linda Kerber, "Separate Spheres, Female Worlds, Woman's Place: The Rhetoric of Women's History," *Journal of American History* 75 (June 1988): 39. An important recent discussion is Mary Ryan, "The Public and the Private Good: Across the Great Divide in Women's History," *Journal of Women's History* 15 (Spring 2003): 10–27.

46. M. Olivia Sage to Hon. E. D. Morgan, May 19, 1882, Edwin D. Morgan Papers, NYSL; emphasis added. Olivia sent greetings to Mrs. Morgan, suggesting a personal connection. Linda Kerber draws attention to the way women and men talked about "spheres" in the late nineteenth century, which she sees as a sign that gender roles were fluid and contested. She writes, "[A]ll the talk about spheres [in nineteenth-century women's writing] is the sound of spheres breaking up"; "Separate Spheres, Female Worlds," 22. Lori Ginzberg suggests that men and women in benevolent associations did identical work and that "spheres talk" served to conceal this fact. Ginzberg, *Women and the Work of Benevolence*, 38.

47. In 1868, the hospital had seventy-five beds. Many more patients were treated as outpatients. McGregor, *Midwives to Medicine*, 80.

48. Rose A. Ourdan to MOS, October 19, 1888; Superintendent to MOS, September 21, 1886, both in RSFR, Box 97, Folder 978. Correspondence shows Sage seeking to admit to a free bed a patient who was needy and deserving. Sage was also informed when patients died, thus freeing space for new admissions.

49. See James T. Patterson, *The Dread Disease: Cancer and Modern American Culture* (Cambridge, Mass.: Harvard University Press, 1987).

50. James Marr Pratt, *Pioneer Surgeons of the Woman's Hospital: The Lives of Sims, Emmet, Peaslee, and Thomas* (Philadelphia, Pa.: F. A. Davis, 1957), 42–43; J. Marion Sims, *The Woman's Hospital in 1874. A Reply to the Printed Circular of Doctors E. R. Peaslee, T. A. Emmet, and T. Gaillard Thomas, Addressed, "To the Medical Profession," May 5th, 1877* (New York: Kent and Co., 1877), 14–16.

51. Vogel, *Invention of the Modern Hospital*; John Harley Warner, *The Therapeutic Perspective: Medical Practice, Knowledge, and Identity in America, 1820–1885* (Cambridge, Mass.: Harvard University Press, 1986); Paul Starr, *The Social Transformation of American Medicine* (New York: Basic Books, 1982).

52. Sage's opposition to the creation of this board is thus deeply contradictory. On gender and professionalization, see Helene Silverberg, ed., *Gender and American Social Science: The Formative Years* (Princeton, N.J.: Princeton University Press, 1998); Morantz-Sanchez, *Sympathy and Science*; Estelle Freedman, "Separatism as Strategy: Female Institution-Building and American Feminism, 1870–1930," *Feminist Studies* 5 (Fall 1979): 512–529.

53. Association, Minutes, 1865, WHP. The costs quoted are for a single room. "Annual Report of the Woman's Hospital [1870]," WHP; McGregor, *Midwives to Medicine*, 198.

54. [Providence Dyeing and Bleaching Company] to MOS, May 3, 1879; [Elise] R. Buell to MOS, January 16, 1880; Mr. L. Vanderbilt to MOS, February 15, 1886. All in RSFR, Box 97, Folder 978.

55. Melavina S. Dodd to MOS, November 11, 1899, RSFR, Box 97, Folder 979.

56. Helen Inslee to MOS, October 8, 1899, RSFR, Box 97, Folder 979; emphasis in the original.

57. Superintendent S. H. LeRoy to MOS, January 6, 1886, RSFR, Box 97, Folder 978.

58. Superintendent S. H. LeRoy to MOS, September 30, 1887, and November 29, 1887. Both in RSFR, Box 97, Folder 978.

59. Superintendent S. H. LeRoy to MOS, January 6, 1886, January 27, 1888, January 30, 1888, February 8, 1888, and March 1, 1888, all in RSFR, Box 97, Folder 978.

60. Register of Cases, Surgeons, WHP, RG 3, Series 12, 1. For Brennan see Emmet, "Reminiscences of the Founders of the Woman's Hospital Association," 374–375.

61. Ross, "Arranging a Doll's House," 97–108; Susan Reverby, *Ordered to Care: The Dilemma of American Nursing, 1850–1945* (New York: Cambridge University Press, 1987); Elizabeth D. Leonard, *Yankee Women: Gender Battles in the Civil War* (New York: Norton, 1994); George M. Fredrickson, *The Inner Civil War: Northern Intellectuals and the Crisis of the Union* (New York: Harper and Row, 1965); Thomas J. Brown, *Dorothea Dix: New England Reformer* (Cambridge, Mass.: Harvard University Press, 1998), 306–308.

62. [Unknown] to MOS, December 3, 1887, RSFR, Box 97, Folder 978; Board of Governors, Minutes of the Woman's Hospital in the State of New York, Minutes of Meeting (handwritten), April 10, 1888, WHP, RG 3, Series 6, Box 137. (Hereafter, Board of Governors, Minutes.) For the development of the nursing profession, see Reverby, *Ordered to Care*; Barbara Melosh, *"The Physician's Hand": Work Culture and Conflict in American Nursing* (Philadelphia, Pa.: Temple University Press, 1982).

63. Frances E. Fowler, Superintendent, to MOS, January 21, 1899, RSFR, Box 97, Folder 979.

64. MOS to Mrs. Jesup, March 12, 1908, RSFR, Box 97, Folder 980.

65. Board of Governors, Minutes, August 17, 1889, WHP; Russell Sage, "The Injustice of Vacations," *Independent* (New York), June 2, 1904.

66. S. H. LeRoy to MOS, March 17, 1888, RSFR, Box 97, Folder 978.

67. Kathleen Waters Sander, *The Business of Charity: The Woman's Exchange Movement, 1832–1900* (Urbana: University of Illinois Press, 1998), 3.

68. Ehrenreich and English set Sims in a historical tradition of misogyny and interpreted the Woman's Hospital's acceptance of poor patients with such

comments as "But it should not be imagined that poor women were spared the gynecologist's exotic catalog of tortures simply because they couldn't pay." Barbara Ehrenreich and Deirdre English, *For Her Own Good: 150 Years of the Experts' Advice to Women* (Garden City, N.Y.: Anchor Press, 1978), 124–125. More recently, historians have retreated to a more nuanced view of the relations between women patients and professional medicine and its practitioners. See L. J. Jordanova, *Sexual Visions: Images of Gender in Science and Medicine between the Eighteenth and Twentieth Centuries* (Madison: University of Wisconsin Press, 1989). Female physicians sometimes advocated the same therapies as their male colleagues, depending on their training and orientation. Regina Morantz-Sanchez writes, "Evidence to support these assumptions about male and female differences [in regard to choice of therapies] is intriguing but inconclusive"; *Sympathy and Science*, 211. See also Regina Markell Morantz and Sue Zschoche, "Professionalism, Feminism, and Gender Roles: A Comparative Study of Nineteenth-Century Medical Therapeutics," *Journal of American History* 67 (December 1980): 568–588; Regina Markell Morantz, "The Perils of Feminist History," *Journal of Interdisciplinary History* 4 (Spring 1974): 649–660; and Morantz's review of J. Barker-Benfield, *Horrors of the Half-Known Life* in *Bulletin of the History of Medicine* 5 (Summer 1977): 307–310; and Irwin H. Kaiser, "Reappraisals of J. Marion Sims," *American Journal of Obstetrics and Gynecology* 132 (December 15, 1978): 878–884.

69. Sims took credit for improving the speculum of the early-nineteenth-century French surgeon Joseph Recamier. Sims, *Story of My Life*, 234; Harris, *Woman's Surgeon*, xviii, 114; Moscucci, *Science of Woman*, 113–117. Debate between medical men about the use of the speculum had "little to do with science, everything to do with morals"; Moscucci, *Science of Woman*, 114.

70. "Register of Cases" [May 1855–January 1862], WHP, Record Group 3, Series 12, Surgeons, no. 230. This case was from November 11, 1861. See Barker-Benfield, *Horrors of the Half-Known Life*; Haller and Haller, *Physician and Sexuality*.

71. McGregor, *Midwives to Medicine*, 186; Moscucci, *Science of Woman*, 141ff.

72. Morantz-Sanchez, *Sympathy and Science*, 184–202.

73. McGregor finds that these operations may in fact have been abortions. If so, they were illegal and thus secret. *Midwives to Medicine*, 140–141, 146–147; Sims quoted on page 201. Regina Morantz-Sanchez finds a similar attitude toward patient consent among late-nineteenth-century doctors of both sexes. Patient consent or its absence was one of the issues in the trial of Dr. Mary Dixon-Jones; Morantz-Sanchez, *Conduct Unbecoming a Woman*.

74. Morantz-Sanchez, *Conduct Unbecoming a Woman*, 105, 107.

75. Ibid.

76. Moscucci, *Science of Woman*, 135.

77. "Woman's Hospital, Third Annual Report," 15–16, cited in McGregor, *Sexual Surgery and the Origins of Gynecology*, 138.

78. Critics accused physicians of "vivisection," or operating on live sub-

jects; of "spaying," since surgery usually led to sterility; of "unsexing" women, since it was believed they took on a masculine appearance after the operation; or simply of being too ready to wield the knife. Moscucci, *Science of Woman,* 157–164. Some of this opposition was clearly conservative complaint against women being rendered sterile, such as the famous remark by Eli Van De Warker—"a woman's ovaries belong to the commonwealth; she is simply their custodian"—or the maternalist concerns expressed by Elizabeth Blackwell. Quoted in Morantz-Sanchez, *Conduct Unbecoming a Woman,* 108ff.

79. Board of Governors, Minutes, May 10, 1887, WHP.

80. Board of Governors, Minutes, April 12, 1886, and May 10, 1887, WHP.

81. Board of Governors, Minutes, July 17, 1887, and August 9, 1887, WHP.

82. The phrase is that of Charles E. Rosenberg; "Florence Nightingale on Contagion: The Hospital as Moral Universe," in *Healing and History: Essays for George Rosen,* ed. Charles E. Rosenberg (New York: Science History Publications, 1979), 116–136. See also James H. Smylie, "The Reformed Tradition," in *Caring and Curing: Health and Medicine in the Western Religious Traditions,* ed. Ronald L. Numbers and Darrel W. Amundsen (New York: Macmillan, 1986), 204–239.

83. For other examples of how nineteenth-century women mystified their work, see Jeanne Attie, "Warwork and the Crisis of Domesticity in the North," in Clinton and Silber, *Divided Houses,* 251.

84. Board of Governors, Minutes, November 10, 1884, and December 8, 1884, WHP. An earlier arrangement had split the responsibility for the salary between the two boards.

85. Board of Governors, Minutes, April 13, 1885, and May 13, 1885, WHP. The Board of Lady Managers appealed to the governors to increase its representation.

86. Board of Governors, Minutes, June 8, 1885, WHP.

87. Sage, "Opportunities and Responsibilities of Leisured Women," 719; Board of Governors, Minutes, June 14, 1886, WHP.

88. The Croton reservoir supplied New York City with water.

89. Board of Governors, Minutes, February 12, 1887, WHP.

90. Emily Johnston was the daughter of railroad president and founder of the Metropolitan Museum of Art, John Taylor Johnston. She married Robert W. de Forest in 1872. James A. Hijiya, "Four Ways of Looking at a Philanthropist: A Study of Robert Weeks De Forest," *Proceedings of the American Philosophical Society* 124 (December 1980): 404.

91. MOS, "Address to the Board of Governors, Woman's Hospital in the State of New York," handwritten, in Minutes of a Conference at the Woman's Hospital, January 6, 1888, RSFR, Box 97, Folder 978.

92. Board of Governors, Minutes, May 8, 1888, WHP; "Act of Incorporation of the Woman's Hospital in the State of New York, passed April 18, 1857, amended April 7, 1858, May 27, 1885, and April 18, 1888," in "Annual Reports of the Woman's Hospital in the State of New York, 1888–1894," WHP.

93. MOS, typed draft of a speech to the Board of Governors, the Woman's Hospital, December 1, 1892, RSFR, Box 97, Folder 982.

The Ladies Assistant Board thus differed both from women's associations that were auxiliaries to societies organized by husbands or male relatives, such as mission boards, and from the separatist, women-only organizations associated with a lively politicized postbellum "women's culture" exemplified by women's colleges, settlements, temperance organizations, women's exchanges, and so on. A now-classic essay describing a theoretical framework for considering separatist organizations is Freedman, "Separatism as Strategy." On missions, a neglected area, see Boyd and Brackenridge, *Presbyterian Women in America.* The women's boards were so successful in collecting money that they were later taken over and merged back into the denominational boards in 1920. Ginzberg, *Women and the Work of Benevolence*, suggests some useful ways of categorizing these associations, as does Scott, "Women's Voluntary Associations."

94. Kerber, "Separate Spheres, Female Worlds," 28.

95. M. Olivia Sage, Chairman Ladies Assistant Board, typed draft of a speech, November 22, 1894, RSFR, Box 97, Folder 982.

96. Mary Putnam Jacobi quotes Sims's account of the reasons for this decision. See Jacobi, "Woman in Medicine," in *Woman's Work in America*, ed. Annie Nathan Meyer (New York: Henry Holt and Company, 1891), 154–155.

Morantz-Sanchez discussed the differences between Jacobi and Elizabeth Blackwell as differences around the meanings of medicine and science. She argues that for Blackwell, medicine was moral renewal as well as cure of disease. Jacobi opposed women's separatism and embraced new bacteriological explanations of disease, while Blackwell and others continued to approach medicine more holistically. Morantz-Sanchez, *Sympathy and Science*, 184–202. Recent scholarship offers a more nuanced analytical framework to replace these dichotomous categories. See Tuchman, "'Only in a Republic,'" 121–142.

97. Morantz-Sanchez, *Conduct Unbecoming a Woman*, 117.

98. Quoted in ibid., 121–122.

99. Emmet, *Incidents of My Life*, 335–336.

100. The books are stamped "Presented by Mrs. Russell Sage, 1879." "Reports of the Woman's Hospital of the State of New York, 1856–1869," WHP. The dedication is in Olivia Sage's handwriting and reads "The Board of Lady Supervisors Present with their Compliments these 2 Volumes of Annual Reports to the Board of Governors, Women's Hospital in the State of New York, 49th Street and 4th Avenue, March 1888." The presentation is recorded later in Board of Governors, Minutes, May 12, 1884, WHP.

101. MOS, speech to the board of governors, Woman's Hospital (typescript), December 1, 1892, RSFR, Box 97, Folder 982.

102. MOS, draft of a speech to the Board of Trustees[?], Woman's Hospital (typescript), November 23, 1893, RSFR, Box 97, Folder 982.

103. MOS, draft report to the Ladies Assistant Board, New-York Woman's

Hospital, January 6, 1888, RSFR, Box 97, Folder 978; MOS, draft of a speech (typed), December 1, 1892 and MOS drafts of speeches (typed), November 22, 1894, and December 2, 1897, all in RSFR, Box 97, Folder 982.

104. Compare Lori Ginzberg's remark that benevolent women "remained loyal to the rhetoric of female benevolence" while at the same time they pursued the remedy of repressive legislation; *Women and the Work of Benevolence*, 210. For the development of the medical profession and health field in this period, see Starr, *Social Transformation of American Medicine*.

105. MOS, draft of a speech (typed), November 21, 1901, RSFR, Box 97, Folder 982. Carroll Smith-Rosenberg discusses these generational transitions in her essay "The New Woman as Androgyne," in Smith-Rosenberg, *Disorderly Conduct: Visions of Gender in Victorian America* (New York: Knopf, 1985), 245–296; see also Theriot, *Mothers and Daughters in Nineteenth-Century America*.

106. "Address of Mrs. Russell Sage," in "Annual Report of the Woman's Hospital [1901]," 22–23, WHP. Sage may have had in mind her own "daughter," Helen Miller Gould, whose mother, also named Helen, had been a lady manager.

107. M. Olivia Sage, Chairman Ladies Assistant Board, draft of a speech (typed), November 22, 1894, RSFR, Box 97, Folder 982.

108. The ledger book containing subscriptions to the building fund is in RSFR, Box 97, Folder 983.

109. Woman's Hospital Ladies Assistant Board, "Annual Report," in "Annual Report of the Woman's Hospital [1899]," WHP.

110. Alice Northrop Snow with Henry Nicholas Snow, *The Story of Helen Gould, Daughter of Jay Gould, Great American* (New York: Fleming H. Revell Company, 1943), 241. But compare with her comment to Mrs. Jesup, fellow lady manager, in 1908, "You are wrong in thinking the Hospital was my 'child.'" MOS to Mrs. Jesup, March 12, 1908, RSFR, Box 97, Folder 980.

111. A payment of $50,000 is noted from Russell Sage in 1899 toward the building fund, Woman's Hospital Ledger Book, RSFR, Box 97, Folder 983.

112. "Annual Report of the Woman's Hospital [1899]," 39, WHP.

113. Mrs. Russell Sage quoted in "Woman's Hospital Plans," newspaper clipping, n.d. [1900], RSFR, Series 10, Box 97, Folder 979.

114. John E. Parsons, "Address to the Woman's Hospital," in "Annual Report of the Woman's Hospital [1897]," 18, WHP.

115. MOS to Mrs. Jesup, March 12, 1908, RSFR, Box 97, Folder 980.

116. The collection of photographs is inscribed "A gift of Mrs. Russell Sage."

117. I thank an anonymous reader for the press for bringing the issue of "fragility and limits" to my attention.

118. "If feminism is to be different, it must acknowledge the ideological and problematic significance of its own past," say Kumkum Sangari and Suresh Vaid in "Recasting Women: An Introduction," in *Recasting Women: Essays in Colonial History* (New Brunswick, N.J.: Rutgers University Press, 1990), quoted

by Nancy Hewitt in Nancy Cott, Gerda Lerner, Kathryn Kish Sklar, Ellen DuBois, and Nancy Hewitt, "Considering the State of U.S. Women's History," *Journal of Women's History* 15 (Spring 2003): 154. McGregor, *Midwives to Medicine*, 67; Louise Michele Newman, *White Women's Rights: The Racial Origins of Feminism in the United States* (New York: Oxford University Press, 1999); Vicki L. Ruiz and Ellen Carol DuBois, eds., *Unequal Sisters: A Multicultural Reader in U.S. Women's History*, 2nd ed. (New York: Routledge, 1994); Nancy A. Hewitt, "Beyond the Search for Sisterhood: American Women's History in the 1980s," *Social History* 10 (October 1985): 299–321.

7. "Some aggressive work"

1. *Third Annual Report of the Emma Willard Association, Chicago Reunion, 1893* (Brooklyn, N.Y.: Press of the Brooklyn Eagle, 1893), 6.

2. Correspondence between Olivia Sage, as president of the Emma Willard Association, and Troy alumnae, many of them retired teachers, leads me to characterize association members as middle class. Much of this correspondence was generated by the alumnae survey of the 1890s. Other letters from the turn of the century and after 1906 can be described as begging letters to Sage. As I describe elsewhere, her secretary, E. Lilian Todd, collected them from her New York home and sent them to the Emma Willard School.

3. Patricia Meyer Spacks, "Selves in Hiding," in *Women's Autobiography: Essays in Criticism*, ed. Estelle C. Jelineck (Bloomington: Indiana University Press, 1980), 112–132.

Voluntary associations proliferated in the years after the Civil War, their goals varying from sociability to civic improvement and reform. Women's separatist organizations provided an arena where unenfranchised middle- and upper-class women could tackle a range of public issues. Some, such as the Women's Municipal League, became directly involved in electoral politics; others, such as the many nativist and patriotic associations, served the educational and cultural needs of members. Kathryn Kish Sklar writes, "Postwar organizations offered their members a constantly expanding range of issues and efforts that filled the civil landscape between the economy and the state"; *Florence Kelley and the Nation's Work: The Rise of Women's Political Culture, 1830–1900* (New Haven, Conn.: Yale University Press, 1995), 73. See also Anne Firor Scott, *Natural Allies: Women's Associations in American History* (Urbana: University of Illinois Press, 1991); and Scott, "Women's Voluntary Associations: From Charity to Reform" and in Nancy A. Hewitt, "Charity or Mutual Aid? Two Perspectives on Latin Women's Philanthropy in Tampa, Florida," both in *Lady Bountiful Revisited: Women, Philanthropy, and Power*, ed. Kathleen D. McCarthy (New Brunswick, N.J.: Rutgers University Press, 1990).

4. The best work to explore this theme is Lori Ginzberg, *Women and the Work of Benevolence: Morality, Politics, and Class in the Nineteenth-Century United States* (New Haven, Conn.: Yale University Press, 1990).

5. Barbara Miller Solomon, *In the Company of Educated Women* (New Haven, Conn.: Yale University Press, 1985), 63, citing Mabel Newcomer, *A Century of Higher Education for American Women* (New York: Harper, 1959), 46.

6. Quoted in Kathleen McCarthy, *Women's Culture: American Philanthropy and Art, 1830–1930* (Chicago: University of Chicago Press, 1991), 61. The exchange charged 10 percent commission on each sale. Scholars disagree in their assessments of this hybrid organization which was part charity, part entrepreneurship. A recent study sees in the exchange movement an example of how nineteenth-century women made resourceful use of the voluntary sphere to obtain employment and run quasi-businesses. Kathleen Waters Sander, *The Business of Charity: The Woman's Exchange Movement, 1832–1900* (Urbana: University of Illinois Press, 1998). McCarthy is more critical in *Women's Culture*, 62–63. See also *Facts concerning the New York Exchange for Woman's Work* (New York: 1898).

7. The rhetoric of "self-support" became widespread among advocates of women's rights in this period. It was adopted by wives as well as working women, including wealthy women such as Harriot Stanton Blatch. For Blatch's founding of the Equality League of Self-Supporting Women in January 1907, see Ellen Carol DuBois, *Harriot Stanton Blatch and the Winning of Woman Suffrage* (New Haven, Conn.: Yale University Press, 1997), 94, 116.

8. Several of the association's printed reports in the New York Public Library bear her *ex libris* ("Mrs. Russell Sage") stamped on them.

9. *New York Exchange for Woman's Work, Annual Report, 1887* (New York: 1887), 24.

10. *New York Exchange for Woman's Work, Report for 1895* (New York: 1895), 7.

11. Olivia's preferred reading is summarized in Irvin G. Wyllie, "Margaret Olivia Sage," *NAW*, 3:222–223. "The educated poor" is in *Facts concerning the New York Exchange for Woman's Work*, 4.

12. *Facts concerning the New York Exchange for Woman's Work*, 8. On male failure in nineteenth-century America, see Scott Sandage, "Deadbeats, Drunkards, and Dreamers: A Cultural History of Failure in America, 1819–1893" (Ph.D. diss., Rutgers University, 1995).

13. *Facts concerning the New York Exchange for Woman's Work*, 13; emphasis in the original.

14. "Russell Sage—A Man of Dollars: The Story of a Life Devoted Solely to the Chill Satisfaction of Making Money for Its Own Sake," *The World's Work* 10 (May 1905): 6031; William S. McFeely, *Grant: A Biography* (New York: Norton, 1981), 488–494.

15. "Reading Some Epitaphs," *New York Times*, July 2, 1887, 5.

16. Denison, "Russell Sage—A Man of Dollars," 6298–6301. Cultural historian Brad Evans describes the use of "types" in magazines at this time. Brad Evans, "Cushing's Zuni Sketchbooks: Literature, Anthropology, and American Notions of Culture," *American Quarterly* 49 (December 1997): 719.

17. "A Bashful Millionaire," *Brooklyn Eagle*, January 17, 1897, 6.

18. "Miss Mattern Dips into Speculation," *New York Times*, March 13, 1887, 3; "Russell Sage's Customer," February 27, 1887, 7, NYSM. Hope Cotton writes, "Gambling women appear as all that is hated and despised, as unnatural mothers, antitheses of virtue, and the causes of men's financial undoing"; "Women and Risk: The Gambling Woman in Eighteenth-Century England" (Ph.D. diss., Auburn University, April 1998), 160. See also T. J. Jackson Lears, *Something for Nothing: Luck in America* (New York: Viking Press, 2002).

19. "Sage Green Appropriate; So Miss Mattern Wears It as Her Legal Garb," *New York Times*, April 10, 1887, 3.

20. "His Motive Known At Last," *New York Times*, April 24, 1887, 3. See also "Was Mr. Sage Mistaken?" *New York Times*, May 1, 1887; "Miss Mattern In Tears," *New York Times*, May 4, 1887, 8; "Miss Mattern's Suit," *New York Times*, May 6, 1887, 2; "Going into Definitions," *New York Times*, May 12, 1887, 8; "Russell Sage's Victory," *New York Times*, June 5, 1887; "Russell Sage's Visitor," *New York Times*, June 9, 1887, 1.

21. Sage countered the suit by stating that he had never owned the property in question. Sarnoff, *Russell Sage, the Money King*, 288–289, 315.

22. "I have in mind the sort of boy that can succeed, and I say to all boys now, there is fame and fortune for them if they are made of the right sort of stuff." Russell Sage, "The Boy That Is Wanted," *Ladies' Home Journal* (November 1891): 8.

23. "Tammany Men at the Seaside: Their Handsome Cottages at Far Rockaway," *New York Times*, July 23, 1893, 1. On the decline of Saratoga and the rise of Newport, see Eric Homberger, *Mrs. Astor's New York: Money and Social Power in a Gilded Age* (New Haven, Conn.: Yale University Press, 2002), 164–172; and Ward McAllister, *Society As I Have Found It* (New York: Cassell Publishing Company, 1890), 335.

24. Cedar Croft is described in "A Talk with Mrs. Russell Sage," *New York Times Illustrated Magazine* (September 26, 1897): 2–3.

25. Elizabeth Cady Stanton, *Eighty Years and More: Reminiscences, 1815–1897* (New York: Schocken, 1971), 450. This visit was in 1892. Cedar Croft was valued in 1918 at a modest $41,700.

26. "A Talk with Mrs. Russell Sage." Caroline Borden to MOS, August 15, 1909, RSFR, Box 66, Folder 590, mentions Olivia's habit of watching the passing ships. In this case, the ship was to carry a Dr. Mary Mills Patrick to the American College for Girls, Constantinople, a college sustained by the donations of Olivia and several wealthy friends.

27. MOS to Nettie McCormick, February 19, 1892, Nettie Fowler McCormick Correspondence, Series 2B, Box 54, WHSA. This nephew, the son of his older brother Henry, had boarded with Russell Sage in Troy while a student at Rensselaer Polytechnic Institute, then worked as a civil engineer on the Milwaukee Railroad, where "under the guidance of his uncle, the young man made his fortune." Sarnoff, *Russell Sage, the Money King*, 271, 279–280.

Russell Sage adopted him after the death of his father. *Troy Directory for the Year Beginning July 1, 1858* (Troy, N.Y.: Adams Company, 1858); *Troy Directory for the Year Beginning July 1, 1859* (Troy, N.Y.: William H. Young, 1859); Marjorie Semerad, "I Decided That Mr. Russell Sage Deserved Another Look," in *Sage Stories: Essays on the Third Quarter Century, 1966–1991*, ed. Coleen Paratore (Troy, N.Y.: The Sage Colleges, 1991), 161–162. See also "Russell Sage, Jr., Very Ill; The Millionaire's Heir Sees Bomb Throwers Everywhere," *New York Times*, December 17, 1891, 1; "Russell Sage, Jr., Dying," *New York Times*, February 2, 1892, 1. He died on February 2, 1892.

28. Of Jay Gould's will, his biographer points out, "not a dime went to anyone outside the family, nothing for servants or charities or public institutions." Maury Klein, *The Life and Legend of Jay Gould* (Baltimore, Md.: Johns Hopkins University Press, 1986), 485. See also Maury Klein, "In Search of Jay Gould," *Business History Review* 52 (Summer 1978): 166–199.

29. Charles Elihu Slocum, *A Short History of the Slocums, Slocumbs and Slocombs of America, Genealogical and Biographical* (Syracuse, N.Y.: Published by the author, 1882), 346; "Col. J. J. Slocum Dies at 91 Years," *New York Times*, October 3, 1924, 21. "Daily contact" documented in Johnston de Forest to Joseph Jermain Slocum, January 18, 1909, EWS.

30. "Mr. Sage in Wall Street: Some of the Characteristics Which Have Made Him Prominent," *New York Times*, December 5, 1891, 2, quotes Sage's doctor as describing him as "not dangerously hurt." See also Sarnoff, *Russell Sage, the Money King*, 272–277; Whittemore, *History of the Sage and Slocum Families of England and America*, 24.

31. Sarnoff, *Russell Sage, the Money King*, 290–302. See also Jane Remsen, "Russell Sage, Yankee," *New England Quarterly* 11, no. 1 (March 1938): 22–25.

32. "Russell Sage Made Love: That, At Least Is the Complaint of Delia Keegan," *New York Times*, July 19, 1893, 2; "Mr. Sage Wants Time to Answer," *New York Times*, July 25, 1893, 1.

33. "The winter has been very trying to all semi-invalids, to which class I believe we both belong"; Harriette Dillaye to MOS, April 5, 1893, 2, EWS.

34. MOS to Nettie McCormick, September 18, 1893, Nettie Fowler McCormick Correspondence, Series 2B, Box 57, WHSA. Charles O. Burgess, "Nettie Fowler McCormick," *NAW*, 2:454–255. Gilbert A. Harrison, *A Timeless Affair: The Life of Anita McCormick Blaine* (Chicago: University of Chicago Press, 1979), though focusing on Nettie's daughter, contains much useful material.

35. Harold Parker, "Russell Sage," *Muncy's Magazine* 12 (1895): 636.

36. Frederic Cople Jaher, "Style and Status: High Society in Late-Nineteenth-Century New York," in *The Rich, The Well-Born, and the Powerful: Elites and Upper Classes in History*, ed. Jaher (Urbana: University of Illinois Press, 1973), 258–284; Eric Homberger, *Mrs. Astor's New York: Money and Social Power in a Gilded Age* (New Haven, Conn.: Yale University Press, 2002); Ward McAllister, *Society As I Have Found It* (New York: Cassell Publishing Company, 1890); Wallace Evan Davies, "Caroline Webster Schermerhorn Astor," *NAW*, 1:62–64; "The Week's

Social Event; Mrs. Astor Entertains Her Hosts of Friends," *New York Times*, February 2, 1892; "The Only Four Hundred: Ward McAllister Gives Out the Official List," *New York Times*, February 16, 1892, 5; "Secrets of Ball-Giving: A Chat with Ward McAllister," *New York Daily Tribune*, March 25, 1888, 11. "Tammany Men at the Seaside: Their Handsome Cottages at Far Rockaway," *New York Times*, July 23, 1893, 1; "A Talk with Mrs. Russell Sage," *New York Times Illustrated Magazine* (September 26, 1897): 2–3.

37. The idea originated with Mrs. Florence Montgomery Taylor of Canton, Illinois, and Mrs. Leon Harvier of New York City; *The Emma Willard Association of Troy Female Seminary, Report of its Organization and First Reunion*, October 15, 1891 (New York, 1892), 1–2. But a one-page printed flyer, now at the Emma Willard School, records a different origin. "The movement to revive the memory of Mrs. Emma Willard began in the 1890s, when some ladies in Troy, N.Y. started the project of erecting the statue of Mrs. Willard, which has since been set up in the Seminary grounds"; "Alumnae and Pupils of Troy Female Seminary," n.d., Emma Willard Association Papers, EWS. See also "Preface," *EWP*, 3.

38. MOS to Nettie McCormick, November 9, 1891, Nettie Fowler McCormick Correspondence, Series 2B, Box 51, WHSA. See also Lynn Gordon, *Gender and Higher Education in the Progressive Era* (New Haven, Conn.: Yale University Press, 1990), 90.

39. On maternalism, see Seth Koven, "Borderlands: Women, Voluntary Action, and Child Welfare," and Sonya Michel, "The Limits of Maternalism: Policies Toward American Wage-Earning Mothers during the Progressive Era," both in *Mothers of A New World: Maternalist Politics and the Origins of Welfare States*, ed. Seth Koven and Sonya Michel (New York: Routledge, 1993), 43–93, 277–320. Useful review essays are Lisa Brush, "Love, Toil, and Trouble: Motherhood and Feminist Politics," *Signs* 21, no. 2 (1996): 429–454; and Felicia Kornbluh, "Review Essay: The New Literature on Gender and the Welfare State: The U.S. Case," *Feminist Studies* 22, no. 1 (1996): 171–197. See also Theda Skocpol, *Protecting Soldiers and Mothers: The Political Origins of Social Policy in the United States* (Cambridge, Mass.: Belknap Press of Harvard University Press, 1992). "Educated women" rhetoric deserves to be explored further.

40. Harriette Dillaye, "Personal Reminiscences of Mrs. Emma Willard," in *Emma Willard Association of Troy Female Seminary*, 16–17; Anne Firor Scott, "The Ever-Widening Circle: The Diffusion of Feminist Values from the Troy Female Seminary, 1822–1872," *History of Education Quarterly* 19 (Spring 1979): 67.

41. "Opposed suffrage" documented in John Lord, *The Life of Emma Willard* (New York: D. Appleton and Company, 1873), 41; Frederick Rudolph, "Emma Hart Willard," *NAW*, 3:610–613. Of Nightingale's position, "it hardly mattered," Mary Poovey writes. "Because her image displaced her own antifeminist sentiments, the name of Florence Nightingale could be enlisted in the feminist cause the woman herself refused to support"; *Uneven Developments: The Ideological Work of Gender in Mid-Victorian England* (Chicago: University of Chicago Press, 1988), 198.

42. Olivia wrote telling Nettie McCormick that she had received a letter from Miss Dillaye "full of valuable suggestions as to scholarships." MOS to Nettie McCormick, February 19, 1892, Nettie Fowler McCormick Correspondence, Series 2B, Box 54, WHSA. Dillaye occupied an honorific position of retired eminence at Ogontz School, Philadelphia, rather like that held by Emma Willard after her own retirement in 1844.

43. Emphasis in the original. Dillaye wrote, "What cream is to milk, what wine is to the grape, what oil is to essence, such is Fellowship to Scholarship," Dillaye to MOS, November 15, 1892; see also Dillaye to MOS, March 9, 1893, both in Margaret Olivia Slocum Sage Collection, EWS. For Emma Willard at Middlebury, see Frederick Rudolph, "Emma Hart Willard," *NAW*, 3:610–613.

44. MOS to Nettie McCormick, October 31, 1895, Nettie Fowler McCormick Correspondence, Series 2B, Box 66, WHSA. Olivia signed off, "I remain with grateful and loving thoughts most sincerely yours, M. Olivia Sage." For "strapped for cash," see "Mrs. Russell Sage on Marriage," *Syracuse Sunday Herald,* June 21, 1903, 29, clipping, "Margaret Olivia Sage," OnHA. "Donated to both funds" is in *Emma Willard Association of Troy Female Seminary,* 12.

45. *Third Annual Report of the Emma Willard Association,* 4.

46. Major studies of the fair are James Gilbert, *Perfect Cities: Chicago's Utopias of 1893* (Chicago: University of Chicago Press, 1991); Robert Muccigrosso, *Celebrating the New World: Chicago's Columbian Exposition of 1893* (Chicago: Ivan R. Dee, 1993); John E. Findling, *Chicago's Great World's Fairs* (New York: St. Martin's Press, 1994); Major Ben C. Truman, *History of the World's Fair* (Philadelphia, Pa.: Mammoth Publishing Co., 1893).

47. Bertha (Mrs. Potter) Palmer to MOS, April 22, 1892, Margaret Olivia Slocum Sage Collection, EWS. Planning of the New York State's Women's Exhibit can be traced in *Minutes of the Board of Women Managers of the State of New York at the World's Columbian Exposition, Held in the Assembly Room Parlors, Capitol, Albany, New York Albany, N.Y.: June 7, 1892–May 22, 1894* (n.p., n.d.); McCarthy, *Women's Culture,* 102–104. The Woman's Pavilion is the subject of Jeanne Madeline Weimann, *The Fair Women* (Chicago: Academy Press, 1981); and Johanna Hays, "The Workings of the Spheres: The Failure of the Woman's Building of the World's Columbian Exposition, 1893," seminar paper, Department of History, Auburn University, 2003. See also Scott, *Natural Allies,* 128–134.

48. MOS to Nettie McCormick, February 19, 1892, Nettie Fowler McCormick Correspondence, Series 2B, Box 54, WHSA.

49. *Third Annual Report of the Emma Willard Association,* 11. This complaint may have been justified: a cursory look through the thousands of items listed in David J. Bertuca, comp., *The World's Columbian Exposition: A Centennial Bibliographic Guide* (Westport, Conn.: Greenwood Press, 1996) turned up no reference to an Emma Willard exhibit.

50. Kate Brannon Knight, *History of the Work of Connecticut Women at the World's Columbian Exposition, Chicago, 1893* (Hartford, Conn.: Hartford Press,

1891), 11, 32–33. For a positive assessment of the fair by a member of the Board of Women Managers of the State of New York for the Columbian Exposition, see "Mrs. Stranahan's Address," in *Third Annual Report of the Emma Willard Association*, 89–92. A useful discussion of women's presence at the Fair is Gail Bederman, *Manliness and Civilization: A Cultural History of Gender and Race in the United States, 1880–1917* (Chicago: University of Chicago Press, 1995), 31–41.

51. *Third Annual Report of the Emma Willard Association*, 25, 12.

52. Alice Northrop Snow, with Henry Nicholas Snow, *The Story of Helen Gould, Daughter of Jay Gould, Great American* (New York: Fleming H. Revell Company, 1943); Klein, *Life and Legend of Jay Gould*, 134, 212–214. Hereafter all references to Helen Gould in the text are to Jay Gould's daughter, not his wife.

53. Mary S. Eddy to MOS, July 12, 1893, EWS. The rolling chairs incident is in Snow and Snow, *The Story of Helen Gould, Daughter of Jay Gould*, 223–225. A photograph of visitors enjoying the rolling chairs is in the delightful volume by Neil Harris, Wim de Wit, James Gilbert, and Robert N. Rydell, *Grand Illusions: Chicago's World's Fair of 1893* (Chicago: Chicago Historical Society, 1993), 130. On the midway, see Robert Rydell, *All The World's a Fair: Visions of Empire at American International Expositions, 1876–1916* (Chicago: University of Chicago Press, 1984), 38–71; John Kasson, *Amusing the Million: Coney Island* (New York: Hill and Wang, 1978), 17–28.

The fair's managers had seen to it that African Americans could not establish a public presence there. In the pamphlet *The Reason Why the Colored American Is Not in the World's Columbian Exposition* (Chicago, 1893), Ida B. Wells called it "literally and figuratively a White City," symbolizing "not the material progress of America, but a moral regression—the reconciliation of the North and South at the expense of Negroes." Wells quoted in Hazel Carby, *Reconstructing Womanhood*, 5.

54. Quoted in *Third Annual Report of the Emma Willard Association*, 66.

55. Ibid., 13–16.

56. MOS to Nettie McCormick, September 19, 1893, Nettie Fowler McCormick Correspondence, Series 2B, Box 57, WHSA.

57. Programs are in the Margaret Olivia Slocum Sage Collection at EWS. The tenth and eleventh meetings (1900 and 1901) were held at Sherry's, the fashionable restaurant. The mangled spelling of "tournado" indicates a word (perhaps also a dish) in transition from the French "tourne-dos" (upside-down) to the American "tornado."

58. "Mrs. Emma Willard's Life and Work in Middlebury," reprinted in George Gary Bush, *History of Education in Vermont* (Washington, D.C.: Government Printing Office, 1900), 130–137, EWS; see also "Announcement of Meeting of the Emma Willard Association, February 13, 1895," EWS.

59. As I show in Chapter 12, disagreement existed about what educational setting was best for women, whether coeducational such as Cornell or Chicago, single-sex such as Wellesley, or coordinate such as Barnard.

60. "The Emma Willard Educational Society," letter to the editor by Mary A. Bennett, *Woman's Journal*, n.d., clipping enclosed by MOS in her letter to McCormick, September 19, 1893. Sage complained that the coverage in the *Journal* was "another of Mrs. Taylor's schemes." MOS to Nettie McCormick, September 19, 1893, Nettie Fowler McCormick Correspondence, Series 2B, Box 54, WHSA. The Emma Willard Association was as much about exclusion of others as about education, as correspondence from the more middle-class Woman's Exchange shows. In 1899, Mary Choate appealed to the association on behalf of the exchange (Olivia was vice president) as its funding was low. Choate suggested that the association might like to rent a room from them, using language in which class resentment was palpable:

> Do you not think it would be rather a nice thing for so respectable
> an association as the Emma Willard Association to help on a band
> of struggling sisters by renting a room of theirs at $45 a month?

The Emma Willard Association subsequently did rent a room from the New York Exchange. "To the Members of the Emma Willard Association," printed notice of annual meeting of the Emma Willard Association, to be held at the New York Exchange for Women's Work, Nov. 9, 1899, signed by Mrs. Russell Sage, president, Emma Willard Association Papers, EWS.

61. "Emma Willard Banquet: Kind Words for the Preceptress of the Famous School," *New York Daily Tribune*, November 11, 1898, 5.

62. Ibid., 19, 22. Nina Baym, "Women and the Republic: Emma Willard's Rhetoric of History," *American Quarterly* 43 (March 1991): 1–23.

63. Historian Bonnie G. Smith has noted, "Fashion served as the most insistent and increasingly popular way of drawing attention to a woman's presence and of speaking about that presence"; *Ladies of the Leisure Class: The Bourgeoises of Northern France in the Nineteenth Century* (Princeton, N.J.: Princeton University Press, 1981), 78.

64. The preface states, "the work of collecting the data was begun under the direction of a committee of which Miss Mary A. Hastings was chairman, and Mrs. Henry L. Palmer, gen. sec., with Mrs. M. M. Fairbanks '45 as editor," *EWP*.

65. When Mrs. Fairbanks died, a Mrs. Lord took over the task of compiling the biographies and organizing the work of publication. The second printing paid belated tribute to Mrs. Fairbanks by listing her as editor on the title page; on the first printing she had been omitted. See "Mary J. Mason [Fairbanks]," *EWP*, 352–354.

66. Mary Jane Fairbanks to MOS, February 27, 189_, Emma Willard Association Papers, EWS. Mrs. Fairbanks's letters to Olivia Sage show the inequality of their positions. In one self-effacing letter, she addressed her patron: "Your duties seem to so over-lap each other that I wonder how you keep pace with them. As I read your name in my *New York Journal*, among the gatherings here, there, and everywhere, I envy your ability, or rather" (she hastily corrected her-

self) "to put it more magnanimously, I congratulate you on your zeal and activity and myself on my interest in what you are doing." She was upset when Olivia did not receive her during a visit to New York: "I feel I cannot return to Providence happy or satisfied without having had my hoped for conference with you." Mary J. Fairbanks to MOS, n.d., Emma Willard Association Papers, EWS.

67. Alice Bryant to Miss E. L. Todd, July 5, 1917, Emma Willard Association Papers, EWS.

68. *Emma Willard Association of Troy Female Seminary*, 12.

69. Mary Jane Fairbanks to MOS, February 4, 1897. Fairbanks ended her letter, "Hopefully and affectionately yours."

70. "Maria Winne," *EWP*, 256.

71. *Harper's Bazaar* (April 29, 1899); "Some New Books," clipping, "Mrs. Sage's Scrapbook, 1891–1897," Margaret Olivia Slocum Sage Collection, EWS.

72. *EWP*, 814. Olivia and Nettie corresponded after the McCormicks moved from New York to Chicago. See also Harrison, *A Timeless Affair*.

73. "Prospectus (for a condensed history of Troy Female Seminary as exemplified in the life of its founder, and in those of its pupils from 1822 to 1872)," Emma Willard Association Papers, EWS.

74. He informed Sage that the estimated cost of printing would be $2,600 for twelve plates and 500 copies of the text. Fairbanks to Russell Sage, June 23, 1896, EWS.

75. ECS to MOS, *Papers of Elizabeth Cady Stanton and Susan B. Anthony*, Reel 39, 709–715. She added, "Perhaps it would be well to wait until you get the edition with all blunders corrected."

76. "Emma Willard Banquet," *New York Daily Tribune*, November 11, 1898, 5.

77. "Wrote themselves into the nation's history" in Gerda Lerner, *The Creation of Feminist Consciousness: From the Middle Ages to 1870* (New York: Oxford University Press, 1993), 115. On memory and history, see Michael Kammen, *Mystic Chords of Memory: The Transformation of Tradition in American Culture* (New York: Alfred A. Knopf, 1991), 93–100. See also Benedict Anderson, *Imagined Communities: Reflections on the Origin and Spread of Nationalism*, rev. ed. (London: Verso Press, 1991); John Bodnar, *Remaking America: Public Memory, Commemoration and Patriotism in the Twentieth Century* (Princeton, N.J.: Princeton University Press, 1992); Genevieve Fabvre and Robert O'Meally, eds., *History and Memory in African-American Culture* (New York: Oxford University Press, 1994). "NAWSA leaders presented to their constituents a sanitized version of the past that robbed the pioneers of much of their color, complexity, and principles," comments Sara Hunter Graham. See "The Suffrage Renaissance: A New Image for a New Century, 1896–1910," in *One Woman, One Vote: Rediscovering the Woman Suffrage Movement*, ed. Marjorie Spruill Wheeler (Troutdale, Ore: New Sage Press, 1995), 169.

78. *Third Annual Report of the Emma Willard Association*, 26.

79. "Emma Willard Association: Its Members 'Count Their Mercies' and Listen to a Paper on the Pilgrim Fathers," unidentified clipping, Emma Willard Association Papers, EWS.

80. Quoted in Theodore Stanton and Harriot Stanton Blatch, eds., *Elizabeth Cady Stanton as Revealed in Her Letters, Diary and Reminiscences* (New York: Harper and Brothers, 1922), 2:301; Lillie Devereux Blake, "Our Forgotten Foremothers," in *The Congress of Women Held in the Woman's Building, World's Columbian Exposition, Chicago, U.S.A., 1893*, ed. Mary Kavanaugh Oldham Eagle (Chicago: American Publishing House, 1893), 32–35.

81. Mark W. Summers, *The Gilded Age: Or, The Hazard of New Functions* (Upper Saddle River, N.J.: Prentice Hall, 1997), 54; Graham, "The Suffrage Renaissance," 166.

82. Emma Willard School, Board of Trustees Minutes, 1886–87, William F. Gurley Papers, EWS. John and Sarah Willard, the founder's son and daughter-in-law, ran the school until 1872, when businessman William Gurley raised $52,000 to buy it for the city of Troy. Emily Wilcox, a great-niece of Emma Willard, was principal from 1872 to 1895. Gurley died in 1887. "History of Troy Female Seminary, from 1872 to 1895," *EWP*, 815–816.

83. William F. Gurley Papers, EWS. "A Noble Gift," *Troy Times Supplement* [1891] and "The Corner Stone Laid," *Troy Daily Press*, June 5, 1891, both clippings in EWS.

84. "Equal Suffrage for Women: Mrs. Russell Sage Gives Her Views on the Subject," *New York Times*, April 15, 1894, 8.

85. "A Notable Golden Anniversary," Margaret Olivia Slocum Sage Collection, EWS; "The First Woman Trustee: Mrs. Russell Sage Now on the Board of Troy Female Seminary," *New York Daily Tribune*, October 19, 1894, 7; "Mrs. Sage's Reminiscences," *Times Sun*, June 20, 1897, clipping, Margaret Olivia Slocum Sage Collection, EWS. Other female members were Mrs. Charles E. Patterson and Mrs. James A. Eddy. Russell Sage was also made a trustee. *Annual Report, Emma Willard School, 1897–98*, 4, 44.

86. Minutes of the Board of Trustees, Emma Willard School, 1893–4, William F. Gurley Papers, EWS; "The Gift of Russell Sage: Fine Dormitory to be Built for the Troy Female Seminary," *New York Daily Tribune*, March 4, 1893, 7.

87. "$120,000 Speech Made by Depew for Mrs. Sage," *Syracuse Post-Standard*, undated clipping [1918?], "Margaret Olivia Sage," OnHA. For this donation see *EWP*, 818. See also *Annual Report, Emma Willard School, 1897–98*, 44.

88. *Report of the Emma Willard Association, Troy Reunion, Unveiling of the Emma Willard Statue and Dedication of Russell Sage Hall, December 1895* (Brooklyn, 1895), 33–34; "The Women's Prophet," clipping, "Mrs. Sage's Scrapbook," Margaret Olivia Slocum Sage Collection, EWS.

89. "Russell Sage Hall: Description of Building and Furniture; Dedicatory Exercises," clipping, May 16, 1895, *Scrapbook, 1891–97*, Margaret Olivia Slocum Sage Collection, EWS; *Report of the Emma Willard Association, Troy Reunion*.

90. "In Memory of Parents," [October 1897]; "Window Dedicated: Ser-

vices at the First Presbyterian Church Yesterday; Mrs. Russell Sage Present," *Syracuse Journal*, October 18, 1897, clippings, Obituaries and Biographical Clippings Collection, OCPL; "Russell Sage's Wife Was Native of Syracuse: Beautiful Memorial Window in First Presbyterian Church Was Her Gift," [June 23, 1906], clipping, Obituaries and Biographical Clippings Collection, OCPL.

91. *Third Annual Report of the Emma Willard Association*, 6.

92. Ibid.

93. MOS to Nettie McCormick, November 9, 1891, Nettie Fowler McCormick Correspondence, Series 2B, Box 51, WHSA.

94. Harriette Dillaye to MOS, September __, 1894, Emma Willard Association Papers, EWS.

95. *Third Annual Report of the Emma Willard Association*, 42–43. This was worded as a resolution and approved by members.

96. Quoted in Scott, "Ever-Widening Circle," 75.

97. Frances Nason to MOS, May 30, 1899, Emma Willard Association Papers, EWS.

98. "Commencement Honors," *Troy Times*, June 10, 1897; "Mrs. Sage's Reminiscences," unidentified clipping, June 20, 1897, both in Margaret Olivia Slocum Sage Collection, EWS. "A Notable Golden Anniversary," *Harper's Bazaar*, June 12, 1897, Emma Willard Association Papers, EWS.

99. "The Emma Willard Association," *New York Mail and Express*, clipping, October 16, 1897, Emma Willard Association Papers, EWS.

100. Linda Kerber, "Separate Spheres, Female Worlds, Woman's Place: The Rhetoric of Women's History," *Journal of American History* 75 (June 1988): 9–39.

101. For example, in a speech on "Emma Hart Willard as an Important Factor in American History," Mrs. Mary Newbury Adams gave her listeners a woman-centered history of the nation where men, rather than being depicted as wise patriarchs, appear as bumblers needing to be bailed out by women. Emma Willard, a "patriotic national woman, appealed to the lawful 'fathers of the State' who by their ignorance and want of appreciation of the value of knowledge caused this great daughter's heart to sorrow and very nearly break." *Emma Willard Association of Troy Female Seminary*, 17.

102. Bederman, *Manliness and Civilization*; Kristin Hoganson, *Fighting for American Manhood: How Gender Politics Provoked the Spanish-American War and Philippine-American Wars* (New Haven, Conn.: Yale University Press, 1998).

103. *Third Annual Report of the Emma Willard Association*, 63.

104. "Mrs. Sage as President," *New York World*, November 11, 1897; "Mrs. Sage Made President," *New York Tribune*, November 11, 1897.

105. Theodore Francis Jones, ed., *New York University, 1832–1932* (New York: New York University Press, 1933), 169–170.

106. MOS to Hon. John W. Burgess, July 19, 1905, John W. Burgess Papers, Columbia; MOS to Hon. Edmund C. Stedman, July 19, 1905, Edmund C. Stedman Collection, Columbia. The University Heights campus of New York Uni-

versity, with its Hall of Fame and library designed by Stanford White, now forms part of the South Bronx Community College. My thanks to urban historian Deborah Gardner, who was my indispensable guide and informant.

107. Ellen Carol Du Bois, *Harriot Stanton Blatch and the Winning of Woman Suffrage* (New Haven, Conn.: Yale University Press, 1997), 106–121; DuBois, "Working Women, Class Relations, and Suffrage Militance: Harriot Stanton Blatch and the New York Woman Suffrage Movement, 1894–1909," *Journal of American History* 74 (June 1987): 34–58; Graham, "Suffrage Renaissance," 157–178.

8. Converted!

Paula Backscheider, Elisabeth Israels Perry, Marjorie Julian Spruill, and my colleague Marie Francois generously read and commented on this chapter.

1. Jessie Ashley, a prominent suffragist and socialist, was the sister of Dean Ashley of the New York University Law School. She entered the law school in 1900 and later became a member of Harriot Stanton Blatch's Equality League of Self-Supporting Women. Virginia Drachman, *Sisters in Law: Women Lawyers in Modern American History* (Cambridge, Mass.: Harvard University Press, 1998), 126. See also Phyllis Eckhaus, "Restless Women: The Pioneering Alumnae of New York University School of Law," *New York University Law Review* 66 (December 1991): 1996–2013; Meredith Tax, *The Rising of the Women: Feminist Solidarity and Class Conflict, 1880–1917* (New York: Monthly Review Press, 1980), 157, 170.

2. Quoted in Mabel Potter Daggett, "Suffrage Enters the Drawing Room," *The Delineator* 75 (January 1910): 37–38.

3. Matthew 25:1–13.

4. Elizabeth Cady Stanton, *The Parable of the Ten Virgins* (n.p., 1897), inscribed, "To Mrs. Russell Sage from her friend Elizabeth Cady Stanton on the occasion of her Graduation from the Troy Female Seminary," EWS. See also ECS/SBA, Reel 37, 591–601.

5. Elizabeth Cady Stanton, *Eighty Years and More: Reminiscences, 1815–1897* (New York: T. Fisher Unwin, 1898), 383; Theodore Stanton and Harriot Stanton Blatch, eds., *Elizabeth Cady Stanton, as Revealed in Her Letters, Diary, and Reminiscences*, 2 vols. (New York: Harper and Bros., 1922); Alma Lutz, *Created Equal: A Biography of Elizabeth Cady Stanton* (New York: John Day Co., 1940), 275. Lutz's biography of Stanton is invaluable because it quotes from sources not found elsewhere. Stanton purged her letters and correspondence, and the two-volume biography by her children Harriot Stanton Blatch and Theodore Stanton was highly edited in an effort to restore their mother to respectability.

Major biographies are Elisabeth Griffith, *In Her Own Right: The Life of Elizabeth Cady Stanton* (New York: Oxford University Press, 1984); and Lois Banner, *Elizabeth Cady Stanton: A Radical for Women's Rights* (Boston: Little, Brown and Co., 1980).

6. "The Solitude of Self" was a speech delivered on January 18, 1892. It is reprinted in *The Elizabeth Cady Stanton–Susan B. Anthony Reader*, ed. Ellen Carol Du Bois (Boston: Northeastern University Press, 1992), 247–254. *The Woman's Bible* signaled "her intellectual freedom from religious authority and the culmination of her personal theology"; Griffith, *In Her Own Right*, 212. A recent study is Kathi Kern, *Mrs. Stanton's Bible* (Ithaca, N.Y.: Cornell University Press, 2001).

7. The resolution, carried by 53 yeas and 41 nays, was passed over Susan B. Anthony's objection. Griffith, *In Her Own Right*, 203–204; "The Bible Resolution and Susan B. Anthony's Comment, NAWSA Convention, Washington, D.C., January 23–28, 1896," in *Concise History of Woman Suffrage*, ed. Mari Jo Buhle and Paul Buhle (Urbana: University of Illinois Press, 1978), 339–340. Press comments on the *Woman's Bible* can be read in *ECS/SBA*, Reel 39, 709–715. On the temperance movement, see Ruth Bordin, *Woman and Temperance: The Quest for Power and Liberty* (1981; repr., Rutgers University Press, 1990); and Ruth Bordin, *Frances Willard: A Biography* (Chapel Hill: University of North Carolina Press, 1986).

8. Stanton, *The Parable of the Ten Virgins*. Stanton had been a vigorous proponent of marriage reform since at least the 1850s. For feminist critiques of marriage, see Amy Dru Stanley, *From Bondage to Contract: Wage Labor, Marriage, and the Market in the Age of Slave Emancipation* (New York: Cambridge University Press, 1998), 175–217.

9. This was at the Academy of Music. For Parkhurst and Talmage, see Edwin G. Burrows and Mike Wallace, *Gotham: A History of New York City to 1898* (New York: Oxford University Press, 1999), 1167–1168, 1203–1205; and "Charles Henry Parkhurst, D.D.," in *Encyclopedia of Social Reform*, ed. W. D. P. Bliss (New York: Funk and Wagnalls Company, 1897), 971–972. De Witt Talmage was one of what scholar Sydney E. Ahlstrom calls the "princes of the pulpit" who rose to prominence in this period; *Religious History of the American People* (New Haven, Conn.: Yale University Press, 1973), 740. See also David Pivar, *Purity Crusade: Sexual Morality and Social Control, 1868–1900* (Westport, Conn.: Greenwood Press, 1973); Alison M. Parker, *Purifying America: Women, Cultural Reform, and Procensorship Activism, 1893–1933* (Urbana: University of Illinois Press, 1997).

10. Helen Miller Gould to "My dear Father," n.d., Helen Miller Gould Shepard Papers, NYHS. She ended, "I am confident there is nothing save the Christian religion that can make good and unselfish men and women everywhere, as we look near us or far away we see unbelief, selfishness, and the love of pleasure." In a subsequent letter, Helen told her father, "I saw Mrs Sage this spring. She wants me to go with them on Sunday night to hear Talmage." HMG to "My dear Father," October 20, 1890, Helen Miller Gould Shepard Papers, NYHS. When Talmage's Brooklyn Tabernacle burned down in 1890, Russell

Sage loaned him $125,000 to rebuild. "He liked Dr. Talmage, he said, and was glad of an opportunity to help him out in securing his new church." Russell Sage made it clear to the reporter that the loan was made on "business principles." "Mr. Sage Drives a Bargain: He Lends Dr. Talmage $125,000 on Very Good Terms," *New York Times*, September 11, 1890, 8.

11. In addition to the works of Bordin, Pivar, and Parker, see Henry F. May, *The Protestant Churches and Industrial America* (1949; repr., New York: Octagon Books, 1963); John Higham, *Strangers in the Land: Patterns of American Nativism, 1860–1925* (New York: Atheneum, 1965); and Paul Boyer, *Urban Masses and Moral Order in America, 1820–1920* (New York: Oxford University Press, 1978), 162–172. The best contemporary statement is Josiah Strong, *Our Country: Its Possible Future and Its Present Crisis* (New York: American Home Missionary Society, 1885).

12. Quoted in Burrows and Wallace, *Gotham*, 1167–1168.

13. David C. Hammack, *Power and Society: Greater New York at the Turn of the Century* (1982; repr., New York: Columbia University Press, 1987), 148–151; Charles W. Calhoun, "The Political Culture: Public Life and the Conduct of Politics," in *The Gilded Age: Essays on the Origins of Modern America*, ed. Charles W. Calhoun (Wilmington, Del.: Scholarly Resources, 1996), 185–214. In *The Lost Promise of Progressivism* (Lawrence: University Press of Kansas, 1994), Eldon J. Eisenach summarizes the Progressive-era eruption of political activity outside the established political parties, calling it "postparty," nonparty, or antiparty politics (8–12). See also Richard L. McCormick, *From Realignment to Reform: Political Change in New York State, 1893–1910* (Ithaca, N.Y.: Cornell University Press, 1981).

14. "Olivia Slocum," *EWP*, 390.

15. HMG to MOS, January 15, 1888, Helen Miller Gould Shepard Papers, NYHS.

16. Suffrage leaders should not be "dazzled by the promise of a sudden acquisition of numbers to our platform with the wide-spread influence of the Church behind them," Stanton wrote earlier. Quoted in Lutz, *Created Equal*, 275.

17. Stanton and Blatch, *Elizabeth Cady Stanton*, 2:340–246, 299.

18. Her diary records, "In June, 1892, at the earnest solicitation of Mrs. Russell Sage, I attended the dedication of the Gurley Memorial Building, presented to the Emma Willard School at Troy, New York." The diary reprints the entire speech. Stanton and Blatch, *Elizabeth Cady Stanton*, 2:340–345.

19. Stanton, *Eighty Years and More*, 449–450. I am grateful to Dr. Natalie Naylor of the Hofstra University Long Island Studies Institute, who helped me find the site where Cedar Croft once stood.

20. Stanton and Blatch, *Elizabeth Cady Stanton*, 2:295, 298.

21. On the failure of "influence," see Carolyn De Swarte Gifford, "Frances Willard and the Woman's Christian Temperance Union's Conversion to Woman Suffrage," in *One Woman, One Vote: Rediscovering the Woman Suffrage Movement*, ed. Marjorie Spruill Wheeler (Troutdale, Ore.: NewSage Press, 1995), 118–133.

22. "Conversion," the term they used to describe this transformation, was "a weighty source of authority for religious behavior," historian Carolyn De Swarte Gifford explains. "Within such a religious climate, if one claimed to receive a changed, reinterpreted image of woman as the content of the conversion experience, the claim would be difficult for another to challenge"; "Frances Willard and the Woman's Christian Temperance Union's Conversion to Woman Suffrage," 124–127. See also Gifford, *"Writing Out My Heart": Selections from the Journal of Frances E. Willard* (Urbana: University of Illinois Press, 1995); Susan Earls Dye Lee, "Evangelical Domesticity: The Women's Temperance Crusade of 1873–74," in *Women in New Worlds: Historical Perspectives on the Wesleyan Tradition*, ed. Hilah Thomas and Rosemary Skinner Keller (Nashville, Tenn.: Abingdon, 1981); Dawn Michele Dyer, "Combating the 'Fiery Flood': The Woman's Christian Temperance Union's Approach to Labor and Socialism" (Ph.D. diss., Auburn University, 1998), 41–83.

I have not been able to verify Olivia's membership in the WCTU.

23. MOS, handwritten fragment, n.d., Margaret Olivia Slocum Sage Collection, EWS.

24. David Kevin McDonald, "Organizing Womanhood: Women's Culture and the Politics of Woman Suffrage in New York State, 1865–1917" (Ph.D. diss., SUNY Stony Brook, 1987), iii–iv; Elinor Lerner, "Immigrant and Working Class Involvement in the New York City Woman Suffrage Movement, 1905–1917: A Study in Progressive Era Politics" (Ph.D. diss., University of California, Berkeley, 1981).

25. Sara Hunter Graham, *Woman Suffrage and the New Democracy* (New Haven, Conn.: Yale University Press, 1996), 21.

The suffrage movement among African American women is the subject of Rosalyn Terborg-Penn, *African-American Women in the Struggle for the Vote, 1850–1920* (Bloomington: Indiana University Press, 1998); Ann D. Gordon and Bettye Collier-Thomas, eds., *African-American Women and the Vote, 1837–1965* (Amherst: University of Massachusetts Press, 1997); Paula Giddings, *When and Where I Enter: The Impact of Black Women on Race and Sex in America* (New York: William Morrow, 1984); and Wanda A. Hendricks, "Ida B. Wells-Barnett and the Alpha Suffrage Club of Chicago," in Wheeler, *One Woman, One Vote*, 263–276.

26. Historians have not been sympathetic to upper-class women's involvement in the suffrage movement, most of them following Eleanor Flexner in *Century of Struggle* (1959) in deploring the New York suffrage movement's turn to women of wealth in the 1890s and after. Flexner, *Century of Struggle: The Woman's Rights Movement in the United States* (1959; New York: Atheneum, 1973), 248–250. A more sympathetic perspective is given in Sara Hunter Graham, "The Suffrage Renaissance: A New Image for a New Century, 1896–1910," in Wheeler, *One Woman, One Vote*, 159–178; see also editor's introduction, 157–158.

Terms are crucial here. While DuBois uses "elite women," "society suffragists," or "women of leisure," Graham refers to the "more conventional women" who had been put off by the movement's association with radicalism. Marilley shows how the so-called doldrums in fact marked progress by NAWSA in appealing to the evangelical women of the WCTU, college women, clubwomen, and others. DuBois, *Feminism and Suffrage*, 109–110; Graham, "The Suffrage Renaissance," in Graham, *Woman Suffrage and the New Democracy*, 21, 159; Suzanne M. Marilley, *Woman Suffrage and the Origins of Liberal Feminism in the United States, 1820–1920* (Cambridge, Mass.: Harvard University Press, 1996), 159–162.

27. Quoted in Tax, *Rising of the Women*, 169; *HWS*, 4:216; National American Woman Suffrage Association, *Proceedings of the National American Woman Suffrage Association, 1893*, 84–85. The convention also adopted a resolution supporting the suffrage for wage-earning women; Buhle and Buhle, *Concise History of Woman Suffrage*, 328.

The era of parlor suffrage was not the first time themes of exclusion had characterized the suffrage movement; elitism shaped suffragist rhetoric as early as the 1848 Declaration of Sentiments, with its call for women's right to vote on the grounds that male governance deprived women of "rights which are given to the most ignorant and degraded men—both natives and foreigners." Graham, *Woman Suffrage and the New Democracy*, 21; Marjorie Spruill Wheeler, *New Women of the New South: The Leaders of the Woman Suffrage Movement in the Southern States* (New York: Oxford University Press, 1993). Nor were elitism and racism in the suffrage movement introduced by or for southern white suffragists, as some have suggested. Marjorie Julian Spruill [Wheeler], personal communication with the author.

28. "An Appeal to the Women of New York," *Woman's Tribune*, January 6, 1894, *ECS/SBA*, Reel 32.

At the end of her long life, Stanton called on legislators to "abolish the ignorant vote." She declared, "There have been various restrictions in the past for men. We are willing to abide by the same for women, provided the insurmountable qualification of sex be forever removed. The popular objection to woman suffrage is that it would double the 'ignorant vote.' The patent answer to this is, abolish the ignorant vote. Our legislators have this power in their own hands." Elizabeth Cady Stanton, "Educated Suffrage," speech given at NAWSA Convention, Washington, D.C., February 12–18, 1903, in Buhle and Buhle, *Concise History of Woman Suffrage*, 347. See also Flexner, *Century of Struggle*, 71–77; and Louise Michele Newman, *White Women's Rights: The Racial Origins of Feminism in the United States* (New York: Oxford University Press, 1999), 57–58.

29. Marilley, *Woman Suffrage and the Origins of Liberal Feminism*, 165 and 263n26. Marilley's source is two unpublished early speeches by Catt, "Subject and Sovereign" and "The American Sovereign." Marilley dismisses handwringing at the illiberalism of the suffrage arguments on the grounds that the suffrage campaign took place in a political environment "that treated racial seg-

regation, white supremacy, and nativist ideologies as respectable" (2–5). See also Robert Booth Fowler, *Carrie Catt: Feminist Politician* (Boston: Northeastern University Press, 1988), 86–89.

30. Rosalyn Terborg-Penn, "African-American Women and the Woman Suffrage Movement," in Wheeler, *One Woman, One Vote*, 137; Newman, *White Women's Rights*, 64.

31. Margaret Olivia Sage, "Views of a Millionaire's Wife," in "Should Women Vote? The Most Notable Symposium of Opinion on This Topic Ever Printed Anywhere," *Press* (New York), April 5, 1894, in Abbé Scrapbooks, vol. 2.

32. The reporter marveled, "There wasn't a pair of stoop shoulders or a badly carried head in the two lines. . . . This may have been due to a total absence of high heels and corsets, that gave free play to every muscle." "The Teachers' Class in Physical Culture: Mrs. Russell Sage a Guest," *New York Recorder*, April 28, 1894, ECS/SBA, Reel 32.

33. Newman suggests that woman suffrage legislation was easier to pass in a western state because it would enfranchise fewer people of color. Newman, *White Women's Rights*, 58.

34. This figure is given in Stanton and Blatch, *Elizabeth Cady Stanton*, 2:307. A much more modest estimate of 134,378 signatures is in Harriette A. Keyser, "New York: New York City Woman Suffrage League," in *Report of the New York State Woman's Suffrage Association*, 1894, 197–198.

35. *Kate Field's Washington* 9, no. 20 (May 16, 1894), n.p., Abbé Scrapbooks, vol. 2. On the antis, see Manuela Thurner, "Better Citizens without the Ballot: American Anti-Suffrage Women and Their Rationale during the Progressive Era," *Journal of Women's History* 5 (Spring 1993): 33–60; and Susan E. Marshall, *Splintered Sisterhood: Gender and Class in the Campaign Against Woman Suffrage* (Madison: University of Wisconsin Press, 1997).

36. Lillie Devereux Blake, "Our New York Letter," *Woman's Journal*, March 10, 1894.

37. "Power of the Movement," Abbé Scrapbooks, vol. 2. See also Ellen Carol DuBois, "Harriot Stanton Blatch and the Transformation of Class Relations Among Woman Suffragists," in *Gender, Class, Race, and Reform in the Progressive Era*, ed. Noralee Frankel and Nancy S. Dye (Lexington: University Press of Kentucky, 1991), 162–179.

38. "Woman and the Suffrage," *New York Sun*, March 31, 1894, Abbé Scrapbooks, vol. 1.

39. "Active Woman Crusaders," *New York Tribune*, April 2, 1894, Abbé Scrapbooks, vol. 2. Lillie Devereux Blake, responding to this canard, denied that society women were "taking up suffrage on an impulse. They have been thinking about these things for years . . . and now, when the time for action has come, they are ready to join the ranks of the great army that is demanding their political freedom." "Mrs. Blake Reports Progress," *New York World*, April 29, 1894, Abbé Scrapbooks, vol. 2.

40. According to Stanton, *Eighty Years and More*, 451. See also Katherine

Devereux Blake and Margaret Louise Wallace, *Champion of Women: The Life of Lillie Devereux Blake* (New York: Fleming H. Revell Co., 1943), 183.

The founding members of the Sherry Committee were Mrs. Henry Sanders, Dr. Mary Putnam Jacobi, Josephine Shaw Lowell, Luria Runkle, Mrs. Robert Abbé, and Adele Field. "Report of the 'Volunteer Committee' in New York City, in *Report of the New York Woman Suffrage Association, 26th Annual Convention, Ithaca, N.Y., November 12–15, 1895* (Boston: Charles Mann, 1895), 217–219. "Political action committee" is Joan Waugh's phrase; "Unsentimental Reformer: The Life of Josephine Shaw Lowell" (Ph.D. diss., UCLA, 1992), 476. See also Robert H. Bremner, "Josephine Shaw Lowell," *NAW*, 2:437–439.

41. "The Lady and the Female: Both Working for Equal Rights But They Don't Pull Together," *New York Evening World,* April 14, 1894, Abbé Scrapbooks, vol. 2. Katherine Grier suggests that the parlor signified "family centered values," but that it was also the family's interface with the public. *Culture and Comfort: Parlor Making and Middle Class Identity, 1850–1930* (Washington, D.C.: Smithsonian Institution Press, 1997).

42. "The Lady and the Female."

43. "Report of the 'Volunteer Committee' in New York City," 219. See also Blake and Wallace, *Champion of Women,* 183.

44. Stanton and Blatch, *Elizabeth Cady Stanton,* 2:304–305.

45. "At *my* house," emphasis in the original; "*during the spring freedom from a great pressure of social engagements,*" emphasis added. "Report of the 'Volunteer Committee' in New York City," 218.

46. "A Meeting at Mrs. Sage's," *New York Sun,* April 15, 1894, and "The Fight for Women," *New York Tribune,* April 16, 1894, both in Abbé Scrapbooks, vol. 1.

47. "A Meeting at Mrs. Sage's," *New York Sun,* April 15, 1894, Abbé Scrapbooks, vol. 2.

48. Abbé Scrapbooks, vol. 2, 42.

49. *New York Times,* April 18, 1894.

50. Margaret Fuller, "Let [women] be sea-captains if you will." S. Margaret Fuller, *Woman in the Nineteenth Century,* a facsimile of the 1845 edition, with an introduction by Madeleine B. Stern (Columbia: University of South Carolina Press, 1980), 159. My thanks to Paula Backscheider for supplying this reference.

51. Rev. Henry A. Boardman, "Public Examinations in Female Schools: Reply to Mrs. Willard," *Troy Daily Times,* December 19, 1857.

52. "Equal Suffrage for Women: Mrs. Russell Sage Gives Her Views on the Subject," *New York Times,* April 15, 1894, 8. On Sage as a Sunday school teacher at West Presbyterian Church, see Marjorie Harrison, *Margaret Olivia Sage: Philanthropist and Friend* (New York: Board of National Missions of the Presbyterian Church in the U.S.A., 1927–1928), 4.

Gerda Lerner memorably traces a 1,000-year tradition of feminist Bible criticism in *The Creation of Feminist Consciousness: From the Middle Ages to 1870* (New York: Oxford University Press, 1993), 138–166. Evelyn Brooks Higginbotham discloses a similar strategy on the part of contemporary black Baptist women: "Working within the orthodoxy of the church, they turned to the Bible to argue for their rights—thus holding men accountable to the same text that authenticated their arguments for racial equality"; *Righteous Discontent: The Women's Movement in the Black Baptist Church, 1880–1920* (Cambridge, Mass.: Harvard University Press, 1993), 121.

53. "A Meeting at Mrs. Sage's."

54. "Equal Suffrage for Women: Mrs. Russell Sage Gives Her Views on the Subject."

55. Ibid.

56. Ibid. She said, "There is a society of women in this city . . . which is trying to pass a bill to have offal removed. Their bill has not been passed." Sage seems to be referring to the Woman's Municipal League.

57. Ibid.; Eleanor Flexner, "Harriot Eaton Stanton Blatch," *NAW*, 1:172–173.

58. "Miss Curtis on Woman Suffrage," Abbé Scrapbooks, vol. 1.

59. Kathleen Waters Sander, *The Business of Charity: The Woman's Exchange Movement, 1832–1900* (Urbana: University of Illinois Press, 1998). Compare with Emmeline Pankhurst's declaration that suffrage work was even more arduous for privileged women than for others because they "have never had to face the struggle for existence." Ellen Carol DuBois, *Harriot Stanton Blatch and the Winning of Woman Suffrage* (New Haven, Conn.: Yale University Press, 1997), 115.

60. Ellen DuBois takes issue with the use by suffrage historians of the term "middle class" for women with independent incomes (DuBois, *Harriot Stanton Blatch,* 89), and Nancy A. Hewitt subtly reworks the categories of class and ethnicity in "Charity or Mutual Aid? Two Perspectives on Latin Women's Philanthropy in Tampa, Florida," in *Lady Bountiful Revisited: Women, Philanthropy, and Power,* ed. Kathleen McCarthy (New Brunswick: Rutgers University Press, 1990), 55–69, and "Varieties of Voluntarism: Class, Ethnicity, and Women's Activism in Tampa," in *Women, Politics, and Change,* ed. Louise A. Tilly and Patricia Gurin (New York: Russell Sage Foundation, 1990), 63–86. See also Stuart Blumin, *The Emergence of the Middle Class: Social Experience in the American City, 1760–1900* (New York: Cambridge University Press, 1989).

61. "Parlor Suffrage Wave," *New York Herald,* April 10, 1894.

62. "The Lady and the Female."

63. Graham, *Woman Suffrage and the New Democracy,* 39.

64. Ruth Crocker, "Unsettling Perspectives: The Settlement Movement, the Rhetoric of Social History, and the Search for Synthesis," in *Contesting the Master Narrative: Essays in Social History,* ed. Jeff Cox and Shelton Stromquist (Iowa City: University of Iowa Press, 1998), 175–209; Suzanne Lebsock, "Women and American Politics, 1880–1920," in Tilly and Gurin, *Women, Politics, and Change,* 48. See also Allen F. Davis, *Spearheads for Reform: The Social Settlements and the Progressive Movement, 1890–1918,* 2nd ed. (New Brunswick: Rutgers University Press, 1984); John Rousmaniere, "Cultural Hybrid in the

Slums: The College Woman and the Settlement House, 1889–1894," *American Quarterly* 22 (Spring 1970): 45–66.

65. When Jane Addams moved into Hull House in 1889, she furnished it with "a few bits of family mahogany." She recalled, "Probably no young matron ever placed her own things in her own house with more pleasure than that with which we first furnished Hull-House"; *Twenty Years at Hull-House, with Autobiographical Notes*, with an introduction and notes by James Hurt (Urbana: University of Illinois Press, 1990), 57.

66. "Creative solution" in Allen F. Davis, *American Heroine: The Life and Legend of Jane Addams* (New York: Oxford University Press, 1973). I use the settlement house for comparison, but the woman's club of this period supplies another parallel. Estelle Freedman, "Separatism as Strategy: Female Institution-Building and American Feminism, 1870–1930," *Feminist Studies* 5 (1979): 512–529.

67. *Demorest's Family Magazine* 30 (January 1894), 183–184, ECS/SBA, Reel 32. Olivia was quoted as being "overjoyed to find that her husband was as thoroughgoing a woman suffragist as herself." "Russell Sage and His Life," *The Troy Record*, July 24, 1906.

68. Elizabeth Cady Stanton to MOS, December 14, [1898], ECS/SBA, Reel 38, 992–993.

69. "New Woman Suffragist," *New York World*, April 19, 1894; "Woman's Right to Vote: Many Prominent Ladies Give Their Reasons for Signing the Petition," *New York Herald*, May 6, 1894, Abbé Scrapbooks, vol. 3.

70. "Woman's Right to Vote: Many Prominent Ladies Give Their Reasons for Signing the Petition."

71. Stanton and Blatch, *Elizabeth Cady Stanton*, 2:307.

72. See Ellen Carol DuBois, ed., *The Elizabeth Cady Stanton-Susan B. Anthony Reader: Correspondence, Writings, Speeches*, rev. ed. (Boston: Northeastern University Press, 1992), 296.

73. The exact date of this subscription is unclear, but her continuing support of the organization is shown in later correspondence. See Mrs. Barclay Hazard to Col. J. J. Slocum, July 11, 1911, RSFR, Box 87, Folder 987. "Will Not Lead the Women. Mrs. Grannis on Dr. Parkhurst's Municipal Campaign," *New York Times*, October 6, 1894, 8.

74. "Will Not Lead the Women"; Burrows and Wallace, *Gotham*, 1167–1168. S. Sara Monoson writes, "The League's electoral activism during the years 1894 to 1905 provides vivid evidence of women's independent, direct, and effective involvement in mainstream politics long before they got the vote"; "The Lady and the Tiger: Women's Electoral Activism in New York City Before Suffrage," *Journal of Women's History* 2 (Fall 1990): 100. See also Maureen Flanagan, "Gender and Urban Political Reform: The City Club and the Woman's City Club of Chicago in the Progressive Era," *American Historical Review* 95 (October 1990): 1032–1050; and Melanie Gustafson, Kristie Miller,

and Elisabeth Israels Perry, eds., *We Have Come to Stay: American Women and Political Parties, 1880–1960* (Albuquerque: University of New Mexico Press, 1999).

75. "Suffrage Pointers," *New York Times*, February 4, 1909, RSFR, Box 98, Folder 995.

76. Ibid. In this interview she claimed that she had supported the suffrage since the 1870s. See also "Mrs. Sage, Now 87, Calls for Vote," *New York Sun*, October 31, 1915, RSFR, Box 99, Folder 997.

77. *Third Annual Report of the Emma Willard Association*, 5; "Degrees for Women: The Struggle at Cambridge; Undergraduates in Battle Array; Jealousy of Oxford," *The Times* (London), May 22, 1894, clipping, Abbé Scrapbooks, vol. 1.

78. These remarks to a Chicago newspaper were reported approvingly in Stanton's diary for November 12, 1899; Stanton and Blatch, *Elizabeth Cady Stanton*, 2:344. See also "Suffrage Pointers."

79. "Suffrage Pointers"; "Mrs. Sage, Now 87, Calls for Vote"; "Mrs. Sage Dies at Her Home," *New York Times*, November 4, 1918, 13.

80. M. Olivia Sage (Mrs. Russell Sage), "Opportunities and Responsibilities of Leisured Women," *North American Review* 181 (November 1905): 719.

81. For the idea of a taxpayer franchise, see "President's Address," in *Reports of the New York State Woman Suffrage Association, 1900, October 29–November 1, 1900* (Rochester, N.Y.: Charles Mann, Printers, 1895), 14–15; *HWS*, 4:860–864. Marjorie Julian Spruill, "Race, Reform, and Reaction at the Turn of the Century: Southern Suffragists, the NAWSA, and the 'Southern Strategy' in Context," in *Votes for Women: The Struggle for Suffrage Revisited*, ed. Jean H. Baker (New York: Oxford University Press, 1992), 102–117. See also Newman, *White Women's Rights*; Ellen Carol DuBois, *Feminism and Suffrage: The Emergence of an Independent Women's Movement in the United States, 1848–1869* (Ithaca, N.Y.: Cornell University Press, 1978); Rosalyn Terborg-Penn, "African-American Women and the Woman Suffrage Movement," in Wheeler, *One Woman, One Vote*, 135–156. Josephine Shaw Lowell, to her credit, denounced "the dangerous and un-American plan of a property qualification"; "Woman Suffrage Expounded," Abbé Scrapbooks, vol. 2.

82. Waugh, "Unsentimental Reformer," 476; Monoson, "'Lady and the Tiger," 128n17.

83. Roy Lubove, "Mary Corinna Putnam Jacobi," *NAW*, 2:263–265; Mary Putnam Jacobi, *The Question of Rest for Women during Menstruation* (New York: G. P. Putnam's Sons, Knickerbocker Press, 1877); Edward H. Clarke, *Sex in Education: or, a Fair Chance for the Girls* (Boston: James R. Osgood, 1873). See also Regina Morantz Sanchez, *Sympathy and Science: Women Physicians in American Medicine* (New York: Oxford University Press, 1985), 55; Virginia G. Drachman, *Hospital with a Heart: Women Doctors and the Paradox of Separatism at the New England Hospital, 1862–1969* (Ithaca, N.Y.: Cornell University Press, 1984), 55–56.

84. Mary Putnam Jacobi, "Woman in Medicine," in *Woman's Work in America*, ed. Annie Nathan Meyer (New York: Henry Holt and Company, 1891), 139–205.

85. Mary Putnam Jacobi, "Address Delivered at the New York Hearing," in New York State Woman Suffrage Party, *Record of the New York Campaign of 1894* (New York, 1895), 19. See also Jacobi, *"Common Sense" Applied to Woman Suffrage: a statement of the reasons which justify the demand to extend the suffrage to women, with consideration of the arguments against such enfranchisement, and with special reference to the issues presented to the New York State convention of 1894* (New York: G. P. Putnam's Sons, 1894). The quote on "hired servants" is in "Parlor Suffrage Meeting," *New York Times*, October 6, 1894, Abbé Scrapbooks, vol. 2.

86. Blake's witty style can be seen in the piece printed in *The Revolution*, where she refers to the "sartorial qualification for suffrage" that voters be "bifurcated" below the waist. Blake and Wallace, *Champion of Women*. The authors (Katherine was a daughter) note that Blake's achievement is not well represented in the four-volume *History of Woman Suffrage*. "Reading that book one would never dream that Mrs. Blake was a leader, an inventor of slogans, a planner of widespread campaigns, during the eleven hard-worked years that she was elected and re-elected president of the lively, powerful Association of New York State" (14). On her estrangement from Susan B. Anthony, Blake and Wallace quote from Blake's diary and indicate that Anthony wanted Blake to drop other issues and concentrate on the vote alone. Blake left journals, a diary, and an unfinished autobiography, and works of fiction; *Champion of Women*, 156–157.

87. "Circular Issued: Stir Created in Woman's Suffrage Association," *Washington Evening Star*, February 10, 1900, ECS/SBA, Reel 40, 896.

88. "To her efforts, mainly, are we in the State of New York indebted for the passage of the laws

    a. Granting school suffrage to women.
    b. Making mother and father joint guardians of their children.
    c. Enabling a woman to make a will without her husband's consent.
    d. Providing that there shall be women as trustees in all public institutions where women are placed.
    e. Providing seats for saleswomen.

The circular noted that "through her efforts, mainly," women were appointed census enumerators in 1880, granted pensions as war nurses, and made eligible for civil service positions and that she "originated and sustained the agitation for the appointment of police matrons." "For President Mrs. Lillie Devereux Blake," draft, typed one-page flyer, Lillie Devereux Blake Papers, Missouri Historical Society.

89. "Mrs. Catt President: Suffragists Choose Susan B. Anthony's Successor," unidentified newspaper clipping [1900], ECS/SBA, Reel 40, 907. Carrie Chapman Catt served as president from 1900 to 1904, followed by Anna Howard Shaw. For a partisan account of this dispute that is bitterly critical of Anthony, see Blake

and Wallace, *Champion of Women*, 204–205. See also Alma Lutz, *Susan B. Anthony: Rebel, Crusader, Humanitarian* (Boston: Beacon Press, 1959), 292.

90. "Being greatly pleased with the truth and the form of statements in the enclosed clipping, I am sending it to you lest it may not come to your notice," Sage wrote. MOS to Susan B. Anthony, May 9th, 1905, quoted in Ida Husted Harper, *Life and Work of Susan B. Anthony* (New York: Arno, 1969), 3:1350–1351. Maren Stein kindly drew this letter to my attention.

91. Ibid.

92. Ibid.

93. DuBois, "Working Women, Class Relations, and Suffrage Militance," in Wheeler, *One Woman One Vote*, names Harriot Stanton Blatch's "view of work as the key to women's independence, dignity and freedom" as the core of her inclusive feminist politics (221–222). I find this consciousness also in Sage, an "elite" woman. Compare with the arguments used by Jane Addams, "Why Women Should Vote," *Ladies Home Journal* (January 1910), and the discussion by Victoria Bissell Brown, "An Introduction to 'Why Women Should Vote,'" in Wheeler, ed., *One Woman One Vote*, 182–195.

94. Sage, "Opportunities and Responsibilities of Leisured Women," 712–713, 719.

95. Ibid, 715. Arthur Huntington Gleason, "Mrs. Russell Sage and Her Interests," *The World's Work* 13 (November 1906): 8184.

96. Quoted in Daggett, "Suffrage Enters the Drawing Room," 37. Alva Belmont's colorful career is painstakingly documented in Peter Geidel, "Alva Belmont: A Forgotten Feminist" (Ph.D. diss., Columbia University, 1993).

97. Marilley, *Woman Suffrage and the Origins of Liberal Feminism*, 164–167, 186; Lori D. Ginzberg, *Women and the Work of Benevolence: Morality, Politics, and Class in the Nineteenth-Century United States* (New Haven, Conn.: Yale University Press, 1990). Sara Graham writes, "Representing themselves to black and immigrant women as potential protectors who would be more trustworthy than any men, they simultaneously asserted their dominance as white, native-born women in a racist and xenophobic society"; *Woman Suffrage and the New Democracy*, 186.

98. Willard Gaylin, Ira Glasser, Steven Marcus, and David Rothman, eds., *Doing Good: The Limits of Benevolence* (New York: Pantheon, 1978). See also Christine Stansell, *City of Women: Sex and Class in New York, 1789–1860* (New York: Alfred A. Knopf, 1986).

9. "Wiping her tears with the flag"

1. M. Olivia Sage (Mrs. Russell Sage), "Opportunities and Responsibilities of Leisured Women," *North American Review* 181 (November 1905): 714.

2. "The Flag An Object Lesson: 'It Cannot Be Too Often Seen,' Says One Patriot," *New York Daily Tribune*, May 30, 1898, 5.

3. My understanding of this remaking of identities has been helped espe-

cially by Nan Enstad's *Ladies of Labor, Girls of Adventure: Working Women, Popular Culture, and Labor Politics at the Turn of the Twentieth Century* (New York: Columbia University Press, 1999). Enstad examines how working-class women, who were barred from the categories "worker" and "lady," shaped what she identifies as "working-class ladyhood." In *Manliness and Civilization: A Cultural History of Gender and Race in the United States, 1880–1917* (Chicago: University of Chicago Press, 1995), Gail Bederman shows the centrality of racial thinking to turn-of-the-century debates over gender. See also James Livingston, *Pragmatism and the Political Economy of Cultural Revolution, 1850–1940* (Chapel Hill: University of North Carolina Press, 1994). Earlier studies slight the gender dimensions of this change.

4. In part, regeneration would come through war. On the gendering of national reconciliation after the Civil War, see Nina Silber, *The Romance of Reunion: Northerners and the South, 1865–1900* (Chapel Hill: University of North Carolina Press, 1993); and Sara M. Evans, "Women's History and Political Theory: Toward a Feminist Approach to Public Life," in *Visible Women: New Essays on American Activism*, ed. Nancy A. Hewitt and Suzanne Lebsock (Urbana: University of Illinois Press, 1993), 128–131.

5. Margaret Olivia Sage, "Response to Welcome, by Mrs. Russell Sage, delivered to the Trustees of the Troy Female Seminary, Mr. Gurley, and Members of the Emma Willard Association," [1896], typescript, Emma Willard Association Papers, Box 3, "Mrs. Russell Sage, Addresses," EWS.

6. *Third Annual Report of the Emma Willard Association, Chicago Reunion, 1893* (Brooklyn, N.Y.: Press of the Brooklyn Eagle, 1893), 36. Sewall's mother was an Emma Willard Association alumna; Clifton J. Phillips, "May Eliza Wright Sewall," *NAW*, 3:269–271.

7. For the literature on the U.S. role in the Spanish-American War, see Lewis L. Gould, *The Spanish-American War and President McKinley* (Lawrence: University Press of Kansas, 1982); David F. Trask, *The War with Spain in 1898* (New York: Macmillan, 1981); Ernest R. May, *Imperial Democracy: The Emergence of America as a Great Power* (New York: Harcourt, Brace and World, 1981).

8. See Kristin L. Hoganson, *Fighting for American Manhood: How Gender Politics Provoked the Spanish-American War and Philippine-American Wars* (New Haven, Conn.: Yale University Press, 1998); Linda K. Kerber, *No Constitutional Right to be Ladies: Women and the Obligations of Citizenship* (New York: Hill and Wang, 1998), 221–302.

9. Hoganson, *Fighting for American Manhood*.

10. Ellen Hardin Walworth, ed., *Report of the Women's National War Relief Association, Organized for the Emergency of the Spanish-American War, March 1898–January 1899* (New York: King Press, 1899), 36. I am grateful to Kristin Hoganson for drawing my attention to this important source and to the Women's Patriotic Relief Association Papers at the New-York Historical Society Library.

11. Sage, "Opportunities and Responsibilities of Leisured Women," 714. On gender and national reconciliation, see Silber, *Romance of Reunion*.

12. The mission project also provided some disturbing new insights among female missionaries regarding the universality of patriarchal rule. On Sage and the language of mission, see Ruth Crocker, "'From Widow's Mite to Widow's Might': The Philanthropy of Margaret Olivia Sage," *American Presbyterians* 74 (Winter 1996): 253–264. Major studies are Patricia Hill, *The World Their Household: The American Woman's Foreign Missionary Movement and Cultural Transformation, 1870–1920* (Ann Arbor: University of Michigan Press, 1985); Jane Hunter, *Gospel of Gentility: American Women Missionaries in Turn of the Century China* (New Haven, Conn.: Yale University Press, 1984). For home missions, see Peggy Pascoe, *Relations of Rescue: The Search for Female Moral Authority in the American West, 1874–1939* (New York: Oxford University Press, 1990); Sarah Deutsch, *No Separate Refuge: Culture, Class, and Gender on an Anglo-Hispanic Frontier in the Southwest, 1880–1940* (New York: Oxford University Press, 1987); Susan A. Yohn, *A Contest of Faiths: Missionary Women and Pluralism in the American Southwest* (Ithaca, N.Y.: Cornell University Press, 1995); and Lois A. Boyd and R. Douglas Breckinridge, *Presbyterian Women in America: Two Centuries of a Quest for Status* (Westport, Conn.: Greenwood Press, 1983).

13. *Brooklyn Daily Eagle*, February 27, 1898, 4.

14. On another occasion, six or seven hundred poor little children from the Home for the Friendless gathered in Madison Square Garden, "every one of them carrying a flag. At a signal from the superintendent they all stood up and waved the flags while they sang the National hymn. . . . I do not believe there was a dry eye in the house." "The Flag An Object Lesson."

15. The appeal was published in the *New York Tribune*, April 2, 1898. Walworth, *Report of the Women's National War Relief Association, 1898–1899*, 33–34.

16. Mrs. Walworth's speech and the accompanying correspondence are in Walworth, *Report of the Women's National War Relief Association, 1898–1899*, 33–48.

17. For Helen Gould's distress at conditions in the camps, see HMG to Frank Gould, August 28, 1898, Women's Patriotic Relief Association Papers, NYHS.

18. Walworth, *Report of the Women's National War Relief Association, 1898–1899*, 56–57. A tragic consequence was that Mrs. Walworth's daughter, a nurse in the camps, contracted typhoid and died on October 18, 1898 (80).

19. HMG to "Dear Frank," August 24, 1898, Helen Miller Gould Shepard Papers, NYHS. She added, "I think it was because we closed at one and she was able to get her lunch instead of dragging on till two."

20. HMG to "Dear Frank," August 28, 1898, Women's Patriotic Relief Association Papers, NYHS.

21. Writing to Sage in February 1907, John Arbuckle, a fund-raiser for the Berry School, Rome, Georgia, recounted how he had taken Helen Gould out in his boat at Lake Mohonk (she was a major donor to the school), "and she

spoke very beautifully about you and that you had been a Mother to her after the death of her own Mother." John Arbuckle to MOS, February 1, 1907, RSFR, Box 70, Folder 628.

22. "From Sihler, *History of New York University* v. 2, 524," typescript in MacCracken Records, "Helen Miller Gould" folder, NYU.

23. Ibid. Ellen Hardin Walworth, writing to Helen Gould, June 21, 1899 from Saratoga, mentions Miss Todd working to complete the Lyndhurst archives. Todd probably came to the attention of Helen Gould as a member of the first NYU Women's Law Class. Personal communication from Lygia Ionnitiu, January 1998.

24. "Mrs. Sage's Hospital Offer," *New York Daily Tribune*, November 17, 1898, 5.

25. "Mrs. Russell Sage's Plea," *New York Daily Tribune*, August 28, 1898, II:7.

26. C. B. Carlisle, "Mrs. Sage's Burden," July 31, 1906, Obituaries and Biographical Clippings Collection, OCPL; HMG to "Dear Frank," August 7, 1898, and HMG to "My dear Brother" [Frank], August 24, 1898, both in Women's Patriotic Relief Association Papers, NYHS. The August 24 letter mentions her return from "the hard trip to Montauk."

27. Carlisle, "Mrs. Sage's Burden."

28. Quoted in Emily S. Rosenberg, *Spreading the American Dream: American Economic and Cultural Expansion, 1890–1945* (New York: Hill and Wang, 1982), 44.

29. "Mrs. Russell Sage's Plea." Emily Rosenberg quotes an advocate of this position in 1901: "The Christian view of politics emphasizes the burden of Government and the responsibility of dominion, and therefore transforms empire from an ambition to an opportunity. Blindly and unworthily, yet, under God, surely and steadily, the Christian nations are subduing the world, in order to make Mankind free." Rosenberg, *Spreading the American Dream*, 43–44. The quote is attributed only to "a missionary."

30. "Emma Willard Banquet," *New York Daily Tribune*, November 11, 1898, 5. On Lowell's work in the Anti-Imperialist League, see Joan Waugh, *Unsentimental Reformer: The Life of Josephine Shaw Lowell* (Cambridge, Mass.: Harvard University Press, 1997), 573–583.

31. George N. Southwick to Col. Mordecai, December 3, 1898, Helen Gould Papers, Lyndhurst, Irvington, New York.

32. "Mrs. Sage to Sailors: Praises Them in Address on the Mayflower at Larchmont," *New York Daily Tribune*, May 20, 1903, 16.

33. "Mrs. Sage Aids Men of the Sea," *New York Observer*, March 21, 1907, 377–378, RSFR, Box 1, Folder 3. Correspondence relating to the American Seaman's Friend Association is also in RSFR, Box 68, Folder 604. Nancy Woloch suggests that women's donations to sailors' homes not only represented an interest in the plight of seamen but also were a gesture of sympathy for the women they abused and abandoned. Nancy Woloch, *Women and the American Experience*, 3rd. edition (New York: McGraw Hill, 2000), 178-183.

34. "I think he better stay at hum," was how the writer conveyed Russell's unpolished speech. "Russell Sage and His Life," *Troy Record*, July 24, 1906, 3.

35. On his earlier career, see "Lieut. Col. Slocum Dies at Age 74," *New York Times*, December 15, 1933, 25. The subtitle reads, "Indian Fighter in West; Commanded Troop Which Surrounded Sitting Bull's Forces When Chief Was Slain." See also Charles Elihu Slocum, *History of the Slocums, Slocumbs and Slocombs of America* (Defiance, Ohio: Quintin Publications, 1908), 2:313.

36. "Mrs. Sage on Debs: Wife of the Wall Street Magnate Talks about the Misguided Agitator," unidentified clipping (Milwaukee, Wisconsin), July 24, 1897, Margaret Olivia Slocum Sage Collection, EWS. On immigration and national identity, see Rivka Lissak, *Pluralism and Progressives: Hull House and the New Immigrants, 1890–1918* (Chicago: University of Chicago Press, 1989).

37. A recent study supports a more sympathetic interpretation of women's patriotic ancestral organizations such as the Daughters of the American Revolution (DAR). Members were not necessarily "reactionaries or politically apathetic socialites," Francesca Morgan argues. They could as well be progressive as reactionary. Francesca Morgan, "Patriotism, Progressivism, and the Daughters of the American Revolution, 1900–1930," paper presented to the Social Science History Association, New Orleans, October 11, 1996, 2, quoted by permission of the author. See also Francesca Morgan, "'Home and Country': Women, Nation, and the Daughters of the American Revolution, 1890–1930" (Ph.D. diss., Columbia University, 1998). See also Stuart McConnell, "Reading the Flag: A Reconsideration of the Patriotic Cults of the 1890s," in *Bonds of Affection: Americans Define Their Patriotism*, ed. John Bodnar (Princeton, N.J.: Princeton University Press, 1996), 102–119; Nancy A. Hewitt, "Charity or Mutual Aid? Two Perspectives on Latin Women's Philanthropy in Tampa, Florida," in *Lady Bountiful Revisited: Women, Philanthropy, and Power*, ed. Kathleen D. McCarthy (New Brunswick, N.J.: Rutgers University Press, 1990), 55–69.

38. In *Romance of Reunion*, Silber writes that "traditional notions of masculine and feminine behavior assumed a special significance in the context of this patriotic upsurge as many saw gender providing a unifying thread, as well as a necessary sense of order, for the country's diverse population" (166). See also Rebecca Edwards, *Angels in the Machinery: Gender in American Party Politics from the Civil War to the Progressive Era* (New York: Oxford University Press, 1997), 152.

39. Margaret Rossiter calls this "an unstated territorial ban on women's attendance." Rossiter provides striking examples of how professional societies deliberately held "smokers" to deter women's attendance. For example, the American Association of Geographers "deliberately held 'smokers' or other important discussions in smoke-filled rooms in order to discourage female attendance and avoid having to consider issues of importance to the women." Rossiter, *Women Scientists in America: Struggles and Strategies to 1940* (Baltimore, Md.:

Johns Hopkins University Press, 1982), 93. Early Progressive-era battles over control of smoking are briefly discussed in Cassandra Tate, *Cigarette Wars: The Triumph of the "Little White Slaver"* (New York: Oxford University Press, 1999).

40. "This Mrs. Sage construes into a snub to herself and as indicating an endeavor on the part of the society to oust the women members." "Mrs. Sage and Mayflower Society Part," *New York Daily Tribune*, November 26, 1902, 7. See also Arthur Huntington Gleason, "Mrs. Russell Sage and Her Interests," *World's Work* 13 (November 1906): 8183.

41. Katherine Devereux Blake and Margaret Louise Wallace, *Champion of Women: The Life of Lillie Devereux Blake* (New York: Fleming H. Revell Co., 1943), 178; *HWS*, 4:873.

42. Blake, *Champion of Women*, 178. See also Theodore Stanton and Harriot Stanton Blatch, eds., *Elizabeth Cady Stanton, as Revealed in Her Letters, Diary, and Reminiscences* (New York: Harper and Bros., 1922), 2:301.

43. "Mrs. Catt Gives Chill to 'Pilgrim Mothers' by Slur on Birth Claims," *New York Journal*, December 23, 1908, Abbé Scrapbooks, vol. 4.

44. Reminiscences of Mrs. Russell Sage quoted in Nancy Boyd Willey, *Built By The Whalers: A Tour of Historic Sag Harbor* (Sag Harbor, N.Y.: The Old Sagg-Harbour Committee, 1945). The invisibility of slavery in New England's understanding of its own history is the subject of Joanne Pope Melish, *Disowning Slavery: Gradual Emancipation and "Race" in New England, 1780–1860* (Ithaca, N.Y.: Cornell University Press, 1998).

45. MOS to Joseph Jermain Slocum, n.d. [1882?], FSW.

46. Conversation with the late Mrs. Florence Slocum Wilson, Pasadena, Calif., July 26, 1994; "Margaret Proctor's Memorabilia," typescript, FSW.

47. "A deep forgetting fell over the twenty thousand Puritans who came to America to build a city on the hill for the spiritual education of their European brethren. Instead the appealing picture of several hundred humble Pilgrims sitting down to dinner with Wampanoag Indians in mutual respect and general thanksgiving came to stand in for the whole gallery of disputatious colonists"; Joyce Appleby, Lynn Hunt, and Margaret Jacob, *Telling the Truth about History* (New York: W.W. Norton, 1994), 107. See also Michael G. Kammen, *Mystic Chords of Memory: The Transformation of Tradition in American Culture* (New York: Knopf, 1991); and John Bodnar, *Remaking America: Public Memory, Commemoration, and Patriotism in the Twentieth Century* (Princeton, N.J.: Princeton University Press, 1992).

48. William Griffith, "The Sage Home on Fifth Avenue," undated clipping [1900?], "Margaret Olivia Sage," OnHA; "A Talk with Mrs. Russell Sage," *New York Times Illustrated Magazine* (September 26, 1897): 2–3. Russell Sage at seventy-eight is described in Harold Parker, "Russell Sage," *Muncy's Magazine* 112 (1895): 634–637.

49. MOS to Nettie McCormick, November 9, 1898, Nettie Fowler McCormick Correspondence, Series 2B, Box 74, WHSA; emphasis added.

50. "Mrs. Russell Sage the Richest Woman in America," July 29, 1906, unidentified clipping, "Margaret Olivia Sage," OnHA.

51. Gleason, "Mrs. Russell Sage and Her Interests," 8183; Irvin G. Wyllie, "Margaret Olivia Slocum Sage," *NAW*, 3:222–223.

52. Gleason, "Mrs. Russell Sage and Her Interests," 8184–8185.

53. Gregory responded that someone had to work or there would be no Monday papers; Elizabeth Hiatt Gregory, *Show Windows of Life* (New York: Wayside Press, Inc., 1944), 70–71. See also "Mrs. Russell Sage at Flying Field: She Did Not See a Flight But Said She's Going to Try Again," *New York Sun*, July 28, 1910; "Mrs. Sage Sees Flights," *New York Sun*, July 29, 1910, 1; "Too Much Wind at Garden City," *New York Herald*, July 28, 1910, 4. My thanks to Lygia Ionnitiu for bringing these references to my attention.

54. Gregory, *Show Windows of Life*, 71.

55. Snow responded, "Mrs. Sage was not a 'common, ordinary teacher.' . . . She taught in a very nice school for young ladies, the Misses Bonney's and Dillaye's on Chestnut Street, Philadelphia." Alice Northrop Snow, with Henry Nicholas Snow, *The Story of Helen Gould, Daughter of Jay Gould, Great American* (New York: Fleming H. Revell Company, 1943), 224–225.

56. Maureen E. Montgomery, *Displaying Women: Spectacles of Leisure in Edith Wharton's New York* (New York: Routledge, 1998), 22–23, 130–135.

57. Snow and Snow, *The Story of Helen Gould*, 239–240; Montgomery, *Displaying Women*, 23. According to Sven Beckert, "The Goulds, Vanderbilts, Morgans, Whitneys, Bakers, and Rockefellers all contributed $10,000 each to incorporate the Metropolitan Opera House Company." This was after William H. Vanderbilt had been refused a box at the Academy of Music, despite offering to buy one for $30,000. Sven Beckert, *The Monied Metropolis: New York City and the Consolidation of the American Bourgeoisie, 1850–1896* (New York: Cambridge University Press, 2001), 247.

58. Snow and Snow, *The Story of Helen Gould*, 239–240.

59. Blake and Wallace, *Champion of Women*, 183.

60. HMG to "My dear Father," April 9, 1891, Helen Miller Gould Shepard Papers, NYHS. The bridegroom was a Demarest who was connected to the president of Rutgers College, a Reformed institution. "The Reformed Tradition," in *The Encyclopedia of American Religious History*, ed. Edward L. Queen II, Stephen R. Prothero and Gardiner H. Shattuck, Jr. (Boston: Facts On File, 1996): 550-552.

61. HMG to "My dear Mrs. Sage," March 10, 1886, Helen Miller Gould Shepard Papers, NYHS. For the *Atalanta*, see Maury Klein, *The Life and Legend of Jay Gould* (Baltimore, Md.: Johns Hopkins University Press, 1986), 318–319, 443.

62. HMG to "My dear Father," April 9, 1891, Helen Miller Gould Shepard Papers, NYHS; emphasis in the original.

63. Lori Ginzberg first suggested this realignment of benevolent women in the late nineteenth century in *Women and the Work of Benevolence*, 198.

64. Nina Baym, "Women and the Republic: Emma Willard's Rhetoric of History," *American Quarterly* 43 (March 1991): 1–23; Nina Baym, *American Women Writers and the Work of History, 1790–1860* (New Brunswick, N.J.: Rutgers University Press, 1995); Anne Firor Scott, "The Ever-Widening Circle: The Diffusion of Feminist Values from the Troy Female Seminary, 1822–72," in Scott, *Making the Invisible Woman Visible* (Urbana: University of Illinois Press, 1984), 86–87n12.

65. Unidentified clipping, *New York Mail and Express*, June 10, 1897, Margaret Olivia Slocum Sage Collection, EWS.

66. Baym, "Women and the Republic," 8; and Nina Baym, "At Home with History: History Books and Women's Sphere before the Civil War," *Proceedings of the American Antiquarian Society* 101, part 2 (1991): 275–295.

67. "Emma Willard Banquet," *New York Daily Tribune*, November 11, 1898, 5.

68. On anxiety about the New Woman, see Ellen Carol DuBois, *Harriot Stanton Blatch and the Winning of Woman Suffrage* (New Haven, Conn.: Yale University Press, 1997). See also Christine Stansell, *American Moderns: Bohemian New York and the Creation of a New Century* (New York: Metropolitan Books, 2000); Sandra Adickes, *To Be Young Was Very Heaven: Women in New York before the First World War* (New York: St. Martin's Press, 1997); Carroll Smith-Rosenberg, "The New Woman As Androgyne," in Smith-Rosenberg, *Disorderly Conduct: Visions of Gender in Victorian America* (New York: Knopf, 1985), 245–290; June Sochen, *The New Woman: Feminism in Greenwich Village, 1900–1920* (New York: Quadrangle Books, 1972); Woloch, *Women and the American Experience*, 275–313. My thanks to my student Catherine Conner, who prompted me to think some more about the New Woman.

69. "Suffragette Audience Hisses President of the United States," unidentified clipping provided by the late Bill Luckham. See also DuBois, *Harriot Stanton Blatch*, 90–91.

70. "Suffragette Audience Hisses President of the United States."

71. "At Emma Willard's Seminary: Mrs. Russell Sage, Fifty Years a Graduate, Makes an Address," *New York Times*, June 11, 1897, 3.

72. MOS, "Presidential Address," *Emma Willard Association, Ninth Annual Report* (November 1899), 14–15.

73. "A Talk with Mrs. Russell Sage."

74. "Mrs. Russell Sage's Opinion: Teaching Women How to Keep House the First Step Toward Solution," *New York Times*, January 20, 1895, 25.

75. Sage, "Opportunities and Responsibilities of Leisured Women," 713.

76. "Mrs. Russell Sage's Opinions: Teaching Women How to Keep House the First Step Toward Solution"; Joanne Meyerowitz, *Women Adrift: Independent Wage Earners in Chicago, 1880–1930* (Chicago: University of Chicago Press, 1988); Dolores Hayden, *The Grand Domestic Revolution: A History of Feminist Designs for American Homes, Neighborhoods, and Cities* (Cambridge, Mass.: MIT

Press, 1982). The valence of "homes," "houses," and variants of these is explored by Wendy Gamber in *Houses, Not Homes: Boardinghouses in Nineteenth-Century America* (forthcoming, Johns Hopkins University Press).

77. "Doing the nation's work" in Kathryn Kish Sklar, *Florence Kelley and the Nation's Work: The Rise of Women's Political Culture, 1830–1900* (New Haven, Conn.: Yale University Press, 1995). For women reformers and state-building, see Robyn Muncy, *Creating a Female Dominion in American Reform, 1890–1935* (New York: Oxford University Press, 1991); Kathryn Kish Sklar, "The Historical Foundations of Women's Power in the Creation of the American Welfare State, 1830–1920," in *Mothers of a New World: Maternalist Politics and the Origins of Welfare States*, ed. Seth Koven and Sonya Michel (New York: Routledge, 1993), 43–93; Maureen Flanagan, *Seeing with Their Hearts: Chicago Women and the Vision of the Good City, 1871–1933* (Princeton, N.J.: Princeton University Press, 2002); Lebsock, "Women and American Politics, 1880–1920," 35–62; and Ellen Fitzpatrick, *Endless Crusade: Women Social Scientists and Progressive Reform* (New York: Oxford University Press, 1990).

78. The years following the Civil War had seen a lively debate over married women's property rights under common law. In common law states, women's rights advocates asserted the separate property rights of wives, while in community property states they emphasized marriage as a partnership where both parties worked together to accumulate property. In both kinds of jurisdiction, the idea was gaining ground that wives contributed to the accumulation of wealth and that therefore property should be owned jointly. Reva B. Siegel, "Home as Work: The First Woman's Rights Claims Concerning Wives' Household Labor, 1850–1880," *Yale Law Journal* 103 (March 1994): 1091–1146. See also Norma Basch, *In the Eyes of the Law: Women, Marriage, and Property in Nineteenth-Century New York* (Ithaca, N.Y.: Cornell University Press, 1982); Joan Hoff, *Law, Gender, and Injustice: A Legal History of U.S. Women* (New York: New York University Press, 1991); Amy Dru Stanley, *From Bondage to Contract: Wage Labor, Marriage, and the Market in the Age of Slave Emancipation* (New York: Cambridge University Press, 1998).

79. I explore the religious roots of Olivia Sage's philanthropy in "'From Widow's Mite to Widow's Might': The Philanthropy of Margaret Olivia Sage," *American Presbyterians* 74 (Winter 1996): 253–264.

80. Mrs. Mary Newbury Adams, quoted in *Third Annual Report of the Emma Willard Association, Chicago Reunion, 1893* (Brooklyn, N.Y.: Press of the Brooklyn Eagle, 1893), 17. For the "tainted money" controversy, see Chapter 10.

81. HMG to MOS, October 28, 1887, Helen Miller Gould Shepard Papers, NYHS.

82. She added, "I did not study the Sunday school lesson very carefully last Sunday for we were out at sea." Helen Gould to "My dear Mrs. Sage," January 13, 1886, Helen Miller Gould Shepard Papers, NYHS.

83. HMG to MOS, May __, 1887, Helen Miller Gould Shepard Papers, NYHS.

84. HMG to MOS, November 15, 1907, Helen Miller Gould Shepard Papers, NYHS.

85. "The founders of the Woman's Law Class had three goals: to provide practical legal knowledge to women who needed either to protect their own personal affairs or to improve their positions in the workplace; to give leisured women the opportunity to expand their education and broaden their minds; and to prepare women who wished ultimately enter a law school." Virginia Drachman, *Sisters in Law: Women Lawyers in Modern American History* (Cambridge, Mass.: Harvard University Press, 1998), 122. See also Phyllis Eckhaus, "Restless Women: The Pioneering Alumnae of New York University School of Law," *New York University Law Review* 66 (December 1991): 1998–1999; *For the Better Protection of Their Rights: A History of the First Fifty Years of the Women's Legal Education Society and the Woman's Law Class: A History of the First Fifty Years of the Women's Legal Education Society and the Woman's Law Class* (New York: New York University Press, 1940). On Emilie Kempin, see Virginia Drachman, *Women Lawyers and the Origins of Professional Identity in America* (Ann Arbor: University of Michigan Press, 1993), 281–283.

86. Theodore Francis Jones, ed., *New York University, 1832–1932* (New York: New York University Press, 1933), 169. The friendship between Helen's brother Frank Gould and Henry MacCracken, Jr., and Helen Gould and Henry's sister Fay is referred to in the text of a speech by Henry MacCracken, Jr., at the dedication in 1954 of the $1.5 million Gould Student Center. Biographical file, "Helen Miller Gould," NYU.

87. Theodore Francis Jones, ed., *New York University, 1832–1932* (New York: New York University Press, 1933), 169. The move to what is now the South Bronx was called the "up-town movement" and involved the new undergraduate college. Other faculties such as education and law were to remain at the Washington Square campus. I am grateful to NYU archivist Nancy Cricco for her explanation of MacCracken and his plans.

88. HMG to Henry MacCracken, April 25, 1898, MacCracken Records, Box 15, Folder 4, 1898–99, NYU. Emphasis in the original.

89. Jones, *New York University*, 169–170, 323. The Hall of Fame is now part of the Bronx Community College.

90. Biographical file, "Helen Miller Gould," NYU.

91. Quoted in J. D. Phelps to Chancellor James Day, May 11, 1906, Papers of Chancellor James Roscoe Day, Box 2, SUA. See also Carlisle, "Mrs. Sage's Burden."

92. Recent scholarship throws doubt on the model of "New York society" created by the well-publicized Ward McAllister, the ambitious social arbiter and gossip, who famously defined the bounded world of New York high society, the so-called Four Hundred: "Why there are only about four hundred people in fashionable New York society," McAllister is supposed to have said. "If you go outside that number you strike people who are either not at ease in a ball room or who make others not at ease." McAllister interview, quoted in Fred-

eric Cople Jaher, "Style and Status: High Society in Late Nineteenth-Century New York," in *The Rich, The Well-Born, and the Powerful: Elites and Upper Classes in History*, ed. Jaher (Urbana: University of Illinois Press, 1973), 263. See also Ward McAllister, *Society As I Have Found It* (New York: Cassell Publishing Company, 1890). My thanks to an anonymous reader for the Press for this point.

93. Edith Wharton, *The Age of Innocence* (1920; reprint, London: Virago Press, 1988), 23. "The Only Four Hundred; Ward McAllister Gives Out the Official List," *New York Times*, February 16, 1892, 5. The Sages were included on a newer list, the 150. For an example of a society event at this time, see "Mrs. Astor Entertains Her Hosts of Friends: Beautiful Decorations Which Testified to the Florist's Art," *New York Times*, February 22, 1892.

94. "Cold, grim hunger" is in Lindsay Denison, "Russell Sage—A Man of Dollars. The Story of a Life Devoted Solely to the Chill Satisfaction of Making Money for Its Own Sake," *World's Work* 10 (May 1905–October 1905), 6301, 6298. See also Maury Klein, *The Life and Legend of Jay Gould* (Baltimore, Md.: Johns Hopkins University Press, 1986), 164, 323.

95. Denison, "Russell Sage—A Man of Dollars," 6299.

96. Sage quoted in Paul Sarnoff, *Russell Sage, the Money King* (New York: Ivan Obolensky, 1965), 343; See also Russell Sage, "The Injustice of Vacations," *Independent* (New York), June 2, 1904; "Death of Russell Sage," *Troy Record*, July 23, 1906.

97. "Russell Sage Is Growing Younger: He Found Yesterday He Could Read without the Aid of Glasses," *New York Times*, July 18, 1895, 14.

98. Denison, "Russell Sage—A Man of Dollars," 6301.

99. MOS to Anna Pratt, November 25, 1901, Richard Henry Pratt Papers, Yale, Beinecke. Erasure in the original.

100. Flora E. Smith, Sec., New York Mission and Tract Society, to MOS, April 3, 1905, RSFR, Box 1, Folder 6. One interpretation is that she had few contacts with the poor and didn't understand what would be useful. Russell Sage's miserliness prevented her from giving substantial gifts either in kind or in cash.

101. Mrs. J. C. Havemeyer to Miss Hunter, November 1904, Emma Willard Association Papers, EWS.

102. "Mrs. Russell Sage on Marriage," *Syracuse Sunday Herald*, June 21, 1903, 29, "Margaret Olivia Sage," OnHA.

103. *Troy Daily Press*, October 1, 1888.

104. Especially Sarnoff, *Russell Sage, the Money King*.

105. His wife, a friend of Helen Gould, had made the Vassar branch the most active auxiliary of the WNWRA during the recent war with Spain. Ellen Hardin Walworth to Helen Gould, June 21, 1899, Helen Miller Gould Shepard Papers, NYHS.

106. The appeal from Vassar is contained in Mrs. A. L. Hadley to MOS, April 30, 1904, RSFR, Box 96, Folder 965. A few weeks later the college

acknowledged a "most kind letter and the cheque for Vassar." Hadley to MOS, June 17, 1904, RSFR, Box 96, Folder 965. Rockefeller's daughter Bessie had attended the college. On President James Monroe Taylor, see Lynn D. Gordon, *Gender and Higher Education in the Progressive Era* (New Haven, Conn.: Yale University Press, 1990), 134–135; and Barbara Miller Solomon, *In the Company of Educated Women: A History of Women and Higher Education in America* (New Haven, Conn.: Yale University Press, 1985), 47–48. Taylor's 1903–1904 campaign raised $350,000, but only three gifts reached $10,000 each. The writer of "Russell Sage and His Life," *The Troy Record*, July 24, 1906, claimed that Olivia had attended Troy Female Seminary with the future wife of Vassar founder Matthew Vassar. I have not been able to verify this.

107. [Radcliffe College] to MOS, March 15, 1906, RSFR, Box 92, Folder 895. Another donation of this transition period was a gift of $50 to the Home for the Friendless, Chicago. The donation was to furnish one room in the new home. William Peck to MOS, RSFR, Box 67, Folder 593.

108. HMG to "My dear Mrs. Sage," March 7, 1903, Helen Miller Gould Shepard Papers, NYHS.

109. Susan W. Duncan to MOS, March 29, 1905, RSFR, Box 91, Folder 891; Olivia's emphasis in the original. Sage already subscribed to this New Jersey charity and it seems that the Jermain connection was genuine. See Henry Whittemore, *History of the Sage and Slocum Families of England and America, Including the Allied Families of Montague, Wanton, Brown, Josselyn, Standish, Doty, Carver, Jermain or Germain, Pierson, Howell* (New York: Published by Mrs. Russell Sage, 1908); Charles Elihu Slocum, *A Short History of the Slocums, Slocumbs and Slocombs of America, Genealogical and Biographical* (Syracuse, N.Y., Published by the author, 1882).

110. Sereno S. Pratt, "Our Financial Oligarchy: The Seventy Six Men Who Make Up the 'Business Senate' of the United States—What They Control—Their Cliques and Parties—Is Their Power Declining?" *World's Work* 10 (October 1905): 6706. Pratt was assistant editor of the *Wall Street Journal*.

111. "Yates Castle," n.d., Obituaries and Biographical Clippings Collection, OCPL.

112. Acknowledgment of the gift is in James Phelps to MOS, July 29, 1907, RSFR, Box 94, Folder 939.

113. To begin with, she requested the name Renwick Hall. She later seems to have changed her mind, though the evidence is partial and confusing. Frank Webb to Chancellor Day, November 4, 1905, and November 6, 1905; Catharine Hunter [secretary] to James R. Day, December __ [1905] and December 6, 1905. All in Papers of Chancellor James Roscoe Day, Box 2, SUA.

Olivia vetoed the names "Slocum College" or "Sage College" and for a time seems to have favored the name "Caroline Longstreet College for Women Teachers." Dean Jacob Street to J. J. Slocum, September 22, 1908, and Henry de Forest to MOS, October 25, 1909, both in RSFR, Box 94, Folder 939.

10. "A kind of old-age freedom"

1. Allison Levy, "The Widow's Cleavage and Other Compromising Pictures," paper presented at the conference "The Widow's Might," Rutgers Center for Historical Analysis, April 2004, 1.

2. The Sages were among several wealthy donors Phelps visited that day. James D. Phelps to James Day, May 11, 1906, Papers of Chancellor James Roscoe Day, Box 2, SUA.

3. Changes in the organization and the purpose of higher education in this period, and in the organization of knowledge, are the subject of many studies, among them George M. Marsden and Bradley J. Longfield, eds., *The Secularization of the Academy* (New York: Oxford University Press, 1992); Ellen Condliffe Lagemann, *The Politics of Knowledge: The Carnegie Corporation, Philanthropy, and Public Policy* (Chicago: University of Chicago Press, 1989); Ellen Condliffe Lagemann, *Private Power for the Public Good: A History of the Carnegie Foundation for the Advancement of Teaching* (Middletown, Conn.: Wesleyan University Press, 1983). See also Thomas L. Haskell, ed., *The Authority of Experts: Studies in History and Theory* (Bloomington: Indiana University Press, 1984); David F. Noble, *America by Design: Science, Technology, and the Rise of Corporate Capitalism* (New York: Knopf, 1977); James A. Smith, *The Idea Brokers: Think Tanks and the Rise of the New Policy Elite* (New York: Free Press, 1991); and Peter Dobkin Hall, *The Organization of American Culture, 1700–1900: Private Institutions, Elites, and the Origins of American Nationality* (New York: New York University Press, 1982).

4. Henry S. Pritchett to James Day, January 28, 1907, and March 6, 1907, both in Papers of Chancellor James Roscoe Day, Box 2, January–April 1907 folder, SUA. Day repeatedly applied to have Syracuse included in the teachers' retirement scheme of the Carnegie Foundation but the application was refused "so long as the formal denominational connection remains." For a hostile description of Syracuse ("the University of Heaven") and its sanctimonious president, see Upton Sinclair, *The Goose-Step: A Study of American Education* (Los Angeles: Published by the author, 1923), 277ff.

5. James L. Barton to Chancellor Day, May 11, 1905. Barton, corresponding secretary to the American Board of Commissioners for Foreign Missions, defended Day's acceptance of Standard Oil money. "I feel it to be my duty as a Christian man and an officer of a benevolent organization to use every means in my power to convert money from idle uses, from secular uses, and even from vicious uses into the service of the Kingdom of God," he wrote to Day; see Papers of Chancellor James Roscoe Day, Box 2, SUA, for this and other letters relating to attacks from alumni and others on Standard Oil, Day's defense of the connection, and the response. For the Standard Oil controversy, see J. Scott Clark to Professor Smalley, December 30, 1909; Day to Thomas Richardson, March 28, 1910. See also J. D. Archbold to Chancellor J. P. Day, September 7 1909, for Archbold's instruction to "draw on me for

$75,000 on account of the campus mortgage." Papers of Chancellor James Roscoe Day, Box 2, SUA. See also Ron Chernow, *Titan: The Life of John D. Rockefeller Sr.* (New York: Random House, 1998), 550–551; Allan Nevins, *A Study in Power: John D. Rockefeller, Industrialist and Philanthropist* (New York: Scribners, 1953), 1:345–348.

6. "I visited Mrs. Russell Sage yesterday remaining at her request nearly an hour." James D. Phelps to James Day, May 11, 1906, Day Correspondence, Box 2, SUA.

7. Ibid.

8. "Russell Sage and His Life," *Troy Record*, July 24, 1906, 3.

9. "Thrifty Old Man of Wall Street Has a Peaceful End: His Remarkable Career," July 23, [1906], Obituaries and Biographical Clippings Collection, OCPL.

10. The fact that Sarnoff got her name wrong (it should have been "Maria") does not inspire much confidence in his version. Yet Sarnoff claimed to have interviewed Dr. Schmuck. "Russell Sage and His Life," *Troy Record*, July 24, 1906, 3; Paul Sarnoff, *Russell Sage, the Money King* (New York: Ivan Obolensky, 1965), 326.

11. Sarnoff, *Russell Sage, the Money King*, 341.

12. Russell Sage had set aside another $10,000 for his sister, Fanny Chapin of Oneida, but she had died two years earlier. "Sage Will a Surprise," *Troy Record*, July 28, 1906; "Mrs. Sage to Get All?" *Troy Record*, July 26, 1906; "The Will of Russell Sage," *Troy Record*, July 28, 1906; "Sage Fortune All for Wife," Obituaries and Biographical Clippings Collection, OCPL.

Estimates of Sage's wealth varied. One report stated that attorneys for Oivia Sage estimated it at between $70 and $80 million, with $30 million in outstanding loans. "Sage Fortune All for Wife." "Sage's Estate at Least $150,000,000," *Troy Record*, August 4, 1906, 8, announced, "In the Sage strong boxes have been found millions of dollars' worth of securities bearing high interest and guaranteed as to principal and income which have been for years unknown to the manipulators of Wall Street."

13. "Sage Fortune All for Wife"; "Thrifty Old Man of Wall Street Has a Peaceful End."

14. "Russell Sage's Estate," *The Outlook* 83 (August 4, 1906), 779.

15. "Mrs. Sage to Get All?"; "Sage Heirs Still Hopeful That Widow Will Settle," *Troy Record*, July 31, 1906, 8. The will was dated February 1901.

16. James H. Sage's comment is reported in "A Preposterous Claim," *The Outlook* 83 (August 11, 1906): 825. See also "Reasons Why Trojan Will Contest Sage Will," *Troy Record*, August 1, 1906, 5; "Statement by Sage Regarding Contest of the Financier's Will," *Troy Record*, August 3, 1906. For this provision of the 1901 will, see "Sage Fortune All for Wife." See also "Mrs. Russell Sage Dies at the Age of Ninety," *Sag Harbor News* [1918], clipping, "Sage and Slocum Book," Jermain Family Collection, JJML.

17. *New York Daily Tribune*, July 25, 1906, 1; "Funeral of Russell Sage Yes-

terday Afternoon," *Troy Record*, July 26, 1906, 5. Among the mourners were Dr. and Mrs. Munn, Maj. Herbert J. Slocum, Mr. and Mrs. Charles Chapin, Dr. Charles Schmuck, and Dr. Lancey Nicholl.

18. James D. Phelps to MOS, January 29, 1907, February 15, 1907, and February 16, 1907, all in RSFR, Box 94, Folder 939.

19. James D. Phelps to MOS, January 29, 1907, RSFR, Box 94, Folder 939.

20. James D. Phelps to MOS, June 26, 1907, RSFR, Box 94, Folder 939.

21. "Russell Sage's Estate," *The Outlook* 83 (August 4, 1906), 779; C. B. Carlisle, "Mrs. Sage's Burden," July 31, 1906, Obituaries and Biographical Clippings Collection, OCPL.

22. "The Will of Russell Sage."

23. "Sage Will a Surprise."

24. I explore the meanings of gifts and charity at the turn of the twentieth century in Ruth Crocker, "'I Only Ask You Kindly to Divide Your Fortune with Me': Begging Letters and the Transformation of Charity in Late Nineteenth-Century America," *Social Politics: International Studies in Gender, State, and Society* 6 (Summer 1999): 131–160. See also Jeffrey Slansky, *The Soul's Economy: Market Society and Selfhood in American Social Thought, 1820–1920* (Chapel Hill: University of North Carolina Press, 2002).

25. Numbers compiled by Michael Donahue. Controversy over Rockefeller's activities would increase again after 1910 when Congress rejected a bill to incorporate the Rockefeller Foundation, which then sought and gained incorporation under the laws of the state of New York. Robert Bremner, *American Philanthropy* (Chicago: University of Chicago Press, 1960), 118–119; Chernow, *Titan*, 550–551.

26. Quoted in Bremner, *American Philanthropy*, 112–113.

The public's reception of Carnegie's philanthropy is described at length in Abigail Van Slyck, *Free to All: Carnegie Libraries and American Culture, 1890–1920* (Cambridge, Mass.: MIT Press, 1995). See also Joseph Frazier Wall, *Andrew Carnegie* (New York: Oxford University Press, 1970). Controversy over Rockefeller philanthropy burst forth a few years later with the work of the Commission on Industrial Relations. See Graham Adams, Jr., *Age of Industrial Violence, 1910–15: The Activities and Findings of the United States Commission on Industrial Relations* (New York: Columbia University Press, 1966); Leon Fink, *Progressive Intellectuals and the Dilemmas of Democratic Commitment* (Cambridge, Mass.: Harvard University Press, 1997), 94–99.

27. "Address of the Hon. Abram S. Hewitt at the Thirty-Seventh Anniversary of the Woman's Hospital, held December 1, 1892," in Woman's Hospital in the State of New York, "Thirty-Seventh Annual Report of the Woman's Hospital [1892]," 37, WHP. The Sages were in the audience for this speech and were probably the target of his remarks.

28. "Wiping her husband's name clear" in Arthur Huntington Gleason, "Mrs. Russell Sage and Her Interests," *World's Work* 13 (November 1905): 8182.

"Your chain of gold" in Caroline Borden to MOS, February 10, 1908, RSFR, Box 66, Folder 590.

29. Carlisle, "Mrs. Sage's Burden." My discussion of the representation of widows was helped by the papers and comments of fellow participants at the conference "The Widow's Might," Rutgers Center for Historical Analysis, Rutgers University, April 2004.

30. MOS to Mrs. Morris Jesup, March 12, 1908, RSFR, Box 97, Folder 980. The Jesups, along with William E. Dodge, Jr., and J. P. Morgan, were among the "merchants, manufacturers, and bankers" who were funders of the early YMCA and the social purity campaign. Andrea Tone, *Devices and Desires: A History of Contraceptives in America* (New York: Hill and Wang, 2001), 9, 12; Paul Boyer, *Urban Masses and Moral Order, 1820–1920* (Cambridge, Mass.: Harvard University Press, 1978), 115–116.

31. "Like a prisoner in her own home" in "Death of Mrs. Russell Sage in the Ninetieth Year of Her Age," unidentified clipping, Troy Scrapbook, Local History Collection, TPL.

32. MOS to Mrs. Nelson Aldrich, October 16, 1907, RSFR, Box 92, Folder 902.

33. Gleason, "Mrs. Russell Sage and Her Interests," 8182–8183.

34. "I am in trouble" quoted in Peter Dobkin Hall, "Inventing the Nonprofit Sector," in Hall, *Inventing the Nonprofit Sector and Other Essays on Philanthropy, Voluntarism and Nonprofit Organizations* (Baltimore, Md.: Johns Hopkins University Press, 1992), 45–46. See also Nevins, *A Study in Power,* 2:291; Raymond B. Fosdick, *The Story of the Rockefeller Foundation* (1952; repr., New Brunswick, N.J.: Transaction Publishers, 1989), 1–13; Sealander, *Private Wealth and Public Life,* 28.

Kathleen McCarthy outlines the role of philanthropic experts in turn-of-the-century Chicago. Examples are Sherman Kingsley, an "inveterate modernizer," who worked with the McCormicks as head of the Elizabeth McCormick Memorial Fund; and Dr. Henry Baird Favill and Frank Billings, physicians who were active in leading antituberculosis and other medical philanthropies. McCarthy, *Noblesse Oblige: Charity and Cultural Philanthropy in Chicago, 1849–1929* (Chicago: University of Chicago Press, 1982), 120–122.

35. William Griffith, "The Sage Home on Fifth Avenue," undated clipping [1900?], "Margaret Olivia Sage," OnHA.

36. Ellen B. Morris to MOS, August 2, 1900, RSFR, Box 97, Folder 979.

37. The de Forest law firm included the brothers Robert W. de Forest, Henry W. de Forest, and Johnston de Forest. Unless indicated, "de Forest" in this work refers to Robert Weeks de Forest, abbreviated RW de F.

38. On Robert de Forest, see "Personalities," Box 153, CSSA, Columbia. Perhaps through her friendship with Emily de Forest, Olivia was induced to give $200 for a lifetime membership in the Metropolitan Museum of Art in 1886, an unusual donation for this early date, especially since Olivia seemed

to have no pretensions as a collector or connoisseur. Emily de Forest's father, John Taylor Johnston, was the museum's first president. Robert de Forest became a trustee in 1889. James Hijiya, "Four Ways of Looking at a Philanthropist: A Study of Robert Weeks De Forest," *Proceedings of the American Philosophical Society* 124 (December 1980): 404, 406.

39. RW de F to Seth Low, January 22, 1894, Seth Low Papers, Columbia. De Forest thanks Low for his subscription to the Provident Loan Society that, together with those from Jacob Schiff, James Speyer, and William E. Dodge, "make $25,000." Hijiya, "Four Ways of Looking at a Philanthropist, 405n8.

40. "Robert W. de Forest," *The Family* (June 1931), 114–115. See also Dawn Greeley, "Beyond Benevolence: Gender, Class and the Development of Scientific Charity in New York City, 1882–1935" (Ph.D. diss., SUNY Stony Brook, 1995), 443. This institution began as the New York Summer School for Philanthropy in 1898. Roy Lubove, *The Professional Altruist: The Emergence of Social Work as a Career, 1880–1930* (1965; repr., New York: Atheneum, 1980), 18.

41. John M. Glenn to the Trustees of the Russell Sage Foundation on the death of RW de F, *The Nation* (May 20, 1931), in "Personalities," Box 153, CSSA, Columbia. On the genteel reformers, see John G. Sproat, *The Best Men: Liberal Reformers in the Gilded Age* (1968; repr., Chicago: University of Chicago Press, 1982); Nancy Cohen, *The Reconstruction of American Liberalism, 1865–1914* (Chapel Hill: University of North Carolina Press, 2002).

42. He would remain the corporate lawyer for this railroad for half a century. Hijiya writes, "At least twice he represented the railroad before the United States Supreme Court in cases involving the Hepburn Act (record: one win, one loss), and for several months he was chairman of the New York Bar Association's Committee on Judicial Nomination." Hijiya, "Four Ways of Looking at a Philanthropist," 404.

43. MOS, Minutes of a Conference at the Woman's Hospital, January 6, 1888, handwritten, RSFR, Box 97, Folder 978. On lawyers as part of the late-nineteenth-century New York bourgeoisie, which called itself a "new business class," see Sven Beckert, *Monied Metropolis: New York City and the Consolidation of the American Bourgeoisie, 1850–1896* (New York: Cambridge University Press, 2001), 253.

44. Donors and their amounts are listed in *Annual Report of the Central Council, New York Charity Organization Society, 1896–97* (New York: Published by the Society, 1897), 137.

45. *Charity Organization,* pamphlet, Abbé Scrapbooks, vol. 3; emphasis in the original. Olivia's brother Jermain was a COS district committee chairman; *Third Annual Report of the Central Council of the Charity Organization Society of the City of New York, April 1, 1885* (New York: Charities Publication Committee, 1885).

46. David C. Hammack, *Power and Society: Greater New York at the Turn of the Century* (1982; repr., New York: Columbia University Press, 1987), 110–111. Beckert's *The Monied Metropolis* also analyzes different factions

among the ruling elites but stresses the growing sense of class identity among merchants and business and professional men.

47. Hammack, *Power and Society*, 116. A description of the Seth Low rally at Cooper Union's Great Hall on October 6, 1897, conveys the tone of this genteel reform movement. "This was a gathering of the wealthy—or at least the well-to-do—but in behavior, in tone, and in the prominent presence of so many women it resembled the annual meeting of the Mission and Tract Society far more than it resembled a meeting of the Union Club, let alone an ordinary political rally"; *New York World*, October 7, 1897. See also Gerald Kurland, *Seth Low: The Reformer in an Urban and Industrial Age* (New York: Twayne, 1971), 207; S. Sara Monoson, "The Lady and the Tiger: Women's Electoral Activism in New York City before Suffrage," *Journal of Women's History* 2 (Fall 1990): 100–135.

Brooklyn was the first major city to abolish outdoor relief. Raymond A. Mohl, "The Abolition of Public Outdoor Relief, 1870–1900: A Critique of the Piven and Cloward Thesis," in *Social Welfare or Social Control? Some Historical Reflections on "Regulating the Poor,"* ed. Walter I. Trattner (Knoxville: University of Tennessee Press, 1983), 35–50.

48. RW de F to Seth Low, May 28, 1902, Seth Low Papers, Columbia. He described his task as "acting practically as Health Commissioner and 'Housekeeper' in cleaning up the old tenements."

49. RW de F to William Harmon, February 12, 1914, and RW de F to Edward Devine, March 22, 1901, both in CSSA, Columbia; RW de F to Low, October 12, 1903, and December 1, 1903, both in Seth Low Papers, Columbia. De Forest forwarded a copy of his report. RW de F to R. Fulton Cutting, September 11, 1903, CSSA, Columbia. The context of urban reform and reformers at this time is given in Roy Lubove, *The Progressives and the Slums: Tenement House Reform in New York City, 1890–1917* (1962; repr., Westport, Conn.: Greenwood Press, 1974); David Ward, *Poverty, Ethnicity, and the American City, 1840–1925: Changing Conceptions of the Slum and the Ghetto* (New York: Cambridge University Press, 1989), 61–79; Jon C. Teaford, *The Unheralded Triumph: City Government in America, 1870–1900* (Baltimore, Md.: Johns Hopkins University Press, 1984). See also Robert de Forest and Lawrence Veiller, eds. *The Tenement House Problem* (New York: Macmillan, 1903).

50. Lori Ginzberg demolished the assumption that nineteenth-century benevolent women disdained business or money-related activities in *Women and the Work of Benevolence: Morality, Politics, and Class in the Nineteenth Century United States* (New Haven, Conn.: Yale University Press, 1990), 36–66. See also Susan Yohn, "'Let Christian Women Set the Examples in Their Own Gifts': The 'Business' of Protestant Women's Organizations," in *Women and Twentieth-Century Protestantism*, ed. Margaret Bendroth and Virginia Brereton (Urbana: University of Illinois Press, 2002), 213–235; Ruth Crocker, "'From Widow's Mite to Widow's Might': The Philanthropy of Margaret Olivia Sage," *American Presbyterians* 74 (Winter 1996): 253–264.

51. [MOS], handwritten note on envelope, n.d., RSFR, Box 1, Folder 7.

Real estate transactions can be followed in the *New York Daily Tribune*. See "Mrs. Sage Lends Again: $1,200,000 on the Hippodrome and $1,650,000 on the Breslin" (December 12, 1906), 1; "Another Big Sage Loan: Financier's Widow Lends $1,500,000 on Wall Street Property" (December 19, 1906), 1; and "Mrs. Sage Lends Half a Million" (December 28, 1906), 7. One provision of the will required the executors to sell all Russell Sage's real estate. Charles W. Osborne, referred to in Russell Sage's will as "long my confidential and trusted assistant," was named an executor.

52. *Third Annual Report of the Charity Organization Society of New York* (New York: Published by the Society, 1885), 33. "How to make the poor better" in Katz, *Improving Poor People*.

53. On the definition of needs, see Nancy Fraser, "Struggle Over Needs: Outline of a Socialist-Feminist Critical Theory of Late Capitalist Political Culture," in *Unruly Practices: Power, Discourse, and Gender In Contemporary Social Theory* (Minneapolis: University of Minnesota Press, 1989), 161–190.

The Charity Organization Society evokes neoconservative "welfare reformers" of our own time. The COS held the poor up to higher standards of morality than its own class, constructed a notion of a "scientific" charity that confused method with science, and called on working people to shun "dependence" while rich corporations (in the case of de Forest, the very corporations that retained him as legal counsel) reaped the rewards of taxpayer-funded support through railroad subsidies, a regressive tax structure, and protective tariffs. Christopher Howard, *The Hidden Welfare State: Tax Expenditures and Social Policy in the United States* (Princeton, N.J.: Princeton University Press, 1997).

54. A critical assessment of the COS is Michael B. Katz, *Improving Poor People: The Welfare State, the "Underclass," and Urban Schools as History* (Princeton, N.J.: Princeton University Press, 1995), 34–36; Michael B. Katz, *In the Shadow of the Poorhouse: A Social History of Welfare in America* (New York: Basic Books, 1986), 36–57. More sympathetic treatments of the COS include Greeley, "Beyond Benevolence"; James Leiby, "Another Look at the COS," *Social Service Review* 58 (December 1984): 523–538; and the useful comparative study by Daniel Levine, *Poverty and Society: The Growth of the American Welfare State in International Comparison* (New Brunswick, N.J.: Rutgers University Press, 1988), 24–36. Roy Lubove notes, "It was ironic that the charity organization societies of the late nineteenth century, which had revolted against the 'officialdom' of existing relief agencies and imbued voluntary service with a semireligious sanctity, were among the leading architects of welfare bureaucracy and professionalization"; Lubove, *Professional Altruist*, 18. Casework can be seen as one kind of surveillance; see Karen Whitney Tice, *Tales of Wayward Girls and Immoral Women: Case Records on the Professionalization of Social Work* (Urbana: University of Illinois Press, 1998). In "Gender and the Economics of the Sentimental Market in Nineteenth-Century America," *Social Politics: International Studies in Gender, State, and Society* 6 (Summer 1999): 105–130, Scott Sandage

looks at the proliferation of surveillance in late-nineteenth-century America through the lens of begging letters from failed businessmen.

55. Edward R. Devine quoted in RW de F to R. Fulton Cutting, February 1, 1896, CSSA, Columbia. Cutting was president of the Association for Improving the Condition of the Poor.

56. "Survey of COS about Whether They Give Relief," 1, Box 154, CSSA, Columbia; Michael Katz, *Poverty and Policy in American History* (New York: Academic Press, 1983), 17–56.

57. *First Annual Report of the Charity Organization of New York* (New York: Published by the Society, 1883), n.p.; RW de F to R. Fulton Cutting, February 1, 1896, CSSA, Columbia. See RW de F to Edward T. Devine, "Outline of a Plan of Co-operation in Relief between the C.O.S. and the AICP," September 28, 1899, Ms. Collection, Columbia. The COS worked with the older New York Association for Improving the Condition of the Poor, a relief-giving agency which shared space in its United Charities Building. See also RW de F to Cutting, December 11, 1908, and Cutting to RW de F, December 15, 1908, and January 18, 1909, all in CSSA, Columbia. I am grateful to Dawn Greeley for clarifying COS relief policy at this time.

58. John Glenn later described the COS as a crusade against the foolish notion that "anyone with a soft heart" could dispense charity. John Glenn, "Memorial Minute," 1931, CSSA, Columbia. For discussion of how the cultural understanding of professionalism as objective and unsentimental affected both the careers of female practitioners of social work and the content of social policy, see Robyn Muncy, "Gender and Professionalization in the Origins of the U.S. Welfare State: The Careers of Sophonisba Breckinridge and Edith Abbott, 1890–1935," *Journal of Policy History* 2, no. 3 (1990): 291–315; Helene Silverberg, ed., *Gender and American Social Science: The Formative Years* (Princeton, N.J.: Princeton University Press, 1998).

59. Greeley, "Beyond Benevolence," 92–93; M. J. D. Roberts, "Reshaping the Gift Relationship: The London Mendicity Society and the Suppression of Begging in England, 1818–1869," *International Review of Social History* 36 (1991): 201; Crocker, "'I Only Ask You Kindly to Divide Some of Your Fortune with Me,'" 133–136.

60. The tripartite division is described in a memo dated February 7, 1907, in which de Forest discusses with Sage "your philanthropic problem" and summarizes the actions taken to date in response to the begging letters from individuals. RW de F to MOS, February 7, 1907, RSFR, Box 2, Folder 11.

61. Edward T. Devine to RW de F, November 30, 1906, CSSA, Columbia. "Russell Sage Foundation. Mrs. Sage's Gifts, 1906–21," Box 159, CSSA, Columbia; [Unknown] to RW de F, April 11, 1914, CSSA, Columbia; RW de F to MOS, February 7, 1907, RSFR, Box 2, Folder 11. Other arrangements were made for letters from farther afield.

62. W. Frank Persons to RW de F, August 1, 1907, and RW de F to W. Frank

Persons, August 3, 1907, both in CSSA, Columbia. This exchange shows Persons, assistant secretary of the New York COS, handling a large number of appeals addressed to Mrs. Sage. By July 31, 1907, Persons informed de Forest that he had received 39,096, of which he had read carefully 14,000 and skimmed 24,000.

63. For example, RW de F to Persons, June 15, 1912, enclosing Mrs. Sage's check for $10,000. Persons to RW de F, October 1, 1914, CSSA, Columbia.

64. Miss E. L. Todd to Mrs. Bertha Bidwell Brown, Manager Vocational Bureau Skilled Workers, January 4, 1915, RSFR, Box 1, Folder 7.

65. See Mabel Schmidt to MOS, February 11, 1910, asking for a job at the Emma Willard School, and Mrs. George Hadley Stewart to MOS, February 15, 1915, trying to persuade Olivia to purchase some letters written by Emma Willard, both in Emma Willard Association Papers, EWS.

66. [W. F. Persons] to RW de F, November 12, 1906, "Preliminary Report on the Sage Letters. Four Weeks Ending October 27, 1906," Box 159, "Russell Sage Foundation. Mrs. Sage's Gifts, 1906–21" folder, CSSA, Columbia.

67. Ibid.

68. [W. F. Persons] to RW de F, November 12, 1906.

69. "Preliminary Report on the Sage Letters. Four Weeks Ending October 27, 1906."

70. [W. F. Persons] to Porter R. Lee, November 24, 1906, Box 159, "Russell Sage Foundation. Mrs. Sage's Gifts, 1906–21" folder, CSSA, Columbia.

71. Persons to Richard H. Lane, February 12, 1907, Box 159, "Russell Sage Foundation. Mrs. Sage's Gifts, 1906–21" folder, CSSA, Columbia.

72. Assistant Secretary, New York Charity Organization Society, to Mary Richmond, October 23, 1906, and W. Frank Persons to RW de F, November 21, 1906, both in Box 159, "Russell Sage Foundation. Mrs. Sage's Gifts, 1906–21" folder, CSSA, Columbia.

73. RW de F to Mr. W. Frank Persons, Superintendent, the Charity Organization Society, October 20, 1910, CSSA, Columbia.

74. RW de F to Edward Devine, January 30, 1902, CSSA, Columbia.

75. Hijiya, "Four Ways of Looking at a Philanthropist," 414. Hijiya interviewed Tousley and other associates of de Forest.

76. Quoted in Gleason, "Mrs. Russell Sage and Her Interests," 8185.

77. [W. F. Persons] to Porter R. Lee, November 24, 1906.

78. De Forest wrote asking Persons to justify the expenditure from the Sage Fund on probation work and a visiting nurse in the Hudson District. RW de F to Persons, January 15, 1908, and Persons to RW de F, January 16, 1908, both in CSSA, Columbia.

79. RW de F to Devine, April 12, 1908, CSSA, Columbia. On the changing views of lack of work signaled by the new term "unemployment," see Alexander Keyssar, *Out of Work: The First Century of Unemployment in Massachusetts* (New York: Cambridge University Press, 1986); Paul T. Ringenbach, *Tramps and Reformers, 1873–1916: The Discovery of Unemployment in New York* (West-

port, Conn.: Greenwood Press, 1973); Hannah Leah Feder, *Unemployment Relief in Periods of Depression: A Study of Measures Adopted in Certain American Cities, 1857 through 1922* (New York: Russell Sage Foundation, 1936); Samuel Rezneck, "Unemployment, Unrest, and Relief in the United States during the Depression of 1893–97," *Journal of Political Economy* 61 (August 1953): 324–345; Joan Waugh, "'Give This Man Work!' The Charity Organization Society of the City of New York, and the Depression of 1893," *Social Science History* 25 (Summer 2001): 217–224.

80. Persons to RW de F, October 1, 1914, and RW de F to Persons, October 5, 1914, both in CSSA, Columbia.

81. "R. M." to Mr. Purdy, August 2, 1918, Box 159, "Russell Sage Foundation. Mrs. Sage's Gifts, 1906–21" folder, CSSA, Columbia.

82. Sarah J. Burrows, assistant superintendent, COS, to Mr. W. F. Persons, April 15, 1908, Box 159, CSSA, Columbia; emphasis added.

83. Olivia's Salvation Army correspondence in RSFR, Box 1, Folder 8, includes several letters thanking her for gifts to that organization. See, for example, Evangeline Booth to MOS, December 31, 1907, acknowledging "your beautiful gift," a check for $2,000. For the Salvation Army's work in urban areas at this period, see Diane Winston, *Red Hot and Righteous: The Urban Religion of the Salvation Army* (Cambridge, Mass.: Harvard University Press, 1999).

84. RW de F, "The 'Christmas Society' and Its Critics," *Charities Review* 1, no. 3 (January 1892), quoted in Hijiya, "Four Ways of Looking at a Philanthropist," 418. Hijiya rather unconvincingly frames this incident as an indication of de Forest's modesty and dislike of ostentation.

85. Evangeline Booth to MOS, December 15, 1913, RSFR, Box 1, Folder 8; emphasis in the original. But a few years later Olivia refused Evangeline Booth's solicitation of $500,000 for a memorial to William Booth, sending only $2,500. Booth to MOS, April 13, 1916, and April 29, 1916, both in RSFR, Box 1, Folder 8.

86. Evangeline Booth to MOS, December 30, 1910, RSFR, Box 1, Folder 8. Age- and health-related reasons prevented Olivia from attending many events in these years.

87. "A Report on the 'Sage' Letters for the Period Ending February 9, 1907," CSSA, Box 159, "Russell Sage Foundation: Mrs. Sage's Gifts, 1906–21" folder, Columbia. The fact that these numbers do not add up (as well as those in the August 1907 report) suggests that the categories the COS established were porous as well as arbitrary.

88. W. F. Persons to RW de F, August 1, 1907, CSSA, Columbia.

89. RW de F to Mr. W. Frank Persons, August 3, 1907, CSSA, Columbia.

90. Carolyn G. Heilbrun, *Writing a Woman's Life* (1988; reprint, New York: Ballantine Books, 1989), 127. Historian Gerda Lerner agrees. "Certain intellectual insights and advances could be made by women only at life-stages when they could be economically and emotionally independent of men," she writes.

Gerda Lerner, *The Creation of Feminist Consciousness: From the Middle Ages to 1870* (New York: Oxford University Press, 1993), 15–16.

91. Forty-five years later, Blatch was still indignant as she described the turn-of-the-century New York suffrage movement she found when she returned from England after the death of her husband. "It bored its adherents and repelled its opponents. Most of the ammunition was being *wasted on its supporters in private drawing rooms* and in public halls where friends, drummed up and harried by the ardent, listlessly heard the same old arguments. Unswerving adherence to the cause was held in high esteem, but, alas, it was loyalty to a rut worn deep and ever deeper"; Harriot Stanton Blatch and Alma Lutz, *Challenging Years: The Memoirs of Harriot Stanton Blatch* (New York: G. P. Putnam's Sons, 1940), 91. Emphasis added.

92. DuBois, *Harriot Stanton Blatch*, 87, 91, 107–119; Flexner, *Century of Struggle*, 250–251; Blatch and Lutz, *Challenging Years*, 93–94; "The Rich Out to Aid Girl Waistmakers," *New York Times*, January 3, 1910, 1. On the WTUL, see Nancy Schrom Dye, *As Equals and as Sisters: Feminism, the Labor Movement, and the Women's Trade Union League* (Columbia, Missouri: University of Missouri Press, 1980); Elizabeth Anne Payne, *Reform, Labor and Feminism: Margaret Dreier Robins and the Women's Trade Union League* (Urbana: University of Illinois Press, 1988); Allen F. Davis, "Margaret Dreier Robins," *NAW*, 3:179–181.

Historian Nancy Woloch writes, "One of the WTUL's major tenets was that women who worked at home without pay ("allies") and women who worked in lofts and factories ("wage-earners") shared the same interests"; *Women and the American Experience*, vol. 2, *From 1860* (New York: McGraw Hill, 1994), 218–219.

93. Several accounts suggest that wealthy suffragists' alliance with working women contributed to the failure of the shirtwaist strike to achieve union recognition and thus helped perpetuate the conditions that led to the tragic Triangle Shirtwaist Fire. For an account that is very critical of the roles of Ann Morgan and Alva Belmont, see Diane Kirkby, "Class, Gender, and the Perils of Philanthropy: The Story of *Life and Labor* and Labor Reform in the Women's Trade Union League," *Journal of Women's History* 4 (Fall 1992): 36–51; Meredith Tax, *Rising of the Women: Feminist Solidarity and Class Conflict, 1880–1917* (New York: Monthly Review Press, 1980), 229–233. See also Anneliese Orleck, *Common Sense and a Little Fire: Women and Working-Class Politics in the United States, 1900–1965* (Chapel Hill: University of North Carolina Press, 1995). Allied to employers by marriage, these wealthy women could never be counted on to support working-class women, these authors suggest.

94. Ellen Carol DuBois, "Working Women, Class Relations, and Suffrage Militance: Harriot Stanton Blatch and the New York Woman Suffrage Movement, 1894–1909," *Journal of American History* 74 (June 1987): 34–58; DuBois, *Harriot Stanton Blatch*, 106–111.

95. The article mentioned as leaders Harriot Stanton Blatch, Carrie Chap-

man Catt, Helen Garrison Villard, and Mrs. Mackay. "Woman Suffrage Made Fashionable by the Four Hundred. May Its Tribe Increase," *New York Evening Journal,* n.d. [1909], Abbé Scrapbooks, vol. 5.

96. Gertrude Foster Brown, "On Account of Sex," unpublished manuscript (1940?), Chapter 4, page 4, Suffrage Collection, Sophia Smith Collection, Smith College, Northampton, Massachusetts. Pagination is inconsistent. See also Margaret Finnegan, *Selling Suffrage: Consumer Culture and Votes for Women* (New York: Columbia University Press, 1999).

97. "Woman Suffrage Made Fashionable"; "Mrs. C. H. Mackay Leads Suffragists," December 23, 1908. Abbé Scrapbooks, vol. 4.

98. "Not a Suffragette: Mrs. Mackay Takes Stand against Militant Methods," April __, 1909; "Mrs. Clarence Mackay Urges Equal Suffrage," *New York Herald,* January __, 1909; "Woman Suffrage Made Fashionable"; "Society Leader Pleading for Women's Suffrage at Hotel Astor Luncheon." All in Abbé Scrapbooks, vol. 5.

99. Brown, "On Account of Sex," Chapter 1, n.p.

100. "Women Suffragists Plan Hot Campaign," *New York Times,* October 25, 1908, 7.

101. "The Suffrage Bazaar," *Woman's Journal,* November 14, 1908, 183. Ellen DuBois's comment is perceptive here: elite women brought not only money to the cause but also "their capacity to signify changing femininity"; *Harriot Stanton Blatch,* 106.

102. "A Hundred Pockets for This Old Lady: Each Containing a Treasure to Bring Funds to the Suffragette Cause," *New York Times,* November 7, 1908, 14; "Many Marvels at Suffragist Bazaar," *New York Herald,* November 7, 1908, 6. My thanks to Irene M. H. Herold for drawing my attention to this event.

103. "The Suffrage Bazaar."

104. "Shall the Women Vote?" *New York Sun,* April __, 1994, in Abbé Scrapbooks, vol. 2.

105. "Women Bury Differences: Suffragists and Suffragettes Unite to Promote their Fair," *New York Times,* November 8, 1908, 3.

106. The Collegiate Equal Suffrage League was an offshoot of Blatch's League of Self-Supporting Women. The Equal Franchise Society later merged into the Woman Suffrage Party; see "Police Guard for Anti-Suffragists," *New York Herald,* December 19, 1908; "Miss Arnold Pleads for Woman Suffrage," *New York Times,* December 19, 1908. In an announcement of the talk, Sage is listed as one of the patronesses. Abbé Scrapbooks, vol. 4. See also Elinor Lerner, "Immigrant and Working-Class Involvement in the New York City Woman Suffrage Movement" (Ph.D. diss., University of California at Berkeley, 1981), 89–91.

107. "College Women on Dr. Abbott's Trail," *New York Times,* December 12, 1908, Abbé Scrapbooks, vol. 4; "College Suffrage League to Meet," January 14, 1909, and "Think Husbands Aren't Mainstays," *New York Times,* January 7, 1909, both in Abbé Scrapbooks, vol. 5.

108. Quoted in DuBois, *Harriot Stanton Blatch,* 101.

109. DuBois, *Harriot Stanton Blatch*, 113–114.

110. Brown, "On Account of Sex," Chapter 9.

111. DuBois, *Harriot Stanton Blatch*, 102; Brown, "On Account of Sex," Chapter 4, page 2; Susan A. Glenn, *Female Spectacle: The Theatrical Roots of Modern Feminism* (Cambridge, Mass.: Harvard University Press, 2000).

112. Brown, "On Account of Sex," Chapter 9.

113. [MOS] to Miss Mary E. Garrett and Miss M. Carey Thomas, April 30, 1907, RSFR, Box 98, Folder 995.

114. She had allowed her name to be on the Suffrage Bazaar letterhead of the Interurban Suffrage Council. Carrie Chapman Catt to MOS October 15, 1908, and Carrie Chapman Catt to MOS, January 10, 1910, and January 17, 1910, all in RSFR, Box 98, Folder 995. Mary Hay to MOS, April 2, 1912, RSFR, Box 98, Folder 996.

115. Carrie Chapman Catt to MOS, January 10, 1910, and January 17, 1910, both in RSFR, Box 98, Folder 995. See also Christopher Lasch, "Alva Erskine Smith Vanderbilt Belmont," *NAW*, 1:126–128; and Peter Geidel, "Alva E. Belmont: A Forgotten Feminist" (Ph.D. diss., Columbia University, 1993). Geidel argues that Belmont was not just a funder but also a strategist for the suffrage campaign.

116. Carrie Chapman Catt to MOS, October 30, 1910, RSFR, Box 98, Folder 996. This suggests that Sage's anonymous donations to the suffrage movement were substantial.

117. Mary Garrett Hay to MOS, April 2, 1912, RSFR, Box 98, Folder 996. Alva Belmont had given the NAWSA a luxurious New York headquarters building costing hundreds of thousands of dollars. "Suffragists' Home Has Club Features," *New York World*, November 26, 1911, Abbé Scrapbooks, vol. 6; Mabel Potter Daggett, "Suffrage Enters the Drawing Room," *The Delineator* 75 (January 1910): 38.

118. Carrie Chapman Catt to MOS, November 2, 1913, RSFR, Box 98, Folder 996. She added, "I know this is much to ask, but thousands of our followers are workers with only dimes to give."

119. Carrie Chapman Catt to E. Lilian Todd, n.d., RSFR, Box 99, Folder 997.

11. Inventing the Russell Sage Foundation

1. Louisa Lee Schuyler to RW de F, March 23, 1907, and RW de F to Louisa Lee Schuyler, March 26, 1907, RSFR, Box 2, Folder 11.

2. Robert Hill, Secretary, New York State Board of Charities to RW de F, March 15, 1907, RSFR, Box 2, Folder 11. The best account of the origins of the RSF is David C. Hammack, "A Center of Intelligence for the Charity Organization Movement: The Foundation's Early Years," in David C. Hammack and Stanton Wheeler, *Social Science in the Making: Essays on the Russell Sage Foun-*

dation, 1907–1972 (New York: Russell Sage Foundation, 1994), 1–34. See also David C. Hammack, "Russell Sage Foundation," in *The Greenwood Encyclopedia of American Institutions: Foundations*, ed. Harold M. Keele and Joseph C. Kiger (Westport, Conn.: Greenwood Press, 1984), 373–380. A recent reappraisal is Alice O'Connor, *Poverty Knowledge: Social Science, Social Policy, and the Poor in Twentieth-Century U.S. History* (Princeton, N.J.: Princeton University Press, 2001), 25–54.

3. Much foundation history was institutional history, focused on individual foundations. However, the following studies are useful because they analyze several foundations or foundations in general: Judith Sealander, *Private Wealth and Public Life: Foundation Philanthropy and the Reshaping of American Social Policy from the Progressive Era to the New Deal* (Baltimore, Md.: Johns Hopkins University Press, 1997), 245; Ellen Condliffe Lagemann, ed., *Philanthropic Foundations: New Scholarship, New Possibilities* (Bloomington: Indiana University Press, 1999); David C. Hammack, "Foundations in the American Polity, 1900–1940," in Lagemann, *Philanthropic Foundations*, 43–69; James A. Smith, *The Idea Brokers: Think Tanks and the Rise of the New Policy Elite* (New York: Free Press 1991), 39; David M. Ricci, *The Transformation of American Politics: The New Washington and the Rise of Think Tanks* (New Haven, Conn.: Yale University Press, 1993); Guy Alchon, *The Invisible Hand of Planning: Capitalism, Social Science, and the State* (Princeton, N.J.: Princeton University Press, 1985); Robert Bremner, *American Philanthropy* (Chicago: University of Chicago Press, 1960); Robert H. Bremner, *From the Depths: The Discovery of Poverty in the United States* (New York: New York University Press, 1956), 154–157. Also important are Barry D. Karl and Stanley N. Katz, "The American Private Philanthropic Foundation and the Public Sphere, 1890–1930," *Minerva* 19 (1981): 236–270; Barry D. Karl and Stanley N. Katz, "Foundations and Ruling Class Elites," *Daedalus* 116 (Winter 1987): 1–40; Barry D. Karl, "Philanthropy and the Social Sciences," *Proceedings of the American Philosophical Society* 129, no. 1 (1985): 14–19; and Peter Dobkin Hall, "Private Philanthropy and Public Policy: A Historical Appraisal," in Robert Payton et al., *Philanthropy: Four Views* (New Brunswick, N.J.: Transaction Books, 1988), 39–72. A lively recent treatment is Mark Dowie, *American Foundations: An Investigative History* (Cambridge, Mass.: MIT Press, 2001). See also the very useful bibliographic essay by Susan Kastan, "Bibliography: Recent Writings about Foundations in History," in Lagemann, *Philanthropic Foundations*, 377–403.

4. Deborah S. Gardner, "Practical Philanthropy: The Phelps-Stokes Fund and Housing," *Prospects: An Annual of American Cultural Studies* 15 (1990): 370, and personal communication with the author.

5. The General Education Board was incorporated by act of Congress in 1903. The initial gift was $1 million, but by 1907 Rockefeller had increased it to $20 million. Raymond Fosdick, *The Story of the Rockefeller Foundation* (New York: Harper and Row, 1952), 9; Waldemar A. Nielsen, *The Big Foundations*

(New York: Columbia University Press, 1972), 334–337. A recent study is Eric Anderson and Alfred A. Moss, Jr., *Dangerous Donations: Northern Philanthropy and Southern Black Education, 1902–1930* (Columbia: University of Missouri Press, 1999).

6. RW de F, "Suggestions for a Possible Sage Foundation," December 10, 1906, RSFR, Box 2, Folder 11.

7. M. Olivia Sage (Mrs. Russell Sage), "Opportunities and Responsibilities of Leisured Women," *North American Review* 181 (1905): 718–719; John F. McClymer, *War and Welfare: Social Engineering in America, 1890–1925* (Westport, Conn.: Greenwood Press, 1980), 50–67.

8. The de Forest family's Huguenot ancestry is recounted in Emily Johnston [Mrs. Robert W.] de Forest, *A Walloon Family in America: Lockwood de Forest and His Forbears, 1500–1848*, 2 vols. (Boston: Houghton Mifflin Co., 1914). See also "Robert Weeks de Forest," *New York Times*, May 7, 1931, 1; "Robert Weeks de Forest," *DAB* 11, Supplement One, to December 31, 1935, 236–237. "A fierce kind of optimism" in Sealander, *Private Wealth and Public Life*, 245. See also Guy Alchon, "Mary van Kleeck of the Russell Sage Foundation," in Lagemann, *Philanthropic Foundations*, 158–159; Dorothy Ross, "Modernist Social Science in the Land of the New/Old," in *Modernist Impulses in the Human Sciences, 1870–1930*, ed. Dorothy Ross (Baltimore, Md.: Johns Hopkins University Press, 1994), 171–189; Richard Hofstadter, *The Age of Reform: From Bryan to FDR* (New York: Vintage Books, 1955); Leon Fink, *Progressive Intellectuals and the Dilemmas of Democratic Commitment* (Cambridge, Mass.: Harvard University Press, 1997), 1–12.

9. As its secretary, Edward Devine moved the COS boldly in this direction. "Personal depravity is as foreign to any sound theory of poverty as witchcraft or demonic possession," he wrote in 1920. "These hardships are economic, social, transitional, measurable, manageable." Edward T. Devine, *Misery and Its Causes* (1920), quoted in James T. Patterson, *America's Struggle against Poverty, 1900–1920* (Cambridge, Mass.: Harvard University Press, 1981), 22. See also Michael B. Katz, *In the Shadow of the Poorhouse: A Social History of Welfare in America* (New York: Basic Books, 1986). The foundation's historian, David Hammack, calls the RSF "a center of intelligence for the Charity Organization Society" in Hammack and Wheeler, *Social Science in the Making*. See also David C. Hammack, *Power and Society: Greater New York at the Turn of the Century* (New York: Russell Sage Foundation, 1982; repr., Columbia University Press, 1987), 78–79, 104; James A. Hijiya, "Four Ways of Looking at a Philanthropist: A Study of Robert Weeks de Forest," *Proceedings of the American Philosophical Society* 124 (December 1980): 404–418.

The best recent treatment of the COS is Dawn Greeley, "Beyond Benevolence: Gender, Class, and the Development of Scientific Charity in New York City, 1882–1935" (Ph.D. diss., SUNY Stony Brook, 1995). See also Paul S. Boyer, *Urban Masses and Moral Order in America, 1820–1920* (Cambridge, Mass.: Harvard University Press, 1978), 223–224; Frank J. Bruno, *Trends in Social Work,*

1874–1956: A History Based on the Proceedings of the National Conference of Social Work (New York: Columbia University Press, 1957); and Roy Lubove, *The Professional Altruist: The Emergence of Social Work as a Career, 1880–1930* (Pittsburgh, Pa.: University of Pittsburgh Press, 1965).

On Devine and his mentor Simon Patten, see Jeff Slansky, *The Soul's Economy: Market Society and Selfhood in American Thought, 1820–1920* (Chapel Hill: University of North Carolina Press, 2002), 171ff.

10. RW de F to Seth Low, December 3, 1904, Seth Low Papers, Columbia; Gerald Kurland, *Seth Low: The Reformer in an Urban and Industrial Age* (New York: Twayne, 1977).

11. Ellen Condliffe Lagemann calls these different "technologies of influence"; *Private Power for the Public Good: A History of the Carnegie Foundation for the Advancement of Teaching* (Middletown, Conn.: Wesleyan University Press, 1983), 57–58; O'Connor, *Poverty Knowledge*, 26–44; Martin Bulmer, Kevin Bales, and Kathryn Kish Sklar, eds., *The Social Survey in Historical Perspective, 1880–1940* (New York: Cambridge University Press, 1991); Margo Anderson and Maurine Greenwald, *Pittsburgh Surveyed: Social Science and Social Reform in the Early Twentieth Century* (Pittsburgh, Pa.: University of Pittsburgh Press, 1996).

12. RW de F to Edward Devine, September 28, 1899; "From a remote camp," RW de F to Devine, August 13, 1902; Edward Devine to RW de F, September 12, 1906; RW de F to Edward Devine, September 20, 1906, all in CSSA, Columbia. See also Clarke A. Chambers, *Paul U. Kellogg and the Survey: Voices for Social Welfare and Social Justice* (Minneapolis: University of Minnesota Press, 1971), 7–8.

In another COS memorandum, dated 1906, he wrote, "[T]he result to the community in eliminating and diminishing some of the more important causes of pauperism is of infinitely greater value than could have been brought about by the same amount . . . of money expended for the relief of individual suffering." John M. Glenn, Lilian Brandt, and F. Emerson Andrews, *Russell Sage Foundation, 1907–1946* (New York: Russell Sage Foundation, 1947), 1:6–7, quoting "Memorandum prepared by Mr. de Forest as president of the Society," *New York Charity Organization Society, Twenty-fifth Annual Report*, 55–56.

13. RW de F to Seth Low, June 2, 1905, Seth Low Papers, Columbia; Stephen Turner, "The Pittsburgh Survey and the Survey Movement: An Episode in the History of Expertise," 35–49; and Martin Bulmer, "The Social Survey Movement and Early Twentieth-Century Sociological Method," 15–34, both in Anderson and Greenwald, eds., *Pittsburgh Surveyed*. See also Robert H. Wiebe, *The Search for Order, 1877–1920* (New York: Hill and Wang, 1967); Thomas L. Haskell, *The Emergence of Professional Social Science: The American Social Science Association and the Nineteenth-Century Crisis of Authority* (Urbana: University of Illinois Press, 1977); Mary Furner, *Advocacy and Objectivity: A Crisis in the Professionalization of American Social Science, 1868–1905* (Lexington: University of Massachusetts Press, 1975); Bulmer, Bales, and Sklar, *The Social Survey in Historical*

Perspective; Helene Silverberg, ed., *Gender and American Social Science: The Formative Years* (Princeton, N.J.: Princeton University Press, 1998); Mark C. Smith, *Social Science in the Crucible: The American Debate Over Objectivity and Purpose, 1918–1941* (Durham, N.C.: Duke University Press, 1994).

14. RW de F to MOS, February 7, 1907, RSFR, Box 2, Folder 11.

15. RW de F to Jeffrey Brackett, October 24, 1906, and Jeffrey Brackett to RW de F, October 26, 1906, both in *The Russell Sage Foundation: Social Research and Social Action in America, 1907–1947*, ed. David C. Maddox (Frederick, Md.: UPA Academic Editions, 1988), 200 H-2.2.

On the social center movement, see Kevin Mattson, *Creating a Democratic Public: The Struggle for Urban Participatory Democracy during the Progressive Era* (University Park: Pennsylvania State University Press, 1998); Patricia Mooney Melvin, *The Organic City: Urban Definition and Neighborhood Organization, 1880–1920* (Lexington: University Press of Kentucky, 1987); Jean B. Quandt, *From the Small Town to the Great Community: The Social Thought of Progressive Intellectuals* (New Brunswick, N.J.: Rutgers University Press, 1970).

16. Jeffrey Brackett to RW de F, October 26, 1906. The Rockefeller Institute for Research in Medicine was established in 1901, the Carnegie Institution in 1902.

17. Edward T. Devine to RW de F, December 16, 1906, CSSA, Columbia. Gilman is identified as one of the Gilded Age political intellectuals, reformers, and "proto-progressive social scientists" who helped "forge the new liberalism" of the twentieth century. Nancy Cohen, *The Reconstruction of American Liberalism, 1865–1914* (Chapel Hill: University of North Carolina Press, 2002), 11.

18. "Suggestions for a Possible Sage Foundation, Memorandum Made by RW de F for Mrs. Sage, December 10, 1906," RSFR, Box 2, Folder 11. See Peter Dobkin Hall, "Private Philanthropy and Public Policy: A Historical Reappraisal," in Robert Payton et al., *Philanthropy: Four Views* (New Brunswick, N.J.: Transaction Press, 1988), 40.

19. "Suggestions for a Possible Sage Foundation."

20. RW de F to MOS, December 10, 1906, RSFR, Box 2, Folder 11. This cover letter accompanied the memorandum of the same date.

21. "Suggestions for a Possible Sage Foundation"; Hijiya, "Four Ways of Looking at a Philanthropist," 413–414.

22. "Suggestions for a Possible Sage Foundation"; Arthur Huntington Gleason, "Mrs. Russell Sage and Her Interests," *World's Work* 13 (November 1905): 8186.

23. Mary Ann Dzuback helped shed new light on the Sage–de Forest relationship. Dzuback to the author, February 2002.

24. Gleason, "Mrs. Russell Sage and Her Interests," 8184. See also Sage, "Opportunities and Responsibilities of Leisured Women," 712–721; William Griffith, "The Sage Home on Fifth Avenue," undated clipping [1900?], "Margaret Olivia Sage," OnHA.

25. Acknowledgments are in J. S. Billings, director, New York Public Library, to MOS, October 5, 1903, and May 6, 1908, and E. H. Anderson to MOS, April 13, 1913, all in RSFR, Box 87, Folder 848.

26. Gleason, "Mrs. Russell Sage and Her Interests," 8185. Parsons, the daughter of English-born stockbroker Henry Clews, moved in the same nouveau riche New York circles as the Sages. Aged twenty-eight in 1906, she was a youngster compared to Olivia, yet Olivia obviously read her work with interest, for she cited it several times. Desley Deacon, *Elsie Clews Parsons: Inventing Modern Life* (Chicago: University of Chicago Press, 1997), 412n32.

27. Sage, "Opportunities and Responsibilities of Leisured Women," 46.

28. Andrew Carnegie, "Wealth," *North American Review* 148 (June 1889): 653–664; Carnegie, "The Best Fields for Philanthropy," *North American Review* 149 (December 1889): 682–698; John D. Rockefeller, *Random Reminiscences of Men and Events* (New York: Doubleday, Doral and Company, Inc., 1933), 184–188. See also Frederick Gates, *Chapters in My Life* (New York: Arno Press, 1977).

29. RW de F to MOS, February 7, 1907, 4, RSFR, Box 2, Folder 11.

30. Ibid., 5–6; emphasis in the original.

31. [RW de F] to MOS, "Sketch of the Russell and Olivia Sage Foundation, organized for good uses," n.d., in Maddox, *Russell Sage Foundation*, 200 H-2.4; RW de F to MOS, February 7, 1907.

32. RW de F to Robert Hill, March 15, 1907; RW de F to Lawrence Veiller, March 16, 1907; RW de F to Frederick Wines, March 23, 1907; RW de F to Ernest Bicknell, March 23, 1907. All in RSFR, Box 2, Folder 11. Frederick Wines, "Causes of Pauperism and Crime," *Proceedings of the National Conference of Charities and Corrections*, 1886 (New York, 1886), 206–214. For Lawrence Veiller, see Roy Lubove, *The Progressives and the Slums: Tenement House Reform in New York City* (Pittsburgh, Pa.: University of Pittsburgh Press, 1963).

33. "Memorandum with Regard to the Sage Foundation," typescript, n.d., in RW de F to Devine, March 12, 1907, and March 16, 1907, CSSA, Columbia. On *Charities and the Commons* and its successor *The Survey*, the authoritative account is Chambers, *Paul U. Kellogg and the* Survey. Devine was editor from 1897 to 1912.

34. "Equal Suffrage for Women: Mrs. Russell Sage Gives Her Views on the Subject," *New York Times*, April 15, 1894, 8; Henry Whittemore, *History of the Sage and Slocum Families of England and America, Including the Allied Families of Montague, Wanton, Brown, Josselyn, Standish, Doty, Carver, Jermain or Germain, Pierson, Howell* (New York: Published by Mrs. Russell Sage, 1908), 39.

35. The minutes refer to "her friend Mr. Robert C. Ogden." Russell Sage Foundation, Minutes, Meeting of Incorporators, 2, in Maddox, *Russell Sage Foundation*, 200 H-2.7; Henry de Forest to RW de F, March 6, 1907, in Maddox, *Russell Sage Foundation*, 200 H-2.10; RW de F to Devine, March 14, 1907, CSSA, Columbia.

Robert Curtis Ogden (1836–1912), like de Forest, was a Yale graduate. He became a trustee after retiring from Wanamaker's in 1907 at the age of seventy-one. Ogden founded the Southern Education Board in 1901 and was its president until his death in 1913. Glenn, Brandt, and Andrews, *Russell Sage Foundation*, 1:229. See also "Robert Curtis Ogden," RSFR, Box 2, Folder 17; "Robert C. Ogden," reprinted from *Metropolitan Magazine* (February 1911), in *The Booker T. Washington Papers*, ed. Louis R. Harlan and Raymond W. Smock (Urbana: University of Illinois Press, 1972–), 10:602–608. See also James D. Anderson, *Education of Blacks in the South, 1860–1935* (Chapel Hill: University of North Carolina Press, 1988); and John H. Stanfield, *Philanthropy and Jim Crow in American Social Science* (Westport, Conn.: Greenwood Press, 1985). Anderson and Moss offer a more sympathetic interpretation of "Ogdenism" than previous studies in *Dangerous Donations*.

For Morton, see Dolores Greenberg, "Levi Morton," *Encyclopedia of American Business History and Biography*, vol. 7, *Banking and Finance to 1913*, ed. Larry Schweikart (New York: Facts on File, 1990), 365–372.

36. Henry de Forest to MOS, February 16, 1907; RW de F to Henry de Forest, March 2, 1907. Both in RSFR, Box 2, Folder 11. The list is handwritten in RW de F to Devine, March 12, 1907, CSSA, Columbia.

37. Gilman died in October 1908 and was replaced by housing expert Alfred Tredway White in February 1909. White served until his accidental death by drowning in January 1921.

38. Tory aristocrat Lord Shaftesbury led the campaign against slavery and child labor in the early nineteenth century. For monied elites in late-nineteenth-century New York City, see Sven Beckert, *The Monied Metropolis: New York City and the Consolidation of the American Bourgeoisie, 1850–1896* (New York: Cambridge University Press, 2001), 75–77; and Hammack, *Power and Society*.

39. For Cleveland Dodge, see RSFR, Box 3, Folder 19, especially "Copy of Material Provided for the National Cyclopedia of American Biography," typescript. Dodge remained a trustee until November 1920.

40. Grace Dodge and Cleveland Dodge to MOS, January 21, 1907, RSFR, Box 101, Folder 1013; Letitia Craig Darlington to MOS, March 16, 1907, RSFR, Box 101, Folder 1010. For Grace Dodge, see Robert D. Cross, "Grace Hoadley Dodge," *NAW*, 1:489–492.

41. Glenn, Brandt, and Andrews, *Russell Sage Foundation*, 1:9; Robert D. Cross, "Louisa Lee Schuyler," *NAW*, 3:244–246. Laurie Ginzberg argues that the efficiency, centralization, and efficiency of Civil War organizations of Schuyler and others marked a radical departure from the scattered, sentimental charitable efforts of their mothers' generation; *Women and the Work of Benevolence: Morality, Politics, and Class in the Nineteenth-Century United States* (New Haven, Conn.: Yale University Press, 1990), 134–161.

42. Homer Folks, "One Hundredth Anniversary Celebration of the Birth of Josephine Shaw Lowell," December 16, 1943, Box 143, CSSA, Columbia.

Harrison claims that Olivia Sage also served on the NYCOS Council, but this claim is unsubstantiated. RW de F, "Brief Characteristics of Trustees of Sage

Foundation," RSFR, Box 2, Folder 11. See also Robert Bremner, *The Public Good: Philanthropy and Welfare in the Civil War Era* (New York: Alfred A. Knopf, 1980), 54–71; Walter I. Trattner, "Louisa Lee Schuyler and the Founding of the State Charities Aid Association," *New-York Historical Society Quarterly* 51 (July 1967): 233–247. I have not been able to trace personal connections between Schuyler and Rice and Sage.

43. HMG to "Dear Mrs. Sage," from Luxor, Egypt, March 3, 1907, Helen Miller Gould Shepard Papers, NYHS.

44. Nancy Hewitt, "Charity or Mutual Aid: Two Perspectives on Latin Women's Philanthropy in Tampa, Florida," in *Lady Bountiful Revisited: Women, Philanthropy, and Power*, ed. Kathleen D. McCarthy (New Brunswick, N.J.: Rutgers University Press, 1990), 67.

45. De Forest's letter to Low thanks him for the pleasurable memory of "that little dinner at the University Club." RW de F to Seth Low, June 30, 1904, in Seth Low Papers, Columbia. Sven Beckert discusses club membership among New York's bourgeoisie. He finds overlapping affiliations—elite men belonged on average to five clubs—which created "dense connections among members of these clubs"; *Monied Metropolis*, 264. Beckert does not discuss women's clubs and club membership.

46. Sklar, "Introduction," in Bulmer, Bales, and Sklar, *Social Survey in Historical Perspective*, xvii. See also Seth Koven, "Borderlands: Women, Voluntary Action, and Child Welfare in Britain, 1840–1914," in *Mothers of a New World: Maternalist Politics and the Origins of the Welfare State*, ed. Seth Koven and Sonya Michel (New Brunswick, N.J.: Routledge, 1993), 94–135; Kathleen D. McCarthy, "Parallel Power Structures: Women in the Voluntary Sphere," in McCarthy, *Lady Bountiful Revisited*, 1–31. For the work of Schuyler, Rice, and their colleagues in the Sanitary Commission, see Judith Ann Giesberg, *Civil War Sisterhood: The U.S. Sanitary Commission and Women's Politics in Transition* (Boston: Northeastern University Press, 2000). See also Joan Waugh, *Unsentimental Reformer: The Life of Josephine Shaw Lowell* (Cambridge, Mass.: Harvard University Press, 1997).

47. [RW de F], "Statement of Mrs. Sage for the Press," typewritten with corrections in pen, RSFR, Box 2, Folder 11. He also wrote to the governor of New York State, Robert Hughes, asking him to sign the bill of incorporation.

48. [RW de F] to Henry de Forest, March 2, 1907, RSFR, Box 2, Folder 11; RW de F to Charles E. Hughes, April 4, 1907, in Maddox, *Russell Sage Foundation*, 200 II-2.9.

49. "My dear Bre'r Rabbit," John Glenn to RW de F, March 10, 1907, in *The Russell Sage Foundation: Social Research and Social Action in America, 1907–1947*, ed. David Maddox (Frederick, Md.: CIS Academic Editions, 1988), 200 H 2.1.3. Shelby Harrison's unpublished biography of John Glenn offers a portrait of this dedicated reformer; "John Mark Glenn—His Pioneer Attack on Social Problems—and First Steps Toward Better Living Conditions," unpublished biography of John Mark Glenn (1966 with some revisions from

1967), v, CSSA, Columbia. Harrison worked on the Pittsburgh Survey. He became director of the Department of Surveys and Exhibits for the Russell Sage Foundation in 1912.

50. Russell Sage Foundation, Minutes of Trustees Meeting, May 10, 1907, 1–2, RS Foundation. The Glenns had recently been married, when he was forty-four, she thirty-three. John Glenn was subsequently reelected to the board of trustees in April 1913. Mary Glenn would succeed Jane Addams as president of the National Conference of Social Work in 1915. Glenn, Brandt, and Andrews, *Russell Sage Foundation*, 1:41.

51. Schuyler to RW de F, March 23, 1907, and RW de F to Schuyler, March 26, 1907, both in RSFR, Box 2, Folder 11; Cross, "Louisa Lee Schuyler."

52. John Glenn (1858–1950), a graduate of Washington and Lee University, earned an LL.B. from the University of Maryland in 1882 and became an attorney and a leader in Baltimore charities. In 1901, he became the president of the National Conference of Charities and Corrections. Jane L. Andrews, "John Mark Glenn," *ANB*, 9:118–119; "John Mark Glenn: A Wise Man with a Loving Heart," *The Survey* (April 20, 1950); Miriam Cohen, "Mary Willcox Brown Glenn," *ANB*, 9:118–119; Louis Dean, "For Immediate Release [obituary of John Glenn]," April __, 1950, RSFR, Box 2, Folder 17. Harrison, "John Mark Glenn," v, xv, 53, 284. The colleague was Joanna Colcord. Glenn, Brandt, and Andrews, *Russell Sage Foundation*, 1:284.

53. David A. Hollinger, "Inquiry and Uplift: Late Nineteenth-Century American Academics and the Moral Efficacy of Scientific Practice," in *The Authority of Experts*, ed. Thomas Haskell (Bloomington: Indiana University Press, 1984), 142–156. On "the religious heritage of social science," see Alchon, "Mary van Kleeck of the Russell Sage Foundation," in Lagemann, *Philanthropic Foundations*, 151–166; Kathryn Kish Sklar, "Hull-House Maps and Papers: Social Science as Women's Work in the 1890s," in Silverberg, *Gender and American Social Science*, 142. Philip J. Ethington stresses the ethical (though not religious) bases of social science reform in "The Metropolis and Multicultural Ethics: Direct Democracy versus Deliberative Democracy in the Progressive Era," in *Progressivism and the New Democracy*, ed. Sidney M. Milkis and Jerome M. Mileur (Amherst: University of Massachusetts Press, 1999), 192–225.

54. Judith Sealander to the author, March 13, 2002. Lively accounts of the Patman Committee and the resulting Tax Reform Law of 1969 are in Waldemar A. Nielsen, *The Big Foundations* (New York: Columbia University Press, 1972), 7–20; Ben Whitaker, *The Philanthropoids: Foundations and Society. An Unsubsidized Anatomy of the Burden of Benevolence* (New York: William Morrow and Company, Inc., 1974), 109–117; Peter Frumkin, "Private Foundations as Public Institutions: Regulation, Professionalization, and the Redefinition of Organized Philanthropy," in Lagemann, *Philanthropic Foundations*, 70–71; and Dowie, *American Foundations*, 15–16.

55. "Constitution of the Russell Sage Foundation," in "Russell Sage Foun-

dation, Minutes," RS Foundation. Hammack characterizes this as "simple and breathtakingly general language"; "A Center of Intelligence for the Charity Organization Movement," 3. Barry D. Karl and Stanley N. Katz point out that many of the early foundations stated their purpose with similar "naivete and ambition." For example, the Rockefeller Foundation's stated purpose was "to promote the well-being of mankind throughout the world." Barry D. Karl and Stanley N. Katz, "Donors, Trustees, Staffs: An Historical View, 1890–1930," in *The Art of Giving: Four Views of American Philanthropy* (Pocantico Hills, N.Y.: Rockefeller Archive Center, 1977), 6–7.

56. RW de F, "Margaret Olivia Sage, Philanthropist," *The Survey* 41 (1918): 151. See also Russell Sage Foundation, "Meeting of Incorporators," in *Minutes of the Trustees*, April 19, 1907, RS Foundation. The incident is repeated in Glenn, Brandt, and Andrews, *Russell Sage Foundation, 1907–1946*, 1:267; Richard Magat, "Safe Harbor for the Social Sciences: The Russell Sage Foundation at 75," *Foundation News* (September–October 1982), 27.

57. Margaret Olivia Sage, "To the Trustees of Russell Sage Foundation," April 19, 1907, RSFR, Box 2, Folder 13. The letter is reprinted in Appendix A of Glenn, Brandt, and Andrews, *Russell Sage Foundation*, 2:667–268. Olivia used wording identical to that of the Phelps-Stokes Fund; see Gardner, "Practical Philanthropy: The Phelps-Stokes Fund and Housing."

58. "I personally think it important from the start to give a national character to our activities," he confided to Devine in May 1907. RW de F to Devine, May 16, 1907, CSSA, Columbia.

59. Quoted in McClymer, *War and Welfare*, 57–58.

60. Ibid.

61. Glenn, Brandt, and Andrews, *Russell Sage Foundation*, 1:42, 43, 49–51. On Veiller's opposition to model tenements and particularly to Forest Hills Gardens, see McClymer, *War and Welfare*, 58–63. See also Grosvenor Atterbury, "Forest Hills Gardens: A Study and Demonstration in Town Planning and Home Building Undertaken by the Russell Sage Foundation at Forest Hills, Long Island," *The Survey* 25 (January 7, 1911): 565.

RSF capital funds were also invested in the National Employment Exchange, a COS project launched in 1909, and in the Chattel Loan Society of New York. Foundation investment in de Forest's Provident Loan Society amounted to $500,000 by 1913. McClymer, *War and Welfare*, 58.

62. Hammack, "Introduction" to *Russell Sage Foundation: Social Research and Social Action in America*, 10; Glenn, Brandt, and Andrews, *Russell Sage Foundation*, 1:272–273. McClymer, *War and Welfare*, 64. Forest Hills Gardens was not intended to produce low-cost housing, a recent study notes; see Susan L. Klaus, *A Modern Arcadia: Frederick Law Olmsted, Jr. and the Plan for Forest Hills Gardens* (Amherst: University of Massachusetts Press, 2002), 124–126, 191n14.

63. Rockefeller philanthropy was feared—no amount of philanthropy would erase the public's view of John D. Rockefeller, Sr., as a predatory capitalist who

was ruthless and calculating. Moreover, Rockefeller made things worse when he coined the name "benevolent trusts" for foundations, recalling Standard Oil and a quarter-century of business takeovers and buyouts. "The Benevolent Trusts—The Value of the Cooperative Principle in Giving," in Rockefeller, *Random Reminiscences of Men and Events*, 165–188. For an account of the Rockefeller charter controversy, see Sealander, *Private Wealth and Public Life*, 218–224. See also Fink, *Progressive Intellectuals and the Dilemmas of Democratic Commitment*, 80–113; Graham Adams, Jr., *Age of Industrial Violence, 1910–1915: The Activities and Findings of the United States Commission on Industrial Relations* (New York: Columbia University Press, 1966).

64. James D. Phelps to MOS, March 14, 1907, RSFR, Box 94, Folder 939. See also William Goodell Frost [president of Berea College] to MOS, March 1, 1907, RSFR, Box 70, Folder 626.

65. "The Russell Sage Foundation: Its Social Value and Importance—Views of Some of Those Actually Engaged in Social Work," *Charities and the Commons* 17 (March 23, 1907): 1079–1085; "What University Men Think of the Russell Sage Foundation: Suggestions in Large Part from the Chairs of Economics, Sociology and Political Economy," *Charities and the Commons* 18 (May 11, 1907): 186–191. See also the collection of press clippings, "Sage Foundation Plans: Its Chief Effort Is to Aid Other Social Workers," *New York Sun*, April 3, 1909; "Russell Sage Foundation Leads War on Tuberculosis," *New York Commercial*, April 3, 1907; "The Scope of the Sage Foundation," *New York Times*, April 3, 1907. All in RSFR, Box 2, Folder 11. See also Daniel Coit Gilman, "Five Great Gifts," *Outlook* (August 1907): 648–657.

66. RW de F to Lawrence Veiller, March 16, 1907, in Maddox, *Russell Sage Foundation*, 200 H-2.16. "Appalled . . . enthusiastic . . . sober," is quoted in Glenn, Brandt, and Andrews, *Russell Sage Foundation*, 1:20. This correspondence, like much else quoted in this source, is now lost. De Forest pleaded exhaustion and longed for "a breathing spell"; RW de F to Devine, May 3, 1907, CSSA, Columbia.

67. "Departments of the Foundation and Their Directors," in Glenn, Brandt, and Andrews, *Russell Sage Foundation*, 2:672.

Glenn, Brandt, and Andrews, *Russell Sage Foundation*, 1:675–701, has the most complete listing of the foundation's activities between 1907 and 1947. Three appendices are especially useful: Appendix C, "Publications of Russell Sage Foundation"; Appendix D, "Grants by Russell Sage Foundation from April 19, 1907 to September 30, 1946"; and "Index to Table of Grants." An outline for a comprehensive history is Deborah S. Gardner, "'A Predominantly Social Point of View': A Century of Social Research, Public Policy and the Social Sciences at the Russell Sage Foundation," typescript. The author kindly shared this unpublished essay with me.

68. Glenn, Brandt, and Andrews, *Russell Sage Foundation*, 1:228–229. The studies were: Elizabeth Beardsley Butler, *Women and the Trades: Pittsburgh 1907–1908* (1909; repr., Pittsburgh, Pa.: University of Pittsburgh Press, 1984);

John Fitch, *The Steel Workers* (1910; repr., University of Pittsburgh Press, 1989); Margaret Byington, *Homestead: The Households of a Mill Town* (1910; repr., Pittsburgh, Pa.: University of Pittsburgh Press, 1996); Crystal Eastman, *Work-Accidents and the Law* (1910; repr., New York: Arno Press, 1969); Paul U. Kellogg, ed., *Wage-Earning Pittsburgh* (1914; repr., New York: Arno Press, 1974); and Paul U. Kellogg, *The Pittsburgh District: Civic Frontage* (1914; repr. New York, Arno Press, 1974). See also Greenwald and Andersen, *Pittsburgh Surveyed,* especially Stephen Turner, "The Pittsburgh Survey and the Survey Movement," 35–49.

69. RW de F, "Memorial Minute," 1918, reprinted in Glenn, Brandt, and Andrews, *Russell Sage Foundation,* 1:269; see also Harrison, "John Mark Glenn," 73.

70. Dorothy Ross writes, "Progressive-era social scientists filled their writings with a sense of discontinuity and turned away from the outmoded past. . . . No sooner did these theorists enter history, as it were, then they turned against the past"; "Modernist Social Science in the Land of the New/Old," 183. The point is also well made in Eldon Eisenach, *The Lost Promise of Progressivism* (Lawrence: University Press of Kansas, 1994).

71. "Mushy philanthropy and self-seeking politics" in RW de F to Devine, March 16, 1907, RSFR, Box 2, Folder 11. See also Hall, "Private Philanthropy and Public Policy: A Historical Appraisal," 59. Dawn Greeley convincingly describes the distaste of charity organization reformers such as de Forest for the sentimental charity, as he saw it, of wealthy but undisciplined donors; see "Philanthropists, Clients, and Charity Workers: The Changing Dynamics of Charity in New York City, 1880–1920," paper delivered at the Social Science History Association, Baltimore, Maryland, November 1993.

72. Quoted in Chambers, *Paul U. Kellogg and the* Survey, 42. "[S]ocial scientists repeatedly cast their scientific enterprise and its goal of rational control in masculine terms"; Ross, "Modernist Social Science in the Land of the New/Old," 179. See also Cohen, *Reconstruction of American Liberalism,* 13, 259–260n21. Kathryn Kish Sklar disputes the idea that a gulf existed between charity, reform, and social science in this period. She shows that Florence Kelley and others could and did practice as social scientists in this period; "Hull-House Maps and Papers: Social Science as Women's Work in the 1890s."

73. RW de F, "Suggestions for a Possible Sage Foundation. Memorandum Made by R.W. de F. for Mrs. Sage, December 10, 1906," typescript, RSFR, Box 2, Folder 11, page 10¹/₂. This page was evidently inserted later between 10 and 11 to include her changes.

74. Schuyler encouraged de Forest to persuade Olivia to name the foundation the Sage Foundation, Schuyler to RW de F, March 23, 1907, and RW de F to Schuyler, March 26, 1907, both in RSFR, Box 2, Folder 11. De Forest and others continued to refer to the foundation by that name. See also Glenn, Brandt, and Andrews, *Russell Sage Foundation,* 1:12.

The late Marjorie Semerad, professor emerita at Russell Sage College,

1962–1983, proposed that the foundation idea may have originated with Russell Sage himself. "In his later years, Russell was asked if there would be a monument in his name. He replied that there would be a 'suitable memorial.' Perhaps the Russell Sage Foundation which Mrs. Sage established . . . was the 'suitable memorial' and he had known of it before he died." Marjorie Semerad, "I Decided That Mr. Sage Deserved Another Look," in *Sage Stories: Essays on the Third Quarter Century, 1966–1991*, ed. Coleen Paratore (Troy, N.Y.: The Sage Colleges, 1991), 163.

75. This is where, for example, the October 25, 1907, meeting took place, with Olivia, de Forest, Gould, and Rice attending (see p. 272 intra).

76. For example, one item from the Executive Committee Minutes, October 25, 1907, reads, "A report by the director was read and its recommendations approved." Typewritten minutes, RS Foundation. Surviving records include the minutes of the foundation's board of trustees between 1907 and 1918; the minutes of the foundation's executive committee (consisting of the president, vice president, and three other trustees) during the same period; and the record of foundation activities during its first decade.

77. Russell Sage Foundation, Executive Committee Minutes, October 25, 1907, typewritten, n.p., RS Foundation. "The following grants, which had been made by the executive committee during the summer recess, were ordered to be reported to the Board of Trustees:

New York Association for the Blind	$12,000
National Association for the Study and Prevention of Tuberculosis	$5,000
For additional expenses of exhibit at Jamestown	$1,000
New York School of Philanthropy for Investigation	$7,500
National Playground Extension	$20,000
Charity Organization Extension	$7,500
Investigation of Canneries in New York	$3,000
School for Social Workers, Boston	$7,500
Chicago Institute for Social Science	$7,500
Homeless Men in Chicago and Minneapolis	$300

78. December 23, 1907, in Minutes, Executive Committee, 1907–1948, Russell Sage Foundation.

79. Glenn, Brandt, and Andrews, *Russell Sage Foundation*, 1:37.

80. Typed note signed "Sec."; Mrs. Arthur C. James to MOS, November 4, 1917, RSFR, Box 100, Folder 1008.

81. Glenn, Brandt, and Andrews, *Russell Sage Foundation*, 1:269, 2:671. There was also a Sag Harbor Social Survey (see p. 273).

82. Luther Gulick to MOS, June 12, 1908, and Joseph Lee to MOS, June 22, 1914, and July 8, 1914. All in RSFR, Box 91, Folder 880. Olivia's response is handwritten on the envelope. Gulick's work at the RSF is described in Glenn,

Brandt, and Andrews, *Russell Sage Foundation*, 1:59–60, 97–101. The best discussion of RSF involvement in the play movement is Sealander, *Private Wealth and Public Life*, 190–197.

83. Though as Judith Sealander points out, "the Great War accomplished in less than a year what the playground movement had failed to achieve in two decades" by revealing that the nation's youth was not fit; *The Failed Century of the Child: Governing America's Young in the Twentieth Century* (New York: Cambridge University Press, 2003), 297–299; Sealander, *Private Wealth and Public Life*, 172, 191. On turn-of-the-century struggles over commercial entertainment, see Kathy Peiss, *Cheap Amusements: Working Women and Leisure in Turn of the Century New York* (Philadelphia, Pa.: Temple University Press, 1983); Dominic Cavallo, *Muscles and Morals: Organized Playgrounds and Urban Reform, 1880–1920* (Philadelphia: University of Pennsylvania Press, 1981); Roy Rosenzweig, *Eight Hours for What We Will: Workers and Leisure in an Industrial City, 1870–1920* (New York: Cambridge University Press, 1983); Mary Odem, *Delinquent Daughters: Protecting and Policing Adolescent Sexuality in the United States, 1885–1920* (Chapel Hill: University of North Carolina Press, 1995); Elisabeth Perry, "'The General Motherhood of the Commonwealth': Dance Hall Reform in the Progressive Era," *American Quarterly* 37 (Winter 1985): 719–733.

84. Glenn, Brandt, and Andrews, *Russell Sage Foundation*, 1:240–241. The school was then absorbed into the public school system in 1910.

85. [RW de F] "Statement of Mrs. Sage for the Press," RSFR, Box 2, Folder 11. Typewritten with corrections in pen.

86. Van Kleeck's industrial studies are summarized in Mary van Kleeck, *Industrial Investigations of the Russell Sage Foundation* (1916); and *Wages in the Millinery Trade* (1914), both conducted by the Department of Industrial Studies, Women's Work, and paid for by the foundation. Guy Alchon, "Mary van Kleeck and Social-Economic Planning," *Journal of Policy History* 3, no. 1 (1991): 1–23.

87. Meg Jacobs, "Constructing a New Political Economy: Philanthropy, Institution-Building, and Consumer Capitalism in the Early Twentieth Century," in Lagemann, *Philanthropic Foundations*, 101–118.

88. John Glenn's much-loved uncle and namesake was blind. Harrison, "John Mark Glenn," 315–320; Gertrude Rice to RW de F, April 27, 1907; Louisa Schuyler to RW de F, April 27, 1907; Louisa Schuyler to John Glenn, May 22, 1907. All in RSFR, Box 2, Folder 11.

89. One of the first grants was to the National Association for the Study and Prevention of Tuberculosis (later, National Tuberculosis Association) "for collection of data on campaign against tuberculosis in the United States; press service; traveling exhibit and field work in southern and western states; contribution to expenses of a conference of the International Union Against Tuberculosis held in New York City." Glenn, Brandt, and Andrews, *Russell Sage Foundation*, 2:686; 1:27.

90. Though Veiller opposed further investment in demonstration housing, including Forest Hills Gardens. See Lawrence Veiller, *Housing Reform* (New

York: Charities Publication Committee, 1910); and McClymer, *War and Welfare*, 59–61. Veiller was never on the payroll of the foundation but he was involved in it over several decades and received "the equivalent of a pension" in the 1940s. Gardner, "A Predominantly Social Point of View," 7–8.

91. Hammack and Wheeler, *Social Science in the Making*, 18.

92. Among the most ambitious of these RSF initiatives were John C. Campbell and Olive Campbell's efforts to improve conditions in the "Southern Highlands." Glenn, Brandt, and Andrews, *Russell Sage Foundation*, 1:115–124, 282. Foundation grants for the Southern Education Board (February 1908, $55,000) and for the Commission on Country Life (October 1909, $5,000) are listed in Glenn, Brandt, and Andrews, *Russell Sage Foundation*, 2:687. See also William Bowers, *The Country Life Movement in America: 1900–1920* (Port Washington, N.Y., 1974); Sealander, *Private Wealth and Public Life*, 73–76. The Division of Education was set up in 1913 after the Department of Child Hygiene was phased out. Glenn, Brandt, and Andrews, *Russell Sage Foundation* 1:65, 85ff.

93. It was agreed that the final decision about a name be postponed "until Mrs. Sage's suggestion or approval could be obtained." Russell Sage Foundation, Minutes of the Board of Trustees, December 10, 1909, RS Foundation.

94. RW de F to Chancellor Day, February 5, 1910, Papers of Chancellor James Roscoe Day, Box 3, SUA. She stayed in Pasadena at the Raymond Hotel, requesting no publicity. Reporters disagreed about whether she was in the best of health or suffering from a nervous complaint. For conflicting accounts, one day apart, see "Mrs. Sage Reported Ill: News of Mrs. Slocum's Death Kept," *New York Sun*, March 25, 1910, and "Mrs. Sage Starts for East," *New York Sun*, March 26, 1910, both in NYSM. The decision to return was made when news came that a niece by marriage (the wife of Herbert Jermain Slocum) had died in an accident in Washington, D.C.

95. MOS to RW de F, May 23, 1910, and RW de F to "Dear Madam" [MOS], May 31, 1911, both in RSFR, Box 83, Folder 800; "List of Navajo Blankets, Formerly the Property of A. C. Vroman of Pasadena, Cal.," typescript, n.d., RSFR, Box 83, Folder 800. It seems that de Forest masterminded both the purchases and the subsequent donations to the museum. "Robert W. de Forest," *Bulletin of the Metropolitan Museum of Art* (1931). In the 1910 letter, de Forest wrote in his capacity as secretary to the Metropolitan Museum of Art, acknowledging the offer of "an ancient Persian jewel bag as a gift to the Museum." In 1913, he became the museum's fifth president.

96. Grace C. Simons to MOS, March 3, 1910, RSFR, Series 10, Box 69, Folder 617; Mrs. Beebe to MOS March 27, 1912, RSFR, Box 101, Folder 1014.

97. RW de F to President Lowell, January 21, 1911, Papers of A. Lawrence Lowell, Harvard.

98. Clipping, *New York World*, May 9, 1912, in "The Sage and Slocum Book," JJML.

99. This is confirmed in RW de F, "Suggestions for a Possible Sage Foun-

dation"; and Minutes for March 30, 1908, April 27, 1908, and April 25, 1910, in Minutes, Executive Committee, 1907–1948, RS Foundation.

100. MOS to Mrs. Morris [Maria] Jesup, March 12, 1908, RSFR, Box 97, Folder 980.

101. Correspondence and documentation relating to the construction and design of the building are in RSFR, Series 3, Boxes 10 and 11, Folders 91–96; Hammack, "Russell Sage Foundation," 4. "She became insistent" is in Glenn, Brandt, and Andrews, *Russell Sage Foundation*, 1:52–53. "Because of the memorial nature of the building, more thought was given to beauty of design, materials, and construction, and more money was spent to obtain it, than otherwise would have been deemed suitable." The authors add tactfully, "It was an advantage also that the Foundation now had a dignified and suitable home of its own" (54).

102. Glenn, Brandt, and Andrews, *Russell Sage Foundation*, 1:197–203, 2:628–634; Frederick Warren Jenkins, *Russell Sage Foundation Library: History, Organization, Scope of Building and Equipment, Methods and Results, Other Collections* (New York: Russell Sage Foundation, 1925). After Shelby Harrison retired in 1947, the trustees sold the building to the Catholic Archdiocese of New York and its library was dispersed; RSFR, Boxes 30 and 31, Folders 233–234. In 1982, the foundation moved into a building designed by Philip Johnson at 112 East 64th Street, where it remains today. Magat, "Safe Harbor for the Social Sciences," 30.

103. Marie Haines Bradwell to MOS, December 20, 1911, RSFR, Box 101, Folder 1013. I have found no correspondence between Olivia and Mary van Kleeck. The executive committee minutes continued to acknowledge Olivia's right to attend, noting as late as January 29, 1917, that "President Sage was excused."

104. Anna Harkness established the Commonwealth Fund in 1918, although, as Judith Sealander notes, "technically it would be more accurate to see the Commonwealth Fund as the creation of Anna Harkness's son, Edward"; *Private Wealth and Public Life*, 12, 139ff. The Milbank Memorial Fund was also established by a woman. For the public health work of these two foundations, see Elizabeth Toon, "Selling the Public on Public Health: The Commonwealth and Milbank Health Demonstrations and the Meaning of Community Health Education," in Lagemann, *Philanthropic Foundations*, 118–130. See also Claude V. Kiser, *The Milbank Memorial Fund: Its Leaders and Its Work, 1905–1974* (New York: Milbank Memorial Fund, 1975); and Kathleen D. McCarthy, *Women's Culture: American Philanthropy and Art, 1830–1930* (Chicago: University of Chicago Press, 1991), 174.

105. Muriel Pumphrey, "Mary Richmond and the Rise of Professional Social Work in Baltimore" (Ph.D. diss., New York School of Social Work, 1956); Muriel Pumphrey, "Mary E. Richmond," *NAW*, 3:152–154; Alchon, "Mary van Kleeck and Social-Economic Planning," 4–5; Eleanor M. Lewis, "Mary Abby Van Kleeck," *NAW*, 3:707–709; Sara Henry Lederman, "From Poverty to Philan-

thropy: The Life and Work of Mary E. Richmond" (Ph.D. diss., Columbia University, 1994); Elizabeth N. Agnew, *From Charity to Social Work: Mary E. Richmond and the Creation of an American Profession* (Urbana: University of Illinois Press, 2004).

106. Crystal Eastman's parents were both ordained Congregational ministers. She graduated from Vassar in 1903 and earned a master's degree in sociology from Columbia in 1904 and a law degree from the New York University Law School in 1907 while working part-time at Greenwich House. She joined Paul Kellogg at the Pittsburgh Survey, publishing *Work Accidents and the Law* in 1910. Allen F. Davis, "Crystal Eastman," *NAW*, 1:543–545; Chambers, *Paul U. Kellogg and the Survey*; Blanche Cook, ed., *Crystal Eastman on Women and Revolution* (New York: Oxford University Press, 1978); "Crystal Eastman," *The Nation* (August 8, 1928), an unsigned obituary by Freda Kirchwey.

107. On the settlements in the 1920s, see Ruth Crocker, *Social Work and Social Order: The Settlement Movement in Two Industrial Cities, 1889–1930* (Urbana: University of Illinois Press, 1992); and Judith Ann Trolander, *Professionalism and Social Change: From the Settlement House Movement to Neighborhood Centers, 1886 to the Present* (New York: Columbia University Press, 1987).

108. Definitions of maternalism vary. For Felicia Kornbluh, it is a belief "that motherhood or potential motherhood was a legitimate basis for women's citizenship"; "Review Essay: The New Literature on Gender and the Welfare State: The U.S. Case," *Feminist Studies* 22 (Spring 1996): 171–197, quote on 178. Others use it to refer to reformers who were committed to sex-specific protective legislation and who emphasized the special needs of mothers rather than the equal rights of women. See Lisa Brush, "Love, Toil, and Trouble: Motherhood and Feminist Politics," *Signs: A Journal of Women in Culture and Society* 21 (1996): 429–454. Judith Sealander points out that despite the fact that maternalist, or pro-motherhood, rhetoric was pervasive in early-twentieth-century foundation and reform literature, state funding of pensions and other supports for mothers and children in this period remained inadequate, patchy, and racially discriminatory. Sealander, *Failed Century of the Child*, 101–105; Sealander, *Private Wealth and Public Life*, 100–116. See also Linda Gordon, *Pitied But Not Entitled: Single Mothers and the History of Welfare* (New York: Free Press, 1994).

109. S. J. Kleinberg, "Seeking the Meaning of Life: The Pittsburgh Survey and the Family," in Greenwald and Anderson, *Pittsburgh Surveyed*, 120–121. Critical of the female reformers for their class and race bias are Gordon, *Pitied But Not Entitled*; Eileen Boris, "Black and White Motherhood," in *Women, The State and Welfare*, ed. Linda Gordon (Madison: University of Wisconsin Press, 1990); and Mimi Abramowitz, *Regulating the Lives of Women: Social Policy from Colonial Times to the Present* (Boston: South End Press, 1988).

110. Guy Alchon writes of van Kleeck, "She personified the promise and agony of a particular type of New Woman: the evangelical Christian as social scientist and social savior"; "Mary van Kleeck of the Russell Sage Foundation,"

153ff.; Alchon, "Mary van Kleeck and Social-Economic Planning," 4–5; Eleanor M. Lewis, "Mary Abby Van Kleeck," *NAW*, 3:707–709.

111. Recent work on Mary van Kleeck by Guy Alchon, on Mary Richmond by Sara Lederman and Elizabeth Agnew, and on Josephine Shaw Lowell by Joan Waugh is helping to make much clearer the lives of these important but neglected reformers and may suggest new categories of analysis. See Guy Alchon, "Mary van Kleeck and Social-Economic Planning," *Journal of Policy History* 3, no. 1 (1991): 1–23; Alchon, "The 'Self-Applauding Sincerity' of Overreaching Theory, Biography as Ethical Practice, and the Case of Mary van Kleeck," in Silverberg, *Gender and American Social Science*, 293–325; Alchon, "Mary van Kleeck of the Russell Sage Foundation: Religion,"119–130; Lederman, "From Poverty to Philanthropy"; Agnew, *From Charity to Social Work*. Mary Richmond's publications include *What Is Social Case Work?* (1922; repr., New York: Russell Sage Foundation, 1971); and *Social Diagnosis* (New York: Russell Sage Foundation, 1917). A never-married woman, Richmond made reform of the age of consent laws her personal crusade. Mary Richmond, *Child Marriages* (New York: Russell Sage Foundation, 1925); Mary Richmond and Fred S. Hall, *Marriage and the State* (New York: Russell Sage Foundation, 1929); Kriste Lindenmeyer, "'Old Before Their Time': Mary Richmond and the Anti-Child Marriage Campaign," paper presented at the Social Science History Association Meeting, Baltimore, Maryland, November 22, 1998.

112. Quoted in Glenn, Brandt, and Andrews, *Russell Sage Foundation*, 1:10; Cross, "Louisa Lee Schuyler"; Lynn McDonald, *The Woman Founders of the Social Sciences* (Ottawa: Carleton University Press, 1994).

113. Ellen Fitzpatrick, *Endless Crusade: Women Social Scientists and Progressive Reform* (New York: Oxford University Press, 1990); Robyn Muncy, *Creating a Female Dominion in American Reform* (New York: Oxford University Press, 1991); Kriste Lindenmeyer, "A Right To Childhood": The U.S. Children's Bureau and Child Welfare, 1912–1946 (Urbana: University of Illinois Press, 1997). These scholars offer finely etched biographical studies of professional women in this period, including their career choices and their institutional settings.

114. The Children's Bureau ended its independent existence in 1946. Lindenmeyer, "A Right to Childhood," 249–253; Muncy, *Creating a Female Dominion in American Reform*, 150–157. See also Estelle Freedman, "Separatism Revisited: Women's Institutions, Social Reform, and the Career of Miriam Van Waters," in *U.S. History as Women's History: New Feminist Essays*, ed. Linda K. Kerber, Alice Kessler-Harris, and Kathryn Kish Sklar (Chapel Hill: University of North Carolina Press, 1995), 170–188.

The RSF institutionalized "the space, outside government and outside the academy, where reform-minded women *and* men could engage in social scientific exploration and have it recognized as such"; O'Connor, *Poverty Knowledge*, 42.

115. Ruth Crocker, "Gender and Social Science at the Russell Sage Foundation, 1907–1930," paper presented at the Social Science History Association Meeting, Baltimore, Maryland, November 2003.

116. Ellen Fitzpatrick found that all of the professional social scientists she studied worked within male-led bureaucracies, defining themselves as professionals first, women second; *Endless Crusade*. See also Muncy, *Creating a Female Dominion*; Silverberg, *Gender and American Social Science*; and Lindenmeyer, *"A Right To Childhood."*

For the professionalization of social work, see Kunzel, *The Professionalization of Benevolence*, 44–48; Fitzpatrick, *Endless Crusade*; Walkowitz, "The Making of a Feminine Professional Identity: Social Workers in the 1920s," *American Historical Review* 95, no. 4 (October 1990): 1051–1075; Daniel Walkowitz, *Working with Class: Social Workers and the Politics of Middle-Class Identity* (Chapel Hill: University of North Carolina Press, 1999); Clarke Chambers, "Women in the Creation of Professional Social Work," *Social Service Review* 60 (March 1986): 8–12; Penina Migdal Glazer and Miriam Slater, *Unequal Colleagues: The Entrance of Women into the Professions* (New Brunswick, N.J.: Rutgers University Press, 1987); and Linda Shoemaker, "'Charity and Justice': Gender and the Mission of Social Work: Social Work Education in Boston, New York, and Chicago, 1898–1930" (Ph.D. diss., Binghamton University, 2001).

117. The best analysis to date is still Robyn Muncy, "Gender and Professionalization in the Origins of the U.S. Welfare State: The Careers of Sophonisba Breckinridge and Edith Abbott," *Journal of Policy History* 2, no. 3 (1990): 290–315.

118. Henry J. Duffy, ed., *A Victorian Wedding in Modern Times* (Elmsford, N.Y.: National Trust for Historic Preservation, n.d.), Shepard was an officer in the Missouri Pacific Railroad. This pamphlet commemorating Helen Gould's wedding also contains Irene Lee Epstein, "Helen Miller Gould, Finley Johnson Shepard: Biographical Sketches." For a list of her organizational activities and memberships as of March 1935, see Addendum to Alice Northrop Snow with Henry Nicholas Snow, *The Story of Helen Gould, Daughter of Jay Gould, Great American* (New York: Fleming H. Revell Company, 1943), 338–340.

119. Anderson and Greenwald, "Introduction," to *Pittsburgh Surveyed*, 8–9.

120. David C. Hammack, "Foundations in the American Polity, 1900–1950," in Lagemann, *Philanthropic Foundations*, 56–58, appreciates the work of foundations in general, but the connection between the Russell Sage Foundation and the Progressive movement has yet to be fully articulated.

121. A useful recent volume is Glenda Gilmore, ed., *Who Were the Progressives?* (New York: Bedford/St. Martin's, 2002).

122. Alchon, *Invisible Hand of Planning*; Smith, *Idea Brokers*; O'Connor, *Poverty Knowledge*.

123. The Last Will of Margaret Olivia Sage, dated October 25th, 1906; First Codicil, Dated February 17, 1908; Second Codicil, dated July 19, 1911, 22, all in FSW. See also "Mrs. Sage Leaves Millions to Charity," *New York Times*, November 14, 1918; "Mrs. Sage's Estate Worth $49,051,045," *New York Times*, November 1, 1919.

Between May 20, 1920, and April 1929, the foundation received a total from

Mrs. Sage's residuary estate of $5,712,854, or seven fifty-second parts of the residuary estate. Glenn, Brandt, and Andrews, *Russell Sage Foundation*, 1:269, 271–272.

124. George Bird Grinnell, "Marsh Island," RSFR, Box 63, Folder 565; RW de F to MOS, February 19, 1912, RSFR, Box 63, Folder 558; Glenn, Brandt, and Andrews, *Russell Sage Foundation*, 1:270, 2:491–492.

12. "Women and education—there is the key"

1. Henry MacCracken to Russell Sage, December 29, 1898, MacCracken Records, NYU.

2. Arthur Huntington Gleason, "Mrs. Russell Sage and Her Interests," *World's Work* 13 (November 1906): 8183.

3. M. Olivia Sage (Mrs. Russell Sage), "Opportunities and Responsibilities of Leisured Women," *North American Review* 181 (November 1905): 720.

4. For an excellent discussion of these millennial hopes for the transformative and progressive potential of women in public life, see Ann Taylor Allen, "Feminism, Social Science, and the Meanings of Modernity: The Debate on the Origin of the Family in Europe and the United States, 1860–1914," *American Historical Review* 104 (October 1999): 1113; and Seth Koven and Sonya Michel, eds., *Mothers of New Worlds: Maternalist Politics and the Origins of Welfare States* (New York: Routledge, 1993).

5. [William Gurley], "Press Release," January 1907, 3; RW de F, "Estimate of Cost—Emma Willard School, Troy, New York," December 18, 1906; William Gurley to RW de F, December 19, 1906; RW de F to William Gurley, January 3, 1907. All in the William F. Gurley Papers, EWS.

6. De Forest advised "as a matter of personal suggestion" not to give or sell the abandoned site to the city of Troy; RW de F to William Gurley, January 3, 1907, William F. Gurley Papers, EWS.

7. J. D. Phelps to Chancellor James Day, May 11, 1906, Papers of Chancellor James Roscoe Day, Box 2, SUA. On women's education, see Thomas Woody, *A History of Women's Education in the United States*, 2 vols. (New York: Science Press, 1929); Barbara Miller Solomon, *In the Company of Educated Women: A History of Women and Higher Education in America* (New Haven, Conn.: Yale University Press, 1985); Lynn D. Gordon, *Gender and Higher Education in the Progressive Era* (New Haven, Conn.: Yale University Press, 1990); William Leach, *True Love and Perfect Union: The Feminist Reform of Sex and Society*, 2nd ed. (Middletown, Conn.: Wesleyan University Press, 1989); Carol Lasser, ed., *Educating Men and Women Together: Coeducation in a Changing World* (Urbana: University of Illinois Press, 1987).

8. Margaret Rossiter, *Women Scientists in America: Struggles and Strategies to 1940* (Baltimore, Md.: Johns Hopkins University Press, 1982), 46–47.

9. Kathryn Kish Sklar, "Who Funded Hull-House?" in *Lady Bountiful Revisited: Women, Philanthropy, and Power*, ed. Kathleen D. McCarthy (New Brunswick, N.J.: Rutgers University Press, 1990), 94–115. See also Mary Lynn McCree,

"Louise deKoven Bowen," *Notable American Women: The Modern Period* (Cambridge, Mass.: Belknap Press of Harvard University Press, 1980), 99–101; James W. Linn, *Jane Addams: A Biography* (New York: Appleton-Century, 1935), 140–144; Allen F. Davis, *American Heroine: The Life and Legend of Jane Addams* (New York: Oxford University Press, 1973). In addition, a "fellowship system" linked wealthy friends to the settlement house through regular monthly donations; Robyn Muncy, *Creating a Female Dominion in American Reform, 1890–1935* (New York: Oxford University Press, 1991), 17–18. Kathryn Kish Sklar writes, "Women reformers of the Progressive era did indeed inhabit a separate political culture—one that gave generously of its own resources in the process of remaking the larger political culture"; "Who Funded Hull-House?" 111.

10. Muncy, *Creating a Female Dominion*, 17–18; Ellen Fitzpatrick, *Endless Crusade: Women Social Scientists and Progressive Reform* (New York: Oxford University Press, 1990); Regina Kunzel, *Fallen Women, Problem Girls: Unmarried Mothers and the Professionalization of Social Work, 1890–1945* (New Haven, Conn.: Yale University Press, 1993); Penina Migdal Glazer and Miriam Slater, *Unequal Colleagues: The Entrance of Women into the Professions, 1890–1940* (New Brunswick, N.J.: Rutgers University Press, 1987); Karen Snedker, "Crossing the Divide: Women's Entry into the World of Policing," paper presented at the Social Science History Association meeting, Fort Worth, Texas, November 1999.

11. Rossiter, *Women Scientists in America*, 42; John D. Rousmaniere, "Cultural Hybrid in the Slums: The College Woman and the Settlement House, 1889–1894," *American Quarterly* 22 (Spring 1970): 45–66. The Association of Collegiate Alumnae was the predecessor of the American Association of University Women.

12. Van Kleeck's scholarship at the New York College Settlement was jointly supported by Smith College Alumnae and the College Settlements Association; Guy Alchon, "'The Self-Applauding Sincerity' of Overreaching Theory, Biography as Ethical Practice, and the Case of Mary van Kleeck," in *Gender and American Social Science: The Formative Years*, ed. Helene Silverberg (Princeton, N.J.: Princeton University Press, 1998), 303.

13. Sarah Knowles Bolton, *Famous Givers and Their Gifts* (New York: Thomas Y. Crowell and Co., 1896), 326–327; Rossiter, *Women Scientists in America*, 46–47; Paul S. Boyer, "Mary Elizabeth Garrett," *NAW*, 2:21–22.

14. Not all such efforts were successful, however. The University of Michigan accepted Dr. Elizabeth Bates's large gift but never carried out its terms. This was an ominous precedent for Sage, as was the failure of Joseph Bennett's gift of $400,000 for an undergraduate college for women at the University of Pennsylvania. And after 1900, large-scale science had become "the realm of professionals, millionaires, big business, and, soon, the big foundations, which few women ever penetrated." Rossiter, *Women Scientists in America*, 47, 88.

15. Mary Roth Walsh, *"Doctors Wanted: No Women Need Apply": Sexual Barriers in the Medical Profession, 1835–1975* (New Haven, Conn.: Yale University Press, 1977), 173–177.

16. Theodore Stanton and Harriot Stanton Blatch, eds., *Elizabeth Cady Stanton as Revealed in Her Letters, Diary and Reminiscences* (New York: Harper, 1922), 1:340–345.

17. The meeting took place at the home of Mrs. Jennings Demorest on East 57th Street; "Woman's Debt to Woman," *New York World*, April 29, 1894, ECS/SBA, Reel 32, 700–701.

18. Stanton and Blatch, *Elizabeth Cady Stanton*, 2:295n1.

19. She adds, "I stood up stoutly for coeducation." Stanton and Blatch, *Elizabeth Cady Stanton*, 2:298. See also Patricia Palmieri, "From Republican Motherhood to Race Suicide: Arguments on the Higher Education of Women in the United States, 1820–1920," in *Educating Women and Men Together: Coeducation in a Changing World*, ed. Carol Lasser (Chicago: University of Illinois Press, 1987).

20. RW de F to MOS, February 7, 1907, and Gertrude Rice to RW de F, April 27, 1907, both in RSFR, Box 2, Folder 11. It was COS doctrine that those who applied for help were usually, by definition, the undeserving.

21. Report of W. F. Persons to RW de F, August 1, 1907, and RW de F to Mr. W. Frank Persons, August 3, 1907, both in CSSA, Columbia. It is not clear whether Persons included educational institutions in this total. For COS handling of Sage's letters, see Ruth Crocker, "'I Only Ask You Kindly to Divide Some of Your Fortune with Me': Begging Letters and the Transformation of Charity in Late Nineteenth-Century America," *Social Politics: International Studies in Gender, State, and Society* 6 (Summer 1999): 131–160.

22. Henry L. Higginson to A. Lawrence Lowell, December 16, 1910, Papers of A. Lawrence Lowell, Harvard.

23. RW de F to Anson Phelps Stokes, Jr., November 20, 1909, Records of the Secretary's Office, Yale, Manuscripts and Archives.

24. Theodore Francis Jones, *New York University, 1832–1932* (New York: New York University Press, 1933), 169–170, 323; Thomas Frusciano and Marilyn Pettit, *New York University and the City: An Illustrated History* (New Brunswick, N.J.: Rutgers University Press, 1997). Gould is estimated to have given the university over $2 million. [Bursar, New York University] to Dr. Elmer Brown, March 19, 1913, MacCracken Records, II. Finances, "Gould-Shepard" folder, Endowments and Trusts: Gould Family Correspondence, 1891–1909, NYU.

25. Phyllis Eckhaus attributes this comment to Columbia Law School dean Harlan Stone, noting that women were admitted to the school only after Stone moved to the Supreme Court in 1941. Phyllis Eckhaus, "Restless Women: The Pioneering Alumnae of New York University School of Law," *New York University Law Review* 66 (December 1991): 1996. For suffrage leader Lillie Devereux Blake's attempt to get women enrolled at Columbia, see Katherine Devereux Blake and Margaret Louise Wallace, *Champion of Women: The Life of Lillie Devereux Blake* (New York: Fleming H. Revell Co., 1943), 110–112.

26. Eckhaus, "Restless Women," 1998–1999; *For the Better Protection of Their*

Rights: A History of the First Fifty Years of the Women's Legal Education Society and the Woman's Law Class (New York: New York University Press, 1940). See also MacCracken Records, "Helen Miller Gould" folder, NYU. On Emilie Kempin, see Virginia Drachman, *Women Lawyers and the Origins of Professional Identity in America* (Ann Arbor: University of Michigan Press, 1993), 281–283.

27. Eckhaus, "Restless Women" 1998–1999. "The University of New York is co-educational in its post-graduate courses and in its Departments of Law, Pedagogy, and Commerce. Its Law Department is celebrated for the prominent women it has graduated"; *HWS*, 4:871.

28. Martha Buell Plum (Mrs. John P.) Munn, "The Law and Liberal Culture," speech to Woman's Law Class, New York University, n.d., James Buell Munn Collection, Box 1, Series 1/C Folder 7, NYU. See also New York University Woman's Law Class Records, NYU.

But this may have been too modest an assessment of the Woman's Law Class. Historian Virginia Drachman writes: "The founders of the Woman's Law Class had three goals: to provide practical legal knowledge to women who needed either to protect their own personal affairs or to improve their positions in the workplace; to give leisured women the opportunity to expand their education and broaden their minds; and to prepare women who wished ultimately to enter a law school"; *Sisters in Law: Women Lawyers in Modern American History* (Cambridge, Mass.: Harvard University Press, 1998), 122.

29. "New York University, Law Lectures to Women" (May 1, 1897) lists the curriculum of four courses on law, describes the Woman's Legal Education Society and the Alumnae Association, and lists the graduates of the 1897 class. James Buell Munn Estate Papers, Series 1/C, Folder 5, MC2, NYU.

30. Guide to the New York University Woman's Law Class Records, 1888–1941, 1983, NYU. The creation of this Advisory Committee was opposed by a number of faculty; Jones, *New York University*, 353.

31. Henry MacCracken to MOS, n.d., RSFR, Box 88, Folder 851; Henry M. MacCracken, "University Heights South," October 31, 1907, marked "Private and Confidential," 1, both in MacCracken Records, Series III, Box 18, Folder 4: University Heights South, NYU.

32. Rossiter, *Women Scientists in America*, 86. See also Gordon, *Gender and Higher Education in the Progressive Era*.

33. "Doctor of Millionaires. The Man Who Cares for Jay Gould's Health," *New York Tribune*, January 3, 1892, clipping, James Buell Munn Estate Papers, NYU. The writer described Munn as Gould's "keeper." See also Paul Sarnoff, *Russell Sage, the Money King* (New York: Ivan Obolensky, 1965), 327–328.

34. Jay Gould and Helen Gould were by far the largest donors. Only a draft remains of this important proposal. MacCracken Records, II. Finances, "Gould-Shepard" folder, NYU; Henry MacCracken to Russell Sage, March 3, 1893, RSFR, Box 88, Folder 850.

35. Minutes of the Executive Committee of the Council of New York University, November 25, 1895, quoted in Taylor, "'No Extra Expense,'" 12–13.

36. Henry MacCracken to Russell Sage, December 29, 1898, MacCracken Records, NYU; emphasis in the original.

37. Ibid.

38. "Pick First Women for Fame's Hall," unidentified newspaper clipping, RSFR, Box 88, Folder 850. See also Henry MacCracken, [Draft of Speech Honoring Emma Willard, 1905], Box 5, Folder 29; "Address to the Emma Willard Society," n.d., McCracken Records, Box 6, Folder 4, [drafts of speeches], NYU.

39. M. Olivia Sage to Chancellor MacCracken, May 31, 1904, McCracken Records, "Honorary Degrees" folder, NYU. Patricia Meyer Spacks has analyzed how women's claims to subjectivity were often made from a concealed position or were elided with claims on behalf of some more famous subject. This certainly seems true of Olivia. See "Selves in Hiding," in *Women's Autobiography: Essays in Criticism*, ed. Estelle C. Jelineck (Bloomington: Indiana University Press, 1980), 112–132.

40. Gustav H. Schwab to Chancellor MacCracken, December 8, 1904, Mac-Cracken Records, "Real Estate, 1892–1908" folder, NYU. This was known as the University Heights property.

41. Henry MacCracken, "Statement," n.d. (1905), MacCracken Records, NYU. This memo begins, "This statement is prepared for the leading benefactors of New York University who have contributed generously to the land and buildings at University Heights."

42. Henry MacCracken, "University Heights South," October 31, 1907, 1–2, MacCracken Records, NYU.

43. Ibid., 2–3. This was $6 million in 2003 dollars. "Gift for the University," *New York Observer*, December 27, 1906; "NYU Takes Title, Acquires Schwab Farm," *New York Daily Tribune*, December 19, 1906, 1; RW de F to Henry MacCracken, October 15, 1906, RSFR, Box 88, Folder 850; RW de F, "Margaret Olivia Sage, Philanthropist," *The Survey* 41 (November 9, 1918): 151.

44. MacCracken, "University Heights South," 3.

45. Ibid., 4.

46. Henry MacCracken, Statement to the Council, October 31, 1907, Mac-Cracken Records, NYU. New York University archivist Nancy M. Cricco kindly helped clarify this correspondence for me. Personal communication to the author, December 12, 1994. "Gift to New York University," typescript, RSFR Box 88, Folder 850.

47. R. H. Pratt to Dr. Elmer E. Brown, December 12, 1913, 1, in Administrative Papers of Chancellor Elmer Ellsworth Brown, Box 62, "Sage, Margaret Mrs. Russell, 1912–1940, 1924" folder, NYU.

48. Dr. Elmer E. Brown to J. J. Slocum, November 20, 1917, Box 62, Folder 1, Administrative Papers of Chancellor Elmer Ellsworth Brown, NYU.

49. R. H. Pratt to Dr. Elmer E. Brown, December 12, 1913, Administrative Papers of Chancellor Elmer Ellsworth Brown, NYU. For the glee club reference I am grateful to Susan Kastan.

50. "Nettie Fowler," *EWP*, 814; Charles O. Burgess, "Nettie Fowler McCormick," *NAW*, 2:454–455. Her son Harold McCormick married Edith, youngest daughter of John D. Rockefeller, Sr. Clarice Stasz, "Edith Rockefeller McCormick's Philanthropy," *Rockefeller Archive Center Research Reports* (Spring 1994): 4–6.

51. Nettie McCormick to MOS, February 7, 1908, Nettie Fowler McCormick Correspondence, Series 1B, Box 12, January–March 1908 file, WHSA.

52. James G. K. McClure to MOS, February 22, 1916, letter of thanks for a $1,000 endowed scholarship at the seminary. In March, McClure wrote thanking Sage for a further $1,500, beginning, "You are an angel, here, now and forever!" James G. K. McClure to MOS, March 15, 1916. Both in RSFR, Box 83, Folder 795.

53. E. Lilian Todd to Mrs. Cyrus H. McCormick, [1913], Nettie Fowler McCormick Correspondence, Series 2B, Box 133, "Todd, E. Lilian" folder, WHSA. In 1915, McCormick thanked Sage for "the 'wireless apparatus,'" a birthday gift, along with another check for $1,000 "for Missions." Nettie McCormick to "My dearest friend" [MOS], [1915], Nettie Fowler McCormick Correspondence, Series 1B, Box 15, Foreign Missions File, WHSA.

54. James D. Phelps to MOS, July 29, 1907 acknowledging "your great gift to Syracuse University" and Dean Jacob Street to J. J. Slocum, September 22, 1908, both in RSFR, Box 94, Folder 939. Correspondence between Olivia and Syracuse University from 1907 to 1909 is in RSFR, Box 94, Folder 939. *Leslie's Weekly*, October 14, 1909, clipping, RSFR, Box 66, Folder 590.

55. Henry de Forest to Chancellor James R. Day, September 3, 1909, Papers of Chancellor James Roscoe Day, Box 3, SUA.

56. James Day to Henry W. de Forest, December 4, 1909, Papers of Chancellor James Roscoe Day Box 3, SUA; Dean Jacob Street to J. J. Slocum, September 22, 1908, RSFR, Box 94, Folder 939; Street to MOS, October 19, 1909, thanking Olivia for permission to use her name, RSFR, Box 94, Folder 939; RW de F to Chancellor Day, February 5, 1910, Papers of Chancellor James Roscoe Day, Box 3, SUA.

57. James R. Day to Henry de Forest, June 17, 1911, Papers of Chancellor James Roscoe Day, Box 3, January–July 1911, SUA.

58. [Unknown] to MOS, June 14, 1912, Papers of Chancellor James Roscoe Day, Box 4, SUA.

59. Peter Dobkin Hall, conversation with the author, November 1999. See also Peter Dobkin Hall, *Inventing the Nonprofit Sector and Other Essays on Philanthropy, Voluntarism, and Nonprofit Organizations* (Baltimore, Md.: Johns Hopkins University Press, 1992).

60. Catharine Hunter [secretary] to Hon. Andrew D. White, July 14, 1910, Andrew Dickson White Papers, Cornell.

61. RW de F to MOS, February 1, 1911, RSFR, Box 92, Folder 894.
At other times, de Forest literally dictated her response. After a visit from

A. Lawrence Lowell of Harvard, she sent a handwritten note, "I have your pleasant visit in mind and will give the matter careful consideration"; MOS to A. Lawrence Lowell, April 7, 1911, handwritten, Papers of A. Lawrence Lowell, Harvard. The note had been drafted by de Forest two days earlier. See RW de F to MOS, April 5, 1911, RSFR, Box 79, Folder 738.

62. RW de F to Anson Phelps Stokes, Jr., May 4, 1907, Records of the Secretary's Office, YRG 4-A, Series 11, "Robert de Forest" folder, Yale, Manuscripts and Archives. The letter was marked "Personal." "Mrs. Sage's 450 Gifts," *New York Herald,* December 20, 1908.

63. Anson Phelps Stokes to RW de F, June 13, 1907, RW de F to Anson Phelps Stokes, June 14, 1907, and Anson Phelps Stokes to RW de F, December 19, 1907, all in Records of the Secretary's Office, Yale, Manuscripts and Archives; Anson Phelps Stokes to MOS, August 30, 1907, RSFR, Box 99, Folder 1001.

64. Anson Phelps Stokes to MOS, April 7, 1908, RSFR, Box 99, Folder 1001.

65. A note from E. H. Anderson, acting director, New York Public Library, acknowledging "a collection of 158 volumes and pamphlets, including College and University Reports, etc." suggests that Olivia had received a lot of solicitations from universities and colleges. E. H. Anderson [to MOS], April 30, 1913, RSFR, Box 87, Folder 848. David A. Hollinger, "Inquiry and Uplift: Late Nineteenth-Century American Academics and the Moral Efficacy of Scientific Practice," in *The Authority of Experts: Studies in History and Theory,* ed. Thomas L. Haskell (Bloomington: Indiana University Press, 1984), 142–156; George M. Marsden, "The Soul of the American University: An Historical Overview," in *The Secularization of the Academy,* ed. George M. Marsden and Bradley J. Longfield (New York: Oxford University Press, 1992), 9–45; Edwin E. Slosson, *Great American Universities* (1910; repr., New York: Arno, 1977).

66. RW de F to Anson Phelps Stokes, Jr., November 20, 1909, Records of the Secretary's Office, Yale, Manuscripts and Archives.

67. Anson Phelps Stokes, Jr., to MOS, December 31, 1909, RSFR, Box 99, Folder 1001. See also *Yale Alumni Weekly,* January 7, 1910.

68. RW de F to Anson Phelps Stokes, Jr., April 14, 1911, and June 17, 1911, Records of the Secretary's Office, Yale, Manuscripts and Archives. She declined the Princeton invitation for the same reason. Mary Boardman had been Olivia's pupil in Philadelphia before her marriage.

69. RW de F to MOS, July 18, 1910, RSFR, Box 75, Folder 690.

70. Mrs. A. L. Hadley to MOS, April 30, 1904; President James M. Taylor to MOS, June 20, 1904, RSFR, Box 96, Folder 965; James Monroe Taylor and Elizabeth Hazleton Haight, *Vassar* (New York: Oxford University Press, 1915), 174–175n2.

71. Helen Hadley to MOS, April 30, 1910; James M. Taylor to MOS, October 1910, both in RSFR, Box 96, Folder 965. On the back of this last letter's envelope, her secretary had written, "Answer—Mrs. Sage will probably contribute $150,000 about January 1, 1910 [*sic*]"; RSFR, Box 96, Folder 965. Pres-

ident James M. Taylor to MOS, July 31, 1911, and August 24, 1911, both in RSFR, Box 96, Folder 965. See also Henry Whittemore, *History of the Sage and Slocum Families of England and America, Including the Allied Families of Montague, Wanton, Brown, Josselyn, Standish, Doty, Carver, Jermain or Germain, Pierson, Howell* (New York: Published by Mrs. Russell Sage, 1908). For Vassar in this period, see Gordon, *Gender and Higher Education in the Progressive Era,* 121–164.

72. James M. Taylor to MOS, August 24, 1911, RSFR, Box 96, Folder 965. On Taylor as a fund-raiser, see Gordon, *Gender and Higher Education in the Progressive Era,* 136.

73. President Caroline Hazard to MOS, February 24, 1908, RSFR, Box 96, Folder 970.

74. Anna Palen to Mrs. Sage, April 3, 1914, RSFR, Box 96, Folder 970.

75. RW de F to MOS, March 25, 1914, RSFR, Box 96, Folder 970; RW de F to MOS, April 5, 1911, RSFR, Box 79, Folder 738.

76. The decision was noted in her hand on the back of an envelope dated April 10, 1914: "Have decided to give $250,000, but am not willing to give building." RSFR, Box 96, Folder 970. Wellesley did receive $800,000 in her will, however.

77. "By 1899, the trustees abolished all the evangelical elements that linked Wellesley with the Mount Holyoke tradition"; Helen Lefkowitz Horowitz, *Alma Mater: Design and Experience in the Women's Colleges from Their Nineteenth-Century Beginnings to the 1930s* (New York: Knopf, 1984), 205, 213–214. Wellesley in this period is the subject of Patricia Ann Palmieri, *In Adamless Eden: The Community of Women Faculty at Wellesley* (New Haven, Conn.: Yale University Press, 1995).

78. Helen Miller Gould to Mary Wooley, 16 May, 1903, quoted in Glazer and Slater, *Unequal Colleagues,* 39 and 255n21.

79. Catharine Hunter [secretary] to Andrew D. White, July 14, 1910, Andrew Dickson White Papers, Cornell; Alice Northrop Snow with Henry Nicholas Snow, *The Story of Helen Gould, Daughter of Jay Gould, Great American* (New York: Fleming H. Revell Company, 1943), 279–280.

80. E. Lilian Todd to G. A. Plimpton, February 25, 1914, in Nancy Slack, "Letters to Margaret Olivia Sage from Rockefeller Archives," in author's possession. I am grateful to Nancy Slack for this reference.

81. Memorandum, "Margaret Olivia Sage. Trustee 1907 to November 1918," typescript, RSFR, Box 1, Folder 1; Frances Hamilton to MOS, December 6, 1915, RSFR, Box 1, Folder 3; Daisy Allen Story, New York Federation of Women's Clubs, to Mrs. Sage, November 8, 1909, RSFR, Box 1, Folder 3. "My heart is so full I cannot find words to thank you," Miss Story wrote.

82. Mary Rutherford Joy to MOS, January 14, 1914, RSFR, Box 90, Folder 869. Gertrude Ely, Secretary, Pennsylvania School of Horticulture for Women, to MOS, February 15, 1916, RSFR, Box 90, Folder 869.

83. "To the Trustees of the Margaret Sage Industrial School, Lawrence,

Long Island," June 16, 1910, SWHA, Box 8, Folder 63: Five Towns Community House, Lawrence, Long Island.

84. E. A. Paddock, President, the Idaho Industrial Institute, to Miss Hunter, March 5, 1908, E. A. Paddock to MOS, May 5, 1910, Mrs. S. B. Dudley to MOS, March 30, 1916, all in RSFR, Box 80, Folder 755.

85. MOS to Mr. W.R. Moody, March __, 1907, RSFR, Box 89, Folder 857. Russell Sage may have been contemplating a bequest to the school shortly before his death. In 1900, he wrote, "I am also considering learning about Mr. Moody's work at Northfield, for future action." Russell Sage, January 6, 1900, RSFR, Box 89, Folder 858. In 1904, Northfield held the first summer school for missions and drew 235 delegates. Patricia R. Hill, *The World Their Household: The American Woman's Foreign Mission Movement and Cultural Transformation, 1870–1920* (Ann Arbor: University of Michigan Press, 1985), 127, 146–147. On the career and significance of Moody, see James F. Findlay, *Dwight L. Moody, American Evangelist, 1837–1899* (Chicago: University of Chicago Press, 1969).

86. Louis Harlan, *Booker T. Washington: The Wizard of Tuskegee, 1901–1915* (New York: Oxford University Press, 1983). A critical view of Tuskegee and Hampton is in James D. Anderson, "Philanthropic Control Over Private Black Higher Education," in *Philanthropy and Cultural Imperialism: The Foundations at Home and Abroad,* ed. Robert F. Arnove (Bloomington: Indiana University Press, 1980), 147–178. Some scholars are now prepared to argue that "industrial education" was more politically astute than it has seemed and that it did not preclude real progress. For women, Tuskegee at this time was a normal school that trained them as teachers. Carolyn Gebhard, "Work in Progress: The Women of Tuskegee," paper presented at the Alabama Women's History Forum, Birmingham, Alabama, March 11, 2000.

87. Andrew Dickson White, letter of introduction for Booker T. Washington, November 13, 1906, and Booker T. Washington to MOS, May 2, 1908, acknowledging a donation of $20,000 for Tuskegee Institute, both in RSFR, Box 95, Folder 952; Last Will of Margaret Olivia Sage (October 25, 1906), First Codicil (February 17th, 1908), and Second Codicil (July 19th, 1911), Surrogates Court of the County of New York, December 11, 1919. A recent analysis of the relationship between Washington and white (male) philanthropists from Washington's side is David Leverenz, "Booker T. Washington's Strategies of Manliness," in *Booker T. Washington and Black Progress,* ed. Fitzhugh Brundage (Gainesville, Fla.: University Press of Florida, 2003). Leverenz writes, "As Washington became the dominant African American of his time by assiduously securing his credit with wealthy whites, he learned that his credit depended on their trust that he could recirculate their surplus wealth for social profit" (163).

88. H. B. Frissell to MOS, May 1, 1913, and March 5, 1914, with attached response from E. Lilian Todd and J. J. Slocum, all in RSFR, Box 79, Folder 737, Todd's emphasis in the original; Last Will of Margaret Olivia Sage, 21.

89. Mrs. I. E. Gibbs to MOS, November 30, 1908, RSFR, Box 70, Folder 626.

90. The files in the Papers of James Roscoe Day for these years document the tensions between the university, parents, and students over undergraduate behavior.

91. Lynn Gordon calls this "intellectual integration and social separatism"; *Gender and Higher Education in the Progressive Era,* 120.

92. Andrew Dickson White to J. J. Slocum, January 21, 1911, Andrew Dickson White Papers, Cornell.

93. J. J. Slocum to Hon. Andrew D. White, February 2, 1911, Andrew Dickson White Papers, Cornell; Andrew D. White to MOS, April 15, 1910, Prudence Risley Log, Department of Manuscripts and University Archives, Cornell University Libraries; "Campus Enlarged by Three Acres," newspaper clipping, n.d., RSFR, Box 75, Folder 690; "Mrs. Sage Guest at Dedication of Risley Hall," newspaper clipping, n.d., OnHA; Andrew D. White to Col. Slocum, February 4, 1911, Andrew Dickson White Papers, Cornell; Andrew D. White to MOS, February 4, 1911, RSFR, Box 75, Folder 690.

94. Andrew D. White to MOS, July 8, 1910, and Catharine Hunter to Hon. Andrew D. White, July 14, 1910, Andrew Dickson White Papers, Cornell.

95. Catharine Hunter [secretary] to Andrew D. White, July 14, 1910; Andrew Dickson White to MOS, October 12, 1910; J. J. Slocum to Andrew D. White, January 18, 1911; Andrew D. White to J. J. Slocum, January 21, 1911; J .J. Slocum to Andrew D. White, February 2, 1911. All in Andrew Dickson White Papers, Cornell. See also "Mrs. Sage Gives $300,000 for Cornell Dormitory," clipping, Papers of A. Lawrence Lowell, "Freshman Dormitories" folder, Harvard. On coeducation at the University of Chicago, see Gordon, *Gender and Higher Education in the Progressive Era,* 85–120.

96. Andrew D. White to MOS, July 8, 1910, Andrew Dickson White Papers, Cornell.

97. Henry de Forest to MOS, October 25, 1909, RSFR, Box 94, Folder 939.

98. The 1906 will contains this stipulation: "It is my desire that each religious, educational, and charitable corporation, which may receive a share of my residuary estate shall use the whole or part of such legacy . . . for some purpose which will commemorate the name of my husband." She added, "But I simply express this as a desire and do not impose it as a condition on my gift." "Mrs. Sage Gives Millions to Charity," *New York Times,* November 14, 1918.

99. James M. Taylor to MOS, October 1910, November 21, 1910, July 31, 1911, and August 24, 1911, all in RSFR, Box 96, Folder 965. See also Kathleen D. McCarthy, *Women's Culture: American Philanthropy and Art* (Chicago: University of Chicago Press, 1991).

100. Henry Lee Higginson to President A. Lawrence Lowell, December 16, 1910, Papers of A. Lawrence Lowell, Harvard.

101. MOS to Trustees of Princeton University, April 7, 1908, and June 19, 1911; W. Wilson to MOS, November 2, 1908; MOS to Mr. John L. Cadwalader, June 3, 1910; RW de F to MOS, January 2, 1912. All in RSFR, Box 99, Folder 1001.

102. Henry L. Higginson to President A. Lawrence Lowell, December 16, 1910, Papers of A. Lawrence Lowell, Harvard; John Cadwalader to MOS, June 3, 1910, RSFR, Box 91, Folder 892.

103. A. Lawrence Lowell to Henry Lee Higginson, December 19, 1910, Papers of A. Lawrence Lowell, Harvard.

104. Henry Lee Higginson to A. Lawrence Lowell, January 21, 1911, Papers of A. Lawrence Lowell, Harvard.

105. "She has decided not to donate the $450,000 which she understands will cover the cost of one dormitory"; Henry de Forest to A. Lawrence Lowell, July 19, 1911, emphasis added. See also A. Lawrence Lowell to MOS, March 28, 1911; A. Lawrence Lowell to J. P. Morgan, July 21, 1911; A. Lawrence Lowell to Henry de Forest, July 21, 1911; MOS to A. Lawrence Lowell, September 13, 1911; and Henry de Forest to President Lowell, September 13, 1911, all in Papers of A. Lawrence Lowell, Harvard.

106. A. Lawrence Lowell to J. P. Morgan, Jr., July 21, 1911, Papers of A. Lawrence Lowell, Harvard, emphasis added.

107. Henry de Forest to A. Lawrence Lowell, July 18, 1912, Papers of A. Lawrence Lowell, Harvard.

108. MOS to A. Lawrence Lowell, August 26, 1912, Papers of A. Lawrence Lowell, "Freshman Dormitories" folder, Harvard.

109. Henry de Forest to President Lowell, July 18, 1912, and A. Lawrence Lowell to Henry de Forest, July 23, 1912, both in Papers of A. Lawrence Lowell, Harvard.

110. MOS to President Lowell, August 26, 1912, Papers of A. Lawrence Lowell, Harvard; President and Fellows of Harvard College to MOS, April 24, 1911; A. Lawrence Lowell to MOS, May 13, 1911; Robert de Forest to President Lowell, July 1912; A. Lawrence Lowell to MOS, September 3, 1912. All in RSFR, Box 79, Folder 739. Despite this large donation, Harvard was not willing to accommodate Sage's subsequent request for a loan for a graduate student, perhaps a relative. Harvard Graduate School of Arts and Sciences to Miss Todd, April 24, 1916, RSFR, Box 79, Folder 738.

111. MOS to President Lowell, September 17, 1912, Papers of A. Lawrence Lowell, Harvard.

112. Palmer Ricketts to MOS, January 1, 1907. This letter confirmed the gift of $1 million as a memorial to her husband. See also Ricketts to MOS, March 5, 1908, February 15, 1909, and June 19, 1909, all in RSFR, Box 92, Folder 896. See also Sarnoff, *Russell Sage, the Money King*, 279–280.

113. Marjorie Semerad, "I Decided That Mr. Russell Sage Deserved Another Look," in *Sage Stories: Essays on the Third Quarter Century, 1966–1991*, ed. Coleen Paratore (Troy, N.Y.: The Sage Colleges, 1991), 161–162.

114. Sage's gift to RPI is acknowledged in Palmer Ricketts to MOS, January 1, 1907, and Ricketts to MOS, March 5, 1908, both in RSFR, Box 92, Folder 896. See also Sarnoff, *Russell Sage, the Money King*, 279–280. For a resolution authorizing the head of the department of electrical engi-

neering to expend "a sum not exceeding $15,000 for the equipment of his depart-
ment in the Sage Laboratory" and another authorizing a $40,000 expenditure
by the mechanical engineering head, see RPI Board of Trustees Minutes, vol.
3, May 6, 1908, 499–500; Minutes of a Regular Meeting of the Board of Trustees
of the Rensselaer Polytechnic Institute, February 6, 1907, RPI Board of
Trustees Minutes, vol. 3, 491–492, 496; RPI Board of Trustees Minutes, September 27, 1911, vol. 4, 35; February 12, 1913, vol. 4, 59. All in RPI, vol. 4,
59, Institute Archives and Special Collections. For Rensselaer Polytechnic,
see Noble, *America by Design*, 20–26. Noble describes RPI as the first modern
engineering school. For engineering education, see David F. Noble, *America
by Design: Science, Technology, and the Rise of Corporate Capitalism* (New York:
Knopf, 1977).

115. RSFR, Box 92, Folder 897; RPI Board of Trustees Minutes, May 5,
1915, vol. 4, 101; RPI Board of Trustees Minutes, September 24, 1913, vol. 4,
73, 75, RPI.

116. Palmer C. Ricketts to MOS, May 2, 1910, RSFR, Box 92, Folder 897.

117. Palmer C. Ricketts to MOS, October 24, 1912, RSFR, Box 92, Folder
897; MOS to Lilian [Todd], May 21, 1915, RSFR, Box 92, Folder 897. Earlier,
Mrs. Sage had requested Ricketts to admit a boy from Sag Harbor. The president replied, "It goes without saying that we are only too glad to help any young
man in whom you are particularly interested"; Ricketts to MOS, June 21, 1910,
RSFR, Box 92, Folder 897.

118. Chancellor James Day, "Report of Chancellor Day to the Honorable
Board of Trustees of Syracuse University, June 13, 1922," 300, Papers of James
Roscoe Day, SUA. "Mrs. Sage Will Build New College Building," "Margaret
Olivia Sage," OnHA. This clipping estimated the cost of the Joseph Slocum
College of Agriculture at between $250,000 and $300,000.

119. J. J. Slocum to Chancellor James R. Day, [September 1912], Papers of
Chancellor James Roscoe Day, Box 4, SUA; J. J. Slocum to Chancellor Day,
September 6, 1913, Papers of Chancellor James Roscoe Day, Box 5, SUA. Jermain wrote, "The eighth of September being the anniversary of Mrs. Sage's
birthday, she requests me to send the enclosed check for $30,000, with her very
sincere regards and best wishes for the success of the Joseph Slocum Division
of Agriculture."

120. Alexandra Oleson and John Voss, eds., *The Organization of Knowledge
in Modern America, 1860–1920* (Baltimore, Md.: Johns Hopkins University
Press, 1979). So complete was the triumph of this new concept of disciplinary
knowledge that the contributors to this anthology do not notice the exclusion
of women from their survey of "knowledge." Compare with Silverberg, ed., *Gender and American Social Science*.

121. David F. Noble, *A World without Women: The Christian Clerical Culture of Western Science* (New York: Knopf, 1992).

122. For a striking modern example, see Rosa Proietto, "The Ford Foundation and Women's Studies in American Higher Education: Seeds of Change?"

in *Philanthropic Foundations: New Scholarship, New Possibilities*, ed. Ellen Condliffe Lagemann (Bloomington: Indiana University Press, 1999), 271–286.

13. "Nothing more for men's colleges"

1. Theodore C. Janeway to Rev. William H. S. Demarest, President, Rutgers College, March 8, 1916, Records of the William H. S. Demarest Administration, Series II, Box 43, Folder 14, Rutgers. Dr. Theodore C. Janeway, a specialist at Johns Hopkins, had attended Russell Sage in his last illness; "Thrifty Old Man of Wall Street Has a Peaceful End," clipping, "Russell Sage," OnHA.

2. James R. Day, Chancellor, to Major J. J. Slocum, September 18, 1912, RSFR, Box 94, Folder 940. But the college yearbooks show the beginnings of a new "disciplinary home" for women in science and agriculture: home economics. Beyond the scope of this story is the history of how women with science degrees were moving into departments of home economics, leaving agriculture and most of the sciences to their male peers.

3. Major Henry Lee Higginson to Pres. A. Lawrence Lowell, January 21, 1911, Papers of A. Lawrence Lowell, Harvard.

4. J. J. Slocum to Grover C. Hart, September 3, 1912, Papers of Chancellor James Roscoe Day, Box 4, SUA; emphasis in the original. Two additional reasons may explain the bluntness and brevity of the letter: Sage's recent row with civic leaders at Sag Harbor and Jermain's limitations as a correspondent.

5. Rutgers' connection with the Reformed Church went back to its origins in 1766 as Queen's College. In 1864, three-fourths of the trustees were required to be communicants of the Reformed Church. Richard McCormick, *Rutgers: A Bicentennial History* (New Brunswick, N.J.: Rutgers University Press, 1966), 126–127.

6. Dr. Bevier Has-Brouck Sleght to Rev. William Demarest, January 6, 1907, Box 33, Folder 33, RG 07/A11/03, Records of the William H. S. Demarest Administration, Series II, Box 43, Folder 14, Rutgers.

7. President Demarest to "My dear Mrs. Sage," n.d. This was a handwritten draft. The final version may have been more polished. Records of the William H. S. Demarest Administration, Series II, Box 43, Folder 14, Rutgers.

8. Andrew Hageman to President Demarest, November 3, 1908, Records of the William H. S. Demarest Administration, Series II, Box 43, Folder 14, Rutgers. For de Forest's response, see RW de F to Mr. Austin Scott, May 11, 1907. Austin Scott was college president from 1891 to 1906 and since stepping down had been Voorhees Professor of History and Political Science. *Catalogue of the Officers and Alumni of Rutgers College, 1766 to 1916* (Trenton, N.J., 1916).

9. RW de F to L. F. Loree, September 28, 1911, Records of the William H. S. Demarest Administration, Series II, Box 43, Folder 14, Rutgers.

10. Rev. Arthur Frederick Mabon of the Collegiate Church reported to Demarest that his colleague Reverend MacLeod did not "know exactly how President Garfield gained access to Mrs. Sage's home—or how she became inter-

ested particularly in Williams College. He thinks that he got there through his name." Mabon to Demarest, February 8, 1916; [Unknown] to Dr. W. H. Demarest, June 13, 1916, Records of the William H. S. Demarest Administration, Series II, Box 43, Folder 14, Rutgers.

11. Janeway to Demarest, March 8, 1916.

12. Hageman to Demarest, September 15, 1916, Records of the William H. S. Demarest Administration, Series II, Box 43, Folder 14, Rutgers.

13. Claudia M. Oakes, *United States Women in Aviation through World War I* (1978; repr., Washington, D.C.: Smithsonian Institution Press, 1985), 10–11.

"A Woman Inventor Who Plans—and Expects—to Fly: Miss Todd and the Coming Trial of Her Aeroplane," *New York Times*, November 28, 1909, 11; Lilian Todd, "How I Built My Aeroplane," *Woman's Home Companion* (November 1909), 11; J. Suche, "At the Mineola Field," *Aeronautics* (December 1910), 197.

14. E. Lilian Todd to Eliza Kellas, January 5, 1916, Margaret Olivia Slocum Sage Collection, Box 5, EWS. The earliest Sage letter signed by E. L. Todd that I have managed to find is to Charles Wolcott, May 13, 1911, Charles D. Walcott Collection, Box 50, Folder 7, Smithsonian. The finding aids to the Margaret Olivia Slocum Sage Collection and the Eliza Kellas Collection do not specifically identify letters from E. Lilian Todd to Kellas or Sage. Since I used these papers before they were catalogued, I am giving Box 5, "Miscellaneous Correspondence about the Emma Willard School and its 'Practical' Offshoot, Russell Sage College," as a location for correspondence by Todd.

15. "I have been in this office seven years today." E. Lilian Todd to Eliza Kellas, January 26, 1918, Margaret Olivia Slocum Sage Collection, Box 5, EWS.

16. E. Lilian Todd to Eliza Kellas, January 5, 1916, Margaret Olivia Slocum Sage Collection, Box 5, EWS.

17. Todd, "How I Built My Aeroplane."

18. Ibid.; Lygia Ionnitiu, "To Conquer the Air: The Dream of E. Lilian Todd," in *The Harriet Quimby Research Conference Journal*. ed. Giacinta Bradley Koontz (Woodland Hills, Calif.: Published by the editor, 2000).

19. Todd, "How I Built My Aeroplane." The text reads, "to evolve a plan," but "plane" seems to be meant.

20. Oakes, *United States Women in Aviation through World War I*, 11.

21. She remained involved with science clubs for young men (for men they all were), the Aero Club, and, later, a radio club. Todd, "How I Built My Aeroplane." See Todd to Kellas, July 1, 1918, Margaret Olivia Slocum Sage Collection, Box 5, EWS, describing "my wireless boys" who "were having a meeting."

22. "Mrs. Russell Sage at Flying Field," *New York Sun*, July 28, 1910.

23. Todd, "How I Built My Aeroplane."

24. E. Lilian Todd to MOS, October 1, 1912; handwritten note on Todd to MOS, November 15, 1912, both in Margaret Olivia Slocum Sage Collection, Box 5, EWS.

25. Elizabeth B. Potwine, *Faithfully Yours, Eliza Kellas* (Troy, N.Y.: Emma Willard School, 1960), 26–27, 37–38, 61. "The son of the family," is quoted on page 26. In "The Women behind Troy's Russell Sage College," *The Sunday Record* (Troy, New York), June 11, 1989, 6–7, historian Helen Upton discussed Sage and Kellas, but not Todd.

26. Eliza Kellas to E. Lilian Todd, April 7, 1918, Eliza Kellas Collection, Folder 3a, EWS.

27. E. Lilian Todd to Eliza Kellas, June 4, 1914, June 5, 1914, June 8, 1914, and June 9th, 1914, all in Margaret Olivia Slocum Sage Collection, Box 6, EWS.

28. E. Lilian Todd to Eliza Kellas, April 30, 1917, Margaret Olivia Slocum Sage Collection, Box 5, EWS.

29. E. Lilian Todd to Eliza Kellas, May 10, 1915, Margaret Olivia Slocum Sage Collection, Box 5, EWS.

30. Quoted in E. Lilian Todd to Eliza Kellas, June 16, 1914, Margaret Olivia Slocum Sage Collection, Box 5, EWS.

31. The report is mentioned in E. Lilian Todd to Eliza Kellas, April 30, 1917, Margaret Olivia Slocum Sage Collection, Box 5, EWS.

32. E. Lilian Todd to Eliza Kellas, November 16, 1915, Margaret Olivia Slocum Sage Collection, Box 5, EWS. By November, Sage must have realized that the project would require more money than she had anticipated, since the three existing buildings would not be sufficient for the planned training college.

33. E. Lilian Todd to Eliza Kellas, November 19, 1915, November 22, 1915, and November 25, 1915, all in Margaret Olivia Slocum Sage Collection, Box 5, EWS.

34. E. Lilian Todd to Eliza Kellas, December 3, 1915, Margaret Olivia Slocum Sage Collection, Box 5, EWS.

35. Eliza Kellas recalled the college's founding in a speech delivered in 1938 to Russell Sage College alumnae at the Tri-City Dinner, Albany, February 17, 1938. Parts of the speech are quoted in Julia Patton, *Russell Sage College: The First Twenty-Five Years, 1916–1941* (Troy, N.Y.: Press of Walter Snyder, 1941), 23. Patton was a professor of English at the college. Her account forms the basis for that of Elizabeth B. Potwine in *Faithfully Yours,* 95. Dr. Helen Upton's account is based on archival research at the Rockefeller Archive Center and elsewhere, but it unfortunately has no reference notes.

36. Patton, *Russell Sage College,* 20–21.

37. Ibid., 22.

38. In Potwine's account, this period of indecision was shorter. She writes that Kellas asked Mrs. Sage for time to consider and returned to Troy, where she spent a night in her office "in prayerful indecision." The next day, she called a group of her teachers together. "Their response was ready and generous. Miss Kellas sent her affirmative decision to Mrs. Sage, the money was promised, and the College was to open in September 1916." Potwine, *Faithfully Yours,* 96.

39. Quoted in E. Lilian Todd to Eliza Kellas, December 17, 1915, Margaret Olivia Slocum Sage Collection, Box 5, EWS.

40. Patton, *Russell Sage College*, 24; Margaret Olivia Sage, "Release of Restrictions Upon Use of Gifts," December 23, 1915, typescript, n.p., Margaret Olivia Slocum Sage Collection, Box 5, EWS.

41. Robert de Forest had insisted on this clause, persuading Kellas to visit these colleges during December to learn how they were organized.

42. Coleen Paratore, ed., *Sage Stories: Essays on the Third Quarter Century, 1966–1991* (Troy, N.Y.: The Sage Colleges, 1991).

43. E. Lilian Todd to Eliza Kellas, November 25, 1915, Margaret Olivia Slocum Sage Collection, EWS.

44. Eliza Kellas to RW de F, September 30, 1916, Eliza Kellas Collection, Folder 3a, EWS.

45. Eliza Kellas to "My dear Mrs. Sage," February 21, 1917, Eliza Kellas Collection, Folder 3a, EWS; Kellas reports that "our College has been progressing most successfully this year." Eliza Kellas to E. Lilian Todd, April 19, 1917, and September 5, 1917, both in Margaret Olivia Slocum Sage Collection, Box 5, EWS.

46. "I have most religiously sought to give you the credit for the idea"; E. Lilian Todd to Eliza Kellas, April 30, 1917, Margaret Olivia Slocum Sage Collection, Box 5, EWS.

47. E. Lilian Todd to RW de F, n.d., Margaret Olivia Slocum Sage Collection, Box 5, EWS.

48. As recounted by Lilian; E. Lilian Todd to Eliza Kellas, April 30, 1917, EWS. The letter was intended to rebut claims by Dr. Odell that the RSC owed its founding to him. See also E. Lilian Todd to Eliza Kellas, April 20, 1918, EWS: "She is returning the money to Troy that Mr. Sage acquired there, possibly with interest."

49. E. Lilian Todd to Eliza Kellas, January 26, 1918, Margaret Olivia Slocum Sage Collection, EWS; Eliza Kellas to E. Lilian Todd, June 19, 1918, Eliza Kellas Collection, Folder 3b, EWS.

50. The issue of the new college was entangled with disputes between the Troy and New York Emma Willard Associations which I have not followed up here. "To the Members of the Emma Willard Association," October 14, 1916 (typed), from Mrs. Russell Sage, President, Margaret Olivia Slocum Sage Collection, Box 1, EWS. See also Nettie Fowler McCormick Correspondence, Series 3B, Box 83 (Emma Willard Association File), WHSA for a proposed new constitution and by-laws for the Emma Willard Association.

51. E. Lilian Todd to Eliza Kellas, October 3, 1916; E. Lilian Todd to Eliza Kellas, January 26, 1918. In June 1918, Kellas thanked Todd "for your efforts to turn Mrs. Sage's attention in our direction"; Eliza Kellas to E. Lilian Todd, June 19, 1918. All in Margaret Olivia Slocum Sage Collection, Box 5, EWS.

52. E. Lilian Todd to Eliza Kellas, January 26, 1918, and April 4, 1918. See also E. Lilian Todd to Eliza Kellas, October 19, 1917. All in Margaret Olivia Slocum Sage Collection, Box 5, EWS.

53. Eliza Kellas to E. Lilian Todd, April 7, 1918, Margaret Olivia Slocum Sage Collection, Box 5, EWS.

54. E. Lilian Todd to Eliza Kellas, January 26, 1918, Margaret Olivia Slocum Sage Collection, Box 5, EWS.

55. E. Lilian Todd to Eliza Kellas, May 8, 1918, Margaret Olivia Slocum Sage Collection, Box 5, EWS.

56. E. Lilian Todd to Eliza Kellas, April 20, 1917, Margaret Olivia Slocum Sage Collection, Box 5, EWS.

57. E. Lilian Todd to Eliza Kellas, January 26, 1918, Margaret Olivia Slocum Sage Collection, Box 5, EWS.

14. "Splendid Donation"

1. Harriet James to MOS, November 4, 1914, RSFR, Box 100, Folder 1008. The writer was the daughter of a friend of Olivia's.

2. Marie Bradwell to MOS, December 20, 1911, RSFR, Box 101, Folder 1013.

3. Sister Paul to MOS, April 17, 1907, RSFR, Box 71, Folder 644. Correspondence relating to disaster relief is collected in Box 76, Folder 694. Correspondence with the Music School Settlement in Harlem is in RSFR, Box 84, Folder 810. The donation to the United Hebrew Charities of New York is acknowledged in RSFR, Box 95, Folder 955. For the New York Peace Society, see RSFR, Box 87, Folder 847. The appraisers of the estate in 1919 put the figure of her lifetime benefaction at $40 million. "Mrs. Sage's Estate Worth $49,051,045," *New York Times*, November 1, 1919.

4. Olivia Sage's letters are in Series 1, Mrs. Russell Sage; Series 3, Early Office Files; and Series 10, Personal Giving. All in RSFR.

5. Newspaper clipping, August 20, 1911, "The Sage and Slocum Book," JJML; Phoenix Fire Company to MOS, May 8, 1907, RSFR, Box 90, Folder 873.

6. Marjorie Harrison, *Margaret Olivia Sage, Philanthropist and Friend* (New York: Board of National Missions of the Presbyterian Church in the U.S.A., [1927–1928]), 8–9; Vol. II, FSW.

7. "Mrs. Russell Sage Restores Ancestral Homestead," *New York Sun*, May 24, 1903; Alison Cornish, et al., "Survey of Sag Harbor Village" was compiled in 1991 as part of the work to expand Sag Harbor's National Register historic district. Alison Cornish kindly shared part of this report with me. Letter to the author, July 2, 1994.

8. "Huntting House," handwritten, n.p., n.d., FSW; Alison Cornish to the author, July 2, 1994.

9. John Jermain, Merchant, and John Godbee, Mariner, both of Sag Harbor, "Agreement to Register the Sloop 'Four Cousins,'" 1801, FSW.

10. MOS to [Unknown], n.d., written from The Laurel House, Lakewood, New Jersey, letter no. 29, FSW.

11. Brearley Service Organization, *The Name in the Case* (Sag Harbor, N.Y.: Joseph Fahy's and Company, n.d.), 10; Arnold Meredith Lewis, "Sag Harbor:

The Study of a Small Community" (M.A. thesis, International Young Men's Christian Association College, Springfield, Mass., 1931).

12. Sage provided $12,000 a year for upkeep of the park; "Mrs. Sage Endows Library," *New York Sun*, July 28, 1912, NYSM.

13. Ladies Village Improvement Society, Sag Harbor, N.Y., *Sag Harbor* (Sag Harbor, N.Y.: LVIS, 1912), 31–33; "The Awakening of the Small Town: What Mrs. Russell Sage Is Doing for Quaint Old Sag Harbor," *Brooklyn Times*, December 30, 1913. For the play movement, see Judith Sealander, *Private Wealth and Public Life: Foundation Philanthropy and the Reshaping of American Social Policy from the Progressive Era to the New Deal* (Baltimore, Md.: Johns Hopkins University Press, 1997), 190–93; Dominick Cavallo, *Muscles and Morals: Organized Playgrounds and Urban Reform, 1880–1920* (Philadelphia: University of Pennsylvania Press, 1981); and John Glenn, Lilian Brandt, and F. Emerson Andrews, *Russell Sage Foundation, 1907–1946*, 2 vols. (New York: Russell Sage Foundation, 1947), 1:32–33, 70–72.

14. Robert K. Atkinson, "Mashashimuet Park and Social Center, Sag Harbor, N.Y., Report for June 1911 and June 1913," Long Island History Collection, East Hampton Library, East Hampton, New York; Dorothy Ingersoll Zaykowski, *Sag Harbor: The Story of an American Beauty* (Sag Harbor, N.Y.: Sag Harbor Historical Society, 1990), 274–277.

15. David Ward, *Poverty, Ethnicity, and the American City, 1840–1925: Changing Conceptions of the Slum and the Ghetto* (New York: Cambridge University Press, 1989), 72; Sealander, *Private Wealth and Public Life*, 190–193.

16. In 1912, a board of trustees was set up and the library was generously endowed. See "Mrs. Sage Endows Library"; Zaykowski, *Sag Harbor*, 278–285.

17. "The Presbyterian Church," May 12, 1911, in "The Sage and Slocum Book," JJML.

18. "Mrs. Sage Aids a School: Will Direct a Movement to Aid the Factory Workers of Sag Harbor, L.I.," *New York Sun*, September 19, 1911.

19. Unidentified newspaper clipping in letter from [name withheld by request] to the author, July 23, 1994; Lewis, "Sag Harbor: The Study of a Small Community," 183–185. There was also a dispute between Olivia Sage and the trustees of the First Presbyterian Church over their contribution to renovation of the steeple in 1910.

20. Marjorie Harrison, *Margaret Olivia Sage: Philanthropist and Friend* (New York: Board of National Missions of the Presbyterian Church in the U.S.A., 1907–1908), 5. This pamphlet must have been reissued later since it deals with World War I.

21. RW de F to MOS February 7, 1907, RSFR, Box 2, Folder 11.

22. Ibid.

23. RW de F to MOS, August 6, 1907, RSFR, Box 72, Folder 648.

24. Arthur Huntington Gleason, "Mrs. Russell Sage and Her Interests," *World's Work* 13 (November 1906): 8185.

25. J. S. Billings to MOS and E. H. Anderson to MOS, April 30, 1913,

both in RSFR, Box 87, Folder 848. See also E. H. Anderson, acting director, New York Public Library, acknowledging "a collection of 158 volumes and pamphlets, including College and University Reports," RSFR, Box 87, Folder 848.

26. Henry L. Higginson to A. Lawrence Lowell, December 16, 1910, Papers of A. Lawrence Lowell, Harvard.

27. "Progress and six percent" in John F. McClymer, *War and Welfare: Social Engineering in America, 1890–1925* (Westport, Conn.: Greenwood Press, 1980), 61.

28. This female world of small-scale urban entrepreneurship is compellingly documented by Wendy Gamber in *The Female Economy: The Millinery and Dressmaking Trades, 1860–1930* (Urbana: University of Illinois Press, 1997).

29. Gleason, "Mrs. Russell Sage and Her Interests," 8185. "Mrs. Russell Sage Could Sew at 4: Tells the Pascal Graduates That She Was Made to Knit Stockings Every Day," *New York Sun,* June 17, 1906.

30. "Mrs. Russell Sage Could Sew at 4"; RW de F to MOS, December 14, 1907, and RW de F to John Glenn, November 18, 1907, both in RSFR, Box 90, Folder 867. The director, Miss Pascal, was still trying to appeal this decision in 1911; see Henry de Forest to Mrs. Laffin, September 19, 1911, RSFR, Box 90, Folder 867.

31. See the numerous invitations to Olivia and *The Ely Club* (pamphlet) [n.p., n.d.], both in RSFR, Box 76, Folder 700.

32. Frances Lyford to Miss Hunter [MOS's secretary], February 26, ____, RSFR, Box 78, Folder 730. This nephew was Stephen L'Hommedieu Slocum. For settlements as social service agencies that also had denominational funding and an evangelical purpose, see Crocker, *Social Work and Social Order,* 111–132.

33. Mrs. Sarah J. Bird to MOS March 12th, 1907, and June 9, 1908, RSFR, Box 78, Folder 729.

34. Adeline Price to MOS, June 20, 1911, RSFR, Box 83, Folder 788. The go-between for this charity seem to have been Olivia's friend Mrs. James Herman Aldrich.

35. E. Lilian Todd, September __, 1915 (handwritten on envelope), RSFR, Box 89, Folder 862; "Mrs. Russell Sage Has Made Big Contribution to Syracuse Institution," May 4, 1907, "Margaret Olivia Sage," Obituaries and Biographical Clippings Collection, OCPL. Olivia's brother Jermain was often referred to as "the Colonel" because of his Civil War service.

36. Mrs. Charles E. Ballou to MOS, May 17, 1910, RSFR, Box 83, Folder 794.

37. Sara Wray to Miss Todd, December 1, 1914, RSFR, Box 76, Folder 699.

38. Woman's Hospital in the State of New York, "63rd Annual Report for the Year Ending September 30, 1918," 14, WHP.

39. Robert Shaw Minturn to MOS, December 24, 1907, and February 20, 1908; Bailey B. Burritt to MOS, January 2, 1915, all in RSFR, Box 1, Folder 5. For the Association for Improving the Condition of the Poor, see Frank

Dekker Watson, *The Charity Organization Movement in the United States* (New York: MacMillan Company, 1922; repr., New York: Arno Press, 1971); Walter Trattner, *From Poor Law to Welfare State,* 5th ed. (New York: Free Press, 1994); Paul Boyer, *Urban Masses and Moral Order, 1820–1920* (Cambridge, Mass.: Harvard University Press, 1978), 86–90; and Robert Bremner, *From the Depths: The Discovery of Poverty in America* (New York: New York University Press, 1976), 51–52. For the COS in New York, see Dawn Greeley, "Beyond Benevolence: Gender, Class, and the Development of Scientific Charity in New York City, 1882–1935" (Ph.D. diss., SUNY Stony Brook, N.Y., 1995).

40. Maria Louise Beebe to MOS, March 7, 1912, and March 27, 1912, RSFR, Box 101, Folder 1014. The fate of this appeal is recorded in an exchange on the envelope. Lilian wrote, "Shall I answer excusing you?" Olivia wrote, "Yes," and Lilian, "So answered."

41. [MOS] handwritten note on envelope, RSFR, Box 104, Folder 1031. See also R. H. Pratt to Miss Hunter, March 15, 1912, RSFR, Box 104, Folder 1031. Pratt later acknowledged her help: "Mr. DeForrest [*sic*], Mrs. DeForrest and Mrs. Sage with some friends, were the little company that always helped me in my work at Carlisle when I was in need." R. H. Pratt to Dr. Elmer E. Brown, December 12, 1913, Administrative Papers of Chancellor Elmer Ellsworth Brown, NYU.

42. Typed note on envelope, February 18, 1915, RSFR, Box 70, Folder 622.

43. Lilian had been asked to act as a go-between for Dr. Cleveland; E. Lilian Todd to MOS, May 15, 1914, RSFR, Box 68, Folder 606.

44. Gleason, "Mrs. Russell Sage and Her Interests," 8185.

45. MOS, handwritten note in pencil on envelope, March 9, 1915, RSFR, Box 70, Folder 622.

46. Last Will of Margaret Olivia Sage (October 25, 1906), First Codicil (February 17th, 1908), and Second Codicil (July 19th, 1911), Surrogates Court of the County of New York, December 11, 1919.

47. MOS to Jane Addams, July 5, 1910, RSFR, Box 80, Folder 752; Anna Beckwith to MOS, May 11, 1914, RSFR, Box 101, Folder 1014.

48. RW de F to Chancellor James R. Day, February 5, 1910, Papers of Chancellor James Roscoe Day, Box 3, SUA.

49. I explore the complex language of appeal and entitlement and suggest ways that this correspondence reflects the changing expectations of petitioners and the changing practice of philanthropic giving at the turn of the century in Ruth Crocker, "'I Only Ask You Kindly To Divide Your Fortune with Me': Begging Letters and the Transformation of Charity in Late Nineteenth-Century America," *Social Politics: International Studies in Gender, State, and Society* 6 (Summer 1997): 131–160. See also Linda Gordon and Nancy Fraser, "A Genealogy of Dependency: Tracing a Keyword of the U.S. Welfare State," *Signs* 19 (1994): 309–336.

50. [Secretary], typed note on envelope, May 2, 1916, RSFR, Box 70, Folder 626. Frost was a significant figure in his advocacy for what would later be called

Appalachia. See Henry D. Shapiro, *Appalachia on Our Mind: The Southern Mountains and Mountaineers in the American Consciousness, 1870–1920* (Chapel Hill: University of North Carolina Press, 1978), 115–116; Nina Silber, *The Romance of Reunion: Northerners and the South, 1865–1900* (Chapel Hill: University of North Carolina Press, 1993), 143–146.

51. RW de F to Chancellor Day, February 5, 1910, Papers of Chancellor James Roscoe Day, Box 3, SUA.

52. Brigadier R. Griffith to E. Lilian Todd, May 1, 1916, RSFR, Box 1, Folder 8.

53. Greeley, "Beyond Benevolence."

54. Marion Spinney to MOS, RSFR, Box 89, Folder 857.

55. E. Lilian Todd to MOS, October 29, 1913, RSFR, Box 79, Folder 745.

56. "On March 17, Mrs. Sage refused to make an appointment with Mrs. Alexander, who said that she wanted a contribution for her hospital. I, therefore, did not send this in to Mrs. Sage." E. Lilian Todd, typed note on envelope, April 8, 1916, and [Unknown] to MOS, March 8, 1914, both in RSFR, Box 87, Folder 846.

57. Mary G. Potter, *Summer Recreation Work: Industrial Membership, Woman's Municipal League*, n.d., pamphlet accompanying Mrs. Barclay Hazard to Colonel Slocum, July 17, 1912, RSFR, Box 98, Folder 987.

58. [Catharine Hunter], typed, undated memorandum (1916?), RSFR, Box 81, Folder 770. See also Berg, *The Remembered Gate*, 226.

59. Alice R. Wilson to MOS, December 14, 1904, December 15, 1905, and December 10, 1905; [E. Lilian Todd], typed memorandum, [1915]. All in RSFR, Box 81, Folder 770. Sage gave $100 in 1913; Elizabeth N. Clark to MOS, June 6, 1913, RSFR, Box 81, Folder 770.

60. [E. Lilian Todd], typed memorandum, [1915].

61. Martha Talmage Wycoff to MOS, [1910], RSFR, Box 76, Folder 700; *The Ely Club*, RSFR, Box 76, Folder 700.

62. Charles D. Walcott to Henry W. de Forest, June 19, 1907, Office of the Secretary, 1907–1924, Box 19, Folder 88, Smithsonian.

63. Charles D. Walcott to Mrs. Sage, January 10, 1908, and Charles D. Walcott to Henry de Forest, January 11, 1908, enclosing four drafts of deeds of gift, Office of the Secretary, 1907–1924, Smithsonian.

64. Charles D. Walcott to Henry de Forest, January 11, 1908, January 30, 1908, and May 28, 1908, Office of the Secretary, 1907–1924, Box 19, Folder 88, Smithsonian.

65. Charles D. Walcott to MOS, October 28, 1908, Box 19, Folder 88; Charles D. Walcott to MOS, February 15, 1909, Box 50, Folder 8; "Herbarium of World Botany: General Statement," Box 50, Folder 7, n.d. All in Office of the Secretary, 1907–1924, Smithsonian.

66. Charles D. Walcott to MOS, December 1, 1909, Office of the Secretary, 1907–1924, Box 50, Folder 8, Smithsonian.

67. RW de F to Charles D. Walcott and T. S. Palmer, September 30, 1912,

and Charles D. Walcott to RW de F, October 4, 1912, both in Office of the Secretary, 1907–1924, Box 19, Folder 9, Smithsonian. See George Grinnell, "Marsh Island," typescript, n.d., and "Deed of Transfer of Marsh Island, October 28, 1911," both in RW de F to MOS, February 19, 1912. See also RSFR, Box 63, Folders 558, 565.

68. Examples are Sunnyside Nursery, RSFR, Box 94, Folder 933; Boy Scouts, RSFR, Box 71, Folder 636; the *New York Tribune* Sunshine Society and Fresh Air Fund, RSFR, Box 88, Folder 849.

69. See Luther Gulick to MOS, March 8, 1912, and May 31, 1917; Luther Gulick to E. Lilian Todd, June 4, 1917. All in RSFR, Box 71, Folder 643.

70. The letter of acknowledgment from President Doggett to MOS in is RSFR, Box 100, Folder 1007.

71. On the Woman's Hospital connection, see MOS, typescript of a speech to the Board of Trustees, New-York Woman's Hospital, December 2, 1897, RSFR, Box 97, Folder 982. Examples of reform commitments passing down from mothers to daughters, and sometimes to granddaughters, are numerous. The YMCA appeal from Harriet James for a "splendid donation" was signed Mrs. Harriet James, "Daughter of Mrs. D. Willis James"; Mrs. Arthur C. James to MOS, November 4, 1917, RSFR, Box 100, Folder 1008.

72. She had visited Pasadena in 1910, and perhaps these other donations resulted from her tour of that year. MOS (?) "Gifts to YWCA," handwritten, RSFR, Box 100, Folder 1008. Grace Dodge and her brother Cleveland Dodge wrote to Mrs. Sage appealing for a donation because the cost of the building on the lot paid for by their mother was running $100,000 over estimate. Grace Dodge to MOS, April 1, 1909. The correspondence with YWCAs is in RSFR, Box 101, Folders 1013, 1014.

73. Several scholars have shown how the cities became home to a workforce of single young women. See especially Joanne Meyerowitz, *Women Adrift: Independent Wage Earners in Chicago, 1880–1930* (Chicago: University of Chicago Press, 1988). New perspectives on the YWCA are offered in Nancy Robertson, "'Deeper Even Than Race'? White Women and the Politics of Christian Sisterhood in the YWCA, 1906–1946" (Ph.D. diss., New York University, 1997).

74. She also made a donation to the Syracuse YWCA, sending $5,000 in May 1915 on her mother's birthday; the letter of acknowledgment is in RSFR, Box 101, Folder 1014.

75. The earliest involvement of Sage in the YMCA that I have found was in a YMCA literary society. "Program for the Literary Society of the Y.M.C.A., Southampton, New York," 1886 and 1887, RSFR, Box 100, Folder 1007.

76. Designing institutions for training and education, meshing these with the needs of employers, creating values in work and leisure—these were part of what scholars have called the organizational revolution. See David Noble, *American by Design: Science, Technology, and the Rise of Corporate Capitalism* (New York: Knopf, 1979).

77. RW de F to MOS, March 28, 1907, and June 26, 1907, RSFR, Box 101, Folder 1010, 1011; RW de F to MOS, RSFR, Box 100, Folder 1007.

78. The Young Men's Christian Association, *Young Men and Their Friends* (New York: Published by the Association, n.d.), 19–20; Thomas Winter, *Making Men, Making Class: The YMCA and Workingmen, 1877–1920* (Chicago: University of Chicago Press, 2002).

79. Richard Morse to MOS, October 19, 1906, December 15, 1906, and March 11, 1907, all in RSFR, Box 100, Folder 1007; Letitia Craig Darlington to MOS, March 16, 1907, RSFR, Box 101, Folder 1010. Olivia's donations to and correspondence with numerous YMCAs are documented in Boxes 100 and 101, RSFR. See, for example, Henry J. McCoy to MOS, October 23, 1906; Cleveland Dodge to Robert de Forest, December 15, 1906; MOS memorandum, March 11, 1907; Winthrop Noyes, Chairman of Building Fund, St. Paul, Minnesota, to MOS, March 23, 1907; Robert de Forest to MOS, May 23, 1907. William E. Dodge, father of Cleveland Hoadley and Grace Dodge, was a founder of the YMCA movement. C. Howard Hopkins, *History of the YMCA in North America* (New York: Association Press, 1951), 105, 108. See Paula Lupkin, "Manhood Factories: Architecture, Business, and the Evolving Urban Role of the YMCA, 1865–1925," in *Men and Women Adrift: The YMCA and the YWCA in the City,* ed. Nina Mjagkij and Margaret Spratt (New York: New York University Press, 1997), 44–45.

80. Letitia Darlington to MOS, March 16, 1907, RSFR, Box 101, Folder 1010.

81. For the St. Paul donation, see Winthrop Noyes to MOS, March 23, 1907; for San Francisco, see Henry McCoy to MOS, October 23, 1906. Both in RSFR, Box 100, Folder 1007.

82. For example, "Miss Gould Spends Busy Day in St. Louis," *St. Louis Daily Globe-Democrat,* October 18, 1907; Clarence J. Hicks to MOS, October 23, 1907, RSFR, Box 100, Folder 1008. Hicks, who was the associate general secretary of the International Committee of the YMCA, reported to Mrs. Sage about his travels with Helen Gould. See also Alice Northrop Snow, *The Story of Helen Gould, Daughter of Jay Gould, Great American* (New York: Fleming H. Revell Company, 1943).

83. Emma Morgan to MOS, April 21, 1914, RSFR, Box 101, Folder 1014.

84. "I know your inclinations do not tend toward any more religious propaganda" in RW de F, "Suggestions for a Possible Sage Foundation," December 10, 1906, 1.

85. De Forest to MOS, July 19, 1917, RSFR, Box 96, Folder 964.

86. Rev. George Ray to MOS, October 18, 1905, August 15, 1910, and June 31, 1911, RSFR, Box 67, Folder 597. Correspondence relating to the A.M.E. Zion church in Sag Harbor is in RSFR, Box 67, Folder 597. A useful source is Alison Cornish, et al., "Survey of Sag Harbor Village," 101; Zaykowski, *Sag Harbor,* 277–286.

87. The firm of architects was Cram, Goodhue, and Ferguson. "First Presbyterian Church" in Raymond Spinzia, Judith Spinzia, and Kathryn Spinzia, *Long Island: A Guide to New York's Suffolk and Nassau Counties* (New York: Hippocrene Books, 1988), 308; *The Russell Sage Memorial: Historical and Descriptive* (n.p., n.d. [1910]); "The First Presbyterian Church of Far Rockaway, New York on The Occasion of the Celebration of the Fiftieth Anniversary of the Founding of the Church, An Historical Address by Rev. J. Milton Thompson, D.D., Pastor Emeritus," typescript, 1938. The funeral service for Russell Sage had been held in the old church. In Patricia Leigh Brown, "Flowing Rivers, Sitting Ducks," *New York Times*, June 17, 1999, B1, 16, the writer discusses the vulnerability of such Tiffany windows. The article features the window Olivia donated.

88. "Potter Pulpit Dedicated," *New York Sun*, September 11, 1916, NYSM.

89. Peter Wosh, *Spreading the Word: The Bible Business in Nineteenth-Century America* (Ithaca, N.Y.: Cornell University Press, 1997).

90. Marion Eager to MOS, October 26, 1915, RSFR, Box 94, Folder 937.

91. RSFR, Box 94, Folder 941, has an acknowledgment of a check for $12 in 1886 for a tea to support Syrian Missions and for dues. See Charlotte Hall to MOS, May 17, 1886, and C. G. Montgomery to MOS, October 8, 1889, both in RSFR, Box 93, Folder 910.

92. Emily Rosenberg, *Spreading the American Dream: American Economic and Cultural Expansion, 1890–1945* (New York: Hill and Wang, 1982).

93. Helen Barrett Montgomery, *Western Women in Eastern Lands: Fifty Years of Woman's Work in Foreign Missions* (1910), quoted in *Women and Religion in America*, ed. Rosemary Radford Ruether and Rosemary Skinner Keller (San Francisco: Harper and Row, 1981), 1:290; "Our Sisters Are Waiting," *Missionary Link for the Woman's Union Missionary Society of America for Heathen Lands* 6 (July 1884), n.p.; Mrs. L. H. Dagett, *Historical Sketches of Woman's Missionary Societies in America and England* (1883; repr., Beltsville, Md.: NCR Corporation, 1977).

94. Annie Montgomery to MOS, n.d., RSFR, Box 93, Folder 910.

95. A. J. Edwards to MOS, n.d. [1913], RSFR, Box 91, Folder 885; Howard Bliss to J. J. Slocum, acknowledging a check for $7,500, RSFR, Box 94, Folder 942; "Other Gifts from Mrs. Sage," *New York Observer*, March 21, 1907, 378; W. Grenfell to MOS, December 30, 1909, RSFR, Box 79, Folder 735.

96. Dr. A. T. Pierson to MOS, May 6, 1911, RSFR, Box 90, Folder 874.

97. "Death of Dr. A. T. Pierson," *The Life of Faith* (clipping), June 7, 1911, 611; Delevan Pierson to MOS, September 29, 1914. Both in RSFR, Box 91, Folder 879.

98. Gertrude Dodd to MOS, April 22, 1911, and Clara E. Masters (Women's Union Missionary Society of America) to MOS, both in RSFR, Box 98, Folder 990.

99. Caroline Borden to MOS, August 15, 1909, RSFR, Box 66, Folder 590. Mary Mills Patrick had earned a doctorate in Berne, Switzerland.

100. Caroline Borden to MOS, n.d. The gifts are acknowledged in E. Harriet Stanwood to MOS, March 4, 1908; Caroline Borden to MOS, February 10, 1908; Mary Mills Patrick to MOS, January 8, 1908; Borden to MOS, August 19, 1911; Borden to MOS, August 19, 1911; Patrick to Mr. Slocum, August 17, 1912. All in RSFR, Box 66, Folders 590, 591.

101. Caroline Borden to MOS, February 10, 1908, RSFR, Box 66, Folder 590.

102. Samuel M. Zwemmer to MOS and Kate Olcott to MOS, September 20, 1912, both in RSFR, Box 89, Folder 856. Helen Gould had given $15,000. Olivia's donation to American Christian Literature for Moslems is in RSFR, Box 66, Folder 589.

103. Susan A. Yohn, *A Contest of Faiths: Missionary Women and Pluralism in the American Southwest* (Ithaca, N.Y.: Cornell University Press, 1995), 1. See also Peggy Pascoe, *Relations of Rescue: The Search for Female Moral Authority in the American West, 1874–1939* (New York: Oxford University Press, 1990); and Sarah Deutsch, *No Separate Refuge: Culture, Class, and Gender on an Anglo-Hispanic Frontier in the American Southwest, 1880–1940* (New York: Oxford University Press, 1987).

104. *New York City Mission Monthly* 1 (March 1888), n.p.; Harrison, *Margaret Olivia Sage*, 4; MOS, Response to the Troy Female Seminary Alumnae Survey, 1893, handwritten, Emma Willard School Archives, EWS; Florence Hayes, *Daughters of Dorcas: The Story of the Work of Women for Home Missions since 1802* (New York: Board of National Missions of the Presbyterian Church in the U.S.A., 1952), 83; M. Katherine Bennett, "Forty Years After," *Home Mission Monthly* 33 (December 1918): 29–30.

105. Last Will of Margaret Olivia Sage (October 25, 1906), First Codicil (February 17, 1908), 21.

106. John Fox to MOS, May 9, 1908, and John Fox to Miss Hunter, December 12, 1908, both in RSFR, Box 66, Folder 588. Correspondence between Robert W. de Forest and the American Bible Society on the subject of Olivia's donation to the Society is in "Robert W. De Forest file (1908–1911)," in the papers of John Fox, Corresponding Secretary, American Bible Society, microfiche, Reel 450. The Russell Sage Endowment Campaign that the ABS began in 1908 in response to Olivia's offer is described in John H. Zimmerman, "Public Relations, Financial Promotion and Support—1901–1930," typescript, April 1967, Essay #17, part V, American Bible Society Archives. The best study of the American Bible Society is Wosh, *Spreading the Word*.

107. James Turner, *Reckoning with the Beast: Animals, Pain, and Humanity in the Victorian Mind* (Baltimore, Md.: Johns Hopkins University Press, 1980), 47–52. For the emergence of a humanitarian sensibility in Western societies, see Thomas L. Haskell, "Capitalism and the Origins of the Humanitarian Sensibility," part 1, *American Historical Review* 90 (April 1985): 339–361, and part 2 (June 1985): 547–566.

108. Alfred Wagstaff to MOS, December 17, 1907, and W. Horton, Gen-

eral Manager, ASPCA, to MOS, July 30, 1910, both in RSFR, Box 68, Folder 607. Mrs. Speyer to MOS, January 3, 1912, RSFR, Box 88, Folder 852; E. L. Todd to Mrs. Speyer, January 23, 1914, and Mrs. Speyer to MOS, May 29, 1914, October 16, 1915, December 3, 1915, and May 18, 1916. All in RSFR, Box 88, Folder 853. See also "$10,000 from Mrs. Sage," *New York Sun*, January 5, 1912, and "Mrs. Sage Aids S.P.C.A.," *New York Sun*, October 27, 1916, both in NYSM.

109. M. Olivia Sage (Mrs. Russell Sage), "Opportunities and Responsibilities of Leisured Women," *North American Review* 181 (November 1905): 720. She also condemned the docking of horses.

110. Ibid. Olivia Sage supported the National Audubon Society as well as Junior Audubon Leagues for children; RSFR, Box 1, Folder 4.

111. "Nine Millionth Member Enrolled in Audubon Junior Club," press release, typed, n.d., RSFR, Box 1, Folder 4; W. T. Hornaday to MOS, May 7, 1914, and E. Lilian Todd to W. T. Hornaday, June 29, 1917, both in RSFR, Box 90, Folder 872.

112. J. J. Slocum to Miss Todd, December 6, 1912, RSFR, Box 88, Folder 854. The bequests are listed in "Mrs. Sage Leaves Millions to Charity," *New York Times*, November 14, 1918, 13.

113. RW de F to MOS, July 3, 1907, and RW de F to John E. Parsons, May 27, 1908, both in RSFR, Box 97, Folder 980. The donation of $50,000 is recorded in Eleanor [illeg.] (Treas., Ladies Board) to MOS, October 30, 1906, RSFR, Box 97, Folder 979.

114. The RSF spent around half a million dollars on tuberculosis prevention and education before 1918. Glenn, Brandt, and Andrews, *Russell Sage Foundation*, 1:225; a useful anthology is Margo Anderson and Maurine Greenwald, eds., *Pittsburgh Surveyed: Social Science and Social Reform in the Early Twentieth Century* (Pittsburgh, Pa.: University of Pittsburgh Press, 1996).

115. Between 1910 and 1916, she gave several large gifts to this Long Island hospital, including $6,000 to remodel a building for a nurses' residence; RSFR, Box 94, Folder 928. Rockaway Beach Hospital, also on Long Island, received $5,000. [Unknown] to MOS, September 10, 1908, September 29, 1911, and August 4, 1913. Sage requested that the gift be listed as coming from "a friend." All in RSFR, Box 92, Folder 900. For Susanna Hospital, Guam, see Mrs. Susan H. P. Dyer to MOS, May 2, 1915, RSFR, Box 94, Folder 935.

116. Leslie Conly, Manager, New York Tribune Fresh Air Fund, to MOS, August 1914. See correspondence from the Robin's Nest, a summer home for crippled children, Tarrytown, New York, to MOS between 1907 and 1909 in RSFR, Box 92, Folder 899. See also "Mrs. Russell Sage Makes $5,000 Gift," April 2, 1907, Obituaries and Biographical Clippings Collection, OCPL. For Southampton Hospital, see RSFR, Box 94, Folder 928.

117. Homer Folks to MOS, June 25, 1907, RSFR, Box 12, Folder 105. Drs. Edward G. and Theodore C. Janeway were directors of the institute. Correspondence regarding the Russell Sage Institute of Pathology is in RSFR, Box 12, Folders 105 and 106.

118. Graham Lusk, M.D., to RW de F, April 5, 1920, and "Mrs. Sage Founds Pathology School," [1907], newspaper clipping, both in RSFR, Box 12, Folder 106. The deed of gift is dated June 8, 1907. Mrs. Sage turned over the institute to the Russell Sage Foundation to be administered jointly with the city of New York. But a dispute soon erupted between the trustees of the institute and the Department of Public Charities and its City Commissioner Drummond. "Sage Institute and City," *Evening Post*, January 5, 1911; "City Hospital Fight Hot," *Morning Sun*, January 5, 1911; "Blames Hospital Controversy on Dr. T. C. Janeway," *New York World*, January 6, 1911; "Drummond to Janeway," *New York Tribune*, January 9, 1911; "Tells Dr. Janeway His Charge Is False," *New York Times*, January 9, 1911; "Sage Institute Out of City Charities," *New York Times*, March 28, 1911. All in RSFR, Box 12, Folder 105.

119. Gertrude Rice to RW de F, April 27, 1907; Louisa Schuyler to RW de F, April 27, 1907; Louisa Schuyler to John Glenn, May 22, 1907. All in RSFR, Box 2, Folder 11. Glenn, Brandt, and Andrews, *Russell Sage Foundation*, 1:231–233; Shelby Harrison, "John Mark Glenn—His Pioneer Attack on Social Problems—and First Steps Toward Better Living Conditions," unpublished biography of John Mark Glenn (1966 with some revisions from 1967) CSSA, Columbia. CSSA See also RSFR, Box 84, Folder 817 for donations to the New York Association for the Blind. For the Orphans' Asylum, see [Unknown] to MOS, January 18, 1909, and January 4, 1911, and "Gift to Aid Orphans Made by Mrs. Sage," *Syracuse Post-Standard* clipping, all in RSFR, Box 89, Folder 861.

120. The volume was Whittemore's *History of the Sage and Slocum Families of England and America*. See also "Mrs. Sage's 450 Gifts," *New York Herald*, December 20, 1908.

121. MOS to Mayor George McClennan, December 10, 1907; RSFR, Box 69, Folder 616. New York's City Hall had been saved from demolition in 1894; see Edwin G. Burrows and Mike Wallace, *Gotham: A History of New York City* (New York: Oxford University Press, 1999), 1084.

122. "Mrs. Sage's Gift to Firemen," *New York Sun* [n.d.], newspaper clipping, NYSM; RW de F, "Margaret Olivia Sage, Philanthropist," *The Survey* 41 (November 9, 1918): 151.

123. RSFR, Box 75, Folder 688 contains correspondence documenting this gift. See also Grace Overmeyer, "Hudson River Bluestockings—The Warner Sisters of Constitution Island," *New York History* 40 (April 1959): 154–155.

124. Indenture between Margaret Olivia Sage and The United States of America, May 25, 1909, U.S. Congress, House, *Joint Resolution to Accept the Gift of Constitution Island, in the Hudson River, New York*, by Mr. Chaney, 60th Cong., 2nd sess. HJ Res. 219. For the gift of Constitution Island, see RSFR, Box 75, Folder 688; J. J. Slocum to Miss Todd, December 6, 1912, RSFR, Box 88, Folder 854. MOS to Capt. Peter Traub, August 14, 1908; Captain Peter E. Traub to Henry de Forest, August 8, 1908; Traub to the Adjutant, U.S. Military Academy, August 9, 1908; MOS to Capt. Traub, August 14, 1908; RW de F to Traub, September 5, 1908; Henry de Forest to MOS, August 25, 1908; MOS

to "The President" [Theodore Roosevelt], September 4, 1908. All in Constitution Island Papers, U.S. Military Academy Archives, NARA, RG 404.

125. The City of New York Fourth of July Committee appealed for $100,000 "to conduct over 300 neighborhood celebrations"; Chairman, Finance Committee, City of New York Fourth of July Committee to MOS, May 29, 1911, and May 14, 1912, both in RSFR, Box 92, Folder 901. In *Eight Hours for What We Will: Workers and Leisure in an Industrial Community, 1870–1920* (New York: Cambridge University Press, 1983), 153–168, Roy Rosenzweig finds that the motives of the reformers in Worcester, Massachusetts, included preventing injuries caused by fireworks, protecting property from mobs, and increasing "Americanism." See also Luther Gulick, "New and More Glorious Fourth," *World's Work* 18 (July 1909): 11784–11787.

126. William Griffith, "The Sage Home on Fifth Avenue," undated clipping [1900?], "Margaret Olivia Sage," OnHA.

127. Hijiya, "Four Ways of Looking at a Philanthropist," 404, 406.

128. Quoted in McCarthy, *Women's Culture*, 121.

129. "Mrs. Sage Makes $100,000 gift to Museum of Art," *New York Herald*, December 20, 1909; Winifred E. Howe, *History of the Metropolitan Museum of Art* (New York: Columbia University Press, 1946), 99; *Fortieth Annual Report of the Metropolitan Museum of Art for the Year Ending December 31, 1909* (New York, 1910), 33; McCarthy, *Women's Culture*, 120–121, 263–264nn17, 19.

130. "Mrs. Sage An Art Patron. May Contribute to Erection of Women's Club in Manhattan," *New York Daily Tribune*, October 12, 1906, 1.

131. "Mrs. Russell Sage Restores Ancestral Homestead," *New York Sun*, May 24, 1903. See also Karen J. Blair, "A Women's Philanthropy of Women's Arts," in *Cultural Leadership in America: Art Matronage and Patronage*, ed. Wanda Corn (Boston: Published by the Isabella Stewart Gardner Museum, 1998).

132. "The Slocum Window," unidentified clipping, October 16, 1898, and "In Memory of the Reverend John Watson Adams," unidentified clipping, May 16, 1907, both in "Margaret Olivia Sage," OnHA.

133. "First Presbyterian Church" in Raymond Spinzia, Judith Spinzia, and Kathryn Spinzia, *Long Island: A Guide to New York's Suffolk and Nassau Counties* (New York: Hippocrene Books, 1988), 308; *The Russell Sage Memorial: Historical and Descriptive* (n.p., n.d. [1910]).

134. "Mrs. Sage Aids Men of the Sea," *New York Observer*, March 21, 1907, 377–378; Men of the British Steamship *Galileo* to MOS, June 1, 1909, RSFR, Box 68, Folder 604.

135. "Distribution of Calendars 1912 for Mrs. Russell Sage," RSFR, Box 100, Folder 1000; Miss Todd [?] to Chaplain George E. T. Stevenson, Navy Dept., July 21, 1917; R. K. Atkinson to Miss Lillian Todd, June 16, 1917, and August 17, 1917, both in RSFR, Box 94, Folder 926. Correspondence in this folder concerns the work of the Soldier Life Activities Committee, Chattanooga, Tennessee. Mrs. Sage was to send a phonograph and twenty-six records.

On the list of approved records, "Dixie Land" had been crossed out and "Let's All be Americans Now" substituted. The national emergency was no time to indulge in regionalism. For World War I–era philanthropy and reform, see Rosenberg, *Spreading the American Dream;* Nancy Bristow, *Making Men Moral: Social Engineering during the Great War* (New York: New York University Press, 1996).

136. John T. Axton, Chaplain, Fort Leavenworth, Kansas to MOS, n.d. [1908?], RSFR, Box 95, Folder 961.

137. Correspondence between Olivia and U.S. Navy chaplains is in RSFR, Box 95, Folder 960. See also "Other Gifts from Mrs. Sage," *New York Observer,* March 21, 1907, 378.

138. MOS to Mrs. Haslett McKim, First Directress, Board of Managers, Association for Relief of Aged and Indigent Females, New York, March 11, 1907, RSFR, Box 68, Folder 619. Records of donations (1907, 1915–1916) to the Syracuse Home Association are in RSFR, Box 94, Folder 937. See also Last Will of Margaret Olivia Sage, dated October 25, 1906, 9.

139. "It is hard for salaried women to face the accumulating of a hundred thousand dollars which is what we must have before we can begin to pay pensions"; Georgia Bellinger to MOS, May 25, 1916, RSFR, Box 91, Folder 890. Olivia also donated to a Teachers' Benefit Society. Its fund-raising literature has remarkable stories of aged, starving, and ill former teachers; RSFR, Box 95, Folder 945.

140. Sage, "Opportunities and Responsibilities of Leisured Women," 712, 719.

141. Miss Potter to MOS, RSFR, Box 96, Folder 968.

142. Dr. McLeod to MOS, March 13, 1912, Dr. McCleod to Miss Todd, November 13, 1916, and Mrs. Potter to MOS, August 22, 1910, all in RSFR, Box 96, Folder 968.

143. Nellie Griesel to MOS, May 19, 1915, RSFR, Box 78, Folder 723.

144. Wilmer Moore, Chairman, Board of Managers, to MOS, June 16, 1917, RSFR, Box 78, Folder 725. The discussion by E. Lilian Todd of what to do when the Music School Settlement sent tickets along with thanks for a donation is in RSFR, Box 84, Folder 810: "There being a dance as part of the entertainment, the feminine attendants will wear 'dance-wear,' which would not be proper for Mr. McCleod, or maybe even Mrs. Glenn."

145. "Free Classes in Manual Training and Domestic Economy," February 17, 1913, RSFR, Box 90, Folder 871.

146. E. Lilian Todd to MOS, July 2, 1913, RSFR, Box 92, Folder 928. The response was drafted and sent to Olivia for her approval.

147. E. Lilian Todd, note on envelope, August 1913, RSFR, Box 66, Folder 591.

148. E. Lilian Todd to Mary Mills Patrick, April 17, 1917; see also Mary Mills Patrick to Mr. Slocum, August 17, 1912, both in RSFR, Box 66, Folder 591.

149. McCarthy, *Noblesse Oblige*, 148.

150. Mrs. Sarah J. Bird to MOS, March 12th, 1907, and June 9, 1908, both in RSFR, Box 78, Folder 729.

151. Miss Lucy Bainbridge, Hon. Superintendent, Aged Pilgrim Fund, to MOS, January 13, 1913, RSFR, Box 1, Folder 6.

152. Ellen Speyer, Secretary, New York Women's League for Animals, May 12, 1911, RSFR, Box 88, Folder 852.

153. Mary M. Calvert, Sec., to MOS, March 15, 1918, RSFR, Box 70, Folder 622.

154. J. J. Slocum to Miss Todd, December 6, 1912, RSFR, Box 88, Folder 854. The bequests are listed in "Mrs. Sage Leaves Millions to Charity."

155. Annie Montgomery to MOS, n.d., RSFR, Box 93, Folder 910.

156. Anna Albee to MOS, July 2, 1914, RSFR, Box 100, Folder 1007. This gift was to the Rutland, Vermont, YMCA.

15. "Send what Miss Todd thinks best"

1. Natalie Zemon Davis, *The Gift in Sixteenth-Century France* (Madison: University of Wisconsin Press, 2000), 10.

2. Emphasis in the original. The letter is addressed to "Dear Lillian [sic]." MOS to E. Lilian Todd, May 21, 1915, RSFR, Box 92, Folder 897.

3. RW de F to A. Lawrence Lowell, January 21, 1911, Papers of A. Lawrence Lowell, Harvard.

4. "I asked Judge Hedges of Bridgehampton in the fall of 1910 if he knew how John Jermain came to Long Island, etc." MOS to [Unknown], n.d., written from the Laurel House, Lakewood, New Jersey, letter no. 29, FSW.

5. Clipping, *New York World*, May 9, 1912, in "The Sage and Slocum Book," Jermain Family Collection, JJML; "Deny Report That Mrs. Sage Is Ill," *New York Herald*, June 5, 1914, NYSM.

6. E. Lilian Todd to Shelby Harrison, July 1, 1937, RSFR, Box 3, Folder 26.

7. E. Lilian Todd to Eliza Kellas, October 3, 1916, Margaret Olivia Slocum Sage Collection, EWS.

8. Nettie McCormick to MOS, September 28, 1912, RSFR, Box 83, Folder 795. Emphasis in the original.

9. Nettie McCormick to MOS, n.d., RSFR, Box 83, Folder 795.

10. Nettie McCormick to MOS, October 2, 1912, RSFR, Box 83, Folder 795. Emphasis in the original.

11. Patricia Giunta, "Helen Gould's Wedding Day," in *A Victorian Wedding in Modern Times*, ed. Henry Duffy (Elmsford, N.Y.: National Trust for Historic Preservation, n.d.) 13–16.

12. The author of "Mrs. Sage's Finest Dress Worth $75," for the *New York Sun* a few years later seemed disappointed to report that Mrs. Sage had "no dress worth more than $75 and no piece of jewelry valued at more than $800" and

that, considering the amount she gave away, her possessions were "not highly expensive." *New York Sun*, November 2, 1919, NYSM.

13. Nettie McCormick to MOS, December 19, 1912, and January 9, 1913, both in RSFR, Box 83, Folder 795.

14. Nettie McCormick to MOS, November 19, 1913, RSFR, Box 83, Folder 795.

15. Nettie McCormick to MOS, April 19, 1913, RSFR, Box 83, Folder 795.

16. Nettie McCormick to MOS, April 1913, RSFR, Box 83, Folder 795. Emphasis in the original.

17. Nettie McCormick to MOS, [February 1915], McCormick Series 1B, Box 15 (Foreign Missions File).

18. Nettie McCormick to MOS February 8, 1915, RSFR, Box 83, Folder 795.

19. Nettie McCormick to MOS, February 8, 1915, RSFR, Box 83, Folder 795.

20. Nettie McCormick to "My very dear friend [MOS]," February 29, 1916, RSFR, Box 83, Folder 795. Emphasis in the original.

21. E. Lilian Todd to Eliza Kellas, May 8, 1918, Margaret Olivia Slocum Sage Collection, EWS.

22. Miss L. Todd to Miss S. Wray, April 2, 1917, RSFR, Box 76, Folder 699.

23. James E. West to E. L. Todd, February 11, 1918, RSFR, Box 71, Folder 636. He promised, "I assure you I shall go into the matter thoroughly."

24. James E. West to MOS, August 29, 1913, and James E. West to E. Lilian Todd, February 11, 1918, both in RSFR, Box 71, Folder 636.

25. [E. Lilian Todd] to Mr. E. Warrington Curtis, President, Southampton Hospital, Long Island, New York, June 13, 1916, RSFR, Box 92, Folder 928.

26. E. Lilian Todd to Colonel Joseph Jermain Slocum, typed note on Robert Grier Cooke to MOS, October 11, 1915, RSFR, Box 76, Folder 707.

27. Lilian Todd, note on envelope, Mrs. McDonald to MOS, November 24, 1912, Margaret Olivia Slocum Sage Collection, Box 1, EWS. Olivia no longer attended these affairs but usually sent a check for the relief fund.

28. This was from the Home for Working Boys, New York. See RSFR, Box 79, Folder 745.

29. "When the doctor told me last Wednesday that he had felt obliged to extirpate several cases of diseased uterus, and not one girl in the institution yet arrived at 18 years—I was next to dumbfounded." Rebecca Latimer Felton to Miss E. L. Todd, December 18, 1915, RSFR, Box 78, Folder 725. In the end, Miss Todd decided that since the letter was mainly a letter of thanks to Mrs. Sage for a $1,000 donation, she would "send it in." Miss Todd's dilemma is recorded on the envelope, typewritten.

30. "But you told me to say 'No' to all the Suffrage folks, and I will—when I get up my courage." [Secretary] to MOS, typescript, November 4, 1913, RSFR, Box 98, Folder 996. See also Carrie Chapman Catt to MOS, November 2, 1913, RSFR, Box 98, Folder 996.

31. E. Lilian Todd to [MOS], n.d. [November 6, 1913], typed draft, RSFR, Box 98, Folder 996. Emphasis in the original.

32. [Secretary] to Carrie Chapman Catt, November 6, 1913, RSFR, Box 98, Folder 996.

33. "I could not pass it" in typed note (by secretary) on envelope, October 27, 1914, RSFR, Box 99, Folder 997. See also Mary Hay, Chairman, Woman Suffrage Party of the City of New York, to Miss E. L. Todd, June 18, 1915; Miss Todd (?) to Carrie Chapman Catt, November 6, 1916, RSFR, Box 98, Folder 996.

34. [Secretary] to Miss [Mary Garrett] Hay, n.d., RSFR, Box 98, Folder 996.

35. "Mrs. Sage, Now 87, Calls for Vote," *New York Sun*, October 31, 1915, clipping, RSFR, Box 99, Folder 997. A valuable discussion of the 1915 march is in Elinor Lerner, "Immigrant and Working-Class Involvement in the New York City Woman Suffrage Movement, 1905–1917" (Ph.D. diss., University of California at Berkeley, 1981), 217.

36. "Mrs. Sage, Now 87, Calls for Vote."

37. In fact, Olivia's financial support of the suffrage formed just one small part of her philanthropic giving to many other institutions and causes. She was not a major donor compared to Alva Belmont or to Mrs. Frank Leslie, who gave over $2 million to the cause. See Madeline Stern, "Miriam Florence Folline Leslie," *NAW*, 2:393–394; Peter Geidel, "Alva Belmont: A Forgotten Feminist" (Ph.D. diss., Columbia University, 1993).

38. [Unknown] to MOS, April 16, 1916, and October 16, 1916, RSFR, Box 99, Folder 997.

39. [MOS], Addendum to "Release of Restrictions Upon Use of Gifts," September 17, 1917, typescript, n.p. The document is notarized by Joseph J[ermain] Slocum, Margaret Olivia Slocum Sage Collection, Box 5, EWS. Paul Cook, Treasurer, to MOS, January 12, 1918, William F. Gurley Papers, EWS. The initial gift to found the college was made (by error) to the Emma Willard School, which was to run the college. This entailed legal difficulties and confusion of all kinds which can be followed in the Todd-Kellas correspondence. See, for example, E. Lilian Todd to Eliza Kellas, April 20, 1917, and E. Lilian Todd to Eliza Kellas, October 19, 1917, both in Margaret Olivia Slocum Sage Collection, Box 5, EWS. See also Dr. Helen M. Upton, "Olivia," in *Sage Stories: Essays on the Third Quarter Century, 1966–1991*, ed. Coleen Paratore (Troy, N.Y.: The Sage Colleges, 1991), 23–24.

40. Eliza Kellas to John Glenn, June 20, 1916, RSFR, Box 34, Folder 272. The foundation had experts in several branches of educational theory. See John Glenn, Lilian Brandt, and F. Emerson Andrews, *Russell Sage Foundation, 1907–1946* (New York: Russell Sage Foundation, 1947) 1:85–96.

41. J. J. Slocum to [Unknown], September 17, 1917. Slocum now sometimes answered correspondence on behalf of the De Forest Brothers law firm.

42. Joseph J. Slocum to General R. H. Pratt, January 16, 1913, Richard Henry Pratt Papers, Box 8, Folder 273, Yale, Beinecke. Emphasis in the original.

43. He wrote from Laredo, Texas, about a scholarship applicant. H. J. Slocum to Kellas, December 9, 1916, Eliza Kellas Collection, Folder 3a, EWS.

44. Eliza Kellas to E. Lilian Todd, April 19, 1917, Eliza Kellas Collection, Folder 3a, EWS.

45. E. Lilian Todd to Eliza Kellas, May 11, 1915, Margaret Olivia Slocum Sage Collection, Box 5, EWS.

46. E. Lilian Todd to Eliza Kellas, May 31, 1915, Margaret Olivia Slocum Sage Collection, Box 5, EWS.

47. Joseph Jermain Slocum to "My dear Sister," [n.d.], RSFR, Box 94, Folder 940.

48. Telephone interview with Mrs. Charles (Lola) Marshall, September 14, 1994. Her mother, whose unmarried name was Laura Ball, was a friend of Olivia Sage.

49. He also advised getting Mr. Shepard [Helen Gould's husband] on the board, "after looking him over and finding out about him." R. H. Pratt to Dr. Elmer E. Brown, Chancellor, New York University, December 12, 1913, Administrative Papers of Chancellor Elmer Ellsworth Brown, Box 62, Folder 1, NYU.

50. E. Lilian Todd to Eliza Kellas, May 3, 1915, Margaret Olivia Slocum Sage Collection, Box 5, EWS. Emphasis in the original.

51. Rev. McCleod to President Demarest, January 23, 1913, Records of the William H. S. Demarest Administration, Box 17, Folder 9, Rutgers. Rev. McCleod was minister of the Collegiate Reformed Church of St. Nicholas.

52. Mrs. Florence Slocum Wilson, interview with the author, March 18, 1996.

53. E. Lilian Todd to Eliza Kellas, July 19, 1916, Eliza Kellas Collection, EWS. Todd may have been miffed because Kellas did not call to see her either.

54. "Speech of John Jermain Slocum at the Pierson Re-Dedication," *Sag Harbor Express,* 1982, incomplete newspaper clipping, FSW.

55. Mrs. Florence Slocum Wilson, conversation with the author, July 26, 1994. At the time of her death in November 1918, Olivia was still paying this monthly allowance of $100 to each of her great-nephews.

56. E. Lilian Todd to Col. Slocum, December 4, 1918, RSFR, Box 106, Folder 1059. This letter lists the "pensioners," relatives and friends who received a regular stipend from Olivia Sage.

57. "Speech of John Jermain Slocum at the Pierson Re-Dedication." He recounted: "Years later, Mrs. John D. Rockefeller, Jr., presented me with the parrot which for a while hung on Eileen's and my dining room wall."

58. Ibid.

59. Ibid. He addressed one to "My dearest Aunty," from Siena, Italy, in June 1912. Herbert Jermain Slocum to MOS, June 27, 1912. See also Herbert Jermain Slocum to MOS, August 12, 1912, and August 21, 1912, all in EGS.

60. "Mrs. Sage's Estate Worth $49,051,045," *New York Times,* November 1, 1919. See also "Lieut. Col. Slocum Dies at Age of 74," *New York Times,* Decem-

ber 15, 1933, 25. The story about "Keep jumping" was told me by Mrs. John (Eileen) Slocum, telephone conversation, January 1, 1995, and also by the late Mrs. Florence Slocum Wilson. It is also in "Speech of John Jermain Slocum at the Pierson Re-Dedication."

61. For a notice of the wedding, see *New York Herald*, February 15, 1899, 10.

62. E. Lilian Todd to Eliza Kellas, May 19, 1916, Margaret Olivia Slocum Sage Collection, Box 5, EWS.

63. E. Lilian Todd to Eliza Kellas, January 26, 1918, Margaret Olivia Slocum Sage Collection, Box 5, EWS. This paragraph of the letter is marked "confidential."

64. My thanks to Jeff Gottlieb of the Central Queen's Historical Association, New York, for this reference and for the photograph.

65. "Services of Burial for Mrs. Sage Will Be Held Thursday," *Syracuse Post-Standard*, clipping, "Margaret Olivia Sage," OnHA.

66. Reminiscence of a Troy citizen of his childhood in Saugus, Massachusetts. "Premature Demonstration: Rumors That Germany Had Accepted Armistice Terms Give Rise to Much Jollification," *Troy Times*, November 8, 1918, 1.

67. Clipping, "Mrs. Sage's Gifts," n.d., Troy Scrapbook, Local History Collection, TPL; "Mrs. Russell Sage Dies at Her Home," *New York Times*, November 4, 1918, 13.

68. E. Lilian Todd to Eliza Kellas, November 4, 1918, Margaret Olivia Slocum Sage Collection, Box 5, EWS.

69. E. Lilian Todd to Eliza Kellas, Margaret Olivia Slocum Sage Collection, Box 5, November 10, 1918, EWS.

70. "Poor boys!" Florence Slocum Wilson (daughter of Myles Standish Slocum), interview with the author, July 28, 1994. "Fifty at Mrs. Sage's Funeral; Body Will Be Taken to Syracuse for Burial," n.d., NYSM.

71. E. Lilian Todd to Eliza Kellas, November 10, 1918, Margaret Olivia Slocum Sage Collection, Box 5, EWS.

72. "Mrs. Sage To Be Laid to Rest in Simple Manner," clipping, "Margaret Olivia Sage," OnHA.

73. E. Lilian Todd to Eliza Kellas, November 10, 1918, Margaret Olivia Slocum Sage Collection, Box 5, EWS.

74. Ibid. Emphasis in the original.

75. This will was found in the 1970s under the eaves of her Sag Harbor home, the Huntting House, by the late George Finckenor, Sag Harbor historian and archivist.

76. Steve (Lt. Col. Stephen L'Hommedieu Slocum [1850–1933]) married Luna Garrison, but they had no children. Herbert Jermain Slocum, Jr., (d. 1948) was married twice, first to Marguerite Spear and then to Anita Desseur of South Carolina. He filed for bankruptcy in 1925 and appealed, but in a 1927 decision by the circuit court of appeals was found liable and made responsible for his debts. At the time of the bankruptcy action, he was said to be living on a scale

of $11,000 a year in Stamford, Connecticut. "H. J. Slocum, Jr. Held Liable for His Debts," *New York Times*, November 2, 1927, 18. He had one son, John Jermain Slocum (1914–1998), who married Eileen Gillespie of Newport, Rhode Island. Myles Standish Slocum (d. 1956), the other grandson and Olivia's grandnephew, married Isobel Bradford and the couple lived in Pasadena, California. They had two daughters, Carolyn and Florence.

77. Margaret Olivia Flint (1900–1978) married Thomas Proctor in 1925. The couple had no children. "Miss Flint to Wed Thomas E. Proctor," *New York Times*, December 20, 1925, 30.

78. The exact amount was $776,586; "Mrs. Sage's Estate Worth $49,051,045."

79. Last Will and Testament of Margaret Olivia Sage (October 1906), First Codicil (February 17th, 1908), Second Codicil (July 19th, 1911), 10–11, Surrogates Court of the County of New York, December 11, 1919.

80. Ibid., 20–21.

81. Ibid., 22; "Over Million Left Syracuse by Mrs. Sage," November 14, 1918, clipping, Obituaries and Biographical Collection, OCPL.

82. Kathleen D. McCarthy, "'Parallel Power Structures': Women and the Voluntary Sphere," in *Lady Bountiful Revisited: Women, Philanthropy, and Power*, ed. Kathleen D. McCarthy (New Brunswick, N.J.: Rutgers University Press, 1990), 1–31. On the decision to fold the auxiliaries into the mainstream denominations, see Lois Boyd and Douglas Breckinridge, *Presbyterian Women in America: Two Centuries of a Quest for Status* (Westport, Conn.: Greenwood Press, 1983), 17, 164.

83. *Forty-Second Annual Report, Woman's Board of Home Missions, Presbyterian Church, USA* (Philadelphia: Woman's Board of Home Missions, May 1921), 65. See also "Mrs. Sage's Estate Worth $49,051,045."

84. "Mrs. Sage's Estate Worth $49,051,045."

85. *Home Mission Monthly* 33, no. 3 (January 1919): 62.

86. RW de F, "Memorial Minute, 1918," reprinted in Glenn, Brandt, and Andrews, *Russell Sage Foundation, 1907–1949*, 1:269. The account continues, "This she did from that time on, up to the close of her long life, not impulsively, but with due regard to helping wisely and permanently; and this she is continuing to do after her death through the provisions of her will." See also "Margaret Olivia Sage, Philanthropist," *The Survey* 41 (1918): 151; James A. Hijiya, "Four Ways of Looking at a Philanthropist: A Study of Robert Weeks de Forest," *Proceedings of the American Philosophical Society* 124, no. 6 (December 1980): 418.

87. Personal communication from Professor Barry D. Karl to the author, January 9, 1990, and February 9, 1998. There was also a move to clear out Sage's letters from the Charities Building as early as 1912. See [John Persons] to RW de F, June 8, 1912, CSSA, Columbia. See also David C. Hammack, "Introduction," in *Russell Sage Foundation: Social Research and Social Action in America, 1907–1947*, ed. David C. Maddox (Frederick, Md.: CIS Academic Editions, 1988).

88. ABS Corresponding Secretary William I. Haven to RW de F, n.d. [1918],

Finance Committee files, American Bible Society Archives. "Bible Society Loses Fight for Sage Money," *New York Sun*, n.d., NYSM. See also Elmer E. Brown to J. J. Slocum, December 21, 1918, inquiring whether the $300,000 lifetime gift to NYU was deductible from the university's legacy, and the response, H. de Forest to Brown, December 26, 1918, that the payment made during Mrs. Sage's lifetime was chargeable against the university's legacy; both in Administrative Papers of Chancellor Elmer Ellsworth Brown, Box 62, NYU. See also "Rensselaer Polytechnic Institute and Emma Willard School Named in the Will of Margaret Olivia Sage," *Troy Record*, November 14, 1918. Another account ("Troy Schools May Not Get Sage Money," *Troy Record*, November 15, 1918) denied the first.

89. Joseph Odell to John Glenn, March 25, 1920, RSFR, Box 34, Folder 272.

90. "Russell Sage College to Install New Head," *New York Times*, February 3, 1929.

91. E. Lilian Todd to Eliza Kellas, Margaret Olivia Slocum Sage Collection, Box 5, November 10, 1918, EWS.

92. Shelby M. Harrison to Mr. Morris Hadley, September 23, 1937, RSFR, Box 3, Folder 26. These beneficiaries were not told that the foundation was paying the pensions. After Lilian's death, the foundation paid the beneficiaries through Ruth Simpson.

93. Lygia Ionnitiu kindly supplied me with a copy of Lilian Todd's death certificate. The full names of both her father and mother were listed as "unknown."

Conclusion

1. As historian Manuela Thurner remarks, "Women's public activities have not always been put to feminist ends." "Better Citizens without the Ballot: American Antisuffrage Women and Their Rationale during the Progressive Era," *Journal of Women's History* 5 (Spring 1993): 50.

2. For current examples, see Marsha Shapiro Rose, "The Women's Funds," *Nonprofit and Voluntary Sector Quarterly* 23 (Fall 1994): 227–242; Rose Proietto, "The Ford Foundation and Women's Studies in American Higher Education," in *Philanthropic Foundations: New Scholarship, New Possibilities*, ed. Ellen Condliffe Lagemann (Bloomington: Indiana University Press, 1999), 271–286; and Kathleen D. McCarthy, ed. *Women, Philanthropy, and Civil Society* (Bloomington: Indiana University Pres, 2000).

3. Catherine Kelly, "Gender and Class Formations in the Antebellum North," in *A Companion to American Women's History*, ed. Nancy A. Hewitt (Malden, Mass.: Blackwell Publishing, 2002), 101.

4. Mary Ryan, "The Public and the Private Good: Across the Great Divide in Women's History," *Journal of Women's History* 15 (Summer 2003): 21–23. For the theme of emergence in women's history, see Manuela Thurner, "Sub-

ject to Change: Theories and Paradigms of U.S. Feminist History," *Journal of Women's History* 9 (Summer 1997): 123–124.

5. "Mrs. Sage Hates Girls to Smoke: Glad the Vanderbilt Tea Room Is Closed and Says the Tobacco Habit Came from Savages Direct," *New York Evening World,* April 15, 1903. My thanks to James McGrath Morris for sending me this reference, which shows Olivia's social conservatism but also comes under the category "the retrieval of facts one does not want to find." See Dee Garrison, "Writing the Biography of Mary Heaton Vorse," in *The Challenge of Feminist Biography: Writing the Lives of American Women,* ed. Sara Alpern, Joyce Antler, Elisabeth Perry, and Ingrid Winter Scobie (Urbana: University of Illinois Press, 1992), 72.

6. "[P]hilanthropy tends to be supply- or donor-led"; Susan A. Ostrander and Paul G. Schervish, "Giving and Getting: Philanthropy as a Social Relation," in *Critical Issues in American Philanthropy,* ed. Jon Van Til and Associates (San Francisco: Jossey-Bass, 1990), 73; Nancy Robertson, "Kindness or Justice? Women's Associations and the Politics of Race and History," in *Private Action and the Public Good,* ed. W. W. Powell and E. Clemens (New Haven, Conn.: Yale University Press, 1998), 202.

7. Robert Bremner, *American Philanthropy* (Chicago: University of Chicago Press, 1960), 116. See also Lawrence Friedman and Mark McGarvie, *Charity, Philanthropy, and Civility in American History* (New York: Cambridge University Press, 2003).

8. Robert Bremner, "Foreword" to Van Til and Associates, *Critical Issues in American Philanthropy,* xiii–xiv.

9. Alan Wolfe, "What Is Altruism?" in *Private Action and the Public Good,* ed. Walter W. Powell and Elisabeth S. Clemens (New Haven, Conn.: Yale University Press, 1998), 36–46.

10. Lawrence Lessig, "Do You Floss? [review of *The Success of Open Source*]," *London Review of Books* 27, August 18, 2005, 24.

Archives Consulted

American Bible Society Archives, New York, New York

Columbia University, Rare Book and Manuscript Library, New York, New York
    Community Service Society Archive
    Seth Low Papers
    Edmund C. Stedman Collection

Cornell University, Department of Manuscripts and University Archives, Ithaca, New York
    Andrew Dickson White Papers, 1832–1919

East Hampton Library, East Hampton, New York
    Long Island History Collection

Emma Willard School Archives, Troy, New York
    William F. Gurley Papers
    Papers of Eliza Kellas
    Margaret Olivia Slocum Sage Collection

Harvard University Archives, Harvard University Library, Cambridge, Massachusetts
    Papers of A. Lawrence Lowell, 1889–1958

Historical Society of Pennsylvania, Philadelphia, Pennsylvania

Huntington Library, San Marino, California
    Papers of Samuel L. M. Barlow, 1776–1905

John Jermain Memorial Library, Sag Harbor, New York
    Jermain Family Collection

Lyndhurst Trust for Historic Preservation, Irvington, New York
    Helen Miller Gould Papers

New-York Historical Society, New York, New York
    Helen Miller Gould Shepard Papers, 1868–1938
    Women's Patriotic Relief Association Papers

New York Public Library, Manuscripts and Archives Division, New York, New York
    United States Sanitary Commission Records, 1861–1872
    New York Sun Morgue Collection
    United States Sanitary Commission Records

New York State Library, New York State Archives, Albany, New York
    Charles Lanman Collection, 1829–1859
    Edwin D. Morgan Papers, 1833–1883

New York University, Elmer Holmes Bobst Library, New York, New York
    Administrative Papers of Chancellor Elmer Ellsworth Brown, 1900–1937

Henry Mitchell MacCracken Administrative Records, 1884–1910, Office
of the Chancellor
James Buell Munn Estate Papers, 1873–1979
New York University Woman's Law Class Records 1888–1923, 1941
Onondaga County Public Library, Syracuse, New York
Obituaries and Biographical Clippings Collection
Onondaga Historical Association, Syracuse, New York
Presbyterian Historical Society, Philadelphia, Pennsylvania
Rensselaer County Historical Society, Troy, New York
Rensselaer Polytechnic Institute, Archives & Special Collections, Troy, New
York
Rockefeller Archive Center, Sleepy Hollow, New York
Russell Sage Foundation Records
Russell Sage Foundation, New York, New York
Papers at the Russell Sage Foundation
Rutgers University Libraries, Special Collections and University Archives, New
Brunswick, New Jersey
Records of the William H. S. Demarest Administration, 1890–1920
Smithsonian Institution Archives, Washington, D.C.
Office of the Secretary, 1907–1924
Sophia Smith Collection, Smith College, Northampton, Massachusetts
Suffrage Collection
St. Luke's-Roosevelt Hospital, Bolling Memorial Medical Library, New York,
New York
Woman's Hospital Papers
Syracuse University Archives and Records Management, Syracuse, New York
Papers of Chancellor James Roscoe Day
Troy Public Library, Troy, New York
Local History Collection
University of Minnesota Libraries, Special Collections and Archives, Minne-
apolis, Minnesota
Social Welfare History Archives
U.S. Military Academy Archives, West Point, New York
Constitution Island Papers, NARA RG 104
Vassar College Archives, Poughkeepsie, New York
Alma Lutz Papers
Wisconsin State Historical Society Archives, Madison, Wisconsin
Nettie Fowler McCormick Papers, 1775–1939
Yale University, Beinecke Rare Book and Manuscript Library, New Haven,
Connecticut
Richard Henry Pratt Papers
Yale University, Manuscripts and Archives, Yale University Library, New Haven,
Connecticut
Records of the Secretary's Office, Yale University, RU 49

Newspapers

Brooklyn Daily Eagle
Morning Star (Carlisle, Pa.)
Red Man (Carlisle, Pa.)
Indian Helper (Carlisle, Pa.)
New York Daily Tribune
New York Herald
New York Sun
New York Times
New York Tribune
New York World
Onondaga Standard (Syracuse, N.Y.)
Sag Harbor News
Troy Record
Woman's Journal

Microforms

Abbé, Mrs. Robert. Scrapbooks of Newspaper Clippings and Other Material Relating to Woman Suffrage, 1894–1921. 26 vols. Microform. New York Public Library.

Holland, Patricia G., and Ann D. Gordon, eds., *The Papers of Elizabeth Cady Stanton and Susan B. Anthony.* 45 microfilm reels. Wilmington, Del.: Scholarly Resources, Inc., 1991.

Maddox, David C., ed. *The Russell Sage Foundation: Social Research and Social Action in America, 1907–1947.* With an introductory essay by David C. Hammack. Frederick, Md.: CIS Academic Editions, 1988.

Primary Sources

Addams, Jane. "The Subtle Problems of Charity." *Atlantic Monthly* 83 (1899): 163–178.

———, et al. *Philanthropy and Social Progress.* New York: Thomas A. Crowell, 1893.

Atterbury, Grosvenor. "Forest Hills Gardens: A Study and Demonstration in Town Planning and Home Building Undertaken by the Russell Sage Foundation at Forest Hills, Long Island." *Survey* 25 (January 7, 1911).

Blake, Katherine Devereux, and Margaret Louise Wallace. *Champion of Women: The Life of Lillie Devereux Blake.* New York: Fleming H. Revell Co., 1943.

Blatch, Harriot Stanton, and Alma Lutz. *Challenging Years: The Memoirs of Harriot Stanton Blatch.* 1940; repr., Westport, Conn.: Hyperion Press, 1976.

Bolton, Sarah Knowles. *Famous Givers and Their Gifts.* New York: Thomas Y. Crowell and Co., 1896.

"A Brief History of Syracuse." In *Syracuse Daily Journal City Register and Directory for 1851–2*. Syracuse, N.Y.: Published at the Journal Office, 1852.

Brown, Arthur Judson. *One Hundred Years: A History of the Foreign Missionary Work of the Presbyterian Church of the U.S.A.* New York: Fleming H. Revell Co., 1936.

Carnegie, Andrew. "The Best Fields for Philanthropy." *North American Review* 149 (December 1889): 682–698.

———. "Wealth." *North American Review* 148 (June 1889): 653–664.

Catt, Carrie Chapman, and Nettie Rogers Shuler. *Woman Suffrage and Politics: The Inner Story of the Suffrage Movement*. New York: Scribner's Sons, 1926.

Chestnut Street Female Seminary, Boarding and Day School, Philadelphia. Philadelphia, Pa.: Henry B. Ashmead, 1855.

Clark, Joshua V. H. *Onondaga; or Reminiscences of Earlier and Later Times*. Syracuse, N.Y.: Stoddard and Babcock, 1849.

Dagett, Mrs. L. H. *Historical Sketches of Woman's Missionary Societies in America and England*. 1883; repr., Beltsville, Md.: NCR Corporation, 1977.

Daggett, Mabel Potter. "Suffrage Enters the Drawing Room." *The Delineator* 75 (January 1910): 37–38.

De Forest, Robert W., and Lawrence Veiller, eds. *The Tenement House Problem*. New York: Macmillan Co., 1903.

Eagle, Mary Kavanaugh Oldham, ed. *The Congress of Women Held in the Woman's Building, World's Columbian Exposition, Chicago, U.S.A., 1893*. Chicago: American Publishing House, 1893.

Emmet, Thomas Addis. *Incidents of My Life Professional-Literary-Social, with Services in the Cause of Ireland*. New York: G. P. Putnam's Sons, 1911.

———. "Reminiscences of the Founders of the Woman's Hospital Association." *The American Gynecological and Obstetrical Journal* (April 1899): 364–365.

Fairbanks, Mrs. A. W., comp. *Emma Willard and Her Pupils, or Fifty Years of Troy Female Seminary, 1822–1872*. New York: Published by Mrs. Russell Sage, 1898.

Fellows, Byron F., Jr., and William F. Roseboom. *The Road to Yesterday: Stories of Syracuse in the Long, Long Ago*. Syracuse, N.Y.: Midstate Offset Printing Corporation, 1948.

First Report of the Woman's Hospital Association, Presented by the Executive Committee. New York: D. Fanshawe, 1856.

Fitch, Charles Elliott. *Encyclopedia of Biography of New York*. Boston: American Historical Association, Inc., 1916.

Fowler, Henry. "The Educational Services of Mrs. Emma Willard." In *Memoirs of Teachers and Educators*, ed. Henry Barnard. 1861; repr., New York: Arno Press, 1969.

Gates, Frederick, *Chapters in My Life*. New York: Arno Press, 1977.

Gilman, Daniel Coit. "Five Great Gifts." *Outlook* (August 1907): 648–657.

Gleason, Arthur Huntington. "Mrs. Russell Sage and Her Interests." *World's Work* 13 (November 1906): 8182–8186.

Glenn, John M., Lilian Brandt, and F. Emerson Andrews. *Russell Sage Foundation, 1907–1946*. 2 vols. New York: Russell Sage Foundation, 1947.

Graham, Abbie. *Grace Dodge: Merchant of Dreams*. New York: The Woman's Press, 1926.

Greene, Jerome D. "The Dormitory Problem." *Harvard Monthly* 40 (April 1905): 39–46.

Guide to Long Branch, the Great Seaside Resort of the United States. Long Branch, N.J.: James B. Morris, 1868.

Harris, Seale. *Woman's Surgeon: The Life Story of J. Marion Sims*. New York: Macmillan Company, 1950.

Harrison, Marjorie. *Margaret Olivia Sage: Philanthropist and Friend*. New York: Board of National Missions of the Presbyterian Church in the U.S.A., 1927–1928.

Harrison, Shelby. "John Mark Glenn—His Pioneer Attack on Social Problems— and First Steps Toward Better Living Conditions." Unpublished manuscript. CSSA, Columbia.

Hopkins, Charles H. *History of the YMCA in North America*. New York: Association Press, 1951.

Jacobi, Mary Putnam. "Women in Medicine." In *Woman's Work in America*, ed. Annie Nathan Meyer, 139–205. New York: Henry Holt and Company, 1891.

Jones, Theodore Francis. *New York University, 1832–1932*. New York: New York University Press, 1933.

King, Moses. *King's Handbook of New York City*. Boston: Moses King, 1892.

Lord, John. *The Life of Emma Willard*. New York: D. Appleton and Company, 1873.

Ludlow, Helen W. "Indian Education at Hampton and Carlisle." *Harper's* 62 (April 1881): 659–675.

Lutz, Alma. *Emma Willard: Daughter of Democracy*. Washington, D.C.: Houghton Mifflin, 1929.

McAllister, Ward. *Society As I Have Found It*. New York: Cassell Publishing Company, 1890.

Maltby, Mrs. Annie C., ed. *Picturesque Oakwood: Its Past and Present Associations*. Syracuse, N.Y.: Fred S. Hills, 1894.

"Margaret Olivia (Slocum) Sage." *The National Cyclopedia of American Biography*. Vol. 10. New York: J. T. White, 1909.

"Margaret Olivia Slocum Sage, Sept. 8, 1828–Nov. 4, 1918." *Dictionary of American Biography*. Vol. 16. New York: C. Scribner's Sons, 1935.

Memorial Service of the Late Mrs. Thomas C. Doremus, the Beloved and Lamented President of the Woman's Union Missionary Society. New York: G. P. Putnam's, 1877.

Meyer, Annie Nathan, ed. *Woman's Work in America*. Introduction by Julia Ward Howe. New York: Henry Holt and Company, 1891.

Montgomery, Helen Barrett. *Western Women in Eastern Lands*. New York: Macmillan, 1911.

Myers, Gustavus. *History of the Great American Fortunes*. New York: The Modern Library, 1936.

Myers, James T., ed. *History of the City of Watervliet, N.Y., 1630–1910*. Troy, N.Y.: Henry Stowell and Sons, 1910.

[New York University]. *For the Better Protection of Their Rights: A History of the First Fifty Years of the Women's Legal Education Society and the Woman's Law Class*. New York: New York University Press, 1940.

Northrup, A. Judd. "History of the First Presbyterian Society in the Village of Syracuse." In *Early Records of the First Presbyterian Church, Syracuse, New York From 1826 to 1850*. Syracuse, N.Y.: The Genealogical Society of Central New York, 1902.

"Our Sisters Are Waiting." *The Missionary Link for the Woman's Union Missionary Society of America for Heathen Lands* 6 (July 1884).

Parker, Harold. "Russell Sage." *Muncy's Magazine* 12 (1895): 634–637.

Patton, Julia. *Russell Sage College: The First Twenty-Five Years, 1916–1941*. Troy, N.Y.: Press of Walter Snyder, 1941.

Potwine, Elizabeth B. *Faithfully Yours, Eliza Kellas*. Troy, N.Y.: Published by the Emma Willard School, 1960.

Pratt, James Marr. *Pioneer Surgeons of the Woman's Hospital: The Lives of Sims, Emmet, Peaslee, and Thomas*. Philadelphia, Pa.: F.A. Davis, 1957.

Pratt, Sereno S. "Our Financial Oligarchy." *World's Work* 10 (October 1905): 6704–6714.

"A Queen Consort of Finance: Mrs. Russell Sage's Long and Noble Life. Suffragist and Patriot." *Ladies Journal*, April 29, 1894.

Remsen, Jane. "Russell Sage, Yankee." *New England Quarterly* 11, no. 1 (March 1938): 3–28.

"Robert W. de Forest." *Bulletin of the Metropolitan Museum of Art* (1931).

Rockefeller, John D., Sr. *Random Reminiscences of Men and Events*. New York: Doubleday, Doral and Company, Inc., 1933.

Rosell, Garth M., and Richard A. G. Dupuis, eds. *The Memoirs of Charles G. Finney*. Grand Rapids, Mich.: Zondervan Publishing House, 1989.

"The Russell Sage Foundation: Its Social Value and Importance—Views of Some of Those Actually Engaged in Social Work." *Charities and the Commons* 17 (March 23, 1907): 1079–1085.

Sage, M. Olivia (Mrs. Russell Sage). "Opportunities and Responsibilities of Leisured Women." *North American Review* 181 (1905): 712–721.

Sage, Margaret Olivia. "Homestead of Colonel Jermain." In Ladies Village Improvement Society, Sag Harbor, Long Island, *Souvenir of Home Coming Week and 25th Anniversary of the Ladies Village Improvement Society, July 2–7, 1912*, ed. Anna Milford. Sag Harbor, N.Y.: LVIS, 1912.

Sage, Russell. "The Boy That Is Wanted." *Ladies' Home Journal* (November 1891): 8.

———. "The Injustice of Vacations." *The Independent*. (New York). June 2, 1904.

————. "Wealth—A Decree of Justice." *The Independent* (New York). May 1, 1902, 1027–1028.

Schenck, J. H. *Album of Long Branch: A Series of Photographic Views.* New York: John F. Trow, 1868.

Scudder, Vida. "Ill-Gotten Gifts to Colleges." *The Atlantic Monthly* 86 (July–December 1900): 675–679.

Sims, J. Marion. *The Woman's Hospital in 1874. A Reply to the Printed Circular of Doctors E. R. Peaslee, T. A. Emmet, and T. Gaillard Thomas, Addressed, "To the Medical Profession," May 5th, 1877.* New York: Kent and Co., 1877.

Sinclair, Upton. *Goose-Step: A Study of American Education.* Los Angeles, Calif.: Published by the author, 1923.

Slocum, Charles Elihu. *A Short History of the Slocums, Slocumbs and Slocombs of America, Genealogical and Biographical.* Syracuse, N.Y., published by the author, 1882.

————. *History of the Slocums, Slocumbs and Slocombs of America.* 2 vols. Defiance, Ohio: Quintin Publications, 1908.

Slosson, Edwin E. *Great American Universities.* 1910; repr., New York: Arno, 1977.

Smith, Matthew Hale. *Sunshine and Shadow in New York.* Hartford: J. B. Burr Publishing Co., 1883.

Snow, Alice Northrop, with Henry Nicholas Snow. *The Story of Helen Gould, Daughter of Jay Gould, Great American.* New York: Fleming H. Revell Company, 1943.

Sparkes, Boyden. *Hetty Green, A Woman Who Loved Money.* Garden City, N.Y.: Doubleday, Doren & Company, 1930.

Stanton, Elizabeth Cady. *Eighty Years and More: Reminiscences, 1815–1897.* 1898; repr., New York: Schocken, 1971.

————, Susan B. Anthony, Matilda Joslyn Gage, eds. *History of Woman Suffrage.* 6 vols. Rochester: Susan B. Anthony, 1881–1922; repr., New York: Arno Press, 1969.

Stanton, Theodore, and Harriot Stanton Blatch, eds. *Elizabeth Cady Stanton as Revealed in Her Letters, Diary and Reminiscences.* 2 vols. New York: Harper and Brothers, 1922.

Stewart, Rhinelander, ed. *The Philanthropic Work of Josephine Shaw Lowell.* New York: Macmillan, 1911.

Stokes, Olivia Phelps. *Letters and Memoirs of Susan and Anna Bartlett Warner.* New York: G. P. Putnam's Sons, 1925.

Suche, J. "At the Mineola Field." *Aeronautics* (December 1910): 197.

Sylvester, Nathaniel Bartlett. *History of Rensselaer County, New York.* Philadelphia, Pa.: Everts and Peck, 1880.

Syracuse, New York, First Presbyterian Church. *Articles of Faith and Covenant Adopted by the First Presbyterian Church in Syracuse. Seventy-Fifth Anniversary of the First Presbyterian Society in the Village of Syracuse, 1824–1899.* Syracuse, N.Y.: Published by the Society, 1899.

————. *A Manual for the Members of the First Presbyterian Church, Syracuse, N.Y.* Syracuse, N.Y.: S. F. Smith and Co., Journal Publishers, 1846.

————. *One Hundredth Anniversary of the First Presbyterian Society in the Village of Syracuse, 1824–1924.* Syracuse, N.Y.: Published by the Society, 1924.

Taylor, James M., and Elizabeth Hazleton Haight. *Vassar.* New York: Oxford University Press, 1915.

To the Children and Children's Children and Family Friends of Mrs. Catharine Ann Jermain . . . Christmas, 1873. Albany, N.Y.: Privately printed, n.d.

Todd, E. Lilian. "How I Built My Aeroplane." *Woman's Home Companion* (November 1909): 11.

Tully, Andrew. *Era of Elegance.* New York: Funk and Wagnalls Company, 1947.

Walworth, Ellen Hardin, ed. *Report of the Women's National War Relief Association, Organized for the Emergency of the Spanish-American War, March 1898–January 1899.* New York: King Press, 1899.

Ware, John F. W. *The Gambling Element in Life, a Sermon Preached in the Music Hall, Boston, October 29, 1871.* Boston: Nichols and Hall, 1871.

Warner, Anna B. *Susan Warner.* New York: G. P. Putnam's Sons, 1909.

Washington, Booker T. "Robert C. Ogden." *Metropolitan Magazine* 35 (February 1911): 636–642.

Weise, A. J. *History of the City of Troy.* Troy, N.Y.: William H. Young, 1876.

"What University Men Think of the Russell Sage Foundation: Suggestions in Large Part from the Chairs of Economics, Sociology and Political Economy." *Charities and the Commons* 18 (May 11, 1907): 186–191.

Whittemore, Henry. *History of the Sage and Slocum Families of England and America, Including the Allied Families of Montague, Wanton, Brown, Josselyn, Standish, Doty, Carver, Jermain or Germain, Pierson, Howell.* New York, published by Mrs. Russell Sage, 1908.

Willard, Emma. *Address to the Public, Particularly to the Members of the Legislature of New York, Proposing a Plan for Improving Female Education.* 2nd ed. 1819; repr., Marietta, Ga.: Larlin Corporation, 1987.

Willey, Nancy Boyd. *Built by the Whalers: A Tour of Historic Sag Harbor.* Sag Harbor, N.Y.: The Old Sagg-Harbour Committee, 1945.

Woody, Thomas A. *A History of Women's Education in the United States.* 2 vols. New York: Science Press, 1929.

Zimmerman, John H. "Public Relations, Financial Promotion and Support—1901–1930." Typescript, April 1967, American Bible Society.

Secondary Sources

Adams, David W. *Education for Extinction: American Indians and the Boarding School Experience, 1875–1928.* Lawrence: University of Kansas Press, 1995.

Agnew, Elizabeth N. *From Charity to Social Work: Mary E. Richmond and the Creation of an American Profession.* Urbana: University of Illinois Press, 2004.

Alchon, Guy. "The 'Self-Applauding Sincerity' of Overreaching Theory, Biography as Ethical Practice, and the Case of Mary van Kleeck." In *Gender and American Social Science: The Formative Years*, ed. Helene Silverberg, 293–325. Princeton, N.J.: Princeton University Press, 1998.

———. "Mary van Kleeck and Social-Economic Planning." *Journal of Policy History* 3, no. 1 (1991): 1–23.

———. "Mary van Kleeck of the Russell Sage Foundation: Religion, Social Science, and the Ironies of Parasitic Modernity." In *Philanthropic Foundations: New Scholarship, New Possibilities*, ed. Ellen Condliffe Lagemann, 151–168. Bloomington: Indiana University Press, 1999.

Allen, Ann Taylor. "Feminism, Social Science, and the Meanings of Modernity: The Debate on the Origin of the Family in Europe and the United States, 1860–1914." *American Historical Review* 104 (October 1999).

Alpern, Sara, Joyce Antler, Elisabeth Perry, and Ingrid Winter Scobie, eds. *The Challenge of Feminist Biography: Writing the Lives of Modern American Women*. Urbana: University of Illinois Press, 1992.

Anderson, Benedict. *Imagined Communities: Reflections on the Origin and Spread of Nationalism*. Rev. ed. London and New York: Verso Press, 1991.

Anderson, Eric, and Alfred A. Moss, Jr. *Dangerous Donations: Northern Philanthropy and Southern Black Education, 1902–1930*. Columbia: University of Missouri Press, 1999.

Anderson, Karen. *Changing Woman: A History of Racial-Ethnic Women in Modern America*. New York: Oxford University Press, 1996.

Anderson, Margo, and Maurine Greenwald, eds. *Pittsburgh Surveyed: Social Science and Social Reform in the Early Twentieth Century*. Pittsburgh, Pa.: University of Pittsburgh Press, 1996.

Andrews, F. Emerson. *Philanthropic Foundations*. New York: Russell Sage Foundation, 1956.

Apparadurai, Arjun. *The Social Life of Things: Commodities in Cultural Perspective*. New York: Cambridge University Press, 1986.

Arnove, Robert F., ed. *Philanthropy and Cultural Imperialism: The Foundations at Home and Abroad*. Boston: G. K. Hall, 1980.

Ascher, Carol, Louise de Salva, and Sara Ruddick, eds. *Between Women: Biographers, Novelists, Critics, Teachers, and Artists Write about Their Work on Women*. Boston: Beacon Press, 1984.

Attie, Jeanie. *Patriotic Toil: Northern Women and the American Civil War*. Ithaca, N.Y.: Cornell University Press, 1998.

Backscheider, Paula R. *Reflections on Biography*. New York: Oxford University Press, 1999.

Baker, Jean H., ed. *Votes for Women: The Struggle for Suffrage Revisited*. New York: Oxford University Press, 2002.

Baker, Paula. "The Domestication of Politics: Women and American Political Society, 1780–1920." *American Historical Review* 89 (June 1984): 620–647.

Barry, Kathleen. *Susan B. Anthony: A Biography of a Singular Feminist*. New York: New York University Press, 1988.

Basch, Norma. *In the Eyes of the Law: Women, Marriage, and Property in Nine-teenth-Century New York*. Ithaca, N.Y.: Cornell University Press, 1982.

Baym, Nina. *American Women Writers and the Work of History, 1790–1860*. New Brunswick, N.J.: Rutgers University Press, 1995.

———. "Women and the Republic: Emma Willard's Rhetoric of History." *American Quarterly* 43 (March 1991): 1–23.

Beckert, Sven. *The Monied Metropolis: New York City and the Consolidation of the American Bourgeoisie, 1850–1896*. New York: Cambridge University Press, 2001.

Bederman, Gail. *Manliness and Civilization: A Cultural History of Gender and Race in the United States, 1880–1917*. Chicago: University of Chicago Press, 1995.

Benhabib, Seyla. *Situating the Self: Gender, Community and Postmodernism in Contemporary Ethics*. New York: Routledge, 1992.

Berg, Barbara. *The Remembered Gate: Origins of American Feminism: The Woman and the City, 1800–1860*. New York: Oxford University Press, 1978.

Blair, Karen J. *The Clubwoman as Feminist: True Womanhood Redefined, 1868–1914*. London and New York: Holmes and Meier, 1980.

———. "A Women's Philanthropy of Women's Arts." In *Cultural Leadership in America: Art Matronage and Patronage*, ed. Wanda Corn, 39–50. Boston: Isabella Stewart Gardner Museum, 1998.

Blanchard, Mary Warner. "Leisure as Work in Turn of the Century Elite Culture." Paper presented at the Social Science Association Meeting, Chicago, November 2001.

———. *Oscar Wilde's America: Counterculture in the Gilded Age*. New Haven, Conn.: Yale University Press, 1998.

Bodnar, John. *Remaking America: Public Memory, Commemoration, and Patriotism in the Twentieth Century*. Princeton, N.J.: Princeton University Press, 1992.

Bordin, Ruth. *Woman and Temperance: The Quest for Power and Liberty*. Philadelphia, Pa.: Temple University Press, 1981.

Boris, Eileen. "The Power of Motherhood: Black and White Activist Women Redefine the Political." In *Mothers of a New World: Maternalist Politics and the Origins of Welfare States*, ed. Seth Koven and Sonya Michel. New York: Routledge, 1993.

Boyd, Lois A., and R. Douglas Brackenridge. *Presbyterian Women in America: Two Centuries of a Quest for Status*. Westport, Conn.: Greenwood Press, 1983.

Boydston, Jeanne. *Home and Work: Housework, Wages, and the Ideology of Labor in the Early Republic*. New York: Oxford University Press, 1990.

Boyer, Paul S. *Urban Masses and Moral Order in America, 1820–1920*. Cambridge, Mass.: Harvard University Press, 1978.

———, Melvyn Dubofsky, Eric H. Monkkonen, Ronald L. Numbers, David M. Oshinsky, and Emily S. Rosenberg, eds. *Oxford Companion to United States History*. New York: Oxford University Press, 2001.

Boylan, Anne. "Timid Girls, Venerable Widows, and Dignified Matrons: Life-Cycle Patterns among Organized Women in New York and Boston, 1797–1840." *American Quarterly* 38 (Winter 1986): 779–797.

Bremner, Robert H. *American Philanthropy*. Chicago: University of Chicago Press, 1960.

———. *From the Depths: The Discovery of Poverty in the United States*. New York: New York University Press, 1956.

———. *The Public Good: Philanthropy and Welfare in the Civil War Era*. New York: Alfred A. Knopf, 1980.

Brumberg, Joan Jacobs. "'Zenanas and Girlless Villages: The Ethnology of American Evangelical Women, 1870–1910." *Journal of American History* 69 (September 1982): 347–371.

Bruno, Frank J. *Trends in Social Work, 1874–1956: A History Based on the Proceedings of the National Conference of Social Work*. New York: Columbia University Press, 1957.

Bulmer, Martin, Kevin Bales, and Kathryn Kish Sklar, eds. *The Social Survey in Historical Perspective, 1880–1940*. New York: Cambridge University Press, 1991.

Burlingame, Dwight F., ed. *The Responsibilities of Wealth*. Bloomington: Indiana University Press, 1992.

Burrows, Edwin G., and Mike Wallace. *Gotham: A History of New York City, to 1898*. New York: Oxford University Press, 1999.

Calhoun, Charles W., ed. *The Gilded Age: Essays on the Origins of Modern America*. Wilmington, Del.: Scholarly Resources, 1995.

Calhoun, Craig, ed. *Habermas and the Public Sphere*. Cambridge, Mass.: MIT Press, 1997.

Casper, Scott E. *Constructing American Lives: Biography and Culture in Nineteenth-Century America*. Chapel Hill: University of North Carolina Press, 1999.

Cayleff, Susan. *Wash and Be Healed: The Water Cure Movement and Women's Health*. Philadelphia, Pa.: Temple University Press, 1987.

Chambers, Clarke A. *Paul U. Kellogg and the Survey: Voices for Social Welfare and Social Justice*. Minneapolis: University of Minnesota Press, 1971.

———. "Women in the Creation of the Profession of Social Work." *Social Service Review* 60 (March 1986): 1–33.

Chambers, Lee. "'Great Was the Benefit of His Death': Maria Weston Chapman and the Construction of Political Widowhood." Paper presented at the conference "The Widow's Might," Rutgers Center for Historical Analysis, April 2004.

Chernow, Ron. *The House of Morgan: An American Banking Dynasty and the Rise of Modern Finance*. New York: Atlantic Monthly Press, 1990.

———. *Titan: The Life of John D. Rockefeller, Sr*. New York: Random House, 1998.

Clemens, Elisabeth S. "Organizational Repertoires and Institutional Change: Women's Groups and the Transformation of U.S. Politics, 1890–1920." *American Journal of Sociology* 98, no. 4 (January 1993): 755–798.

Clinton, Catherine and Nina Silber, eds. *Divided Houses: Gender and the Civil War*. New York: Oxford University Press, 1992.

Clotfelder, Charles, ed. *Who Benefits from the Nonprofit Sector?* Chicago: University of Chicago Press, 1992.

Cohen, Nancy. *The Reconstruction of American Liberalism, 1865–1914*. Chapel Hill: University of North Carolina Press, 2002.

Collier, Robert H. *A History of the Jermain Memorial Church Congregation of Watervliet, New York, 1814–1974*. Albany, N.Y.: Argus-Greenwood Inc., 1976.

Cott, Nancy, Gerda Lerner, Kathryn Kish Sklar, Ellen DuBois, and Nancy Hewitt. "Considering the State of U.S. Women's History." *Journal of Women's History* 15 (Spring 2003): 145–163.

Cotton, Hope. "Women and Risk: The Gambling Woman in Eighteenth-Century England." Ph.D. diss., Auburn University, 1998.

Crocker, Ruth. "From Gift to Foundation: The Philanthropic Lives of Mrs. Russell Sage." In *Philanthropy, Charity, and Civility in American History*, ed. Lawrence Friedman and Mark McGarvie, 199–215. Bloomington: Indiana University Press, 2003.

———. "'From Widow's Mite to Widow's Might': The Philanthropy of Margaret Olivia Sage." *American Presbyterians* 74 (Winter 1996): 253–264.

———. "Gift, Gender and Performance in the Career of Mrs. Russell Sage." Paper presented at the Southern American Studies Association meeting, Atlanta, Georgia, February 2001.

———. "The History of Philanthropy as Life-History: A Biographer's View of Mrs. Russell Sage." In *Philanthropic Foundations: New Scholarship, New Possibilities*, ed. Ellen Condliffe Lagemann, 318–328. Bloomington: Indiana University Press, 1999.

———. "'I Only Ask You Kindly to Divide Your Fortune with Me': Begging Letters and the Transformation of Charity in Late Nineteenth-Century America." *Social Politics: International Studies in Gender, State, and Society* 6 (Summer 1999): 131–160.

———. "Philanthropy." In *Poverty in the United States: An Encyclopedia of History, Politics, and Policy*, ed. Gwendolyn Mink and Alice O'Connor. New York: ABC-CLIO, 2004.

———. *Social Work and Social Order: The Settlement Movement in Two Industrial Cities, 1890–1930*. Urbana: University of Illinois Press, 1992.

———. "'Unrepresentable in Our Narratives': Women's History and Female Philanthropists." Paper presented at the Western Association of Women Historians, Asilomar, California, June 1997.

———. "Unsettling Perspectives: The Settlement Movement, the Rhetoric of Social History, and the Search for Synthesis." In *Contesting the Master Narrative: Essays in Social History*, ed. Jeff Cox and Shelton Stromquist, 175–209. Iowa City: University of Iowa Press, 1998.

Cross, Whitney R. *The Burned-Over District: A Social and Intellectual History of*

Enthusiastic Religion in Western New York, 1800–1850. 1950; repr., New York: Harper and Row, 1965.

Daniels, Arlene Kaplan. *Invisible Careers: Women Civic Leaders from the Volunteer World.* Chicago: University of Chicago Press, 1988.

Davidoff, Leonore, and Catherine Hall. *Family Fortunes: Men and Women of the English Middle Class, 1780–1850.* Chicago: University of Chicago Press, 1987.

Davis, Allen F. *Spearheads for Reform: The Social Settlements and the Progressive Movement, 1890–1918.* 2nd ed. New Brunswick, N.J.: Rutgers University Press, 1984.

Davis, Natalie Zemon. *The Gift in Sixteenth-Century France.* Madison: University of Wisconsin Press, 2000.

Deacon, Desley. *Elsie Clews Parsons: Inventing Modern Life.* Chicago: University of Chicago Press, 1997.

Delegard, Kirsten. "Women's Movements, 1880s–1920s." In *A Companion to American Women's History,* ed. Nancy A. Hewitt. Malden, Mass.: Blackwell Publishing, 2002.

Deutsch, Sara. "'Learning to Talk More Like a Man': Boston Women's Class-Bridging Organizations, 1870–1940." *American Historical Review* 97 (April 1992): 379–404.

———. *No Separate Refuge: Culture, Class, and Gender on an Anglo-Hispanic Frontier in the Southwest, 1880–1940.* New York: Oxford University Press, 1987.

Douglas, Mary. "No Free Gifts." Foreword to Marcel Mauss, *The Gift: The Form and Reason for Exchange in Archaic Societies,* trans. W. D. Halls. New York: W.W. Norton, 1990.

Dowie, Mark. *American Foundations: An Investigative History.* Cambridge, Mass.: MIT Press, 2001.

Drachman, Virginia. *Women Lawyers and the Origins of Professional Identity in America.* Ann Arbor: University of Michigan Press, 1993.

DuBois, Ellen Carol. *Feminism and Suffrage: The Emergence of an Independent Women's Movement in America, 1848–1869.* Ithaca, N.Y.: Cornell University Press, 1978.

———. *Harriot Stanton Blatch and the Winning of Woman Suffrage.* New Haven, Conn.: Yale University Press, 1997.

———. "Politics and Culture in Women's History: A Symposium." *Feminist Studies* 6 (Spring 1980): 26–64.

———. "Working Women, Class Relations, and Suffrage Militance: Harriot Stanton Blatch and the New York Woman Suffrage Movement, 1894–1909." *Journal of American History* 74 (June 1987): 34–58.

Duffy, Henry J., ed. *A Victorian Wedding in Modern Times.* Elmsford, N.Y.: National Trust for Historic Preservation, n.d.

Eckhaus, Phyllis. "Restless Women: The Pioneering Alumnae of New York University School of Law." *New York University Law Review* 66 (December 1991): 1996–2013.

Eisenbach, Eldon J. *The Lost Promise of Progressivism*. Lawrence: University Press of Kansas, 1994.

Enstad, Nan. *Ladies of Labor, Girls of Adventure: Working Women, Popular Culture, and Labor Politics at the Turn of the Twentieth Century*. New York: Columbia University Press, 1999.

Epstein, Barbara Leslie. *The Politics of Domesticity: Women, Evangelism and Temperance in Nineteenth-Century America*. Middletown, Conn.: Wesleyan University Press, 1981.

Fink, Leon. *Progressive Intellectuals and the Dilemmas of Democratic Commitment*. Cambridge, Mass.: Harvard University Press, 1997.

Finnegan, Margaret. *Selling Suffrage: Consumer Culture and Votes for Women*. New York: Columbia University Press, 1999.

Fitzpatrick, Ellen. *Endless Crusade: Women Social Scientists and Progressive Reform*. New York: Oxford University Press, 1990.

Flanagan, Maureen. *Seeing with Their Hearts: Chicago Women and the Vision of the Good City, 1871–1933*. Princeton, N.J.: Princeton University Press, 2002.

Flexner, Eleanor. *Century of Struggle: The Woman's Rights Movement in the United States*. 1959; repr., New York: Atheneum, 1973.

Fosdick, Raymond. *The Story of the Rockefeller Foundation*. New York: Harper and Row, 1952.

Foucault, Michel. *The History of Sexuality: An Introduction*, vol. 1. 1978; repr., New York: Vintage Books, 1990.

Frankel, Noralee, and Nancy S. Dye, eds. *Gender, Class, Race, and Reform in the Progressive Era*. Lexington: University of Kentucky Press, 1991.

Fraser, Nancy. "From Redistribution to Recognition? Dilemmas of Justice in a 'Postsocialist' Age." In Fraser, *Justus Interruptus: Critical Reflections on the "Postsocialist" Condition*. New York: Routledge, 1997.

———. *Unruly Practices: Power, Discourse, and Gender in Contemporary Social Theory*. Minneapolis: University of Minnesota Press, 1989.

Frederickson, George. *The Inner Civil War: Northern Intellectuals and the Crisis of the Union*. New York: Harper and Row, 1965.

Freedman, Estelle. "Separatism as Strategy: Female Institution-Building and American Feminism, 1870–1930." *Feminist Studies* 5 (Fall 1979): 512–529.

———. "Separatism Revisited: Women's Institutions, Social Reform, and the Career of Miriam Van Waters." In *U.S. History as Women's History*, ed. Linda K. Kerber, Alice Kessler-Harris, and Kathryn Kish Sklar, 170–188. Chapel Hill: University of North Carolina Press, 1995.

Friedman, Lawrence, and Mark McGarvie, eds. *Philanthropy, Charity, and Civility in American History*. New York: Cambridge University Press, 2003.

Furner, Mary, and Barry Supple, eds. *The State and Economic Knowledge: The American and British Experiences*. New York: Cambridge University Press, 1990.

Gamm, Gerald, and Robert D. Putnam. "The Growth of Voluntary Associations in America, 1840–1940." *Journal of Interdisciplinary History* 29 (Spring 1999): 511–557.

Gardner, Deborah S. "Practical Philanthropy: The Phelps-Stokes Fund and Housing." *Prospects: An Annual of American Cultural Studies* 15 (1990): 359–411.

———. "'A Predominantly Social Point of View': A Century of Social Research, Public Policy, and the Social Sciences at the Russell Sage Foundation." Unpublished manuscript.

———, ed. *Vision and Values: Rethinking the Nonprofit Sector in America.* PONPO Working Paper #251. New York: Nathan Cummings Foundation, 1998.

Gaylin, Willard, Ira Glasser, Steven Marcus, and David Rothman, eds. *Doing Good: The Limits of Benevolence.* 1978; repr., New York: Pantheon, 1981.

Geidel, Peter. "Alva Belmont: A Forgotten Feminist." Ph.D. diss., Columbia University, 1993.

Giesberg, Judith Ann. *Civil War Sisterhood: The U.S. Sanitary Commission and Women's Politics in Transition.* Boston: Northeastern University Press, 2000.

Gilcreast, Everett. "Richard Henry Pratt and American Indian Policy, 1877–1906: A Study of the Assimilation Movement." Ph.D. diss., Yale University, 1967.

Ginzberg, Lori D. *Women and the Work of Benevolence: Morality, Politics, and Class in the Nineteenth-Century United States.* New Haven, Conn.: Yale University Press, 1990.

Glazer, Penina Migdal, and Miriam Slater. *Unequal Colleagues: The Entrance of Women into the Professions.* New Brunswick, N.J.: Rutgers University Press, 1987.

Gordon, Beverly. *Bazaars and Fair Ladies: The History of the American Fundraising Fair.* Knoxville: University of Tennessee Press, 1998.

Gordon, Lynn. *Gender and Higher Education in the Progressive Era.* New Haven, Conn.: Yale University Press, 1990.

Graham, Sara Hunter. *Woman Suffrage and the New Democracy.* New Haven, Conn.: Yale University Press, 1996.

Greeley, Dawn. "Beyond Benevolence: Gender, Class, and the Development of Scientific Charity in New York City, 1882–1935." Ph.D. diss., SUNY Stony Brook, 1995.

Greenwald, Maurine, and Margo Anderson, eds. *Pittsburgh Surveyed: Social Science and Social Reform in the Early Twentieth Century.* Pittsburgh, Pa.: University of Pittsburgh Press, 1996.

Griffith, Elisabeth. *In Her Own Right: The Life of Elizabeth Cady Stanton.* New York: Oxford University Press, 1984.

Hall, Jacqueline Dowd. "Open Secrets: Memory, Imagination, and the Refashioning of Southern Identity." *American Quarterly* 50 (March 1998): 109–124.

———. "'You Must Remember This': Biography as Social Critique." *The Journal of American History* 85 (September 1998): 439–465.

Hall, Peter Dobkin. *Inventing the Nonprofit Sector and Other Essays on Philanthropy, Voluntarism, and Nonprofit Organizations.* Baltimore, Md.: Johns Hopkins University Press, 1992.

———. *The Organization of American Culture, 1700–1900: Private Institutions, Elites, and the Origins of American Nationality*. New York: New York University Press, 1982.

Hammack, David C. *Power and Society: Greater New York at the Turn of the Century*. New York: Russell Sage Foundation, 1982; repr., New York: Columbia University Press, 1987.

———. "Toward a Political History of American Foundations." *History of Higher Education* 10 (1990): 91–101.

———, and Stanton Wheeler. *Social Science in the Making: Essays on the Russell Sage Foundation*. New York: Russell Sage Foundation, 1994.

Harrison, Gilbert A. *A Timeless Affair: The Life of Anita McCormick Blaine*. Chicago: University of Chicago Press, 1979.

Haskell, Thomas L. *The Emergence of Professional Social Science: The American Social Science Association and the Nineteenth-Century Crisis of Authority*. Urbana: University of Illinois Press, 1977.

———, ed. *The Authority of Experts: Studies in History and Theory*. Bloomington: Indiana University Press, 1984.

Hayden, Dolores. *The Grand Domestic Revolution: A History of Feminist Designs for American Homes, Neighborhoods, and Cities*. Cambridge, Mass.: MIT Press, 1982.

Hays, Johanna. "The Failure of the Woman's Building of the World's Columbian Exposition, Chicago, 1893." Unpublished seminar paper, History Department, Auburn University, 2003.

Heath, Sarah. "Negotiating White Womanhood: The Cincinnati YWCA and White Wage-Earning Women." In *Men and Women Adrift: The YMCA and YWCA in the City*, ed. Nina Mjagkij and Margaret Spratt. New York: New York University Press, 1997.

Heilbrun, Carolyn. "Non-Autobiographies of 'Privileged' Women: England and America." In *Life/Lines: Theorizing Women's Autobiography*, ed. Bella Brodzki and Celeste Schenck. Ithaca, N.Y.: Cornell University Press, 1988.

———. *Writing a Woman's Life*. New York: Ballantine Books, 1988.

Hewitt, Nancy A. "Charity or Mutual Aid? Two Perspectives on Latin Women's Philanthropy in Tampa, Florida." In *Lady Bountiful Revisited: Women, Philanthropy, and Power*, ed. Kathleen D. McCarthy, 55–69. New Brunswick, N.J.: Rutgers University Press, 1990.

———, ed., *A Companion to American Women's History*. Malden, Mass.: Blackwell Publishing, 2002.

———. *Women's Activism and Social Change: Rochester, New York, 1822–1872*. Ithaca, N.Y.: Cornell University Press, 1982.

———, and Suzanne Lebsock, eds. *Visible Women: New Essays on American Activism*. Urbana: University of Illinois Press, 1993.

Higham, John. *Strangers in the Land: Patterns of American Nativism, 1860–1925*. 2nd ed. New Brunswick, N.J.: Rutgers University Press, 1988.

Hijiya, James. "Four Ways of Looking at a Philanthropist: A Study of Robert Weeks de Forest." *Proceedings of the American Philosophical Society* 124 (December 1980): 404–418.

Hilkey, Judy. *Character Is Capital: Success Manuals and Manhood in Gilded Age America*. Chapel Hill: University of North Carolina Press, 1997.

Hill, Patricia. *The World Their Household: The American Woman's Foreign Missionary Movement and Cultural Transformation, 1870–1920*. Ann Arbor: University of Michigan Press, 1985.

Hine, Darlene Clark. "'We Specialize in the Wholly Impossible': The Philanthropic Work of Black Women." In *Lady Bountiful Revisited: Women, Philanthropy, and Power*, ed. Kathleen D. McCarthy, 70–93. New Brunswick, N.J.: Rutgers University Press, 1990.

Hoff, Joan. *Law, Gender, and Injustice: A Legal History of U.S. Women*. New York: New York University Press, 1991.

Hofstadter, Richard. *The Age of Reform: From Bryan to FDR*. New York: Vintage Books, 1955.

Hoganson, Kristin L. *Fighting for American Manhood: How Gender Politics Provoked the Spanish-American War and Philippine-American Wars*. New Haven, Conn.: Yale University Press, 1998.

———. "Garrisonian Abolitionists and the Rhetoric of Gender, 1850–1860." *American Quarterly* 45 (December 1993): 558–595.

Hollinger, David. "Inquiry and Uplift: Late Nineteenth-Century American Academics and the Moral Efficacy of Scientific Practice." In *The Authority of Experts*, ed. Thomas Haskell, 142–156. Bloomington: Indiana University Press, 1984.

Homberger, Eric. *Mrs. Astor's New York: Money and Social Power in a Gilded Age*. New Haven, Conn.: Yale University Press, 2002.

Horowitz, Helen Lefkowitz. *Alma Mater: Design and Experience in the Women's Colleges from Their Nineteenth-Century Beginnings to the 1930s*. New York: Knopf, 1984.

Hunter, Jane. *Gospel of Gentility: American Women Missionaries in Turn of the Century China*. New Haven, Conn.: Yale University Press, 1984.

———. *How Young Ladies Became Girls: The Victorian Origins of American Girlhood*. New Haven, Conn.: Yale University Press, 2002.

Hyde, Lewis. *The Gift: Imagination and the Erotic Life of Property*. 1979; repr., New York: Random House, 1983.

Ionnitiu, Lygia M. "To Conquer the Air: The Dream of E. Lilian Todd." In *The Harriet Quimby Research Conference Journal*, ed. Giacinta Bradley Koontz. Woodland Hills, Calif.: Published by the editor, 2000.

Jacobs, Meg. "Constructing a New Political Economy: Philanthropy, Institution-Building, and Consumer Capitalism in the Early Twentieth Century." In *Philanthropic Foundations: New Scholarship, New Possibilities*, ed. Ellen Condliffe Lagemann, 101–118. Bloomington: Indiana University Press, 1999.

Jaher, Frederic Cople. "Style and Status: High Society in Late Nineteenth-Century New York." In *The Rich, The Well-Born, and the Powerful: Elites and Upper Classes in History.* Urbana: University of Illinois Press, 1973.

Janiewski, Dolores. "Learning to Live 'Just Like White Folks': Gender, Ethnicity, and the State in the Inland Northwest." In *Gendered Domains: Rethinking Public and Private in Women's History,* ed. Dorothy O. Helly and Susan Reverby, 167–180. Ithaca, N.Y.: Cornell University Press, 1991.

Juster, Susan. *Disorderly Women: Sexual Politics and Evangelicalism in Revolutionary New England.* Ithaca, N.Y.: Cornell University Press, 1994.

Kammen, Michael. *Mystic Chords of Memory: The Transformation of Tradition in American Culture.* New York: Alfred A. Knopf, 1991.

Kaplan, Amy. "Manifest Domesticity." *American Literature* 70 (September 1998): 581–606.

Kaplan, Amy, and Donald Pease. *Cultures of United States Imperialism.* Durham, N.C.: Duke University Press, 1993.

Karl, Barry D., and Stanley N. Katz. "The American Private Philanthropic Foundation and the Public Sphere, 1890–1930." *Minerva* 19 (Summer 1981): 236–270.

———. "Donors, Trustees, Staffs: An Historical View, 1890–1930." In *The Art of Giving: Four Views of American Philanthropy.* Pocantico Hills, N.Y.: Rockefeller Archives Center, 1979.

———. "Foundations and Ruling Class Elites." *Proceedings of the American Academy of Arts and Sciences* 116 (Winter 1987): 1–41.

———. "Philanthropy and the Social Sciences." *Proceedings of the American Philosophical Society* 129, no. 1 (1985): 14–19.

Kastan, Susan. "Bibliography: Recent Writings about Foundations in History." In *Philanthropic Foundations: New Scholarship, New Possibilities,* ed. Ellen Condliffe Lagemann, 377–403. Bloomington: Indiana University Press, 1999.

Katz, Esther. "Grace Hoadley Dodge: Women and the Emerging Metropolis, 1856–1914." Ph.D. diss., New York University, 1980.

Katz, Michael B. *Improving Poor People: The Welfare State, the "Underclass," and Urban Schools as History.* Princeton, N.J.: Princeton University Press, 1995.

———. *In the Shadow of the Poorhouse: A Social History of Welfare in America.* New York: Basic Books, 1986.

———. *Poverty and Policy in American History.* New York: Academic Press, 1983.

Kendall, Diana. *The Power of Good Deeds: Privileged Women and the Social Reproduction of the Upper Class.* Lanham, Md.: Rowman & Littlefield, 2002.

Kerber, Linda. *No Constitutional Right to Be Ladies: Women and the Obligations of Citizenship.* New York: Hill and Wang, 1998.

———. "Separate Spheres, Female Worlds, Woman's Place: The Rhetoric of Woman's History." *Journal of American History* 75 (June 1988): 9–39.

Kessner, Thomas. *Capital City: New York City and the Men behind America's Rise to Economic Dominance, 1860–1900.* New York: New York University Press, 2003.

Kirkby, Diane. "Class, Gender, and the Perils of Philanthropy: The Story of *Life and Labor* and Labor Reform in the Women's Trade Union League." *Journal of Women's History* 4 (Fall 1992): 36–51.

Klaus, Susan L. *A Modern Arcadia: Frederick Law Olmsted, Jr. and the Plan for Forest Hills Gardens.* Amherst: University of Massachusetts Press, 2002.

Klein, Maury. "The Boys Who Stayed Behind: Northern Industrialists and the Civil War." In *Rank and File: Civil War Essays in Honor of Bell Irvin Wiley,* ed. James I. Robertson, Jr., and Richard M. McMurry, 137–156. San Rafael, Calif.: Presidio Press, 1976.

———. *The Life and Legend of Jay Gould.* Baltimore, Md.: Johns Hopkins University Press, 1986.

Koven, Seth. "Borderlands: Women, Voluntary Action and Child Welfare in Britain, 1840–1914." In *Mothers of a New World: Maternalist Politics and the Origins of the Welfare State,* ed. Seth Koven and Sonya Michel, 94–135. New York: Routledge, 1993.

Kunzel, Regina. *Fallen Women, Problem Girls: Unmarried Mothers and the Professionalization of Social Work, 1890–1945.* New Haven, Conn.: Yale University Press, 1993.

Lagemann, Ellen Condliffe. *The Politics of Knowledge: The Carnegie Corporation, Philanthropy, and Public Policy.* Chicago: University of Chicago Press, 1989.

———. *Private Power for the Public Good: A History of the Carnegie Foundation for the Advancement of Teaching.* Middletown, Conn.: Wesleyan University Press, 1983.

———, ed. *Philanthropic Foundations: New Scholarship, New Possibilities.* Bloomington: Indiana University Press, 1999.

Laqueur, Thomas. *Making Sex: Body and Gender from the Greeks to Freud.* Cambridge, Mass.: Harvard University Press, 1990.

Leach, William. *True Love and Perfect Union: The Feminist Reform of Sex and Society.* 2nd ed. Middletown, Conn.: Wesleyan University Press, 1989.

Lears, T. J. Jackson. *Something for Nothing: Luck in America.* New York: Viking, 2003.

Lebsock, Suzanne. "Women and American Politics, 1880–1920." In *Women, Politics and Change,* ed. Louise A. Tilly and Patricia Gurin. New York: Russell Sage Foundation, 1990.

Lederman, Sarah Henry. "From Poverty to Philanthropy: The Life and Work of Mary E. Richmond." Ph.D. diss., Columbia University, 1994.

Lerner, Elinor. "Immigrant and Working-Class Involvement in the New York City Woman Suffrage Movement, 1905–1917." Ph.D. diss., University of California at Berkeley, 1981.

Lerner, Gerda. *The Creation of Feminist Consciousness: From the Middle Ages to 1870.* New York: Oxford University Press, 1993.

Levy, Allison. "The Widow's Cleavage and Other Compromising Pictures." Paper presented at the conference "The Widow's Might," Rutgers Center for Historical Analysis, April 2004.

Lewis, Arnold Meredith. "Sag Harbor: The Study of a Small Community." M.A. thesis, International Young Men's Christian Association College, Springfield, Mass., 1931.

Lindenmeyer, Kriste. "Old Before Their Time: Mary Richmond and the Anti-Child Marriage Campaign." Paper presented at the Social Science Association meeting, November 1998.

Lubove, Roy. *The Professional Altruist: The Emergence of Social Work as a Career, 1880–1930.* 1965; repr., New York: Atheneum, 1980.

———. *The Progressives and the Slums: Tenement House Reform in New York City.* Pittsburgh, Pa.: University of Pittsburgh Press, 1963.

MacDonald, Dwight. *The Ford Foundation: The Men and the Millions.* New York: Reynal, 1956.

Magat, Richard. "Safe Harbor for the Social Sciences: The Russell Sage Foundation at 75." *Foundation News* (September–October 1982): 27–32.

Marilley, Suzanne M. *Woman Suffrage and the Origins of Liberal Feminism in the United States, 1820–1920.* Cambridge, Mass.: Harvard University Press, 1996.

Marsden, George M., and Bradley J. Longfield, eds. *The Secularization of the Academy.* New York: Oxford University Press, 1992.

Matthews, Becky. "Interaction of Crow and Euro-American Women, 1880–1945." Ph.D. diss., Auburn University, 2002.

Mauss, Marcel. *The Gift: The Form and Reason for Exchange in Archaic Societies.* Trans. W. D. Halls. 1950; repr., New York: W.W. Norton, 1990.

McCarthy, Kathleen. *Noblesse Oblige: Charity and Cultural Philanthropy in Chicago, 1849–1929.* Chicago: University of Chicago Press, 1982.

———. "'Parallel Power Structures': Women and the Voluntary Sector." In *Lady Bountiful Revisited: Women, Philanthropy, and Power*, ed. Kathleen McCarthy. New Brunswick, N.J.: Rutgers University Press, 1990.

———. *Women's Culture: American Philanthropy and Art.* Chicago: University of Chicago Press, 1991.

———, ed. *Lady Bountiful Revisited: Women, Philanthropy, and Power.* New Brunswick, N.J.: Rutgers University Press, 1990.

———, ed., *Women, Philanthropy, and Civil Society.* Bloomington: Indiana University Press, 2000.

McCloskey, Robert Green. *American Conservatism in the Age of Enterprise, 1865–1910.* New York: Harper Torchbooks, 1951.

McClymer, John F. *War and Welfare: Social Engineering in America, 1890–1925.* Westport, Conn.: Greenwood Press, 1980.

McConnell, Stuart. "Reading the Flag: A Reconsideration of the Patriotic Cults of the 1890s." In *Bonds of Affection: Americans Define Their Patriotism*, ed. John Bodnar, 102–119. Princeton, N.J.: Princeton University Press, 1996.

McCormick, Richard L. *From Realignment to Reform: Political Change in New York State, 1893–1910.* Ithaca, N.Y.: Cornell University Press, 1981.

McCormick, Richard P. *Rutgers: A Bicentennial History.* New Brunswick, N.J.: Rutgers University Press, 1966.

McCusker, John J. "Comparing the Purchasing Power of Money in the United States (or Colonies) from 1665 to 2003." Economic History Services, 2004. Available online at http://www.eh.net/hmit/ppowerusd.

————. *How Much Is That in Real Money? A Historical Commodity Price Index for Use as a Deflator of Money Values in the Economy of the United States.* 2nd. ed. Worcester, Mass.: American Antiquarian Society, 2001.

McDonald, David Kevin. "Organizing Womanhood: Women's Culture and the Politics of Woman Suffrage in New York State, 1865–1917." Ph.D. diss., SUNY Stony Brook, 1987.

McDonald, Lynn. *The Woman Founders of the Social Sciences.* Ottawa, Ontario: Carleton University Press, 1994.

McGregor, Deborah Kuhn. *Sexual Surgery and the Origins of Gynecology: J. Marion Sims, His Hospital, and His Patients.* New York: Garland Publishing, Inc., 1989. Revised as *From Midwives to Medicine: The Birth of American Gynecology.* New Brunswick, N.J.: Rutgers University Press, 1998.

Melish, Joanne Pope. *Disowning Slavery: Gradual Emancipation and "Race" in New England, 1780–1860.* Ithaca, N.Y.: Cornell University Press, 1998.

Meyerowitz, Joanne. *Women Adrift: Independent Wage Earners in Chicago, 1880–1930.* Chicago: University of Chicago Press, 1988.

Minow, Martha. *Making All the Difference: Inclusion, Exclusion, and American Law.* Ithaca, N.Y.: Cornell University Press, 1990.

Mjagkij, Nina, and Margaret Spratt, eds. *Men and Women Adrift: The YMCA and YWCA in the City.* New York: New York University Press, 1997.

Monoson, S. Sara. "The Lady and the Tiger: Women's Electoral Activism in New York City Before Suffrage." *Journal of Women's History* 2 (Fall 1990): 100–135.

Montgomery, Maureen E. *Displaying Women: Spectacles of Leisure in Edith Wharton's New York.* New York: Routledge, 1998.

Morantz, Regina Markell, and Sue Zschoche. "Professionalism, Feminism, and Gender Roles: A Comparative Study of Nineteenth-Century Medical Therapeutics." *Journal of American History* 67 (December 1980): 568–588.

Morantz-Sanchez, Regina. *Conduct Unbecoming a Woman: Medicine on Trial in Turn-of-the-Century Brooklyn.* New York: Oxford University Press, 1999.

Morgan, Francesca. "'Home and Country': Women, Nation, and the Daughters of the American Revolution, 1890–1930." Ph.D. diss., Columbia, 1998.

Muncy, Robyn. *Creating a Female Dominion in American Reform, 1890–1935.* New York: Oxford University Press, 1991.

————. "Gender and Professionalization in the Origins of the U.S. Welfare State." *Journal of Policy History* 2, no. 3 (1990): 290–315.

Murolo, Priscilla. *The Common Ground of Womanhood: Class, Gender, and Working-Girls' Clubs, 1884–1928.* Urbana: University of Illinois Press, 1997.

Newcomer, Mabel. *A Century of Higher Education for American Women.* New York: Harper, 1959.

Newman, Louise Michele. *White Women's Rights: The Racial Origins of Feminism in the United States.* New York: Oxford University Press, 1999.

Nickliss, Alexandra. "Phoebe Apperson Hearst." Ph.D. diss., University of California at Davis, 1994.

———. "Phoebe Apperson Hearst's Gospel of Wealth, 1883–1901." *Pacific Historical Review* 71 (November 2002): 575–605.

Nielsen, Waldemar A. *The Big Foundations.* New York: Columbia University Press, 1972.

Nielson, Kim. "Doing the 'Right' Right." *Journal of Women's History* 16, no. 3 (2004): 168–172.

Oakes, Claudia M. *United States Women in Aviation through World War I.* 1978; repr., Washington, D.C.: Smithsonian Institution Press, 1985.

O'Connor, Alice. *Poverty Knowledge: Social Science, Social Policy, and the Poor in Twentieth-Century U.S. History.* Princeton, N.J.: Princeton University Press, 2001.

Odendahl, Teresa. *Charity Begins at Home: Generosity and Self-Interest among the Philanthropic Elite.* New York: Basic Books, 1990.

Oleson, Alexandra, and John Voss, eds. *The Organization of Knowledge in Modern America, 1860–1920.* Baltimore, Md.: Johns Hopkins University Press, 1979.

Ostrander, Susan A., and Paul G. Schervish. "Giving and Getting: Philanthropy as a Social Relation." In *Critical Issues in American Philanthropy: Strengthening Theory and Practice,* ed. Jon Van Til and Associates, 67–98. San Francisco: Jossey-Bass, 1990.

Ostrower, Francie. *Why the Wealthy Give: The Culture of Elite Philanthropy.* Princeton, N.J.: Princeton University Press, 1995.

Overmeyer, Grace. "Hudson River Bluestockings—The Warner Sisters of Constitution Island." *New York History* 40 (April 1959): 137–158.

Painter, Nell Irvin. "Writing Biographies of Women." *Journal of Women's History* 9 (Summer 1997): 154–163.

Palmieri, Patricia. *In Adamless Eden: The Community of Women Faculty at Wellesley.* New Haven, Conn.: Yale University Press, 1995.

———. "From Republican Motherhood to Race Suicide: Arguments on the Higher Education of Women in the United States, 1820–1920." In *Educating Women and Men Together: Coeducation in a Changing World,* ed. Carol Lasser. Chicago: University of Illinois Press, 1987.

Paratore, Coleen, ed. *Sage Stories: Essays on the Third Quarter Century, 1966–1991.* Troy, N.Y.: The Sage Colleges, 1991.

Parry, Jonathan, and Maurice Bloch, eds. *Money and the Morality of Exchange.* New York: Cambridge University Press, 1989.

Pascoe, Peggy. *Relations of Rescue: The Search for Female Moral Authority in the American West, 1874–1939.* New York: Oxford University Press, 1989.

Payton, Robert. *Philanthropy: Four Views.* New Brunswick, N.J.: Transaction Books, 1988.

Poovey, Mary. *Making A Social Body: British Cultural Formation, 1830–1864.* Chicago: University of Chicago Press, 1995.

————. *Uneven Developments: The Ideological Work of Gender in Mid-Victorian England.* Chicago: University of Chicago Press, 1988.

Powell, Walter W., and Elisabeth Clemens, ed. *Private Action and the Public Good.* New Haven, Conn.: Yale University Press, 1998.

Rezneck, Samuel. "Mr. and Mrs. Russell Sage (1816–1918), A Money-Maker and His Philanthropic Wife." In *Profiles Out of the Past of Troy, New York, since 1789,* 193–197. Troy, N.Y.: Greater Troy Chamber of Commerce, 1970.

Ricci, David M. *The Transformation of American Politics: The New Washington and the Rise of Think Tanks.* New Haven, Conn.: Yale University Press, 1993.

Roberts, M. J. D. "Reshaping the Gift Relationship: The London Mendicity Society and the Suppression of Begging in England, 1818–1869." *International Review of Social History* 36 (1991): 201–231.

Robertson, Nancy. "'Deeper Even Than Race'? White Women and the Politics of Christian Sisterhood in the Y.W.C.A., 1906–1946." Ph.D. diss., New York University, 1997.

————. "Kindness or Justice? Women's Associations and the Politics of Race and History." In *Private Action and the Public Good,* ed. W. W. Powell and E. Clemens. New Haven, Conn.: Yale University Press, 1998.

Rose, Marsha Shapiro. "The Women's Funds." *Nonprofit and Voluntary Sector Quarterly* 23 (Fall 1994): 227–242.

Rosenberg, Charles E. "Florence Nightingale on Contagion: The Hospital as Moral Universe." In *Healing and History: Essays for George Rosen,* ed. Charles E. Rosenberg, 116–136. New York: Science History Publications, 1979.

Rosenberg, Emily S. *Spreading the American Dream: American Economic and Cultural Expansion, 1890–1945.* New York: Hill and Wang, 1982.

Rosenzweig, Roy, and Elizabeth Blackmar. *The Park and the People: A History of Central Park.* Ithaca, N.Y.: Cornell University Press, 1992.

Ross, Dorothy. "Modernist Social Science in the Land of the New/Old." In *Modernist Impulses in the Human Sciences, 1870–1930.* Baltimore, Md.: Johns Hopkins University Press, 1994.

Rossiter, Margaret W. *Women Scientists in America: Struggles and Strategies to 1940.* Baltimore, Md.: Johns Hopkins University Press, 1982.

Ruegamer, Lana. "Female Moral Authority in Nineteenth-Century America: Toward the Matriarchal Moment, 1993." Paper presented at the Berkshire Conference on the History of Women, Vassar College, June 1993.

Russett, Cynthia. *Sexual Science: The Victorian Construction of Womanhood.* Cambridge, Mass.: Harvard University Press, 1989.

Ryan, Mary P. *Cradle of the Middle Class: The Family in Oneida County, New York.* New York: Cambridge University Press, 1981.

————. "Gender and Public Access: Women's Politics in Nineteenth-Century America." In *Habermas and the Public Sphere,* ed. Craig Calhoun, 259–288. Cambridge, Mass.: MIT Press, 1992.

Ryan, Susan M. *The Grammar of Good Intentions: Race and the Antebellum Culture of Benevolence.* Ithaca, N.Y.: Cornell University Press, 2003.

Sandage, Scott. A. *Born Losers: A History of Failure in America*. Cambridge: Harvard University Press, 2005.

Sander, Kathleen. *The Business of Charity: The Woman's Exchange Movement, 1832–1900*. Urbana: University of Illinois Press, 1998.

Sangari, Kumkum, and Suresh Vaid, eds. *Recasting Women: Essays in Indian Colonial History*. New Brunswick, N.J.: Rutgers University Press, 1990.

Sarnoff, Paul. *Russell Sage, the Money King*. New York: Ivan Obolensky, 1965.

Schervish, Paul G., Platon E. Coutsoukis, and Ethan Lewis. *Gospels of Wealth: How the Rich Portray Their Lives*. Westport, Conn.: Praeger, 1994.

Schweikart, Larry, ed. *Encyclopedia of American Business History and Biography*. Vol. 7, *Banking and Finance to 1913*. New York: Facts on File, 1990.

Scott, Anne Firor. "The Ever-Widening Circle: The Diffusion of Feminist Values from the Troy Female Seminary, 1822–1872." In Scott, *Making the Invisible Woman Visible*, 64–88.

———. *Making the Invisible Woman Visible*. Urbana: University of Illinois Press, 1984.

———. *Natural Allies: Women's Associations in American History*. Urbana: University of Illinois Press, 1991.

———. "What, Then, Is the American: This New Woman?" In *Making the Invisible Woman Visible*, 3–25. Urbana: University of Illinois Press, 1984.

Sealander, Judith. *The Failed Century of the Child: Governing America's Young in the Twentieth Century*. New York: Cambridge University Press, 2003.

———. *Private Wealth and Public Life: Foundation Philanthropy and the Reshaping of American Social Policy from the Progressive Era to the New Deal*. Baltimore, Md.: Johns Hopkins University Press, 1997.

Semerad, Marjorie. "I Decided That Mr. Sage Deserved Another Look." In *Sage Stories: Essays on the Third Quarter Century, 1966–1991*, ed. Coleen Paratore. Troy, N.Y.: The Sage Colleges, 1991.

Shammas, Carole, and Michel Dahlin. *Inheritance in America from Colonial Times to the Present*. New Brunswick: Rutgers University Press, 1987.

Shaw, Stephanie J. *What a Woman Ought to Be and to Do: Black Professional Women Workers during the Jim Crow Era*. Chicago: University of Chicago Press, 1996.

Shoemaker, Linda. "'Charity and Justice': Gender and the Mission of Social Work: Social Work Education in Boston, New York, and Chicago, 1898–1930." Ph.D. diss., Binghamton University, 2001.

Silverberg, Helene, ed. *Gender and American Social Science: The Formative Years*. Princeton, N.J.: Princeton University Press, 1998.

Sklar, Kathryn Kish. *Catharine Beecher: A Study in American Domesticity*. New Haven, Conn.: Yale University Press, 1973.

———. *Florence Kelley and the Nation's Work: The Rise of Women's Political Culture, 1830–1900*. New Haven, Conn.: Yale University Press, 1995.

———. "Hull-House Maps and Papers: Social Science as Women's Work in the 1890s." In *Gender and American Social Science: The Formative Years*, ed.

Helene Silverberg, 127–155. Princeton, N.J.: Princeton University Press, 1998.

———. "Who Funded Hull-House?" In *Lady Bountiful Revisited: Women, Philanthropy, and Power*, ed. Kathleen D. McCarthy, 94–118. New Brunswick, N.J.: Rutgers University Press, 1990.

Skocpol, Theda, and Marshall Ganz. "A Nation of Organizers: The Institutional Origins of Civic Voluntarism in the United States." *American Political Science Review* 94 (September 2000): 527–546.

Slack, Charles. *Hetty: The Genius and Madness of America's First Female Tycoon*. New York: Ecco/Harper-Collins Publishers, 2004.

Slansky, Jeffrey. *The Soul's Economy: Market Society and Selfhood in American Social Thought, 1820–1920*. Chapel Hill: University of North Carolina Press, 2002.

Smith, James Allen. *The Idea Brokers: Think Tanks and the Rise of the New Policy Elite*. New York: Free Press, 1991.

Smith-Rosenberg, Carroll. *Religion and the Rise of the American City: The New York City Mission Movement, 1812–1870*. Ithaca, N.Y.: Cornell University Press, 1971.

Solomon, Barbara Miller. *In the Company of Educated Women: A History of Women and Higher Education in America*. New Haven, Conn.: Yale University Press, 1985.

Spacks, Patricia Meyer. "Selves in Hiding." In *Women's Autobiography: Essays in Criticism*, ed. Estelle C. Jelineck, 112–132. Bloomington: Indiana University Press, 1980.

Spruill, Marjorie Julian. "Race, Reform, and Reaction at the Turn of the Century: Southern Suffragists, the NAWSA, and the 'Southern Strategy' in Context." In *Votes For Women: The Struggle for Suffrage Revisited*, ed. Jean H. Baker, 102–117. New York: Oxford University Press, 2002.

Stanley, Amy Dru. "Beggars Can't Be Choosers: Compulsion and Contract in Postbellum America." *Journal of American History* 78 (March 1992): 1265–1293.

———. *From Bondage to Contract: Wage Labor, Marriage, and the Market in the Age of Slave Emancipation*. New York: Cambridge University Press, 1998.

Stansell, Christine. *American Moderns: Bohemian New York and the Creation of a New Century*. New York: Metropolitan Books, 2000.

———. *City of Women: Sex and Class in New York, 1789–1870*. New York: Knopf, 1986.

Stasz, Clarice. "Edith Rockefeller McCormick's Philanthropy." *Rockefeller Archive Center Research Reports* (Spring 1994): 4–6.

Strathern, Marilyn. *The Gender of the Gift: Problems with Women and Problems with Society in Melanesia*. Berkeley, Calif.: University of California Press, 1988.

Summers, Mark Wahlgren. *The Gilded Age: Or, The Hazard of New Functions*. New York: Prentice Hall, 1997.

Taylor, Teresa R. "No Extra Expense: The Exclusion of Women from New York

University, 1870–1918." Unpublished seminar paper, New York University, January 1988.

Theriot, Nancy M. "Women's Voices in Nineteenth-Century Medical Discourse: A Step toward Deconstructing Science." *Signs* 19 (Autumn 1993): 1–3.

Thompson, Victoria. *The Virtuous Marketplace: Women and Men, Money and Politics in Paris, 1830–1870.* Baltimore, Md.: Johns Hopkins University Press, 2000.

Thurner, Manuela. "Subject to Change: Theories and Paradigms of U.S. Feminist History." *Journal of Women's History* 9 (Summer 1997): 122–146.

Tilly, Louise A., and Patricia Gurin, eds. *Women, Politics, and Change.* New York: Russell Sage Foundation, 1990.

Tompkins, Jane. *Sensational Designs: The Cultural Work of American Fiction, 1790–1860.* New York: Oxford University Press, 1985.

Trattner, Walter I. "Louisa Lee Schuyler and the Founding of the State Charities Aid Association." *New York Historical Association Quarterly* 51 (July 1967): 233–247.

Trennert, Robert A. "Educating Indian Girls at Nonreservation Boarding Schools, 1878–1920." *Western Historical Quarterly* 13 (July 1982): 169–190.

Turner, Paul Venable. *Campus: An American Planning Tradition.* New York: Architectural History Foundation and MIT Press, 1984.

Van Slyck, Abigail. *Free To All: Carnegie Libraries and American Culture, 1890–1920.* Chicago: University of Chicago Press, 1995.

Vicinus, Martha. *Independent Women: Work and Community for Single Women, 1850–1920.* London: Virago Press, 1975.

Walkowitz, Daniel. "The Making of a Feminine Professional Identity: Social Workers in the 1920s." *American Historical Review* 95 (October 1990): 1051–1075.

Wall, Joseph Frazier. *Andrew Carnegie.* New York: Oxford University Press, 1970.

Walker-McNeal, Pearl Lee. "The Carlisle Indian School: A Study in Acculturation." Ph. D. diss., American University, 1979.

Walton, Andrea, ed. *Women and Philanthropy in Education.* Bloomington: Indiana University Press, 2004.

Wanken, Helen M. "'Woman's Sphere' and Indian Reform: The Women's National Indian Association, 1879–1901." Ph.D. diss., Marquette University, 1981.

Waugh, Joan. *Unsentimental Reformer: The Life of Josephine Shaw Lowell.* Cambridge, Mass.: Harvard University Press, 1998.

Weimann, Jeanne Madeline. *The Fair Women.* Chicago: Academy Press, 1981.

Weiner, Annette. *Women of Value, Men of Renown: New Perspectives on Trobriand Exchange.* Austin: University of Texas Press, 1976.

Wellman, Judith. "The Seneca Falls Women's Rights Convention: A Study of Social Networks." *Journal of Women's History* 3 (Spring 1991): 9–33.

Welter, Barbara. "The Cult of True Womanhood." *American Quarterly* 18 (1966): 151–174.

———. "'She Hath Done What She Could': Protestant Women's Missionary Careers in Nineteenth-Century America." In *Women in American Religion*, ed. Janet Wilson James. 111–125. Philadelphia: University of Pennsylvania Press, 1980.

Wexler, Laura. *Tender Violence: Domestic Visions in an Age of U.S. Imperialism*. Chapel Hill: University of North Carolina Press, 2000.

Wheatley, Stephen C. *The Politics of Philanthropy: Abraham Flexner and Medical Education*. Madison: University of Wisconsin Press, 1988.

Wheeler, Marjorie Spruill, ed. *One Woman, One Vote: Rediscovering the Woman Suffrage Movement*. Troutdale, Ore.: NewSage Press, 1995.

Wosh, Peter. *Spreading the Word: The Bible Business in Nineteenth-Century America*. Ithaca, N.Y.: Cornell University Press, 1994.

Yohn, Susan A. *A Contest of Faiths: Missionary Women and Pluralism in the American Southwest*. Ithaca, N.Y.: Cornell University Press, 1995.

———. "'Let Christian Women Set the Examples in Their Own Gifts': The 'Business' of Protestant Women's Organizations." In *Women and Twentieth-Century Protestantism*, ed. Margaret Bendroth and Virginia Brereton, 213–235. Urbana: University of Illinois Press, 2002.

Zaykowski, Dorothy Ingersoll. *Sag Harbor: The Story of an American Beauty*. Sag Harbor, N.Y.: Sag Harbor Historical Society, 1990.

Index

Page numbers in italics refer to illustrations.

RUTH CROCKER grew up in Southampton, England, and attended St. Anne's College, Oxford, where she earned a degree in Modern History. She subsequently earned an M.A. and Ph.D. at Purdue University in U.S. History. She holds the title of alumni professor in the Department of History at Auburn University, where she is also director of the Women's Studies Program. She is author of *Social Work and Social Order: The Settlement Movement in Two Industrial Cities* (1992).